INTRODU

BUSINESS MANAGEMENT

EIGHTH EDITION

INTRODUCTION TO BUSINESS MANAGEMENT

EDITORS

Prof. G.S. DU TOIT | Prof. B.J. ERASMUS | Prof. J.W. STRYDOM

AUTHORS

Prof. J.A. Badenhorst-Weiss | Prof. T. Brevis-Landsberg | Prof. M.C. Cant
Prof. G.S. du Toit | Prof. B.J. Erasmus | Prof. L.P. Krüger
Mr R. Machado | Prof. J. Marx | Prof. R. Mpofu | Prof. S. Rudansky-Kloppers
Prof. R. Steenkamp | Prof. J.W. Strydom | Ms. M. Vrba

CONTRIBUTORS

Ms. T. Cohen | Dr D. Geldenhuys | Ms. J. Geldenhuys | Prof. R. Pellisier
Ms. P. Ringane | Dr S. Pienaar | Dr E. Swanepoel | Prof. P. Venter

OXFORD
UNIVERSITY PRESS
SOUTHERN AFRICA

OXFORD
UNIVERSITY PRESS

SOUTHERN AFRICA

Oxford University Press Southern Africa (Pty) Ltd

Vasco Boulevard, Goodwood, Cape Town, Republic of South Africa
P O Box 12119, N1 City, 7463, Cape Town, Republic of South Africa

Oxford University Press Southern Africa (Pty) Ltd is a subsidiary of
Oxford University Press, Great Clarendon Street, Oxford OX2 6DP.

The Press, a department of the University of Oxford, furthers the University's objective of excellence in research, scholarship, and education by publishing worldwide in

Oxford New York

Auckland Cape Town Dar es Salaam Hong Kong Karachi
Kuala Lumpur Madrid Melbourne Mexico City Nairobi
New Delhi Shanghai Taipei Toronto

With offices in

Argentina Austria Brazil Chile Czech Republic France Greece
Guatemala Hungary Italy Japan Poland Portugal Singapore South Korea
Switzerland Turkey Ukraine Vietnam

Oxford is a registered trade mark of Oxford University Press
in the UK and in certain other countries

Published in South Africa
by Oxford University Press Southern Africa (Pty) Ltd, Cape Town

Introduction to Business Management
Eighth edition
ISBN 978 0 19 599251 9

First published 2010
Eighth impression 2012

Publishing manager: Alida Terblanche
Assistant commissioning editor: Marisa Montemarano
Managing editor: Lisa Andrews
Editors: Louise Banks and Jeanne Maclay-Mayers
Designers: Brigitte Rouillard and Oswald Kurten
Cover design: Judith Cross
Indexer: Adrienne Pretorius
Cover image: iStockphoto

Set in Photina MT Std 10 pt on 12 pt by Barbara Hirsch
Printed and bound by ABC Press, Cape Town
118069

Acknowledgements
The authors and publisher gratefully acknowledge permission to reproduce copyright material in this book. Every effort has been made to trace copyright holders, but if any copyright infringements have been made, the publisher would be grateful for information that would enable any omissions or errors to be corrected in subsequent impressions.

ABRIDGED TABLE OF CONTENTS

CONTENTS

PREFACE

This book focuses on the management of business organisations in the South African business environment. It describes how managers should manage resources and activities to enable organisations to operate as profitably as possible, thereby increasing the wealth of society and the country in general.

This eight edition of *Introduction to Business Management* marks a milestone in introductory business-management texts in South Africa as it is one of the few introductory business-management texts to have shown consistent growth over an extended period. The first edition was published in 1984 and now, 26 years later, the eighth edition is ready for publication! Since the publication of the first edition, more than half a million students at many universities and other institutions have used *Introduction to Business Management* as the foundation on which to build their careers in the business world.

Organisation of the text

Part 1 of the book introduces the reader to the world of business management. It describes the role of the entrepreneur and manager in the business world, the business organisation as the subject of study and the South African business environment. It also focuses on the growing importance of corporate social responsibility for South African businesses.

Part 2 contains an exposition of the management process and a survey of general management principles on which the functional management areas discussed in Part 3 are based.

Part 3 deals with operations management, human-resources management, marketing management, financial management, and purchasing and supply management.

Part 4 provides an integration of the previous work and shows how it is applied in the strategic-management process.

Changes from previous editions

The eighth edition follows the same value-chain approach that was used in the seventh edition. Supply chains and value chains are complementary and focus on the flow of products and services in one direction, and the value that is generated in the eyes of the customer flowing back. Creating a profitable value chain requires a careful alignment between what the customer wants (through the demand or value chain) and what is delivered via the supply chain.

In this edition, the authors have endeavoured to retain all the elements that have contributed to the success of the book. Comments by students and academics were extremely useful and were incorporated where possible in the new layout and contents.

The eighth edition of *Introduction to Business Management* offers many improvements in style, content and presentation to make the text even more effective and enjoyable. This edition includes substantial new and improved material, especially regarding the functional areas of business, where each functional area is now discussed in its own chapter. Separate chapters on corporate social responsibility and strategic management have also been included. Each chapter includes a case study that places the core elements in a practical perspective, and integrates theory and practice. Chapters also include challenges in the form of short case studies that require students to think critically about the concepts and the applications thereof. Key terms, multiple-choice questions and questions for discussion are included in each chapter to help students in their preparation for assignments and the examination.

In addition to the textual revisions, new and existing authors have contributed to the contents of this edition. The combined experience of the editors and authors further enhances the quality and the relevance of the text.

Acknowledgements

This book benefitted from the ideas contributed by a wide range of colleagues who teach from it in a number of tertiary institutions. Their ideas and suggestions were extremely useful and were incorporated, where possible, in the new layout and contents.

We continue to welcome constructive comments from colleagues at universities, as well as from managers in business practice, in an attempt to make future management education in South Africa even more relevant and meaningful.

We would like to acknowledge the work done by Dr M.D.C. Motlatla in ensuring that the text is Africa oriented and culture sensitive.

We would like to cite the work of the following colleagues who contributed to the updating of certain chapters:

Ms. T. Cohen
Ms. J. Geldenhuys
Ms. P. Ringane
Dr E. Swanepoel
Prof. P. Venter
Prof. R. Pellisier
Dr S. Pienaar

The editors

Prof G.S. Du Toit
Prof B.J. Erasmus
Prof J.W. Strydom

PART 1

The business world and the place of

BUSINESS MANAGEMENT

The eighth edition of the textbook *Introduction to Business Management* follows a value-chain approach. In developing this process, some of the supply-chain concepts that are used today were considered. Supply chains and value chains are complementary views that show the flow of products and services in one direction, and the value that is generated in the eyes of the customer flowing back. Creating a profitable value chain therefore requires a careful alignment between what the customer wants (through the demand or value chain) and what is delivered via the supply chain.

The value-chain model used for this book is depicted in the figure below. It indicates the relationship between the different areas of the book that build up the value-chain concept as we understand it.

The value chain distinguishes between the two types of activity in an organisation: primary activities and secondary activities. The primary activities are activities that are involved in the physical production of the product, while the secondary activities provide the infrastructure that allows the primary activities to take place.

As can be seen from the figure, the support activities are grouped in Chapters 1, 2, 3, 5, 6, 7, 8, 9 and 15. As in any organisation, we need to do a strategic evaluation of the business environment in which the business operates (Chapter 4). Having done this, we move on to the primary activities of the value chain, which are covered in Chapters 10, 11, 12, 13 and 14.

This model will be repeated at the beginning of each part of the book to reflect the progress made by the student in understanding the value-chain concept.

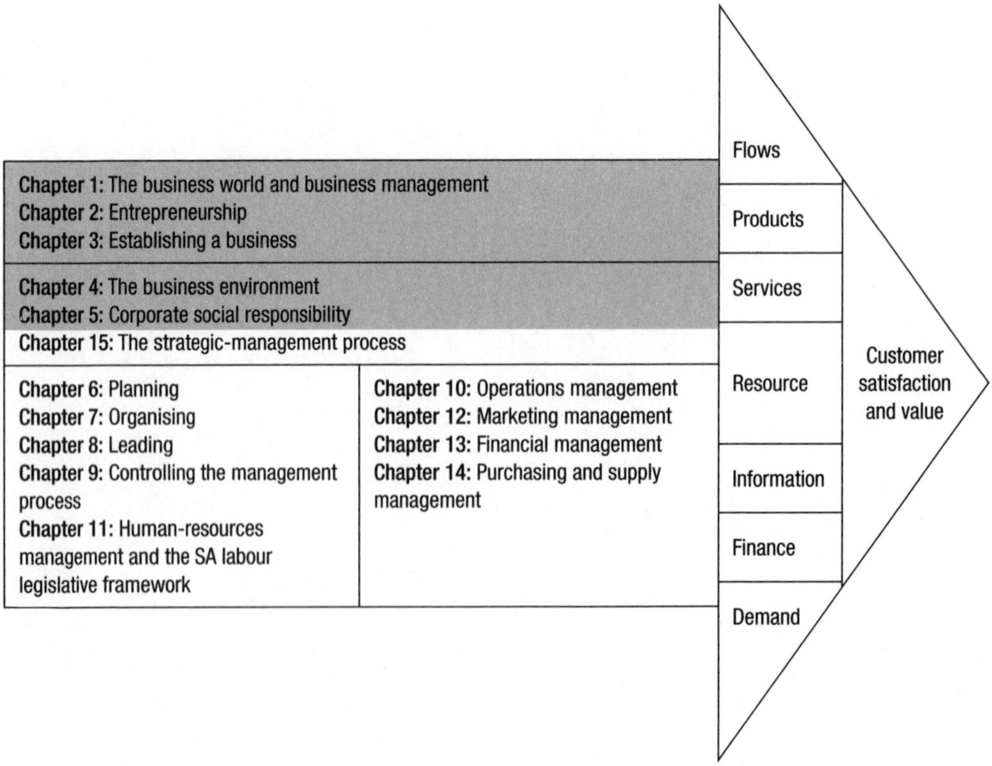

Source: Adapted from Mentzer, T. J. (ed.). 2001. *Supply Chain Management.* London: Sage, pp. 22–23.

CHAPTER

1

THE BUSINESS WORLD AND BUSINESS MANAGEMENT

The purpose of this chapter

This chapter discusses the role of business in society and explains how a business organisation in a market economy employs the various resources of a nation (its natural resources, human resources, financial resources and entrepreneurship) in order to satisfy the need for products and services. The chapter gives an overview of the prevailing economic systems in the world and explains how the business organisation functions in a market economy.

Learning outcomes

On completion of this chapter you should be able to:

- explain the role the business organisation plays in making available the products and services society must have to exist and thrive
- describe the needs of society and how a business organisation satisfies those needs in a market economy
- distinguish between the world's three main economic systems
- explain the interface between a business organisation and a market economy
- describe the nature and purpose of business management as a science, where the enabling factors, methods and principles of the business are studied to ensure the efficient functioning of a business organisation
- comment on the development of business management as a science
- distinguish between and comment on the different management functions.

1.1 Introduction

In a market economy, the business world can be seen as a complex system that involves transforming resources into products and services. These products and services must meet the **needs** of people in exchange for a profit. This description of business emphasises four different elements:

- human activities
- production
- exchange
- profit.

These elements are discussed in detail in section 1.2, but first consider the case study below. This case study provides an illustration of how, in a market economy such as that of South Africa, businesses can grow into industries with their own sets of rules and dynamics, all with the view of striving for the ultimate business goal: making a **profit**.

Case study

External forces impacting on profit-driven enterprises: Turbulence in the South African Airline Industry

The terrorist attacks that occurred on 11 September 2001 in the United States resulted in a global downturn in air travel, and had a significant impact on the American and European airline industries. United States airlines posted net losses in excess of USD7 billion and 80 000 jobs were lost in the United States alone as a direct result of the attacks.

Between January 2001 and December 2005, United States airlines as a group lost nearly USD35 billion[1], although this was not completely owing to the 2001 terrorist attacks. Globally, the airline industry was hit by unprecedented price increases in jet fuel as well as health scares. These health scares were responses to illnesses such as the Severe Acute Respiratory Syndrome (SARS), which started in Asia in 2002, and Swine Flu (a strain of the H1N1 virus), which spread globally through flights out of Mexico in early 2009[2]. These are examples of unparalleled events that occurred outside the airlines' control, and outside the control of the airline industry as a whole. Such events resulted in decreased demand for air traffic. This then led to a fall in revenue and consequently a decline in profits and, in many cases, losses.

Amidst this global downturn, air travel to and from South Africa increased as there was a change in what tourists and business people perceived as a "safe destination"[3]. In 2007, in excess of nine million foreigners visited South Africa (an 8,3% increase since 2006)[4] where 2,5 million visitors entered the country by air travel (the second most frequently used mode of travel in South Africa after road transport)[5]. The Airports Company South Africa (ACSA) recorded that more than 36 million departing and arriving passengers (domestic and international) were handled on the ACSA network during the 2007/2008 financial year[6].

In anticipation of the 2010 FIFA World Cup, ACSA invested in excess of R19 billion for the construction of infrastructure. This capital injection put pressure on the company's current cash flow. However, the capital invested was essential to provide the required capacity for the expected traffic demand of 2010 (a target of ten million) and to meet forecasted future growth[7]. The infrastructure costs include the costs of upgrading the Cape Town International Airport and La Mercy Airport, as well as the cost of building the brand-new King Shaka Airport near Durban.

The growth in the South African airline industry since 2002 has been phenomenal. Climbing at 8% per annum between 2002 and 2007, this growth has been far faster than the growth of the gross domestic product (GDP), which averaged in the region of 3% to 4% per year during that period.

South Africa's largest domestic and international airline, state-owned South African Airways (SAA), carries an average of seven million domestic, regional and international passengers a year. However, although SAA has benefited from the growth in air travel to and within South

Africa, the airline faces stiff competition. SAA's net profit for 2005 was R65 million, down from over R2 billion in 2001[8]. Moreover, the airline revealed a loss of R883 million in the 2006 financial year. Pulling itself back up, the airline posted a net profit of R123 million for the 2007 financial year. However, this profit excluded the restructuring costs of R1,35 billion, which was required to turn the airline around to regain its position and profits[9].

While for many years SAA dominated the aviation scene in Southern Africa (and the rest of Africa), in recent years its position in the airline industry has been seriously challenged. Despite the relatively small air-travel market in South Africa and the impact of the global economic slowdown, the country's airline industry is still growing and remains highly competitive. While still having to compete with traditional rival airlines such as British Airways and Lufthansa in the international arena, SAA faced a growing challenge in the domestic airline market. Following considerable deregulation of the South African airline industry, a number of smaller low-cost domestic airlines entered the market, the first of which was kulula.com in July 2001 (growing the domestic airline market by approximately 10% within just two years of its launch[10]), followed by 1time Airlines in 2004.

In a very short time, these low-cost carriers (LCCs) were able to leverage their resources, particularly technological resources, and capitalise on the opportunities that were presented in South Africa's growing market economy. Kulula.com was the first airline in South Africa to introduce the concept of e-ticketing, allowing for savings in commission and agents' fees of between 12% and 15%. Further savings were achieved through the airline's "no-frills" strategy. Other LCCs followed suit with similar "least-cost systems". Within a few short years, the smaller airlines revolutionised the way South Africans book and pay for their air tickets, and at the same time changed the competitive dynamics of the South African airline industry. Particularly in domestic air travel, it would appear as though price is fast becoming one of the main decision-making criteria for many consumers.

In 2003, SAA had made the following statement to Business Day: "SAA is not a low-cost carrier and therefore has no reason to change its market positioning. Most of its passengers are discerning business people who value the frequency, convenience, punctuality and reliability of flights the most."[11] However, in 2006, SAA introduced, amidst a cloud of controversy, its own LCC, Mango, to compete directly with kulula.com and 1time. Two years later, SAA experienced extreme losses, and needed the help of an expensive turnaround strategy to restructure its organisation towards profits, while low-cost carriers were cruising in the market.

In 2007, South Africa's Nationwide Airlines, originally a full-service carrier (FSC) like SAA, changed its operating model and joined the attractive realm of successful LCCs in South Africa. In November that year, the airline was temporarily suspended after an engine fell off one of its Boeing 737-200s during take-off at the Cape Town International Airport. Soon after, during March and April 2008, the airline experienced a 30% rise in its fuel costs and, perhaps as result of its accident, a decrease in passenger numbers[12]. Adding to this, a Black Economic Empowerment (BEE) deal, which could have helped alleviate the plight of Nationwide Airlines, fell through. As a result of all the above-mentioned factors, the airline had no choice but to cease all flight operations, thus leading to its liquidation[13].

The South African airline industry has also not been exempt from the impacts of the global financial crisis. South Africa fell victim to the global economic slowdown in the second half of 2008. In the first half of 2009, the country was declared to be in recession as it had experienced two quarters of negative growth in its GDP. So, while profit is, of course, the major objective for South African airlines, consumers have tighter wallets and businesses' budgets are almost exhausted, which affects leisure and business air travellers respectively. Therefore at this stage the ultimate aim of the organisations is survival.

While the fight for market share has stirred much-needed competition in the airline industry, only time will tell how long the South African airline industry will be able to keep up its aggressive and sustained price war. Will the 2010 FIFA World Cup come just in time to give further impetus to the race for profits or will it merely be a saving grace for the South Africa airline industry?

1.2 The role of business in society

The **business world** is a complex system of individuals and business organisations that, in a market economy, involves the activity of transforming resources into products and services in order to meet peoples' needs. These products and services are offered to the market in exchange for profit. This description of business emphasises four different elements:

- Firstly, business involves human activities. Business organisations are managed by people. While businesses may own property, machines and money, all of these are managed or operated by people.
- Secondly, business involves production. Production is the **transformation** of certain **resources** into products and services, as illustrated in Figure 1.1. This may be, for example, the conversion of flour, sugar and butter into bread, or the conversion of bricks, sand, cement, wood and steel into a house. Indeed, even services are produced. A hospital provides an example of this: labour, beds and medicine are converted into a health service. The South African airline industry offers another example: passengers are transported safely and efficiently to their required destinations, and as this happens, the passengers (consumers) become part of the transformation process.
- Thirdly, business involves exchange. Businesses produce products and services, not for their own use, but to exchange for money or for other products and services.

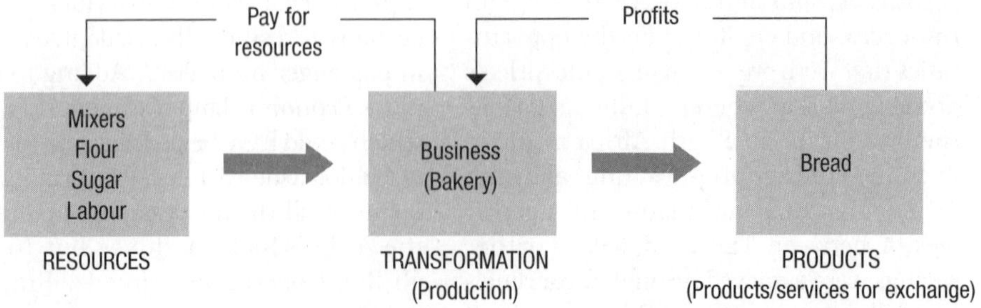

Figure 1.1: How entrepreneurs transform a nation's resources into products and services

- Finally, business involves profit. Few individuals or business organisations can continue producing products and services without earning a profit. Profit is the reward for meeting the needs of people, and it enables businesses to pay for resources and to make a living. That is why the airline industry case study ends by raising the question of how long the price war between the various airlines can be sustained. Without profits being generated, some of the airlines might cease to exist.

Some businesses produce tangible products such as bread, cars, houses or bicycles. Other businesses produce services such as entertainment, communication, insurance or transport (see the case study of the airline industry on pages 4–6).

Business is the means by which society endeavours to satisfy its needs and improve its standard of living. At the heart of all business activity are entrepreneurs, who start new ventures and thereby create jobs, economic growth and, it is hoped, prosperity. No-one invented the business world. It is the result of activities related to meeting the needs of people in a market economy.

The most important characteristic of the business world in the developed countries of the West and Asia is the freedom of individuals to establish any business of their choice and to produce, within limits, any product or service the market requires. This system, in which individuals themselves decide what to produce, how to produce it and at what price to sell their product, is called a **market economy** (or **market system**). This is the prevailing economic system in South Africa.

The market economy is a complex system comprising various types of small and large business organisations that collectively mobilise the resources of a country to satisfy the needs of its inhabitants. These businesses group together to form **industries**. Figure 1.2 shows the composition of the South African business world in terms of major industry sectors and their contribution to the economy.

The business world or economic structure of South Africa resembles that of many industrialised countries. Large businesses such as Standard Bank, Vodacom, Anglo American, Barloworld and many other large public corporations – over 400 of which are listed on the Johannesburg Securities Exchange (JSE) – are responsible for most of South Africa's economic activity.

Large businesses in South Africa contribute to about 64% of the country's economic activity, while small and medium-sized enterprises (SMEs), which are mostly family or individually owned, contribute to about 30% of economic activity. Micro-enterprises,

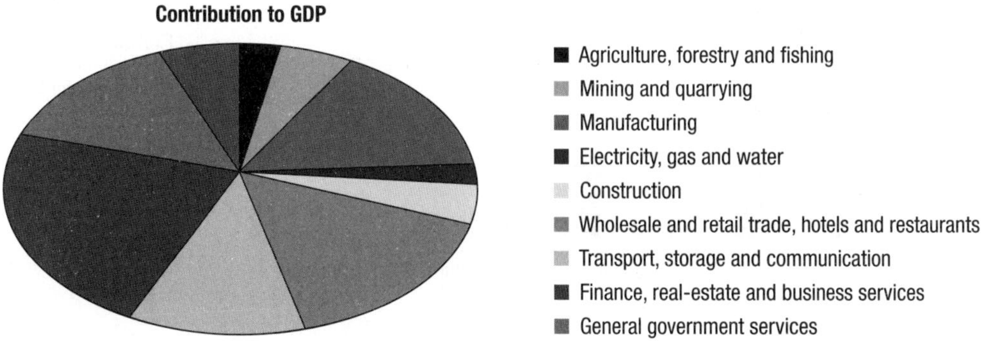

Figure 1.2: The composition of the South African business world in terms of contribution to GDP

Source: Statistics South Africa. 2009. "Gross Domestic Product" (*Statistical release P0441*), Second quarter.

consisting of one-person businesses, contribute to 6% of economic activity.

However, strictly speaking, micro-enterprises (the informal sector) are not regarded as part of the formal economy because the people involved in these enterprises live primarily on a subsistence or survival basis. Moreover, such people put pressure on the infrastructure of inner-city areas and contribute nothing in the form of income tax.

The variety of needs that a country has determines the complexity of its business environment. In First World countries, businesses are the primary source of products, services and employment. Figure 1.3 shows the importance of the South African business world in providing employment in South Africa.

Business creates wealth, is a catalyst for economic growth and is credited with bringing about the high standard of living in developed countries. Take, for example, the role business has played in the United States. In the space of two centuries, the United States went from being a relatively undeveloped nation to a leading industrial nation, which at that time owned nearly 40% of the world's wealth with only 6% of the world's population. (Of course, business and industry environments, and hence economies, are constantly changing, and much has changed for the United States and the rest of the world since the economic turmoil of 2008.)

Business also serves the community indirectly by means of technological innovation, research and development, and improvements to infrastructure. It plays a crucial role in supporting, in various ways, education, the development of human resources, the arts, conservation, sport and other activities that improve the quality of life of a community.

The business world and society both depend on and influence each other. At the heart of the business world is the entrepreneur or businessperson. In the pursuit of profit, entrepreneurs constantly search for new ideas, new products and new technologies. In so doing, they initiate innovation and bring

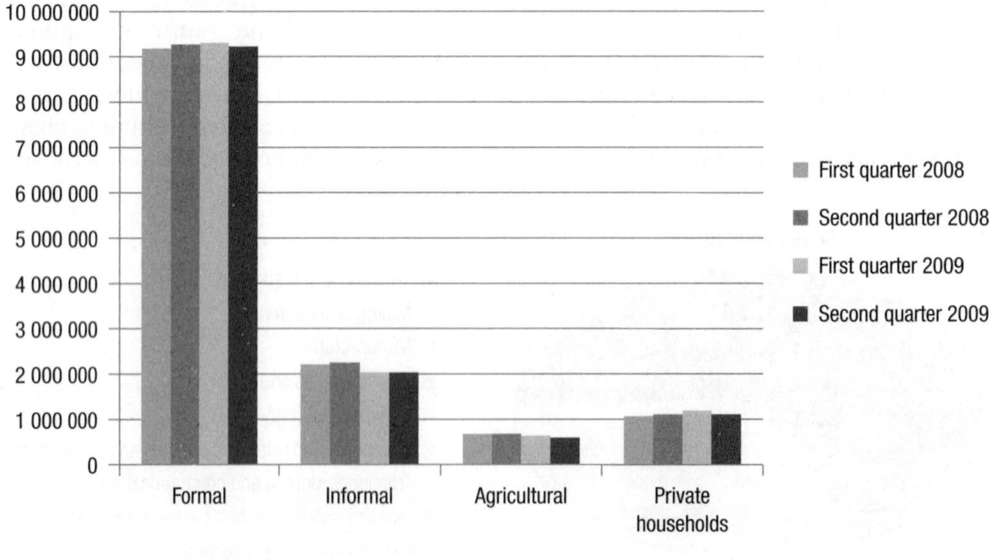

Figure 1.3: The contribution of the business sector to employment in South Africa

Source: Statistics South Africa. 2008. *Labour Force Survey* (Second quarter) & Statistics South Africa. 2009. *Labour Force Survey* (Second quarter).

about change. Their decisions on investment, production and employment influence not only the state of the economy, but also the prosperity of whole communities.

Consider, for example, the influence of the local entrepreneur, Mark Shuttleworth, and the positive effect that his company, HBD Venture Capital, has had on many growing, early-stage South African companies. HBD, established in 2000, invests in companies that have just started generating revenue and have positive growth prospects globally. Three such company's on HBD's portfolio are Moyo (the African food, art, music and retail business), OrderTalk (a company that provides software for internet-based ordering to the restaurant, fast-food and hospitality industries) as well as the taxi operator, SA Cab[14].

Conversely, society exerts its influence on business in a number of ways. If businesses fail to abide by the expectations and desires of the community (for example, by employing fraudulent or unethical practices, by polluting or degrading the environment, or by indulging in profiteering and monopolistic exploitation), the community will often react by instituting regulations and legislation to curb such practices. Consider an example relating to the airline industry: in 2006 at OR Tambo International Airport in Johannesburg, more than a million litres of jet fuel was accidentally allowed to leak from the airport into the nearby Blaauwpan Dam. Residents in the neighbouring suburbs did not sit by idly, but rather chose to put pressure on the Airports Company of South Africa (ACSA) to take responsibility for the disaster. An example relating to fraudulent and unethical practices is the bread scandal of 2007. Tiger Brands and other bread producers were accused of fixing the price of bread, an allegation that was brought to the attention of the Competition Commission by a small-business owner. Tiger Brands admitted to the price-fixing and received a fine of almost R100 million[15]. The price-fixing had abused not only the retailers and smaller businesses selling the basic commodity, but also the ultimate consumers, especially the poor. This, as well as the milk price-fixing scandal of 2008, is an example of a cartel that exploited the community and which, in effect, can further impoverish poorer consumers and ultimately an economy. To eliminate such anti-competitive behaviour, in April 2009 the presidency assented to the Consumer Protection Act (No. 68 of 2008) to, among many other objectives, prohibit unfair business practices and promote a consistent legislative and enforcement framework to protect consumers[16].

The attitude of society towards the business world is by no means consistent, for in a changing environment the community will, at different times, have different expectations of the business world. If the business world fails to respond to the expectations of the community, the attitude of the community towards the business world is likely to change. Consider, for example, the issue of equity in South African organisations. When South Africa became a democracy in 1994, businesses were obliged to include Black people in their organisations. Because of the slow rate of response to this call, however, society reacted through government by instituting legislation that forces the business world to transform its organisations so that Black people are included at all levels. The Employment Equity Act (No. 55 of 1998), as well as the Broad-Based Black Economic Empowerment Act (No. 53 of 2003), are examples of society's response to the exclusion from business of people of colour, women and people with disabilities.

Most Western countries have, over the years, come to regard the business sector as a valuable social institution because it has helped to realise society's needs and also to raise the standard of living. In the closing decades of the twentieth century, however, most Western nations decided that a high standard of living amid a deteriorating physical environment and inadequate social progress does not make sense. The business world is thus under continuous and often increasing pressure with regard to social responsibility, affirmative action, business ethics, consumerism and environmental damage. A discussion of these factors will follow.

The **social responsibility** of business is a concept that originated in media revelations of malpractice by businesses and the resultant insistence of society on restricting such malpractice through regulation. Historically, the social responsibility of a business has been measured by its contribution towards employment opportunities and by its contribution to the economy. But while these factors remain important, many other factors are nowadays included in assessing the social performance of a business. These other factors are the provision of a responsible and safe workplace, the provision of housing, concern about health issues, involvement with community issues, environmental awareness and the empowerment of previously disadvantaged individuals, both economically and managerially. (Social responsibility is discussed in more detail in Chapter 5.)

Affirmative action (equity regarding an organisation's workforce) is aimed at creating equal employment opportunities for all by ensuring that workforces are composed in roughly the same proportions as the groups

The growth of broad-based BEE in South Africa

The research group Empowerdex examined a broad spectrum of empowerment issues. An important finding was that by 2006, at least 10% of South Africa's top 40 companies had sold in excess of 25% of their shares to Black shareholders. In the decade up until 2006, approximately 1 360 BEE transactions worth R285 billion had taken place.

A further indicator of the impact of broad-based BEE in South Africa, as highlighted by Empowerdex, is the number of Black directors on the boards of JSE-listed companies. In 1992, South Africa had 15 Black directors on the boards of JSE-listed companies. In 1997, there were 98. In 2003, that increased to 207 and in 2006, there were more than 400 Black directors holding 556 board seats at JSE-listed companies. In 2008, there were 487 Black individuals holding 714 directorship positions, where these individuals held 24% of all directorship positions of the top 100 JSE-listed companies.

In 2009, the top five empowerment companies, according to Empowerdex, were as follows:

- Adcorp Holdings Ltd (Company Empowerment score: 88,71%)
- Hosken Consolidated Investments Ltd (Company Empowerment score: 84,63%)
- Nedbank Group Ltd (Company Empowerment score: 82,45%)
- Kelly Group Ltd (Company Empowerment score: 82,28%)
- Gijima Ast Group Ltd (Company Empowerment score: 80,92%).

Broad-based BEE has come a long way in South Africa since the Broad-Based Black Economic Empowerment Act (No. 53 of 2003) came into effect. However, of the above figures, the majority of the Black shareholders are in non-executive directorship positions. Therefore, more Black males and females still need to be appointed in executive directorship positions. In 2008, of the 1 023 executive directors, only 118 were Black individuals (and of these only 16 were female). The codes of good practice on broad-based BEE set a target of 50% of Blacks at the level of executive director, and a target of 25% of Black females at this same level.

Sources: Empowerdex. 2006. "Top Empowerment Companies Survey". Johannesburg: Empowerdex.; Empowerdex. 2009. "Top Empowerment Companies Survey". [Online] Available: http://www.empowerdex.co.za Accessed 20 November 2009 & Jack, V. 2008. "Black directors at listed companies inch up to 24%" in *Business Report* [Online] Available: http://www.busrep.co.za/index.php?from=rss_Business%20Report&ArticleId=4631422.

that make up the population as a whole. In South Africa, the Employment Equity Act became law in 1998. The stated intention of the Act is to eliminate unfair discrimination, ensure employment equity and achieve a diverse workplace that is broadly representative of the country's demographic realities. The inclusion of Black people and other designated groups at management level is of crucial importance to South Africa's economy.

The South African government's Accelerated and Shared Growth Initiative for South Africa (AsgiSA) strategy aimed for an economic-growth target of 4,5% per year for 2005 to 2009, and of 6% per year thereafter. However, while South Africa's GDP grew by approximately 5,1% in 2007, it only grew by 3,1% in 2008[17], and then followed the rest of the world into recession. By June 2009, South Africa's GDP had decreased by an annualised rate of 6,4%[18].

For the South African economy to grow at the much-needed level of 4,5% or higher, there must be enough skilled managers to drive the economy. It is widely recognised that a moderate real economic growth rate of 2,7% per year will require an additional 100 000 managers each year for the foreseeable future.

Since the traditional source of managers (the population of White males) has been exhausted, most of the managers that are required will have to come from the Black population. Since 1994, there has been a steady increase in the number of Black people in management, yet, despite this, White people, especially White males, remain over-represented in management structures. According to the Commission for Employment Equity, in South Africa in 2007/2008, 12,6% of senior managers were Black men and 50% were White men. Females of all colours accounted for only 24,9% of senior managers[19]. Regarding middle managers and professionally qualified and experienced specialists, 15,5% were Black men and 38,7% were White men. White and Black females represented 18,5% and 8,6% of this category respectively.

Business ethics is a concept that is closely related to social responsibility[20], except that business ethics focuses specifically on the ethical behaviour of managers and executives in the business world. Managers, in particular, are expected to maintain high ethical standards. (Chapter 5 will focus on social responsibility and business ethics.)

While there are business concepts regulating the business environment, its employees and society as a whole, specific reference should be made to the concept of consumerism.

Consumerism is a social force that protects consumers against unsafe products and malpractice by exerting moral and economic pressure on businesses. In South Africa, the South African National Consumer Union acts as a watchdog for consumers. A recent example would be the introduction of the Consumer Protection Act (No. 68 of 2008), as mentioned above in the Tiger Brands price-fixing scandal. Social pressure on businesses often results in increased government regulation to force compliance with social requirements and norms. Ultimately, the will of the community is seen to prevail.

People have also become concerned about the **environmental damage** that can be caused by businesses. Businesses are frequently responsible for air, water and soil pollution, and for the resultant detrimental effects on fauna and flora. Citizens often form pressure groups to protect the environment. For example, because of pressure from the community, the construction of a new plant that Iscor had planned to establish at Saldanha was delayed for 17 months. Iscor eventually had to build the plant eight kilometres away from the initial site, so as to avoid possible damage to the ecology. Another South African example is the 2006 jet-fuel leak from OR Tambo International Airport, which was mentioned above. This leak resulted in massive ecological damage to aquatic and bird life.

The business world is so interconnected with society that it may be defined as a process that uses a country's means of production to produce products and services to satisfy the needs of the people. The primary purpose of business in a free-market system is to make a profit while satisfying the needs of the people. (A brief overview of the needs of communities, and of the means of satisfying these needs, is given below to explain not only the purpose of business in a market system, but also the extent of the field of **business management**, which is the focus of this book.)

1.3 Needs and need satisfaction

1.3.1 The multiplicity of human needs

The continued existence of humans depends upon the constant satisfaction of numerous needs, both physical and psychological. The work that every member of a community performs is directly or indirectly related to need satisfaction. Even in the most remote inhabited areas, certain products and services are needed.

Needs may be very simple and few, as in the case of a rural and under-developed community in which individuals or families, with the help of nature, find the resources necessary to satisfy a simple need structure. For example, the traditional lifestyle of the San people of the Kalahari depends on the satisfaction of the most basic necessities for survival. However, in highly industrialised communities, needs may be numerous and may therefore require large and complex organisations to satisfy them.

A need may have a physical, psychological or social origin, but no matter what form it takes, it requires satisfaction. The number of identifiable needs is infinite. Some needs, particularly those that are physiological, are related to absolutely basic necessities, such as the satisfaction of hunger and thirst. These needs have to be satisfied for the sake of survival. Other needs, particularly those that are psychological, relate to things that make life more pleasant, but that are not essential to survival. These needs include needs for holidays, video machines, dishwashers,

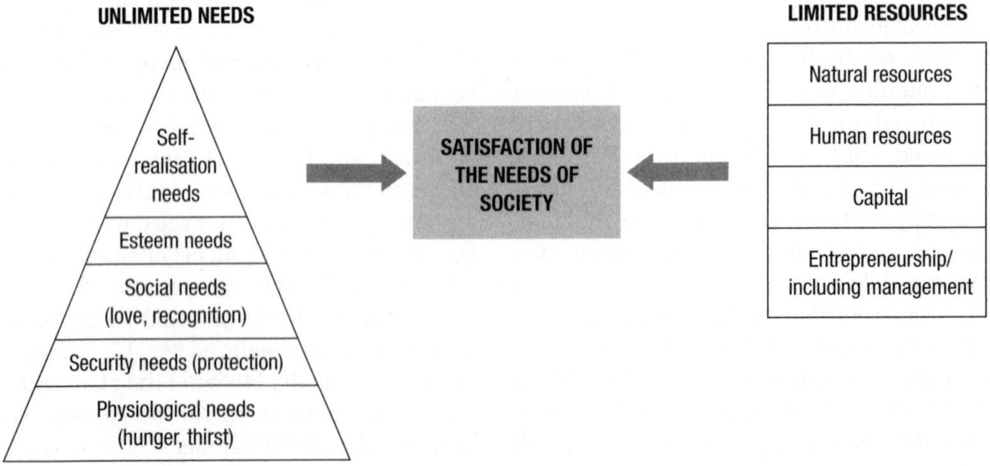

Figure 1.4: The needs and resources of the community

Source: Based on "The pyramid of human needs" from Maslow, A.H. et al. 1954. *A theory of human motivation*. New York: Harper, pp. 35–47. Reprinted by permission of Ann Maslow Kaplan.

tennis courts, luxury cars, and innumerable products and services of a similar nature.

Basic physical and psychological needs may also overlap. For example, people do not wear clothes merely for warmth and protection, but also to be fashionable. Some people enjoy expensive delicacies accompanied by fine wines in luxurious restaurants, and in this way simultaneously satisfy survival needs and psychological needs.

Abraham Maslow (1908–1970) was an American clinical psychologist who explained variable and unlimited human needs by means of a hierarchy of needs. According to Maslow, human needs range, in a definite order, from the most essential for survival to the least necessary. The left-hand side of Figure 1.4 on page 12 shows **Maslow's hierarchy** of needs.

It is clear from Figure 1.4 that the need hierarchy is composed in such a way that the order of importance ranges from basic physiological needs, which have to be satisfied for survival, to psychological needs, with which the higher levels of the hierarchy are mainly concerned. Because humans are social beings who live in communities, they also have collective needs, such as protection and education. An individual, a family or a community first satisfies the most urgent needs, and then, when this has been done, moves up to the next level until the higher psychological levels are reached. With changing circumstances, individuals not only desire more possessions, but also continually want still newer and better products and services. For example, radio offers entertainment, but black-and-white television is believed to offer better entertainment, and colour television still better entertainment. Once these products and services have been acquired, however, the need arises for a

Table 1.1: Expenditure patterns of South African households for the 2005/2006 tax year

Products and services bought	Total expenditure (%)
Food and non-alcoholic beverages	14,4
Alcoholic beverages and tobacco	1,2
Clothing and footwear	5,0
Housing, water, electricity, gas and other fuels	23,6
Furnishings, household equipment and routine maintenance of the house	6,9
Health	1,7
Transport	19,9
Communication	3,5
Recreation and culture	4,6
Education	2,4
Restaurants and hotels	2,2
Miscellaneous products and services	14,4
Other unclassified expenses	0,3
Total	100

Source: Statistics South Africa. 2008. *Income and expenditure of households 2005/2006: Analysis of results.* [Online] Available: http://www.statssa.gov.za/Publications/Report-01-00-01/Report-01-00-012005.pdf Accessed 30 August 2009.

DVD player, more television channels – as evidenced in the phenomenal growth of DSTV – and more and better programmes. And so it goes on. As society satisfies one need, a new one comes into existence, and there is no end to the constantly increasing number of human needs.

Table 1.1 on page 13 indicates some of the needs people have. It is interesting to note that in 2005/2006, South African households spent on average 14,4% of their income on food, which satisfies one of the most basic needs. *Per capita* spending, however, has dropped substantially since 2000.

It is important to keep in mind that the percentages given in Table 1.1 are of average household consumption. Since South Africa has a diverse population of people, it also has diverse needs and consumption patterns.

1.3.2 Society's limited resources

If one considers the multiple and unlimited needs of humans, especially in highly developed societies, it is clear that there are only limited resources available to satisfy all their needs. Although Western countries, most notably the United States, possess very impressive means of production, they do not have unlimited resources. Consider, for example, the increases in crude oil prices that have occurred over the past few years. These increases have been brought about by the fact that the world has a limited supply of oil. It is estimated that there were originally around 2 000 gigabarrels of oil on earth. Society has already used up 45–70% of this precious resource, using half in just the last 40 years[21]. In 2008 alone, global oil reserves fell by 3 billion to 1,258 billion barrels. Analysts believe that it will take 42 years to rebuild the stock to the previous level[22]. This illustrates the impact that society has had on the world's already scarce natural resources in just one year. The impact of these increases also hit the airline industry hard: in 2005, SAA's fuel bill increased from R1,7 billion to R4,9 billion, and this increase has remained a challenge to the airline. By 2008, the cost of jet fuel, SAA's biggest cost contributor, constituted 30% of the airline's operating costs, and the airline consumed approximately 750 thousand barrels (120 million litres) of jet fuel per month[23].

A country has only a certain number of people in its workforce to operate a certain number of machines, and a certain number of factories, hospitals and offices to produce a certain quantity of products and services. In other words, the resources of any community are scarce, and can easily be exceeded by its needs. Resources are therefore the basic inputs in the production of products and services, and they are also known as production factors.

Figure 1.4 on page 12 shows those resources society possesses in limited quantities only and which it uses to satisfy its needs: natural resources, human resources, capital and entrepreneurship. These resources are discussed in more detail below.

1.3.2.1 Natural resources

Natural resources, also known as the production factor of land, include agricultural land, industrial sites, residential stands, minerals and metals, forests, water and all such resources that nature puts at the disposal of humankind. The most important characteristic of natural resources is that their supply cannot be increased. In other words, the amount of natural resources any one country possesses is given, and therefore in most cases is scarce. Moreover, human effort is usually necessary to process these resources into need-satisfying products, for example, in the transformation of forests into timber and paper, or, in the case of the airline industry, the refining of oil to produce the jet fuels that aeroplanes need to fly.

1.3.2.2 Human resources

Human resources, also known as the production factor of labour, include the physical and mental talents and skills of people employed to create products and services. People receive wages for their labour. The size of the labour force of any country, and therefore, in a sense, the availability of that production factor, is determined by, among other things, the size of the population, the level of its education and training, the proportion of women in the labour force and the retirement age. For the manufacturing processes of a country to be of any value, the country's labour force has to be trained for certain periods and to certain levels of skill to be able to produce the products and services required. Training periods will differ depending on the skill being learnt. For example, the training period of a flight attendant will be considerably shorter than the training period of a pilot. The combination of human skills is of particular importance, for without this combination, natural and financial resources cannot be utilised productively.

1.3.2.3 Capital

Capital is represented by the buildings, machinery, cash registers, computers and other products produced, not for final human consumption, but for making possible the further production of final consumer products. Capital products usually have a long working life, for example, office buildings, factories, machinery and other equipment may be used over and over again in the production process. In the airline industry, capital usually has an exceptionally long working life, but also comes at a very high price. The reason for the scarcity factor of capital is that a community takes years to build up its stock of capital. Every year it spends a certain amount on things such as roads, bridges, mineshafts, factories and shopping centres, and there is always a shortage of these things. The owners or suppliers of capital are usually remunerated in the form of interest or rent.

Case study

Going green – influencing sustainability and profitability

In the last decade, sustainable business practice has become an important concept for business organisations.

'Project Green' is an initiative that was launched by kulula.com in 2007. A central aspect of the project is creating public awareness of the issues relating to carbon emissions. Kulula's users are invited to play a part in making a difference. Since the launch of the initiative, Kulula has raised over one million rand, which will be spent planting indigenous trees and grass at schools and rural communities throughout South Africa in partnership with Food & Trees South Africa.

The Project Green initiative:

- increases biodiversity and the natural ecosystem
- creates work opportunities by offering jobs on tree-planting projects
- develops small-business opportunities
- educates society on the importance of greener living and where to start.

Kulula's new fleet of Boeing 737s are more fuel efficient (burning 26% less fuel) and less harmful to the environment than the old fleet of MD82s.

The airline industry is leaving a huge carbon footprint in the world's atmosphere. Kulula's green initiative is a good example to illustrate what a business organisation can do to lessen the environmental harm it does, help the community and rejuvenate the natural environment. At the same time, the business organisation helps itself by creating a sustainable and profitable business environment in which to operate.

Source: kulula.com. 2010. "Project Green". [Online] Available: https://www.kulula.com/info/projectgrinfo.aspx Accessed 11 February 2010.

1.3.2.4 Entrepreneurship

Entrepreneurship is the fourth factor of production. It refers to the collective capacity of entrepreneurs, who are those individuals who accept the risks involved in providing products and services for their society. The airline 1time, mentioned in the airline industry case study at the start of this chapter, was started by four entrepreneurs: Gavin Harrison, Glenn Orsmond, Rodney James and Sven Petersen. Entrepreneurs are rewarded with profits for the risks they take and the initiative they show, but they suffer losses for errors in judgement. The production factor of entrepreneurship is scarce in the sense that not everybody in a community is prepared to take the risks that are inevitable when providing products or services, or has the ability to manage an organisation successfully. Although the contemporary focus on entrepreneurship is mainly on small and medium businesses, entrepreneurs are not limited to these. A large or corporate business is also a place for entrepreneurship.

1.3.3 Need satisfaction: A cycle

To be able to satisfy the needs of the community, entrepreneurs have to utilise scarce resources in certain combinations in order to produce products and services. Economic value is created in the course of the production process by combining production factors in such a way that final products are produced for consumers. A nation's survival depends on the satisfaction of its people's needs. Striving for need satisfaction with the limited resources available is an incentive for economic progress.

Given its unlimited needs but limited resources, society is confronted with the fundamental **economic problem**: how to ensure the highest possible satisfaction of needs with these scarce resources. This is also known as the **economic principle**. Society cannot always get what it wants, so it must choose how it will use its scarce resources to the maximum effect in order to satisfy its needs. In short, it has to make a decision about solving the following economic issues:

- Which products and services should be produced, and in what quantities? (How many capital products should be produced? How many consumer products should be produced? Should railways or trucks, houses or flats be built? If flats are chosen, how many should be built?)
- Who should produce these products? (Should the state or private individuals take charge of production? Or should this responsibility be shared, as in the case of South Africa's airline industry?)
- How should these products and services be produced, and what resources should be used? (There are various methods of production and types of resources that should be considered. For example, should a production-line method be chosen? Should a labour-intensive approach be used?)
- For whom are these products and services to be produced? (Will the products cater largely for the needs of the rich or the poor? Will services be aimed at business clients or families?)

The answers to address the economic issues listed above are given by the community. The **community** decides which **institutions** should be responsible for the production and distribution of products and services, as well as the role that each institution has to play.

Figure 1.5 on page 17 shows how, against the background of its needs and by means of its political process, the community determines the **economic system** in which the necessary need-satisfying institutions are established.

In a market economy, need-satisfying institutions, including business organisations and **government organisations**, offer products and services on the market in return for profit. If the community is not satisfied with the way in which these organisations provide for its

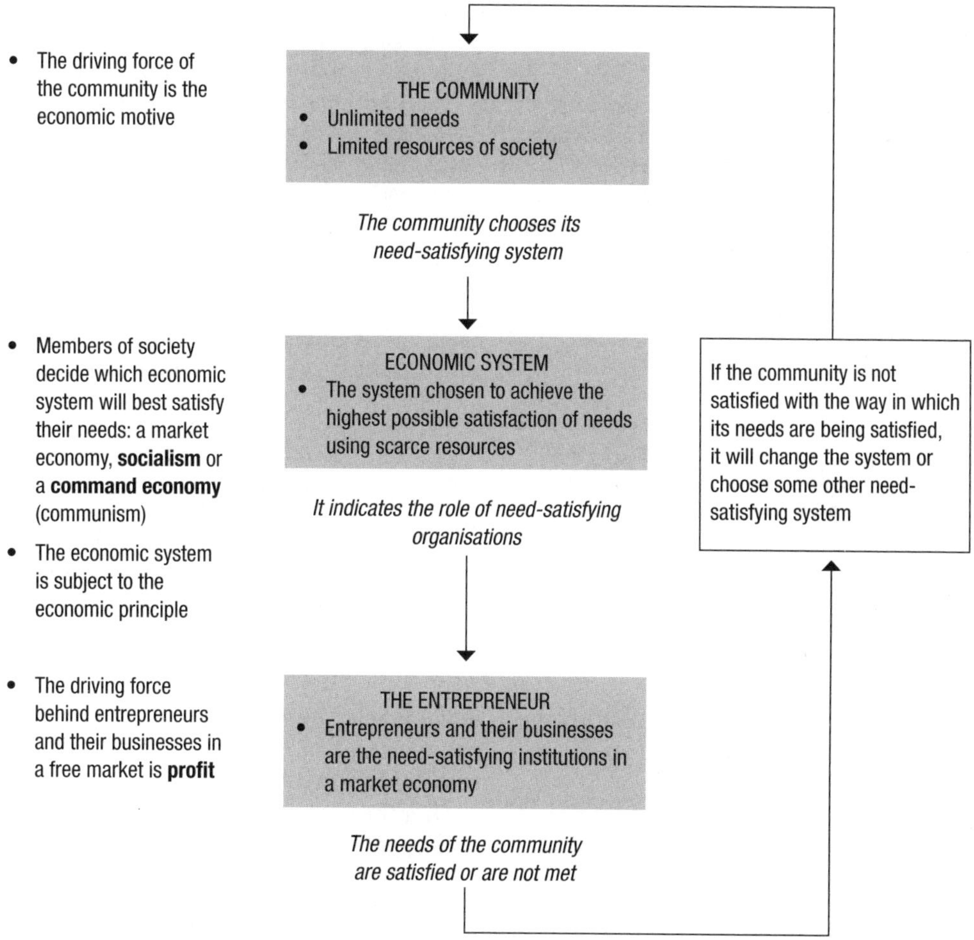
• The driving force of the community is the economic motive
THE COMMUNITY
• Unlimited needs
• Limited resources of society
The community chooses its need-satisfying system
• Members of society decide which economic system will best satisfy their needs: a market economy, socialism or a command economy (communism)
• The economic system is subject to the economic principle
ECONOMIC SYSTEM
• The system chosen to achieve the highest possible satisfaction of needs using scarce resources
It indicates the role of need-satisfying organisations
If the community is not satisfied with the way in which its needs are being satisfied, it will change the system or choose some other need-satisfying system
• The driving force behind entrepreneurs and their businesses in a free market is profit
THE ENTREPRENEUR
• Entrepreneurs and their businesses are the need-satisfying institutions in a market economy
The needs of the community are satisfied or are not met

Figure 1.5: The cycle of need-satisfaction in a community

needs, it will change the economic system or choose a new need-satisfying system. The appearance of new businesses and the disappearance of others are examples of this cycle of need satisfaction in the community.

Another example of this cycle at work that illustrates the community getting what it wants occurred in the form of South African businesses offering longer shopping hours from 1965 onwards. This change occurred because of the large-scale urbanisation of South African society and the participation of women in the labour markets. These women found the opportunity to shop on Saturday afternoons and Sundays very useful.

Over the years, different communities have developed different approaches in order to satisfy their needs, and different economic systems have been tried and tested. Each of these systems, as chosen by various communities to satisfy specific needs, has its own approach to the fundamental economic problem of what products and services should be provided by whom and for whom.

The study of these systems constitutes the field of economics as a social science and examines the means used to satisfy innumerable human needs with limited resources. Business management, in contrast, is concerned with the institutions that are

The need for communication

The needs of society ultimately culminate in products or services that satisfy particular needs. A case in point is cellphones. People have a basic need to communicate, and where this is possible, to communicate with individuals over a fair distance. During most of the last century, the only way this could be done was by means of the telephone, where the caller first had to call a specific building (house or office) and then wait for the relevant person to be found by whoever answered the phone. The cellphone was, therefore, a response to the need to communicate immediately with a specific individual, without the inconvenience of having to locate the person first or the frustration of dealing with inoperative telephone lines.

As consumer needs have evolved, so did the design and functionality of the cellphone. Cellphones are no longer just a means of communication. Nowadays, cellphones have high-megapixel cameras, radios, MP3 players, memory cards, e-mail and internet access, geographical positioning systems (GPS), touch-screen activation and much more. One can even do banking from one's cellphone.

It is interesting to note how important cellphones are to many South Africans, even among those who have a low income or no income[24]:

- People with a monthly household income of R1 600 or less collectively spent about R260 million on cellphone expenses each month during 2008.
- Among urban adults who do not receive an income, 76% say that they personally own, rent or have use of a cellphone.

created in the economic system to satisfy the needs of a community, and these are mainly **business organisations**.

To provide some necessary background to the study of business management and the role of business organisations in society, a brief overview of the different economic systems now follows.

1.4 The main economic systems

1.4.1 The community and its economic system

Every community is engaged in a struggle for survival that is necessitated by scarcity. Therefore each community needs to have a complex mechanism that is constantly dealing with the complicated task of ensuring that the production and distribution of products occurs. Each country is confronted with the fundamental economic problem of which economic system to choose to solve the problem of what products should be produced and marketed by which producers for which consumers. Each country must decide on some system to solve that problem.

Over the years, countries and communities have approached need satisfaction in different ways. There are three main approaches that are still followed by present-day communities for the solution of their fundamental economic problems. They are the market economy, the command economy and socialism. While these economic systems are often incorrectly referred to as "political ideologies", they should rather be described as "economic systems influenced by politics". It is necessary to take a brief look at these systems to understand the origin and role of business organisations in society. As none of these economic systems is ever found in a pure form, the discussion that follows is merely an exposition of the basic premises of each system.

1.4.2 The market economy

One of the economic systems adopted by humans for the solution of their economic problems is the market economy, also known as the **free-market economy** or free-enterprise system. It is a system in which most products and services demanded by a community are supplied by private organisations seeking profits. It functions on the following assumptions:

- Members of a community may possess assets and earn profits on these.
- The allocation of resources is affected by free markets.
- Members of the community can freely choose between products, services, places of residence and careers.
- The state keeps its interference in the system to a minimum.

In the market economy, particular value is attached to the right of individuals to **possess property** such as land, buildings, equipment or vehicles, including the right to earn an income from this property. This right is also the driving force of the market economy: it stimulates individuals and entrepreneurs to acquire more and to make a profit through the productive utilisation of their assets or their capital. In the pursuit of maximum profits, this **capital**, which is nothing other than the resources of the community, is applied as productively as possible.

This aspect also affects the **distribution of resources** through free markets. The private possession of capital has an important influence on the manner in which resources are allocated or employed in a market economy, as the decisions about what products should be produced by which producers rest with those who own the resources.

This means that farmers, factory owners, industrialists and individuals are free to do what they like with their assets. However, in their decisions concerning production and marketing, they have to take account of the tastes, preferences and other demands of consumers if they want to make a profit. Thus, the question of which consumers' needs should be met (for whom?) is answered. Such decisions in a market economy are not taken by some central body but by a system of free markets, which indirectly puts a price on every production factor or consumer product.

Free markets also imply the third characteristic of this system: **freedom of choice**. The producers are able to decide whether or not they can profitably produce their products at the prices set by the market. This is the producers' free choice. Likewise, the consumer is free to choose whether to buy the product at that price. The consumer is also free to live where he/she wishes and to study and train for whatever career he/she wants to follow. A system of free markets therefore necessarily entails freedom of choice. Private owners of property are free to own what they like and to do with it as they please: rent it out, sell it, exchange it or even give it away. People with businesses are free to produce what they wish and to employ whomever they choose. Similarly, workers, who own their labour, can use this human resource as they choose. In this way, **competition** comes into operation in a system of free markets.

The final characteristic of a free-market economy is **minimum state interference** in markets. The assumption is that the state should merely ensure the proper maintenance of the system without excessive regulation of, or even participation in, the business world.

1.4.3 The command economy

The second type of economic system is a command economy or a centrally directed economic system. Adopted by some countries as an alternative to a market economy, it was until recently known as communism. Its main characteristic is that the state owns and controls the community's resources or factors of production.

A command economy is a system of communal ownership of a country's factors of production in which the individual owns no property, with the exception of private domestic assets. This means that individuals own no land, factories or equipment. The

A free economy creates wealth

The fewer restrictions on economic activity, the wealthier a country's citizens. The Heritage Foundation and *Wall Street Journal's* 2009 Index of Economic Freedom measures how well 183 countries score on an analysis of ten specific components of economic freedom. These components include business freedom, trade freedom, fiscal freedom, government size, monetary freedom, investment freedom, financial freedom, property rights, freedom from corruption and labour freedom. Taken cumulatively, these factors offer an empirical snapshot of a country's level of economic freedom.

Scores are given out of 100, where 100 and 0 represent the maximum and minimum freedom of an economy respectively. The results demonstrate beyond doubt that countries with the highest levels of economic freedom also have the highest living standards.

Out of all the regions, Sub-Saharan Africa scored the lowest on the 2009 Index of Economic Freedom, with an average of 53,1. (This score excluded Zimbabwe, whose hyperinflation was estimated at over 10 000 percent, which would distort the regional average and the world average.) Mauritius scored 74,3, making it the 18th freest economy in the world and the leader in Sub-Saharan Africa. Botswana came second in the region and was rated 34th in the world. South Africa came third in the region with a score of 63,8 and came 61st in the world.

South Africa also scored below the world average in fiscal freedom, making it a relatively poor country, although it is a moderately free economy.

Countries with high scores on the Index of Economic Freedom, such as Hong Kong, which is listed as the freest economy in the world, have an average *per capita* income of USD39 062. Countries with lower scores, such as South Africa, earn a mere USD9 087 *per capita*. It is also quite clear that a country's level of economic freedom is strongly related to its economic performance and has a direct impact on its standard of living, as can be seen in Figure 1.6.

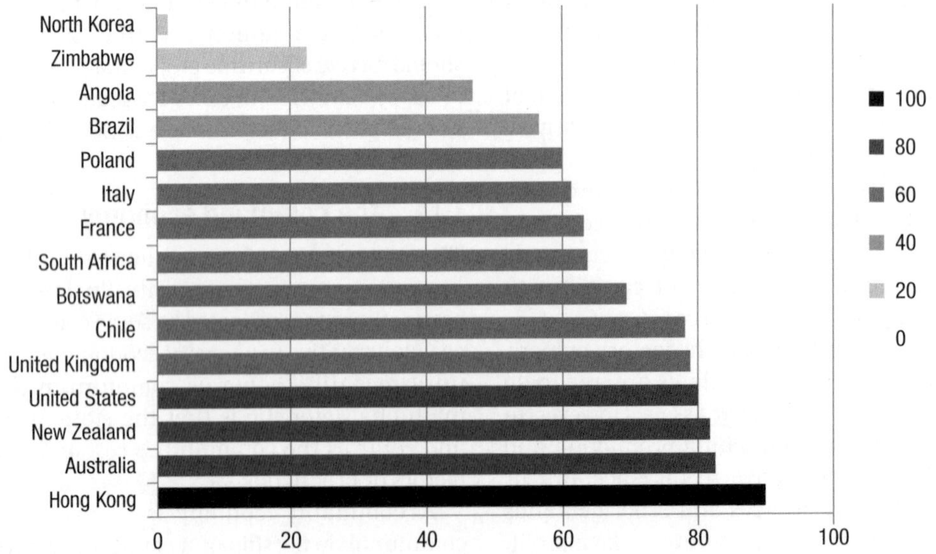

Figure 1.6: Current ratings of economic freedom for various countries

Source: The Heritage Foundation and *Wall Street Journal*. 2009. "Index of Economic Freedom". [Online] Available: http://www.heritage.org/Index/Explore.aspx Accessed 23 November 2009.

state assumes complete responsibility for the production and distribution of products and services, and all decisions about what should be produced – and about how, by whom and for whom it should be produced – rest with a central government.

The choices of products and services are therefore limited to what the state offers; the design of these products falls entirely outside the control of ordinary individuals. It is the state that decides what the needs of the community are, how and where the desired products will be obtainable, and in what quantities they may be used. In the absence of free consumer choice, the profit motive is also absent, as is the competition factor, because, as mentioned above, the state owns the organisations that produce the products and services.

In most countries that adopted a command economy, the system failed because it robbed individuals of the initiative to produce products and services, and it prevented the creation of wealth. The poverty of the Soviet Union and other East European countries and their collapse in the late twentieth century is evidence that the system did not create wealth. Command economies are, nevertheless, still officially adhered to in China, Cuba and some African states.

1.4.4 Socialism

Socialism is the third economic system, and may be regarded as a **compromise** between a pure market economy and a pure command economy. Under socialism, the state owns and controls the principal (generally strategic) industries and resources, such as manufacturers of steel, transportation, communications, health services and energy. Less important and smaller matters such as trade and construction, as well as the production of materials and services of lesser strategic importance, are left to private initiative. In socialism, the fundamental assumption is that strategic and basic resources should belong to every member of the community. For the rest, businesses and consumers operate within free markets in which they are at liberty to make decisions without restriction. Although consumers in a socialist economy have greater freedom of choice than those under a command economy, the provision of the basic products and services by the state is a limiting factor in the creation of wealth.

1.4.5 Mixed economies

None of the three main economic systems in use occurs in a pure form anywhere. They occur as **mixed economies**, with the dominant system incorporating certain characteristics of the other systems. Thus China, which officially has a command economy, employs private initiative, while growing state intervention in the major market economies of the world is no strange phenomenon.

Figure 1.7 on page 22 shows the relative success of various countries with different economic systems. The gross national income (GNI) *per capita* of 2008 of some of the world's poorest countries (for example, Mozambique, Ethiopia, Tanzania, Zambia and Zimbabwe) is compared with that of some of the richest (for example, Switzerland, Japan, the United States, France and the United Kingdom).

Countries such as South Africa, Brazil, Hungary, Namibia and Argentina, each of which has a unique economic system, rate about midway between the richest and poorest countries of the world. Several factors, including education, culture and work ethic, affect the prosperity of any particular country, but Figure 1.7 shows that countries with market economies are wealthier than others.

1.4.6 The state and economic systems

The fact that under both the market system and socialism the state intervenes to help solve the economic problem does not mean that there is necessarily a tendency to move

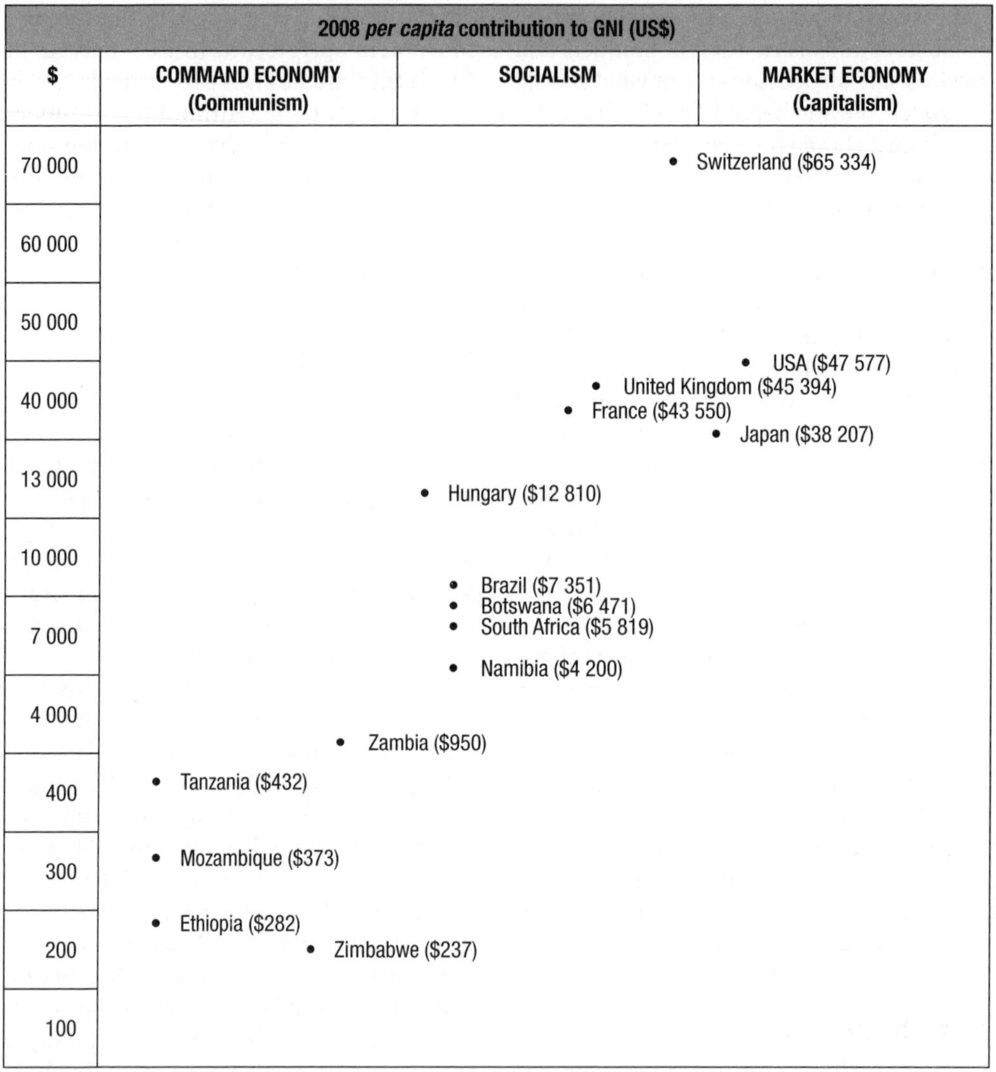

Figure 1.7: A comparison of the economic contributions of people in a variety of economic systems

Source: Adapted from information in the report of the International Bank for Reconstruction and Development/The World Bank. 2009. *Doing Business 2010: Reforming through difficult times.* Washington, DC: The World Bank, IFC and Palgrave MacMillan. [Online] Available: http://www.doingbusiness.org/documents/fullreport/2010/DB10-full-report.pdf Accessed 27 January 2010.

in the direction of a command or centrally directed economy. Any intervention by the state should be seen as necessary. On the one hand, the state provides the essential collective products and services such as roads, education, water, power, health care and justice, and on the other hand, the state maintains the economic system.

In particular, this means government intervention in market mechanisms and the so-called "freedom of entrepreneurs". Examples here are the protection of natural resources by preventing pollution, the restriction of monopolistic practices by ensuring competition, and the protection of consumers against false or misleading information and exploitation. The state also helps business by stimulating the economic system (through the promotion of exports, by encouraging the creation of small businesses, by assisting research and by granting subsidies). Furthermore, through the application of its monetary and fiscal policies, the state creates a climate conducive to economic growth and productivity. In a nutshell, government intervention in the economic system aims at encouraging economic growth and stability by managing recession and inflation, and effecting greater equity in the distribution of incomes[25].

A much-debated form of government intervention takes place when the state does not limit itself to the above-mentioned activities, but acts as an entrepreneur in its own right. The state does this in the areas of transport services, electricity supply, arms manufacture, broadcasting and television services, and many other industries in South Africa. For example, consider the Gautrain, the state-of-the-art rapid-rail project of the Gauteng Provincial Government, which is discussed in the box below.

The main reasons usually advanced for government intervention in these spheres is that the private entrepreneur is not interested in these activities and may not even be capable of carrying them out. This is because of the enormous scale of the businesses that produce services such as transport and electricity, and the corresponding risks attached to them. It is also argued that some organisations are of such strategic importance to the community that they cannot be left to profit-seeking private entrepreneurs.

However, these arguments do not entirely justify a regular and continuous entrepreneurial role played by government. If any such intervention by the state is carried to excess, the result is a bureaucracy that affects national productivity adversely by limiting private competition.

There are divergent opinions about what the proper role of government in a country's economy should be.

1.4.7 Final comments on different economic systems

Different communities use different economic systems to meet their needs using their available resources. Each system thus has its own peculiar characteristics (as can be seen from Table 1.2 on page 24) and each democratic country arranges its economic system in such a way that it solves its wealth problem as effectively as possible in accordance with the wishes of its inhabitants. Bearing in mind the fact that pure forms of

Mobility – the key to future economic growth

As a public transport service, the Gautrain links three anchor stations in Gauteng: stations at the OR Tambo International Airport, Tshwane and Johannesburg. The Gautrain project is managed by the Gauteng Department of Transport and is a project of the Gauteng Provincial Government. Upon its completion, it will act as a need satisfier by providing a commuter service between the OR Tambo International Airport and business hubs in Johannesburg and Tshwane.

This multi-billion-rand initiative, designed in line with global practice, is aimed at enhancing and supporting economic growth in the Gauteng Province, as well as generating employment. Furthermore, the Gautrain project supports many other government objectives and is a part of a longer-term vision that involves creating and sustaining a new culture of public-transport usage.

Source: Gauteng Provincial Government. 2009. "About Gautrain". [Online] Available: http://www.gautrain.co.za/index.php?fid=1&fp=0 Accessed 20 February 2010.

Table 1.2: A comparison of the main economic systems

	Market economy	Socialism	Command economy
Main characteristics	• There is private ownership of the factors of production. • There is freedom of choice.	• Basic industries are owned by the state. • There is freedom of choice.	• The state owns and controls all industries and agriculture.
Markets	• Free competition exists.	• Limited competition exists as a result of state industries.	• No competition exists.
Driving force	• Profit and reward are achieved according to individual ability.	• The profit motive is recognised. • Employees' pay in state-owned concerns is based on workers' needs.	• Profit is not allowed. • Workers are urged to work for the glory of the state.
Management	• Private businesses create the management environment. • Managers are free to make decisions. • People are free to choose their careers.	• The management environment comprises state-owned as well as private businesses. • Decisions are restricted to government policy in state-owned organisations.	• The state creates the management environment. • There is no freedom of decision. • Managers are also party members.
Labour	• Workers are independent and free to choose their jobs and their employer. • They are free to join unions and to strike.	• Workers are free to choose their jobs and their employers. • There is a limited right to strike in state organisations.	• There is a limited choice of jobs. • Unions are controlled by the state.
Consumers	• There is freedom of choice in free markets. • Spending is only limited by income.	• There is freedom of choice, except in respect of the products of state organisations, the prices and quality of which have to be accepted.	• Rationing of products occurs. • There is a very limited choice. • Prices of products and income levels are set by the state.
Advantages	• Private initiative occurs. • There is economic freedom.	• There is the possibility of full employment. • The state stabilises economic fluctuations.	• The state can concentrate resources towards particular ends.
Disadvantages	• The environment is unstable. • Cyclical fluctuations occur. • There are high social costs.	• There is little incentive in state organisations. • State organisations can be unproductive.	• There is low productivity. • There is a low standard of living. • Planning is difficult or impossible.

the different economic systems almost never exist, the most appropriate description of the prevailing economic system in South Africa is that it is a mixture between the market system and the socialist system. More precisely, the South African economic system can be defined as one that is moving towards a market-oriented economy, yet that presently has a high degree of government participation in and control of the economy[26]. South African consumers thus enjoy a high degree of freedom to buy what they want and to shop where they want.

In South Africa, the individual entrepreneur must judge which products and services the consumer wants, and then offer these at a price the consumer is prepared and able to pay. A complex network of organisations evolves out of the interaction between needs and the entrepreneurs who satisfy these needs. In a market economy, this network is termed the "business world".

The South African economy

The economic systems of Western countries, with which South Africa associates itself, are combinations of a market economy and socialism. Despite the defects and shortcomings of the more-or-less free-market order in South Africa, most inhabitants believe that this economic system satisfies their needs better than any system that might be based on pure socialism or a command economy.

Since 1994, South Africa has steadily moved to an increasingly market-oriented position with less and less government intervention and control. This move has undoubtedly had a positive effect on the South African economy, as can be seen in the figures below.

In 2004, South Africa's GDP figure stood at R1 404 billion and GDP per capita was R30 129. Consumer price inflation was at its lowest level in 40 years (3,4%) and producer price inflation was at a 58-year low (1,9%). South Africa had become an important role-player in global exports, hence the global economy.

By 2007, economic stability was evident in South Africa. With GDP growth of 5,1% for the year, the country's economy was at its strongest in over two decades.

However, South Africa was not able to avoid the effects of the global meltdown in 2008, when the country's GDP grew by only 3,1%. By June 2009, GDP had decreased by 6,4%, pulling South Africa's economy into recession.

Nonetheless, today South Africa still leads its continent in industrial output and mineral production, generating 40% and 45% respectively of Africa's total output[27].

South Africa's exports were valued at R292,3 billion and its imports at R304,7 billion, with major exports being minerals, precious metals, machinery, vehicles, automotive components, pulp and paper.

South Africa has more telephones, cellphones, autobanks and computers than the all rest of the countries on the continent of Africa put together. South Africa also has more than 15 times the African average of paved roads, and half the electricity and energy capacity in the whole of Africa.

Certain factors make South Africa a favourable investment destination and other factors deter investors from the country.

Positive factors include:

- sound macro-economic policies
- 100% ownership permitted
- a large, growing domestic market in South Africa
- modern transport and communication systems
- rich natural resources
- modern banking and financial services.

Negative factors include:

- high rates of crime
- extensive exchange controls, although these are being eased
- major skills shortages, particularly in management roles.

1.5 The need-satisfying institutions of the market economy

1.5.1 Business organisations

The workings of a market economy are affected by its **need-satisfying institutions**, which are the private business organisations that, for the most part, satisfy the needs of the community. The business world therefore consists of a complex system of inter-dependent organisations that mobilise the resources of a country to satisfy the country's needs at the risk of a loss and in the pursuit of profit.

Such are the conditions under which a private business exists in a market economy. Under such a system, an organisation has to make a profit to be able to survive. This can happen only if it satisfies the needs or wishes of the consumer, and hence the community.

By meeting the needs of the consumer, business organisations therefore solve the fundamental economic problem: which products and services should be produced, and how and for whom.

Figure 1.8 shows how businesses, as the main need-satisfying institutions under this

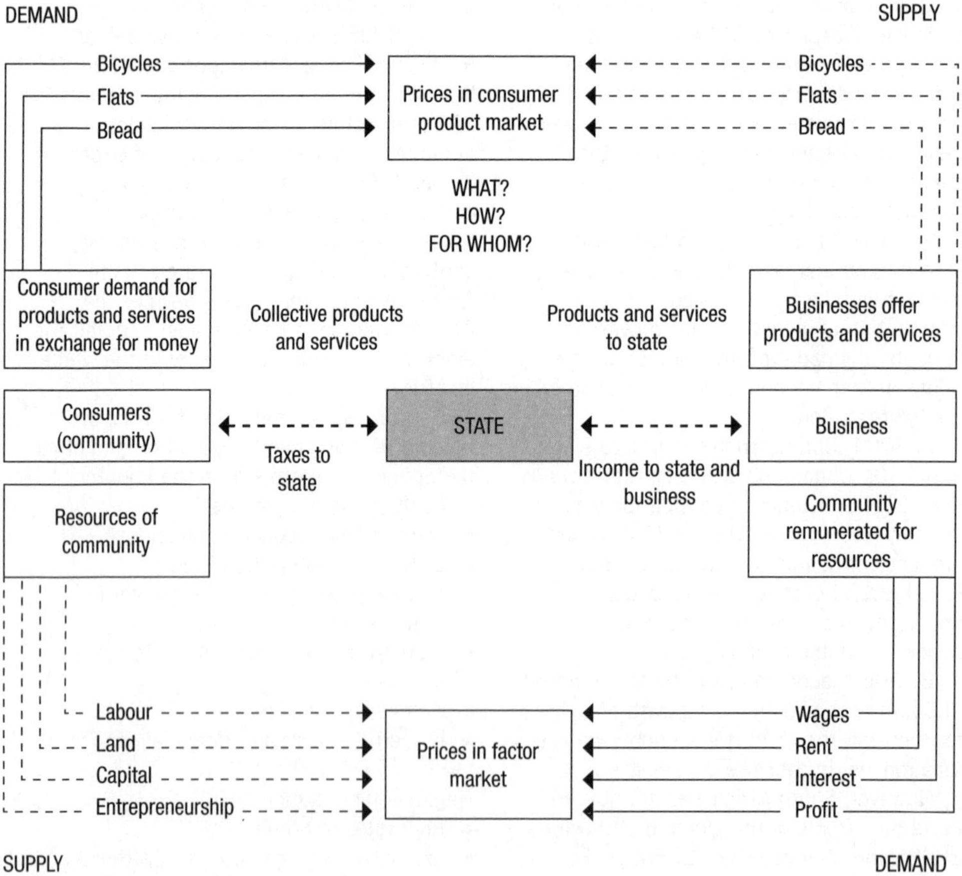

Figure 1.8: Products and services offered in the market system

Source: Adapted from Samuelson, P.A. & Nordhaus et al. 1980. *Economics*. 11th ed. New York: McGraw-Hill Company, p. 41. Reprinted with permission of the McGraw-Hill Companies.

system, use the resources of society to produce products and services for consumers.

Consumers' needs culminate in the demand for consumer products and services offered on the market by businesses (in department stores, boutiques, car salesrooms, pharmacies and so on). Therefore, consumer demand helps to determine what products and services need to be provided and for whom.

To be able to produce products and services, business organisations need resources, so a demand arises for production factors, which are offered in the factor market by the community. Business organisations pay salaries and wages to the community in exchange for production factors, and consumers in turn pay for their products and services with that money. Competition in both markets determines how the products and services are to be produced so that the entrepreneur can continue to make a profit.

In order to make a profit, the enterprise must therefore take the initiative and accept certain risks in mobilising the resources of the community before items can be produced. The owner of a bicycle factory, for example, has to erect or rent a building, install machinery, buy raw materials and components, and employ people to manufacture bicycles as productively as possible to satisfy the needs of consumers. The transport contractor has to transport products to places where there is a need for them. The retailer has to present a range of products conforming to consumers' needs in as convenient a way as possible. A banker does not produce a physical article, but provides a service in the form of finance placed at the disposal of manufacturers, dealers and numerous other entrepreneurs and consumers. And these are but a few examples of the innumerable activities carried out in the business world by business organisations – large and small, local and multi-national – that play an indispensable part in South African society.

Business organisations may be defined as those private need-satisfying institutions of a market economy that accept risks in pursuit of profit by offering products and services on the market to the consumer. Business organisations assume one of a variety of forms: a sole proprietorship, a partnership, a close corporation, a private company or a public company (as will be discussed in Chapter 3).

While a business organisation is a **private enterprise** (one owned by private entrepreneurs), in a mixed-market economy there are government and non-profit-seeking organisations that satisfy community needs in addition to profit-seeking businesses.

1.5.2 Government organisations

In the discussion of the various economic systems, several principles of a market economy were identified. One principle was the condition that government should intervene as little as possible with market mechanisms, and when it does, it should confine itself to the protection and creation of collective non-profit-seeking facilities and services such as those concerned with health care, education, justice and defence. The government departments responsible for such state functions may also be regarded as need-satisfying organisations. (However, because the profit motive is absent and the services provided are collective, such government institutions fall under the subject of public administration rather than business management.)

The discussion of the various economic systems also mentioned that the pure market economy exists only in theory and that several mixed systems are in fact to be found, including the South African system, which was defined as a market-oriented economy with a high degree of state intervention. The intervention specifically indicates the large number of government organisations in South Africa, which are also known as state-owned enterprises (SOEs), parastatals or public corporations. Unlike the collective systems that produce products and services on a non-profit-seeking basis, these public corporations offer products and services for profit, and sometimes in competition with other businesses in the market. Sometimes these public corporations may be regarded as business organisations, but with this difference: they are owned and controlled by the state and not by a private entrepreneur. Eskom, Transnet and SAA are examples of such public corporations, and there are many others.

These public corporations may also be regarded as need-satisfying institutions through which the state creates products and services believed to be of strategic, economic or political importance to the community, especially as regards self-sufficiency in transport, energy, military equipment and armaments. There is, however, a growing trend in South Africa towards the privatisation of major government organisations. The state sold Sasol in 1979, in 1998 ACSA was privatised, and then in 2003 Telkom was listed on the JSE and the New York Stock Exchange.

Critical thinking

In the South African economy, both government organisations and private businesses act as society's need-satisfying institutions.

Government organisations and private businesses: Servicing the needs of South Africans

Students often ask: "How is it possible that government organisations act as need-satisfying institutions?" and: "How is it possible for government organisations and private businesses to service similar needs?"

The answer to the first question is that government organisations very definitely act as need-satisfying institutions in that they provide an array of both products and services to their citizens. In most cases, these products and services are exchanged for rates and taxes. The key difference between government organisations and private businesses lies, however, in the fact that private businesses seek to make profits through the fulfilment of society's needs, whereas this is not the case with government institutions.

Regarding the ways that government organisations and private businesses service similar needs, there are two examples that are particularly relevant in the South African situation:

- The first example is society's need for a safe and secure environment. South Africa has a particularly high crime rate compared to the crime rates of other developed countries. In response to this, both government organisations and private businesses seek to address society's security needs. The government does this through the provision of policing services, an efficient judicial system and effective facilities for correctional services. In doing this, the government seeks to address society's needs, although not with a profit orientation. At the same time, many business organisations provide products and services to address the security needs of society. Examples of such products include electric fencing, burglar alarms and security gates, while examples of services include private security, vehicle-tracking and short-term insurance. In contrast to the government organisations, businesses providing these products and services do so in exchange for profits.
- Another good example in South Africa is health care. Both government and private businesses seek to address society's need for health care. Government seeks to provide health-care services to its citizens through public hospitals, clinics and emergency services, without a focus on profit. At the same time, private companies such as Netcare, Medi-Clinic and Intercare seek to offer the same services, but with the goal of providing quality services in exchange for profit.

Many more examples exist in South Africa in the areas of education, transport and social security.

Although the productivity levels of government organisations are suspect, those that seek profits also fall within the scope of business management.

1.5.3 Non-profit-seeking organisations

Non-profit-seeking organisations are the other group of need-satisfying institutions that offer services, and, to a lesser extent, products not provided by private enterprise or government organisations. Examples of non-profit-seeking organisations are sports clubs, cultural associations and welfare organisations, and associations of organised business such as the National African Federated Chamber of Commerce (NAFCOC) and the South African Chamber of Business (SACOB). These organisations differ from other need-satisfying organisations in that they provide their services without seeking profit.

The continued existence of such organisations therefore depends on the financial support of those members of the community who require their services. Although such organisations do not set profit-making as their primary objective, they often function on the same basis as a business organisation, seeking a surplus of income over expenditure, or at least a balance of income and expenditure. These organisations – especially the larger ones – therefore employ management principles. And despite their small share in the economy, the study of such organisations also falls within the field of business management.

1.6 The nature of business management

1.6.1 Economics and business management as related sciences

A society is constantly faced with the problem of how to use its scarce resources to satisfy its needs as efficiently as possible. **Economics** is a social science that studies how humans choose different ways of using their scarce resources to produce products and services. It is therefore a study of the economic problem and related variables, with the improved well-being of the community as its preconceived goal. The variables that economics studies include prices, money, income and its distribution, taxes, productivity, government intervention and economic growth, as well as many other economic questions affecting the well-being of a country.

Business management is an applied science that is concerned with the study of those institutions in a particular economic system that satisfy the needs of a community. In a mixed-market economy, as is found in South Africa, private business organisations are therefore the main area of study.

While economics examines the entire economic system of a country, business management limits its studies to one component of the economic system: the individual organisation, whether it be a private business, a public corporation or, to a lesser extent, a non-profit-seeking organisation. For example, economics examines the problem of inflation against the background of its implications for the national economy, while business management is more concerned with the effects of inflation on individual businesses.

1.6.2 The purpose and task of business management

The discussion of the cycle of need satisfaction indicated that the primary human endeavour is to achieve the highest possible satisfaction of needs with scarce resources. This endeavour follows the economic principle, to which every economic system is subject. It follows that any component of an economic system, including a business organisation, is also subject to the economic principle. Where the individual business organisation is concerned, this entails achieving the highest possible output with the lowest possible input of production factors[28].

The **purpose of business management** is to produce the most units of products or services at the lowest possible cost.

From this emerges the **task of business management**, which is to determine how an organisation can achieve the highest possible output (products and services) with the least possible input (human resources, natural resources and capital). More specifically, the task of business management entails an examination of the factors, methods and principles that enable a business to function as efficiently and productively as possible in order to maximise its profits. In short, it is a study of those principles that have to be applied to make a business organisation as profitable as possible. It may also include a study of the environmental factors that could have an effect on the success of an organisation, its survival or its profitability.

Examples of approaches, principles and methods studied by business management with the purpose of making an organisation function as productively as possible

General approaches to management methods, which have been tested over the years, include the following:

- The mechanistic approach, introduced at the turn of the century, emphasises mass production, especially under the management of engineers.
- The human-relations approach originated in the 1930s and emphasises the motivation of workers.
- The contingency approach of the 1950s argues that the management approach is prescribed by the prevailing situation.
- Strategic management, the most recent approach, makes a special study of how management should act in an unstable environment.

Various supplementary approaches and developments, such as organisation design, the management of change, information management, corporate culture and the management of diversity are still being studied.

In the field of **marketing management**, research into experimentation with approaches and methods has also contributed to the more productive operation of businesses. These include the following:

- The marketing concept replaced the production approach in management philosophy to enable businesses to adjust their resources more effectively to the needs of consumers.
- Market research, as an instrument of marketing philosophy, has developed many methods of studying the needs of consumers.
- Methods of studying and determining consumer habits and segmenting markets, as well as strategic management aids, have also stimulated marketing management to higher productivity.

Financial management as an area of business management has also tested many methods, especially financial ratios. The following are some examples:

- ratios to access the financial performance of businesses
- capital budgets and capital-budget techniques, in particular to evaluate potential investment possibilities
- approaches to dividend policy
- approaches to and methods of financing growth and expansion as profitably as possible.

In the same way, numerous methods, principles, approaches and problems in other areas of business management (such as production and operations, purchasing, human-resources management and external relations) have been researched and tested.

The sum total of this sustained study of, and experimentation with, management approaches and methods, and research on management problems, constitutes the body of knowledge known as business management.

The purpose and task of business management

- The economic principle consists of the human endeavour to satisfy unlimited needs with limited resources. All economic systems are subject to it.
- In a mixed-market economy, a business organisation as a need-satisfying institution is a component of the economic system, and is therefore also subject to the economic principle.
- According to the economic principle, a business organisation always has to endeavour to obtain the highest possible output (products and services) at the least possible input (lowest cost). This is the purpose of business management.
- The business organisation is the subject studied by business management.
- The task of business management is to examine factors, methods and principles that enable a business organisation to maximise its profits and achieve its objectives.

The **study of business management** entails comprehensive and ongoing research and the examination of management problems, the testing of approaches and principles, experimentation with methods and techniques, and the continuous weighing up of environmental variables. The result is an applied science that indicates how business organisations can best be directed towards realising their objectives.

Therefore, in the case of business organisations, the economic principle is defined as the endeavour to achieve the highest possible income in the market at the lowest possible cost, with profit as the favourable difference between the two[29]. This principle is also applicable to government organisations and non-profit-seeking organisations. The only difference is that in the case of government organisations and non-profit-seeking organisations, the difference between inputs and outputs is not measured in profit, but rather in terms of surplus, savings or higher productivity.

In a business organisation, the economic principle and the profit motive coincide, making profits the driving force, and so the task of business management becomes one of maximising profits[30]. However, this does not mean that the task of business management is to maximise profits at the cost of everything else, especially the well-being of society. In today's business environment, the objective is rather to maximise profits through good management and care of employees, customers, investors and society in general.

To summarise, the task of business management is to study those factors, principles and methods that will lead a business organisation, as a component of the prevailing economic system, to reach its objectives. In a mixed-market economy, this primarily – though not exclusively – means making a profit.

1.6.3 Is business management an independent science?

Business management is a young subject and its scientific basis is still the subject of lively debate. There is no easy answer to the question of whether business management is an independent science, as there are many diverse opinions as to what exactly constitutes a science.

The most common definitions of a science emphasise different characteristics. Business management is continually being tested in the light of these characteristics to determine whether it merits the status of a science:

- The most outstanding characteristic of an independent science is a **clearly distinguishable subject of study** that forms the nucleus of a discipline[31]. Business management completely satisfies this condition, particularly with regard to the business organisation, which, as a component of the market economy, is its subject of study.

- A fundamental characteristic of a science, which supplements the one mentioned above, is that it should be **independent of other sciences**. As we have already pointed out, business management has its own identifiable subject of study, and from this point of view may be regarded as a science. However, it should be clearly understood that a business organisation can be studied by other sciences for other reasons. People are social animals who organise themselves into groups to fulfil purposes that are too big or too complex for a single individual. A business organisation comprises people who wish to attain certain personal and organisational goals. Business organisations may also, therefore, form a subject of study for sciences such as sociology, psychology and medicine. However, the way in which business management views an organisation is indicated by the purpose of the study. This is to examine those things that may guide businesses as effectively as possible towards their objective, which is primarily to make a profit. This essential characteristic also allows business management to qualify as a science because, unlike other sciences, it is concerned mainly with ways of maximising the profitability of a business.
- A third characteristic of a science is that it is a **uniform, systematised body of knowledge of facts and scientific laws**, and that its laws and principles are constantly **tested in practice**[32]. In this regard, business management encompasses a great deal of systematised knowledge found worldwide in the comprehensive literature on the subject. It also contains numerous rules and principles that may successfully be applied in practice, even though they are not as exact as those in the natural sciences. This leads to the view that management is a normative science, which means that it constantly endeavours to establish norms or guidelines for management with a view to maximising profits.
- It is also said that the final purpose of a science should be to produce a **generally accepted theory**. In this regard, business management does not yet satisfy the requirements of an independent science. Because of the rapidly changing environment in which business organisations exist, it is doubtful whether this stage will ever be reached. It should also be borne in mind that the involvement of people in the management process and the influence of uncontrollable variables make it difficult, if not impossible, to explain management problems with any single uniform theory.

While it is still debatable whether business management can be regarded as an independent science, this examination at least provides an insight into its nature. To summarise, business management is a young applied science that sets out to study the ways in which a business can achieve its prime objective, which is to make a profit. However, this does not mean that the application of management principles and approaches should always be done in a scientific way, nor does it require that the intuition and experience of managers should be summarily dismissed. Successful management is often regarded as an art as well as a science.

1.6.4 The interfaces between business management and other sciences

Throughout the discussion of the scientific status of business management, it was held that the business organisation, as the subject of study, is the most important entity. However, one should bear in mind that businesses are also studied by other disciplines for other reasons. Business management, in its task of studying and examining those things that help a business to attain its goals as efficiently as possible, constitutes a young, developing science that frequently makes use of the knowledge gathered by other disciplines on the functioning of the business organisation, even though these disciplines may not be interested in the profitability of organisations. In short, business science takes from other disciplines what it can use to help businesses to accomplish their goals.

Many current management concepts originated in other sciences and now form an integral part of the body of knowledge of business management. For example, the concept of strategy was borrowed from military principles, sociological knowledge and principles help explain the behaviour of an organisation, engineering principles are applied to improve productivity in the manufacture of products, and mathematical models and computer science are used to help management make decisions. Furthermore, advertising frequently uses psychology, the arts and communication principles and techniques – all, of course, from the viewpoint of profitability.

Table 1.3 on page 34 provides a self-explanatory exposition of the multi-disciplinary nature of business management. In view of the constantly changing environment in which contemporary businesses operate, business management is likely to make more, rather than less, use of other sciences in future.

1.7 Classifying the study material of business management

In order to decide on appropriate study material relating to business management, it is useful to follow a **guideline** that will offer a broad basis upon which knowledge of business management can be built. This guideline can be formed around **questions** that arise in response to phenomena that influence costs or profits for the business. This is where the task of management arises: to examine those things that will best improve the profitability of the business organisation to ensure its success.

The various **activities** that management must undertake to make a business organisation work can also be seen to constitute the field of business management:

- Markets must be researched to determine whether there is a need for a particular product.
- Raw materials must be purchased to produce such products.
- Staff and equipment must be acquired to manufacture the products.
- Money has to be obtained to pay for the materials and the equipment, as well as to remunerate staff.
- These often disparate activities have to be co-ordinated or managed.

To give scientific direction to the study of these interrelated activities, the total field of business management is divided into seven **functions**. Each function (or **management area**) comprises all aspects of a specific group of activities. (See Table 1.3 and the discussion that follows.)

The main reason for dividing the field of business management into different functional areas is the need to systematise the large body of knowledge. The multi-disciplinary nature of the subject also makes division necessary. The training and skills required for the various functions are highly diverse, and on occasion each function makes use of different disciplines to achieve its management purpose. Financial management makes use of computer science, risk management and accountancy concepts, while human-resources management uses a great deal of psychological knowledge and social theory.

Some degree of specialisation in a specific management function is necessary to make management as productive as possible. In this book, however, the functions are distinguished only for analytical purposes, to provide a better understanding of each and to explain its relation to the others.

Table 1.3: Interfaces between other sciences and business-management functions

	General management	Marketing management	Financial management	Production and operations management	Purchasing management	Human-resources management	Public-relations management
Anthropology	• Cultural relationships and organisational behaviour • Management of diversity	• Cultural determinants of demand • Behavioural structures				• Employee behaviour • Management of diversity	• Behaviour of external groups
Economics	• Environmental scanning	• Market analysis of, for example, consumer expenditure	• Influence of financial strategy • Behaviour of financial markets	• Location problems	• Market analysis of availability and stockpiling • Evaluation of competition in the market	• Labour-market analyses • Remuneration structures	• Economic influence of external groups
Engineering		• Product development		• Erection of factories • Factory outlay	• Value analysis	• Safety of employees	
Law (especially mercantile law)	• Format of an organisation	• Misleading practices • Product safety • Packaging	• Takeovers • Mergers	• Pollution by factories	• Representations • Law of contracts	• Conditions of employment • Negotiation with unions • Labour laws	• Misleading messages • Sponsorship contracts
Computer science	• Information management • Planning models	• Marketing research • E-marketing	• Financial models	• Optimal outlays	• Materials-requirement planning • Manufacturing-resource planning	• Labour-information systems • Labour research	• Public-relations research
Accounting	• Control systems • Budgets	• Marketing audit • Sales and cost analyses	• Interpretation of financial statements	• Cost analysis	• Valuation of inventory • Cost analysis	• Human-asset accounting	• Budgets
Psychology	• Leadership • Motivation • Negotiation	• Consumer behaviour • Communication			• Negotiation	• Testing • Performance analysis	• Communication • Persuasion
Sociology	• Organisational behaviour • Interfaces between the organisation and the environment	• Socio-demographic classification • Group influences			• Business ethics	• Organisational behaviour	• Group influences
Mathematics and statistics	• Decision models • Planning models	• Market research • Market forecasting • Market measuring	• Financial models • Deviations		• Inventory forecasting	• Human-resources planning models	• Pre- and post-testing of programs

The function of general management includes an examination of the management process as a whole: the planning that management has to do, the organisation that it has to establish to carry out its plans, the leadership and motivation needed to get things done, and the control that has to be exercised over the whole process. This requires a survey of the different management approaches that may be adopted. General management is the overall function through which top management develops strategies for the whole business. It cuts through all the other functions because they are carried out at the top level as well as in each functional area.

The operations function concerns all those activities that mobilise the resources (such as raw materials, capital and human resources) of a business organisation to create the finished products and services that can be distributed to meet the needs of its customers.

The human-resources function entails the management of a variety of activities involved in driving employees within a business organisation to achieve their maximum potential for the organisation and themselves. In so doing, this function guides employees towards the accomplishment of the objectives and vision set out by general management.

The marketing function is responsible for marketing the products or services of the business. This includes assessing the market and the needs of consumers, as well as developing a strategy to satisfy those needs profitably.

The financial function includes the acquisition, utilisation and control of the money that the business needs to finance its activities, raw materials and equipment in such a way that its profits are maximised without endangering its liquidity or solvency.

The purchasing and supply function is responsible for the acquisition of all products and materials required by the business to function profitably – raw materials, components, tools, equipment and, in the case of wholesalers and retailers, the inventory to be purchased. Purchasing managers have to be in contact with suppliers so that they are aware of new products and know the prices at which products can be bought. They also have to keep inventory up to date in order to ensure continuity of functioning.

Ultimately, the functions form a synergistic whole that directs the business organisation towards its goal and its objectives.

1.8 The arrangement of this book

Business management comprises a broad body of knowledge. For logical flow in this book, the body of knowledge has been divided into four parts as follows:

- Part 1: Chapters 1–5
- Part 2: Chapters 6–9
- Part 3: Chapters 10–14
- Part 4: Chapter 15.

Chapter 1, the introduction to business management, has set the scene for Part 1 and the rest of the book. Chapter 2 discusses the entrepreneur and entrepreneurship, while Chapter 3 looks at the establishment of the business organisation in greater detail. The environment within which a business operates is examined in Chapter 4. Chapter 5 addresses the issue of corporate social responsibility.

Part 2 of this book reviews the management process, the developments in management theory and some approaches to management. Chapter 6 and Chapter 7, which examine planning and organising respectively, form the starting point for an examination of the management process. The nature of motivation and leadership in an organisation is discussed in Chapter 8, while Chapter 9 deals with control, the final part of the management process.

The functional areas of a business are examined in Part 3 of the book. Chapter 10 looks at operations management, which concerns the management of the physical production of products and services. Chapter 11 looks at how an organisation can manage what are arguably its most important resources: its employees. Chapter 12 provides an overview of the marketing function and the public-relations function of a business. Chapter 13 discusses financial management, investment management and financing decisions. The last chapter of Part 3, Chapter 14, provides an overview of the purchasing and supply function, as well as the sourcing activities.

Part 4 is the concluding section of the book. This part deals with relevant topics in today's business world: business strategy, decision-making and the strategic-management process.

1.9 Summary

This chapter has explained the business organisation's role in society. It has also considered the interaction between society and the business organisation as a social process that transforms a country's means of production so that products and services can be produced that will satisfy the needs of society. This process was explained in greater detail in the discussion of a business organisation as a component of the economic system, where it was specifically shown how, as a need-satisfying institution of the market economy, the business organisation provides for the needs of people. Lastly, this chapter examined the task of business management.

Key terms

business management	industries
business organisation	institutions
business world	market economy
capital	market system
command economy	Maslow's hierarchy
community	mixed economies
competition	natural resources
economic principle	needs
economic problem	needs-satisfying
economic system	profit
entrepreneurship	resources
free-market economy	socialism
government organisation	social responsibility
human resources	transformation

Questions for discussion

Reread the case study on pages 4–6 and answer the following questions:

1. Do you think the fact that South Africa is moving more towards a market economy has had an impact on the South African airline industry? If you do, give your reasons by saying how this impact has occurred.
2. An airline is a different type of business compared to a production company, for example, the global paper business Sappi. How might the resources, transformation process and outputs of SAA and Sappi differ?
3. It is clear from the case study that price is one of the key competitive factors in the airline industry. However, is price the only factor on which airlines compete? Give reasons for your answer.
4. As a result of the unprecedented increase in the price of jet fuel, the domestic airline industry felt the brunt of the global financial crisis long before many industries in South Africa. In early 2009, South Africa's economy officially entered a recession. What impact do you think this had on the domestic airline industry? Provide reasons for your answer.

5. ACSA has invested billions of rands in the upgrading and construction of infrastructure for the 2010 FIFA World Cup. In your opinion, how has this affected South Africa's economy, and will it be sustainable in the long-term? Explain your answer.

? Multiple-choice questions

1. Which of the following statements are correct?
   i. In a market economy, the business world is a complex system of individuals and business organisations who transform resources into products and services with their only aim being the benefit of their own enterprises.
   ii. Society, especially in highly developed countries, has a limited number of needs.
   iii. The primary purpose of business in a market economy is to make a profit while satisfying the needs of people.
   iv. The market economy is a complex system that is comprised of various types and sizes of businesses that together mobilise the resources of a country to satisfy the needs of its inhabitants.
      a. i, ii
      b. ii, iv
      c. ii, iii
      d. iii, iv
2. Which of the following statements about socialism is true?
   a. There is minimum state interference in markets.
   b. The state owns and controls the principal industries such as communication, health services and transportation.
   c. People with businesses are free to use their resources as they choose.
   d. The state assumes complete responsibility for the production and distribution of products.
3. A business's endeavour to achieve the highest possible satisfaction of needs at the lowest possible cost given the limited resources available is known as __________.
   a. the production factor
   b. wealth creation
   c. the economic principle
   d. need satisfaction
4. What is the key purpose of business management?
   a. To examine the factors, methods and principles that enable a business to function as efficiently and productively as possible to maximise profits.
   b. To produce the most units of products and services at the lowest possible cost.
   c. To study, understand and determine how to satisfy the needs of consumers.
   d. To identify problems management may encounter and provide solutions for effective management.
5. Which of the following characteristics relates to a market economy?
   a. There is private ownership of production factors and freedom of choice.
   b. There is freedom of choice and the basic industries are owned by the state.
   c. There is freedom of choice, and the state owns and controls all the industries.
   d. There is private ownership of production factors and the basic industries are owned by the state.

Answers to multiple-choice questions

1. d
2. b
3. c
4. b
5. a

References

1. Maxon, T. 2006. "Airlines are still struggling long after impact of 9/11". *The Dallas Morning News*, 9 December. [Online] Available: http://www.azstarnet.com/sn/byauthor/146186 Accessed 25 November 2009.
2. BBC News. 2009. "Q & A: Advice about swine flu". [Online] Available: http://news.bbc.co.uk/2/hi/health/8021958.stm Accessed 25 November 2009.
3. Morrell, P.S. & Alamdari, F. 2002. "The impact of 11 September on the aviation industry: Traffic, capacity, employment and restructuring". Geneva: International Labour Office.
4. *South Africa.info*. 2008. "South Africa's tourism industry". [Online] Available: http://www.southafrica.info/business/economy/sectors/tourism-overview.htm#growth Accessed 25 November 2009.
5. Statistics South Africa. 2008. "Key findings". [Online] Available: http://www.statssa.gov.za/PublicationsHTML/Report-03-51-022008/html/Report-03-51-022008_4.html Accessed 25 November 2009.
6. Airports Company South Africa. 2008. "Annual Report". [Online] Available: http://www.acsa.co.za/home.asp?pid=3726 Accessed 25 November 2009.
7. South Africa 2010. 2008. "Transport: Government's promise". [Online] Available: http://www.sa2010.gov.za/transport Accessed 25 November 2009.
8. South African Airways. 2006. "Annual report". [Online] Available: http://www.pmg.org.za/minutes/20061030-south-african-airways-2006-annual-report Accessed 10 February 2010.
9. South African Airways. 2008. "Annual Report: Restructuring towards profitability". [Online] Available: http://www.flysaa.com/pv_obj_cache/pv_obj_id_2B9D7FEEBE79435FF1BB18CEF503BCF0F53B0900/filename/Financial_Report2008_Restructuring_towards_profitability.pdf Accessed 25 November 2009.
10. Buhalis, D. & Egger, E. 2008. *eTourism case studies*. Burlington: Butterworth-Heinemann, p. 283.
11. Phasiwe, K. 2003. "New no-frills no competition says SAA". *Business Day*, 11 November.
12. South African Press Association. 2008. "Airline's crash on the cards". [Online] Available: http://www.iol.co.za/index.php?set_id=1&art_id=vn20080430105107457C838463 Accessed 6 August 2008.
13. Sibanyoni, M. 2008. "Buyers lining up for Nationwide". [Online] Available: http://www.fin24.com/articles/default/display_article.aspx?ArticleId=1518-24_2316288 Accessed 25 November 2009.
14. HBD Venture Capital. 2009. "About HBD: The Company". [Online] Available: http://www.hbd.com/about-hbd/the-company Accessed 25 November 2009 & HBD Venture Capital. 2009. "Our investments: HBD Fund 2". [Online] Available: http://www.hbd.com/our-investments/fund-2 Accessed 25 November 2009.
15. Flanagan, L., Smillie, S. & Tromp, B. 2007. "The great bread scandal", *The Star*, 13 November. [Online] Available: http://www.thestar.co.za/index.php?fArticleId=4125886 Accessed 25 November 2009.
16. Parliament of the Republic of South Africa. 2009. "Consumer Protection Act, 2008", *Government Gazette*, No. 32186 (Vol. 526), 29 April.
17. Statistics South Africa. 2008. *Key findings: P0441 – Gross Domestic Product (GDP)* (Fourth quarter). [Online] Available: http://www.statssa.gov.za/publications/statskeyfindings.asp?PPN=p0441&SCH=4339 Accessed 25 November 2009.
18. BBC News. 2009. "South Africa goes into recession". 26 May. [Online] Available: http://news.bbc.co.uk/2/hi/business/8068126.stm Accessed 25 November 2009.
19. Department of Labour. 2008. *Commission for Employment Equity: Annual Report 2007–2008*. [Online] Available: http://www.info.gov.za/view/DownloadFileAction?id=90058 Accessed 25 November 2009.
20. Cowan, K.R. 1992. "Business ethics in South Africa: An investigation of managerial perceptions and attitudes" (A paper presented at the Fourth Conference of the South African Institute of Business Scientists, Vista University, Bloemfontein). June.
21. British Petroleum. 2006. "BP Statistical Review of World Energy (XLS)". 8 December. [Online] Available: http://www.bp.com/liveassets/bp_internet/switzerland/corporate_switzerland/STAGING/local_assets/downloads_pdfs/b/statistical_review_of_world_energy_full_report_2007.pdf Accessed 10 February 2010.

22. British Pretroleum. 2009. "Oil reserves". [Online] Available: http://www.bp.com/sectiongenericarticle.do?categoryId=9023769&contentId=7044915 Accessed 25 November 2009.
23. South African Airways. 2008. *2008 Annual report: Restructuring towards profitability*. [Online] Available: http://www.flysaa.com/Shared/Downloads/Financials/Financial_Report2008_Restructuring_towards_profitability.pdf Accessed 25 November 2009.
24. Eighty20. 2008. *Fact-a-day*. [Online] Available http://www.eighty20.co.za/blog/?s=%27household+income%27+%27cell+phone%27.; http://www.eighty20.co.za/blog/?s=%2776%25%27+%27cell+phone%27 Accessed 10 February 2010.
25. Lombard J.A., Stadler J.J. & Haasbroek, P.J. 1987. *Die ekonomiese stelsel van Suid-Afrika*. Pretoria: HAUM, p. 34.
26. Lombard J.A., Stadler J.J. & Haasbroek, P.J. 1987. *Die ekonomiese stelsel van Suid-Afrika*. Pretoria: HAUM, p. 34.
27. Department of Trade and Industry. "Why Invest in SA?" [Online] Available at: http://www.thedti.gov.za/whyinvestinsa.htm Accessed 10 February 2010.
28. See also: Radel, F.E. & Reynders, H.J.J. (Eds). 1980. *Inleiding tot die bedryfsekonomie*. Pretoria: J.L. van Schaik, p. 2.
29. Radel, F.E. & Reynders, H.J.J. (Eds). 1980. *Inleiding tot die bedryfsekonomie*. Pretoria: J.L. van Schaik, p. 4.
30. Radel, F.E. & Reynders, H.J.J. (Eds). 1980. *Inleiding tot die bedryfsekonomie*. Pretoria: J.L. van Schaik, p. 5.
31. Lucas, G.H.G. *et al.* 1979. *Die taak van bemarkingsbestuurder.* Pretoria: J.L. van Schaik, p. 11.
32. Radel, F.E. & Reynders, H.J.J. (Eds). 1980. *Inleiding tot die bedryfsekonomie*. Pretoria: J.L. van Schaik, p. 2. See also: Marx, F.W. & Churr, E.G. 1981. *Grondbeginsels van die bedryfsekonomie*. Pretoria: HAUM, p. 24.

CHAPTER

2

ENTREPRENEURSHIP

The purpose of this chapter

This chapter examines entrepreneurship as the creative and driving force behind the business organisation. It is basically the entrepreneur who decides what, how, by whom and for whom products and services should be produced to satisfy the needs and wants of society. This chapter examines the nature of entrepreneurship, and the role of entrepreneurs and small businesses in the economy. In addition, it looks at the entrepreneurial process, as well as the different ways of entering the business world: by starting a new business and growing it, by buying an existing business and growing it, by entering into a franchise agreement or through corporate entrepreneurship. Finally, the feasibility of new venture opportunities is discussed.

Learning outcomes

On completion of this chapter you should be able to:

- define the term "entrepreneur"
- discuss the concept of entrepreneurship and the entrepreneurial process
- describe the roles of entrepreneurs and small businesses in the economy
- explain how to become an entrepreneur
- comment on the skills and resources required to become an entrepreneur
- identify and describe the different ways of entering the business world
- present recommendations regarding the choice of a business opportunity
- elaborate on what a feasibility study is and its value to the entrepreneur.

2.1 Introduction

The previous chapter revealed that the science of business management examines how to improve the performance of a business organisation, and it focused on how business organisations transform a nation's resources into products and services to meet the needs and wants of its people. However, in order to understand how the business organisation satisfies the needs and wants of a nation in a market economy, one needs to understand the driving force behind the business organisation: the entrepreneur.

It is the **entrepreneur** who decides what, how, by whom and for whom products and services should be produced. An entrepreneur is someone who starts a **business** with the intention of making a profit and assumes the risk of losing all of his/her resources if the venture fails. (Managers, in contrast, are not entrepreneurs for they assume relatively little risk for the success or failure of the business.)

The entrepreneur is the source of one of the four main factors of production discussed in Chapter 1: natural resources (land), human resources (labour), financial resources (**capital**) and entrepreneurship. Entrepreneurship is the factor that mobilises the other three resources (land, labour and capital) and harnesses them in different combinations to meet the needs and wants of society.

Entrepreneurship is the process by which individuals pursue opportunities without regard to resources they currently control[1].

The process of starting a new business, of sometimes failing and sometimes succeeding, is entrepreneurship. Entrepreneurship is constituted by those individuals in society who use their initiative and take the risk of harnessing the factors of production to provide products and services. The entrepreneur's reward for taking the initiative and taking risks is profit. The entrepreneur's punishment for making the wrong decisions is financial loss.

By knowing what drives entrepreneurs, and how they identify and assess business opportunities and enter the business world, the student of business management will have a better understanding of how business organisations function. This is essential even if the student plans to become a manager, as managers play a key role in the success or failure of business organisations, and need to know how the entrepreneurial process works.

2.2 Different concepts of what an entrepreneur is

The first question that arises in the quest for a scientifically based definition of the notion of an "entrepreneur" concerns identity: Who or what is an entrepreneur? Is the owner of a suburban filling station, the local estate agent or the owner of a Nando's franchise an entrepreneur? Are there entrepreneurs in schools, government projects and large enterprises?

There is no hard-and-fast rule here, nor is there a formal classification or register of entrepreneurs. Moreover, scientists have different views on whom or what exactly an entrepreneur is:

- Economists subscribe to the view that entrepreneurs combine different resources in specific combinations to generate products and services so as to make a profit. Their focus is on what entrepreneurs do. Entrepreneurs, to them, are people who are driven primarily by the profit motive.
- Behaviourists (psychologists and sociologists) tend to view entrepreneurs from the behavioural perspective. Psychologists describe entrepreneurs according to their characteristics, for example, the achievement orientation of entrepreneurs and their propensity towards creativity and risk-taking.
- Marxists regard entrepreneurs as exploiters.
- Corporate managers see entrepreneurs as small operators who lack the potential to manage a large enterprise.
- Proponents of a market economy see entrepreneurs as the economic force responsible for the prosperity of a country.

In addition, simply in the field of management and entrepreneurship, writers give differing definitions of what an entrepreneur is. Entrepreneurs have been described as people who:

- have innovative ideas (because business involves new products, new processes, new markets, new materials and new ways of doing things)
- identify opportunities (created by the unlimited needs of people and trends that appear in the environment)
- find resources (natural resources, human resources, financial resources and entrepreneurship) to pursue these opportunities for personal gain (profit)

- take financial risks (run the risk of potential loss or failure of the businesses they start)
- bring about change, growth and wealth in the economy (winning nations have entrepreneur-driven economies)
- re-energise economies and create jobs (desperately needed in South Africa)
- start, manage and grow small businesses (the owner of a business starts and manages the business and re-allocates the business resources in such a way that the business makes a profit and grows).

An entrepreneur is usually a creative person who scores high on achievement motivation, is willing to take calculated risks and views a challenge as a new **opportunity**. The term "entrepreneur" tends to be associated with the founding of a new business or the owning and managing of a small one.

2.3 The renaissance of entrepreneurship

Entrepreneurs throughout the world are stirring up a revolution that is revitalising economies because the establishment of new businesses and the growth of existing ones are responsible for most of the products and services that are changing people's lives. Furthermore, entrepreneurs generate jobs. The traditional providers of job opportunities, namely large enterprises and government organisations, have been replaced by small businesses as the main providers of jobs. In the United States, small and medium-sized enterprises (SMEs) employ 85% of the workforce, and in Central and Eastern Europe, millions of new entrepreneurs are endeavouring to reform and transform the liberated communist economies.

Critical thinking

The term "entrepreneur" is often coupled with a new business or a small business, or with businesses that start as a result of an invention.

Are entrepreneurs found in large corporations?
Entrepreneurship is the process of mobilising and risking resources (financial resources, human resources and natural resources) to utilise a business opportunity or introduce an **innovation** in such a way that the needs and wants of society for products and services are satisfied, jobs are created and the owner of the business profits from it. This process includes new as well as existing businesses, but the emphasis is usually on new products or services and new businesses.

However, the fact that the term "entrepreneur" is associated with founding a new business or owning and managing a small one does not mean that entrepreneurs are not found in large corporations. In fact, most of South Africa's large corporations were started from small beginnings by people who went on to become illustrious entrepreneurs. The following people are well-known entrepreneurs:

- Anton Rupert, founder of Rembrandt, Remgro and Richemont
- Raymond Ackerman, founder of Pick n Pay
- Patrice Motsepe of African Rainbow Minerals, Armgold
- Tokyo Sexwale of Mvelaphanda Holdings
- Mark Shuttleworth of Thawte
- Annetjie Theron, founder of the Annique Skin Care and Cosmetic range
- Bill Venter of Altech and Altron
- Herman Mashaba, founder of Black Like Me
- Cyril Ramaphosa, founder of Shanduka
- Richard Maponya, owner of Maponya Mall, Soweto's first mega-regional up-market shopping centre, which opened in 2009.

Entrepreneurs are also transforming China and Cuba, the last bastions of communism.

Worldwide, countries are debating ways and means of addressing the problems of unemployment. **Employment** is closely linked to the state of the economy. When there is no growth in the economy, fewer employment opportunities are available.

2.4 Entrepreneurship in South Africa

Growth in the South African economy has declined over the past few decades. In the 1960s, growth of the gross domestic product (GDP) averaged nearly 6% per year. During the 1980s, GDP growth decreased to 2,2%, followed by no growth in the 1990s. In 2006, GDP growth averaged 4,9%, but this decreased again, to –3%, in the second quarter of 2009[2].

In order to sustain and improve the economic development of the country, a GDP growth rate of 6% should be attained within the next few years. The contribution of entrepreneurs will be relied on for a large part of the prospective 6% growth. While it is the combination of all businesses – small, medium and micro-enterprises (SMMEs) and large national and international businesses – that determines the state of the economy, it is high-potential entrepreneurs who are focused on growing their businesses who are responsible for growth and employment creation in the economy. An economic growth rate of about 12% per year is needed to achieve an employment growth rate of 3%, which will help to combat the high unemployment rate of 23,6%[3].

There are many reasons for South Africa's high unemployment level, but one reason in particular is the labour law. Statistics reveal that the more flexible the labour market is (the freer it is from government intervention), the lower the unemployment rate is. Another significant reason for South Africa's high unemployment is that South Africa does not have enough businesspeople involved in small businesses to create employment. The current interest in the phenomenon of entrepreneurship is therefore very understandable.

Yet entrepreneurship is a scarce resource, as born out by the results of the Global Entrepreneurship Monitor (GEM) survey. The Total Early-stage Entrepreneurial Activity (TEA) index is calculated based on this GEM survey, and shows the percentage of people aged between 18 and 64 who are actively involved in starting a business or managing a business that they wholly or partly own and that is fewer than three and a half years old. The GEM provides the TEA index to offer useful data on both the extent and nature of entrepreneurial activity in South Africa. In 2008, South Africa ranked 23rd out of 43 countries, with a TEA rate below the average rate of all participating countries (10,6%). South Africa's TEA rate of 7,8% is significantly lower than the average for all efficiency-driven economies (11,4%), as well as being below the average for all middle- to low-income countries (13,2%). Since 2001, South Africa's performance in terms of relative position has consistently been below the median and this trend continued in 2008. The 2008 GEM survey therefore confirms the findings of previous GEM reports that, given its *per capita* income, South Africa's rates of entrepreneurial activity are lower than would be expected. According to the GEM data, a country at South Africa's stage of economic development would be expected to have a TEA rate in the order of 13%, almost double South Africa's actual rate of 7,8%[4].

However South Africa has many successful entrepreneurs, and an example of such an entrepreneur appears in the case study on page 45. This study shows how a South African entrepreneur, Mr Ebrahim, managed to raise seed capital to start his own business, an investment company called Oasis Group Holdings. At first, he appointed too many employees at too high a cost, but he managed to set this right. In spite of many restrictive

Case study

Entrepreneurship in action: Exploiting restrictive rules

Buying shares in a company run by one of the finalists in this year's World Entrepreneur Awards helped finalist Adam Ismail Ebrahim – CEO and CIO of Oasis Group Holdings – fund his company.

"In 1997 – when I realised that my time as an employee was coming to an end – I sold shares that I had bought in Naspers a year before its listing at R1,45, for R50," says Ebrahim, whose brothers, Mohamed Shaheen (chairman) and Nazeem (deputy chairman), pooled resources with him to start an investment company.

They wanted to provide a particular service not previously offered to Muslims, both in terms of savings and retirement. Muslims have the dilemma that their religious rules prohibit them from benefitting from the proceeds of companies involved in alcohol, tobacco, financial services, entertainment and pork products as well as companies that are highly leveraged. The use of derivatives is also prohibited.

Oasis began with seed capital of R3 million, with a strong focus on developing the niche market of investments that complied with Shariah religious law. It has since grown to be the leader worldwide in Shariah-compliant investments. Both its global funds were rated AA by Standard & Poor's and its Crescent Global Fund received a five-star rating from MorningStar.

Ebrahim, who hails from District Six, holds a BSoc (Hons) from UCT. He later studied accounting, completed his articles at Deloitte and was seconded to the firm's London office in September 1986.

"It was an interesting time, with new regulations being implemented in the financial-services sector. On top of first-hand experience of changes in the regulatory environment, I witnessed the stock-market crash the following year," says Ebrahim, who gained insight into the world of investment while witnessing the contrast between "absolute euphoria caused by booming market conditions and utter depression" when the tide turned.

He returned to South Africa in 1988 and joined Allan Gray as an analyst, but was soon promoted to being the partner responsible for training managers. "Until 1996 things went very well and I felt that I was living my dream," says Ebrahim, who later found it "increasingly difficult" to get motivated by his environment.

"When I resigned to start out on my own, Allan Gray offered to fund my business. However, I felt that it would be inappropriate and that I wouldn't really be independent. I wanted the freedom to paddle my own boat, to follow my own philosophy and target untapped markets with my own resources. Thus we became competitors after I had eight good years with Allan Gray, gaining confidence and an understanding of the industry.

"But then I made a huge mistake," says Ebrahim. "I believed people who made promises of vast amounts of money that they'd invest in the new business. On the strength of that I made the next mistake: I hired 16 people – six being highly paid CAs.

"We had no revenue, no assets, an expensive salary bill and a very expensive cost structure – and the losses just kept mounting. To make matters worse, two weeks after getting our first institutional client, markets were hit by the Asian crisis. I know it has since become a sensitive image to use, but it was like a toddler taking his first steps along the beach just when a tsunami hits ...

"But we survived – on the foundations of an investment philosophy of no volatility, which, combined with our ethical offering, proved to be a very definite and successful niche.

"I fired everybody after realising they were having a ball doing nothing. We started managing the money we did have very strictly, our performance improved, losses disappeared and the company – and each of its operating subsidiaries – has never made a loss again," says Ebrahim.

"After having made every mistake possible, and having learnt very expensive lessons, performance started picking up and we decided to enter the retail market, which provided the breakthrough the company needed. People started coming to us, whereas before we had to call on people trying to convince them to invest R300 a month. Up to 65% of our sales were based on that direct model, which has led to our having the lowest churn ratio in the industry and proving how important personal relationships are in business. We now have 30 000 direct retail clients."

The Oasis Crescent Equity Fund, its flagship fund, has been the best performing equity fund since its inception in August 1998: R100 000 invested in that fund is now worth more than R1,1 million and the fund has now crossed the R2 billion mark.

December 2000 was another landmark for the group, when it registered its first global fund, the Crescent Global Equity Fund. That has since established itself as the world's best performing Shariah-compliant equity fund.

The retail retirement business was launched in 2002, providing all investors access to Shariah-compliant and ethical retirement savings not previously available. "We find that 30% of our clientele aren't Muslims," says Ebrahim. Oasis also launched the first Shariah-compliant prudential unit trust in April last year and the first listed Shariah-compliant property fund in November last year.

Ebrahim ascribes the success of the business – voted best collective investment-scheme manager in South Africa for the past two quarters – to an owner-based culture and adherence to global regulatory and ethical standards. He says the Oasis model is also built on selling a product tailored to what people need and not so much on what they want, a result of building up a personal relationship with a client.

Oasis has more than R25 billion of assets under management, and employs 140 people in South Africa and Ireland. Through a joint venture in Malaysia, the group has exposure to Singapore, Indonesia and Brunei.

"We see SA as a great investment destination and intend to run our global business from our head office in Cape Town," says Ebrahim.

In February 2007, Oasis opened associate offices in Dubai. In that same year, Oasis reached the USD4 billion mark in assets under management. In June 2007, it celebrated its tenth birthday. In February 2008, Oasis opened its office in Dublin to further the growth of its global portfolio-management capabilities. It continues to expand its product range.

Sources: Adapted from Naudé, C. 2006. "Exploiting restrictive rules", *Finweek*, 9 November, pp. 69–70. Reprinted by permission of Gallo Images/IMAGES24.co.za/Finweek.

rules pertaining to investments in his market, he managed to identify investments complying with the requirements of his clients. His Cape Town-based business then became very profitable, and by 2008 it had two overseas branches, one in Dubai and one in Dublin[5].

2.5 The role of entrepreneurs and small-business owners in society

Chapter 1 described how businesses, owned and driven by entrepreneurs, satisfy needs and wants by mobilising a country's natural, human and financial resources to produce much-needed products and services. In the process, wealth is created for society (in the form of jobs) and for the entrepreneur (in the form of profits). Entrepreneurial activity is the essential source of economic growth and social development, and the key role played by this factor of production was under-estimated for many decades. Entrepreneurship is the spark that brings the other factors of production into motion. However, it is also imperative to realise that entrepreneurship is in turn mobilised by the self-efficacy, creativity, skills and expectations of individuals. If the entrepreneurial spirit is absent, the production machine does not go into action.

People with entrepreneurial talents and skills and an entrepreneurial orientation are able to achieve more than others in mobilising productive resources by starting enterprises that will grow. People with entrepreneurial qualities are rare and valuable. They constitute a resource that greatly contributes to, if not causes, the production of products and services. They set in motion the creation of employment opportunities.

True entrepreneurs differ dramatically from **small-business owners** who are satisfied with some autonomy and earning a reasonable income for themselves and perhaps a few employees, but who have no intention of growing and developing their business entrepreneurially. Therefore not all small businesses are entrepreneurial. There is a distinct difference between entrepreneurial businesses and some, or perhaps even the majority of, SMMEs, which are not entrepreneurial. SMMEs often exist as a way of earning income that is an alternative to working as an employee. They satisfy their owner's need for independence or the lifestyle needs of their owner.

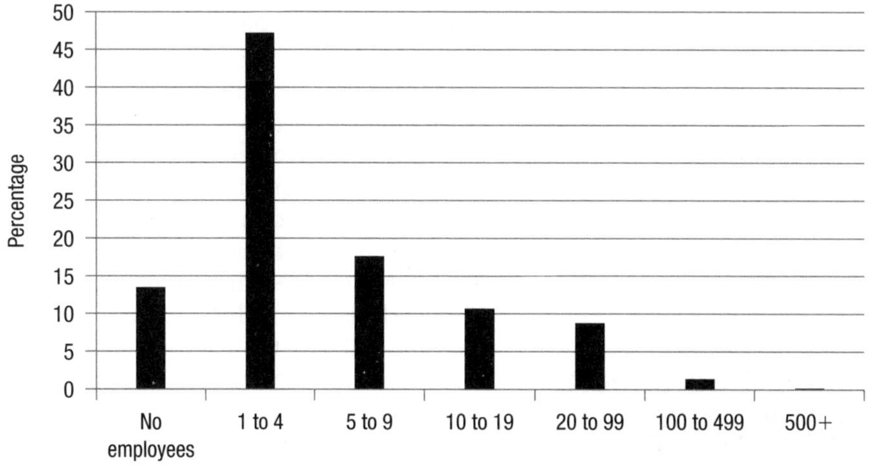

Figure 2.1: Employment size of businesses in the United States

Source: US Census Bureau. 2004. "Statistics of US Businesses". [Online] Available: http://www.census.gov/epcd/www/smallbus.html Accessed 3 September 2009.

Mr Ebrahim, the subject of the case study on pages 45–46, is a true entrepreneur. He not only started his own business in 1997, but also managed to grow it over fewer than ten years to become a medium to large business, and he still remains entrepreneurial. He continuously adds new products, such as the Oasis Crescent Equity Fund in 1998, the Crescent Global Equity Fund in 2000, Oasis's retail retirement business in 2002, and a prudential unit trust as well as a property fund in 2005. By 2009, the company had 21 funds including various equity, property and retirement funds.

However, while high-growth entrepreneurs are vital for any economy, this does not mean less entrepreneurial SMMEs are not important. In South Africa, the sector including SMMEs comprises about 95% of all enterprises, accounts for almost 75% of employment in the country and contributes approximately 56% to the country's GDP[6].

Similarly, in the United States, nearly 80% of businesses have fewer than ten employees, and 47% of businesses employ between one and four employees, as is shown in Figure 2.1 on page 47.

Cognisance should be taken of the fact that the definition of a small business can vary from country to country. In South Africa, the National Small Business Amendment Act (No. 29 of 2004) defines a "small business" as a company with a labour force of fewer than 50 employees[7]. In developed economies such as the United States, "small businesses" are defined as businesses that employ up to 500 people.

2.6 Why do entrepreneurs do what they do?

As well as examining what an entrepreneur is and what an entrepreneur does, a succinct overview of why entrepreneurs enter the world of business will add to an understanding of the complex concept of entrepreneurship. However, a full understanding of why entrepreneurs do what they do has eluded researchers for many years. Comparative studies have indicated that roughly one-third of a nation's people enter into business, while the other two-thirds are professionals, government employees, employees of businesses and the unemployed. But what is it about the entrepreneur that causes him/her to enter into the world of business?

The decision to enter into business is influenced by many variables, which differ from country to country. However, three broad categories of reasons for individuals initiating ventures are their traits and characteristics, their skills and industry **experience**, and the opportunities arising owing to international trends towards outsourcing.

2.6.1 Entrepreneurs' traits and characteristics

The following **traits and characteristics** are typical of entrepreneurs.

2.6.1.1 Achievement motivation

The most researched and possibly the most essential trait of an entrepreneur is **achievement motivation**. In pioneering studies by the researcher David McClelland[8], entrepreneurs are described as people with a higher need to achieve than people who are not entrepreneurs. Achievement motivation is characterised by actions of intense, prolonged and repeated effort to accomplish something that is difficult. The person with achievement motivation will also work single-mindedly towards his/her goal and will have the determination to win and to do everything well. He/she will enjoy competition.

Achievement motivation goes hand-in-hand with ambition and competitiveness. People with a high need to achieve are attracted to jobs that challenge their skills and their problem-solving abilities. They avoid goals that they think would be almost impossible to achieve or ones that would guarantee success. They prefer tasks in which the outcome depends upon their individual efforts.

An entrepreneur or would-be entrepreneur's high need for achievement also includes the following other needs:

- the need to be personally responsible for solving problems
- the need to set one's own goals and reach these goals through one's own efforts
- the need to have feedback on the degree of success with which tasks are accomplished
- the need to have personal accomplishments
- the need to have control over one's own time, and to use time and money creatively (entrepreneurs who start a new business usually desire independence and do not want to be controlled by someone else).

From the case study, it is clear that Mr Ebrahim of Oasis Group Holdings has a need for achievement. Once he had reached his dream of becoming a partner in Allan Gray, he realised that he had other goals to achieve and started his own business. He demonstrated a definite need to be independent by refusing funding from his former employer. He used his own time and money (resources) to enter a new market, which is evidence of his ability to identify an opportunity. He wanted the freedom "to paddle [his] own boat, to follow [his] own philosophy and target untapped markets with [his] own resources".

2.6.1.2 An internal locus of control

The second significant characteristic of an entrepreneur is a strong internal locus of control as opposed to an external locus of control. An **internal locus of control** indicates a person's need to be in charge of his/her own destiny, whereas an external locus of control indicates that a person believes that the outcome of an event is primarily out of his/her personal control. People with an external locus of control regard luck and fortune, rather than personal ability and hard work, as the reasons for success. People with a strong internal locus of control believe that the outcome of an event is determined by their own actions. They believe that they have control over their own behaviour, are successful in persuading and motivating other people, actively seek relevant information and knowledge, are well informed about their careers, perform well on skills-related tasks and process information efficiently. Luck, chance or fate is therefore of little relevance to an entrepreneurial personality.

In the case study, Mr Ebrahim clearly acknowledged his own mistakes, including believing in promises made by people and hiring a workforce that was too expensive. He took personal control by getting rid of superfluous employees, by starting to manage the company's money personally and by initiating an investment policy of no volatility.

2.6.1.3 Innovation and creativity

Successful entrepreneurs and owners of small businesses are innovative and creative. **Innovation**, or the production of something new or original, results from the ability to conceive of and create new and unique products, services or processes. Entrepreneurs identify opportunities in the marketplace and visualise creative new ways to take advantage of them. Innovation is usually included in any definition of creativity. Although not all entrepreneurs develop new products or services, or discover new resources, every person who establishes an enterprise, and who adds value and ensures that an enterprise continues to exist (thereby developing job opportunities) is involved in economic creation.

"**Creativity**" refers to the creation of something new, for example, the creation of a new business by developing a new product or service, building an organisation by financial manipulation, reshaping an existing business, or creating a business that will survive on its own and generate a financial fortune as testimony to the entrepreneur's skill. Basically, creativity involves new ideas, and any application of these new ideas is based on innovation.

However, as well as involving the identification of opportunities and solutions, creativity can also involve the adjustment or refinement of existing procedures or products. Although entrepreneurs understand the importance of innovation, they often view the risk and the high investment that the development of innovative products or services requires as being out of proportion to the potential profit. This explains why entrepreneurs often creatively adapt innovations of competitors by, for example, product adjustments, imaginative marketing and client service. Thus their creativity finds expression on the continuum of innovation and adaptation.

From the case study, it follows that Mr Ebrahim had the ability to be innovative. He developed a savings and retirement service, an equity fund, a prudential unit trust and a property fund not previously offered to a particular target market, namely Muslim people. By ensuring compliance to Shariah religious laws (that prohibit Muslim people from benefitting from the proceeds of companies involved in alcohol, tobacco, financial services, entertainment, pork products, high-leverage operations and the use of derivatives), he made it possible for this target market to save and invest for retirement.

2.6.1.4 Risk-taking

Most researchers agree that entrepreneurial behaviour involves the taking of risks in one way or another. In the business world, many variables such as interest rates, currency fluctuations, new laws and so on are beyond the control of the entrepreneur. The successful entrepreneur correctly interprets the risk situation and then determines actions that will minimise the risk; he/she does not take chances, but sometimes feels it is necessary to take **calculated risks**. Unsuccessful entrepreneurs, in contrast, do not take any risks, or else they take expensive, impulsive decisions that they do not think through. Entrepreneurs investigate the critical variables of the situation and calculate the probable results before they take decisions. Successful entrepreneurs avoid opportunities where there is a high probability that they will be unsuccessful, regardless of the reward.

Entrepreneurs manage the risk of their enterprises by accepting control and being involved in the basic aspects of the enterprise. They control their enterprises by getting access to information. They reduce their exposure to financial loss by involving investors, often with the risk of losing control. They shorten the time between the conceptualisation of an idea and availability of the product or service in the market. This is one way of limiting the risk of competition.

The conclusion can be drawn that, before embarking on a venture, successful entrepreneurs take calculated risks based on applicable research, the analysis of information and the investigation of the probable results of an opportunity. As part of this process, they undertake tasks such as feasibility studies, market research, and research and development.

In the case study, Mr Ebrahim knew that he had experience in the business that he planned to pursue. He was also willing to invest his own money (by the sale of his shares in another company) as well as money provided by his brothers (who were to become shareholders in the business). He determined the cost, his available funds and his own knowledge before starting the business. Yet this was not sufficient proof that the business would be a success. He first had to learn various other lessons in the business before he became successful. The establishment of any business involves some risks. Personal mistakes, as well as environmental factors such as volatile financial markets, contributed to the risks of Oasis Group Holdings, but Mr Ebrahim overcame them through entrepreneurial skills and knowledge of the industry.

2.6.1.5 Other traits

The other traits of entrepreneurs include high levels of energy, confidence, future orientation, optimism, the desire for feedback, high tolerance for ambiguity, flexibility/adaptability and commitment.

2.6.2 Entrepreneurs' skills and industry experience

Some people can exploit **opportunities** more successfully than others. **Skills and** knowledge, an identified opportunity and the quest for independence are among the most significant **reasons for people becoming entrepreneurs**. Experience, training and education in a specific field contribute to the success of an entrepreneur in identifying an opportunity, establishing a business and managing it.

Job termination and job dissatisfaction can also lead people to become entrepreneurs. In South Africa, the experience of being unemployed may trigger some people into becoming entrepreneurs. These entrepreneurs are known as **necessity entrepreneurs** and are usually less successful than **opportunity entrepreneurs**.

Entrepreneurship is not necessarily an opportunity for the unemployed because only a few unemployed people have the four main factors of production: natural resources (land), human resources (labour), financial resources (capital) and entrepreneurship. Experience, access to resources and an identified opportunity (which usually comes with experience and exposure in business) are essential for successful entrepreneurship. For example, Mr Ebrahim, featured in the case study on pages 45–46, is qualified in accounting and knew the financial-services sector well owing to extensive exposure and employment in it for ten years. He also had access to capital (his own savings in the form of shares and the savings of his brothers) and, most importantly, he had the desire and ability to create a new business instead of continuing to be employed.

2.6.3 Opportunities arising owing to outsourcing

Outsourcing occurs when work is done for a company by people other than the company's full-time employees[9]. For example, South African Breweries (SAB) previously used large trucks to distribute the beer that the company brewed to customer outlets. Now the distribution of beer has been outsourced to owner-drivers of trucks. Drivers and employees of SAB were empowered to purchase trucks and set up their own businesses. They receive contracts from SAB to deliver beer to clients in demarcated areas[10].

Outsourcing usually takes place when a company defines activities that can be completed by other companies that are particularly skilled at and experienced in completing such activities. In cases where the other company could not deliver a better-quality activity, but the same quality of activity, outsourcing would be considered if the activity could be delivered at a lower cost.

Government departments, government organisations and large businesses outsource many of the services and components they need. In this way, they reduce personnel costs and gain access to special skills. In this process, once again, entrepreneurs play a critical role. They are responsible for the formation of new businesses, to which non-core functions are outsourced, often taking over or buying sections of larger organisations that otherwise would have been closed down.

According to a survey conducted in the United States by the International Facility Management Association[11], the services that are most often outsourced are (in order):

- architectural design
- trash and waste removal
- housekeeping
- facility systems
- landscape maintenance
- property appraisals
- major moves

- hazardous-materials removal
- major redesigns
- furniture moves
- food services.

Outsourcing is seen as part of a company's strategic plan. The reasons for outsourcing services, according to most of the facility managers, is to acquire specialty skills that are unavailable in-house or are not cost-efficient to handle in-house. Furthermore, they outsource services so that they can focus on their core competencies. Other reasons to outsource include acquiring access to specialty tools and equipment, adding flexibility to work fluctuations, enhancing quality and improving customer satisfaction[12]. In South Africa, owing to labour laws and other complicated issues in the environment, human-resources functions are often outsourced.

2.6.4 Other reasons for entrepreneurship

While employees of large businesses are often laid off, SMMEs continue to be established and to grow. Retrenched employees either become self-employed or become employed by new SMMEs that are formed when large businesses sell off some of their sections to function as SMMEs. For example, three employees of a large mining group that unbundled a few years ago bought two mines that would have been closed down. They had experience in the mining industry, developed a plan, took some risks, started off with a loan, took over the operations, restructured and made some crucial changes. They have been extremely profitable, are growing, and are in the process of buying additional mines and providing employment to many. The worldwide privatisation of government organisations has also resulted in employees becoming entrepreneurs.

While the brief overview above gives some of the main reasons for people becoming entrepreneurs, it does not cover the exhaustive list that may be found in many textbooks. It must also be remembered that entrepreneurs and owners of small businesses come in every shape, size and colour, and from all backgrounds.

2.7 The small business

The concept of entrepreneurship is strongly associated with the establishment of a small business or the owning of one, and therefore attention is drawn to the distinction between entrepreneurship and small business by defining "a small business" and explaining its role in the economy.

2.7.1 Defining "a small business"

It is difficult to formulate a universal definition of a small business because the economies of countries differ and people adopt particular standards for specific purposes. South African towns typically have a variety of small businesses, such as the local hairdressing salon, the greengrocer, the video shop and the hardware store.

An example of a small business would be a restaurant started by a woman who was previously an employee at a different restaurant, where she learnt and gained knowledge about the restaurant business. However this woman eventually started her own restaurant after identifying a need for a specific type of restaurant, for example, one specialising in organic food. This owner is now satisfied with the success of her restaurant and the income she earns from it, and has no plans or inclination to expand or open other restaurants.

What may be considered a small business is also relative to one's frame of reference. A local supermarket regarded by some people as big may actually be small in comparison with a business such as Pick n Pay. Likewise, medium and even large businesses in South Africa may be small in comparison with their overseas counterparts. In most countries, it is therefore accepted practice to make use of quantitative criteria when attempting to define a small business enterprise.

Examples of quantitative criteria in defining a small business are:

- the number of employees
- the sales volume
- the value of the assets
- the market share.

In the National Small Business Amendment Act (No. 29 of 2004), micro-businesses in the eleven different sectors are defined as businesses with five or fewer employees and a turnover of up to R200 000. Very small businesses employ up to 10 or 20 employees, depending on the sector. Small businesses employ up to 50 employees, and have a total annual turnover ranging between R3 million and R32 million, depending on the sector in which the business is classified, and with a total gross asset value ranging between R1 million and R6 million, again depending on the sector[13]. Medium-sized businesses usually employ up to 100 or 200 people (depending on the sector), and the maximum turnover varies from R5 million in the Agricultural Sector to R51 million in the Manufacturing Sector, and to R64 million in the Wholesale Trade, Commercial Agents and Allied Services Sector[14].

A comprehensive definition of a small and medium-sized enterprise (SME) and a small, micro and medium-sized enterprise (SMME) in South Africa is therefore any enterprise with one or more of the following characteristics:

- fewer than 200 employees
- an annual turnover of less than R64 million
- capital assets of less than R23 million
- direct managerial involvement by owners.

Oasis Group Holdings, the subject of the case study on pages 45–46, is an example of an entrepreneurial business that began as a small business with limited funds but that, through the entrepreneurial flair of its owner, developed and grew to be a medium-sized to large business.

2.7.2 The role of small businesses in the economy

In developed economies, the entrepreneur is recognised as a key factor in the process of economic development. Entrepreneurs innovate, take risks and employ people. They create markets and serve consumers by combining materials, processes and products in new ways. They initiate change, create wealth and develop new enterprises. More specifically, the strategic role of small business in any economy revolves around the production of products and services, innovation, the aiding of big business and job creation.

2.7.2.1 The production of products and services

Small businesses combine the resources of society efficiently to produce products and services for the society in which they operate. Small businesses are less inhibited by large bureaucratic decision-making structures, and are more flexible and productive than many large firms. In advanced economies, they not only employ the majority of the workforce, but also produce most of the products and services.

2.7.2.2 Innovation

Small businesses have been responsible for most of the innovation worldwide. Statistics show that many scientific breakthroughs in the United States originated with small organisations and not in the laboratories of large businesses. The following are some examples of the new products created, developed or invented by entrepreneurs:

- photocopiers
- jet engines
- insulin
- helicopters
- vacuum tubes
- colour film
- penicillin
- ballpoint pens
- zips

- personal computers
- velcro.

More recently, the following technology-related products and services have been created, developed or invented by entrepreneurs:

- cellphones
- the internet
- search engines such as Google
- microchips
- MP3 players such as the iPod
- internet-safety software
- MXIT
- drag-and-draw digital paint sets.

2.7.2.3 The aiding of big business

Any country needs large enterprises to be able to function competitively in local and, especially, in international markets. The Japanese mega-corporations, for example, compete internationally as world players and have conquered markets that earn them billions of foreign currency for domestic development. In the process, they provide millions of local suppliers with orders. It is the efficiency of the local suppliers, however, that enables the big corporations to compete internationally. Small businesses not only act as suppliers to large businesses, but also distribute their products.

2.7.2.4 Job creation

As was previously stated, small businesses provide many of the new job opportunities needed by a growing population. In fact, they create jobs, whereas large corporations are shedding jobs.

The small business is often entrepreneurially driven. It is this entrepreneurial spirit that is in particular encountered in the smaller enterprise that is the catalyst for economic development and job creation. Small businesses tend to stimulate competition and thereby improve productivity.

2.8 The entrepreneurial process

Entrepreneurship is the process of identifying, creating or sensing an opportunity where others do not see it, and of finding and combining resources (often owned by

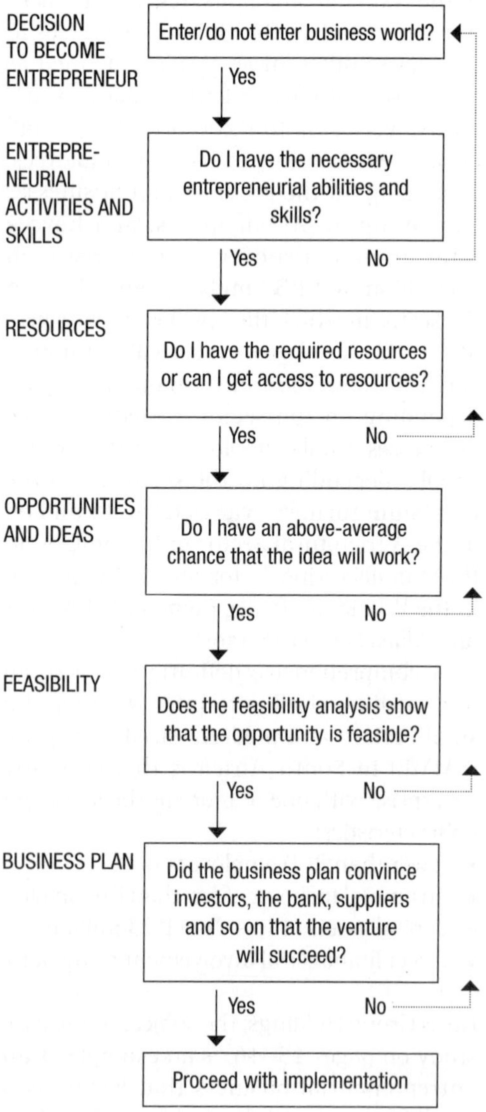

Figure 2.2: The entrepreneurial process: A framework for decision-making about new ventures

someone else) to pursue the opportunity until it becomes a successful established business. Of the thousands of business ventures that entrepreneurs launch every year, many never get off the ground, while others have a spectacular start. Much of the success in establishing a new business depends on how well the entrepreneur has done his/her homework. This is a difficult process because the range of problems and options confronting the entrepreneur is vast, and differs from one opportunity to the next.

For example, although Holiday Inn and City Lodge compete in the same industry, they did not evolve in the same way. Their room rates and the range of services available to customers differ.

The options that are appropriate for one entrepreneurial venture may be completely inappropriate for another. Entrepreneurs must make a bewildering number of decisions – and they must make the right decisions or their businesses will perish.

By following a scientific decision-making framework as illustrated in Figure 2.2 on page 54, the entrepreneur has a better chance of success. This framework or entrepreneurial process of entering the business world follows a logical sequence and clarifies many of the questions the entrepreneur is faced with.

The **entrepreneurial process** involves the following issues to be resolved or phases to be worked through:

- The **personal characteristics, abilities and skills** of the new owner of a business have a profound influence on the success or failure of the new venture. Before entering the business world, any potential entrepreneur should first clarify whether he/she has what it takes to do so.
- Another key factor in the creation of a new venture is the question of resources, or rather **access to resources**. Without access to entrepreneurship and the financial, natural and human resources necessary for the establishment of a business, the new venture is doomed.
- A critical aspect of the entrepreneurial process is the realistic and objective assessment of the **opportunity** that the entrepreneur is pursuing.
* Once the opportunity has been identified and defined, the entrepreneur needs to find out if it can be turned into a successful venture. This calls for a **feasibility study**.
- When the entrepreneur has some certainty about the **feasibility** of the venture, he/she needs to compile a **business plan**.
* After the feasibility has been established and the resources have been acquired, the entrepreneur must **launch and manage** the new business.

These phases of the entrepreneurial process can also be perceived as a framework for decision-making. In each of the phases in the process, the entrepreneur is faced with many questions that must be clarified before he/she can proceed to the next phase.

Yet the framework given above does not guarantee that a new venture will be successful. Rather, it provides a logical sequence of steps or phases in the entrepreneurial process. In each phase, there is a multiplicity of issues that need to be carefully assessed if the new idea is to be implemented successfully.

Figure 2.3 on page 56 summarises the dynamics of the entrepreneurial process. The entrepreneurial process is the creation of new value through the entrepreneur identifying new opportunities and using his/her leadership skills to build an organisation that fits the opportunity, and attracts and manages a configuration of resources with the focus on exploiting the opportunity[15]. During this dynamic process, the entrepreneur continuously learns through success and failure. From this process, entrepreneurial behaviour, characteristics and/or skills that contribute to success may become apparent.

The sections that follow offer a closer examination of the first four phases of the entrepreneurial process.

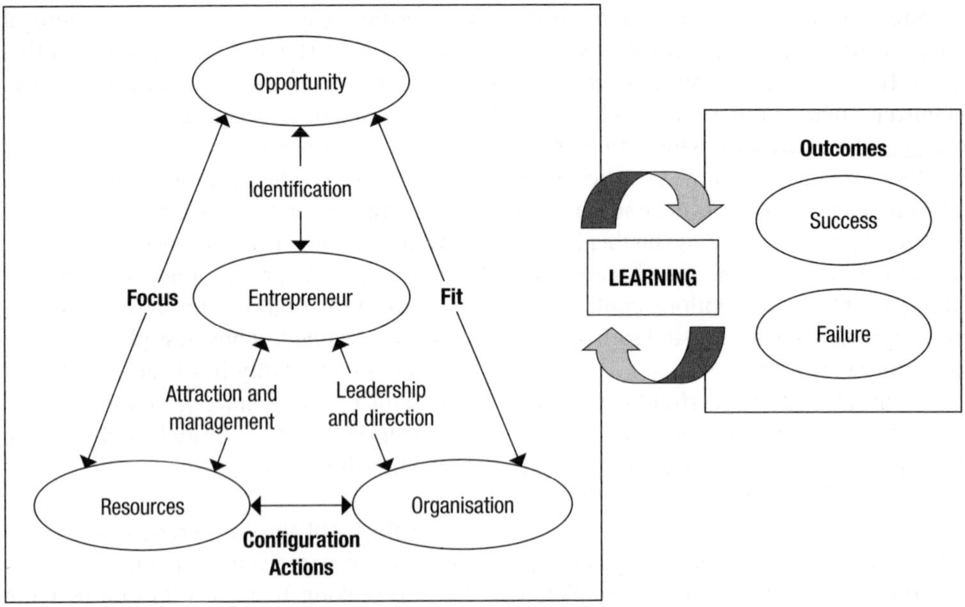

Figure 2.3: The dynamics of the entrepreneurial process

Source: Wickham, P.A. 2004. *Strategic entrepreneurship.* 3rd ed. Harlow: Prentice-Hall – Financial Times, pp. 134, 138–139.

2.8.1 Skills required for entrepreneurship

A skill is simply knowledge that is demonstrated through action. Potential entrepreneurs therefore need knowledge about the particular environments and industries in which they want to operate, plus considerable management skills, such as the following:

- **Strategy skills** involve the ability to consider the business as a whole and to understand how it fits within its marketplace, how it can organise itself to deliver value to its customers and the ways in which it does this more effectively and efficiently than its competitors.
- **Planning skills** involve the ability to consider what the future might offer, how this will impact on the business, and what resources and actions are necessary to prepare for it.
- **Marketing skills** involve the ability to evaluate the offerings of the business and their features, to determine how they satisfy customers' needs and wants, and to establish why customers find them attractive. Marketing skills also involve the pricing, promotion and distribution of the products or services. In the case study on pages 45–46, Mr Ebrahim invested in a model of direct selling based on a personal relationship with investors. This model ensured the lowest churn ratio in the investment industry, resulting in 30 000 direct retail clients. The product was tailored to the needs of the people and not so much to what they wanted. This was determined by Oasis through personal relationships with clients.
- **Financial skills** involve the ability to manage money – to be able to keep track of expenditure and to monitor cash flow – and to assess investments in terms of their potential and their risks.
- **Project-management skills** involve the ability to organise projects, to set specific objectives, to draw up schedules and to

ensure that the necessary resources are in the right place at the right time, in the right quantity and the right quality.

- **Human-relations skills** involve the ability to deal with people, and include leadership skills, motivational skills and communication skills.

All these management skills are needed in entrepreneurship, and the more favourably a person is endowed with these skills, the greater his/her chances for success. These skills are discussed in Parts 2 and 3 of this book.

2.8.2 Resources needed to start a business

An entrepreneur must have an adequate amount of resources to start a business, or he/she must have access to resources to be able to enter into business. In many ventures, entrepreneurs do not necessarily want to own the resources that will enable them to start a business, but they may seek control of the resources they use. The emphasis is therefore not on what resources the entrepreneur owns, but rather on what access to and control of resources he/she has.

Entrepreneurs acquire resources from the economy and transform these into need-satisfying products and services for the community. Resources are therefore the inputs that the business combines to create the outputs it delivers to its customers. In broad terms, there are three kinds of resources that entrepreneurs need to build their ventures: financial resources, human resources and operating or physical resources.

An opportunity can be exploited only if the entrepreneur has money or has access to money. **Financial resources** can take the form of cash, a bank overdraft, loans, outstanding debtors or investment capital. Financial resources include basic resources that can readily be converted into cash.

Human resources are people such as the management team, lawyers, accountants, and technical and other consultants. Human resources basically include people with knowledge and skills that contribute to the success of the venture.

Operating resources or **physical resources** are assets such as offices, vehicles, equipment, raw materials and, in the case of larger small businesses, buildings, machinery and the plant.

Prospective entrepreneurs must realise that the acquisition of resources implies risk, especially if the expected profits and return on investments do not materialise. If the entrepreneur has used his/her savings to finance the business or used his/her house as security against a loan, that entrepreneur is the one who carries the risk and who stands to lose the savings or the house if the venture is unsuccessful.

If using investors as a source of finance, prospective entrepreneurs must know that investors always compare alternative investments with the anticipated return on the investment and the risks involved.

Although a prospective entrepreneur may have the right experience and the right personal traits to become an entrepreneur, he/she cannot successfully exploit an opportunity without the necessary resources or without access to these resources. This is the most difficult hurdle to cross in becoming the owner of a small business.

2.8.3 Business opportunities

Establishing a new business usually involves an idea that the entrepreneur pursues enthusiastically. Finding a good idea is therefore the first step in converting an entrepreneur's creativity into a business opportunity. The danger, however, is that the attractiveness of the idea is often over-rated. In other words, having the best idea is by no means a guarantee of success. Unless the entrepreneur has the capacity and capability to transform the idea into a product or service that captures a significant share of the market, the idea is of little value.

But where do new ideas for a business start-up come from? Research in both the United States and other countries points to the fact that prior work experience, an understanding of the industry and knowledge of the market account for most new venture ideas. For example, in the case study on pages 45–46, it was clear that Mr Ebrahim had extensive experience in the financial-services industry and he also had a very good knowledge of the market, namely the people of the Muslim community and their needs, as well as the Shariah restrictions that apply to them. This knowledge and experience resulted in 70% of the clients of Oasis being Muslims bound by Shariah.

The scientific way to search for ideas involves a thorough search of the business environment for ideas and patterns that emerge from various environmental trends. The business environment is examined in more detail in Chapter 4.

2.8.3.1 New venture ideas

The environment referred to includes everything that happens around the entrepreneur. Trends in the environment include economic, political and **social trends**, fashions that change over time, new ways in which products are distributed, new services that are offered and so on.

Topical trends in South Africa include economic and social trends:

- When the exchange rate favours foreigners (that is when the rand is weak against the dollar, pound and euro), this makes South Africa a very attractive tourist destination and most activities associated with tourism could provide entrepreneurial opportunities.
- The high unemployment rate combined with a police force that appears incapable of enforcing the law results in violent crime being rampant in South Africa. This fact threatens, for example, foreign investment and tourism, but offers many ideas and opportunities for the protection of individuals and their property. It has resulted in a high demand for the services of businesses that install burglar bars, security fences, security gates, alarm systems and security services such as guards.
- Changing social trends over the past decade have contributed to changing food consumption and distribution patterns, and the outcome is a proliferation of fast-food outlets and pubs.
- Among the new services that have sprung up in the wake of privatisation of government organisations are mail and courier services.

In searching the environment for entrepreneurial ideas, entrepreneurs must remember that industries, like fashions, go through various life-cycle stages, as illustrated by Figure 2.4 on page 59.

Virtually everything changes according to a **life cycle**, going through the stages of introduction (embryo), growth, maturity and decline. When examining a new venture idea, it is important to know what stage the relevant industry is in, because a different strategy is needed for each stage.

Industries in the maturity stage are, for example, very competitive, resulting in high marketing costs. It is clear from the life-cycle diagram that the car (automobile) industry as a whole is very mature. Nonetheless, some of its segments are in a developing phase, for example, mini-vans, sports models and upmarket imports. Convertibles are back in fashion, and in the suburbs young mothers drive around in 4×4s. Despite increasing traffic jams, people still drive, and the cars they drive reflect changing lifestyles.

Where can you find gaps in the life-cycle diagram in Figure 2.4? Ideas can be generated at any point in the **life-cycle stages** of industries. They may emerge even in those industries that fall into the decline category. This is evident from the revival of cigar smoking. There is even a magazine in South Africa that specifically targets cigar smokers. In addition, hula hoops are making a comeback.

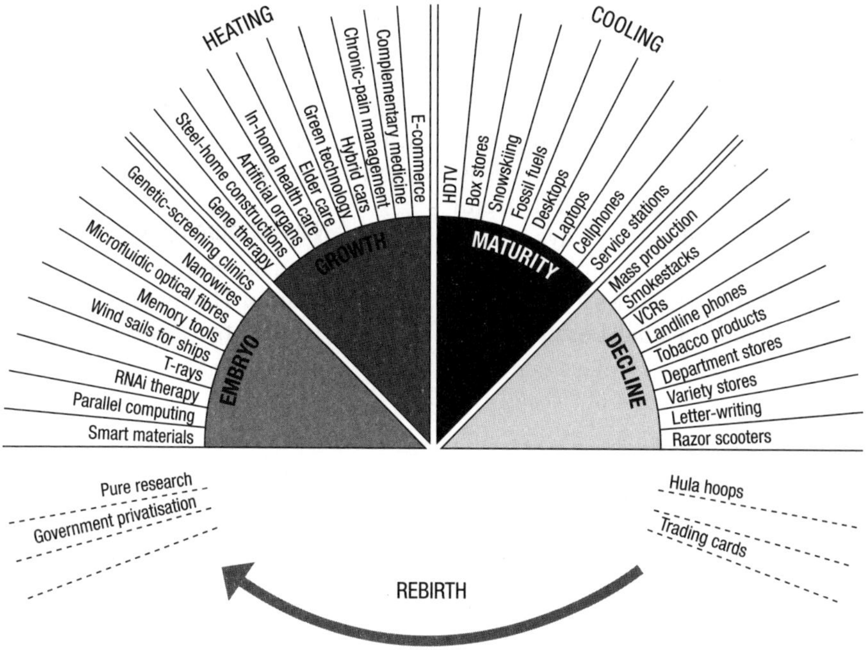

Figure 2.4: The life-cycle stages of industries

Source: Adapted from Ryan, J.D. 1989. *Small Business: An Entrepreneur's Business Plan.* 2nd ed., p. 32. South-Western, a part of Cengage Learning, Inc. www.cengage.com/permissions.

South African industries can also be classified into the categories that appear in Figure 2.4, but prospective entrepreneurs should take a close look at the following industries, which could, in the African landscape, be labelled growth industries:

- **Education.** The government's main priority is to educate all South Africans. Proof of this is the fact that the budget for education comprises the largest portion of the annual budget. The importance of education, combined with the inability of government to reach its educational objectives, has resulted in many opportunities in private education, from elementary education to technical and tertiary education.
- **Health care.** Most government hospitals perform poorly. Thus numerous opportunities exist for entrepreneurs to start health-care ventures, especially home health care. In addition, opportunities such as the development of generic medicine and other health-care products can be pursued.
- **Tourism.** This has the potential to provide thousands of new jobs. Very little start-up capital is needed to become a tour guide, for example, or to establish a bed-and-breakfast in an existing personal residence. South Africa is becoming a destination for international conferences and sporting events, which open up many opportunities. Examples include academic conferences, visits by international sports teams and the 2010 Soccer World Cup.
- **Privatisation of government and semi-government services.** Worldwide and in South Africa, government services are being privatised. Entrepreneurs have the opportunity to acquire these organisations or parts of them.

Other sources of ideas include advertisements, retailers, competitors, trade shows, industry associations, contracts, consultants, patents and research institutes. The creative ability of the prospective entrepreneur is imperative in the generation of new ideas. A truly creative person will find useful ideas in a variety of different ways and by various means. Ideas, however, have to be transformed into opportunities if they are to result in the creation of small businesses.

The case study on this page shows how the entrepreneur Paul Anley found the resources to establish the South African business Pharma Dynamics in 2001, which in 2008 was still a fast-growing company with a growth rate of 41%[16].

2.8.3.2 New venture opportunities

Good ideas can be turned into successful new ventures. However, a good idea is not necessarily the same thing as a good

Case study

Seizing an opportunity in the health-care industry

Pharma Dynamics, established by Paul Anley, is a very strong business in the field of generic medicines for chronic cardiovascular illnesses, especially hypertension.

Anley says, "We benefitted hugely by entering a very young industry with an experienced management team and sales force." He says that was a definite contributing factor to the company being profitable from day one.

Based on research by IMS, the world's leading provider of business intelligence and strategic consultancy services for the pharmaceutical and health-care industries, Pharma Dynamics has been South Africa's fastest-growing pharmaceutical company since its inception in 2001, growing more than 50% in 2005. Anley is confident that it will achieve a turnover figure of R270 million by 2010.

The company, with its head office in Cape Town and a regional office in Sandton, north of Johannesburg, employs 53 people, 33 being sales staff who sell to 2 500 retail pharmacies, private practitioners and specialist physicians, especially in the cardiovascular field, throughout South Africa.

Anley says, "One of our strengths is the fact that we focus on 17 products instead of hundreds, which means that the reps can spend quality time with doctors. It's also important to be the first to market a new product, and this we achieve by obtaining the South African marketing rights for every pharmaceutical product expiring over the next three years.

"In the early days, it was difficult for us as a small company to be the first to market with generics, because you're constantly coming up against huge multi-nationals," says Anley, who had to mortgage his house to get seed capital. "However, it also helped that I cashed in some Warner Lambert share options granted in US dollars when the rand was trading at USD1/R12."

Apart from its strength in the field of cardiovascular generics, Pharma Dynamics also focuses on the growth of biogenerics. Because a very large portion of the population of South Africa suffers from diabetes, it has formed a joint venture with Wockhardt, a leading biopharmaceutical company in India. After its products have been submitted to the necessary regulatory procedures, the first generic insulin products will hopefully be brought to South Africa in the next couple of years.

Source: Naudé, C. 2006. "A dose of confidence". *Finweek*, 9 November, pp. 72–73. Reprinted by permission of Gallo Images/IMAGES24.co.za/Finweek.

opportunity. It may be a good idea, for example, to freeze a swimming pool during the short South African winter to save pool chemicals and to provide a home ice rink for children. But the idea cannot be transformed into a new venture opportunity because research has shown that South African pool owners do not find the idea persuasive as pool surfaces are too small. Moreover, because of the costs involved, the idea is not feasible.

A good idea is also not necessarily a good investment opportunity. Many people tend to become infatuated with an idea. They under-estimate the difficulty involved in developing it into a product or service that will be desirable to the market. Ultimately, the market determines whether an idea has potential as an investment opportunity.

The following are some of the fundamental requirements for a **good investment opportunity**:

- There must be a clearly defined market need for the product or service. The most successful entrepreneurs and investors are market focused; they start with what customers and the market want, and they do not lose sight of this.
- The opportunity must be able to achieve a sustainable competitive advantage.
- The opportunity must have the potential to grow.
- The opportunity must be rewarding to the investor and/or the entrepreneur.
- The timing of the opportunity must be right. A window of opportunity must exist. (For example, the window of opportunity for the delivery of a wedding cake closes on the day of the wedding. If the wedding cake is delivered on the morning after the wedding, it is worthless.)

Thus good opportunities are those that satisfy a market need, are well timed and reward the entrepreneur.

However, generating a good idea and starting a new venture from scratch is not the only way to enter the business world. Buying an existing business or procuring a franchise can reduce many of the uncertainties faced when starting a business.

2.8.3.3 Buying an existing business

There are several advantages to buying an existing business when compared with other strategies for entering the business world. Since customers are used to doing business with the company at its present address, they are likely to continue doing so once it has been taken over by a new owner. If the business has been making money, the new owner will break even sooner than if he/she started the business from scratch. Planning for an

Table 2.1: Advantages and disadvantages of buying an existing business

Advantages	Disadvantages
Customers will be familiar with the business location.	The business location may be undesirable or threatened with becoming undesirable.
There will be an established customer base.	The image of the business will be difficult to change.
Experienced employees will come with the business.	Employees are inherited rather than chosen.
Planning can be based on known historical data.	There may be difficulties in changing the way the business is run.
Supplier relationships will already be in place.	There may be liabilities for past business contracts.
Inventory and equipment will be in place.	The inventory and equipment may be obsolete.
Financing may be available from the owner.	Financing costs could drain the cash flow and threaten the survival of the business.

ongoing business can be based on previous financial records, rather than having to rely on projections, as with a start-up business. An inventory, equipment and suppliers are already in place, and the business is managed by employees who know from experience how to keep the business going. In addition, it may be possible to obtain financing from the previous owner.

If the timing of the deal occurs when the entrepreneur is ready to buy a business and the owner needs to sell for a legitimate reason, this may be the best way of entering the business world. There may be disadvantages, however, in buying an existing business, as Table 2.1 on page 61 shows. In addition, one cannot simply buy an existing business in the hope that it is or will be an ongoing success. The business remains an opportunity for which a feasibility analysis will be necessary.

2.8.3.4 Franchising

Another way of entering the business world is through the acquisition of a **franchise**. The franchise concept gives an entrepreneur the opportunity of starting a business that has been proven in the marketplace. The entrepreneur then becomes a **franchisee**. The **franchisor** gives the franchisee the right to operate a business, using the franchise company's name, products and systems. In return, the franchisee pays the franchise company for this right on an ongoing basis.

However, while the franchisor is an entrepreneur, it is perhaps more correct to view the franchisee as an intrapreneur, who possibly initiates innovative ideas in the franchise system. Franchisees do not have the freedom to experiment, operate and market their businesses based on their own vision of how things should be done. Instead, they must usually adhere strictly to the plans of the franchisor. However, a recent study proved that franchisees do show an entrepreneurial orientation in certain situations, such as multiple-outlet franchisees[17]. Franchisors in many sectors have recognised the benefit of multiple-unit franchisees[18] and this is seen as an entrepreneurial continuation of the franchise trend.

Franchisors usually fall in the medium-sized to large business category, as the more successful franchisors usually manage large numbers of franchises as part of their business, apart from the overall management of the franchise group.

The Standard Bank Franchise Factor® survey of 2008 identified 531 franchise systems in South Africa, an increase of 15% from 470 in 2006. The full effect of the contribution of franchise systems to the economy is evident in the net growth in business units with 3 567 new units, an increase of over 14% to 28 620. Of the units, 32% are owned by previously disadvantaged individuals (PDIs). The franchising sector has seen excellent growth over the past two years, with a significant turnover of R256,46 billion, marking a 37% increase in turnover and the creation of 67 000 new jobs. The sector also enjoys a staggeringly high sustainability rate of almost 96%. The sector's contribution to the GDP was 12,57%[19]. However, South Africa has franchises in only 17 business sectors, whilst the United States has franchises in over 70, the UK and Canada in over 50 and Australia in over 25[20].

In South Africa, most reputable franchises are registered with the Franchise Association of Southern Africa (FASA). The purpose of this organisation is to ensure that franchising in southern Africa is a quality concept that can enable entrepreneurs to start new businesses. FASA is an excellent source of information on franchises.

2.8.3.5 Corporate entrepreneurship

Corporate entrepreneurship (also known as **intrapreneurship**) is entrepreneurship in an existing business. It happens when a person or team develops a new corporate business within a business through identifying a new opportunity or business idea. Corporate entrepreneurship is a method by which a corporation or large business introduces new and diversified products or services to an existing business. This is done through internal processes and by using the corporation's resources. Corporate entrepreneurship creates opportunities for a corporation to diversify, as well as for the creation of new industries. In addition, corporate entrepreneurship enables investment and profits through the establishment of new businesses within a business.

Corporate entrepreneurs are also valuable wealth creators in an economy. The advantage of new businesses established in this manner is that sufficient funding or seed capital is usually available for the capital-intensive establishment phase and the growth phase that follows.

The case study on this page illustrates corporate entrepreneurship by focusing on Koos Bekker, a true corporate entrepreneur. He initiated a totally new concept in the 1980s: pay television in the form of M-Net, within an existing company Naspers, a conventional publishing house responsible for publication of newspapers and magazines. Thus, an existing business diversified by adding a totally new product, pay television. The new product was a new concept that developed into MultiChoice, which, after further development, now provides pay television to 50 African countries. Bekker then added another new and diversified product, cellphones, and established MTN. MWEB, an internet company, was also launched through

Case study

The advantages of corporate entrepreneurship

In the mid-1980s, Mr Koos Bekker (currently CEO of Naspers) and two friends approached Ton Vosloo, chairman of Naspers, a publishing company for magazines and newspapers, to determine whether he would be interested in the concept of pay television. It was at the time of the start of pay television in America, but television was still relatively new in South Africa. Eventually a consortium of all the publishers of daily newspapers was established to finance M-Net, which was started in September 1986.

At first, the venture was catastrophic. The initial target market of M-Net, namely hotels and flat complexes, was not interested and neither were advertisers. Six months later, the business was losing R3,5 million per month on a turnover of R500 000. When decoders were introduced to single houses, the product started to sell. Two years later, the company started to break even and then it became profitable. M-Net then led to the establishment of various companies, such as MultiChoice in 1990, and today provides pay television channels to 50 African countries.

MultiChoice then introduced the cellphone concept to South Africa. Mr Bekker and his team presented a business plan to the entire board of Telkom's predecessor, which saw it as ridiculous to hope that 300 000 people would buy cellphones. Nevertheless, MultiChoice proceeded with the development of the project. After many delays, the government and the ANC decided that two licences would be granted: one to MultiChoice and its partners Nail and Transnet, and another to Telkom and its associates (Vodacom). In retrospect, the figure MultiChoice initially supplied was almost as much of an underprediction as Telkom's estimate of cellphone buyers. Today more than 20 million people own cellphones in South Africa.

When the role of the internet in the economy became clear, MultiChoice also established MWEB.

Source: Naude, C. 2006. "Die begin is die lekkerste". *Finweek*, 9 November, p. 71. Reprinted by permission of Gallo Images/IMAGES24.co.za/Finweek.

corporate entrepreneurship by Naspers. Thus, from within a publishing business, various other business opportunities were identified and established.

2.8.4 The feasibility of the idea or opportunity

Many small businesses result from an idea that has been converted into a useful application. Ideas have little value until they are converted into new products, services or processes. However, as was discussed in previous sections, not all ideas can be converted into feasible ventures. An idea must therefore be subjected to a feasibility test to prove that it has value. Aspiring entrepreneurs often find that the idea has already been developed or that competitors already exist. The same applies to opportunities that entrepreneurs may recognise. The entrepreneur should therefore also do a feasibility analysis of any apparent opportunity.

Even buying an existing business or recognising a franchise opportunity does not necessarily mean that the new or existing venture will be an instant success. No matter how promising the idea or opportunity may appear, the entrepreneur should determine whether it is feasible as soon as possible. Doing a feasibility analysis in good time may prevent the entrepreneur from losing valuable resources on an idea or opportunity that in fact offers little hope of success.

A feasibility study is the collection of data that helps forecast whether an idea, opportunity or venture will survive. The feasibility study gives the entrepreneur an information profile that should enable him/her to take a definite decision on whether or not to go ahead with the venture. A feasibility study is not the same as a business plan. It precedes the business plan and consists mainly of gathering data to enable the entrepreneur to take a decision on whether to go ahead with the idea, opportunity or new venture. Once the feasibility of an idea has been assessed, the entrepreneur can commit to implementing the idea or abandon the idea altogether, depending on the outcome.

When an idea appears feasible, the entrepreneur can proceed to determine how to make the idea work. In other words, the entrepreneur must now decide how to translate the idea into reality. This stage entails the drawing up of a **business plan**. Because of its significance to the entrepreneurial process, the business plan will be discussed more fully in Chapter 3.

2.9 Summary

This chapter addressed the concept of entrepreneurship and the idea that the entrepreneur is the driving force behind the business organisation. The role of entrepreneurs in the economy was examined, as were the reasons for people becoming entrepreneurs. Following this, the various aspects and phases of the entrepreneurial process were explored, including an assessment of the entrepreneur's unique abilities and skills, access to resources, the search for opportunities and the feasibility study.

Key terms

achievement motivation	job creation
business	life-cycle stages
business plan	locus of control
capital	managing a business
corporate entrepreneurship	marketing skills
creativity	necessity entrepreneur
employment	operating resources
entrepreneur	opportunities
entrepreneurial process	opportunity entrepreneur
experience	outsource
feasibility	physical resources

feasibility study	planning skills
financial resources	project-management skills
financial skills	resources
franchise	skills
growing a business	small, medium and micro-enterprises (SMMEs)
human-relations skills	social trends
human resources	starting a business
innovation	strategy skills
intrapreneurship	traits

? Questions for discussion

Reread the case study on pages 45–46 and answer the following questions:

1. What do you regard as the three main reasons for the success of Oasis Group Holdings? Explain why you chose each reason.
2. Do you think Mr Ebrahim was an entrepreneur or an owner of a small business after he started the business? Give reasons for your answer.
3. How do Mr Ebrahim and his company contribute to the economy of South Africa?
4. Do you think Mr Ebrahim is a necessity entrepreneur or an opportunity entrepreneur? Give reasons for your answer.
5. Why was Mr Ebrahim's business idea a good opportunity? Discuss and give reasons for your answer.

? Multiple-choice questions

1. Scientists have different views on whom or what exactly an entrepreneur is. Which one of the following is the view of an economist?
   a. The entrepreneur is an exploiter.
   b. The entrepreneur is a small-business owner who lacks the potential to manage a large company.
   c. The entrepreneur combines different resources in specific combinations to generate products and services at a profit.
   d. The entrepreneur is a person with an achievement orientation and a propensity towards creativity and risk-taking.
2. Writers on management and entrepreneurship have different views on entrepreneurship. Which one of the following descriptions of an entrepreneur is false?
   a. The entrepreneur has innovative ideas.
   b. The entrepreneur identifies opportunities.
   c. The entrepreneur exploits resources.
   d. The entrepreneur takes impulsive decisions.
3. From a psychological perspective, an entrepreneur exhibits certain characteristics, one of which is a need for achievement. With regard to the need for achievement, which one of the following statements is false?
   a. A person with a high need for achievement will work single-mindedly towards his/her goal with the determination to win.
   b. A person with a high need for achievement is attracted to jobs that challenge his/her skills and problem-solving abilities.
   c. A person with a high need for achievement pursues goals that he/she thinks will be almost impossible to achieve.
   d. A person with a high need for achievement prefers tasks in which the outcome depends upon his/her individual efforts.
4. The entrepreneurial process is the creation of new value through the entrepreneur identifying new

opportunities and using his/her leadership skills to build an organisation that fits the opportunity, and attracts and manages a configuration of resources with the focus on exploiting the opportunity. Which option shows the order in which the entrepreneurial process occurs?
   a. The opportunity, the feasibility study, the business plan, abilities and skills, access to resources, managing the business
   b. Abilities and skills, access to resources, the opportunity, the feasibility study, the business plan, managing the business
   c. The business plan, abilities and skills, access to resources, the opportunity, the feasibility study, managing the business
   d. The feasibility study, the opportunity, abilities and skills, access to resources, managing the business, the business plan
5. Instead of starting a new business, an entrepreneur may consider buying a business. There are several advantages and several disadvantages to buying a business. Which of the following statements is a disadvantage of buying a business?
   a. The entrepreneur inherits the employees, the inventory and equipment may be obsolete, and the existing image may be difficult to change.
   b. Planning can be based on historical data, the customers are familiar with the location and employees are experienced.
   c. The entrepreneur inherits the employees, the inventory and equipment may be obsolete, the customers are familiar with the location and the existing image may be difficult to change.
   d. The inventory and equipment may be obsolete, the existing image may be difficult to change and planning can be based on historical data.

Answers to multiple-choice questions

1. c
2. d
3. c
4. b
5. a

References

1. Barringer, B.R. & Ireland, R.D. 2008. *Entrepreneurship: successfully launching new ventures*. 2nd ed. Upper Saddle River, New Jersey: Pearson International, p. 6.
2. Statistics South Africa. 2009. *Gross Domestic Product*. Statistical release P044, Quarter 2, 2009. [Online] Available: www.statssa.gov.za Accessed 2 September 2009, p. 4.
3. Statistics South Africa. 2009. *Quarterly Labour Force Survey*. Statistical release P0211, Quarter 2, 2009. [Online] Available: www.statssa.gov.za. Accessed 2 September 2009, p. 4.
4. Herrington, M., Kew, J. & Kew, P. 2008. *Global Entrepreneurship Monitor*, South African Report 2008. Cape Town: University of Cape Town, Graduate School of Business, Centre for Innovation and Entrepreneurship, p. 4.
5. Oasis Group Holdings. 2009. "Oasis Milestones". [Online] Available: http://www.oasis.co.za Accessed 13 November 2009.
6. DTI (Department of Trade and Industry). 2005. *Annual review of small business in South Africa – 2004*. Pretoria: DTI, Enterprise Development Unit. [Online] Available: http://www.dti.gov.za/seda Accessed 31 January 2006, p. 10.
7. National Small Business Amendment (No. 29 of 2004).
8. McClelland, D.C. 1986. "Characteristics of successful entrepreneurs". *Journal of Creative Behavior*, Vol. 21, No. 3, pp. 219–233.
9. Barringer, B.R. & Ireland, R.D. 2008. Entrepreneurship: successfully launching new ventures. 2nd ed. Upper Saddle River, New Jersey: Pearson International, p. 412.
10. SAB Ltd. 2006. *30 years of empowerment*. Johannesburg: CSR Department, Corporate Affairs, SAB, p. 27.

11. International Facility Management Association. 1999. *Research Report 20*. [Online] Available: www.ifma.com Accessed 3 September 2009.
12. International Facility Management Association. 1999. *Research Report 20*. [Online] Available: www.ifma.com Accessed 3 September 2009.
13. National Small Business Amendment Act (No. 29 of 2004).
14. National Small Business Amendment Act (No. 29 of 2004).
15. Wickham, P.A. 2004. *Strategic entrepreneurship*. 3rd ed. Harlow: Prentice-Hall – Financial Times, pp. 132–141.
16. Pharma Dynamics. 2009. "Business highlights". [Online] Available: http://www.pharmadynamics.co.za Accessed 11 November 2009.
17. Maritz, P.A. 2005. "Entrepreneurial service vision in a franchised home entertainment system" (an unpublished DCom thesis in business management for the University of Pretoria).
18. Johnson, D.M. 2004. "In the mainstream, multi-unit and multi-concept franchising". *Franchising World*, April.
19. Cape Business News. 2008. "Franchising grows employment, GDP and turnover". 20 October. [Online] Available: http://www.cbn.co.za/dailynews/3280.html Accessed 3 September 2009.
20. Franchiseek South Africa. 2009. "Franchise statistics". [Online] Available http://www.franchiseek.com/SouthAfrica/Franchise_South_Africa_Statistics.htm Accessed 3 September 2009.

CHAPTER

3

ESTABLISHING A BUSINESS

The purpose of this chapter

This chapter focuses on the different forms of enterprise or legal ownership that are available to the entrepreneur. It covers the characteristics, advantages and disadvantages of the sole proprietorship, the partnership, the close corporation, the business trust and the company. Each of these forms is discussed in order to enable learners to compare them and make informed decisions. Once the entrepreneur knows what the available options are, he/she will be able draw up a business plan for the new business. The location factors are also discussed here.

Learning outcomes

On completion of this chapter you should be able to:

- understand and discuss the key considerations that are applicable when a form of business has to be chosen
- distinguish the different forms of enterprise found in South Africa
- explain the objectives, importance and need for a business plan
- evaluate a business plan
- give an overview of a business plan
- identify the location factors of a business.

3.1 Introduction

This chapter focuses on the different forms of enterprise that are available to the entrepreneur. It explains the factors that should be taken into account in selecting the appropriate form of enterprise for a particular business. The characteristics of the sole proprietorship, the partnership, the close corporation, the company and the business trust are explained, and the relative advantages and disadvantages of each are highlighted.

Some very important changes have resulted from the current South African corporate-law reform. These changes could affect the choice of emerging entrepreneurs significantly. The future position of business forms that will be affected by the enactment of the Companies Act (No. 71 of 2008) is briefly highlighted under the discussion of each type of enterprise.

An entrepreneur who is aware of the various enterprise forms and their implications can make an informed decision about the structure of his/her business.

Once the entrepreneur understands what the available options are, he/she can draw up a business plan for the new business. The basic content of such a business plan and the different issues that should be evaluated are also discussed in this chapter. In addition, the location factors of a business are examined.

3.2 The legal form of ownership[1]

3.2.1 Introduction to the legal form of ownership

An entrepreneur can conduct business through various forms of enterprise. An enterprise is an organisational structure through which business is conducted. Several options are available to the entrepreneur. There are, however, many issues that should be considered when deciding on the form of ownership. To what extent does the entrepreneur want to be liable for financial and legal risk? Who will have a controlling interest in the business? How will the business be financed?

It is clear that one of the first issues facing an entrepreneur about to enter a business undertaking is the selection of the type of enterprise. This decision can have a tremendous impact on almost every aspect of the business. As a business changes over time, a different business form may become more fitting. Therefore, knowledge of the different enterprise forms is crucial in planning for the possible future growth or transfer of a business.

Many factors may influence the entrepreneur's choice of the form of enterprise to use for his/her business. Considerations include the size of the business, the nature of the proposed business activities, the participation style, the management structure, the financing needs, the accountability of participants, and tax and legal implications. The key to choosing the "right" form of ownership lies in understanding the features of each enterprise and how it will influence an entrepreneur's specific business and personal circumstances. A characteristic of the business form that can be considered decisively beneficial for one business may be viewed as a distinct drawback in another business. Although, generally speaking, there is no best form of enterprise, there may well be one form best suited to each entrepreneur's specific circumstances.

The characteristics of each of the enterprise forms will be explained with reference to a number of key considerations: independence, liability, control, compliance, taxation and transferability.

3.2.2 Considerations in choosing a form of enterprise

From a legal point of view, the most pertinent consideration in choosing a form of business is whether or not the enterprise will have **legal (or juristic) personality**. A juristic person exists independently from its members. It is recognised as a legal subject alongside natural persons or individuals. It has its own rights, assets and obligations. Its existence is not affected by changes in its membership. This provides the business with continuity. Therefore the business can potentially exist forever. The members are usually not liable for the debts or obligations of the juristic person. Members enjoy limited liability as they stand to lose only the capital they have contributed to the entity.

Limited liability means the protection afforded by the juristic person to its members or owners in the event of it being sued. Claims are, for example, made against a company and the assets for payment of the company debts, and not against the personal estates of the company's members or directors.

However, despite the fact that limited liability is closely associated with separate legal personality, it is not an automatic consequence of being a juristic person. Despite the fact that trusts are generally not considered to be juristic persons as the trust assets are held in the trustee's personal estate, trusts enjoy limited liability in the sense that only the assets in the trust estate according to the trust deed are used to settle trust debts.

Companies and close corporations are juristic persons, while sole proprietorships and partnerships are not. In trusts, the position is more complicated. Generally trusts are not viewed as juristic persons, but in terms of certain legislation such as the Income Tax Act, the Deeds Registry Act, the Transfer Duty Act, the Insolvency Act and the Companies Act (No. 71 of 2008), trusts are considered to be juristic persons.

The extent of the liability of the business owner is a very important consideration. Ideally, an entrepreneur would like to insulate his/her personal assets from the business creditors so that the entrepreneur will not lose everything should the business be unsuccessful. The members of companies and close corporations are usually not liable for the debts of the enterprise. In contrast, sole proprietors and partners are liable in their personal capacities for the debts of the business. The trustee or beneficiary of a business trust is in principle not liable for the payments of trust debts. According to our law, the trustee is considered to have two separate estates, one being his/her personal estate and one for the trust assets. Trust debts are usually only paid out of the separate trust estate.

The degree of **control** or management authority the entrepreneur will be able to exercise over the activities of the business is another factor to consider. A broad range of options exists in this regard. A sole proprietor enjoys total management autonomy with respect to the business he/she owns. Companies are, however, characterised by a formal division between ownership and control. The participative management structures of partnerships and close corporations fall in between these two. Although a business trust is administered or managed by the trustee, the trust deed can apportion control between the trustee, the establisher of the business trust and the trust beneficiaries.

Also of relevance is the potential for **capital acquisition**. Some businesses are extremely capital intensive and this factor may be decisive. In other businesses, capital may be of lesser importance owing to the business activities involved. A public company is ideally suited to the raising of large sums of capital. In other enterprise forms, the capital is provided by a limited number of persons and their own financial positions are thus important. Factors such as the number of participants, their exposure to risk and their say in the management play a role in financing decisions.

Compliance with legal formalities and regulations can impose a considerable administrative and financial burden on an enterprise. The requirements for and the cost of the establishment, management and dissolution of each form of enterprise differ. Irrespective of the particular enterprise form adopted, a business can be subject to a multitude of other legal and regulatory requirements that often depend on size-related factors such as turnover and number of employees. So, for example, employers who employ more than 50 employees or have a turnover exceeding the amount stipulated by the minister (currently R5 million), would have to comply (in addition to all other applicable legislation) with the obligations imposed by the Employment Equity Act, whereas other employers would be exempt.

Taxation is also an important consideration. The rates for income tax, capital-gains tax and transfer duty vary depending on the kind of taxpayer. Value-added tax (VAT), which is levied at a standard rate of 14%, is applied irrespective of the enterprise form.

At the time of writing, companies and close corporations were taxed at a fixed rate of 28% on their taxable income. Small-business corporations are taxed on a sliding scale, with the maximum marginal rate set at 28%. Micro-businesses with an income of less than R1 million are taxed at a lower rate of between 0% and 7% on amounts exceeding R750 001. Secondary tax on companies (STC) is payable at a rate of 10% on the net dividend distributed to members. South African branches of foreign-resident companies are exempted from paying STC. Individuals are taxed on a sliding scale, with the maximum marginal rate set at 40%. Business trusts are taxed at a flat rate of 40% on the income retained in the trust.

Capital-gains tax is charged on the net capital gain of a taxpayer in the tax year. In the case of natural persons, some exclusions apply, after which a maximum of 10% of the net capital gain is included in the taxable income of the individual and taxed at the normal rates. An annual exclusion of R17 500 on capital gain or loss is granted to individuals. The inclusion rate for companies is 14% and for business trusts it is 20% of the net capital gain. This included part will be taxed at the normal rates for companies and trusts.

Transfer duty is levied at a flat rate of 8% on the value of fixed property acquired by companies, close corporations and trusts. Natural persons pay no transfer duty in respect of property up to a value of R500 000, thereafter 5% of the value of property of R500 001 and above. On property above R1 million in value, natural persons pay R25 000 plus 8% of the value exceeding R1 million.

Many factors will influence the total income tax burden of an enterprise. For this reason, no single enterprise form can be said to be the most advantageous from a tax perspective. The total income tax will depend on the amount of the taxable income (or loss) generated in the business (whether or not the enterprise is a separate taxpayer), the tax status and taxable income of the business owners, and the extent of distributions made to them. It is sometimes said that double taxation arises with respect to companies and close corporations. Although it is true that income that has already been taxed in the hands of the company or close corporation is taxed again when it is distributed to members as dividends or payments, the effect is offset

Case study

The importance of location

Thabang Molefi is a young up-and-coming entrepreneur from Soweto. Thabang used all the money she saved while working as a beauty therapist on a passenger liner to open a beauty spa in a township. Her Roots Health and Beauty Spa in Diepkloof was so successful that she decided to open another spa in Spruitview. The R190 000 that she won in the SAB Kickstart entrepreneurship competition provided the funding to open four more Roots Health and Beauty spas in other townships four years after the first spa was opened in Diepkloof in 2002.

"One of the most important factors of a successful venture, particularly in my business, is a good location. I was very fortunate to have obtained such a position when I started. It is a lesson that I still remember," says Thabang.

As so many young entrepreneurs do, Thabang found it difficult to obtain financing from conventional sources and she admits that the prize money from the SAB Kickstart competition saved her business.

"It was impossible to obtain finance from anybody when I started because the business was considered to be too risky and unconventional," she says.

Today she has three investors, two with a share of 10% each and one with a 5% share, who meet her financing needs.

Source: Jekwa, S. 2007. "Black Beauty". *Finweek*, 11 January, p. 48. Reprinted by permission of Gallo Images/IMAGES24.co.za/Finweek.

by the specific tax rates imposed on income and distributions respectively. The income of a sole proprietorship and a partnership is taxed in the hands of the sole proprietor or partners. The income retained in a business trust is taxed in the hands of the trustee as representative taxpayer, while the beneficiaries are taxed on the income distributed to them during the tax year. Securities-transfer tax for transfer of shares in companies or member's interest in close corporations is currently one-quarter of a per cent.

The ease with which the business or the entrepreneur's interest in the business can be **transferred** should also be considered when the most appropriate enterprise form is being selected. There may be many reasons why an entrepreneur may wish to, or have to, transfer his/her business or parts of it. Shares in public companies, especially if they are listed on an exchange, are very easily transferable and the most liquid form of investment in a business. In private companies, close corporations and partnerships, the transfer of an interest is dependent on the approval of the remaining members or partners. Beneficiaries of a business trust may transfer their rights in accordance with the trust deed.

The sections that follow will address the main characteristics of sole proprietorships, partnerships, close corporations, companies and business trusts in terms of these key considerations.

> **Critical thinking**
>
> Taking tax considerations into account, which form of enterprise would you recommend as most suitable for Thabang's Beauty Spas?

3.2.3 The sole proprietorship

The **sole proprietorship** is a business that is owned and managed by one individual. This is a very popular of business because it is very easy and inexpensive to set up.

A sole proprietorship is not a separate legal (juristic) person. It does not exist independently of the owner or proprietor. The lifespan of the business is linked to the lifespan or the legal capacity of the owner. The owner's legal capacity is his/her capacity to act under the law, for example, to enter into contracts. If the owner dies, becomes insolvent or otherwise legally incapable, this usually means the end of the business. If the business is discontinued, even temporarily following the death or incapacity of the sole proprietor, it may be difficult for the heir or transferee to resume the business.

There is no legal separation of the personal and business assets of the owner. Practically, it is preferable to keep separate books in respect of the business, but all the assets used in the business belong to the owner alone. Any profit of the business belongs to the owner in his/her personal capacity, even if it is kept in a separate business account or invested in business assets.

The owner does not enjoy any limitation of liability and therefore risks losing all his/her personal possessions if the business is unable to meet its obligations. The owner is personally liable for all the debts and claims arising from the running of the business. Personal creditors can claim against business assets and *vice versa*.

The owner has direct control and authority over the activities of the business. The owner usually manages the business and is free to take decisions concerning the running of the business. The business is therefore able to adjust readily to changes. However, a sole proprietorship can, depending on the circumstances, make exceptionally high demands on the management ability and personal freedom of the owner. The proprietor may delegate some or all management functions or decisions to employees or agents.

The capital-acquisition potential of the sole proprietorship depends on the owner's financial strength and creditability. The owner may already have sufficient assets or could rely on debt financing (loans). A sole proprietor may encounter difficulty in obtaining sufficient funds, especially when the business reaches a stage of expansion. Financiers often limit their risk by insisting on some measure of control or supervision over the business operations. Therefore, a sole proprietor may have to relinquish authority and freedom in exchange for funding.

There are very few formalities and legal requirements for the establishment of a sole proprietorship. As a result, it is the least-expensive enterprise form. Apart from the prescriptions of the Business Names Act (No. 27 of 1960), there are no particular legal requirements for the establishment, management or dissolution of a sole proprietorship.

As far as tax liability is concerned, as mentioned above, the entire income of the business belongs to the owner even if the income is kept in the business. Accordingly, the income is taxable in the hands of the owner as an individual taxpayer. Depending on the owner's taxable income and the tax rates at any given time, sole proprietorship may be advantageous or disadvantageous compared to other enterprise forms. If the business suffers a loss, this can be set off against the proprietor's other income, resulting in a reduction of his/her total taxable income.

From a legal perspective, transfer of ownership of a sole proprietorship is reasonably simple. The owner may at any time decide to sell the business, close down the business, or transfer the business or assets to someone else. However, it may be a problem to find a buyer. The business may be so closely associated with the personality of the proprietor that it may be difficult to place a value on the goodwill of the business. In some instances, the proprietor or executor may have to sell the business assets individually at a price that compares very unfavourably to the value of the business as a going concern.

A sole proprietorship offers the following advantages:

- It is simple to create.
- It is the least-expensive way of beginning a business.
- The owner has total decision-making authority.
- There are no special legal restrictions.
- It is easy to discontinue.

A sole proprietorship has the following disadvantages:

- The owner is personally liable without limitation.
- Limited diversity in skills and capabilities is available.
- The owner has limited access to capital.
- There is lack of continuity.

In the course of time, it has become evident that if two or more sole owners join forces, they are able to bring about a stronger unit because their combined financial and other resources are then at their disposal. This has led to the development of the partnership as another form of business available to the entrepreneur. The partnership is possibly one of the oldest commercial institutions known to humankind.

3.2.4 The partnership

In many respects, a **partnership** is similar to a sole proprietorship and the two business forms share several of the same disadvantages. A partnership may be described as a contractual relationship between two or more (but usually not more than 20) persons, called partners, who operate a lawful business with the object of making a profit. Partners may be natural or juristic persons. This means that a company or a close corporation may be a partner. The essential characteristics of a partnership are that each partner has to contribute something to the partnership, the partnership must be carried on for the joint benefit of the partners and each partner should have the expectation of sharing in the profit. Owing to the fragility in terms of the continuation of partnerships and the risks associated with this particular business form, a relationship of utmost good faith is required between partners.

A partnership does not have a legal personality. The partners in their personal capacity, rather than the partnership as such, jointly enter into all transactions or contracts. The assets contributed to or accumulated by the partnership belong to all the partners jointly as co-owners. The partners are also jointly liable for all the partnership debts.

Although a partnership is not a juristic person, the law nevertheless regards a partnership as an entity for certain limited purposes:

- Firstly, the partners may institute legal proceedings in the name of the partnership rather than all the partners jointly. The partners may also be sued in the name of the partnership, for example, "Du Buisson and partners" or "Smith and Brown Financial Advisers".
- Secondly, the law treats the partnership estate as a separate estate for purposes of sequestration. Although the estates of the partners will also be sequestrated when the partnership estate is sequestrated, the partnership creditors will have to prove their claims against the partnership estate and not against the estates of the individual partners.

The continued existence of a partnership depends on the continued involvement of the partners. It is also largely dependent on the legal capacity of the partners. Should a partner be declared insolvent or insane, the partnership would usually be terminated. Whenever there is any change in the membership of the partnership, for example, through the death or withdrawal of a partner or the admission of a new partner, the partnership dissolves automatically. It is, however, possible for the remaining partners to form a new partnership. In most cases, the partnership agreement will provide for such a "continuing" of a partnership between the existing partners.

During the existence of the partnership, the partners are jointly liable for all claims against the partnership, regardless of who was responsible for bringing about the claim. A creditor must either sue all the partners jointly or sue in the name of the partnership. If the partnership assets are insufficient to meet the claim of the creditor, the partners are liable for the debt out of their personal estates. The personal possessions of the partners are therefore not protected against any claim. Once a partnership has been dissolved, the partners are jointly and severally liable for partnership debts. This means that a creditor can recover the full debt from one partner only, leaving it to the partner who settled the debt to claim the necessary proportionate contributions from his/her co-partners.

The partners have joint control and authority over the business. However, the partners can adjust the control and authority aspect in their partnership agreement. For example, one or more partners can be excluded from representing or participating in the management of the partnership. This would, however, not necessarily exclude liability in terms of transctions concluded by a partner who has been excluded in this way. The principle of mutual mandate provides for liability of the partners for contracts concluded by any partner in the name of the partnership if the transaction falls within the scope of the partnership business. Therefore the partners will, during the existence of the partnership, be held jointly liable in terms of any transaction concluded by a partner if the contract is not outside the scope of the business. A partner who has been excluded from participating in management who concludes a contract within the scope of the partnership will, however, be in breach of his/her fiduciary duty to his/her co-partners.

The joint management of the partnership can lead to problems if the partners have different opinions or work ethics. A partnership may even be terminated as a result of the personal circumstances of its partners or their incompatibility in running the business. In this respect, the partnership is less adaptable to changing circumstances than a sole proprietorship. However, the partnership's broader authority can mean improved management ability because the business draws on the knowledge, experience and expertise of a greater number of people. It also allows for division of labour and specialisation, with the additional advantage that individual partners are exposed to less pressure than a sole proprietor.

A partnership usually has better capital-acquisition potential than a sole proprietorship because there are more people who can contribute and who can provide security for credit. It is a requirement for a valid partnership that each partner must make an initial contribution to the partnership. A contribution can consist of anything that has a monetary (economic) value, including money, property, services, knowledge or skill. If the partnership contract does not specify how the profits will be divided, the division will be done in proportion to the value of each partner's contribution.

A partnership is established by concluding a contract. There are no formal requirements for setting up a partnership.A partnership contract may be concluded orally, in writing or even tacitly (that is, through certain behaviour). However, it is customary and preferable for the contract to be in writing. The contract makes provision for matters such as the nature and goals of the business, capital contributions by individual partners, profit-sharing, management and dissolution.

A partnership is not a separate taxpayer. Since the partnership income belongs to all the partners jointly in specific proportions, each partner is taxed individually on his/her share of the income. The partners also deduct the partnership expenses in the same proportion as the income. The income tax payable on each partner's share of the partnership income will depend on his/her tax status and other income.

In general, transfer of ownership is more complicated in partnerships than in sole proprietorships because more people are involved and because the stipulations or provisions of the partnership contract have to be complied with. However, it can be easier for a partner to sell his/her interest in a partnership than it is to sell a sole proprietorship. One reason for this is that the remaining partners may opt to buy out the partner. Often partners take out life insurance policies that will enable the remaining partners to acquire a deceased partner's interest. Some entrepreneurs may also prefer to buy an interest in a business rather than buying a whole business.

To summarise, the partnership offers the following advantages:

- ease of formation
- diversification of skills and abilities of partners
- increased opportunity for accumulation of capital
- minimal legal formalities and regulation.

The partnership has the following disadvantages:

- the personal liability of partners
- the relative difficulty in disposing of an interest in the partnership
- the potential for conflict between partners
- lack of continuity (can be overcome by agreement).

3.2.4.1 How partnerships are affected in terms of the Companies Act (No. 71 of 2008)[2]

The Companies Act (No. 71 of 2008) has still not been implemented as serious problems with it are currently being rectified. It will most probably be enacted in the next year or so. The discussion of it in this chapter includes the most recent information available.

Previously, partnerships were not permitted to have more than 20 partners. This rule could only be relaxed in exceptional circumstances. In terms of the Companies Act (No. 71 of 2008), there is no limit to the number of partners. This could lead to greater diversification of skills and abilities.

However, the disadvantages applicable to this business form remain unchanged. Increasing the number of partners could, in fact, hold a greater risk of personal liability for debts and social-compatibility problems.

3.2.5 The close corporation

A **close corporation** has characteristics of both a partnership and a company. It has the advantage of being a legal (or juristic) person that exists separately from its members. A close corporation may have one or more members, but not more than ten. Juristic persons may not be members of a close corporation, except in certain very limited circumstances, specified in the Close Corporations Act (No. 69 of 1984), where they may be members in the capacity of an official representative.

The core characteristic of the close corporation is that it is "closed" in the sense that the members both own and control the close corporation. The interest of a member is expressed as a percentage and the total interest of members must always amount to 100%. The name of a close corporation must end with the abbreviation "CC" or its equivalent in any other official language of the Republic of South Africa.

As a juristic person, a close corporation has its own rights, assets and liabilities. A close corporation has the capacity and powers of a natural person in as far as this may apply to a juristic person. Therefore, a close corporation is even entitled to certain fundamental rights as set out in the Constitution of the Republic of South Africa, 1996.

Because the close corporation has legal personality, its continued existence is not influenced by the withdrawal or entry of members. It can also withstand changes in the personal circumstances and legal status of its members.

The members of a close corporation are generally not liable for the debts and liabilities of the close corporation. Therefore the members' personal assets in their private estates are not at risk of being lost in the business. However, the Close Corporations Act (No. 69 of 1984) imposes personal liability on members for certain violations of its provisions. Personal liability is also imposed for carrying on the business of the corporation recklessly, fraudulently or with gross negligence, or for abusing the juristic personality of the corporation.

The members share the management and control of a close corporation on an equal basis. The Close Corporations Act (No. 69 of 1984) regulates the internal operation of the close corporation. The Act provides that certain persons, such as minors or insolvents, may not participate in the management of a close corporation. Decisions are generally taken by majority vote, but in some specific instances, a majority of 75% or even the consent of all the members is required.

If the corporation has two or more members, they may enter into an association agreement that alters certain aspects of the internal functioning of the corporation. An association agreement may, for example, provide that only certain members will participate in the management of the corporation or that authority to conclude contracts on behalf of the close corporation will depend on the percentage of each member's interest. Notwithstanding the existence of such agreement, any member of the close corporation who contracts with a non-member is regarded as an agent who is able to bind the close corporation to any contract, even if such a contract falls outside the scope of business of the corporation. The close corporation will only escape liability if the non-member knew or should reasonably have known that he/she did not have the authority to represent the corporation. This arrangement protects third parties contracting with the corporation, but it exposes the members of the corporation to risk. Therefore it is important that members are selected carefully. Any member of the close corporation who acts without authority will be liable to the corporation as a result of his/her breach of his/her fiduciary duties towards the close corporation. Members are expected to carry out their duties honestly and in good faith, and not to exceed their powers.

The capital-acquisition potential of a close corporation is higher than in a partnership, mainly because members may be more inclined to contribute to a corporation knowing that they do not stand to lose more than what they have invested. Each person who becomes a member of a close corporation must make a contribution with a monetary (economic) value. This could be in money, property or even services in connection with the formation of the corporation. Services are, however, not an acceptable contribution for a new member joining an existing corporation. The members' contributions and their interest in the corporation need not be in direct proportion to each another. Two members who have contributed the same amount of money to a corporation may, for example, agree that one of them will hold a 60% member's interest and the other one will hold a 40% member's interest. A close corporation can also use loan capital and members are often required to bind themselves as sureties for credit incurred by the corporation. Although this in effect removes the advantage of limited liability, it enables the corporation to obtain increased funding.

A close corporation may not make any payments to members in their capacity as members (for example, profit distribution or repayment of contributions) unless the solvency and liquidity tests are satisfied. The solvency test means that after payment, the corporation's assets must still exceed its liabilities, based on a reasonable valuation. A corporation meets the liquidity test if, after the payment is made, it will still be able to pay its debts as they become payable in the ordinary course of business.

As stated above, close corporations are currently regulated by the Close Corporations Act (No. 69 of 1984). The legal prescriptions contained herein are not strict and the corporation can be registered at very little cost. A close corporation is created by the registration of a single founding document, called a founding statement. The founding statement contains details such as the proposed name of the corporation, the nature of the business, the personal details of members and their interests in the corporation. The founding statement is similar to the memorandum of association of a company. Although a founding statement is registered, it is not open for public inspection and nobody is deemed to know its contents.

A close corporation is a separate taxpayer. For purposes of the Income Tax Act, close corporations are treated as companies and the distributions they make to their members are regarded as dividends. The taxable income of a close corporation is therefore taxed either at a fixed rate of 28%, or if it qualifies as a small business, at a lower scale according to income. STC of 10% is payable on the net "dividend" distributed to members. The total income tax payable by the corporation and by the members on the profits generated by the corporation will thus be influenced by the extent to which income is retained in the close corporation or distributed to members. This flexibility can be used to the advantage of members.

A member's interest can be transferred to another individual who will then become a member of the corporation. New members can also acquire a member's interest directly from the corporation by making a contribution, followed by an adjustment to the percentages held by the other members. A member may also sell his/her member's interest to the corporation if it satisfies the solvency and liquidity criteria. In such a case, the relative percentages of the remaining members will also be adjusted. Transfers or acquisitions of members' interests must be in accordance with the association agreement or, if there is no such agreement, with the approval of all the members of the corporation. A transfer of member's interest does not affect the existence of the corporation. Therefore, a member's interest is more easily transferable than a partnership interest. However, unrestricted transferability is limited by the "closed" nature of a close corporation.

A close corporation has the following advantages:

- It has the advantages attached to separate legal (juristic) personality.
- It is reasonably cheap and simple to form.
- Members have limited liability.
- There is increased capital-acquisition potential.
- Management is relatively simple.
- It has continuity.

A close corporation has the following disadvantages:

- Membership is limited to ten.
- Juristic persons may not be members.

3.2.5.1 How close corporations are affected in terms of the Companies Act (No. 71 of 2008)[3]

The Companies Act (No. 71 of 2008), which was promulgated in April 2009, is expected to come into operation in mid-2010. Many changes will result from the incorporation of this piece of legislation. One of the main results relevant to our discussion is that the option of registering a new close corporation will no longer be available to new entrepreneurs once the Act (and in particular section 13 thereof) comes into operation. This is very unfortunate, especially because registration statistics evidence a tendency to incorporate close corporations rather than companies. Of the number of close corporations registered, the figures also reveal a relatively high subsistence rate when compared to that of all forms of companies. However, the Act aims to make companies a more favoured option by introducing a simpler registration process. It is envisaged that close corporations may eventually be phased out if the simplifications introduced prove workable for smaller businesses.

The Companies Act (No. 71 of 2008) amends and repeals various sections of the Close Corporations Act (No. 69 of 1984). It is aimed at levelling the playing fields between close corporations and private companies. Identical regulation requirements will forthwith apply to close corporations and private companies.

The following aspects, which were previously only applied in respect of companies, will be made applicable to close corporations:

- The criteria for names and the new voluntary procedure for the reservation of names will apply.
- The "disqualification" and "probation" rules for company directors will likewise be applicable to "managing members".
- Certain provisions relating to annual financial statements will apply. In particular, they must be prepared within six months of the end of the financial year to which they relate (this was previously nine months). Annual financial statements must be audited if required by regulations that are still to be published. Alternatively, these statements must either be audited voluntarily at the option of the corporation or reviewed independently, unless the close corporation is specifically exempted.
- Close corporations are given the option of opting to comply with the enhanced transparency and accountability requirements in Chapter 3 of the Companies Act (No. 71 of 2008). As it is not compulsory, however, it is doubtful whether close corporations would comply voluntarily.
- The business-rescue procedure will apply to close corporations in financial distress.
- The new definition of "control", and hence the terms "related" and "interrelated" persons as used in the Companies Act (No. 71 of 2008) will also apply to close corporations.

- Provisions relating to the dissolution and winding-up of companies will be the same for close corporations.
- The complaints, investigations and adjudication procedures before the Takeover Regulation Panel or Companies Tribunal will be on par for companies and close corporations.

Existing close corporations will continue to exist indefinitely, but will have to comply with both the legal requirements of the Companies Act (No. 71 of 2008) as well as the remaining provisions of the Close Corporations Act (No. 69 of 1984). Close corporations will therefore be subjected to more onerous administrative duties and arrangements. The benefit of simple regulation in close corporations will be negated by the requirement to adhere to both the Close Corporations Act (No. 69 of 1984) and the Companies Act (No. 71 of 2008). In addition, it will become impossible to convert any type of company into a close corporation.

Members of a close corporation may decide to convert the business into a company should they wish to do so. This can be done by lodging a notice of conversion, a certified copy of a special resolution by the members approving the conversion and a new Memorandum of Incorporation (the founding document for a company) with the Registrar. A filing fee will have to be paid and notice of the conversion must be published. The Registrar of Deeds must effect necessary changes resulting from the conversion and any resultant name changes. The effect of conversion from a close corporation to a company will be as follows:

- Each member of the close corporation will have an option to become a shareholder of the company.
- The juristic person that existed as a close corporation will continue to exist in the form of a company.
- All the assets, liabilities, rights and obligations of the close corporation will vest in the company.
- If any legal proceedings were instituted before the registration as a company by or against the close corporation, they may be continued by or against the company.
- The conversion would naturally place both an administrative as well as a financial strain on the members of the close corporation.

3.2.6 The company

The **company** developed to meet business people's need to obtain more capital than they could through a sole proprietorship or partnership. Companies as business forms also bridged many of the deficiencies and undesirable features of partnerships. People eventually came to accept the notion that, from a legal point of view, there could be a fictitious person with rights and duties who is able to participate in commercial life and whose existence would not depend upon the life of a natural person or persons. Business people could obtain large sums of money through such a separate legal entity so that they could undertake commercial ventures that individuals could not afford, to the benefit of the entire community. Companies enjoy all the benefits attached to a separate legal (juristic) personality as well as potentially unlimited capital-generating capacity.

The company is characterised by the separation of ownership and control. This means that a formal distinction is made between the members or shareholders of the company and its managers or directors.

The Companies Act (No. 61 of 1973) provides for the incorporation of two types of companies:

- companies with a share capital
- companies limited by guarantee.

An incorporated association not for gain, or a section 21 company as it is commonly known, is a type of company limited by guarantee. The members of a company limited by guarantee agree to contribute a specific amount if the company is liquidated. Such companies are not often used for conducting a business. They are usually incorporated for a humanitarian purpose such as the promotion of a specific sport, cultural activity or charity. Associations not for gain do not issue any of their profits to their members, but use these profits to promote the specific purpose for which the company was formed. The aim is therefore not to make a profit for personal benefit.

The most common type of company is the company with a share capital. The discussion that follows will be restricted to this type. A company with a share capital can be either a public company or a private company.

A company is a legal (juristic) person and thus has its own rights, assets and liabilities. A company exists independently from its members or shareholders and has the potential for perpetual existence. Therefore the personal estates of shareholders remain unaffected when claims are instituted against a company. Unlike a close corporation, which has unlimited capacity and powers, a company exists only for the purpose for which it was formed, as determined by the main object set out in its memorandum of association. However, it has become practice to formulate the main object very widely so that capacity does not present a problem.

The shareholders and directors are generally not personally liable for the debts of the company. The shareholders enjoy limited liability as they stand to lose only the consideration they paid in exchange for their shares. In exceptional circumstances, the directors and controlling shareholders may be held personally liable for debts of the company if the juristic personality of the company has been abused or if the company's business has been conducted recklessly. This is referred to as "piercing the corporate veil".

As has been stated, a distinction is made between **ownership** and **control**. A company has two organs:

- **The general meeting of members.** The general meeting makes broad policy decisions and exercises control over the company's affairs through its right to appoint and remove directors, and to amend the company's articles of association, which govern the internal operation of the company. The voting rights of shareholders are linked to the number of shares they hold in the company. Decisions at meetings are normally taken by means of a vote.
- **The board of directors.** The administration of the company is entrusted to its directors. The precise division of powers between the board of directors and the general meeting is determined by the articles of association. The day-to-day management of the company is usually delegated to the board of directors. Directors are usually appointed by the general meeting, and their functions and powers are defined in the articles of association. These functions are jointly exercised by the directors (as the board of directors) by means of a majority vote. The board can, if it is empowered to do so by the articles of association or the general meeting, delegate some of its functions and powers to a managing director.

The structure of a company facilitates the appointment of specialised managers with diverse areas of expertise and experience. This is usually an advantage, but there is always a risk of decision-making being delayed owing to differences of opinion.

A company's capital is made up of share capital, representing the consideration the company receives in exchange for the shares it issues, as well as accumulated funds and loan capital. As far as the potential for capital acquisition is concerned, the company, and particularly the public company, has a distinct advantage over the sole proprietorship, partnership and close corporation. This is because the general public can be invited to invest capital and acquire shares in a public company.

The features of limited liability, free transferability of shares and the existence of specialised management all facilitate diversification of shareholders. The shares of public companies may further be listed on a stock exchange, which increases the ability to raise capital even further. The strict regulation of companies, coupled with compulsory financial disclosure, also makes financial institutions more willing to provide loan capital to a company than to other forms of enterprise. The capital-acquisition potential of a company can be further enhanced if shareholders or directors are prepared to provide additional loan security in their personal capacities. This often happens in practice, especially in the case of private companies.

A shareholder's interest in the company is represented by the number of shares he/she holds in the company. Shareholders share in the profits of a company when a dividend is declared or a payment by virtue of shareholding is authorised. Distributions by the company are subject to compliance with the criteria of solvency and liquidity.

A company is currently subject to many more legal prescriptions than the other forms of enterprises, which translates into increased costs as well. As discussed above, this is subject to change upon the inception of the new Companies Act (No. 71 of 2008). The legal prescriptions for close corporations will then become equivalent to those applicable to private companies.

Companies are currently regulated by the Companies Act (No. 61 of 1973). The Securities Services Act (No. 36 of 2004) regulates aspects of listed companies. The Companies Act (No. 61 of 1973) requires that a company register a constitution (the founding documents) with the Registrar of Companies. The constitution is made up of two documents: the memorandum of association, which governs the external relationships of the company, and the articles of association, which govern the internal affairs of the company. These documents also contain the name, main objectives and internal management rules, among other things. Any person dealing with the company is presumed to be aware of the contents of these public documents.

A company is a taxpayer. It is currently taxed at a fixed percentage of 28% on its taxable income. Small companies with a limited income are taxed on a sliding scale up to a specific limit. Secondary tax for distributions made by the company is set at 10% of net dividends distributed.

In public companies, the transfer of ownership takes place through the unlimited and free transfer of shares. Ownership is transferred through the private sale of shares or, in the case of a listed company, through transactions on the stock exchange. The transfer of shares usually has no influence on the activities of the company and the company therefore has an unlimited lifespan.

Shares in a private company are not freely transferable. The method of transfer is laid down in the company's articles of association. Transfer is usually subject to the approval of the board of directors. A shareholder who wants to sell his/her shares therefore has to find a buyer who is acceptable to the board. In most instances, a shareholder has to offer the shares to the remaining shareholders first in proportion to their existing shareholding. The shareholder may only transfer the shares to an outsider if the other members are not prepared to acquire them at the same price. In other words, a pre-emptive right exists in favour of other shareholders for transfer of shares in a private company. Despite these limitations, the transfer of shares in a private company is unlikely to influence its activities or the continued existence of the business.

To summarise, the advantages of a company are:

- limited liability
- the ability to raise large amounts of capital
- separation of ownership and control
- continuity
- transferability of shares.

The disadvantages are:
- a high degree of legal regulation
- high operational costs.

3.2.7 Differences between the public company and the private company

The main differences between a private company and a public company are as follows:
- The number of members (shareholders) of a private company ranges from one person to 50 people. A public company must have at least seven members, but there is no maximum, provided the number of shares authorised in the memorandum at any given time is not exceeded.
- A private company must have at least one director while a public company must have at least two directors.
- The articles of association of a private company must contain some restriction on the transferability of its shares. The shares in a public company are freely transferable.
- The general public cannot subscribe to the shares of a private company. A private company can therefore not list its shares on the stock exchange. Public companies may raise capital by issuing shares to the public. The public can be invited to buy shares in the company by means of a prospectus. A public company is also eligible to list its shares on the stock exchange.
- The name of a private company must end with the words "(Pty) Ltd" or "(Proprietary) Limited", for example, "Maxi Removals (Pty) Ltd". There is also another type of private company: the incorporated company or section 53(b) company. The name of an incorporated company must end in the word "Incorporated" ("Inc."), for example, "Andersons Incorporated". Certain professions allow their members to form this type of company instead of practising in a partnership. The members, who usually have to be directors as well, are jointly and individually liable for the contractual debts of the company. The name of a public company must end in the word "Ltd" or "Limited", for example, "Moroko Traders Limited".
- While both types of company are subject to a number of legal regulations, a private company is not as strictly controlled as a public company.

3.2.7.1 How companies are affected in terms of the Companies Act (No. 71 of 2008)[4]

The introduction of the Companies Act (No. 71 of 2008) is set to change the face of South African companies completely. Upon its enactment, the whole of the Companies Act (No. 61 of 1973) will be repealed. It is impossible to show all the changes that will result, but some significant changes that are material in respect of the choice of business form for up-and-coming entrepreneurs will be highlighted.

The Act is aimed at simplifying the registration procedure in respect of companies. Instead of the current two constitutive documents, registration of a single document called a Memorandum of Incorporation is required. Reservation of a name for the business for purposes of registration will become optional and companies will be permitted to register a business under a registration number instead until they find a suitable name. Despite the requirement that the Memorandum of Incorporation be registered and held at the company's business premises for public inspection, outsiders dealing with the company will no longer be deemed to have knowledge of the contents of the public document.

The classification of companies will change. There will be only two types of company: profit companies and non-profit companies. Profit companies can further be divided into state-owned companies, private companies, personal-liability companies and public companies.

The distinctive characteristics of private and public companies respectively will largely remain the same. However, public companies will have to comply with even stricter requirements concerning accounting records, financial reporting, auditing, minutes of meetings, registers of shareholders and annual returns than required in terms of the Companies Act (No.61 of 1973). These requirements will be applied less stringently for private companies and non-profit companies.

The Companies Act (No. 71 of 2008) will have far-reaching effects in terms of corporate governance. The following highlights are of importance:

- The powers and responsibilities of directors will be increased.
- The burden of the office of director will be increased as duties and liabilities of directors have been extended.
- The rights of shareholders to hold directors accountable and even remove directors have been extended.
- The duties of directors are codified in the legislation. However, these duties do not exclude any of the common-law duties already applicable in respect of directors. These duties are in addition to the existing duties of directors.

Previously, the powers of the board of directors of a company were balanced with those of the general meeting of members of the company. However, with the new Companies Act (No. 71 of 2008) and its regulations, the effective governance of corporations and liability for non-compliance has been placed squarely upon the shoulders of the board of directors.

Owing to the uncertainties of the application of the new Companies Act and the major shift evidenced by its new concepts and rules, it can be expected that a reasonable transitional period during which existing companies can adapt to the new rules and procedures will follow after the promulgation of the new legislation.

The simplification of processes of registration and decision-making in companies may be a positive change. However, the harsh penalties for non-adherence connected to the onerous duties of directors may diminish the pool of qualified, suitable and perhaps even willing directors. This could prove counterproductive in the quest for advancement of entrepreneurship and growth of profitable, efficient South African companies.

3.2.8 The business trust

The **business trust** is becoming an increasingly popular enterprise form. It developed out of the ordinary trust. A trust is established when the founder of the trust places assets under the control of a trustee to be administered for the benefit of the beneficiaries. The trust assets and the beneficiaries must be clearly identified. There is no limit on the number of beneficiaries. Beneficiaries may be natural or juristic persons. A business trust is a trust that has the object of conducting a business in order to generate a profit.

A trust is a seperate entity from its trustees and beneficiaries, much like a company or a close corporation. A trust is also not owned by anyone. It does not terminate unless by agreement or if it is sequestrated as a result of its inability to pay debts. Trusts are, however, not creatures of statute. They are not registered with the Registrar of Companies like companies or close corporations. A trust is a product of a legal contract called a trust deed.

A trust does not have juristic personality. The trustee owns the trust assets in an official representative capacity and is also liable for the debts of the trust in his/her capacity as trustee. However, since the trustee is liable only out of the trust assets and not in his/her personal capacity, the effect is similar to limited liability. A trustee is considered to have two separate estates: a personal estate out of which his/her personal debts are paid and the trust estate, which is liable for trust debts only. A trust can be set up for any period of time and is thus capable of perpetual existence. The existence of a trust does not depend on the identity of the trustee or its beneficiaries.

The management of a trust is in the hands of the trustees who have to exercise their duties in accordance with the trust deed and in good faith. The trust founders are able to exercise control over the trustees by their right to amend the trust deed. In a private business trust, the same persons are usually founders, trustees and beneficiaries of the trust. This means the management structure is similar to that of a partnership.

The capital of a trust is provided by the trust founder or founders. A trust has limited potential for capital acquisition. Loan capital may be obtainable, usually in exchange for security provided by the parties to the trust. The distribution of profits to members will generally be left to the discretion of the trustees, affording the parties maximum flexibility with regard to retention or distribution of funds.

It is easy and cheap to establish a trust. All that is required is a trust deed identifying the trust property, trustees and beneficiaries, and setting out the powers of the trustees. This trust deed is often in the form of a contract or a will. There is very little regulation of trusts compared with regulation of other enterprise forms. Trusts that take investments from the public (for example, unit trusts) are, however, subject to specific regulation. The lack of regulation of trusts can be a disadvantage if the trust deed has not been formulated properly and if trustees are not selected carefully.

A trust is regarded as a separate taxpayer. The trustee is seen as a representative taxpayer. Income tax on trust income is allocated according to the conduit principle. In other words, income that accrues to the beneficiaries is taxed in their hands, while income retained in the trust is taxed in the hands of the trustee as representative taxpayer. Where the entitlement of beneficiaries to income is not pre-determined in the trust deed, but is left to the discretion of the trustees, great flexibility in tax-planning and structuring is possible. Transfer of the interest of a beneficiary can be achieved by a variation of the trust deed.

The advantages of a private business trust are the following:

- ease of formation
- limited liability
- extreme flexibility
- absence of legal regulation
- continuity.

The disadvantages of a business trust are:

- limited access to capital
- potential for conflict between parties.

3.2.8.1 How trusts are affected in terms of the Companies Act (No. 71 of 2008)[5]

The Companies Act (No. 71 of 2008) also includes trusts under its definition of juristic persons. What exactly was intended by this inclusion is unclear. It could possibly be that the legislature intends to prevent avoidance of corporate law principles by trusts that are associated with groups of companies. At the time of writing, the insolvency stipulations that will be applied in corporations were still under review. For these purposes, it may be a prudent step to include trusts under the definition of juristic person, as the position of the assets held in such trusts (which would generally be excluded to the disadvantage of the creditors as they form part of the trustee's private estate) would be clear.

3.2.9 Other forms of enterprise

Various other enterprise forms are possible in South Africa, although the forms that have been discussed are the most common.

Co-operative societies should be mentioned briefly. Although some co-operatives are restricted to agriculture and farming activities, trading co-operatives can be used for various kinds of businesses. Co-operative societies are similar to private companies in many respects. The Co-operatives Act (No. 91 of 1981) applies to co-operatives, but is to be replaced by the Co-operatives Act (No. 14 of 2005), which has not yet been put into operation. Co-operatives attempt to achieve certain economic advantages for their members through joint action on the members' part. In South Africa, co-operatives are found mainly in farming communities as organisations selling and/or supplying products or products and services. Because of their distinctive features, co-operatives are not usually real alternatives to the forms of business we have mentioned.

Mention should also be made of **joint ventures**. "Joint venture" is a generic term designating some sort of co-operation between persons or businesses. It does not refer to a specific legal construction with unique consequences. In each instance, the legal consequences depend on the specific agreement between the parties. The term is most often used to denote a partnership between two or more companies, in which case ordinary partnership principles apply to the joint venture.

3.2.10 Summary of legal forms of ownership

Once entrepreneurs have identified their opportunity and evaluated it, they basically have three options for entering the business world (as discussed in Chapter 2):

- entering into a franchise agreement
- buying an existing business
- establishing a business from scratch.

In all of these cases, the entrepreneur's choice of a form of business is very important.

In choosing a form of enterprise, entrepreneurs must remember that there is no single "best" form of enterprise. Each form has its own advantages and disadvantages. An entrepreneur's choice must reflect his/her particular situation. There may be a business form that is best for the entrepreneur's individual circumstances. Understanding the forms of enterprise, and the characteristics, advantages and disadvantages of each one, is the entrepreneur's key to selecting the form of ownership that best suits him/her.

In this section, we have discussed the different forms of enterprise available to the entrepreneur. We have compared the characteristics, advantages and disadvantages of the sole proprietorship, the partnership, the close corporation, the company and the business trust. Some of the changes that will become effective upon enactment of the Companies Act (No. 71 of 2008) in respect of partnerships, close corporations, companies and trusts were also highlighted.

Once the entrepreneur knows what the available options are, he/she can put everything together by drawing up the business plan for the new business.

3.3 Developing a business plan for the new business

In this section, the development of the business plan for the new venture will be examined.

3.3.1 The objectives of a business plan

For the entrepreneur starting a new venture, a **business plan** is a written document that accomplishes certain basic objectives. The most important objective is to identify and describe the nature of the business opportunity or the new venture.

The second objective is to present a written plan of how the entrepreneur plans to exploit the opportunity. Here, the business plan explains the key variables for the success or failure of the new venture. It is a guideline to the things that must be done to establish and operate the new venture. It provides a large number of instruments (such as the mission, goals, objectives, target markets, operating budgets, financial needs and so on) that the entrepreneur and managers can draw on to lead the venture successfully.

These instruments, which help managers to keep the venture on track, constitute the key components of the business plan. A business plan is therefore also a valuable managerial tool that helps the entrepreneur and his/her team to focus on charting a course for the new business.

A third objective of the business plan is to attract investors, or to persuade a bank, other institution or person who provides financial resources, to lend the entrepreneur the money he/she needs to establish the new business. Careful preparation can make the difference between success and failure when shopping in the capital market.

Apart from the above-mentioned main objectives, a business plan provides many other benefits:

- systematic, realistic evaluation of the new venture's chances of success in the market
- a way of identifying the key variables that will determine the success of the new venture, as well as the primary risks that may lead to failure
- a game plan for managing the business successfully
- a management instrument for comparing actual results against targeted performance
- a primary tool for attracting money in the hunt for financial resources.

3.3.2 Importance and necessity of the business plan

The overall importance of the business plan lies in its planning activities. Planning is the fundamental element of management that pre-determines what the business organisation proposes to accomplish and how this is to be accomplished. Planning, and thus the idea of a business plan, is hardly something new. Big businesses have long been turning out annual business plans by the thousand, especially for marketing new products, buying new businesses or expanding globally. What is new, however, is the growing use of such plans by small entrepreneurs. These entrepreneurs are, in many cases, forced by financial institutions to draw up a business plan before any financial support will be considered.

The business plan is important not only to the entrepreneur, but also to his/her employees, potential investors, bankers, suppliers, customers and so on. Each group of stakeholders in the business will study the business plan from a different perspective. It is therefore clear that any business, but especially a new venture, needs to have a business plan to answer questions that various stakeholders in the venture may raise.

There are eight reasons for an entrepreneur to write a business plan:

- **To sell the business to him-/herself.** The most important stakeholders in any business are its founders. First and foremost, the entrepreneur needs to convince him-/herself that starting the business is right for him/her, from both a personal point of view and an investment viewpoint.
- **To obtain bank financing.** Up until the late 1980s, writing a business plan to obtain bank financing was an option left up to the entrepreneur. Bankers usually took the approach that a business plan helped the entrepreneur to make a better case, though it was not an essential component in the bank's decision-making process. However, banks now require entrepreneurs to include a written business plan with any request for loan funds. As a consequence, obtaining money from a bank is tougher than it has ever been and a business plan is an essential component of any campaign to convince banks about a new business.
- **To obtain investment funds.** For many years now, the business plan has been the "ticket of admission" to venture capital or "informal" capital from private investors.
- **To arrange strategic alliances.** Joint research, marketing and other efforts between small and large companies have become increasingly common in recent years, and these require a business plan.

- **To obtain large contracts.** When small companies seek substantial orders or ongoing service contracts from major corporations, the corporations often respond (perhaps somewhat arrogantly) as follows: "Everyone knows who we are, but no-one knows who you are. How do we know you'll be around in three or five years to provide the parts or service we might require for our product?" For this reason, entrepreneurs are required to have a business plan.
- **To attract key employees.** One of the biggest obstacles that small, growing companies face in attracting key employees is convincing the best people to take the necessary risk, and to believe that the company will thrive and grow during the coming years.
- **To complete mergers and acquisitions.** No matter which side of the merger process the entrepreneur is on, a business plan can be very helpful if he/she wants to sell the company to a large corporation.
- **To motivate and focus the management team.** As smaller companies grow and become more complex, a business plan becomes an important component in keeping everyone focused on the same goals.

3.3.3 Stakeholders in a business plan

There are internal as well as external stakeholders. Each category is discussed in the sections that follow.

3.3.3.1 Internal stakeholders

New venture management

A written business plan is essential for the systematic coverage of all the important features of a new business. It becomes a manual to the entrepreneur and his/her management team for establishing and operating the venture. The following aspects are of primary importance to the entrepreneur and his/her team:

- the vision that the entrepreneur has for the new business
- the mission that defines the business
- an overview of the key objectives (this is derived from the mission statement)
- a clear understanding of the overall strategy to accomplish the objectives, as well as a clear understanding of the functional strategies (marketing strategy, financial strategy, human-resources strategy and so on) that form substantial parts of the business plan.

Employees

From the employees' point of view, there is also a need for a business plan. More specifically, employees need to have a clear understanding of the venture's mission and objectives to be able to work towards attaining the objectives. A business plan also serves to improve communication between employees and to establish a corporate culture. A well-prepared plan provides employees with a focus for activities. The business plan also helps prospective employees to understand the emerging culture of a young business. It is important that managers and employees contribute to the development of the business plan to establish "ownership" of the plan among them.

> **Critical thinking**
>
> Consider the case study at the start of this chapter. Who are the internal stakeholders in Thabang Molefi's Roots Health and Beauty Spa?

3.3.3.2 External stakeholders

The business plan is even more important to outsiders, on whom the entrepreneur depends for the survival and success of the venture. Indeed, the importance of the business plan may be said to revolve around "selling" the new business to outsiders, who may include the customers, investors and banks.

Customers

When small businesses seek substantial orders or ongoing service contracts, major customers always want assurance that the business will still be around in three or five years' time to provide the parts or service they might require for the product. Customers are almost always impressed by a business plan, since it proves to them that the entrepreneur has thought about the future.

Investors

Almost everyone starting a business faces the task of raising financial resources to supplement their own resources (personal savings, investment in shares or property and so on). Unless the entrepreneur has a wealthy relative who will supply funds, he/she will have to appeal to investors or bankers to obtain the necessary funds. Very few investors or financial institutions will consider financial assistance without a well-prepared business plan.

Investors have a different interest in the business plan from the interest of other stakeholders, and if the entrepreneur intends to use the business plan to raise capital, he/she must understand the investor's basic perspective. A prospective investor has a single goal: to earn a return on the investment, while at the same time minimising risk. While many factors may stimulate an investor's interest in the venture, certain basic elements of a business plan attract (or repel) prospective investor interest more than others.

The matrix in Figure 3.1 presents an evaluation of business plans from the investor's point of view. Only certain basic indicators have been included.

Banks

Banks are a common source of debt capital for small businesses. To improve the chance of obtaining bank loans or what is known in South Africa as "overdraft facilities", the entrepreneur should know what it is that banks look for in evaluating an application for such a loan. Most banks use the four Cs to evaluate a loan application: capital, collateral, character and conditions.

- **Capital.** A small business must have a stable equity base of its own before a bank will grant a loan. The bank expects the small business to have an equity base of investment by the owner/s before it will make a loan. South African banks generally insist on at least 50% equity.
- **Collateral.** This includes any assets the owner pledges to a bank as security for repayment of the loan. Bankers view the

High ↑ RETURN ON INVESTMENT	• Product or service fully developed • Some markets established • Acceptance by users • Acceptable level of own equity • Patent protection • Experienced management team	• Product or service fully developed • High sales in some markets • Acceptance by users • High level of borrowed funds • Financial projections out of line with industry • Management team without track record
↓ Low	• Product or service idea only • Acceptance not tested • Markets assumed • Patent protection • Acceptable track record of entrepreneur and team	• Product or service idea only • Acceptance not tested • Markets assumed • Market projections out of touch with reality • Single entrepreneur without track record

Figure 3.1: Matrix for the evaluation of business plans

owner's willingness to pledge collateral (personal or business assets) as an indication of the entrepreneur's dedication to making the venture a success.

- **Character.** Aspects of the owner's character (such as honesty, competence, determination, ability and a good track record) play a critical role in the bank's decision to grant a loan.
- **Conditions.** The conditions surrounding a loan request also affect the bank's decision. Banks will consider factors relating to the business operation, such as potential market growth, competition and form of ownership, as well as the current state of the economy.

3.3.4 The scope of the business plan: How much planning is needed?

The level of commitment to the writing of a business plan varies greatly among entrepreneurs. Should it be one page long or one hundred pages long? Considerations that determine the amount of planning include the following:

- style and ability
- the preferences of the management team
- the complexity of the product or service and of the business
- the competitive environment
- the level of uncertainty.

The depth and detail in the business plan therefore depend on the size and scope of the proposed new venture. An entrepreneur planning to market a new portable computer nationally will need a comprehensive business plan, largely because of the nature of the product and the market pursued. In contrast, an entrepreneur who wants to manufacture burglar bars and steel gates for the local market will not need such a comprehensive plan. The difference in the scope of the business plan may depend on whether the new venture is a service, involves manufacturing, or is an industrial product or consumer goods. The size of the market, competition and many other environmental factors may also affect the scope of the business plan.

3.3.5 Components of the business plan

While it is important that the primary components of a solid business plan be outlined, every small entrepreneur must recognise that such a plan should be tailor-made, emphasising the particular strengths of the new venture. Two issues are of primary concern when preparing the business plan:

- the basic format of the written presentation
- the content or components of the business plan.

3.3.5.1 The format of the business plan

The first question that comes to mind when thinking about writing the business plan is: Who should write the plan? Many small-business managers employ the professional assistance of accountants, attorneys and marketing consultants. However, experts agree that the entrepreneur may consult professionals, but should in the end write the plan him-/herself. To help determine whether or not to use a consultant, the entrepreneur may use a table similar to Table 3.1 on page 91 to make an objective assessment of his/her own skills.

Through such an assessment, the entrepreneur can identify what skills are needed and who should be consulted to help prepare the business plan.

There are no rigid rules regarding the format of the business plan. However, whatever format is eventually decided on, the plan should have an attractive appearance.

The length of the business plan will depend on the venture, but it can vary from five to twenty pages, excluding annexures and substantiating documents.

Table 3.1: Skills assessment for writing a business plan

Skills	Excellent	Good	Fair	Poor
Planning				
Market research				
Forecasting sales				
Accounting charges				
Operational issues				
Labour law				
Management issues				
Product design				
Legal issues				

3.3.5.2 The content of the business plan

As has already been mentioned, the business plan for each venture is unique. Although no single standard list of business-plan components exists, there is considerable agreement as to what the content of the business plan should be. The following are the most important components of the business plan:

- the executive summary
- the general description of the venture
- the products-and-services plan
- the marketing plan
- the management plan
- the operating plan
- the financial plan
- the supporting materials.

By now, it may be assumed that the value of a business plan is understood and the entrepreneur is ready to prepare one.

Apart from the fact that the business plan begins with the cover page, the huge amount of information that is available on the business makes it difficult to decide what to include under the headings of the various business-plan components listed above. The beginner needs a conceptual scheme to identify the important segments of a good business plan. Table 3.2 on page 92 provides an overview of such a plan.

Table 3.3 on page 92 provides a more detailed outline for each section of a good business plan. Once each of these phases has been completed by the entrepreneur, he/she will have a simple but complete draft of a business plan.

In developing a comprehensive plan, the simple plan will be supplemented by an exhaustive set of questions that should be considered. The examination and consideration of each component of the comprehensive business plan will be discussed in more detail below.

> **Critical thinking**
>
> Consider once again the case study at the start of this chapter. Given the nature of the business of Roots Health and Beauty Spa, to which component of the business plan should Thabeng pay the most attention when preparing a business plan?

3.3.6 Description of a new venture

The next step in the preparation of the business plan is a description of the venture. This step is an extension of the feasibility analysis discussed in Chapter 2. The entrepreneur analyses the entrepreneurial

Table 3.2: Overview of a business plan

Executive summary	A one- to three-page overview of the total business plan. Written after the other sections are completed, it highlights their significant points and, ideally, creates enough excitement to motivate the reader to read on.
General company description	Explains the type of company and gives its history if it already exists. Says whether it is a manufacturing, retail, service or other type of business. Shows the type of legal organisation.
Products-and-services plan	Describes the product and/or service and points out any unique features. Explains why people will buy the product or service.
Marketing plan	Shows who will be the business's customers and what type of competition the business will face. Outlines the marketing strategy and specifies what will give the business a competitive edge.
Management plan	Identifies the "key players": the active investors, management team and directors. Cites the experience and competence they possess.
Operating plan	Explains the type of manufacturing or operating system the business will use. Describes the facilities, labour, raw materials and processing requirements.
Financial plan	Specifies financial needs and contemplated sources of financing. Presents projections of revenues, costs and profits.

Table 3.3: Outline of a simple business plan

General company description	• Name and location • Nature and primary product or service of the business • Current status (start-up, buy-out or expansion) and history (if applicable) • Legal form of organisation
Products and/or services	• Description of products and/or services • Superior features or advantages relative to competing products or services • Any available legal protection, for example, patents, copyrights or trademarks • Dangers of technical or style obsolescence
Marketing plan	• Analysis of target market and profile of target customer • How customers will be identified and attracted • Selling approach, type of sales force and distribution channels • Types of sales promotion and advertising • Credit and pricing policies
Management plan	• Management-team members and their qualifications • Other investors and/or directors and their qualifications • Outside resource people and their qualifications • Plans for recruiting and training employees
Operating plan	• Operating or manufacturing methods used to produce the product or service • Description of operating facilities (location, space and equipment) • Quality-control methods to be used • Procedures used to control inventory and operations • Sources of supply and purchasing procedures
Financial plan	• Revenue projections for three years • Expense projections for three years • Necessary financial resources • Sources of financing

environment to assess the new idea or venture, the factors that might improve his/her chances of success and factors that could work negatively against the proposed venture. This analysis of the environment assists the entrepreneur in taking a rational decision about whether to implement the idea or abandon it. If the entrepreneur decides to implement the idea, he/she must describe it in detail and prepare a business plan for the new idea or venture.

3.3.6.1 A general description of the new venture

Bearing in mind the needs and requirements of banks and investors for a successful business plan (that it should not be too long, and that it should be concise and accurate), a brief but accurate description of the new venture is necessary.

The body of the business plan begins with a brief description of the new venture itself. If the business is already in existence, its history is included. This section informs the reader, for example, whether the business is engaged in tourism, retailing, construction or some other line of business, and also where the business is located and whether it serves a local or an international market. In many cases, issues noted in the legal plan, especially the form of organisation, are incorporated into this section of the plan. Some important

Description of Calabash Guided Tours and Transfers

Name and location of the new venture

Calabash Guided Tours and Transfers is a proposed extension of a successful existing small venture called Tshwane Airport Shuttle. Tshwane Airport Shuttle has been operating for three years, transferring mainly tourists from Johannesburg International Airport to Pretoria and back. It now wants to expand into guided tours for tourists. Calabash Guided Tours and Transfers will be a partnership between Mthombeni Mahlangu and Jacques du Toit. They can both be contacted at 444 Nicolson Street, Brooklyn, Pretoria, 0181, which is also the existing premises of Tshwane Airport Shuttle. Tel. 012-444 4444.

Nature and primary product or service of the business

During the past twelve months, the two partners have studied trends in the transfer and transportation of tourists, mainly in the Gauteng area of South Africa. They have identified a need by tourists for safe transfers, safe day trips and longer tours in a crime-ridden South Africa, where tourists have come to be included in robbery and murder statistics. Because of their three years' of experience in transferring tourists and business people from OR Tambo International Airport to Pretoria, offering guided transfers, trips and tours will form a natural extension of their existing small business. They expect to satisfy their customers by providing a safe and quality guided tour service in the upmarket segments of the tourism industry in Gauteng.

Current status

The new business, Calabash Guided Tours and Transfers, will be started at the beginning of the new year, assuming that adequate funding can be found in the next four months.

Legal form of organisation

The new business will begin operation as a partnership between Mthombeni Mahlangu and Jacques du Toit. Both partners agree to enter into a formal partnership agreement based on a 50–50 decision concerning workload, profits and responsibilities, and how the new venture is funded. Should the source of funding necessitate a close corporation or a limited company, the two persons also agree to restructure the legal form of the new venture to accommodate any requirements a bank or private investor may have.

questions to be addressed in this section of the plan may include the following:

- Is this a start-up, buy-out or expansion?
- Has this business begun operation?
- What is the firm's mission statement?
- Where was this business started?
- What are the basic nature and activity of the business?
- What is its primary product or service?
- What customers are served?
- Is this business in manufacturing, retailing, service or another type of industry?
- What are the current and projected states of this industry?
- What is the business's stage of development? For example, has it begun operations? Is it producing a full product line?
- What are its objectives?
- What is the history of this company?
- What achievements have been made to date?
- What changes have been made in the structure or ownership of the existing business?
- What is the firm's distinctive competence?

Again, there are no fixed issues that should be considered in the general description of the new venture or existing business. Some entrepreneurs may emphasise a successful history, while others may concentrate on the new business's competitive advantage. The general description of a business called Calabash Guided Tours and Transfers on page 93 highlights four critical aspects that should be included in the general description.

3.3.7 Analysing the market

Certain activities that form the basis of the business plan take place simultaneously. Strictly speaking, the description of the new venture's strategy can only be finalised once the entrepreneur has completed a market analysis to find out if a market for the product exists and, if so, how he/she will exploit the market. In other words, once the entrepreneur is convinced that there is good market potential in a particular segment of the market, he/she must work out how the product will reach the market and what marketing strategy to adopt.

Entrepreneurs often become infatuated with their product or service and believe or hope that there is a market for it. This euphoria can be very costly, if not devastating, to the new venture with its limited resources. The analysis of the new venture's market and the development of a marketing strategy involve the following key items:

- concepts
- the identification of a target market
- research and forecasting in the target market
- a marketing plan or strategy for the selected market segment/s.

Chapter 12 deals with these aspects in detail.

3.3.8 Determining the financial needs of the new venture

The entrepreneur or potential investors need answers to certain crucial financial questions to determine whether the new venture is not only attractive, but also feasible. The financial analysis constitutes a further crucial component of the business plan. The entrepreneur's projections of a new venture's profits, its required assets and its financial requirements over the next one to five years should be supported by substantiated assumptions and explanations about how the costs, profits and financial requirements are determined. In order to make the necessary financial projections, the entrepreneur must first have a good understanding of financial statements and how to interpret them.

The key issues in this section are therefore:

- an understanding of how financial statements work
- an understanding of how profitability is assessed
- an ability to determine a venture's financial requirements.

Chapter 13 deals with these aspects in detail.

3.4 The location of the business

3.4.1 The choice of location

The choice of geographical location for premises is of extreme importance for all kinds of business, although it may be more important for some businesses than for others. For certain businesses, location may be a crucial factor. Depending on the nature of the proposed product or service to be offered, the entrepreneur should decide, for example, whether the business needs to be located near its market, near its sources of raw materials, near to other competitors, in the city centre, in the suburbs, in a rural area, in existing industrial areas or according to personal preference.

The **location factors** that have to be considered when making this choice are briefly analysed in section 3.4.2.

3.4.2 Location factors

The most important location factors are the following:

- **Sources of raw materials.** Where, in what quantity, of what quality and at what prices can these materials be obtained?
- **Availability of labour.** Where and at what cost is the required labour available in terms of, for example, quantities, levels of training, development potential and productivity?
- **Proximity of and access to the market.** This includes aspects such as the potential advantages over present competitors, the current extent and potential development of the market, the perishability of products, the needs of consumers and users regarding, for example, delivery, after-sales services and personal contact, and the possible entry of competitors into the market.
- **Availability and cost of transport facilities.** This includes aspects such as the availability of rail, air, road and water transport facilities, the transport costs of raw materials in relation to finished products and the possibility of the entrepreneur using his/her own transport (road links and limitations on private transport).
- **Availability and costs of power and water.** These must satisfy the needs of the prospective business.
- **Availability and costs of a site and buildings.** Buildings need to comprise units of the required size and appearance, with the necessary facilities and expansion possibilities. Consideration should also be given to accessibility for suppliers of raw materials, customers and employees.
- **Availability of capital.** This does not necessarily affect the choice of a specific location, but can still play a role when the suppliers of capital set specific conditions or express certain preferences in this regard, for example, or when capital is such a limiting factor that it necessitates the choice of the cheapest location.
- **Attitude, regulations and tariffs of local authorities.** These comprise, for example, the attitude of local authorities to industrial development, including possible concessions that encourage location, health regulations, building regulations, property rates, water and electricity tariffs, and the availability and costs of other municipal services.
- **The existing business environment.** This could influence the establishment of the proposed business by, for example, the provision of repair and maintenance services, as well as the availability of spares, and banking, postal and other communication facilities.
- **The social environment.** This concerns the provision of satisfactory housing and educational, medical, recreational and shopping facilities for employees of the proposed business.

- **Climate.** Some production processes require a particular type of climate. Climate can also influence the acquisition, retention and productivity of personnel.
- **Central government policy.** This may encourage or discourage the establishment of certain types of business in specific areas in a direct or indirect manner through, for example, tax concessions.
- **Personal preferences.** These relate to the area or areas that entrepreneurs and their families prefer to live in.

Critical thinking

Recall the case study at the start of this chapter. Should Thabeng extend her business into the CBD of Johannesburg? Would she be just as successful there?

3.5 Summary

In this chapter, the legal forms of a business that are available to the entrepreneur were discussed. This discussion covered the characteristics, advantages and disadvantages of the sole proprietorship, the partnership, the close corporation, the company and the business trust. In addition, the development of the business plan for a new venture was examined. The final section of the chapter dealt with the most important location factors.

Key terms

business plan	joint venture
business trust	location factor
close corporation	partnership
company	sole proprietorship
co-operative society	

Questions for discussion

1. Why is a business plan important? Consider this question from the perspectives of both internal and external users.
2. What are the key sections of a business plan?
3. What are the factors to consider in choosing the legal forms of a business or organisation?
4. What are the advantages and disadvantages of a business trust?
5. What are the factors to consider when deciding on the location of a new family restaurant?
6. In considering the case study at the start of this chapter, assume that Thabang is married to an up-and-coming businessman, JJ, who owns two business properties in the CBD of Johannesburg. The couple also own a house, which is registered in JJ's name. They are married in community of property.

   How will this information affect Thabang's choice of the form of enterprise for her beauty spas?

Multiple-choice questions

1. Members of a business usually enjoy limited liability in the business. Which of the following statements about this limited liability is not correct?
   a. The members stand to lose all their capital if the business is sued.
   b. The members stand to lose only the capital that was invested in the business.
   c. Limited liability means that the members or owners are protected from being sued in their private capacity.
   d. Trusts also enjoy limited liability.
2. Which of the following are not juristic persons?
   a. sole proprietorships

   b. trusts according to the Companies Act (No. 71 of 2008)
   c. companies
   d. close corporations
3. The business format selected by the entrepreneur has a lot to do with the legal personality of the business. Which one of the following statements is incorrect?
   a. The business as a legal person exists independently from its members.
   b. It is perceived by the law that a legal person is similar to a natural person.
   c. A legal personality has its own assets and obligations, such as the repayment of loans.
   d. The business existence is affected by changes in the number of people who are members of the business.
4. Which of the following statements is wrong?
   a. Members of companies and close corporations are usually not liable for the debts of the business.
   b. Sole proprietors enjoy total management autonomy.
   c. Partnerships and close corporations have participative management structures.
   d. Companies are ideally suited to raise large sums of money.
5. Look at the list below.
   i. employees
   ii. customers
   iii. banks
   iv. investors

   Which of the individuals and institutions listed above are stakeholders of the business?
   a. i
   b. i, ii
   c. i, ii, iii
   d. i, ii, iii, iv

Answers to multiple-choice questions

1. a
2. a
3. d
4. a
5. d

References

1. Havenga, P.H. et al. 2004. *General principles of commercial law.* 5th ed. Cape Town: Juta, pp. 285–303.
2. Delport, P. *The New Companies Act Manual* as contained in Benade, M.L. et al. *Entrepreneurial Law: Incorporating the New Companies Act Manual.* Special edition. LexisNexis, pp. 1–12, 41, 49–51, 139–144.
3. Delport, P. *The New Companies Act Manual* as contained in Benade, M.L. et al. *Entrepreneurial Law: Incorporating the New Companies Act Manual.* Special edition. LexisNexis, pp. 1–12, 41, 49–51, 139–144.
4. Delport, P. *The New Companies Act Manual* as contained in Benade, M.L. et al. *Entrepreneurial Law: Incorporating the New Companies Act Manual.* Special edition. LexisNexis, pp. 1–12, 41, 49–51, 139–144.
5. Delport, P. *The New Companies Act Manual* as contained in Benade, M.L. et al. *Entrepreneurial Law: Incorporating the New Companies Act Manual.* Special edition. LexisNexis, pp. 1–12, 41, 49–51, 139–144.

CHAPTER

4

THE BUSINESS ENVIRONMENT

The purpose of this chapter

This chapter introduces the environment in which a business functions and explains how the environment influences the development of a business organisation. This includes treatment of the following related topics:

- the concept of environmental change
- the composition and characteristics of the business environment
- the impact of the different environmental variables (the components of the sub-environments) on the daily operation of a business
- threats and opportunities that transpire owing to an interaction of the variables in the external environment
- the need to monitor the business environment
- how a business organisation can respond to the influences of the environment.

These topics are illustrated in the case study on De Beers on pages 102–103.

Both entrepreneurs and established organisations must consider the internal and external environmental factors that can help or hinder the development of their business. These environmental factors are the fundamental foundation of the strategies implemented by the organisation[1]. This chapter discusses various kinds of strategies that a business is likely to find effective.

Learning outcomes

On completion of this chapter you should be able to:

- understand the meaning of environmental change
- explain the composition and characteristics of the business environmental model
- discuss each of the subenvironments of the environmental model
- explain how each of the environmental variables in the micro-, market and macro-environments can influence an industry or individual business
- explain the difference between opportunities and threats in the external environment
- discuss environmental scanning as a means of managing change in the business environment.

4.1 Introduction

Society depends on **business** organisations for most of the products and services it needs, including the employment opportunities that businesses create. Conversely, business organisations are not self-sufficient, nor are they self-contained. They obtain resources from the society and environment in which they operate. Therefore business organisations and society (or, more specifically, the environment in which the businesses function) depend on each other.

This mutual dependence entails a complex relationship between business organisations and their environment. This relationship increases in complexity when certain variables in the environment (such as technological innovation or political developments) bring about change that impacts in different ways on the business organisation.

The importance and influence of **environmental change** on the successful management of an organisation became acutely apparent in the last few decades when environmental forces brought about unforeseen change. The 1970s were characterised by extreme energy- and oil-price increases. In the 1980s, there was a shift from local to global business, and many countries experienced fierce competition from Japan and other Asian countries. The 1990s heralded a new age of connectivity, with the emergence of the internet and the World Wide Web, both of which revolutionised the operations of business organisations. Businesses could now take their digital material and send it anywhere at very little cost. The spread of the commercial web browser allowed individuals and companies to retrieve documents or web pages stored in websites and display them on any computer screen in an easy-to-use manner[2]. During the latter part of the 1990s, Western countries enjoyed the longest-ever economic boom, which ended on 11 September 2001 with the terrorist strike on the World Trade Center in New York. This incident heralded a new era in world history, introducing a new world order with new alliances and new enemies. Then, in 2008, the stock-market crash on New York's Wall Street signalled the beginning of a global financial crisis, which led to economic recession in many countries.

South Africa, after experiencing many years of macro-economic stability and a global commodities boom, was not exempt from this crisis. The economy began to slow in the second half of 2008 owing to decreased demand and commodity prices[3]. After experiencing two consecutive quarters of negative growth on its gross domestic product (GDP), South Africa officially entered an economic recession in the first half of 2009.

Although 2009 was a trying year for South Africa's economy, the country is privileged to be hosting the 2010 FIFA World Cup. This mega-event will boost the country's economy. It is hoped that South Africa's economy will expand by 3,7% in 2010 and by 4% in 2011[4].

Global events and South Africa's own political and cultural changes have all combined to make the South African management environment more challenging[5]. Both the previous decades of instability and then the new era of rapid change and uncertainty have increased business organisations' need to stabilise the impact of environmental change. The result of this is a greater awareness of environmental influences on management decisions, and the development of an approach to investigate and monitor change in the environment.

4.2 The organisation and environmental change

It has been said that change has become the only constant reality of our time and that it is the only definite phenomenon in management[6]. In the management sciences particularly, change is a difficult concept to define. The *South African Pocket Oxford*

Dictionary defines change as "moving from one system or situation to another"[7]. Expressed simply, change refers to any alteration in the *status quo*. This implies a change from a condition of stability to one of instability, a shift from the predictable to the unpredictable or from the known to the unknown. Change cannot be measured, and it causes insecurity. No single factor can be held responsible for it, and it occurs in different ways and at a different rate depending on the place and community in which it occurs. Moreover, the rate of change often has a greater effect on the environment than the direction of change.

The rapid rate of change

To understand the rapid rate of change, consider this extract from a famous speech made by former United States president John F. Kennedy in 1962:

> No man can fully grasp how far and how fast we have come, but condense, if you will, the 50 000 years of man's recorded history in a time span of but a half-century. Stated in these terms, we know very little about the first 40 years, except at the end of them advanced men had learnt to use the skins of animals to cover themselves. Then about ten years ago, under this standard, man emerged from his caves to construct other kinds of shelter. Only five years ago, man learnt to write and use a cart with wheels. Christianity began less than two years ago. The printing press came this year, and then less than two months ago, during this whole 50-year span of human history, the steam engine provided a new source of power. Newton explored the meaning of gravity. Last month, electric lights and telephones and automobiles and airplanes became available. Only last week did we develop penicillin and television and nuclear power ...

Source: Lowne, C. (Compiler). 2005. *Speeches that changed the world.* London: Bounty Books, p. 73.

At the beginning of the twenty-first century, the rapid rate of change is even more staggering. Today the rise of a "knowledge economy" is characterised by an explosion of technologies (for example, blogging, online encyclopaedias and podcasting), with knowledge and resources connecting all over the world. Computers, e-mail, fibre-optic networks, teleconferencing and dynamic new software allow more people than ever before to collaborate and compete in real time with other people on different kinds of projects from different corners of the planet and on a more equal footing than at any previous time in history[8].

Figure 4.1 shows the three subenvironments of the business environment. Environmental variables (the components of each subenvironment) increasingly affect the environment in which business organisations operate and make decisions regarding investments and strategies.

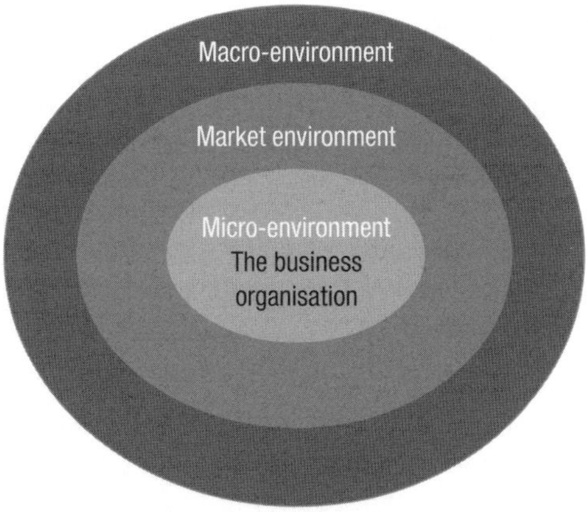

Figure 4.1: The business environment

Environmental variables that are constantly changing the environment in which business organisations operate include technological innovations (such as secure online-payment systems), economic fluctuations (such as changes in exchange rates and interest rates), new laws (such as South Africa's labour laws) and social factors (such as increased urbanisation and changing social values).

During the past 16 years, the structure of South African society and its lifestyles, values and expectations have changed visibly, in particular since 27 April 1994, when a "new" South Africa was formally established.

South Africa's democratically elected government brought about drastic changes, in particular a new social order. The democratisation of South Africa also normalised the country's international relations, but at the same time exposed South African businesses to a borderless world in which they have to compete. Another notable transformation was the steady economic growth that was achieved under the former president, Thabo Mbeki, and the former finance minister, Trevor Manual.

However, in the first quarter of 2008, business confidence fell to a seven-year low[9] as a result of higher inflation and the weakening of the rand, among other variables. Confidence rose again slightly in 2009 with a range of positive developments that materialised early in the year. Nonetheless, there is much instability in South Africa while the global economy continues to deteriorate with economic growth contracting in many countries[10]. In working towards economic stability in South Africa, President Jacob Zuma and Finance Minister Pravin Gordhan have a mighty challenge ahead.

In addition, South Africa is experiencing accelerating urbanisation, increased poverty, an influx of unskilled immigrants and high crime rates, all of which will affect the South African business environment.

The case study below looks at a big player in the South African economy: De Beers. It shows how De Beers has experienced radical changes in the last few decades, both in South Africa and in the rest of the world.

Worldwide, business organisations are restructuring, outsourcing and trimming workforces. Without these major changes, business organisations would not be able to align themselves with the realities of the changing external environment. And without adapting to these changes, they would not be fit to compete in the new global economy.

Other changes that affect the business organisation include changes in monetary and fiscal policy, which impact on financial management. Changing consumer needs, often the result of economic and technological

Case study

The business environment in action: De Beers faces a challenging but promising outlook

De Beers was established in 1888. Today it is the world's leading diamond company, producing approximately 40% of the world's supply of rough diamonds. In its early years, when the company produced over 90% of the world's diamonds, it was able to control the production and hence the supply of diamonds almost at will. Then, from the early 1900s, when competitors began to challenge its prominence, De Beers used its position to co-ordinate and regulate the supply of diamonds in pursuit of price stability and consumer confidence. During the 1990s, the diamond industry experienced dramatic swings in the supply of diamonds, the world economy moved onto a low inflationary path and the industry experienced a period of pricing pressure, causing De Beers to rethink its business model and strategy. De Beers is now very aware of competition from companies in Australia, Canada and Botswana.

The year 2008 marked the 120th anniversary of De Beers. The company has experienced many global crises in the past and in every instance, De Beers has emerged better equipped to make the most of the inevitable recovery. This longevity is a reflection of an ability to adapt to changing situations, a long-term approach that is required to be successful in the diamond business and a sophisticated approach to sustainability that lies at the heart of its business model.

De Beers' openness to change and innovation has assisted the company in achieving certain milestones in the year of its 120th anniversary. During 2008 alone, De Beers opened three new mines (two in Canada and one in South Africa) and launched the Diamond Trading Company in Botswana as well as the Forever brand in Asia. The decision was also made to sell a number of marginal mines, including the South African Cullinan Mine, which was sold to Petra Diamonds Limited.

Voorspoed in the Free State province was one of the three new mines of 2008. All employees of the mine have a minimum of a Grade-12 education (a rather unique achievement in South Africa) and Voorspoed is also breaking new ground in women's empowerment by implementing plans to place women in 50% of all technical positions by the end of 2009. The mine also entered into a broad-based Black Economic Empowerment (BEE) partnership, whereby it plans to include historically disadvantaged South Africans in its management structure.

During the first quarter of 2008, each constituent member of the De Beers family of companies re-evaluated growth plans in favour of right-sizing, cost reductions and cash conservation. This was done in response to the rapidly emerging economic crisis, which proved to be as dramatic as it was unprecedented. The response was fast, targeted and measured, with strategies launched globally to conserve cash, reduce diamond production in line with client demand, stimulate consumer demand and ensure staffing levels that would correspond with operation requirements. Unfortunately the lower levels of production forecast unavoidable job losses.

During the year, De Beers produced 48,1 million carats, a decline on the 51,1 million carats produced in 2007. This slow-down was partly deliberate owing to the lower client demand in the last quarter of 2008 (luxury products are not immune from the effects of the global economic crisis), as well as being partly a consequence of the divestiture of various mines.

De Beers Consolidated Mines (DBCM) is part of the global De Beers family of companies, and it experienced an added challenge that negatively affected its operations: the South African power shortages. This "load-shedding" was another reason why DBCM produced only 12 million carats in 2008, which was 3 million carats less than in 2007.

However, De Beers has achieved much in recent years in reshaping the business, seeking cost and capital efficiencies, and driving profitability. Tough decisions made in the good times helped De Beers prepare its portfolio for less favourable trading conditions. The company will continue to reduce capital expenditure and off-mine costs substantially.

Serving as a beacon during difficult times, the De Beers commitment is to "live up to diamonds". This defines not only what De Beers is and what it stands for, but it also provides a framework for ensuring that the company emerges from the current economic downturn with an enhanced reputation and commitment to sustainability.

Sources: Robinson, T. 2004. "The double-decker diamond mine". *South African Process Engineer*, No. 6, Cape Town: Johnnic Communications, p. 36; De Beers. 2008. "Report to Society 2008. Living up to diamonds: From natural resources to shared national wealth". [Online] Available: http://www.debeersgroup.com/ImageVault/Images/id_1847/ImageVaultHandler.aspx Accessed 11 February 2010 & De Beers. 2008. *Operating and financial review 2008*. [Online] Available: http://www.debeersgroup.com/ImageVault/Images/id_1709/ImageVaultHandler.aspx Accessed 11 February 2010.

change, make new demands on marketing management (as in the De Beers' case study). Existing methods of production can change suddenly because of technological advances, and the introduction of new raw materials can cause established industries to disappear. Moreover, trade unions, through strikes and forced absenteeism, are making increasing demands on human-resources management.

The interaction between the environment and a business organisation is an ongoing process that often results in a new environment with new **threats** and new opportunities. Management should align its organisation with the environment in which it operates in such a way that it can identify in advance the opportunities and threats environmental change brings. It is only when management is fully prepared that an organisation can fully utilise the opportunities and deal with possible threats. To be able to do this, managers must first understand the composition and nature of the business environment.

4.3 The composition of the business environment

In the latter half of the twentieth century, it became very clear that the effective management of the business organisation required management to take careful note of environmental changes. This was partly the result of the systems approach to management, which argued that an organisation is an integral part of its environment and that management should therefore adopt a policy of "organisational Darwinism" to ensure

Critical thinking

It is crucial to pay careful attention to the constant changes in the business environment.

Urgent need to keep up with environmental change

Why is environmental change so important in a business context? If you scrutinise the chairman's report or economist's statement in an annual report of your choice, you will find various trends mentioned. Some of these trends will have had a positive impact on the business's operations, while others might have affected performance in a negative way. To illustrate this point, consider the following excerpt from the 2008 group economic review of First National Bank by the bank's chief economist, Cees Bruggemans:

> In South Africa, economic activity slowed throughout the financial year. Just as domestic expenditure had been the driver of the strong expansion of the economy over the previous four years, it subsequently became the reason for a weakening in activity from late 2007. The impact of high borrowing costs, slower growth in real disposable incomes and weaker house price inflation saw consumers cut back sharply on discretionary spending such as on motor vehicles, other durable products and new homes. Activity in the mining and manufacturing sectors was particularly severely impacted by electricity outages in the early part of 2008. Considering weakening household expenditure, deteriorating global growth and a higher cost of capital, growth in private-sector fixed investment held up well, except in residential construction. Investment by the public sector accelerated as part of the government's drive to address infrastructure bottlenecks.

Source: Bruggemans, C. 2008. *FirstRand Group Annual Report 2008.* [Online] Available http://www.firstrand.co.za/AnnualReport2008/FirstRand-Annual-Report-full.pdf Accessed 26 November 2009, pp. 4–5.

that its business does not become extinct in a rapidly changing world in which only the fittest can survive.

The rising instability in the environment made it increasingly necessary to study environmental change and influences. But the question was what exactly to look for in the environment. It would have been hopelessly confusing to have to take every single factor into consideration without any framework to organise information. A variety of influences, ranging from spiritual and cultural values to purely natural influences, may be identified as determinant variables in the business environment[11].

The **business environment** is therefore defined as all the factors or variables, both inside as well as outside the business organisation, which may influence the continued and successful existence of the business organisation. In other words, the business environment refers to the internal as well as the external factors that impact on the business organisation, and that largely determine its success.

4.3.1 The three subenvironments

In order to recognise the environmental variables that influence a business, a realistic classification is necessary. Classification makes it possible to identify distinct trends in each of the classes, which enables further analysis of these trends.

Figure 4.2 on page 106 shows the composition of the business environment with its various subenvironments. It is a visual model of the interaction between a business organisation and its environment. According to this model, the business environment consists of the three distinct subenvironments described below.

4.3.1.1 The micro-environment

The **micro-environment** consists of the business itself, over which management has complete control. This includes variables in this environment, such as the **vision** of the business organisation, the various **business functions** and the **resources** of the business, which are under the direct control of management. The decisions made by management will influence the market environment through the strategy employed to protect, maintain or increase the business's share of the market. For example, management might apply a marketing strategy, using pricing and advertising, to increase market share.

An analysis of the micro-environment allows managers to determine the capabilities, and the strengths and weaknesses, of the organisation[12]. Knowing the organisation's strengths and weaknesses allows management to utilise opportunities and counter threats in the external environment.

The micro-environments of many business organisations worldwide have been subjected to changes relating to re-engineering, restructuring and the trimming of workforces. Without these major changes, businesses would no longer be able to align themselves with a changing environment.

4.3.1.2 The market environment

The **market environment** is encountered immediately outside the business organisation (see Figure 4.1 on page 101). In this environment, all the variables depicted in Figure 4.2 become relevant for every organisation, because they determine the nature and strength of competition in any industry. The key variables in this environment are:

- **consumers** with a particular buying power and behaviour
- **competitors**, including new and potential competitors who want to maintain or improve their position
- **intermediaries**, who compete against each other to handle the business's product
- **suppliers**, who supply, or do not wish to supply, raw materials, products, services and finance to the business organisation.

All these variables give rise to particular opportunities and threats. It is in the market environment that management finds its most

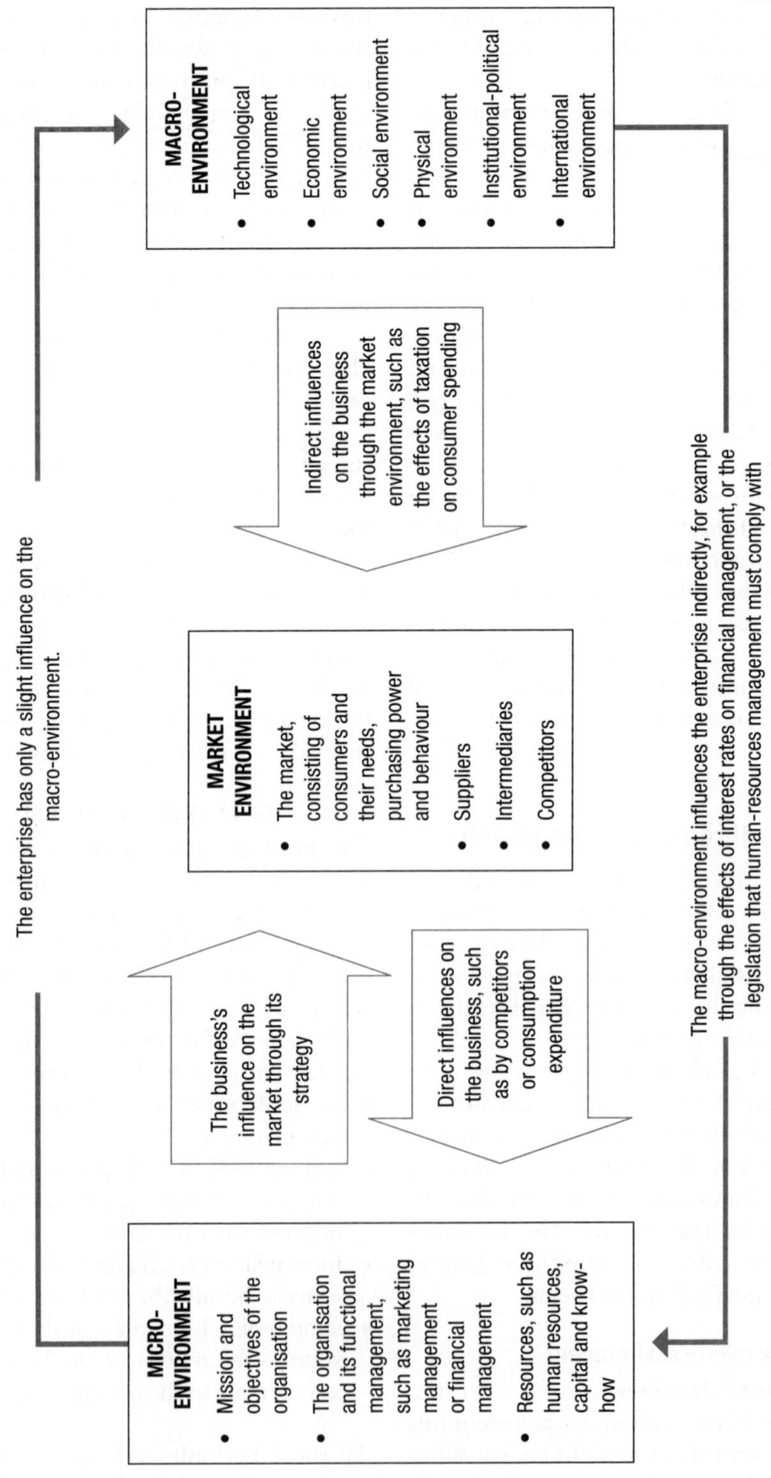

Figure 4.2: The composition of the business environment

important tasks: to identify, assess and take advantage of opportunities in the market, and to develop and adapt its strategies to meet competition. For these reasons, the market environment is often called the "**task environment**".

Management has no control over the components of the market environment, although management may influence the variables concerned through its strategy. However, the market environment continually influences a business.

For example, a new competitor with sufficient resources could start a price war, or a competitor could market a new product protected by patents. In the case study on De Beers, it was noted that De Beers is very aware of competition from companies in Australia, Canada and Botswana. Conditions such as consumer buying power and consumer boycotts can also affect a business. (The fictional movie *Blood Diamond* reflects an increased consumer awareness of the unethical trading of diamonds sourced from war-torn countries.)

Both the market environment and the micro-environment are affected by developments in the macro-environment.

4.3.1.3 The macro-environment

The **macro-environment** is the subenvironment that is external to both the organisation and the market environment. Threats and opportunities may occur in the macro-environment, but, as the individual business organisation has little or no control over the macro-environment, its influence on these threats and opportunities is insignificant.

The macro-environment consists of six distinct components or variables:

- the **technological environment**, which continuously brings change and innovation
- the **economic environment**, in which factors such as inflation, exchange rates, recessions, and monetary and fiscal policy influence the prosperity of the business organisation
- the **social environment**, in which consumer lifestyles, habits and values (formed by culture) make certain demands on the business organisation, particularly through consumerism
- the **physical environment**, which consists of natural resources such as mineral wealth, flora and fauna, and manufactured improvements such as roads and bridges
- the **institutional environment**, with the government and its political and legislative involvement as the main components
- the **international environment**, in which local and foreign political trends and events affect the business organisation (micro-environment) as well as the market environment.

Just as there is interplay between the three subenvironments, there is also interplay between the variables peculiar to each subenvironment (for example, the interplay between the technological and social environments). These interactions will be elaborated on in sections 4.4 to 4.6.

4.3.2 Characteristics of the business environment

The most important characteristics of the business environment are the interrelatedness of the environmental variables, the increasing instability, the environmental uncertainty and the complexity of the environment. A discussion of each of these will show why it is necessary for management to monitor these characteristics continuously.

- **The interrelatedness of the environmental factors or variables** means that a change in one of the external factors may cause a change in the micro-environment and, similarly, a change in one external factor may cause a change in the other external factors. For example, the crash in August 1998 of the Johannesburg Stock Exchange (JSE) – Africa's largest securities exchange – caused a 30% decline in the value of the rand against foreign currencies. This, in turn, resulted in more economic change, including extremely high interest rates, which reduced the purchasing power of consumers and, in turn, led to depressed property and car sales. Yet export businesses benefitted from this change in the macro-environment. A similar incident occurred on a smaller scale a decade later. In 2008, the JSE crashed owing to a technological problem, and consequently brokers and companies lost revenue. In less than a day, approximately R7 billion was lost because of this[13].

- **Increasing instability and change** comprise one of the consequences of interdependence in the environment. However, although the general rate of change in the environment accelerates, environmental fluctuation is greater for some industries than for others. For example, the rate of change in the pharmaceutical and electronics industries may be higher than in the automobile-component and bakery industries.
- **Environmental uncertainty** is dependent on the amount of information that management has about environmental variables, and on the confidence that management has in such information. If there is little information available, or if the value of the information is suspect, the uncertainty of management about the environment will increase, and *vice versa*.

Critical thinking

Business organisations should be proactive in continuously monitoring the many variables that may influence the state of the business environment in which they operate. By doing this, organisations minimise the risk of being caught off-guard and maximise their ability to deal effectively with the challenges that are posed.

The intricacy of the business environment – inflation illustrated

In considering the characteristics of the business environment, the economic variable of inflation is a good example to illustrate the interrelatedness, uncertainty, instability and complexity of the business environment. What are the various environmental variables that might influence inflation in South Africa?

Inflation in South Africa is being influenced by the following environmental variables[14]:

- **The physical environment**: Billions of rand are being invested in the economy to bolster South Africa's infrastructure capacity, for example, South Africa's R650-billion infrastructure rollout, which is occurring from 2009 to 2012. Of this amount, almost R14 billon was allocated to prepare the transport system for the 2010 FIFA World Cup. In addition, there is the R7,7-billion taxi-recapitilisation program, R22 billion for airport development and R27 billion for the Gautrain[15].
- **Consumer buying power**: An increase in consumer spending is a result of, among other things, economic growth, low interest rates and the growth of the Black middle class (also known as the Black Diamonds). Conversely, a decrease in consumer spending is a result of slower economic growth and higher interest rates, and therefore a slower growth of previously high-potential markets.
- **The international environment**: The rise in the crude-oil price affects the price of fuel. This then causes increases in the price of food and other basic commodities.
- **The economic environment**: A depreciation of the rand's exchange rate, interest-rate hikes and a high unemployment rate are contributing factors.

All of the variables listed above are likely to lead to acceleration in inflation in the short term.

- **The complexity of the environment** indicates the number of external variables to which a business organisation has to respond, as well as variations in the variables themselves. A bakery, for example, has fewer variables to consider in its business environment than a manufacturer of computers, and therefore has a less complex environment. It is one of the advantages of businesses with less complex environments that they need less environmental information to make decisions.

These few exceptional characteristics of the environment show how important it is for management to know and understand the environment within which the business organisation operates.

4.4 The micro-environment

As explained earlier, the micro-environment comprises the internal environment of the business. The micro-environment may be viewed as an environment with three sets of variables:

- the vision, mission and objectives of the business
- its management
- its resources[16].

These variables are responsible for the outputs of the business, and they are under the direct control of management. An analysis of these variables will lead to the identification of the organisation's strengths and weaknesses. Each of the variables in the micro-environment is linked to the external environment in some way.

The **vision, mission and objectives** of the enterprise are the reason for its existence. A **vision statement** answers the question: What do we want to become? A **mission statement** is developed after the vision statement and answers the question: What is our business? A mission statement is an "enduring statement of purpose that distinguishes one business from other similar firms"[17]. The mission statement serves as the foundation for the development of long-term objectives, which are the specific results an organisation seeks to achieve[18]. (Without specific objectives to strive for, there would be no need for an organisation.) Examples of a mission statement and strategic objectives are given below.

The vision, mission statement and strategic objectives of SABMiller

Vision
To be the most admired company in the global beer industry

Mission statement
To own and nurture local and international brands that are the first choice of the consumer

Strategic objectives
Our success will depend on the rigorous implementation of four strategic priorities:

- creating a balanced and attractive global spread of business
- developing strong, relevant brand portfolios in the local market
- constantly raising the performance of local businesses
- leveraging our global scale.

Source: SABMiller. 2009. "SABMiller 2009 – Business overview". [Online] Available: http://www.sabmiller.com/files/pdf/corporate_presentation.pdf Accessed 26 November 2009, pp. 4–5.

An organisation's objectives and mission statements such as those given above are influenced by the external environment. For example, unlikely as it now may seem, a drastic decrease in the demand for beer owing to changes in South African consumer preferences would force SABMiller to reconsider its mission. If this turned out to be a prolonged social trend, the organisation might shift its strategic focus to hotels and gaming.

The different areas of management or business functions and the way in which an organisation is structured constitute another set of variables in the micro-environment that have certain interfaces with the external environment. For example, marketing is the business function that is in close contact with the market: marketing management keeps an eye on consumers and their preferences as well as on the activities of competitors so that it can develop strategies to counter any influences from the market environment. Similarly, financial management keeps an eye on levels of taxation and rates of interest that could influence the financial position of the business. Human-resources management may influence the environment through its employment policy, just as trade unions, strikes, the availability of skilled labour, wage demands and new labour laws may affect its decisions. A business organisation should be structured in such a way that it is able to deal with influences from the environment and still operate productively within the environment, especially the market environment.

The resources of a business comprise the last set of internal variables that have certain interfaces with external environments. These resources include the following:

- **tangible resources**, such as production facilities, raw materials, financial resources, property and computers
- **intangible resources**, such as brand names, patents and trademarks, the company reputation, technical knowledge, organisational morale and accumulated experience
- **organisational capabilities**, which refer to the ability to combine resources, people and processes in particular ways[19].

The resources of a business organisation can be at risk from threats or they can benefit from opportunities presented by environmental variables. For example, an important tangible resource such as a particular production process may be threatened by a new technology or a new invention. Alternatively, special skills or knowledge (an intangible resource) can be employed to exploit an opportunity in the environment, such as when a business with knowledge and experience of exporting takes advantage of a devaluation in the rand to make a profit.

This also illustrates that while some business organisations are threatened by a specific variable in the external environment, it may appear to be an opportunity for other organisations. Furthermore, this shows that the micro-environment varies from one business organisation to the next.

4.5 The market environment

The market environment (or task environment) is immediately outside the business organisation, as shown in Figure 4.1 on page 101 and Figure 4.2 on page 106. It consists of the market, suppliers, intermediaries and competitors, which are sources of both opportunities and threats to a business. More precisely, this environment contains those variables that revolve around competition. In order to understand clearly the interaction between the enterprise and its market environment, it is necessary to examine the variables in the market environment more closely.

4.5.1 The market

Several meanings can be attached to the term "market", but in this context, it refers to people who have needs to satisfy and have the financial means to do so. In other words, the market, as a variable in the market environment, consists of people with particular demands who manifest certain forms of behaviour in satisfying those demands. (This subject is discussed more fully in Chapter 12.) If a business wants to achieve success with a strategy of influencing consumer decisions in its favour in a competitive environment, management needs to be fully informed about all aspects of consumer needs, purchasing power and buying behaviour.

Critical thinking

How does a mission statement differ from vision and objectives? Study the excerpt about the Coca-Cola Company below and see if you can answer this question.

Vision and Mission of the Coca-Cola Company

The world is changing all around us. To continue to thrive as a business over the next ten years and beyond, we must look ahead, understand the trends and forces that will shape our business in the future and move swiftly to prepare for what's to come. We must get ready for tomorrow today. That's what our 2020 Vision is all about. It creates a long-term destination for our business and provides us with a "Roadmap" for winning together with our bottler partners.

Vision statement

Our vision serves as the framework for our Roadmap and guides every aspect of our business by describing what we need to accomplish in order to continue achieving sustainable, quality growth.

- **People:** Be a great place to work where people are inspired to be the best they can be.
- **Portfolio:** Bring to the world a portfolio of quality beverage brands that anticipate and satisfy people's desires and needs.
- **Partners:** Nurture a winning network of customers and suppliers. Together we create mutual, enduring value.
- **Planet:** Be a responsible citizen that makes a difference by helping build and support sustainable communities.
- **Profit:** Maximise long-term return to shareowners while being mindful of our overall responsibilities.
- **Productivity:** Be a highly effective, lean and fast-moving organisation.

Mission statement

Our Roadmap starts with our mission, which is enduring. It declares our purpose as a company and serves as the standard against which we weigh our actions and decisions.

- To refresh the world ...
- To inspire moments of optimism and happiness ...
- To create value and make a difference.

In theory, a vision statement and objectives focus on the future and answer the question: What do we want to become? The mission statement concerns the present, the reality of daily operations and answers the question: What is our business?

Source: The Coca-Cola Company. 2009. "Our Company: Mission, vision & values". [Online] Available: http://www.thecoca-colacompany.com/ourcompany/mission_vision_values.html Accessed 29 November 2009.

Management also has to understand that these conditions are directly influenced by variables in the macro-environment: demographic trends influence the number of consumers, economic factors such as high interest rates determine the buying power of consumers and cultural values exert certain influences on the buying behaviour. Management should also understand that this continuous interaction between market variables and the variables in the macro-environment gives rise to changes in both environments.

South African businesses operate in a complex market environment, characterised by a heterogeneous population. To determine the market for its market offering, management analyses the total number of consumers in a specific area or market segment and the purchasing power of those consumers.

Purchasing power is represented specifically by consumers' personal disposable income. Personal disposable income is the portion of personal income that remains after direct taxes plus credit repayments (loans from banks, shops and other institutions) have been deducted, and is available for buying consumer products and services. Purchasing power therefore also serves as an interface between the macro-environment and the micro-environment. (Other characteristics of the consumer market that influence purchasing patterns, such as language, gender distribution and size of family, are discussed in more detail in Chapter 12.)

Purchasing power and consumer spending in South Africa[20]

In part owing to stable economic growth up until 2008, consumer spending in South Africa grew exceptionally fast at a rate of between 6% and 7% per year. This, in turn, influenced buying behaviour – in August 2006 almost 45 000 new passenger vehicles were sold and annual sales were up more than 17%.

The increase in purchasing power and consumer spending seems to have been bolstered by the inexorable march of Black families up the income ladder. In 2008, there were approximately three million Black Diamonds in South Africa, accounting for 40% of the country's consumer spending power, an increase of R70 billion since 2007. One of the many factors leading to the increase in purchasing power includes the availability of credit, as well as the movement of the Black Diamonds from the townships to the suburbs[21].

However, during February 2009, only 20 406 new passenger vehicles were sold in South Africa, a decrease of 33% compared to February the year before[22]. This indicated reduced purchasing power and consumer spending in South Africa. Consumers were feeling the pinch of an unstable economy.

The **consumer market** can further be subdivided according to the products that are bought:

- durable products (for example, furniture, domestic appliances and motor cars)
- semi-durable products (for example, food and tobacco)
- services (for example, insurance, rental and communication).

This classification enables management to analyse specific segments of the market according to what products were purchased.

Besides the market in consumer products, there are also industrial markets in which products and services are supplied by manufacturing enterprises for the production of further products and services. Government markets involve the purchase of products and services by the central government, provincial governments and local authorities. International markets relate to foreign buyers, including consumers, manufacturers, resellers and governments.

Large and complex, the market environment must be continuously analysed by the business organisation in order for this business organisation to function successfully. Moreover, variables in the macro-environment, such as economic factors, political trends and upheavals, as well as population growth and urbanisation, also influence the market environment and, eventually, the products and services that the business offers to the market.

4.5.2 Suppliers

According to the systems approach, a business organisation is regarded as a system that receives inputs from the environment and converts these into outputs in the form of products or services for sale in the market environment. The inputs required are mainly materials (including raw materials, equipment and energy), capital and labour. Suppliers provide these items to businesses. When one considers that approximately 60 cents out of every rand spent goes into purchases from suppliers, the importance of suppliers in the market environment becomes clear. If a business cannot obtain the right inputs of the necessary quality in the right quantity

Challenging economic times[23]

Consumers cut discretionary spending during the challenging economic times, according to the findings of the July 2009 MasterCard Worldwide Survey. During the 2008 and 2009 period, South African consumers changed their purchasing priorities. The survey found that consumers were paying more attention to assets of long-term value (these include retirement savings, investments and renovations) and holding back on their discretionary spending for that time period. This does not mean that South African consumers would not spend at all. The top three items consumers would still spend their discretionary income on included fashion and accessories, entertainment and dining, and buying or upgrading property. When participants were asked if they would still donate part of their income to charities, only 45% of the respondents said yes, and said that their donations would only be up to 2% of their annual income.

Based on the above information, Rodger George, Consumer Business Industry Leader for Deloitte South Africa, stated, "During times like these, consumers tend to buy downwards in terms of product and price selection, and they often trade-off products within their available spend basket. Value becomes a key driver for purchase decisions that are often prioritised according to needs, and in some cases 'feel-good' sentiments."

and at the right price for the production of its products, then it cannot achieve any success in a competitive market environment. The interaction between a business organisation and its supplier network is a good example of the influence of environmental variables on the business.

In the case of materials, practically every business, whether it is in manufacturing, trading or contracting, depends on regular supplies. The whole question of materials management, the scanning of the environment with regard to suppliers and relations with suppliers as environmental variables is dealt with in Chapter 14.

In addition, a business organisation depends not only on suppliers of raw materials, but also on suppliers of capital. Banks and shareholders are such suppliers. They are discussed in Chapter 13. Small businesses in particular find it difficult to raise capital.

Businesses also need a supply of human resources. Many business organisations first turn to labour brokers such as employment agencies to fill this need. Trade unions and other pressure groups can also be regarded as "suppliers" of human resources, and enterprises, especially in the manufacturing and mining sectors, have complex relationships with these "suppliers". The scanning of the environment, particularly with regard to human-resources problems, is discussed in greater detail in Chapter 11.

4.5.3 Intermediaries

Apart from the consumers and competitors with whom marketing management has to deal in the market environment, **intermediaries** also play a decisive role in bridging the gap between the manufacturer and the consumer. Intermediaries include wholesalers and retailers, agents and brokers, representatives and, in townships, spaza shops. They also include bankers, asset managers and insurance brokers, who, from a financial perspective, are also involved in the transfer of products and services.

Decision-making by management in respect of intermediaries is complicated by the **dynamic and ever-changing nature** of intermediaries. New trends and markets are responsible for the development of new kinds of intermediaries. Contemporary trends in South Africa in this regard are, for example, extended shopping hours, increased advertising by shopping centres, the escalating importance of Black retailers in Black residential areas, the increase in the number of franchises and spazas, and the shift of power from the manufacturer to large retailers because of bar-coding and own brand names (the retail chain stores such as Pick n Pay, Woolworths and Shoprite/Checkers are well known for their "no-name" or generic brands).

Relationships with intermediaries also complicate management's decision-making as they often involve entering into long-term agreements that may have certain implications for marketing strategy. The power of large retailers also has certain implications for price and advertising decisions.

New trends among intermediaries provide management with certain opportunities, but also hold out the possibility of threats.

4.5.4 Competitors

Since the fall of communism, most organisations operate in market economies that are characterised by competition in a market environment. This means that every business that tries to sell a product or service in a market environment is constantly up against competition, and that it is often **competitors** that determine how much of a given product can be sold and what price can be asked for it.

Moreover, businesses compete for a share of the market and also compete with other businesses for labour, capital and materials. As a variable in the market environment, competition may be defined as a situation in the market environment in which several businesses, offering more or less the same kind of product or service, compete for the patronage of the same consumers. The result of competition is that the market mechanism keeps excessive profits in check, stimulates higher productivity and encourages technological innovation. But while the consumer benefits from competition, it is a variable that management has to take into account in its entry into, and operations in, the market.

The nature and intensity of competition in a particular industry are determined by the following five factors (also see Figure 4.3):

- the possibility of new entrants (or departures)
- the bargaining power of clients and consumers
- the bargaining power of suppliers
- the availability or non-availability of substitute products or services
- the number of existing competitors.

These factors should be taken into account when marketing management assesses competition.

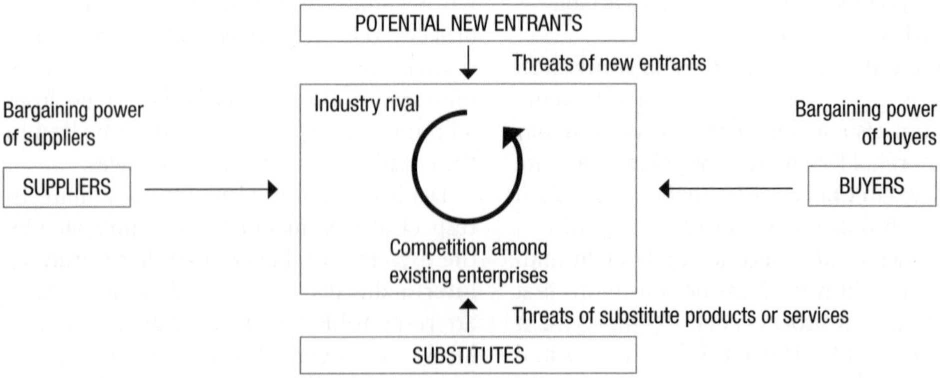

Figure 4.3: The competitive forces in an industry

Source: Griffin, R.W. 1999. *Management.* Houghton Mifflin Company, p. 87. © South-Western, a part of Cengage Learning, Inc. Reproduced by permission. www.cengage.com/permissions.

Figure 4.3 illustrates the five **competitive forces** responsible for competition in a particular industry. The collective strength of these five forces determines the competitiveness in the industry, and therefore the profitability of participants in the industry. Competition varies from intense, in industries such as tyres and retailing, to moderate in the mining and cooldrink industries. The weaker the five forces are, the better the chances are of survival and good performance. Digital technologies and the internet, although not yet in full swing in South Africa, have also contributed to an increase in competition. E-commerce reduced entry barriers, widened the geographical span of markets and increased price transparency. It is therefore an important task of management to find a position in the market where the business organisation can successfully defend itself against the forces of competition. The alternative would be to find a position where the business can influence the forces of competition in its favour.

Continuous monitoring of competition provides the basis for the development of a strategy. It emphasises the critical strengths and weaknesses of the business, gives an indication of the positioning strategy that should be followed, singles out areas in which strategy adjustments can contribute to higher returns, and focuses on industry trends in terms of opportunities and threats.

The scanning of the market environment for opportunities and threats entails an examination of variables such as the economy and the technology in the macro-environment, as well as trends in the variables within the market environment, namely those factors that influence consumer spending, suppliers and competition in the market.

4.5.5 Final comments on the market environment

In the market environment, the interaction between a business and its suppliers, consumers and competitors can result in opportunities or threats to a business. Management must be aware of the trends in the market environment so that the business can exploit opportunities profitably and avoid threats in good time. Environmental scanning, market research and information management are the proper instruments with which to do this (see Chapter 12).

4.6 The macro-environment

4.6.1 The composition of the macro-environment

Apart from the market environment, which has a direct influence on the fortunes of a business, there is a wider macro-environment within which a business also operates. This wider macro-environment has variables that directly or indirectly exert an influence on a business and its market environment. These variables constitute the uncontrollable forces in the external environment that are sometimes referred to as "**mega-trends**".

As Figure 4.2 on page 106 shows, the macro-environment is divided into six variables or components that a business organisation has to observe and respond to: the technological environment, the economic environment, the social environment, the physical environment, the institutional-political environment and the international environment.

Macro-variables (variables that exist in the macro-environment) have an effect not only on the market environment and on decision-making by management, but also on each other, and this constantly causes change in the business environment. In a democratically elected state, the community (which is also the consumer), with its particular culture and values, decides what government it wants, and gives the government a mandate to form a certain political structure, which in turn determines the affairs of the community. Therefore, politics is interwoven with the economy and is influenced by the policies adopted and the economic measures taken to achieve political ends. The result is a certain standard of living for the community.

Stimulated by the needs of the community, and with the support of the economy and the government, it is technology that is mainly responsible for the rate of change in the business environment. Social trends also influence politics and the economy. The international environment acts as a considerable force for change in the other variables and therefore in the total business environment. The result of this interaction is often a new business environment, with new opportunities and new threats.

In studying the macro-environment, the emphasis is on change caused by the uncontrollable macro-variables and the implications for management.

4.6.2 The technological environment

Change in the environment is generally a manifestation of technological innovation or the process through which human capabilities are enlarged. Technological innovation originates in research and development (R&D) by, mainly, business, universities and government. This technological innovation results not only in new machinery or products, but also in new processes, methods, services and, even, approaches to management, which bring about change in the environment. Table 4.1 illustrates how the moving assembly line in car manufacturing (a new production process) enlarged human capabilities and brought about widespread change.

The introduction of the moving assembly line by Henry Ford in 1913 resulted in a radical reduction in manufacturing effort. Between 1908 and 1913, improved productivity enabled the price of the Model-T Ford to be cut from USD850 to USD360. Consequently the car was no longer only available to the wealthy elite, but also to a broader section of society.

A rapidly changing macro-environment

With the exception of a few basic products, most of the things bought and sold today came into existence in the last 60 years. Aeroplanes, radio, television and nuclear power were unknown in the time of Dingane, while Albert Luthuli never knew antibiotics, personal computers, photocopy machines or space flights. Steve Biko did not know of robot factories, ordinary citizens as space travellers or the silicon protein molecules that have already made the silicon chip obsolete. And when former president Nelson Mandela was inaugurated as State President, cellphones were not yet in operation. One reason for the constant rate of acceleration of technological innovation is the fact that 90% of all the scientists who have ever lived are alive today.

Technological innovation also affects other environmental variables. The economic growth rate, measured in terms of GDP, is influenced by the number of new inventions.

Table 4.1: Craft versus mass production at Ford (1913–1914)

Assembly time	Craft production 1913 (minutes)	Mass production 1914 (minutes)	Reduction in effort (%)
Engine	594	226	62
Magneto	20	5	75
Axle	150	26,5	83
Components into vehicle	750	93	88

Source: Smith, D. 2006. *Exploring innovation.* McGraw-Hill Education, Maidenhead, Berks., p. 25. Reproduced by kind permission of the McGraw-Hill Publishing Company.

Technology and changes in lifestyle

- Early in the nineteenth century, railways opened up the hinterlands of America and England.
- In the nineteenth century, electricity began to revolutionise people's lifestyles.
- Since the beginning of the twentieth century, the motor car has brought radical changes to the development of cities and the workplace.
- The advent of the passenger jet in the 1950s transformed tourism into the world's major industry within two decades.
- People are now experiencing the impact of micro-electronics. What used to be a room-sized computer is now a pocket model. The effect of micro-electronics is that it results in ever-smaller units of production that nevertheless yield the same returns.
- Advances in nanotechnology are now dramatically changing industries such as health care and mining.
- Cellphones have revolutionised communication.
- The internet has created opportunities for real-time social networking across the globe by means of web-based applications such as Facebook (which has over 250 million active users) and Twitter (which more and more business executives are using to boost their firms).

Social change, in which the appearance of a new product (such as satellite television, the internet or cellphones) brings about a revolution in people's lifestyles, is also partly the result of technology. Conversely, these variables influence technology, and so the process of innovation and change is repeated. The Sony Walkman example in the box below illustrates how innovation and change are repeated, and how an innovation can bring about social change.

Technological breakthroughs such as cellphones, fibre optics, arthroscopic surgery, bullet trains, voice-recognition computers and the internet result in new products and services for consumers, lower prices and a higher standard of living. But technology can also make products obsolete, as in case of the Sony Walkman.

Every new facet of technology and every innovation creates opportunities and threats in the environment. Television was

The Sony Walkman and social change

When it first came out, the Walkman was a highly innovative product. The personal stereo was an audio product that enabled its young, mobile users to listen to music whenever and wherever they wanted to, without being harassed by older generations concerned about noise. The Walkman was a huge commercial success, selling 1,5 million units in just two years. As well as securing Sony's future as a consumer-electronics manufacturer, it had a much wider impact on society. It was soon copied by other manufacturers, but, more significantly, it changed the behaviour of consumers. Young people found they could combine a healthy lifestyle while continuing to listen to music. So the Walkman may be said to have helped promote a whole range of activities, including jogging, walking and gym usage.

But consumer needs evolve and change is inevitable. CDs wiped out the market for cassette tapes. Portable audio-tape players were replaced by portable audio-CD players.

Then Apple introduced the popular iPod digital music player and the iTunes website for the sale and download of music. Now 670 000 of South Africa's adults download music from the internet, and 82% of these users are under the age of 35[24].

It seems that the Walkman is forever a thing of the past.

Nanotechnology

Nanotechnology is the engineering of functional systems at the molecular scale. It potentially holds the key to new materials that could improve South African's quality of life, as well as the position of the country to compete on a global level.

In promoting nanotechnology, the United States National Science Foundation proposes that people imagine:

> ... a medical device that travels through the human body to seek out and destroy small clusters of cancerous cells before they can spread. Or a box no larger than a sugar cube that contains the entire contents of the Library of Congress. Or materials much lighter than steel that possess ten times as much strength[25].

It is said that, in advanced form, nanotechnology will have significant impact on almost all industries and all areas of society. According to the Centre for Responsible Nanotechnology, it will offer "better-built, longer-lasting, cleaner, safer and smarter products for the home, for communications, for medicine, for transportation, for agriculture, and for industry in general".

The economic and social benefits of nanotechnology have been proven internationally. Realising this, South Africa invested R170 million in nanotechnology research for the period 2006 to 2009 and developed a nanotechnology strategy. The strategy explores nanotechnology socially (dealing with water and energy research) and industrially (dealing with mining and minerals research).

Source: Center for Responsible Nanotechnology. 2006. "General purpose technology". [Online] Available: http://www.crnano.org/whatis.htm Accessed 29 November 2009 & Naidoo, B. 2008. "Nanotechnology holds many socioeconomic challenges". [Online] Available: http://www.engineeringnews.co.za/article/nanotechnology-holds-many-socioeconomic-challenges-2008-05-30 Accessed 29 November 2009.

a threat to films and newspapers, but at the same time it presented opportunities for satellite communications, advertising and instant meals. The opportunities created by computers and the internet in banking, manufacturing, transport and practically every other industry are innumerable. Moreover, technological innovation often has unpredictable consequences. For example, the contraceptive pill meant smaller families, more women at work, and therefore more money to spend on holidays and luxury articles that would previously not have been affordable. The most outstanding characteristic of technological innovation is probably the fact that it constantly accelerates the rate of change.

A further characteristic of technological innovation that impacts on management is the fact that inventions and innovations are unlimited. Technology influences the entire organisation. The most basic effect is probably higher productivity, which results in keener competition. The ability to produce more and better products threatens organisations with keener competition, compelling them to re-assess factors such as their mission, strategy, organisational structures, production methods and markets. Superior management of technology within the organisation can be an important source of competitive advantage.

Continued assessment of the technological environment should include the following:

- the identification of important technological trends
- an analysis of potential change in important current and future technology
- an analysis of the impact of important technologies on competition
- an analysis of the organisation's technological strengths and weaknesses
- a list of priorities that should be included in a technology strategy for the organisation.

Business and water technology

Consider how a large multi-national organisation like SABMiller is utilising technology to ensure best practices in efficient production processes.

SABMiller is creating awareness of sustainable water management through an initiative with the World Wildlife Fund (WWF) called the Water Footprint Network. An aim of this initiative is that SABMiller reduces water consumption in its operations to an average of 3,5 litres to make a litre of beer. This will help SABMiller save 20 billion litres of water per year by 2015[26].

In a developing country such as South Africa, managers should continually assess technology trends that revolve around the following:

- **Water technology.** South Africa's water resources can sustain only 80 million people. SABMiller is a prime example of an organisation that is managing its natural resources efficiently. The world's consumption of water has grown at about twice the rate of its population in the past century alone.
- **Mineral technology.** South Africa has vast mineral resources, and new ways to improve the processing of its mineral treasures should continually be assessed.
- **Marine technology.** This is needed to utilise South Africa's vast coastal and oceanic resources.
- **Agricultural and veterinary technology.** South Africa is one of a few countries that allow the genetic modification of crops. Genetically modified (GM) maize and corn can, for example, make crops more drought resistant, but they also pose threats to biodiversity. Technology in this area therefore needs to be assessed continually to find a balance between providing food to the African continent while still preserving Africa's wildlife and tourism.
- **Medical technology.** This is needed to prevent epidemics and to support the sports industry.
- **Transport technology.** This is needed to provide transport for people. Transport in South Africa is an increasingly important issue, especially as 500 000 overseas tourists are expected to visit the country in 2010 for the FIFA Soccer World Cup.
- **Power technology.** This is needed to harness cheaper and environmentally friendly forms of power, such as solar power. The need for power or electricity in South Africa has increased exponentially since the 1994 election. South Africa's current infrastructure cannot support the increased demand, and power failures have become a standard occurrence. Apart from causing inconvenience, power failures cause losses of millions of rands to businesses.

Technological progress affects a business as a whole, including its products, its life cycle, its supply of materials, its production process and, even, its approach to management. These influences all require management to be increasingly on the alert regarding technological change.

4.6.3 The economic environment

After technology, which is primarily responsible for change in the environment, there is the economy, which is influenced by technology, politics, and the social and international environments, while in turn also influencing these variables. These cross-influences continuously cause changes in, for example, the economic growth rate, levels of employment, consumer income, the rate of inflation, interest rates and the exchange rate. Ultimately, these economic forces have implications for management.

The economic well-being of a country, or its economic growth rate, is measured by the range and number of products and services it produces. Expressed in monetary

Critical thinking

The management of a particular organisation, especially an organisation that is relied on heavily, can have repercussions on the day-to-day livelihood of all role-players in society.

South Africa's energy crisis

Inadequate power supply and production?[27]

Eskom has the monopoly in electricity generation in South Africa. In the last few years, Eskom has found itself in a position where the demand for electricity has exceeded the available supply. In attempt to manage the energy shortage and try to meet demand, Eskom used a last-resort measure that interrupted supply to certain areas of South Africa. This was termed "load-shedding". Eskom's load-shedding programs reached a climax in the first quarter of 2008, severely affecting South Africa's economy and productivity, especially in the manufacturing and mining sectors. Load-shedding not only affected businesses and industries, but it also had a negative effect on South African households and the economy in general.

During the load-shedding period, businesses and households invested in alternative energy supplies (such as solar power and generators), while Eskom implemented a recovery project including power-purchase programs and the installation of energy-efficient technologies to address the short-, medium- and longer-term supply needs.

During the financial year that ended in June 2009, Eskom reported the biggest loss in its history: R9,7 billion. A tariff hike of 31,3% was granted to Eskom by the National Energy Regulator of South Africa (NERSA) as of June 2009. This will increase the financial burden on consumers.

If Eskom were to apply for another tariff increase, do you think this would be the solution to Eskom's financial problems? What effect will the tariff hikes have on the economy, and which industries will be worst hit?

terms, this standard is known as the **gross domestic product (GDP)**, which is the total value of all the products and services finally produced within the borders of a country in a particular period (usually one year)[28].

A high economic growth rate of around 7–8% per year in real terms signals an economy that grows fast enough to create jobs for its people, one that exports more products than it imports to sustain a positive trade balance and a stable currency, and one that can provide its people with an improved standard of living. A low economic growth rate, especially one that is below the population growth rate, usually lowers the people's standard of living.

Between 1999 and 2006, South Africa saw the longest period of uninterrupted economic growth in its history. In fact, during the second quarter of 2006, the GDP grew at an annualised rate of 4,9%, one of the highest rates in the world. Although South Africa needs a growth rate of over 7% per year in real terms to provide jobs for the millions in the unemployment queue, the economic story over the last 12 years is overall a good one[29].

A country's economic growth rate influences consumers' purchasing power, which can, in turn, give rise to changes both in spending behaviour and in the type of products or services purchased.

Management must take note of structural changes in the incomes of different consumer groups and adjust its strategies accordingly. In addition to monitoring the economic growth rate, management must also monitor the business cycle very carefully. The correct assessment of upswing and downswing phases in the economy is essential to the strategy of any business. If management expects a recession, it can, for example, reduce its exposure by decreasing inventory, thereby avoiding high interest-rate costs. Any plans for expansion can also be deferred. In an upswing (or boom period), the right strategy may be to build up sufficient inventory in good time and to carry out whatever expansion is necessary.

Inflation, like economic growth, is an economic variable that affects the decisions management has to make. During the 1960s, South Africa had a very low inflation rate, but from the mid-1970s, double-digit inflation became a regular phenomenon. From 1974 to 1992, the average annual rate of consumer price increases amounted to 13,8%. But since 1993, single-digit price increases, comparable to those of the early 1970s, were again recorded because of improved monetary discipline. However, owing to rising oil prices and a depreciation in the rand's exchange rate, inflation was 11,3% for 2008[30].

The costs and effects of inflation on a business need to be analysed and managed on a permanent basis. Inflation increases the costs for exporting industries and also for local industries competing against imported products. When a country's inflation rate is higher than that of its major trading partners and international competitors, there is a reduction in its international competitiveness. This is still the case with South Africa because its inflation rate is still higher than most of the world's important trading countries.

Another economic variable affecting a business and its market environment is the government's **monetary policy**. This influences the money supply, interest rates and the strength of the currency, and therefore has important implications for management. High interest rates result in a high cost of credit, which tends to modify behaviour and results in a subsequent decline in consumer spending and fixed investment.

The government's **fiscal policy**, in contrast, affects both businesses and consumers through taxation and tax reforms. The fiscal policy is also reflected in the annual National Budget, which is normally communicated in February of each year. In the 2008/2009 National Budget, former Finance Minister Trevor Manuel announced that when setting the gross tax-revenue target of R659 billion for the year ahead, the need to provide relief to households and encouragement to the business sector was taken into account. Manuel also proposed adjustments to the schedules for personal income tax, which he stated would provide relief of R13,6 billion to individual taxpayers. This would compensate for the effects of inflation while providing further relief, mainly to lower- and middle-income earners. Education,

Facts about inflation in South Africa[32]

- From 1946 to 1997, the average level of consumer prices rose by 4 638% over the entire period, or at an average rate of 8,7% per annum.
- This means that an item that cost R100 in 1946 cost R4 638 in 1997.
- Expressed in terms of purchasing power, R1 in 1997 could purchase only about one-fiftieth of the products and services it could buy in 1946.
- The average inflation rate of 6,9% in 1998 was the lowest since 1973, when it was 6,5%.
- The average annual rate of consumer price increases from 1974 to 1992 was 13,8%. At this rate, prices doubled every five years.
- In 2006, consumer inflation was within the South African Reserve Bank's range of 3–6%.
- In 2007, inflation went up to 6,5% and inflation for 2008 had dramatically increased to 11,3%[33].

key to reducing poverty and accelerating long-term economic growth, has the largest share of expenditure (R140,4 billion) in the budget, an amount that has grown by 14% per year[31].

The economies of surrounding countries also affect the economic variables of a country. The South African economy operates in a region where most of the world's poor people live. Of Africa's 53 countries, at least 24 are among the poorest in the world. In addition, Africa has nearly 16% of the world's population, but sadly has an insignificant share in global wealth, producing less than 4% of the world's GDP[34].

The economic trends discussed above demand constant examination by management.

4.6.4 The social environment

The environmental variable that is probably most subject to the influence of other variables (especially technology and the economy) is the social environment. This affects management indirectly in the form of consumers and directly in the form of employees.

Humans are largely products of their society. As members of a particular society, they accept and assimilate their society's language, values, faith, expectations, laws and customs. The way of life of a group of people influences the individual's way of life, and so consumption cannot be explained solely in economic terms. Consumption is also a function of culture and social change.

A rise in interest rates bound to curb consumer spending[35]

High interest rates that surpass 25% (as the rate briefly did in 1998) seem to be a thing of the past. For many years, South Africa experienced low interest rates. Of growing concern, however, was the high growth in consumer spending and consumer indebtedness. Consumer spending raises the inflation rate. Consumer indebtedness, which can be defined as household debt relative to annual income, grew to 68% (the highest in South African history) in 2006. In an attempt to curb consumer spending, the South African Reserve Bank raised the repo rate by 0,5% to 7,5% in June 2006 and then to 8% in August 2006. Another one percentage-point rise occurred in 2007. Inflation reached a high of 11,3% in 2008 and by May 2009, the prime lending rate (the interest rate experienced by the end consumer) was 12%[36]. Increased interest rates send a signal to the market that the cost of credit is rising. This, in turn, restrains consumer spending, and purchases in certain product categories, such as cars, might decrease.

However, this does not always necessarily restrain the ongoing credit turmoil experienced on a global scale. The economic slowdown, increasing retrenchments and credit contraction illustrate the impact of the 2008/2009 financial crisis on South Africa. South Africa's "new" National Credit Act (NCA) was implemented in 2007. It was intended to regulate the credit-granting industry, curb reckless lending and ensure that consumers are protected from harmful lending practices. The strict NCA proved a positive example globally during the period of the credit crunch. Many African and European countries sought advice from South Africa with the aim of hardening their own credit legislation and restricting irresponsible lending.

In South Africa during the period from March 2008 to March 2009, credit granted to consumers contracted by 42% (with mortgages and motor-vehicle finance contracting most sharply). This is an indication of the impact of curbed consumer spending based on inflation, stricter credit legislation and the general financial crisis[37].

South Africa: A mixed society[38]

South Africans are a complicated combination of races, languages, religions, colours and cultures. South Africa's indigenous cultures include those of the Basotho, Tswana, Xhosa, Swazi, Ndebele, San, Venda, Nama, Zulu, Pedi and Tsonga people. Apart from the majority of indigenous cultures, there are also three other large groups: Indian people, White people and Coloured people. Each culture is influenced by the others.

A culture is not static. Over time, a society's values, expectations, habits and way of life change. It is up to the business organisation to keep up with these changes in culture and the subsequent changes in consumer needs.

4.6.4.1 Demographic change

Demographic change is change in the growth and composition of populations. Demographic change is probably the social variable that causes the most change in the market. It does so by altering people's ways of life.

Societies in the developed world are characterised by falling population-growth rates and shrinking families, with the emphasis on smaller consumer units. There are growing numbers of one-person households, and consequently a growing demand for services. There is also a growing population of ageing, affluent people, whose needs give rise to special business opportunities, such as in the tourism industry.

In the developing world, population growth and poverty remain prominent issues, causing great concern to politicians and environmentalists.

The concerns surrounding high population-growth rates in developing countries revolve around poverty, pollution and degradation of the environment, as well as illness and famine. A third of the world's population (two billion people) is in danger

Population patterns

- Almost half of all people live in six countries: China (1 324 million), India (1 149 million), the United States (304 million), Indonesia (239 million), Brazil (195 million) and Pakistan (172 million).
- In 2009, the world's population stood at 6,8 billion. It is expected to reach the seven billion mark towards the end of 2011.
- The world's population growth is almost entirely concentrated in the world's poorer countries.
- About 81% of the world's population lives in developing countries and 90% of births are in developing and less developed countries.
- While the world's total population is still rising, there are signs that, worldwide, growth is slowly coming under control.
- The average annual population growth rate in developed countries is 0,2% per year, while it is 1,4% in less developed countries and as high as 2,5% in parts of Africa.
- Developed regions also have a lower fertility rate, averaging 1,7 children per woman, less than the "replacement level" target of 2. In the developing world, this rate is 2,7 and can even increase to 8 in the poorest countries.
- It is forecasted that nine out of ten youths (ages 15–24) will be in developing countries by the year 2050. A major question is whether the economic conditions of these countries will be able to meet the rising expectations of their citizens.

Source: 2004. *Wêreld-Atlas vir Suid-Afrikaners.* Johannesburg: Jonathan Ball, pp. 11–12; Nations Online. 2008. "Countries of the World". [Online] Available: http://www.nationsonline.org/oneworld/world_population.htm Accessed 29 November 2009 & Population Reference Bureau. 2009. World population data sheet. [Online] Available: http://www.prb.org/pdf09/09wpds_eng.pdf Accessed 29 November 2009, pp. 1, 3, 6.

of starving. All of these concerns have a profound effect on business, especially in Africa, where 55 million people (including a large percentage of employees) are expected to die of Aids by 2020.

South Africa's annual population-growth rate has declined since 2001 with the estimated rate being 1,38% in 2001 and 1,07% in 2009. The total population of South Africa (49,3 million people in 2009) is expected to increase to 54,4 million in 2025. The proportion of Black people, which was 69,5% in 1951, increased to 79,4% in 2009, while that of White people, at 19,1% in 1951, decreased to 9,1% in 2009[39]. South Africa also hosts many illegal immigrants. Figures as high as 12 million immigrants have been quoted.

Overall, the projected growth rates of the various population groups in South Africa are due to decline, with the rate of decline greatest among White people, followed by Asian people, Coloured people and Black people. With the average annual decline of the population-growth rate, the White population could possibly approach zero population growth by the year 2011. This has many implications for the producers of products and services for traditionally White market segments.

Changes in population-growth patterns, as well as age and composition patterns, have an effect on the needs, income and behaviour of consumers, and also on employment patterns.

4.6.4.2 Urbanisation

Changes in population-growth patterns are influencing the geographical distribution and mobility of the world's population.

The movement of people from rural areas towards cities is known as **urbanisation**. Urbanisation is one of the foremost trends of the world's population. Estimates of the future spread of urbanisation are based on the observation that by 2008, more than 70% of the populations in Europe, North America and other regions with richer developed nations already lived in urban areas. Although Africa and Asia compare weakly with 39% and 41% respectively living in urban areas, the highest growth rate in urban populations is found in developing regions. In 2009, the proportion of the global population living in urban areas had increased to 50% and it is expected to rise to 70% (6,4 billion people) by the year 2050, with millions of people joining the towns and cities in Asia and Africa[40]. Urbanisation therefore affects businesses in many ways, especially in the areas of housing, sanitation, slum control and health services.

4.6.4.3 Level of education

Another social trend that will greatly affect management is the level of education of the population. Where the level of education is increasing, this will, on the one hand, raise the level of skills of both managers and workers, and, on the other hand, will result in an increased demand for books, magazines, newspapers and online resources.

Furthermore, better education and training will mean a more sophisticated consumer, with definite demands being made on management regarding the quality of products, advertisements and working conditions.

However, in South Africa, the educational level of all consumers is no longer rising. The matriculation pass rate in 2008 was 62,5%, which was 2,5% lower than in 2007, and 6,4% lower than 2002[41]. Of the 565 744 students who passed matric in 2007, only 85 000 students passed with a university endorsement. Just 25 000 students had a higher-grade mathematics pass, and only 8 000 received marks that were high enough to enter engineering or science degree programs[42]. This is one example illustrating the skills shortage in South Africa.

Furthermore, Joe Makhafola, spokes-person of South Africa's Department of Communication, stresses the problem of skill shortages within the Information and Communication Technology (ICT) sector in South Africa. This skills shortage is prevalent owing to the lack of access to education and training, and the trend of skilled professionals migrating to other countries[43].

4.6.4.4 The changing role of women

Another social variable with clear implications for management is the **changing role of women in developed societies.** As recently as 17 years ago, 60% of American women believed that a woman's place was in the home. Now only 22% are of that opinion.

The proportion of economically active White South African women increased from 19% in 1960 to 36,7% in 2004. The proportion of economically active Coloured women stood at 34,6% in 2007. The involvement of Asian women in economic activities also increased sharply, from 5% in 1960 to about 25% in 2004. The proportion of economically active Black women nearly doubled to 27,3% in 2007, a percentage that is still expected to show a marked rise.

Of the economically active population in South Africa, women constitute 45,8%. This is broken down as follows: African females (34,4%), Coloured females (5%), Indian females (1%) and White females (5,4%). African and White women contribute 5,9% and 9,8% to top management respectively[44].

Although women make up a minority of top management positions in South Africa, women are still being appointed in high-status positions at large institutions. For example, in 2009 Gill Marcus was appointed as the first female Reserve Bank governor and Cheryl De La Rey was appointed as the first female vice-chancellor of the University of Pretoria.

4.6.4.5 Consumerism

A further social trend to be considered is **consumerism**, the social force that protects the consumer by exerting legal, moral, economic and even political pressure on management. This movement is a natural consequence of a better educated public that resists such things as misleading advertisements, unsafe products, profiteering and other objectionable trade practices, and presses for the so-called "rights of the consumer". In a market system, these rights are generally recognised as the following:

- the **right to safety**, which entails protection against products that may be dangerous or detrimental to life or health
- the **right to be informed**, which means objective information is provided to enable the consumer to make rational choices
- the **right to freedom of choice**, which entails giving the consumer access to competitive products or substitutes, and protects against monopolies
- the **right to be heard**, which means that consumers are given the assurance that their interests will receive attention from government and related parties.

The South African Consumer Union endeavours to protect the consumer, to act as a watchdog, and to be in direct contact with manufacturers, suppliers and distributors of consumer products whenever this is in the consumer's best interests. This union also monitors legislation that may affect the consumer and, where necessary, campaigns for the amendment of existing laws or advocates for new legislation to protect the consumer. The new Consumer Protection Act (No. 68 of 2008) is an example of such an Act.

4.6.4.6 Social responsibility and business ethics

Another important aspect of the social environment is the pressure that society exerts on business organisations, forcing them to seek legitimacy by being **socially responsible.** This means that business organisations should not only seek to maximise the value for their shareholders, but also constantly consider the consequences of their decisions and actions on society. Well-known management scholars Ghoshal, Bartlett and Moran maintain that organisations should seek compatibility of their own interests with the interests of society while striving for overall value creation[45]. Consumers are realising that although businesses produce much of what is good in our society, they also cause great harm. Management is mostly criticised for misleading advertising, dangerous products, pollution of the environment, lay-offs, industrial accidents, exploitation of the consumer and other consequences[46]. Organisations are therefore called upon to be socially responsible.

Corporate social responsibility (CSR) can be defined as "the broad concept that businesses are more than just profit-seeking entities and, therefore, also have an obligation to benefit society"[47].

While profits and employment remain important, these days many other factors are included in assessing the performance of a business. These include equity or the empowerment of designated groups (economically and managerially), housing, response to environmental concerns, provision of a responsible and safe workplace, care about health issues and involvement with community issues.

Some businesses perform an annual social audit to measure their social performance. Based on the results of the social audit, a business can review its social responsibility. However, the crux of social responsibility is the community's insistence that a business should be a "good corporate citizen" in every respect, one that produces profit for owners and investors, but simultaneously markets safe products, combats pollution, respects the rights of employees and consumers, and assists the disadvantaged. In short, businesses are expected to promote the interests of society.

In South Africa, corporate social responsibility seems to play an especially important role. Government alone cannot be expected to rectify the inequities of the past at a rate that is fast enough to alleviate poverty. Though South African businesses spend millions on social investment, they remain under pressure to uplift the disadvantaged. In future, in South Africa and elsewhere, pressure will intensify and may even give rise to a more regulatory environment.

Table 4.2 on page 127 shows the various aspects according to which society judges the social performance of a business.

As a concept, **business ethics** is closely related to social responsibility, except that business ethics has to do specifically with the ethics or the ethical behaviour of managers and executives in the business world.

Ethics can be defined as "a guide to moral behaviour based on culturally embedded definitions of right and wrong"[48]. Managers, in particular, are expected to maintain high ethical standards.

At issue here is the integrity of entrepreneurs and managers, and the degree to which their decisions conform to the norms and values of society. Business ethics revolves around the trust that society places in people in business and the obligations these people have towards society.

Greed, the exploitation of workers and consumers, and the abuse of positions of trust have caused the business ethics of entrepreneurs and managers to be criticised. In 2002, for example, only 17% of Americans regarded business executives' ethics as high or very high. Pfizer, the world's largest drugmaker, was given a criminal fine of $2,3 billion in September 2009, the largest amount in United States history, for what government lawyers described as fraudulent marketing of 13 drugs[49]. Such an allegation not only has an affect on the revenue of the company, but it can also destroy a brand's share value if the company's reputation is compromised through reports of unethical behaviour.

Yet, despite the many unethical practices that take place globally, a provider of solutions that promote corporate ethics and responsibility in the workplace reported that 94% of employees surveyed in 2007 said that it is "critical" or "important" that the company they work for is ethical[50].

In South Africa, examples of unethical and corrupt conduct by executives include the

Table 4.2: The social responsibility of business

Area of social responsibility	Issues in social responsibility	Laws/regulations pertaining to social responsibility
Social responsibility to employees (workplace responsibility)	• Equal employment opportunities • Developing a quality workforce (training and the skills-development levy) • Gender inclusion • Access for disabled persons • Sexual-harassment awareness • Respect for diversity • Safe working conditions	• Employment Equity Act (No. 55 of 1998) • Skills Development Act (No. 97 of 1998) • Gender Equality Act (No. 39 of 1996) • Mine Health and Safety Act (No. 29 of 1996) • Public Service Amendment Act (No. 30 of 2007)
Social responsibility to the consumer and customers	• Safe products and services • No misleading advertising and communication • Proper information about products and services	• Consumer Protection Measures Act (No. 95 of 1998) • Consumer Protection Act (No. 68 of 2008)
Responsibility to the investor and financial community	• No deceptive accounting reports • Accuracy of financial reporting • No insider trading • No bribes to customs or other government officials	• South African Statement of Generally Accepted Accounting Practice (GAAP), as approved by the Accounting Practice Board • The "Code of Corporate Practices and Conduct" representing the principles of good governance, as set out in the *King Report III* of 2009, which supersedes the *King Report II* of 2002
Social responsibility to the general public	• Natural-environment issues, including conservation and pollution control • Public-health issues such as HIV/Aids • Housing for the poor • Philanthropic donations • Social welfare • Avoiding unlawful competition	• World Heritage Convention Act (No. 49 of 1999) • Housing Act (No. 107 of 1997) • Welfare Laws Amendment Act (No. 106 of 1996)

controversial arms deal, the Saambou affair and the misuse of funds at LeisureNet.

Corporate governance was institutionalised by the publication of the King Report on Corporate Governance (*King Report I*) in November 1994. This was superseded by the 2002 King Report on Corporate Governance in South Africa *(King Report II)*. The purpose of the "Code of Corporate Practices and Conduct" contained in these reports is to promote the highest standards of corporate governance, and therefore business ethics, in South Africa. The *King Report on Corporate Governance* (*King Report III*) of 2009 updated the earlier reports and incorporated a number of important changes, and takes effect from March 2010[51].

Many South African organisations have responded to the call for socially responsible and ethical behaviour. SABMiller, for example, has a sustainability framework and clearly communicates its responsibility towards the communities in which it operates.

Sustainable development targets at SABMiller

SABMiller has taken a number of steps in working towards sustainable development. On its website, the business records that it has:

- set a target to improve its water efficiency by 25%, reducing consumption from 4,6 hl/hl to 3,5 hl/hl by 2015
- set a target to reduce fossil-fuel emissions from energy use on its sites by 50% per hectolitre of lager produced by 2020
- developed a comprehensive internal alcohol-education program, currently being rolled out across the business
- launched the TalkingAlcohol.com website to provide accurate and balanced information about its products to parents, retailers, medical and health experts, policy-makers and consumers.

Source: SABMiller. 2009. "Business Overview". [Online] Available: http://www.sabmiller.com/files/pdf/corporate_presentation.pdf Accessed 1 December 2009 p. 21.

Chapter 5 discusses ethics and social responsibility in more detail.

4.6.4.7 HIV/Aids

HIV/Aids is a huge social problem. So far, more than 25 million people have died of Aids. At least 25 million may follow in the next few years. In 2007 alone, there were 33 million people in the world living with HIV. Of this number, young people between the ages of 15 and 24 years account for an estimated 45% of new HIV infections.

This disease is devastating families and communities and destroying hope, particularly in Sub-Saharan Africa. Sub-Saharan Africa has the largest number of people living with HIV/Aids in the world, accounting for 67% of all people living with HIV and for 75% of Aids deaths in 2007. In South Africa, there are an estimated 5,7 million people living with HIV, with nearly a thousand Aids deaths occurring daily[52]. Table 4.3 shows the frightening statistics of

Table 4.3: Regional statistics for HIV and Aids, end of 2008

Region	Adults and children living with HIV/Aids	Adults and children newly infected	Adult prevalence*	Deaths of adults and children
Sub-Saharan Africa	22,4 million	1,9 million	5,2%	1,4 million
North Africa and the Middle East	310 000	35 000	0,2%	20 000
South and South-East Asia	3,8 million	280 000	0,3%	270 000
East Asia	850 000	75 000	<0,1%	59 000
Oceania	59 000	3 900	0,3%	2 000
Latin America	2,0 million	170 000	0,6%	77 000
Caribbean	240 000	20 000	1,0%	12 000
Eastern Europe and Central Asia	1,5 million	110 000	0,7%	87 000
North America	1,4 million	55 000	0,4%	25 000
Western and Central Europe	850 000	30 000	0,3%	13 000
Global total	33,4 million	2,7 million	0,8%	2 million

* Proportion of adults aged 15–49 who were living with HIV/Aids.

Source: Adapted from information in UNAIDS. 2009. "UNAIDS/09.36E/JC1700E". AIDS epidemic update December 2009, p.11 & Avert. 2008. "World Wide HIV/AIDS statistics". [Online] Available: http://data.unaids.org/pub/Report/2009/JC1700_Epi_Update_2009_en.pdf Accessed 1 December 2009.

HIV prevalence, both around the globe and in Sub-Saharan Africa.

The concerns that potential investors, and especially human-resources managers, have about the epidemic involve the fact that organisations will soon have to deal with a workforce of which up to 40% is infected with HIV/Aids[53], and with a situation in which an organisation could lose key people. Because organisations are legally obliged to support HIV/Aids-positive employees, few investors are interested in entering labour-intensive industries such as transport, mining and manufacturing. HIV/Aids could cause a loss of approximately 1,5% of the GDP of the worst affected countries, such as South Africa. This means that over 25 years, the GDP would be 31% smaller than it would otherwise have been. To individual businesses, the cost of HIV/Aids includes the costs of absenteeism, lost productivity, health-care expenditures and the replacement (recruitment and training) of workers. These expenses could cut profits by at least 6%[54].

Management urgently needs to develop strategies and programs to deal adequately with HIV/Aids in the workplace.

4.6.4.8 Culture

Culture is another social variable that influences organisations in a number of ways. In South Africa, new cultural values are emerging among young urban Black people. For example, the extended family living under one roof is viewed with disfavour, women have become more independent, and negative attitudes towards marriage and large families are frequently expressed. The shape of the market, the influence of the culture that currently enjoys political power and the attitude of the workforce are only a few of the numerous ways in which culture can affect an organisation.

Social problems such as the HIV/Aids epidemic and poverty bring about developments that cause change in the environment. Management cannot afford to ignore these social influences.

4.6.5 The physical environment

The physical environment refers to the physical resources that people (and businesses) need to support life and development, such as water, air, climate, the oceans, rivers, forests and so on. Environmentalists warn that if the biomass, which maintains a life-sustaining balance, is damaged beyond repair, human beings will simply cease to exist. With approximately 6,8 billion people relying on the resources of the same planet, governments and businesses are now beginning to realise that the plundering of physical resources may endanger countries and even continents.

Currently, the numbers of domestic stock are too high, and the amount of crops and other biomaterial that people extract from the Earth each year exceeds by an estimated 20% what the planet can replace.

Regarding the physical environment, the issues of most concern include[55]:

- **Population and health patterns.** Despite a slow-down in population growth, the number of people is still rising. In poor countries, mostly in Asia and Africa, population growth leads to land degradation, pollution, malnutrition and illness.
- **Food.** Two billion people (one-third of the planet's population) are in danger of starving.
- **Water.** The growth in water usage is outpacing the supply thereof, and agricultural run-off and urban discharge are polluting the rivers. Within the next 25 years, two-thirds of humanity may live in countries that are running short of water. Only 2,5% of the Earth's water is fresh, and only a fraction of that is accessible, despite the fact that each person needs 50 litres per day for drinking, cooking, bathing and other needs. At present, slightly more than one billion people lack access to clean drinking water and 2,6 billion people lack adequate sanitation.

- **Energy and climate.** The demand for energy is growing worldwide, but about 2,5 billion people still have no access to modern energy sources. Most of South Africa's power is provided by Eskom, whose production capacity is currently strained. In general, the world is overly dependent on fossil fuels, such as oil and coal, which result in heavy air pollution. Air pollution promotes global warming and climate disruptions. The realisation that people need a safe, clean, affordable, diverse supply of energy has led to billions being invested in energy research and development.
- **Biodiversity.** More than 17 000 known species of animals and plants are threatened with extinction. Many vanishing species provide humans with both food and medicine.

The physical environment influences business simply because it is the environment from which business obtains its physical resources. It is also the environment into which business discharges its waste. The following interfaces with the physical environment present opportunities as well as threats to a business organisation:

- **The cost of energy.** Fluctuations in oil prices directly affect the business organisation's environment and dramatically affect the political and economic landscape. As a consequence, this presents threats to, and opportunities for, business. The increasing cost of energy has launched the most widespread drive for technological innovation the energy sector has ever seen[56]. Research on solar power, wind power and nuclear power has been intensified, and offers many opportunities to entrepreneurs. Using their surplus maize yield, South African farmers are currently investigating the production and use of ethanol as an alternative energy source.
- **The growing cost of pollution.** Pollution costs the community a great deal in

Critical thinking

How do social trends influence management decision-making? Before answering this question, consider the following information.

Convenience: A main driver of food consumption in South Africa

Social trends play an important role in consumers' focus on convenience. The Bureau for Food and Agricultural Policy, in a report entitled "SA Agricultural Outlook", found that the main requirements are for portable and prepared food products, and for availability at convenient shopping locations. These needs are driven by social changes such as longer working hours, more women entering the workforce and the lack of efficient public transport in South Africa.

An example of the convenience trend is online retail shopping. Online shopping volumes were up by 40% for the period 2006 to 2007, a trend that is on the rise as the range of products available online and the connection options increase. As consumers have less flexible schedules, time is of the essence, and online shopping is very convenient. In 2008, approximately R1,2 billion was spent shopping online, excluding purchases of cars and airline tickets. Online shopping is growing as more people are becoming comfortable with the online environment.

Sources: Adapted from Sherry, S. 2006. "Consumer trends – the quick and the healthy". *Financial Mail*, 28 July. [Online] Available: http://secure.financialmail.co.za/06/0728/business/cbus.htm Accessed 25 February 2007 & Fin24. 2009. "Online shoppers on the up". [Online] Available: http://www,fastmoving.co.za/news-archive/retailer-news/online-shoppers-on-the-up/?searchterm=online%20retail%20growth Accessed 1 December 2009.

terms of destroyed living space, as well as expenses related to the prevention and remedying of pollution. Complying with laws designed to minimise pollution can also be expensive. Here opportunities present themselves, for example, in the form of new methods of producing and packaging products to keep pollution to a minimum.

- **Environmentalism.** Many opportunities for entrepreneurs exist in the fields of conservation and ecotourism.
- **Scarce resources.** A broad range of resources that are becoming increasingly scarce (for example, certain raw materials) are a matter of concern to entrepreneurs. Shortages affect the supply of products and can cause severe price rises. However, shortages also create opportunities, since they often necessitate different methods of production or substitute products.

Destruction of natural vegetation in South Africa

Approximately 80% of rural households in South Africa depend on firewood as their main source of energy as they do not have access to electricity. Roughly 11,2 million tons of firewood is used every year in South Africa, with individual households using between 1 and 7 tons per annum[57]. At least 12 million people (one-third of the population) still rely on firewood as their main source of energy.

The daily gathering of wood is uneconomical and time-consuming, and it also has far-reaching consequences for the environment. In addition, it is mainly indigenous and natural vegetation that is destroyed in this way, and such vegetation is not regenerated.

The destruction of the natural habitat has had dire consequences all over South Africa. Soil erosion is one of the most visible results of the over-exploitation of natural resources.

Businesses should respond to the vulnerability of the physical environment by taking timeous steps to limit any harmful effects on the community. If managers do not show clear signs of a sense of social and environmental responsibility, they should not be surprised if hostile relations develop that may threaten the survival of the business.

Various industries have taken steps to limit their damage on the physical environment. For example, the soap industry is carrying out research on less harmful chemicals, the fast-food industry is developing containers to reduce litter and the motor industry is being compelled by legislation to design emission systems to minimise pollution.

4.6.6 The institutional-governmental environment

Management decisions are continually affected by the course of politics, especially the political pressures exerted by the ruling administration and its institutions. As a component of the macro-environment, the government affects the business environment and business enterprises in a regulating capacity (as explained in Chapter 1). The government intervenes in the macro-environment on a large scale and influences it by means of legislation, the annual budget, taxation, import control (or a lack of it), the promotion of exports, import tariffs to protect certain industries against excessive foreign competition, price controls for certain products and services, health regulations, incentives to encourage development in a specific direction and so on.

Furthermore, the government influences the market through government expenditure. Whenever the government acts as a producer, as in the case of numerous businesses (for example, Eskom), it competes with private enterprise for labour, materials and capital. To an increasing extent, it is the task of management to study the numerous and often complex activities of government, as well as legislation and political developments, to determine their influence on the profitable survival of the business.

An overhaul for South Africa's corporate law[58]

For over three decades, companies in South Africa felt that they were being regulated by legislation that was out of touch with the needs of a modern business. The philosophical approach spelt out by the Department of Trade and Industry (DTI) is that "company law should promote the effectiveness and development of the South African economy". The new Companies Act (No. 71 of 2008) aims to increase flexibility and efficiency in South Africa's company law, while at the same time strengthening transparency, corporate governance and protection for stakeholders, according to Astrid Ludin, Deputy-General at the DTI.

The new political dispensation in South Africa, with its new form and philosophy of government, resulted in new power bases, with far-reaching consequences for the South African business environment. The new labour laws and the Employment Equity Act (No. 55 of 1998) are examples of how the new government influences the management of businesses.

One of the most critical tasks facing businesses is to retain well-qualified, skilled employees in order to carry out the Employment Equity Act (EEA). Tito Mboweni, the former governor of the Reserve Bank, pointed out the difficulty of this in the following reported comment: "I have sought to recruit many competent Black people, and no sooner have we trained them than they leave."[59]

A major development in the institutional environment was the release of the Companies Act (No. 71 of 2008). This bill replaces the Companies Act (No. 61 of 1973) and amends the Close Corporations Act (No. 69 of 1984). Some of the reasons for implementing the Companies Act (No. 71 of 2008) include:

- to replace the outdated legislation of the original Acts
- to define the relationship between companies and their respective shareholders or members and directors
- to respond to globalisation and the advent of democracy
- to simplify company registration and maintenance[60].

4.6.7 The international environment

While each of the factors discussed so far exerts, to a greater or lesser extent, an influence on the business environment, the situation is rendered even more complex, with even more opportunities and threats, if an international dimension is added. Businesses that operate internationally find themselves in a far more complex global business environment because every country has its own peculiar environmental factors, technology, economy, culture, laws, politics, markets and competitiveness, and each is different from those of every other country.

International and multi-national organisations are susceptible to all kinds of international currents and trends. For example, De Beers is vulnerable to changes in the market environment of the countries in which it mines and sells diamonds. The De Beers case study showed how the organisation is exposed to price pressures and increased competition.

The new economic order taking shape worldwide is indicative of the increasing globalisation of the world economy. Globalisation and the trend towards a borderless world continually affect businesses in new ways. However, globalisation does not only present opportunities – it also poses threats. Management must therefore constantly assess possible global threats to its markets and products.

4.7 Opportunities and threats in the market environment and the macro-environment

The changes brought about in the market environment by the respective variables and their interactions, as well as the trends that constantly develop in the macro-environment, may be classified into two groups:

- changes that offer an opportunity
- changes that pose a threat.

An "**environmental opportunity**" may be defined as a favourable condition or trend in the market environment that can be exploited to the business's advantage by a deliberate management effort. However, it should be clearly understood that the possibilities inherent in an opportunity always have to be assessed against the background of the organisation's resources and capabilities (the micro-environment). Without the necessary capabilities and resources, an opportunity cannot be properly exploited. The success of a business in making good use of an opportunity therefore depends on its ability to satisfy the requirements for success in that particular market.

In contrast to an environmental opportunity, an "**environmental threat**" may be defined as an unfavourable condition or trend in the market environment that can, in the absence of a deliberate effort by management, lead to the failure of the business, its products or its services. In view of the constant changes in the market environment, it is the task of management to identify such threats, both actual and potential, and to develop a counter-strategy to meet them.

Knowledge of trends in the environment, along with the identification of those issues that largely determine a business's course of development, is also necessary to make the decisions that will maximise profitability. For this, scanning the environment is a necessary management task. It enables management to identify threats and demands from the environment and, wherever possible, to turn these into opportunities.

4.8 Environmental scanning

The degree to which the environment influences the management of a business depends largely on the type of business, and the goals and objectives of its management. Moreover, environmental influences differ from one management area to the next, and even at different levels of management. This means that the importance, scope and method of **environmental scanning** – that is, the process of measurement, projection and evaluation of change regarding the different **environmental variables** – differ from one organisation to the next.

The importance of environmental scanning may be summarised as follows[61]:

- The environment is continually changing, therefore purposeful monitoring is necessary to keep abreast of change.
- Scanning is necessary to determine what factors and patterns in the environment pose threats to the present strategy of a business.
- Scanning is also necessary to determine what factors in the environment present opportunities for the more effective attainment of the goals and objectives of a business.
- Businesses that systematically scan the environment are more successful than those that do not.
- In the 50 years between 1920 and 1970, almost half of the 100 largest organisations in the United States failed because they did not scan the environment adequately and adapt themselves to change accordingly.

The extent of environmental scanning is determined by the following factors:

- the basic relationship between a business and its environment
- the nature of the environment within which a business operates and the

demands made by the environment on a business (the more unstable the environment and the more sensitive the business is to change, the more comprehensive the scanning has to be; increasing instability usually means greater risk)
- the source and extent of change (the impact of change is rarely so compartmentalised that it affects only one or two areas of an organisation; change has an interactive and dynamic effect on several aspects of a business).

The best method of environmental scanning is a much-debated subject. It will largely be determined by the importance the business attaches to the environment and by the amount of scanning required. The following are a few guidelines that may be followed:
- The most elementary form of scanning is to update relevant secondary or published information obtainable from a wealth of sources such as the media, the organisation's own data, professional publications, financial journals, statistics, associates in other organisations, banks, research institutions, records in the organisation's own filing system and employees.
- The more advanced form of scanning is the addition of primary information or special investigations on particular aspects of the environment. Such investigations can be carried out by members of the organisation's own staff or by outside consultants.
- Scanning at a much more advanced level could mean the establishment of a scanning unit within the business. The unit should have its own staff, who monitor a broad range of environmental variables and make forecasts about some of these (such as technological predictions by industrial analysts, and economic predictions and market assessments by economists using a number of models). Such a scanning unit is usually located in management's planning department.

The question that then arises is how all the collected information can be brought to the attention of the relevant manager. There are many different opinions about this, the most common being that information about the environment forms the foundation of strategic planning since it influences the types of strategies likely to be successful. Strategic planning is the responsibility of top management. (It is discussed in greater detail in Chapter 6.)

4.9 Summary

A business and the environment in which it operates, including the community that it serves, depend on each other for survival. Together they form a complex dynamic business environment where change in the environmental variables continually determines the success or failure of a business. Because these variables are often beyond the control of management, it is management's task to adapt the organisation to change in the environment. At times, management acts proactively by anticipating events, thereby also accelerating change. Knowledge of a changing environment by means of sustained environmental scanning is a prerequisite for taking advantage of opportunities and averting threats.

Key terms

business	intangible resources
competitive forces	intermediaries
competitors	international environment
consumerism	macro-environment
consumer market	market environment
corporate social responsibility	micro-environment
economic environment	organisational capabilities
environmental change	physical environment

environmentalism	purchasing power
environmental opportunity	social environment
environmental scanning	suppliers
environmental threat	tangible resources
environmental variables	task environment
ethics	technological environment
gross domestic product (GDP)	threat
inflation	urbanisation
institutional environment	

Questions for discussion

Reread the case study on pages 102–103 and answer the following questions:

1. a. What were the most dramatic changes that forced De Beers to reconsider its business model?
   b. Can you think of any other changes in South Africa that might influence De Beers' strategic decision?
2. What environmental variables would influence the operation of the new mine in Voorspoed?
3. Do an internal and external environmental analysis on De Beers in the following areas:
   a. the micro-environment
   b. the market environment
   c. the macro-environment.
4. Do you think De Beers wields some bargaining power as a supplier of diamonds? Explain your point of view.
5. Describe the competitive situation in the diamond industry. Refer to the five competitive forces in the market.
6. What is the difference between an opportunity and a threat? Explain this using examples from the case study.
7. a. What scope of environmental scanning does a company such as De Beers need?
   b. What methods of environmental scanning would you recommend to De Beers?

Multiple-choice questions

1. South Africa entered a recession in the first quarter of 2009. Businesses, industries and the economy as a whole were affected by this. This is an example of a situation in the __________ environment, which forms part of the __________ environment, over which managers in an organisation have __________ control.
   a. institutional, macro, indirect
   b. economic, macro, no
   c. technological, macro, indirect
   d. economic, market, no
2. Which of the following options is most true regarding the micro environment?
   a. It is defined as all the variables, both inside and outside the business organisation, that may influence the existence of the business organisation.
   b. It consists of three subenvironments, where internal factors impact the business organisation.
   c. It consists of the business itself, where business capabilities are determined by management.
   d. It entails all the tasks of identifying, assessing and taking advantage of the opportunities that influence a business.
3. Which of the following options is reflective of the market environment?
   a. Billions of rands are being invested in the economy to improve upon South Africa's infrastructure.
   b. There is a massive increase in consumer spending and the growth of the Black Diamonds.
   c. Intangible resources exist, such as brand names, trademarks and company reputation.

d. The strategic objectives of a business include gaining an advantage over its competitors.

4. During an interview for an internship position at a large consulting firm in Johannesburg, you are asked about the main factors to consider in the macro-environment. Which of the following options would best describe the possible content of your answer?
   a. An overview of the competitors, suppliers and intermediaries of the consulting firm
   b. The possibility of new entrants and the availability or non-availability of substitute products or services that may provide threats or opportunities for the consulting firm
   c. The impact of economic changes, technological advances, social and demographic issues, political and legislative changes, environmental imperatives and international developments for the consulting firm
   d. The demographic profile of the firm's customers, and the effect of the economic changes on consumer buying power and spending patterns
5. Which of the following statements about environmental scanning is correct?
   a. Environmental scanning is necessary to keep abreast of change, to determine which factors pose threats to existing goals and to determine which factors represent opportunities to promote current goals.
   b. Environmental scanning is necessary to keep abreast of change, to determine which factors represent opportunities to promote current goals and because businesses that systematically scan the environment are guaranteed success.
   c. Environmental scanning is necessary to impede change, to counteract threats to existing goals and to determine which factors represent opportunities to promote current goals.
   d. Environmental scanning is necessary to keep abreast of change, to determine which factors pose threats to existing goals, to determine which factors represent opportunities to promote current goals and because businesses that systematically scan the environment are guaranteed success.

Answers to multiple-choice questions

1. b
2. c
3. b
4. c
5. a

References

1. Friedman, T.L. 2006. *The world is flat: The globalised world in the twenty-first century.* London: Penguin.
2. Friedman, T.L. 2006. *The world is flat: The globalised world in the twenty-first century.* London: Penguin.
3. Central Intelligence Agency. 2009. "South Africa" in *The World Fact Book.* [Online] Available: https://www.cia.gov/library/publications/the-world-factbook/geos/sf.html Accessed 1 December 2009.
4. Kew, J. 2010. "South African economy may expand 3,7% in 2010, Old Mutual says". 19 January. [Online] Available: http://www.bloomberg.com/apps/news?pid=20601116&sid=agItIvU_mDyU Accessed 24 January 2010.
5. Ehlers, T. & Lazenby, K. 2004. *Strategic management: Southern African concepts and cases.* Pretoria: Van Schaik.
6. BBC News. 2009. "South Africa goes into recession". 26 May. [Online] Available: http://news.bbc.co.uk/2/hi/business/8068126.stm Accessed 1 December 2009.
7. Soanes, C. (Ed.) 2002. *South African Pocket Oxford Dictionary.* 3rd ed. Cape Town: Oxford University Press, p. 141.
8. Friedman, T.L. 2006. *The world is flat: The globalised world in the twenty-first century.* London: Penguin.

9. *Mail & Guardian*. 2008. "SA business confidence down to seven-year low". [Online] Available: http://www.mg.co.za/article/2008-06-11-business-confidence-dips-to-sevenyear-low Accessed 1 December 2009.
10. SA Goodnews. 2009. "SA consumer confidence rises against gloomy global trends". [Online] Available: http://www.sagoodnews.co.za/economy/sa_consumer_confidence_rises_against_gloomy_global_trends.html Accessed 3 September 2009.
11. Van Wyk, R.J. 1985. "Environmental change and the task of the human resource manager" in *SA Journal of Business Management*, Vol. 16, No. 2, p. 72.
12. Smit, P.J. 2003. *Strategic management: Study Guide for STRBES-C*. Pretoria: University of South Africa.
13. Finn, C. 2008. "Learning a lesson from the JSE crash". [Online] Available: http://www.ioltechnology.co.za/article_page.php?iSectionId=2886&iArticleId=4554858 Accessed 1 December 2009.
14. Van den Heever, J. 2006. "A good story to tell" in *Finweek, Survey*, 21 September, p. 10.
15. Fin24. 2009. "The great economic challenge". [Online] Available: http://www.fin24.com/articles/default/display_article.aspx?ArticleId=2549582&SurveyId=Transport%20Infrastructure%202009&SurveyCategory=surveys_this_week Accessed 11 December 2009.
16. See also Hodge, B.J. & Anthony, W.P. 1984. *Organization theory*. Boston: Allyn & Bacon, Ch. 3.
17. David, F.R. 2007. *Strategic management: Concepts and cases*. 11th ed. Upper Saddle River, New Jersey: Pearson, p. 11.
18. David, F.R. 2007. *Strategic management: Concepts and cases*. 11th ed. Upper Saddle River, New Jersey: Pearson, p. 11.
19. Pearce, J.A. & Robinson, R.B. 2005. *Strategic management*. 9th ed. New York: McGraw-Hill, p. 151.
20. Bisseker, C. 2005. "The black middle class" in *Financial Mail*, 16 December. [Online] Available: http://free.financialmail.co.za/05/1216/ecomark/aecomark.htm Accessed 11 February 2010.
21. The UCT Unilever Institute of Strategic Marketing. 2008. "Black diamond woman". [Online] Available: http://www.unileverinstitute.co.za/index.php?option=com_content&task=view&id=448&Itemid=91 Accessed 1 December 2009.
22. *Bizcommunity.com*. 2009. "New vehicle sales still on the skids". [Online] Available: http://marketing.bizcommunity.com/Article/196/140/33395.html Accessed 1 December 2009.
23. *Fastmoving.co.za*. 2009. "SA consumers cut discretionary spending". [Online] Available: http://www.fastmoving.co.za/news-archive/sa-economy/sa-consumers-cut-discretionary-spending Accessed 1 December 2009.
24. Eighty20. 2009. *Fact-a-day*. [Online] Available: http://www.eighty20.co.za/databases/index.cgi Accessed 3 September 2009.
25. Centre for responsible Nanotechnology. 2008. "What is Nanotechnology?" [Online] Available: http://www.crnano.org/whatis.htm Accessed 11 February 2010.
26. SABMiller & WWF-UK. 2009. "Water footprinting: Identifying & addressing water risks in the value chain". [Online] Available: http://www.sabmiller.com/files/reports/water_footprinting_report.pdf Accessed 1 December 2009.
27. Eskom. Not dated. "What is load shedding?" [Online] Available: http://www.eskom.co.za/live/content.php?Item_ID=5608 Accessed 1 December 2009.
28. Mohr, P.J., Fourie, L.J. & Associates. 1995. *Economics for South African students*. Pretoria: J.L. van Schaik, p. 91.
29. Van den Heever, J. 2006. "A good story to tell" in *Finweek, Survey*, 21 September, p. 10.
30. Van den Heever, J. 2006. "A good story to tell" in *Finweek, Survey*, 21 September, p. 10.
31. National Treasury. 2009. "Budget Speech 2009 by the Minister of Finance, Trevor A. Manuel", 11 February. [Online] Available: http://www.info.gov.za/speeches/2009/09021114561001.htm Accessed 1 December 2009.
32. South African Reserve Bank. 1998. "South African Reserve Bank statistics" in Quarterly Bulletin, September. Available: http://www.resbank.co.za/Economics/stats.html & Van den Heever, J. 2006. "A good story to tell" in *Finweek, Survey*, 21 September, p. 10.
33. Van den Heever, J. 2006. "A good story to tell" in *Finweek, Survey*, 21 September, p. 10.
34. Kumo, W. 2009. "Root causes of African underdevelopment and opportunities for revival". [Online] Available: http://www.afroarticles.com/article-dashboard/article.php?id=172848&act Accessed 1 December 2009.

35. Van den Heever, J. 2006. "A good story to tell" in *Finweek, Survey*, 21 September, p. 10.
36. The rand today.com. 2009. "Prime lending rate drops to 12%". [Online] Available: http://www.therandtoday.com/2009/04/30/prime-lending-rate-drops-to-12/ Accessed 1 December 2009.
37. National Credit Regulator. 2009. "Annual Report 2008/2009, CEO's overview". [Online] Available: http://www.ncr.org.za/pdfs/ANR2009/NCR%20REPORT%202009.pdf Accessed 11 February 2010 & National Credit Regulator. 2010. "Should a need arise, borrow wisely – cautions the Credit Regulator". [Online] Available: http://www.ncr.org.za/press_release/borrow2010.pdf Accessed 11 February 2010.
38. 2004. *Wêreld-Atlas vir Suid-Afrikaners.* Johannesburg: Jonathan Ball, pp. 11–12.
39. Statistics South Africa. 2009. "Mid-year population estimates" (Statistical release P0302). [Online] Available: www.statssa.gov.za Accessed 3 September 2009, pp. 7–8.
40. United Nations. 2008. "World population increasingly urban". [Online] Available: http://www.cbsnews.com/stories/2008/02/26/world/main3880698.shtml Accessed 1 December 2009 & Population Reference Bureau. 2009. "World population data sheet". [Online] Available: http://www.prb.org/pdf09/09wpds_eng.pdf p.10 Accessed 31 August 2009.
41. *Mail & Guardian.* 2009. "Matrics achieve 62.5% pass rate in 2008". [Online] Available: http://www.mg.co.za/article/2008-12-30-matrics-achieve-625-pass-rate-in-2008 Accessed 1 December 2009.
42. ITWed. 2008. "ICT skills shortage shock". [Online] Available: http://www.itweb.co.za/sections/business/2008/0809171100.asp?S=Training%20and%20e-Learning&A=ELR&O=google Accessed 1 December 2009.
43. It News Africa. 2009. "South Africa addresses ICT skills shortage". [Online] Available: http://www.itnewsafrica.com/?p=2426 Accessed 1 December 2009.
44. Department of Labour. 2008. "8th Commission for employment equity: Annual Report". Pretoria: Department of Labour.
45. Ghoshal, S., Bartlett, C.A. & Moran, P. 1999. "A new manifesto for management" in *Sloan Management Review*, Spring, pp. 9–20.
46. Werther, W.B. Jr. & Chandler, D. 2006. *Strategic corporate social responsibility: Stakeholders in a global environment.* Thousand Oaks, CA: Sage.
47. Werther, W.B. Jr. & Chandler, D. 2006. *Strategic corporate social responsibility: Stakeholders in a global environment.* Thousand Oaks, CA: Sage, p. 7.
48. Werther, W.B. Jr. & Chandler, D. 2006. *Strategic corporate social responsibility: Stakeholders in a global environment.* Thousand Oaks, CA: Sage, p. 7.
49. O'Reilly, C. & Capaccio, T. 2009. "Pfizer agrees to record criminal fine in fraud probe". [Online] Available: http://www.bloomberg.com/apps/news?pid=20601103&sid=a4h7V5lc_xXM Accessed 1 December 2009.
50. Teen, M.Y., Teo, D. & Lander, D. 2009. "Employees' perceptions of ethics: Promoting an ethical climate in Asia-Pacific organizations". [Online] Available: http://www.watsonwyatt.com/asia-pacific/pubs/perspecitve/docs/Feb2009/09Winter_Ethics.pdf Accessed 1 December 2009.
51. The Times. 2009. "Public input adds value to King III". [Online] Available: http://www.timeslive.co.za/thetimes/article 68897.ece Accessed 1 December 2009.
52. UNAIDS. 2008. "Report on the global AIDS epidemic 2008". [Online] Available: http://www.unaids.org/en/KnowledgeCentre/HIVData/GlobalReport/2008/2008_Global_report.asp Accessed 1 December 2009.
53. SME Toolkit South Africa. 2009. "Implementing a workplace HIV/AIDS programme – why and how?" [Online] Available: http://southafrica.smetoolkit.org/sa/en/content/en/4972/Implementing-a-Workplace-HIV-AIDS-Programme-why-and-how- Accessed 1 December 2009.
54. Avert. 2009. "The impact of HIV & AIDS in Africa: The impact on enterprises and workplaces". [Online] Available: http://www.avert.org/aidsimpact.htm Accessed 1 December 2009.
55. Time. 2002. "Special report: How to save the earth", 2 September, pp. 18–22 & Bodman, S.W. 2006–2007. "This needs to change" in *Newsweek Special Issue*, December 2006–February 2007, p. 20.
56. Yergin, D. 2006–2007. "A great bubbling" in *Newsweek Special Issue*, December 2006–February 2007, p. 30.

57. ProBec. Not dated. "Basic energy facts, South Africa". [Online] Available: http://www.probec.org/displaysection.php?czacc=&zSelectedSectionID=sec1194875816 Accessed 1 December 2009.
58. McNulty, A. 2007. "Corporate Law: Back in touch with business" in *Financial Mail*, 23 February.
59. Israelstam, I. 2006. "Employees are victims of 'Affirmative Auction'" in *The Star*, 16 October. [Online] Available: http://www.highbeam.com/doc/1G1-152807434.html Accessed 11 February 2010.
60. Department: Trade and Industry, Republic of South Africa. 2008. "Companies Bill". [Online] Available: http://www.info.gov.za/view/DownloadFileAction?id=92510 Accessed 1 December 2009 & Department: Trade and Industry, Republic of South Africa. 2008. "Companies Bill, 2008." [Online] Available: http://www.anc.org.za/pbf/sp/cobill-presentation.pdf Accessed 1 December 2009.
61. Glueck, W.F. 1980. *Business policy and strategy management*. Tokyo: McGraw-Hill, pp. 89–93.

CHAPTER

5

CORPORATE SOCIAL RESPONSIBILITY

The purpose of this chapter

Corporations operate within particular societies and countries. The impact (good or bad) of their presence and operations on communities and the environment is huge. They exert tremendous financial power and influence upon all sectors of society. Corporations have the power to influence policy, and lobby both government and civil society to further their own selfish interests, maximising profit for their shareholders. They can do so to the detriment of society and the environment. Business also has the power to transform society for the better by acting responsibly in its pursuit of profit. This chapter will explore the role of business as an agent of change for the common good. It will do so by defining and exploring the following interrelated concepts: "corporate social responsibility", "corporate governance", "stakeholder engagement" and "sustainable development".

Learning outcomes

On completion of this chapter you should be able to:

- explain what "corporate social responsibility" (CSR) is
- give a brief overview of the historic development of CSR
- explain why a company would consider implementing CSR programs
- define "corporate governance"
- explain who the stakeholders of a company are
- give reasons why a company should engage with its stakeholders
- describe how a company would go about engaging with its stakeholders
- define the concept "sustainable development"
- describe the contribution of CSR to sustainable development.

5.1 Introduction

The development and implementation of corporate social responsibility (CSR) frameworks, policies and practices in companies is an ongoing process. It calls for vision and commitment from the leadership and management of the company, in other words, the board of directors and the senior management team.

Most medium- to large-sized corporations grasp some of the concepts and are implementing CSR to a certain extent. Few companies, however, have "institutionalised" corporate social responsibility in their corporate practices and culture. BHP Billiton is a shining example of how corporate social responsibility can be entrenched in the core business of an organisation, driving both profits as well as development.

Case study

BHP Billiton: Resourcing the future

BHP Billiton is the world's largest diversified resource company. The company employs 41 000 people in more than 100 operations in 25 countries. The BHP businesses produce oil and gas, alumina and aluminium, copper, energy coal, iron ore, nickel, manganese and metallurgical coal, as well as uranium, gold, zinc, lead and silver. BHP acknowledges the significant socio-economic impact of the resources industry and the company's shared responsibility with governments, local suppliers, contractors and employees for ensuring that wealth generated from natural resources helps to drive sustainable economic development and poverty reduction. BHP Billiton was awarded a 'Big Tick' in the Impact on Society category and was shortlisted for the Company of the Year award at the Business in the Community Awards (United Kingdom) in 2008.

In the summary of the full Sustainability Report 2008, which was prepared in accordance with the Global Reporting Initiative (GRI) G3 Sustainability Reporting Guidelines, company CEO Marius Kloppers refers to the positive contribution of BHP Billiton to emerging economies. This contribution includes providing higher living standards and greater opportunities for millions of people. Kloppers also highlights the challenges faced by a global company such as BHP Billiton in an increasingly complex world. The company believes the sustainability challenges could potentially have a serious impact on its business and ongoing success. Some of these challenges include attracting competent people to work for the company in tight labour markets, climate change, serious health problems such as malaria and HIV/Aids, human rights and the loss of life in the workplace.

BHP Billiton has responded positively to these challenges. The CEO has committed himself to eliminating hazards and ensuring that all of the company's employees go home safely at the end of each work day. Kloppers recognises that production and financial results can never come before safety. Current health priorities include the promotion of the consistent use of personal protection equipment, the reduction of employee exposure to a range of workplace risks, fatigue management, and maintenance or improvement of the general health and fitness of employees.

The company has set five-year targets that reflect its intention to slow climate change by further reducing the energy and greenhouse-gas intensity of the business. BHP Billiton is also working with other interested parties in the search for technological solutions to help manage its emissions and to address the impact of its products on global climate change.

The company sees itself as an important role-player in social development through the creation of employment and training opportunities, provision of infrastructure, development of local business, and payment of taxes and royalties in its host countries. BHP Billiton invests one per cent of its pre-tax profits in community-based projects. This meant a total investment of USD141 million during the 2008 financial year. Major resources were channelled to improving access of local people to quality education and helping to tackle major health issues such as malaria and HIV/Aids. The company also runs a Matched Giving Program, in which a portion of the company's **social investment** is directed to organisations about which employees are passionate. BHP Billiton believes that recognising and supporting their employees' community activities is an important part of attracting and retaining skilled people, despite tight employment conditions across the resources sector.

In the report, BHP Billiton also talks about the importance of **stakeholder engagement**, from one-on-one meetings and multi-stakeholder forums to cross-sector partnerships and industry initiatives such as the International Council of Mining and Metal's Sustainable Development Framework. This engagement provides valuable advice and challenges the company's views on broad issues related to **sustainable development**. The company's participation in several voluntary initiatives (for example, the **United Nations Global Compact**, the Voluntary Principles of Security and Human Rights, and the **Global Reporting Initiative**) encourages better corporate understanding of stakeholder views. It also earns the company a **licence to operate** from the communities and governments in whose countries it functions. BHP Billiton believes that adherence to **voluntary standards** and implementation of initiatives designed to promote sustainable social, environmental and economic development can make a company a more attractive business partner for governments and local communities. At the same time, adherence to these standards and implementation of these initiatives has a positive impact on operational performance and efficiency, thus improving the company's bottom line.

The company believes its bottom line depends on access to resources and its licence to operate. Maximising its bottom line means recognising the value-protection and value-add achieved by enhancing non-financial or sustainability dimensions. One of these dimensions is aspiring to Zero Harm to people, host communities and the environment. Other dimensions include **effective governance** and **risk-management processes**, being **socially responsible** and contributing to sustainable development, and ensuring that the broader economic contributions of the company's operations are injected into the regions where it operates. Beyond the business case for corporate social responsibility are also many societal benefits that flow from integrating sustainability into BHP Billiton's business: improved standards of living and self-sustaining communities, enhancing economic contributions, resource conservation and biodiversity, and improving stakeholder trust. In addition, the company believes that its business goals can best be attained through honesty, fairness and integrity in everything it does.

The summary of the Sustainability Report 2008 also refers to the **corporate governance** processes that manage the broader affairs of the company. Various systems and supporting documents to implement BHP Billiton's commitment to sustainable development have been put in place. The Sustainability Committee of the Board continues to oversee the group's sustainability strategy, policy, initiatives and activities. Management holds primary responsibility for the company's health, safety, environment and community performance, and for driving its commitment to Zero Harm.

The **Code of Business Conduct**, which is built around the idea of working with integrity, applies to every member of the workforce, regardless of job or location, and provides a behavioural framework for decision-making. It is based on the values contained in the company's charter and highlights the fact that the company cares as much about how results are obtained as it does about delivering good results. The Health, Safety, Environment and Community (HSEC) Management Standards provide the basis for developing and applying management systems at all levels of the company. These standards drive the company's contribution to sustainable development. A Business Conduct Helpline and a Fraud Hotline operated by Group Audit Services respond to issues related to equality in employment, conflict of interest, gifts and hospitality, fraud and theft.

Source: BHP Billiton. 2008. "Resourcing the future: Sustainability Summary Report 2008". [Online] Available: http://www.bhpbilliton.com/bbContentRepository/docs/bhpb_sustainability_2008.pdf Accessed 27 January 2010.

5.2 Introducing corporate social responsibility

5.2.1 What is corporate social responsibility?

The term "**corporate social responsibility**" (CSR) is not mentioned once in the Sustainability Summary Report of BHP Billiton, yet this report discusses the company's CSR policies and practices. What is CSR?

Corporate agents exert tremendous power upon the world. According to the World Bank, 95 of the world's 150 largest economic entities are corporations such as Wal-Mart, Exxon and Mobil. Often, this economic power allows corporations to cause real (but legal) harm to human health, human society, political governance and the natural environment. But corporations can also use their power, influence and the markets to contribute to the **common good**. They can do so through **partnerships** with government, business, communities or by themselves, providing equitable and safe job opportunities to the poor, investing in small and medium enterprises (SMMEs) through their supply chains and building infrastructure as BHP Billiton does. Industry can innovate new technologies on energy efficiency or develop products to provide the poor with access to markets. Businesses can also mitigate their impact on societies and the environment or even contribute to social development. How then should the capacities of business organisations to meet essential needs without dishonouring community values be defined?

Definitions of CSR vary by virtue of, amongst other things, the different practical orientations of corporations towards their responsibilities. Different companies also give varying emphasis to different aspects of CSR (for example, community involvement, socially responsible products and processes, and socially responsible employee relations) to realise their business objectives. The general consensus is that CSR is an umbrella concept that recognises the following points:

- Companies have a responsibility for their impact on society and the natural environment. This responsibility may extend beyond legal compliance and the liability of individuals.
- Companies have a responsibility for the behaviour of others with whom they do business (for example, within supply chains).
- Business needs to manage its relationship with wider society, whether for reasons of commercial viability or to add value to society.

5.2.1.1 Corporate citizenship and corporate social investment

Some literature uses the terms "corporate citizenship", "corporate social investment" and "corporate social responsibility" interchangeably. Although corporate social responsibility and corporate citizenship both refer to business's conduct in society, the former focuses solely on the responsibility aspect of business while the latter focuses on business being a social player by virtue of both its rights and its responsibilities as a citizen. Some explanation as to why the term "corporate social responsibility" is preferred above the term "corporate citizenship" in this book is given below. Note that corporate social investment refers only to one very specific aspect of corporate social responsibility. This will also be briefly explained below.

Corporate citizenship

The term "**corporate citizenship**" recognises corporations as legal persons with certain rights and responsibilities in the same way as individual citizens have rights and responsibilities as members of a community. As a legal entity, a corporation has certain rights and is bound by some responsibilities. These include the right to govern internal affairs, the right to enter into contracts, the right to hold assets, the right to hire, and the right to sue and be sued. Corporate personhood means that corporations are granted constitutional rights.

By implication, corporations are therefore able to use their constitutional rights to define the law and to resist local communities who would rather eliminate harm than regulate and legalise some of it. The managers of a cellphone corporation are, for example, able to use civil-rights claims to force a township government to site a cellphone tower in opposition to the townspeople for the purpose of maximising the corporation's profit. The term "corporate citizenship" is fraught with controversy because of two assumptions that it makes: that property deserves rights, and that property interests are equal or even superior to human rights. Corporations are not natural persons as a result of the respect, rights or dignity that civil society currently grants to them. Rather, corporations are legal fictions; they are tools for human use.

"Corporate social responsibility", with its focus on the responsibilities of corporations, is therefore a preferred term to "corporate citizenship" although they are uncritically equated with the same meaning by some authors.

Corporate social investment (CSI)

In the northern hemisphere, **corporate social investment** is also called corporate philanthropy. In the case study on BHP Billiton, CSI is the company's commitment to invest one per cent of its pre-tax profits in community-based projects. Although this means that a substantial amount of money is contributed to community-based projects, CSI does not refer to a company's contribution to society through its **core business activities** (in this case, the creation of employment and training opportunities) or local business development. Neither does it refer to a company's contribution through its engagement in public policy, an important contribution recognised by the World Economic Forum Global Corporate Citizenship Initiative[1].

5.2.2 An historic overview of the development of CSR[2]

The relationship between industry, government and society has been at issue since industry first began. History shows that CSR developed as a response by corporations to growing public concern about their impact on society. CSR is also the result of the devastation brought about by wars and market failures, which resulted in people losing their homes and jobs. CSR developed as a response to address such crises. Advances in technology mean that entities have better access to information and to each other. Individuals, civil-society groups and the media are joining hands globally to develop targeted and sector-specific standards, tools and frameworks that hold business to new levels of accountability and transparency. It has become obvious that CSR should be more than a reactive response to public outcry and government regulation in order for business to survive and thrive. The global financial crisis of 2008 has been a wake-up call for business to redefine itself in terms of values and ethics.

5.2.2.1 Growing public concern (1800–1900)

The factory system was introduced during the Industrial Revolution. This system moved production away from the craft model and toward large-scale, highly differentiated and often inhumane workplaces. These were the kind of working conditions to which Karl Marx objected in the mid-nineteenth century. Today's mega-companies began to emerge during the 1870s. Their activities increasingly affected other realms of society, creating a demand for petroleum and railroads. Growing public concern and debate about the monopoly status of some corporations and the appropriateness of their actions resulted.

5.2.2.2 Government intervention and the beginnings of CSR programs (1890–1914)

The period between 1890 and the beginning of World War 1 in 1914 is frequently characterised as the peak of economic globalisation and colonialism, with corporate behaviour crossing national boundaries. Laws were passed in the United States and Western Europe addressing emerging business issues such as the formation of trusts, the use of child labour and safety in a range of industries. More legislation was passed in the first 20 years of the twentieth century. However, ordinary people were not satisfied with government regulation as the only response to the negative impact of industrialisation on community and family life. They wanted social transformation. In response to this populist demand, many large corporations started developing industrial welfare programs. These programs provided for the education, recreation and socialisation of workers.

5.2.2.3 CSR develops as a coherent position (1929–1945)

On 29 October 1929, a day that became known as Black Tuesday, the stock market crashed in the United States. The roll-on effect was a worldwide economic downturn, the Great Depression. Globalisation meant that the depression had a devastating effect on virtually every country in the world. International trade, personal income, tax revenue, prices and profits plummeted. World War II started in 1939. Further interest in social controls in various fields (for example, labour protection, banking reform and public utility controls) abounded as a result of the devastation wreaked by the Great Depression and World War II. The public participated vigorously in policy-related debates on these issues and on the more general nature of the corporation–society relationship. The concept "corporate social responsibility" emerged as a coherent idea shortly after World War II.

5.2.2.4 CSR conceptualised (1945–1970)

A variety of conceptions of CSR were developed after the end of World War II in 1945. These conceptions urged business to produce social benefits such as higher standards of living, widespread economic progress and security, order, justice, freedom and the development of the individual person. One of the common ways of fulfilling social responsibilities in the United States at the time was through corporate philanthropy. Government regulators emerged, holding corporations to a new level of accountability.

In September 1970, **Milton Friedman**, Nobel Prize Laureate in Economics, published an essay titled "The Social Responsibility of Business is to Increase Its Profits" in the *New York Times Magazine*. This became one of the most debated essays on CSR of all time. According to Friedman, the doctrine of CSR required accepting that "political mechanisms, not market mechanisms, are the appropriate way to determine the allocation of scarce resources"[3]. For Friedman, CSR was more firmly grounded in socialism than in capitalism. Consequently, he was highly critical of the idea of expanding the responsibilities of business beyond the basic responsibility of making money for its shareholders. Although Friedman did assert that executives should conform to the basic rules of society, embodied in law and ethical custom, he explained that acting in a socially responsible manner at the expense of shareholders was akin to spending someone else's money for the social interest. In response to Friedman, scholars such as Archie Carroll moved the discussion about CSR beyond the economic bottom line and the question of legal compliance to the range of contemporary social issues that may concern the public at any time.

During the 1970s, the focus shifted from corporate responsibility to corporate responsiveness, emphasising what companies could do to improve the world rather than to ensure their own survival. During this period, the term "corporate social responsibility" became so fashionable that its acronym (CSR) could stand alone.

5.2.2.5 CSR eroded by the power of the market (1980–1990)

In the 1980s, there was an ideological shift towards a free-market economic system in which businesses operate without government control in matters such as pricing and wage levels. The underlying assumption of this model is that when the market is left to its own devices, it is absolutely efficient in terms of allocating resources to fulfil unlimited human needs. Any interference in the market from the state or other social constructs would be an impediment to the efficient allocation of resources. State-owned enterprises were nationalised and financial markets were deregulated. With this came a change in the relationship between government and corporations, with far less government regulation and investment in social upliftment. Many developing countries had this Western model forced upon them as a condition for receiving loans by the structural adjustment policies of the International Monetary Fund and the World Bank.

By the late 1980s, the negative social impacts of neo-liberalism were becoming apparent in those countries that had undergone radical transformation. Unemployment rose, the gap between rich and poor grew dramatically, and environmental damage incurred by corporations operating outside their home countries increased. Financial deregulation and the development of computer technology allowed investors to move capital freely from one country to another. This created economic instability in the developing world and bestowed unprecedented power upon corporations over governments, reducing the influence of civil society.

5.2.2.6 Growing activism and intensified discussions on CSR (1990–2007)

During the early to mid-1990s, increasing numbers of **corporate scandals** and associated societal discontent with corporate behaviour and with neo-liberalism itself began to emerge. The most famous of these scandals were Royal Dutch Shell's attempted sinking of the Brent Spar oil storage platform in the North Sea, and the Nigerian government's hanging of activist Ken Saro-Wiwa and eight associates who were protesting against environmental damage caused by oil extraction and the government's failure to return oil revenue for community development. Shell was blamed for not intervening to stop the execution. The company suffered particularly from the Brent Spar incident as it sparked consumer boycotts of Shell products. In Germany alone, Shell experienced drops of up to 40% in sales. Shell later announced that it would in future consult NGOs on such issues as the environment and human rights before deciding on development options.

In 1994, John Elkington coined the term **"triple bottom line (TBL)"**[4]. The TBL agenda focuses corporations on the economic value that they add as well as on the environmental and social value they add or destroy. The late 1990s saw this term take off, with more and more companies using TBL thinking and accounting to build a business case for profit on all three elements.

In June 1999, organised demonstrations against globalisation and the World Trade Organization (WTO) began in London and spread to cities across the world. Some centre-left governments recognised the failed legitimacy of *laissez-faire* economics and called for a "Third Way" that constituted a better balance between government, the economy and civil society.

The UN Global Compact (UNGC) was first proposed in 1999 by the UN Secretary-General Kofi Annan in an address to the World Economic Forum (WEF), which is a meeting of some of the world's most important economic leaders. In his address, the Secretary-General challenged business leaders to join this international initiative that would bring companies together with UN agencies, labour and civil society to support nine (now ten) principles in the areas of human rights, labour, the environment and the fight against corruption.

The development of radically different information technologies such as satellite

The ten principles of the Global Compact

These principles enjoy universal consensus and are derived from:

- the Universal Declaration of Human Rights
- the International Labour Organization's Declaration on Fundamental Principles and Rights at Work
- the Rio Declaration on Environment and Development
- the United Nations Convention Against Corruption.

The Global Compact asks companies to embrace, support and enact, within their sphere of influence, a set of core values in the areas of human rights, labour standards, the environment and anti-corruption.

Human rights

- **Principle 1:** Businesses should support and respect the protection of internationally proclaimed human rights.
- **Principle 2:** Businesses should make sure that they are not complicit in human-rights abuses.

Labour standards

- **Principle 3:** Businesses should uphold the freedom of association and the effective recognition of the right to collective barganing.
- **Principle 4:** Businesses should work to eliminate all forms of forced and compulsory labour.
- **Principle 5:** Businesses should support the effective abolition of child labour.
- **Principle 6:** Businesses should support the elimination of discrimination in respect of employment and occupation.

Environment

- **Principle 7:** Businesses should support a precautionary approach to environmental challenges.
- **Principle 8:** Businesses should undertake initiatives to promote greater environmental responsibility.
- **Principle 9:** Businesses should encourage the development and diffusion of environmentally friendly technologies.

Anti-corruption

- **Principle 10:** Businesses should work against corruption in all its forms, including extortion and bribery.

Source: United Nations Global Compact. "The Ten Principles". [Online] Available: http://www.unglobalcompact.org/AbouttheGC/TheTENPrinciples/index.html Accessed 1 February 2010.

and the internet led to the collapse of many forms of traditional authority. This meant that a wide range of different stakeholders increasingly demanded information on what business was planning to do. In 2001, the Global Reporting Initiative (GRI), built on TBL foundations, was inaugurated as one of the most powerful symbols of this trend.

Other initiatives and standards on CSR were introduced during the late 1990s and early 2000s. These include the AA1000 Series of Standards, the Global Sullivan Principles, the ISO 14000 Series of Standards, the Forest Stewardship Council (FSC), the OECD Guidelines for Multinational Enterprises and SA8000.

The discussions on CSR intensified during the 1990s and 2000s. This coincided with the corporate meltdown of a number of high-profile American-based corporations (for example, Enron, Adelphia Communications, Arthur Andersen LLP, WorldCom and Tyco International) in the early 2000s. The understanding of CSR was expanded to develop more nuanced arguments concerning issues such as corporate social performance, sustainability, stakeholder theory, green marketing and business ethics. New instruments, frameworks and standards were developed to measure and monitor corporate performance and impact on the triple bottom line.

The new millennium also ushered in new institutional champions of change: public-private partnerships (PPPs). PPPs are hybrids of the industrialised state of the 1960s, and the free-market forces and non-governmental organisations of the 1980s and 1990s. PPPs are generally defined as initiatives where public-interest entities, private-sector companies and/or civil-society organisations enter into an alliance to achieve a common practical purpose, pool core competencies, and share risks, responsibilities, resources, costs and benefits. Only time will tell if these partnerships are any better at solving the complex and interconnected social, economic and environmental challenges of the twenty-first century.

5.2.2.7 The future of CSR (2008 onwards)

In 2008, the global economy was faced with its worst crisis since the Great Depression of 1929. Loose credit extension and large fiscal deficits in the United States had increased the debt of households and governments, and debt levels had become unsustainable. The increase of interest rates in the United States in 2006 and 2007 caused many debtors to default, putting the value of all housing loans at risk. This uncertainty resulted in the share price of financial and non-financial companies falling, affecting lending operations between banks. Financial institutions involved in property, such as Northern Rock, failed, while other institutions experienced increasingly large losses on their investment in the housing market. Losses of USD200 billion were predicted in the early days of the crisis.

In late 2008, estimated losses stood at USD1,4 trillion. Central banks in advanced economies responded by announcing co-ordinated action to address short-term funding markets, establishing temporary currency swap arrangements and injecting liquidity into the markets. Sovereign wealth funds were tapped for funding for UBS, Morgan Stanley and Merrill Lynch. Interest rates were cut sharply. These interventions did little to stem the tide. Investment banks in the US failed (Lehman Brothers), were bought for a song (Bear Sterns) or circumvented regulations to access a deposit base (Goldman Sachs and Morgan Stanley). The US Federal Reserve provided AIG, a large insurance company, with support of approximately USD150 billion, made up of an initial equity stake of USD40 billion and the difference in various liquidity support measures. Governments committed about USD4 trillion to support financial institutions around the world. About USD661 billion of write-downs and losses had been acknowledged at the time of writing. General Motor's share price fell 88% in 2008. Chrysler, Ford and General Motors requested a bailout of USD25 billion. Economic conditions deteriorated worldwide.

The head of the International Monetary Fund, Dominique Strauss-Kahn, predicted that the global economic crisis would have such a severe impact on Africa that it threatened to unravel the continent's economic and social success of the last decade and throw millions of people back into poverty. He stressed that the impact of the crisis on Africa could be so great that it could lead to civil unrest and even war.

Mervyn King, head of the committee that produced the three King reports on good governance, ascribed much of the crisis to failures in corporate governance, greed and dishonesty. At the time of writing, voices were calling with renewed vigour for a movement towards redefining values, and placing norms and responsibilities at the core of corporate agendas. This ethical crisis will once again reshape the CSR agenda for the future.

Read the following extract from a blog posted on 4 November 2008 by Wayne Visser, CEO of Corporate Social Responsibility International, in which he draws links between the global financial crisis and CSR, and predicts its impact on the future of CSR. Note that Visser distinguishes between the old CSR (corporate social responsibility, which he calls CSR 1.0) and the new CSR (corporate sustainability and responsibility, which he calls CSR 2.0[5]). In this extract, Visser begins by examining the links between CSR and the current global economic crisis. He then addresses the impact that this crisis will have on CSR.

CSR and the financial crisis: Taking stock

The blame for the financial crisis may be laid on a lack of responsibility in several places:

- **Irresponsible banking.** I'd like to suggest a multi-level approach to this. At the first and most obvious level, we can say the financial crisis is a direct result of irresponsible banking. According to the Mortgage Bankers Association, the number of subprime loans offered to risky borrowers increased more than 15 times since 1998. Essentially, the banks got greedy and compromised good banking practices of credit-risk assessment.
- **Irresponsible financial markets.** At another level, the crisis is the predictable consequence of irresponsible financial markets. Since the deregulation of the 1980s, the derivatives market has grown to around USD600 trillion, almost ten times the value of global GDP. This speculative trading (which some call the "casino economy") is meant to hedge risk, but it also increases the volatility and systemic risk of financial markets. We would do well to recall economist John Maynard Keynes' warning: "Speculators may do no harm as bubbles on a steady stream of enterprise. But the position is serious when enterprise becomes the bubble on a whirlpool of speculation. When the capital development of a country becomes a by-product of the activities of a casino, the job is likely to be ill-done."
- **Irresponsible corporations.** Others argue that the crisis is the inevitable consequence of irresponsible corporations. This is linked to the short-termism of shareholder-value-driven public companies.
- **Irresponsible executives.** The financial crisis has been further inflamed, some claim, by irresponsible executives, as evidenced by their outrageous pay packages. In 2007, the CEO of a Standard & Poor's 500 company received, on average, USD14,2 million in total compensation, according to The Corporate Library. United for a Fair Economy reports that, in 2006, CEOs received more than 364 times the pay of the average worker in the United States (up from 42 times in 1980). More specifically, it seems the leaders of Wall Street's top banks are still in line

to receive pay deals worth more than USD70 billion in 2008, a substantial proportion of which is expected to be paid in discretionary bonuses. "Many critics of investment banks," reports *The Guardian*, "have questioned why firms continue to siphon off billions of dollars of bank earnings into bonus pools rather than using the funds to shore up the capital position of the crisis-stricken institutions."

- **Irresponsible capitalism.** Some would even go so far as to say that the current financial crisis represents a systemic failure of shareholder-driven, free-market capitalism. Among such critics is European Central Bank President Jean-Claude Trichet, who argues that the current financial crisis is partly a result of the demise of the original Bretton Woods' agreement after deregulation since the 1970s. Trichet's conclusion is unequivocal: "It's absolutely clear that financial markets need discipline: macro-economic discipline, monetary discipline, market discipline." British Prime Minister Gordon Brown and French President Nicolas Sarkozy agree, stating that the turmoil has shown the world's post-World War II financial architecture is not fit for the task of controlling today's global financial system.

Irrespective of its causes, it is likely that the financial crisis will have a substantial impact on CSR. The question is: How will this impact play out? Who will win and who will lose? According to a poll run on the CSR International blog during October, 44% of CSR professionals believe that CSR will increase as a result of the crisis. A further 26% believe it will change, while 22% think it will weaken. This is a slightly surprising result that may mask a more complex answer. In my opinion, the impact on CSR will vary depending on the type of CSR being practised:

- Philanthropic CSR will be worst hit. I have little doubt that those who have adopted an immature version of CSR, in which CSR is primarily about philanthropy (sponsorship, donations, charity and employee volunteering), will suffer substantial cutbacks during the coming recession. Irrespective of the fact that those most in need of charity will be worst hit by the crisis, companies around the world will be forced into cost-cutting, and philanthropy budgets will be among the first to be trimmed.
- Strategic CSR will be less affected. It is likely that Michael Porter and Mark Kramer's concept of strategic CSR will pay dividends for its followers in the aftermath of the financial crisis. They argue that "the more closely tied a social issue is to a company's business, the greater the opportunity to leverage the firm's resources – and benefit society." Hence, companies that have aligned their philanthropic and broader CSR efforts with their core business are more likely to protect these initiatives, even during the recession. For example, the commitment Coca-Cola has made to become a water-neutral company is so closely tied to its core business (which is, after all, mostly about selling huge volumes of sugar water) that the company cannot afford to abandon this as a superfluous CSR program. Management knows that if it is not perceived to be managing the scarce water resources of the communities in which it operates responsibly, its business will ultimately fail (as the company has already found to its detriment in India).
- Embedded CSR will be largely unaffected. CSR can only be resilient if it is part of the DNA of an organisation. In other words, CSR will only survive the vagaries of fickle markets, fluctuating profits, financial crises and leadership whims if it is totally embedded in the corporate culture, strategy and governance systems. The impending recession will be the ultimate DNA-test for companies. A year from now, we will have a much better idea of who has driven CSR deep into the heart of their business and who has simply been wearing it as a mask. One example may be the United Kingdom's Co-operative

Bank. Although it will not emerge from the financial crisis completely unscathed, its deeply ingrained ethical approach to banking – introduced in 1992 – is unlikely to change and may even have contributed to its robustness over the past 12 months. As Jonathan Porritt, Chairman of the UK's Sustainable Development Commission, says, "At the very least, the relative resilience of this business model should prompt both Treasury and the sector's regulators to think again about alternative ownership and governance structures in the financial services sector."

- CSR 2.0 will continue to strengthen. For those companies that are alive to the opportunities of the CSR 2.0 revolution, even the recession will present large opportunities for business growth and financial profits. This is because CSR 2.0 is all about the creation of scalable solutions to the world's most urgent and intractable problems, such as water stress and climate change. Unlike the defensive, incremental, risk-based CSR of the past (CSR 1.0), CSR 2.0 rides the wave of emerging responsible and sustainable markets. For example, the demand for renewable energy and low-carbon technologies now far exceeds the supply. And given the escalating costs of climate change, the high oil price and ambitious political targets (of up to an 80% reduction in greenhouse-gas emissions by 2050), companies that have strategically positioned themselves as clean technology-solutions providers will continue to benefit from this USD284 billion market, which is expected to grow to over USD1,3 trillion by 2017.

What is the relationship between the financial crisis and CSR? The answer is that it depends. It depends on your beliefs about how deep the irresponsibility behind the economic meltdown runs. Is it banks simply over-extending themselves, or a far more systemic failure in the corporate, financial and capitalist models?

How will CSR be affected by the financial crisis? Similarly, the answer depends on how deep CSR runs within the organisation. Is it superficial philanthropic CSR, something more strategic or embedded, or even the more revolutionary CSR 2.0 version? Either way, the recession ahead will not only be an acid test for companies' CSR commitment, but for CSR itself. It may very well be that the time has come for CSR to adapt or die.

Source: CSR International. 2008. "CSR and the Financial Crisis: Taking Stock". [Online] Available: http://csrinternational.blogspot.com/2008/11/csr-and-financial-crisis-taking-stock.html Accessed 1 February 2010.

5.2.3 Why would a company implement CSR programs?

Companies today do CSR for multiple reasons. Some companies use CSR (and very specifically CSI) as a marketing or public-relations tool to project an image of being socially responsible. Others do CSR because the founder of the organisation believed in philanthropic giving and the culture of the organisation is built on the founder's beliefs. As is the case with BHP Billiton, however, most CSR programs are driven by a combination of reasons.

5.2.3.1 Social drivers

No company would wish to have the reputation of being socially irresponsible. It is desirable for an organisation or an activity to be thought of as socially responsible. Some consumers prefer socially responsible products and services, and employees increasingly choose to work for companies with a reputation for being socially responsible. BHP Billiton recognises CSR as a driver for attracting and retaining skilled people by acknowledging and supporting employees' community activities. There is also a small growth in dedicated socially responsible investor (SRI) funds, particularly in the United States and the United Kingdom, but also in continental Europe. Mainstream investment funds and stock exchanges are addressing CSR objectives. Primary mechanisms for these are the Dow Jones Sustainability Index in New York, the FTSE4Good in London and more recently South Africa's JSE Socially Responsible Investment Index.

Civil-society organisations and other groups have worked with companies and governments to develop voluntary standards or guidelines as to how socially responsible corporations should act. Examples of these guidelines include the ten principles of the United Nations Global Compact discussed on page 148, the **Equator Principles**, which aim to improve the social and environmental aspects of banks' project finance, and the **Extractive Industry Transparency Initiative (EITI)**, which aims to improve the revenue transparency from extractive industries and their host governments.

Thus it becomes obvious that many companies engage in CSR because society expects it of them. The companies want to protect their reputation by meeting these societal expectations.

5.2.3.2 Governmental drivers

Most governments enforce local and national legal systems with which companies have to comply in order to operate in that country. These systems include legislation about companies, labour relations and environmental management. Many governments also show considerable interest in encouraging business involvement in social issues through CSR. The government of the United Kingdom even has a cabinet minister for CSR, and a variety of policies and initiatives to coax corporations to be more socially responsible. Governments can also facilitate CSR through the provision of organisational support. This can even be extended to subsidies for CSR organisations and activities. Governments may also introduce so-called soft regulation to encourage corporations to be more socially responsible. Legislation encourages corporate behaviour that is socially and environmentally responsible, as well as ethical reporting.

In CSR, compliance stretches beyond the letter of the law to the spirit of the law. If a company complies only with the letter of the law, this means it is doing the bare minimum to avoid sanction. It is possible to comply with the letter of the law in such a way that the objectives of the legislation are not achieved. Complying with the spirit of the law means that the company is doing what can be reasonably expected to further the objectives of the legislation.

5.2.3.3 Market drivers

CSR does not only represent costs for companies. It can also result in various advantages such as reduced costs or increased revenues. Companies can reduce cost through CSR by:

- avoiding fines
- avoiding legal costs
- using resources efficiently, for example, reducing use of energy or paper means lower energy or paper costs
- using alternative raw material sources such as recycled materials
- reducing recruiting costs
- increasing staff retention
- reducing the cost of capital.

Companies can also increase revenue through CSR by ways of:

- developing new products or services, for example, carbon credit trading
- growing markets for services, through general programs such as job creation and social development, or more specific interventions such as bridging the digital divide
- improving access to markets, for example, government procurement
- avoiding boycotts
- exploiting the CSR premium (we have already referred to consumers who prefer to buy products and services from

companies that are socially responsible; some consumers are prepared to pay a premium for products and services that they consider socially responsible).

Many companies see CSR as part and parcel of their competitive edge. By integrating economic strategies with CSR strategies, they can achieve a competitive advantage. In other words, companies receive a financial reward for addressing social, environmental and economic problems.

The **business case** plays a dominant role in motivations for companies to do CSR. What, however, happens to social, economic and environmental issues for which a business case cannot be made? There are also many factors such as the company's visibility, location, size, ownership structure, and the sector and market segments in which it operates that influence whether or not there is a business case to be made. Despite the many claims made on its behalf, there is also no empirical evidence for the business case for CSR.

5.2.3.4 Ethical drivers

Generally speaking, **ethics** is about deciding between right and wrong conduct. **Business ethics** is a subset of ethics that focuses on deciding between right and wrong at the workplace and in business generally.

Responsibility can be seen as an ethical value. Hence, it goes beyond individual considerations and is oriented towards the common good. Some thinkers might see the market system as a subsystem to the social system, and thus believe that enterprises have a social responsibility as well as a legal and economic responsibility. Companies might feel ethically responsible for damage resulting from production, for example, harm inflicted on the environment. They might also feel responsible for the communities in which they operate, and thus do more than simply comply with the law, especially in countries with inadequate bureaucratic regulation. For some companies, CSR is the right thing to do.

The ethical responsibility of business does not only apply to external damage. It also

Ten myths about business ethics

Ethics in the workplace is about prioritising moral values and ensuring that behaviours are aligned with those values. Myths about business ethics abound. Some of these myths arise from general confusion about the notion of ethics. Other myths arise from narrow or simplistic views of ethical dilemmas. Here are ten common myths about business ethics. Each myth is followed by an explanation that debunks it.

- **Myth 1: "Business ethics is more a matter of religion than management".** Diane Kirrane[6] asserts that "altering people's values or souls isn't the aim of an organisational ethics program – managing values and conflict among them is."
- **Myth 2: "Our employees are ethical so we don't need to pay attention to business ethics".** Most of the ethical dilemmas faced by managers in the workplace are highly complex. Kirrane mentions that when the topic of business ethics comes up, people are quick to speak of the golden rule of honesty and courtesy. But when presented with complex ethical dilemmas, most people realise there's a wide grey area to deal with when trying to apply ethical principles.
- **Myth 3: "Business ethics is a discipline best led by philosophers, academics and theologians".** Lack of involvement of leaders and managers in business ethics literature and discussions has led many to believe that business ethics is a fad or a movement, having little to do with the day-to-day realities of running an organisation. They believe business ethics is primarily a complex philosophical debate or a religion. However, business ethics is a management discipline with a programmatic approach that

includes several practical tools. Ethics management programs have practical applications in other areas of management areas, as well.

- **Myth 4: "Business ethics is superfluous. It only asserts the obvious: 'Do good!'".** Many people feel that codes of ethics or lists of ethical values to which an organisation aspires are superfluous because they represent values to which everyone should naturally aspire. However, the value of a code of ethics to an organisation is its priority and focus about certain ethical values in that workplace. For example, it's obvious that all people should be honest. However, if an organisation is struggling with issues of deceit in the workplace, prioritising honesty is very important, and honesty should be listed in that organisation's code of ethics. Note that a code of ethics is an organic instrument that changes with the needs of society and the organisation.
- **Myth 5: "Business ethics is a matter of the good guys preaching to the bad guys".** Some writers do seem to claim a moral high ground while lamenting the poor condition of business and its leaders. However, people who are well versed in managing organisations realise that good people can take bad actions, particularly when stressed or confused. (Stress and confusion are not excuses for unethical actions – they are reasons.) Managing ethics in the workplace includes all of us working together to help each other remain ethical and to work through confusing and stressful ethical dilemmas.
- **Myth 6: "Business ethics is the new policeperson on the block".** Many people believe business ethics is a recent phenomenon because of increased attention to the topic in popular and management literature. However, business ethics was written about by Cicero 2 000 years ago. Business ethics has been given more attention recently because of the social responsibility movement that started in the 1960s.
- **Myth 7: "Ethics can't be managed".** Actually, ethics is always managed, but, too often, it is managed indirectly. For example, the behaviour of the organisation's founder or current leader is a strong moral influence on the behaviour of employees in the workplace. Strategic priorities (profit maximisation, expanding market share, cutting costs and so on) can be very strong influences on morality. Laws, regulations and rules directly influence behaviours to be more ethical, usually in a manner that improves the general good and/or minimises harm to the community. Some people are still sceptical about business ethics, believing that you can't manage values in an organisation. Donaldson and Davis[7] note that management is, after all, a value system. Sceptics might consider the tremendous influence of several "codes of ethics" such as the Ten Commandments in Christian religions or the Constitution of the United States. Codes can be very powerful in smaller organisations as well.
- **Myth 8: "Business ethics and social responsibility is the same thing".** The social responsibility movement is only one aspect of the overall discipline of business ethics. Corporations also need to consider how business ethics can be managed. Writings about social responsibility often do not address practical matters of managing ethics in the workplace, for example, developing codes, updating polices and procedures, approaches to resolving ethical dilemmas and so on.
- **Myth 9: "Our organisation is not in trouble with the law, so we're ethical".** It is possible to be unethical, yet operate within the limits of the law. Examples include withholding information from superiors, fudging on budgets and constantly complaining about others. However, breaking the law often starts with unethical behaviour that has gone unnoticed. The "boil the frog" phenomenon is a useful parable here: if you put a frog in hot water, it immediately

jumps out. If you put a frog in cool water and slowly heat up the water, you can eventually boil the frog. The frog doesn't seem to notice the adverse change in its environment.

- **Myth 10: "Managing ethics in the workplace has little practical relevance".** Managing ethics in the workplace involves identifying and prioritising values to guide behaviours in the organisation, and establishing associated policies and procedures to ensure those behaviours are conducted. This could be called "values management". Values management is also important in other management practices, for example, managing diversity, Total Quality Management and strategic planning.

Source: Free Management Library. "Ten Myths About Business Ethics". [Online] Available: http://managementhelp.org/ethics/ethxgde.htm#anchor29959 Accessed 28 January 2010. © Carter McNamara, MBA, PhD, Authenticity Consulting, LLC.

applies to responsible business dealings and conduct in the workplace. However, there is much confused and incorrect thinking about business ethics.

The global financial meltdown of 2008/2009 took an enormous economic and social toll on the international community in terms of lost jobs, loss of personal savings, impoverishment, and loss of trust in both corporations and governments. It has reinforced the importance of CSR, in particular the moral and ethical drivers of CSR. The crisis is the result of several failures, but ultimately they all come down to the failure of governance systems and ethics. As a result, companies all around the world are working to embed their ethical behaviour in codes of conduct.

5.3 Corporate governance

5.3.1 Corporate governance defined

Governance generally refers to the way in which an organisation or group makes decisions about how to manage its affairs. Essentially corporate governance is the system by which companies are managed and controlled. A corporation is a legal entity recognised by law. It therefore has to adhere to the statutory principles of corporate governance as prescribed by law.

There are also numerous frameworks, standards and codes available to guide companies towards good governance. Examples include the OECD Principles of Corporate Governance and the three **King Committee reports on corporate governance**. It is, however, impossible to stop dishonesty or to legislate morality in companies. Morality, whether corporate or individual, is driven by a certain mindset. In this sense, corporate governance is essentially about leadership that is transparent. The leadership of a company must be seen to be answerable and accountable to that company's stakeholders.

5.3.1.1 Roles and responsibilities within a company in terms of good governance

Corporations are "artificial persons". This artificial personhood allows a corporation to enter into contracts and do business. It can own assets and owe money to others, and it can sue and be sued in its own name in law. An artificial person cannot run a company. Only a natural person (human being) can ensure that the interests of the company are looked after. The **board of directors** is a group of people assembled to lead and control the company so that it functions in the best interests of its shareholders. The rights and responsibilities of directors are conferred on them by various acts, the articles of association of the company and common law. A director stands in a **fiduciary relationship** to the company (the term "fiduciary" is derived from the Latin *fiduciarius*, meaning "of trust") and is bound by fiduciary responsibilities. The board is the focal point of the corporate governance system. Management is primarily responsible for implementing strategy as defined by the board.

In order to enable the board to discharge its duties and responsibilities, as well as fulfil its decision-making process effectively, it may delegate some of its functions to board committees. However, delegating authorities to board committees or management does not in any way reduce the board's collective accountability and responsibility for the performance and affairs of the company.

Boards are composed of both **executive** and **non-executive** directors. Executive directors are those members of the management team who are appointed to the board. They are full-time employees of the company. Executive directors have a fiduciary role as directors of the company on the one hand. They also have a role as senior management. Non-executive directors are not involved in the day-to-day operation of the business of the company and do not receive any remuneration other than their director's fees. They are independent of management and should be free from any significant business or other relationship with the company that could materially hamper their independence. Non-executive directors should be in a position to provide independent judgement on issues facing the company, assist in objectively monitoring and reviewing management's performance against budget and company strategy, and ensure adequate protection of the interests of the company where these may conflict with the personal interests of the (executive) directors. An independent director is a non-executive director who has no existing or prior business, employment, consultancy or other relationship with the company.

There are two separate and very distinct tasks at the top of every company that must be performed by two separate individuals to ensure a balance of power and authority. The chairman of the company is responsible for the running of the board and the chief executive officer is responsible for running the company's business. It is also recommended (and sometimes required) that the chairman be an independent non-executive director.

5.3.2 How does corporate governance relate to CSR?

5.3.2.1 Good corporate governance is an important aspect of CSR

The impact of corporate misconduct and unlawful acts is demonstrated in the box on page 158. Such scandals are harmful to the reputation of corporations competing globally for customers and talents. They also harm investors, shareholders, employees and the public, who are all affected by failures in corporate governance. CSR recognises the responsibility of corporations for their impact on society.

The downfall of Enron and the WorldCom and Xerox scandals (see page 158) are good examples of the impact that corporate governance failures have on society.

5.3.2.2 CSR has evolved as an aspect of good corporate governance

Instead of the boards of corporations only asking questions about shareholder value (the bottom line) and the pay packets of "fat cat" directors, boards should also ask questions like: What is business for? What are our core values? Who should have a say in how companies are run? What is the appropriate balance between shareholders and stakeholders? And what balance should be struck at the level of the triple bottom line?

Sir Adrian Cadbury redefined corporate governance in this sense as " ... concerned with holding the balance between economic and social goals and between individual and communal goals ... the aim is to align as nearly as possible the interests of individuals, corporations and society.[8]"

The notion that companies do not operate in a vacuum, but that they are responsible

Another week, another corporate catastrophe!

Whilst world markets were still coming to terms with the collapse of Enron, the US dollar tumbled to its worst level against the euro in two and a half years in the wake of the accounting scandals that emerged at WorldCom and Xerox in June 2002. Accounting irregularities at WorldCom and Xerox are anticipated to total over USD7 billion.

Xerox admitted to have overstated four year's worth of profits to the tune of some USD3 billion. The WorldCom fraud, described by the Securities and Exchange Commission (SEC) as "of unprecedented magnitude", comes amidst a crisis of confidence in United States capitalism, after a series of other accounting scandals at Enron, Tyco International and Global Crossing.

The Enron scam came to light in October 2001 after a senior female employee expressed her reservations about the company's accounting practices. Enron admitted to having grossly inflated its profits and concealed many millions of dollars in debts so that they did not show on company accounts. Two of the most respected banks in the United States, JP Morgan Chase and Citigroup, were found to have aided and abetted the deception.

Sources: Naidoo, R. 2002. *Corporate Governance.* Cape Town: Double Storey Books, pp. 3, 26 & Stones, L. & Bain, J. 2002. "Markets may face another rough ride this week". *Business Day,* 1 July.

for their impact on society and the natural environment, was broached in the King reports with a call for companies to account for their financial performance as well as their social and environmental performance. Increasing requirements for accounting on the triple bottom line has become particularly evident in the last decade as another aspect of good corporate governance.

5.3.2.3 CSR finds expression in corporate governance

If corporate governance is a leadership challenge and if CSR has evolved as an aspect of good corporate governance, it follows that the chairperson and his/her board, which are the focal point of the corporate governance system, should govern CSR programs. They have to monitor risks and opportunities, engage with stakeholders, formulate policies and strategies to be implemented, and monitor this implementation. Management is responsible for implementing and managing the CSR program. In this sense, the optimum structure for CSR mirrors the structure relating to financial governance: a separation between the day-to-day management of these issues, on the one hand, and monitoring and assurance (the independent checking on performance) on the other hand.

A CSR program should be embedded in a specific board-level structure such as a CSR committee. This committee should have a good understanding of CSR. There are three ways in which the board and the CSR committee can determine how to establish the corporate policy for CSR:

- A values-based system, where the CSR policy is aligned to the company's own vision, mission, values and guiding principles, is used when a company addresses CSR in a proactive manner.
- A **stakeholder-engagement process**, which allows stakeholders to determine what they want from the company and what they consider to be the issues and culture of the company, is a reactive approach.
- A combination of both values-based and stakeholder-engagement processes, which often emerges from an original emphasis on a values-based approach, develops when the company has moved from setting its own objectives aligned to its values to involving its stakeholders. This allows

the company to ensure that its strategy satisfies its own needs as well as the needs of its stakeholders.

The policy statement of the CSR committee should cover the company's vision, commitment, goals and targets for CSR. Once the board and the CSR committee have established a policy and strategy for CSR, it will need to be implemented throughout the company. Each company will have a different way of ensuring the implementation of the CSR strategy within the management structures of the company, but generally speaking, especially in the case of large companies with multiple operating units, it is often necessary to have a dedicated department that focuses on CSR.

In conjunction with the relevant board committee, the CSR department is responsible for identifying the appropriate key performance indicators (KPIs) for implementing the CSR policy and for measuring company performance with respect to these indicators. This information will need to be collected regularly and systematically, and it will need to be reported on to the board committee so that this committee can monitor the implementation of the policy.

The CSR department will also need to ensure that the various business units and line departments such as human resources know about the CSR policy and are doing what they can to implement it. The CSR department is also responsible for stakeholder engagement.

5.4 Stakeholder engagement

The concept of a "stakeholder" has already been mentioned a couple of times in this chapter. You have learnt that one of the ways in which the board and the CSR committee can determine how to establish the corporate policy for CSR is a stakeholder-engagement process.

Other reasons why companies engage with stakeholders include the following:

- Responsible companies want to understand and respond to society's expectations of what it means to be, for example, a responsible manufacturer, marketer and employer.
- Engagement is a means to help build better relationships with all parties, resulting in improved business-planning and performance.
- Engagement helps provide opportunities to align business practices with societal needs and expectations, helping drive long-term sustainability and shareholder value.

5.4.1 Defining "engagement"

The different levels of engagement are set out in Table 5.1 on page 160. The level of engagement is determined by the goals aspired to through the interaction with stakeholders, the mode of communication with stakeholders, the nature of the relationship between the company and its stakeholders, and the engagement approach used with the stakeholders.

5.4.2 Defining "stakeholders"

Stakeholders are persons or groups that are potentially affected by or affect the business activity of a company. As a result, stakeholders impose various responsibilities on the company. External stakeholders beyond the narrow shareholder and owner group (for example, customers, employees, the community, the environment, suppliers, regulators, non-governmental organisations and so on) are included here. All stakeholders are important, but the degree to which they are prioritised by the company may change depending on the issue, and factors such as influence, knowledge, credibility and legitimacy.

At a basic level, there are two kinds of stakeholders. **Primary stakeholders** are stakeholders whose ongoing support for the

Table 5.1: Levels of engagement

Level	Goal	Communication	Nature of relationship	Engagement approaches
Remain passive	• No goal • No engagement	• No active communication	• No relationship	• Stakeholder concern expressed through protest, letters, media, websites and so on, or pressure on regulatory bodies and other advocacy efforts
Monitor	• Monitor stakeholders' views	• One-way communication: Stakeholder to company	• No relationship	• Media and internet tracking • Second-hand reports from other stakeholders possibly via targeted interviews
Inform	• Inform or educate stakeholders	• One-way communication: Company to stakeholder • No invitation to reply	• Short- or long-term relationship with stakeholders "We will keep you informed"	• Bulletins and letters • Brochures, reports and websites • Speeches, conferences and public presentations • Open houses and facility tours • Road shows and public displays • Press releases, press conferences, media advertising and lobbying
Transact	• Work together in a contractual relationship where one partner directs the objectives and provides funding	• Limited two-way communication: Setting and monitoring of performance according to terms of contract	• Relationship terms set by contractual agreement "We will do what we said we would" or "We will provide the resources to enable you to do what we agree"	• Public-private partnerships, grant-making (donor agreements for funding of non-governmental organisations) and cause-related marketing (marketing activities of companies that promote NGO causes as well as the company product)
Consult	• Gain information and feedback from stakeholders to influence decisions made internally	• Limited two-way communication: Company asks questions and the stakeholders answer	• Short- or long-term involvement "We will keep you informed, listen to your concerns, consider your insights and provide feedback on our decision"	• Surveys • Focus groups • Workplace assessments • One-to-one meetings • Public meetings and workshops • Standing stakeholder advisory forums • Online feedback and discussion

Level	Goal	Communication	Nature of relationship	Engagement approaches
Involve	• Work directly with stakeholders to ensure that their concerns are fully understood and considered in decision-making	• Two-way or multi-way communication between company and stakeholders • Learning takes place on both sides • Stakeholders and company take action individually	• May be one-off or longer-term engagement "We will work with you to ensure that your concerns are understood, to develop alternative proposals and to provide feedback about how stakeholders' views influenced the decision-making process"	• Multi-stakeholder forums • Advisory panels • Consensus-building processes • Participatory decision-making processes
Collaborate	• Partner with or convene a network of stakeholders to develop mutually agreed solutions and joint plan of action	• Two-way or multi-way communication between company/ companies and stakeholders • Learning, negotiation and decision-making take place on both sides • Stakeholders work together to take action	• Long-term relationship "We will look to you for direct advice and participation in finding and implementing solutions to shared challenges"	• Joint projects, voluntary two-party or multi-stakeholder initiatives and partnerships
Empower	• Delegate decision-making on a particular issue to stakeholders	• New organisational forms of accountability: Stakeholders have formal role in governance of an organisation or decisions are delegated out to stakeholders	• Long-term relationship "We will implement what you decide"	• Integration of stakeholders into governance structure (for example, as members, shareholders or on particular committees)

Source: Krick, T., Forstater, M., Monaghan, P. & Sillanpää, M. 2005. *The Stakeholder Engagement Manual*, Vol. 2: *The Practitioner's Handbook on Stakeholder Engagement*, p. 60. [Online] Available: http://www.accountability21.net/uploadedFiles/publications/Stakeholder%20Engagement%20 Handbook.pdf *The Stakeholder Engagement Manual*. Accessed 29 January 2010.

Applying the concept: "One-way communication", "consultation" and "dialogue"

It is worthwhile specifically differentiating between these three terms because they are often used interchangeably, but mean completely different things when referring to stakeholder engagement.

Communication generally means to provide information of some kind. Here, accuracy and timeliness are vital. Vehicles for communication include brochures, newsletters, reports, briefings, press releases, presentations, displays and websites.

Consultation is the process of gathering information, guidance and advice from stakeholders. It may occur through formal or informal meetings. The organisation arranges the consultation, sets the terms and takes decisions as it sees fit. Consultation can improve decision-making and performance by providing perspective or feedback on a current issue, community needs and expectations, or impacts, services or performance. Vehicles for consultation include surveys, focus groups, *ad hoc* advisory meetings and feedback mechanisms such as response forms.

Dialogue involves a two-way exchange of views and opinion. Participants in a dialogue seek to understand and learn from each others' perspectives and experiences. They do not seek to defend their own perspectives, as in a debate. Open dialogue based on mutual respect leads to learning, trust and co-operation. Dialogue often involves long-term relationships. It requires a high degree of transparency and trust. Both parties must be willing to listen, overcome their bias, suspend judgment and take the other party's views seriously. Dialogue often aims at finding agreements for future action. Trade-offs and compromise may be necessary. Vehicles for dialogue include multi-stakeholder forums, long-term advisory panels, leadership summits, one-on-one meetings, round-table sessions and workshops.

Source: Eccles, N. & Anderson G. 2009. *Study Guide to Corporate Citizenship.* [Unpublished Unisa study guide] pp. 96–97.

company is vital for its survival. These stakeholders commonly have some contractual or financial relationship with the company. Most importantly, primary stakeholders include shareholders and employees. A company cannot survive if shareholders or employees withdraw their support for the company. In many instances, government is also a primary stake holder. For example, government would be a primary stakeholder in a mining company because the company would depend on government permission to mine. A local community could also be a primary stakeholder of a mining company, especially if that community owned the land that the company needed. Local community protest or sabotage can make a mine's operation impossible.

Secondary stakeholders are stakeholders who have a less direct impact on the company. Secondary stakeholders could include environmental NGOs or the media, for example. However, there is no clear distinction between primary and secondary stakeholders. A secondary stakeholder can become a primary stakeholder if the conditions change. For example, a local group that is small and powerless probably has little impact on a company, but if it gets more local support or if it has a convincing legal argument, it can quickly become a primary stakeholder.

5.4.3 Principles for stakeholder engagement

Several important approaches to guide and govern the entire stakeholder-engagement process are described below. Note that different companies will apply these approaches differently with each stakeholder issue.

Key approaches of the stakeholder-engagement process

A company that has grasped the importance of actively developing and sustaining relationships with affected communities and other stakeholders throughout the life of its project will reap the benefits of improved risk management and better outcomes on the ground. On the other hand, a company that is perceived as engaging with stakeholders only when engagement suits its purposes or when it wants something from those stakeholders may be undermining its own interests.

Remember these five key words throughout the stakeholder-engagement process:

- **Involvement.** Encourage broad involvement by welcoming interested parties and respecting their roles. Build existing relationships and find new participants to enrich dialogue.
- **Candour.** Be comprehensive. Make sure that you consider every issue. Build trust by creating an environment where different opinions are welcome. Be candid. Disclose your agenda, assumptions, goals and boundaries.
- **Relevance.** Make the process relevant by focusing on the issues of greatest importance. Share knowledge so that all participants have access to pertinent information. Ensure that the process is timely and that the process takes place when new information can influence decisions and actions.
- **Learning.** Uncover new perspectives. Seek mutual understanding and identify mutually beneficial solutions to problems. Focus on the future. Emphasise what can be done to resolve issues.
- **Action.** Act on results by applying what has been learnt to improve business planning and decision-making. Provide stakeholders with evidence of how the results of the process will be used.

Source: International Finance Corporation. 2007. *Stakeholder Engagement: A Good Practice Handbook for Companies Doing Business in Emerging Markets.* [Online] Available: http://www.ifc.org/ifcext/enviro.nsf/AttachmentsByTitle/p_StakeholderEngagement_Full/$FILE/IFC_StakeholderEngagement.pdf Accessed 29 January 2010.

5.4.4 The stakeholder-engagement process

The information that follows provides a framework for the stakeholder-engagement process.

Steps in the process

Today, the term "stakeholder engagement" is emerging as a means of describing a broader, more inclusive and continuous process between a company and those potentially impacted that encompasses a range of activities and approaches, and spans the entire life of a project. The change reflects broader changes in the business and financial worlds, which increasingly recognise the business and reputational risks that come from poor stakeholder relations, and place a growing emphasis on corporate social responsibility and transparency and reporting. In this context, good stakeholder relations are a prerequisite for good risk management.

The stakeholder-engagement process can be implemented by following the six basic steps explained below:

- **Prepare.** Identify and understand the territory to be explored through the engagement process with stakeholders. Determine the most important issues where stakeholder engagement might be helpful and what kinds of stakeholders might be considered for engagement.
- **Plan.** Set objectives and parameters for the engagement process, and identify and prioritise stakeholders with whom

to engage. Decide how an adequate objective for the engagement process can be set and how the process can be kept within bounds. Consider who should be accountable for engaging and how to determine exactly which stakeholders should be involved. Decide on the best mode of discussion to have and how to measure the success of the process.
- **Design.** Co-develop the engagement plan, including the agenda and logistics, to meet the engagement objectives. Determine how and when to extend an invitation to explore whether engagement is possible and what objectives might be mutually agreed to for the engagement. Consider the best way to conduct the sessions, whether an independent third-party facilitator will be required, and what logistics and rules must be in place. Decide whether it is necessary to verify or audit the engagement.
- **Engage.** Successfully meet the objectives through execution of the engagement plan with stakeholders. Before doing this, establish whether the correct background information, materials and training to begin the engagement are available. Decide on the steps or actions that will follow the engagement.
- **Evaluate.** Assess the outcomes of engagement for both the company and stakeholders against specific objectives. Decide if further engagement sessions are necessary and use the pre-determined criteria to assess whether the engagement was successful. Consider the outcomes and establish whether the process was helpful.
- **Apply.** Share information and integrate the outcomes of the engagement process appropriately into business practices. Decide how to ensure that the results of the engagement reach the right internal decision-makers and how to inform stakeholders about follow-up from the engagement session.

Source: International Finance Corporation. 2007. *Stakeholder Engagement: A Good Practice Handbook for Companies Doing Business in Emerging Markets.* [Online] Available: http://www.ifc.org/ifcext/enviro.nsf/AttachmentsByTitle/p_StakeholderEngagement_Full/$FILE/IFC_StakeholderEngagement.pdf Accessed 29 January 2010.

5.5 Sustainable development

5.5.1 Defining "sustainable development"

The concept of "sustainability" means different things to different people. As a result, there are many definitions of the term. In 1987, the Brundtland Commission supplied the following definition: "Sustainable development is development that meets the needs of the present without compromising the ability of future generations to meet their own needs."[9]

This definition encapsulates two key concepts:

- the concept of **needs**, in particular the essential needs of the world's poor, to which over-riding priority should be given
- the idea of **limitations** imposed by the state of technology and social organisation on the environment's ability to meet present and future needs.

The Brundtland Commission's definition contributed to the understanding that sustainable development encompasses a number of areas and highlights sustainability as the idea of **environmental, economic and social progress and equity**, all within the limits of the world's natural resources.

The International Institute for Sustainable Development (IISD) explains sustainable development in terms of systems thinking. All definitions of sustainable development require that we see the world as a system – a system that connects space and a system that connects time. When the world is considered as a system over space, it is easy to see that air pollution from North America affects air quality in Asia, and that pesticides sprayed in Argentina could harm fish stocks off the coast of Australia. When the world is considered as a system over time, it becomes obvious that the decisions made by previous generations about how to farm the land continue to affect agricultural practice today and that the economic policies endorsed today will have an impact on urban poverty in years to come.

Quality of life can also be seen as a system. Physical health is important, but so is access to education. The value of a secure income is diminished for a person living in an area where the air is polluted. Freedom of religious expression is important, but a person whose family is starving has little interest in this freedom.

The concept of sustainable development is rooted in this sort of systems thinking. The problems that the world faces are complex and serious, and cannot be addressed in the same way as they were created.

5.5.2 The history of sustainable development

People have always expressed their concerns about development and the environment in various ways, including through protests, publications and dialogue. The global-development dialogue today revolves mainly around the development of strategies to solve the interrelated economic, social and environmental challenges of our world. This dialogue originated as the environmental movement and the post-World War II international development community merged.

The devastation left by the Great Depression in 1929 and World War II in 1945 ushered in an era of unprecedented organised development. However, this development was not good from an environmental point of view.

Silent Spring[10] by Rachel Carson was published in 1962. This book brought the close link between the environment and development to the attention of many people. The book pointed out that levels of agricultural pesticides were extremely high, with the potential to cause damage to humans and other animal species. The environmental movement was officially born in 1971 with the formation of the environmental NGO Greenpeace. In 1972, a group of scientists known as the Club of Rome published a report entitled "The Limits to Growth"[11]. The report concluded that the world's social and economic system would collapse before 2070 unless drastic changes were made soon.

There was a growing awareness during the 1970s that the development undertaken post-World War II was unsustainable. In 1980, the International Union for the Conservation of Nature (IUCN), together with the United Nations Environment Programme (UNEP) and the World Wildlife Fund (WWF) published a report entitled "World Conservation Strategy: Living Resource Conservation for Sustainable Development"[12] that called for a new approach to development.

Half a century ago, modern technology was perceived to be the panacea to all the world's problems. Today, people have a much more realistic understanding of the reasons behind the state of the world.

Interested readers can find a timeline of the development of the concept of "sustainable development" at http://www.iisd.org/rio+5/timeline/sdtimeline.htm.

5.5.3 International conferences and agreements on sustainable development

The term "sustainable development" has consequently been explored and defined at many intergovernmental conferences and in many agreements, especially within the United Nations system. Major international meetings have brought sustainable development to the mainstream.

5.5.3.1 The Rio Earth Summit (1992)

The first of these international meetings was the UN Conference on Environment and Development, also known as the Earth Summit, which was held in 1992 in Rio, Brazil. 152 world leaders attended the conference and sustainability was enshrined in **Agenda 21**, a plan of action and a recommendation that all countries should produce national sustainable development strategies.

In the years to come, some groups argued that business, in particular, has not contributed sufficiently to Agenda 21. In the years since Rio, there has been little change in poverty levels, inequality or sustainable development.

5.5.3.2 The United Nations Global Compact (1999)

The UN Global Compact (UNGC) was first proposed in 1999 by the UN Secretary-General Kofi Annan as a result of corporations' limited contribution to Agenda 21. The ten principles of the Global Compact were discussed on page 148.

5.5.3.3 The Millennium Development Goals (2000)

Countries were also slow on delivering on the objectives of sustainable development. In 2000, the UN General Assembly, which includes all member states, agreed on a new set of ambitious objectives that are directly related to sustainable development: the **Millennium Development Goals (MDGs)**. World leaders vowed to work towards achieving these eight goals by the year 2015:

1. Eradicate extreme hunger and poverty.
2. Achieve universal primary education.
3. Promote gender equality and empower women.
4. Reduce child mortality.
5. Improve maternal health.
6. Combat HIV/Aids, malaria and other diseases.
7. Ensure environmental sustainability.
8. Develop a global partnership for development.

Progress since Rio

In the ten years since Rio, sustainable development hasn't been very high on international agendas. In the words of UN Secretary General Kofi Annan: "Progress towards the goals established at Rio has been slower than anticipated and in some respects conditions are worse than they were ten years ago." In many countries – rich and poor – this is often because of a perception that sustainability is expensive to implement and ultimately a brake on development.

Poor countries ... usually lack the physical infrastructure, ideas and human capacity to integrate sustainability into their development planning. Besides, they are often quite sceptical about rich countries' real commitment to sustainable development and demand a more equitable sharing of environmental costs and responsibilities. Many people also believe that environmental problems can wait until developing countries are richer. ...

Ten years on, there is still no widely shared vision of what sustainable development might mean in practice. India sees the idea of a light ecological footprint as part of its cultural heritage. Japan, on the other hand, is debating whether the emphasis should be on the "sustainable" or on the "development" half of the equation.

Source: LEAD International and Panos London. 2002. "Roads to the Summit: Reports from six countries on progress towards Sustainable development". [Online] Available: http://www.bvsde.paho.org/bvsacd/cd21/summit.pdf Accessed 31 January 2010.

5.5.3.4 The World Summit on Sustainable Development (2002)

In 2002, the **World Summit on Sustainable Development (WSSD)** was held in Johannesburg, South Africa. The WSSD was crucial in raising awareness of the need for business to contribute to sustainable development. It put the issues of corporate social responsibility and corporate accountability firmly on the international agenda. One of the key outcomes was the Johannesburg Declaration on Sustainable Development. This declaration highlighted that is not just the multi-national corporations that need to respond to this call. All business will have to be a part of the broad shift towards sustainable development at local and global levels.

Calls for public-private partnerships have been a feature of key sustainable development conferences, including the Rio Earth Summit and the WSSD. During the WSSD, partnerships were identified and agreed upon as a complement to the formal intergovernmental agreements. The MDGs also explicitly call for a partnership for sustainable development (see goal 8).

5.5.4 The contribution of CSR to sustainable development

The private sector has finances, management expertise and the technology to contribute to sustainable development through CSR. A corporation with an interest in ecological issues might extend this interest to the business interest in sustainable development. An example of this is Coca-Cola's interest in conserving freshwater resources (see the case study below).

Another example is the substantial power that business enjoys in many issues of sustainable development. This includes

Case study

Converging on Water: An Innovative Conservation Partnership

The Coca-Cola Company and the World Wildlife Fund are combining our international strengths and resources to help conserve and protect freshwater resources throughout the world.

Water is vital to both WWF and The Coca-Cola Company. Beverages are The Coca-Cola Company's business, and water is the main ingredient in every product we make. Safe water also is vital to the sustainability of the communities we serve. WWF's mission is the conservation of nature and the protection of natural resources for people and wildlife. Protecting freshwater ecosystems is a top priority in WWF's work. Now, through a partnership announced on June 5, 2007, we are combining our international strengths and resources to support water conservation throughout the world.

Here is what we will do together:

- Measurably conserve seven key watersheds.
- Improve the efficiency of the Coca-Cola system's water use.
- Support more efficient water use in the Company's agricultural supply chain, beginning with sugarcane.
- Decrease the Coca-Cola system's carbon-dioxide emissions and energy use.
- Inspire a global movement by uniting industries, conservation organisations and others in the conservation and protection of freshwater resources around the world.

Source: The Coca-Cola Company. 2007. "Converging on Water: An Innovative Conservation Partnership". [Online] Available at: http://www.thecoca-colacompany.com/citizenship/conservation_partnership.html Accessed 31 January 2010.

the power to self-regulate and to regulate its supply chains to enhance sustainable development.

But there are also limits to the extent to which corporations can be held responsible for sustainable development. Many negative contributions to sustainable development stem from the behaviour of individual members of society. For example, some practices exclude sections of society from the benefits of development, thus threatening social conflict. The failure to adopt sustainable waste-disposal practices and the excessive consumption of public resources such as water are also contrary to sustainable development. Many threats to sustainable development stem from governmental deficits, such as the failure to develop and implement global limits to carbon emissions or the failure to inhibit the destruction of diminishing natural resources such as forests.

Responsible business is therefore a requirement of sustainable development, but it is not sufficient to ensure sustainable development. Corporations, communities, governments and individuals need to work together to achieve this goal.

5.5.4.1 Think global, act local

"Think global, act local" was a prominent slogan after the 1992 Rio Earth Summit. It means that many sustainable development challenges, such as poverty or climate change, need to be considered at the global level and in international agreements, but that we need to act at the local level.

The local implementation of the recommendations of Agenda 21 has been guided by an initiative called Local Agenda 21. Different countries have implemented Local Agenda 21 in different ways. For example, South African local government authorities are required to prepare **integrated development plans (IDPs)** in a way that supports sustainable development. CSR requires that South African companies contribute to the development and implementation of IDPs.

5.6 Summary

This chapter began by introducing corporate social responsibility (CSR) and the related concepts of corporate social investment and corporate citizenship. It explored CSR by giving an historic overview of its development, followed by a discussion on the social, governmental, market and ethical drivers of CSR programs, and the importance of implementing CSR. The chapter looked at the people responsible for taking the leadership on CSR, and for formulating policies and frameworks, and the people who are responsible for legislating policies and frameworks, and implementing programs. Corporate governance and its relation to CSR were examined. In a discussion on stakeholder engagement, the term as well as its principles and processes were defined and explored. The chapter ended by defining sustainable development and looking at the contribution of CSR to sustainable development.

Key terms

Agenda 21	Millennium Development Goals (MDGs)
business ethics	Rio Earth Summit
corporate citizenship (CC)	stakeholder engagement
corporate governance	sustainability report
corporate social investment (CSI)	sustainable development
corporate social responsibility (CSR)	triple bottom line (TBL)
Global Reporting Initiative (GRI)	United Nations Global Compact (UNGC)
integrated development plans (IDPs)	voluntary standards
King Report I, II and III on Corporate Governance	World Summit on Sustainable Development (WSSD)

? Questions for discussion

Reread the case study at the beginning of the chapter and answer the following questions:

1. In your opinion, what are the main drivers of BHP Billiton's CSR program? Explain your answer.
2. Give an example of BHP Billiton's contribution to sustainable development.
3. Explain what is meant by the term "corporate social investment" (CSI). Use a CSI project of BHP Billiton to support your explanation.
4. How does a sustainability report differ from a financial report?
5. Explain how BHP Billiton's CSR program finds expression in its corporate governance.

? Multiple-choice questions

1. Look at the list of parties that may have caused the development of corporate social responsibility below.
   i. Irresponsible citizens
   ii. Government regulation
   iii. Growing public concern
   iv. The devastation of wars and markets
   v. Profitability

   Now select the combination of parties that caused the development of social responsibility.
   a. i, ii, iii
   b. i, iii, iv
   c. ii, iii, iv
   d. ii, iii, v
2. Read the statements about business ethics below.
   a. The ethical responsibility of business applies to externalities.
   b. The ethical responsibility of business applies to conduct in the workplace.
   c. The ethical responsibility of business is only about "doing good".
   d. The ethical responsibility of business extends to compliance with laws.
   e. The ethical responsibility of business applies to business dealings.

   Now select the combination of statements that are correct.
   a. i, iii, iv
   b. ii, iii, v
   c. i, ii, iv, v
   d. iii
3. Which of the following statements represents good corporate-governance practices in company H?
   a. The executive chairperson is responsible for the running of the board.
   b. The chief executive officer is an independent director.
   c. The chairperson manages the CSR program.
   d. The chairperson provides leadership for the CSR program.
4. Which one of the following statements is not true?
   a. Stakeholders can potentially affect the business activities of a company.
   b. The term "stakeholders" is synonymous with the term "shareholders".
   c. Primary stakeholders can also become secondary stakeholders.
   d. The environment can be classified as a stakeholder.
5. Which of the following concepts does not relate to the discourse on sustainable development?
   a. The United Nations Global Compact
   b. The UN Conference on Environment and Development
   c. The Millennium Development Goals
   d. None

Answers to multiple-choice questions

1. c
2. c
3. d
4. b
5. d

References

1. World Economic Forum. 2010. "Corporate Global Citizenship". [Online] Available: http://www.weforum.org/en/initiatives/corporatecitizenshipindex.htm Accessed 29 January 2010.
2. May, S., Cheney, G. & Roper, J. (eds.). 2007. Overview. In *The Debate over Corporate Social Responsibility*. New York: Oxford University Press, pp. 15–29.
3. Friedman, Milton. 1970. "The Social Responsibility of Business is to Increase Its Profits". *New York Times Magazine*, September, pp. 32–33, 122–126.
4. Elkington, J. 1994 "Towards the sustainable corporation: Win-win-win business strategies for sustainable development". *California Management Review* 36, no. 2, pp. 90–100.
5. CSR International 2010. "Welcome to CSR International – the incubator for CSR 2.0". [Online] Available: http://www.csrinternational.org/ Accessed 28 January 2010.
6. Kirrane, D. 1990. "Managing Values: A Systematic Approach to Business Ethics". *Training and Development Journal*, November, pp. 53–60.
7. Donaldson, J. & Davis, P. 1990. "Business Ethics? Yes, but What Can it Do for the Bottom Line?" *Management Decision*, Vol. 28, No. 6.
8. World Bank. 1999. *Corporate Governance: A Framework for Implementation – Overview*. [Online] Available: World Bank Report http://www.systemiclogic.net/artifacts/PUB/governance/gcgfbooklet.pdf Accessed 29 January 2010.
9. Brundtland Commission. 1987. "Report of the World Commission on Environment and Development". [Online] Available: http://www.un.org/documents/ga/res/42/ares42-187.htm Accessed 30 January 2010.
10. Carson, R. 1962. *Silent Spring*. New York: Houghton Mifflin.
11. Club of Rome. 1972. "The Limits to Growth". [Online] Available: www.clubofrome.org/docs/limits.rtf Accessed 30 January 2010.
12. International Union for Conservation of Nature and Natural Resources. 1980. "World Conservation Strategy: Living Resource Conservation for Sustainable Development". [Online] Available: http://data.iucn.org/dbtw-wpd/edocs/WCS-004.pdf Accessed 31 January 2010.

Websites: www.unglobalcompact.org
www.globalreporting.org
www.equator-principles.com
www.eitransparency.org
http://www.iisd.org/sd/
www.un.org/millenniumgoals

PART 2

The business

ORGANISATION AND MANAGEMENT

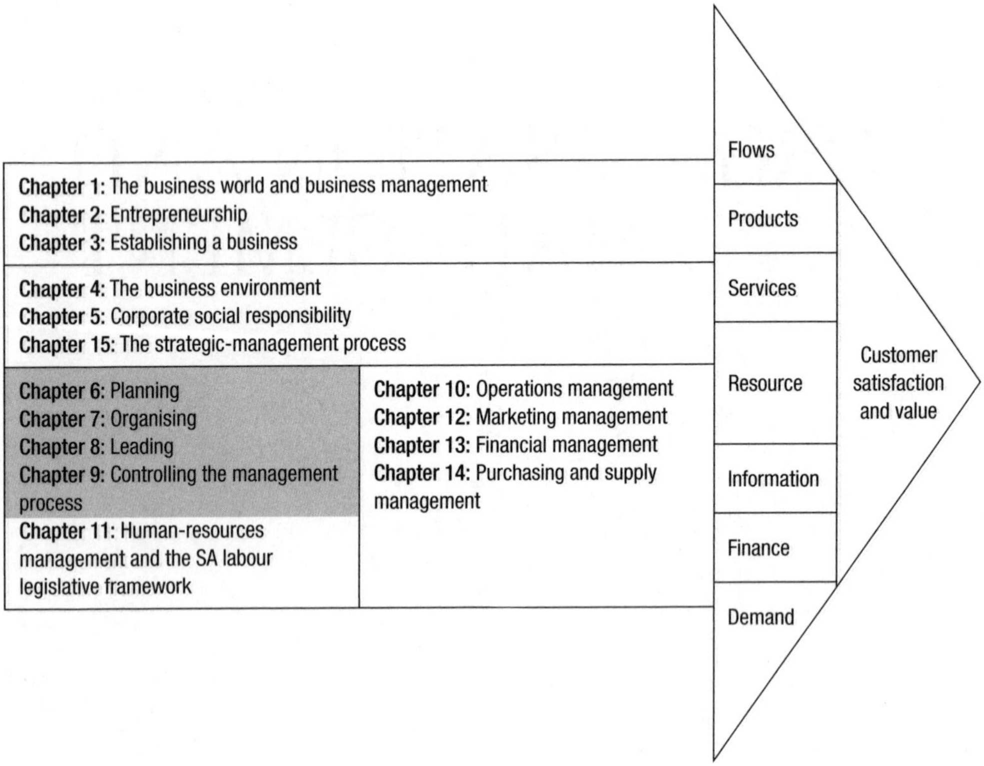

Source: Adapted from Mentzer, T. J. (ed.). 2001. *Supply Chain Management.* London: Sage, pp. 22–23.

CHAPTER

6

PLANNING

The purpose of this chapter

The purpose of this chapter is to explore the concept of planning as the first of four management functions, as defined by the management process. Planning is the basis for the rest of the management functions, and incorporates goals and plans. Plans specify how the organisation will achieve its goals. The management process takes place in the context of the environment in which the organisation operates.

Learning outcomes

On completion of this chapter you should be able to:

- explain the nature of planning as a management task
- describe the importance of planning as the first step in the management process
- describe the planning process
- interpret goals meaningfully
- describe the different organisational goals
- depict the hierarchy of goals
- differentiate between strategic, functional and operational planning
- differentiate between different strategies to accomplish different goals.

6.1 Introduction

Planning gives direction to the organisation. It forces managers to be future-oriented and enables the organisation to deal with changes in the business environment. This chapter briefly explains the benefits and costs of planning in organisations. It then focuses on the two components of planning, namely goals and plans, and explains the planning process. This chapter also discusses the focus of planning at the organisation's three levels.

No small beer empire

SA Breweries (SAB) started as Castle Brewing in 1895, with Castle Lager being the first beer it produced. Its first major acquisitions were Ohlsson's and Chandlers Union Breweries in the 1950s, when it changed its name to SAB. It also acquired the rights to bottle and distribute Coca-Cola through Amalgamated Beverages. It listed on the then Johannesburg Stock Exchange in 1987.

When SA Breweries' head office was still located in Jan Smuts Avenue, Johannesburg, the top managers often discussed a global strategy around boardroom tables. However, in the days of apartheid, the company was unable to invest globally. Like most big South African companies, SAB was stuck at home and forced to invest in other unrelated organisations such as hotels, retail and manufacturing.

The obvious choice for SAB's first cross-border expansion was Africa. In the 1980s, SAB invested in Botswana, Lesotho and Swaziland before moving further afield when apartheid began to unravel. Its strategic alliance with family-owned French beverage group Castel in 2001 allowed it to invest in countries like Algeria and Morocco, where Castel was strong.

With the symbolic dismantling of the Berlin Wall in 1989 and the beginning of the demise of apartheid, SAB recognised an emerging market in Eastern and Central Europe. "We recognised the growth potential in those emerging markets and identified the less established players that operated there. We were in a strong position to enter the emerging markets," says Financial Director Malcolm Wyman. "Post-communist Central European countries were looking for skills and breweries were being privatised. We were a very small African brewer and knew that we had to get into these countries ahead of the large multi-nationals in order to have a competitive advantage."

In 1999, SAB moved its primary listing to the London Stock Exchange. Soon afterwards, SAB bought three breweries in the Czech Republic and faced the challenge of managing the integration of three independently run, formally competing brewers. Despite the retrenchment of 20% of the workforce, the Czech business grew profits from USD20 million to USD120 million in three years. "We set about introducing SAB methods, such as segmenting the market and rationalising the brands," SAB stalwart – now SABMiller (SA) chief executive – Tony van Kralingen says.

The Czech Republic is just one of 60 countries on six continents in which (the renamed) SABMiller now operates, but the approach it followed back in 1999 is typical of its subsequent approach to acquisitions, and with a few exceptions, it was always successful. The SAB model, which they transported to various parts of the world, aims for a dominant market position in the target country, then to buy competitors and invest in brands. SABMiller now boasts a portfolio of more than 200 brands and is the world's largest brewer in terms of volume.

The architects of the strategy that transformed SAB into a global player are the group's chief executive Graham Mackay and Malcolm Wyman, the financial director. "He is the best strategic chess player in corporate business I know," says researcher Julian Wentzel of Mackay. "He has a vision and a map well ahead of anyone else." Mackay says he identifies patterns and looks for what will happen next. "One of the advantages I have is the ability to see things from a global perspective," he says. "I travel to many different markets and see what is happening in many different areas of the world."

Wyman, on the other hand, is the corporate finance brains behind the strategy, and he introduced the famous SAB mergers and acquisitions (M&A) methodology that has determined the process and formulation of each of its 30 large deals. Wyman is able to look at the macro-environment and, at the same time, he has an unbelievable eye for detail.

However, according to Mackay, strategy is only as good as its execution. To get that right, SAB built the best M&A team and implemented stringent and ruthless acquisition criteria. "We have been told that our M&A teams are the best in their class," Wyman says. The other part of their strategy is the ability to choose from a wide selection of experienced managers to deploy to operations around the world.

The 1999 London listing and access to far larger amounts of capital helped push SAB into the big league. Its global profile changed and it was able to make far bigger acquisitions on the world stage.

In 2002, SAB followed the 1999 Czech deals with another transformative deal. Moving away from South Africa, SAB bought Miller Brewing from Phillip Morris, the second-largest brewer in the United States by volume. SAB's name changed to SABMiller. The Miller acquisition was a shift from the SAB strategy of identifying opportunities in emerging markets and marked the change from a large emerging-market brewer to a global brewer.

In 2005, SABMiller consolidated its position in Latin America, where it had already bought a few small brewers, by buying a majority interest in Bavaria, South America's second-largest brewer. In 2008, SABMiller formed a joint venture with Molson Coors Brewing to combine the United States and Puerto Rico operations of Miller and Coors Brewing. The new company, MillerCoors, with its complementary brands and locations, has a bigger distribution network and is able to increase competitiveness by reducing overheads to achieve cost savings.

Two other important acquisitions in developed markets were the purchase of Italy's Peroni and the Dutch-based Grolsch. The ownership of a portfolio of well-known brands – Peroni, Pilsner, Urquell, Grolsch and Miller Genuine Draft – is part of the next phase of SABMiller's strategy: to develop an international brand portfolio and sell these brands in all the markets where it operates, alongside the local mainstream brands. SABMiller decided to focus on premium brands mostly because of growing global wealth and the aspirational identity attached to premium beers. The attraction for SABMiller is the higher prices, wider margins and faster growth that premium brands offer.

Mackay sees yet another trend developing, and SABMiller is already investigating and planning to act on this trend. "There is a fragmentation of brands at the top end. There is a search for more authentic brands as opposed to the blockbuster international premium ones," he says. According to him, there is a move towards unique beers from small brewers as well as to unknown foreign beers in the United States and United Kingdom.

The brewer is not about to stop making further acquisitions. The first Asian country in which SABMiller set up operations was China. The company also acquired Narang Breweries in India and it bought Australian brewer Bluetongue at the end of 2007. The market is huge in India and China, with both countries having populations of over one billion people.

In China, SABMiller's Snow is the country's top-selling beer and one of the fastest-growing brands in the world. Although SABMiller achieved significant volumes in China, profits are low. "Historically, that is the tradition in China. Pricing and margins are sacrificed for volume, and if you get that wrong, it is market share that is gone," says Wayne Hall, finance director of SABMiller in China. On the other hand, Australia's beer market is fairly developed, but the margins are extremely high, often around 38%. However, the perception is that this market will have strategic advantages.

In South Africa, SABMiller owns The South African Breweries Ltd (100%), Appletiser South Africa (Pty) Ltd (100%), Distell Group Ltd (29%), Coca-Cola Canners of Southern Africa (Pty) Ltd (32%) and Tsogo Sun Holdings (Pty) Ltd (49%).

The top managers of SABMiller see the organisation as a "global consolidator" and expect another big acquisition between now and 2012. "We see ourselves as a contender for any attractive major deal that may arise," says SABMiller Financial Director Wyman. He adds that SABMiller's ambition is not necessarily to be the number one brewer in the world, but rather to be the world's best global brewer.

There are various choices. If speculation is true that a handful of global beer giants could start merging, SABMiller would be in a position to make a bid for one of them.

The size and influence SABMiller enjoys in many of its markets make it imperative that it behaves responsibly and improves the lives of the less fortunate. SABMiller invests millions in social programs. Mackay says, "We believe the best way to help society is to succeed as a business by providing products that people enjoy, creating jobs and wealth, contributing taxes and helping others to advance economically."

"While our products contribute to people's quality of life, we also have a responsibility to make sure they are used sensibly. We therefore have a range of educational and research programs in areas such as under-age drinking and road safety. Under the title "The Responsible Way", we've also adopted a new group-wide policy on alcohol together with a code of conduct covering all our commercial communications," says Mackay.

Source: Adapted from *Financial Mail*. 2008. "No small beer empire". February 15, pp. 31–39; SABMiller. 2005. "SABMiller Annual Report"; SABMiller. 2009. "SABMiller Annual Report" & SABMiller. 2009. "SABMiller 2009 – Business Overview". [Online] Available: http://www.sabmiller.com/files/pdf/corporate_presentation.pdf Accessed 2 December 2009.

6.2 The benefits and costs of planning

There is a saying that if you do not know where you want to go, any road will take you there. Managers need to know which way to go. Planning provides that direction.

For example, Meyer Kahn, the chairman of SABMiller, stated that despite a worldwide recession, SABMiller was able to deliver good results in 2009[1]. He attributes the company's success to a clear, consistent strategy and operational strength built up over many years. He mentions that SABMiller measures its progress against a range of key performance indicators. By planning to attain specific performance indicators through a process of reconciling the threats in the business environment with the organisation's own operational strengths, SABMiller was able to produce positive results in a challenging business environment.

6.2.1 The benefits of planning

Planning has many **benefits**, and the more turbulent the environment, the greater the necessity for planning. How do managers plan for the future in an environment characterised by constant change, such as the environment at the beginning of the second decade of the twenty-first century?

Managers cannot predict the future, the planning exercise cannot change the business environment and no plan can be perfect. However, managers can plan to steer the organisation in the best possible direction, taking into consideration the organisation's internal strengths and weaknesses. Good managers understand that although they are leading the organisation in a pre-determined direction, they should anticipate change in the environment, and adjust their goals and plans accordingly when necessary. Since 2008, the world economy has spiralled into a serious recession, yet some organisations managed to produce creditable results in 2009. How did they do it? Some of the benefits of planning are listed below, and examples from the SABMiller Annual Report of 2009 illustrate how this global organisation has used the benefits of planning to its advantage, even in the bleak circumstances of 2009.

6.2.1.1 Planning provides direction

The most important function of planning is that it gives **direction** to the organisation in the form of goals and plans. By creating a blueprint of where the organisation is heading (goals) and formulating plans to attain these goals, managers ensure that the organisation is both effective (providing products or services that the market wants) and efficient (providing products and services at the lowest cost).

Through careful planning, SABMiller has grown into a global organisation, and developed a balanced and attractive portfolio of businesses since listing on the London Stock Exchange in 1999[2].

6.2.1.2 Planning reduces the impact of change

The process of goal-setting and planning is by definition future oriented. Managers continually scan the environment to anticipate change that may affect the organisation in the future. They plan for the organisation to benefit from opportunities and to avoid threats, thereby reducing uncertainty, guesswork and the risks caused by change.

According to SABMiller Chairman, Meyer Kahn, 2009 was a good year for SABMiller. He explained, "In difficult economic conditions, we have drawn on our strengths, addressed the many opportunities in our markets and produced a creditable set of results."[3]

6.2.1.3 Planning promotes co-ordination

Planning focuses all activities in an organisation in one direction: to attain the organisation's goals effectively and efficiently. If all the members of the organisation are aware of the goals they have to meet, they can co-ordinate their activities. This will foster co-operation and teamwork.

According to SABMiller Chief Executive, Graham Mackay, "We continue, consistently and relentlessly, to tighten our efficiency and raise the performance of each local business. We also seek to gain maximum value from our global scale by transferring skills and proven ways of working across the organisation."[4]

6.2.1.4 Planning ensures cohesion

The increasing complexity of organisations and the interdependence of all the parts of the organisation (individuals, sections, departments, teams and so on) emphasise the necessity of planning to ensure cohesion. Planning enables top management to see the organisation as a total system in which the goals of all the different parts of the organisation are reconcilable with each other as well as with the primary goals of the organisation as a whole.

6.2.1.5 Planning facilitates control

Control is the process by which management ensures that the actual organisational activities are compatible with the pre-determined goals and planned activities. Control enables management to measure the actual performance against the set goals and plans, and to take corrective action if significant deviations occur.

During the planning process, managers formulate organisational goals and plans at various levels of the organisation. These goals and plans later facilitate control. Without planning, control cannot take place.

In SABMiller, key performance indicators are used to monitor the progress achieved regarding each of the organisation's four strategic priorities[5]:

- creating a balanced and attractive global spread of business
- developing strong, relevant brand portfolios in the local market
- constantly raising the performance of local businesses
- leveraging their global scale.

6.2.2 The costs of planning

Despite the obvious benefits of planning, it can also result in the following **costs** to the organisation[6].

6.2.2.1 Planning may create rigidity

Managers may not be inclined to deviate from set plans, even when changes in the environment may require flexibility in terms of planning.

6.2.2.2 Planning consumes management time

Planning is time consuming and may require a substantial portion of the valuable time and energy of managers.

6.2.2.3 Formal plans may replace intuition and creativity

The formal planning process can turn into a programmed routine and subsequently diminish the vital role of creativity and intuition in planning.

6.2.2.4 Planning could cause delays in decision-making

Planning could shift the focus in an organisation from performing to evaluating, resulting in a delay in making crucial decisions regarding environmental changes that influence the organisation.

6.3 Managerial goals and plans

If one intends to travel from Johannesburg to Cape Town, it would be sensible to buy a map. The map would enable one to set goals for reaching Cape Town. The most important, primary goal would be to reach Cape Town on a specific date. Secondary goals could be that one should reach Bloemfontein before it gets dark on the first day of the journey and that the trip should not cost more than R2 000. In this way, one could formulate several plans to achieve the main goal of reaching Cape Town.

On a personal level, most people are quite familiar with setting goals and formulating plans. The managerial function of planning in organisations is similar as it comprises the same two components.

Firstly, managers need to ask the question: Where do we want this organisation to be at a specific future date? (This will entail setting goals.) Secondly, they need to ask: How will the organisation achieve its goals? (This will entail formulating plans.) Thus, the concept of planning incorporates two components: determining the organisation's goals and developing plans to achieve these goals.

Against this background, an **organisational goal** (or objective) can be defined as "a desirable state of affairs that an organisation aims to achieve at some point in the future".

An **organisational plan** can be defined as "the means by which the goal is to be realised". The concepts of goals and plans are interrelated.

6.3.1 The nature of goals

Organisational goals are the starting point of the planning process. Goals flow directly from the mission statement, but are more specific.

Organisations have **multiple goals**, and the type of goal that is set is influenced by the organisational level at which it is set. Goals range from strategic goals formulated by top-level managers to operational goals formulated by lower-level managers.

The **focus of goals** differs because different goals pertain to different aspects of the organisation, such as finances, the environment, participants and survival. Strategic goals are holistic in that they apply to the whole organisation. For example, the strategic goal of SAB was to become the biggest brewer in the world. However, the organisation also has goals pertaining to the environment and social responsibility, and many other goals concentrating on all the different areas of the organisation.

The **time period** of goals may be short term, intermediate or long term.

Goals may be **publicly stated or not**. The degree of openness is concerned with whether the goals are official or operative. Official goals are formally and publicly declared (in the annual reports and the media), whereas operative goals represent the private goals of an organisation. Companies listed on the Johannesburg Securities Exchange (JSE) have to make their annual results public because shareholders (people who buy the company's shares on the stock exchange) have a right to know about the financial and managerial state of the companies in which they invest. They do not have to make public other goals, such as operational and strategic goals relating to, for example, the company's competitive advantage.

6.3.2 The importance of goals

It is crucial for managers to establish where the organisation is heading. Goals are important in this regard for the following reasons:

- Goals provide guidance and agreement on the **direction** of the organisation, and they steer all the employees and the activities they perform in the same direction. Without goals, a business is like a ship without a rudder.
- Clearly formulated, unambiguous goals facilitate effective planning in terms of **resource deployment**.
- Goals can inspire and **motivate** employees, especially if the employees can perceive a specific link between their performance in terms of goal achievement and the rewards they receive.
- Goals provide the basis for the effective evaluation of employee and organisational performance, and for the **control** of organisational resources.
- From the above, it is clear that effective goal-setting plays an important part in the **success** of organisations. To ensure that goals are as effective as possible, they should adhere to specific criteria.

6.3.3 Criteria for effective goals

To improve the chances of successfully achieving goals, managers should ensure that goals are not ambiguous. The **SMART framework** states that goals should be specific, measurable, attainable, relevant and time bound. Managers can follow this framework in order to formulate goals properly:

- When a goal is "**specific**", it indicates what the goal relates to, the period to which the goal refers and the specific desired results of the goal.
- When a goal is "**measurable**", this means that the manager has stated the goal in such terms that the result can be evaluated objectively and in quantified terms. Managers must be able to see if the goals are satisfied when they compare actual results with pre-determined goals. This is especially true for tactical and operational goals. To say, for example, "Market share should be increased" is too vague and not measurable, whereas to say, "Market share should increase by 10% over the next two years in Gauteng" is precise and measurable.
- When a goal is "**attainable**", it is realistic, yet it should still provide a challenge. Furthermore, managers should assign the responsibility for reaching goals to specific individuals. Each manager generally has responsibilities for setting goals at his/her level in the organisation. This means that the relationship between the expected results and the people responsible for the results should be clearly stated so that managers fully understand the aims and goals, and are in no doubt about what they have to do to achieve them.
- When a goal is "**relevant**", this means that it relates to the organisation's mission and strategic goals. It follows that the various goals in an organisation should be compatible with each other because they all derive from the same mission and strategic goals. "Horizontal consistency" refers to the compatibility of the objectives of various departments with one another. If, for example, the marketing department proposes to extend its line of products, the costs of production will increase, and therefore the production division will find

it difficult to embark on cost-cutting as one of its goals. "Vertical consistency" means that departmental goals are compatible with those of subsections. For example, if marketing sets a target of an 8% increase in sales, this has to be compatible with the sales objectives set for the geographical markets of the business (in other words, the total increase in sales for the particular regions should add up to 8%).

- When a goal is "**time bound**", it has a specific time limit. People are likely to ignore goals with no time limit because there is no sense of urgency associated with them. So instead of saying, "Increase production by 1 000 units," managers should rather say, "Increase production by 1 000 units by the end of December this year."

6.3.4 A goal-setting technique: Management by objectives

Management by objectives (MBO) is a technique designed to achieve the integration of individual and organisational goals in organisations. Management by objectives is a system whereby managers and employees define goals for every department, project and person, and use them to monitor subsequent performance[7].

The assumptions underlying the successful implementation of an MBO program is that it should have the support of top management and that employees should understand the process. All employees must have a clear understanding of the organisation's **purpose**, mission, long-term goals and strategy. Individual employees' goals derive from the goals of the department, section, group or team to which they belong, which in turn derive from the organisation's mission and long-term goals.

The process goes as follows:

- The manager and the employee have an initial discussion that results in the formulation of a clear job description and key performance areas for the employee.
- The employee establishes potential key performance targets in the pre-determined areas of responsibility for a forthcoming period. The employee and the manager meet to develop a set of goals for the employee to which both are committed.
- The employee and manager mutually establish checkpoints to measure the employee's progress.
- Evaluation of the degree of goal attainment takes place at the end of the pre-determined period. The evaluation focuses on the analysis of the achieved results compared with the pre-determined goals.

Management by objectives has many advantages and some disadvantages for an organisation. These are listed in Table 6.1.

Table 6.1: Advantages and disadvantages of the management-by-objectives technique

Advantages of MBO	Disadvantages of MBO
• The efforts of managers and employees focus on attaining organisational goals. • The organisation's performance can improve. • Employees are motivated. • Individual goals align with organisational goals.	• Constant change in the environment can cause frequent changes in organisational goals, thereby disrupting MBO. • Poor relations between managers and employees reduce the effectiveness of MBO. • Operational goals may displace strategic goals. • The organisational culture may discourage effective use of MBO. • MBO can result in too much paperwork.

Source: Adapted from Daft, R.L. 2010. *The New Era of Management.* 9th ed, p. 170. Canada: South-Western, a part of Cengage Learning, Inc. Reproduced by permission. www.cengage.com/permissions.

When used correctly, management by objectives can be an effective tool to align individual and organisational goals. However, it can do more harm than good when it is reduced to an annual process of filling in forms, which are then filed and forgotten, as this has a negative effect on employee motivation.

6.3.5 The nature of plans

While a goal is a desired future state that the organisation attempts to achieve, a plan is the "blueprint" for goal achievement. It indicates how the goals are going to be reached by specifying the resources that will be used, the period in which the plans must be implemented and all the other actions that will be necessary to achieve the goals.

When formulating plans to achieve the organisation's goals, managers consider **several alternative plans of action** and ultimately select the alternative (or alternatives) that has the best chance of leading to the achievement of the pre-determined goals.

Various factors influence managers when they develop alternative plans, such as external factors, the organisation's strengths and weaknesses, and the costs associated with plans.

External factors, such as market factors, legislation or economic trends, influence the business environment and subsequently the ability of the organisation to achieve its goals. Such environmental influences occur in the form of opportunities to exploit or threats to avert (see Chapter 4 on environmental scanning). Managers consider these opportunities and threats when making alternative plans.

Managers also take cognisance of the **strengths and weaknesses** in the organisation's internal environment when they develop alternative plans. They aim to capitalise on the organisation's strengths, such as particular skills, a patent, capital, the image of the organisation, or possession of a raw-material source or a marketing channel. At the same time, alternative plans should not expose the weaknesses of the organisation to threats in the environment.

Managers weigh the costs of alternative plans against their respective advantages and through this process develop rational plans.

6.4 The planning process

6.4.1 The planning context

Several factors determine the **context** in which planning takes place. These variables set the **parameters** within which managers can formulate realistic organisational goals and plans. Managers cannot set goals and make plans that are unattainable in terms of either the environment in which the organisation operates or the resources at the disposal of the organisation. For example, the corner café cannot have a goal such as, "To gain 50% of the market share in selling groceries in Soweto this year." Such a goal is unrealistic in terms of the café's planning context. On the other hand, SABMiller's strategy to enter emerging markets in 1989 was an excellent decision because the company was in a strong position to enter the emerging markets ahead of the large multi-nationals, thus obtaining a valuable competitive advantage.

The five variables that set the parameters for organisational planning are the purpose of the organisation and the environment, the organisation's mission statement, the organisation's environment, the managers' values and the managers' experience.

The **purpose** of the organisation includes its obligation to society (for example, providing safe products at reasonable prices) and its obligation to its stakeholders (for example, to make a profit) or a combination of these factors. In the SABMiller case study, Mr Mackay clearly stated the purpose of the organisation when he said that the best way to help society is to succeed as a business by providing products that people enjoy, creating jobs and wealth, contributing taxes and helping others to advance economically.

The **mission statement** sets out the unique purpose that distinguishes the organisation from other organisations of its type. The mission statement guides the goal-setting and planning in organisations.

The **environment** is one of the most crucial variables that influence planning. In Chapter 4, it was emphasised that organisations are open systems that have specific interactions with their environments. To survive, organisations must plan to take advantage of external opportunities and to avoid threats in the environment. During the strategic-planning process, organisations set long-term goals and formulate strategic plans to reconcile their internal strengths and weaknesses with external opportunities and threats. Managers at different levels of the organisation transform the strategic goals and plans into tactical, operational plans, and individual goals and plans.

The **values of managers** influence and cement the organisation's culture, strategy and structure. They also determine the organisation's commitment to social responsibility. In the case study, Mr Mackay remarked that the size and influence SABMiller enjoys in many of its markets make it imperative that it behaves responsibly and improves the lives of the less fortunate. SABMiller invests millions into social programs. The values of the group appear in the box below. These group values reflect the values of the top managers and contribute to the planning context at SABMiller.

SABMiller values

Our group values:

- Our people are our enduring advantage.
- Accountability is clear and personal.
- We work and win in teams.
- We understand and respect our customers and consumers.
- Our reputation is indivisible.

Source: SABMiller. 2009. "SABMiller 2009 – Business Overview". [Online] Available: http://www.sabmiller.com/files/pdf/corporate_presentation.pdf Accessed 2 December 2009.

The **experience of management** is also important because it influences the planning performance of managers. The architects of the strategic plans that transformed SAB into a global player are the group's chief executive, Graham Mackay, and its financial director, Malcolm Wyman. A researcher remarked that Mackay is the best strategic "chess player" in corporate business, commenting that he has a vision and a map well ahead of anyone else. Mackay says he identifies patterns and looks for what will happen next. Clearly, Mackay's experience is a major advantage in terms of strategy formulation at SABMiller.

6.4.2 Steps in the planning process

Planning is a process. By expanding on the example of travelling from Johannesburg to Cape Town, the planning process becomes apparent.

If one's goal is to travel by car from Johannesburg to Cape Town, many roads will lead one there, and one can therefore develop alternative plans (Johannesburg–Durban–Cape Town, Johannesburg–Beaufort West–Cape Town and Johannesburg–Knysna–Cape Town, for example). However, associated with each route are specific variables that can help make one of the options more attractive than the others. For example, travelling from Johannesburg to Cape Town via Beaufort West is much shorter than travelling from Johannesburg to Cape Town via Durban. To travel via Knysna to Cape Town is another option, but while this route is scenic, there are cost and time implications.

One must decide on a plan within a certain planning context, for example, one has only two days to get to Cape Town, and one has only R2 000 to pay for the trip (including petrol, accommodation and food). The decision will then be reached by evaluating each of the alternative plans in terms of the planning context and other criteria that are important, such as the dangers of travelling on South African roads in the dark. Only after one has evaluated all the alternatives should a plan be selected (travelling via Beaufort West in two days).

The next step is to implement the plan by booking a car service for a week before the trip and making a reservation to sleep over somewhere halfway through the trip.

The final step is to travel to Cape Town, sleeping over in Colesberg. However, if, when one reaches Bloemfontein, one hears a traffic report on the radio warning motorists that the authorities have closed the road from Colesberg to Beaufort West owing to flooding, one will have to implement reactive planning and change one's route by travelling via Graaf-Reinet instead of Beaufort West.

This example illustrates that planning comprises a number of steps, which follow each other in a specific sequence, thus forming a process. **The steps in the planning process are**:

- Establish goals.
- Develop alternative plans.
- Evaluate alternative plans
- Select a plan.
- Implement the plan.
- Do reactive planning, if necessary, when changes occur in the environment.

Figure 6.1 illustrates the planning process.

The managers at the various **levels** of the organisation all follow the steps of the planning process, but each level has a different focus:

- **Top-level** managers formulate long-term strategic goals and strategic plans for the entire organisation.
- **Middle-level** managers use strategic goals and strategic plans as inputs to develop medium-term tactical goals and tactical plans for their functional departments.
- **Lower-level** managers use tactical goals and tactical plans to develop short-term operational goals and operational plans for their sections.

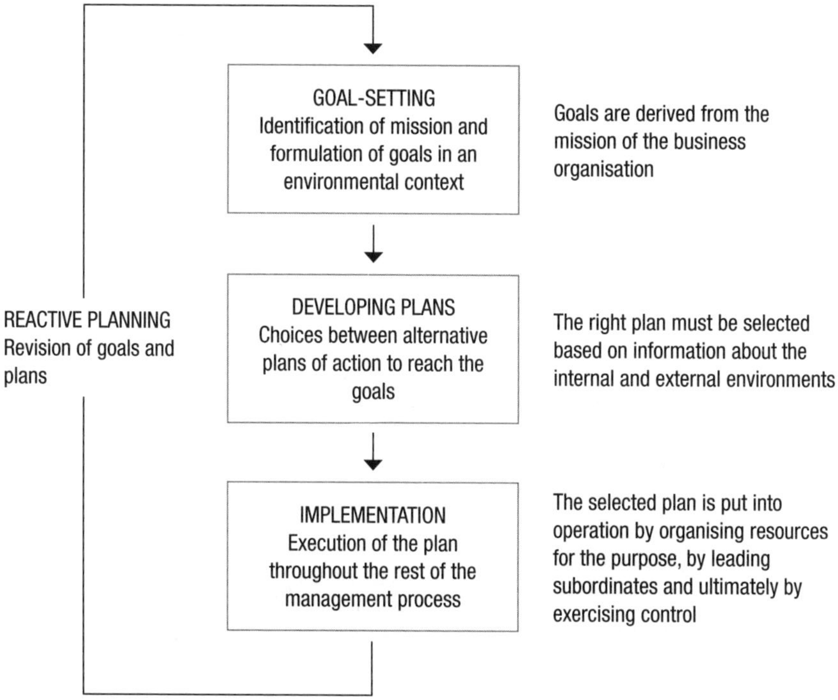

Figure 6.1: The planning process

Figure 6.2 illustrates the planning process as goals and plans cascade down from the strategic level to the operational level.

6.4.3 Strategic goals and plans

The first half of the twentieth century was characterised by stable business environments with low and stable rates of interest, few raw-material shortages, a slow and steady rate of technological innovation, and a general economy in which inflation was practically unknown. In such a stable environment, organisations were able to sell their products or services without being too concerned about the future. The assumption was that future environments would be more or less the same as prevailing ones, so that a mere extension or projection of previous plans was adequate to ensure profitable survival.

However, since the 1950s, the business environment has been changing at an unprecedented rate. Managers have had to look for new approaches because old ones have proved to be of little use in an unstable environment. At the same time, organisations have become larger and more complex. In these circumstances, long-term planning came into being during the late 1950s in an attempt to take countermeasures against instability in the business environment. In the 1960s and 1970s especially, managers used the general concept of strategic planning in an effort to keep abreast of change in the business environment and to develop long-term or strategic plans. Strategic planning is a popular management tool, and organisations ranging from government departments and not-for-profit organisations to global organisations use it to help them operate in the business environment of the twenty-first century, of which the first decade has been characterised by systemic change.

6.4.3.1 Strategic goals

Top managers formulate strategic goals that apply to the organisation as a whole over the long term. Strategic goals include a vision, a mission statement and long-term goals.

A **vision** implies that managers need to think about new possibilities that will carry their organisation into the future. A vision promotes change and provides the foundation for a strategic plan. The vision is the picture of the future the organisation seeks to create. Organisations with clear vision statements generally outperform organisations without a vision. When there is a clear vision, decision-making focuses on the important issues and

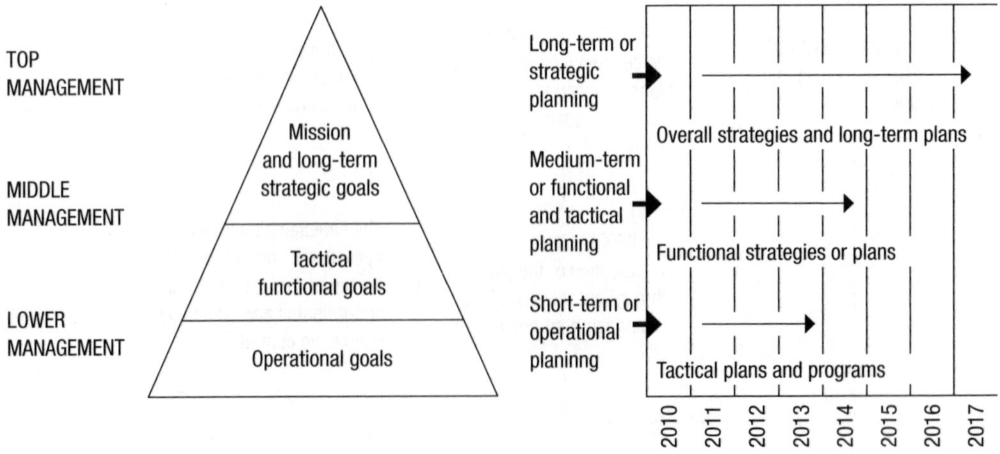

Figure 6.2: The levels of goals and plans and their time frames

individuals are motivated because they can see how their efforts contribute to the success of the organisation.

SABMiller's vision

SABMiller's vision is to be "the most admired company in the global beer industry". SABMiller explains that it wants to be the investment of choice, the employer of choice and the partner of choice[8].

The **mission statement** spells out the mission or over-arching goal of the organisation. The mission statement sets the organisation apart from other organisations operating in the same industry by defining it in terms of its unique combination of products, customers and technology. In the mission statement, the organisation answers three important questions:

- What is our business (products and services)?
- Who are our customers (markets)?
- How do we provide our products or services (technology)?

The mission statement may also include the organisation's intention to secure its survival through sustained growth and profitability. In addition, the organisation may use it to make a statement about the organisation's culture, public image, self-concept, social responsibility and the quality of its products. The mission statement sets the stage for strategic, tactical and operational planning in the organisation.

Long-term strategic goals derive from the organisation's mission statement. They are complex and deal with the organisation as a whole. While their focus is long term, the exact period may vary from organisation to organisation, depending on the industry.

In considering long-term goals, top managers usually include goals in such critical areas as profitability, productivity, competitive position, human-resources development, human relations, technological leadership and social responsibility. Strategic goals should be clear, since tactical goals derive from them.

SABMiller's long-term strategic goals

In the case of SABMiller, Mackay and the other top managers formulated strategic goals for SABMiller that resulted in strategies such as moving into new markets, acquiring (or merging with) breweries all over the world, and becoming a global operation with a balanced and attractive portfolio of businesses.

6.4.3.2 Strategic plans

In order to achieve the organisation's strategic goals, top managers develop strategic plans. These plans focus on the organisation as a whole and not on a specific function or operation, although the ultimate aim is to create synergy.

SABMiller's mission statement

SABMiller's mission is to "own and nurture local and international brands that are the first choice of the consumer"[9].

SABMiller's mission statement defines the organisation in terms of the following core components:

- product: local and international beer brands
- market: local and international beer consumers
- technology: owning and nurturing local and international beer brands (breweries).

This mission sets SABMiller apart from other organisations competing in the national and international beer market.

Top managers tasked with developing strategic plans have access to the necessary information about the organisation and its business environment. While formulating the strategic plans, these top managers interpret the opportunities and threats in the business environment and determine their potential impact on the organisation. The process requires managers to think conceptually, integrating the consequences of alternative strategic plans with the needs and resources of the organisation in order to create a competitive advantage.

Strategic plans usually refer to a period of more than five years, but this depends on the industry in which the organisation operates. Strategic plans filter down in the organisation to form the basis for tactical plans, and subsequently for operational plans.

There are two levels of strategic plans (or strategies): corporate strategies and business strategies.

Corporate strategies (or grand strategies) identify what businesses the organisation should be in, thus focusing on the scope of the organisation and how managers deploy resources. They also determine whether the organisation will expand its present business, buy or start other businesses, or reduce operations by selling or closing parts of the business.

SABMiller's corporate strategy

SABMiller's **corporate strategy** is to create a balanced and attractive global spread of businesses.

The following are examples of specific corporate strategies:

- A **market-development** strategy means that the organisation plans to develop existing markets for its present products more intensively or else to develop new markets for existing products. In the latter case, the organisation considers new regions or the export market. For example, SABMiller has used a market-development strategy in creating brewing interests and distribution agreements across six continents.
- A **product-development** strategy is when an organisation develops new products for existing markets or modifies existing products to win greater approval among consumers. For example, in the 1990s, SAB introduced Castle Lite to the existing market to satisfy beer drinkers' needs for a light beer.
- A **concentration-growth strategy** normally entails a business directing all its resources and skills to the profitable growth of a single product in a single market. In short, the business concentrates all that it has on what it does best to realise its mission. SA Breweries started as Castle Brewing in 1895. The first beer it produced was Castle Lager. The company directed all its resources to Castle Lager in the South African market until the 1950s, when it started expanding.
- An **innovation** strategy entails an organisation constantly improving products to take advantage of the initial high profitability of a better product. For example, SABMiller investigates and plans to act on new trends such as the demand for unique beers from small brewers.
- A **horizontal-integration** strategy involves taking over similar organisations. This strategy gives access to new markets and gets rid of competition. For example, SAB bought three breweries in the Czech Republic and combined them.
- In the case of a **vertical-integration** strategy, the organisation takes over other businesses, such as those providing raw materials or acting as outlets, with the purpose of ensuring a supply source or a distribution channel.
- A **joint-venture** strategy is when two or more firms embark on some project that is too big for one firm to tackle on its own. The advantage of such a strategy lies mainly in the pooling of resources and skills. For example, in 2008, SABMiller

formed a joint venture called MillerCoors with Molson Coors Brewing Company to combine their United States and Puerto Rico operations.
- A **diversification** strategy is when an organisation chooses to take over other firms and so enter into new activities or when it sets up a completely new entity. This strategy spreads risk, results in synergy and can achieve quicker growth or higher profits. For example, SABMiller has hotel and gaming interests through Tsogo Sun, the largest hotel and gaming group in South Africa.
- A **turnaround** strategy is a strategy that organisations follow during difficult times, when they may find their profits declining and they are compelled to cut costs by terminating unprofitable products, getting rid of unprofitable assets, and, in particular, improving ineffective management.
- A **divestiture** strategy usually involves selling a business or parts of it in line with its mission.
- A **liquidation** strategy occurs when an organisation admits failure and wants to keep shareholders' losses to a minimum.

Business strategies determine how best to compete in a particular industry or market. For example, SABMiller uses a different business strategy in China and in Australia. In China, SABMiller's Snow is the country's top-selling beer, yet profits are low because a business will lose market share if it tries to increase its profit margins. However, in Australia, SABMiller competes differently because the margins are extremely high.

6.4.4 Tactical goals and plans

The strategic goals and plans serve as input for middle managers to formulate tactical goals and plans (also called functional goals and plans). Tactical goals and plans are set at the level of middle management by the managers in each functional area. Tactical goals and plans focus on how to carry out those tasks necessary for the achievement of strategic goals.

6.4.4.1 Tactical goals

Tactical goals are medium-term or short-term goals derived from the long-term goals. For example, in order to increase market share from 10% to 20% over the next five years (a long-term goal), sales in an organisation will have to increase by 18% a year and the organisation will have to appoint additional staff (short-term goals).

6.4.4.2 Tactical plans

Tactical plans have a more specific focus when compared to strategic plans because they deal with people and actions. Middle-level managers who are department heads (such as marketing managers or operations managers) formulate medium-term plans for their various functional areas to realise tactical goals.

Tactical plans take into consideration strategic goals and plans, tactical goals, resource allocation, time issues and human-resources commitments.

Table 6.2 on page 188 shows examples of tactical or functional plans.

6.4.5 Operational goals and plans

Middle-level and lower-level managers develop operational goals and plans.

6.4.5.1 Operational goals

Operational goals (or short-term goals) refer to a period of no longer than one year. Operational goals deal with the day-to-day activities of an organisation and the allocation of resources. They take the form of unit goals and operational standards. Operational plans are executed by first-line managers.

6.4.5.2 Operational plans

Operational plans (or short-term plans) refer to a period of no longer than one year. The purpose of operational plans is to achieve operational goals. Two basic forms of operational plans are single-use plans and standing plans.

Single-use plans are developed to achieve a set of goals that are not likely to be repeated in future.

- A **program** is a set of plans for attaining a one-time organisational goal. An example of a program is the building of a new shopping mall.
- A **project** is also a set of plans for attaining a one-time organisational goal, but it is smaller in scope and complexity than a program. It is often part of a larger program. An example of a project could be the installation of the air-conditioning system for a new shopping mall.
- A **budget** is a numerical plan for allocating financial, human, physical and informational resources to specific activities.

Standing plans are ongoing plans that provide direction for tasks that are performed repeatedly in the organisation:

- **Policies** are broad in scope and are derived from the organisation's overall goals. Policies define the boundaries for decision-making to ensure that decisions are consistent with the organisation's goals. Examples of policies are: "The customer is always right" and: "We pay our employees competitive wages." They are broad guidelines on managerial action. First-line managers rarely make policies. Instead, they interpret and apply them. Managers must use their judgement within the limits set by policies. For instance, a policy of: "We pay our employees competitive wages" does not tell a manager what to pay a new employee. However, if the industry rate for this specific job were in the R100–R150 per hour range, the policy would clarify that offering an hourly starting rate of either R50 or R200 is not acceptable.
- A **rule** is a statement that prescribes to employees what they may or may not do in a specific situation. Managers often use rules when they confront a recurring problem to ensure consistency. For example, rules about lateness or absenteeism permit managers to make disciplinary decisions quickly and fairly.
- **Standard procedures** and methods define a precise series of steps to attain certain goals. Examples are procedures for handling employees' grievances and methods of issuing refunds.

6.6 The implementation of plans

Implementing the chosen plan involves developing a framework for its execution, leadership to set the plan in motion and the exercise of control to determine whether the performance of the activities is going according to plan. If there is a deviation from

Table 6.2: Tactical or functional plans

Functional-management areas	Key aspects to be considered
Marketing	Product line, market position, distribution channels, market communication and prices
Finance	Policy on debtors, dividends, asset management and capital structure
Production and operations	Improvement of productivity, location problems and legislation
Human resources	Labour relations, labour turnover, training of human resources and equity considerations
Purchasing	Suppliers, policy on creditors and sources of raw materials

the plan, control will reveal this and **reactive planning** will be necessary. This implies that managers may need to reconsider the goal and the resources required in order to fit the new information about the environment.

6.7 Summary

Planning is the starting point of the management process. It determines the "what" and "how" of planning. The "what" of planning refers to the various goals of the organisation and the "how" of planning describes the organisation's plans to achieve these goals. Goals and plans can be strategic, tactical or operational, and the period they refer to can be long term, medium term or short term respectively. To implement the plans, managers organise, lead and control organisational resources to achieve the long-term, medium-term and short-term goals of the organisation. The next three chapters deal with the functions of organising, leading and control.

Key terms

attainability	operational goals and plans
budget	planning context
business strategy	policies
concentration-growth strategy	product-development strategy
corporate strategy	program
diversification strategy	project
divestiture strategy	purpose
environment	relevancy
horizontal-integration strategy	rule
implementation of plans	single-use plan
innovation strategy	specificity
joint-venture strategy	standard procedure
liquidation strategy	standing plan
management by objectives	strategic goals and plans
managers' experience	tactical goals and plans
managers' values	time bound
market-development strategy	turnaround strategy
measurability	vertical-integration strategy
mission statement	vision

Questions for discussion

Reread the case study on pages 174–176 and answer the following questions:

1. What examples from the case study illustrate the benefits of planning?
2. What is the difference between planning, goals and plans?
3. Discuss the nature of goals and find an example in the case study to substantiate your arguments.
4. Explain what the planning context entails and use examples from the case study to illustrate your answer.
5. What examples of strategies were evident in the case study, but were not discussed elsewhere in this chapter?

Multiple-choice questions

Lower-level, middle-level and top-level managers perform the same management functions, but the focus of their activities is different. Consider the following statements and answer Questions 1, 2 and 3:

i. Focus on creating and maintaining a competitive advantage for the organisation.
ii. Develop plans focused on functional areas.
iii. Focus planning narrowly with short time horizons.

iv. Perform the management functions of planning and control.
v. Create a vision of the future for the organisation.
vi. Use standing plans.
vii. Use information that is specific and quantitative when planning.
viii. Set tactical goals.
ix. Focus on the entire organisation.
x. Implement strategic plans.

1. Statements __________ describe the work of lower-level managers.
   a. i, iv, v, ix
   b. ii, iv, vii, x
   c. iii, iv, vi, vii
   d. iv, v, vi, vii
2. Statements __________ describe the work of middle-level managers.
   a. i, iv, v, ix
   b. ii, iv, viii, x
   c. iii, iv, v, vi
   d. iv, v, vi, vii
3. Statements __________ describe the work of top-level managers.
   a. i, iv, v, ix
   b. ii, iv, vii, x
   c. iii, iv, v, vi
   d. iv, v, vi, vii
4. The core components of the mission, described in the mission statement, are __________.
   a. product, philosophy and market
   b. product, market and technology
   c. market, technology and strategy
   d. technology, product and vision
5. A strategy aimed at increasing market penetration within existing customer groups is a __________ strategy.
   a. market-development
   b. product-development
   c. concentric-diversification
   d. backward vertical-integration

Answers to multiple-choice questions

1. c
2. b
3. a
4. b
5. b

References

1. SABMiller. 2009. "SABMiller Annual Report", p. 4.
2. SABMiller. 2009. "SABMiller Annual Report", p. 2.
3. Kahn, M. 2009. "Chairman's statement" in "SABMiller Annual Report", p. 4.
4. Mackay, G. "Chief Executive's review" in "SABMiller Annual Report", p. 11.
5. Mackay, G. "Chief Executive's review" in "SABMiller Annual Report", p. 8.
6. Brevis, T. & Vrba, M.J. 2007. *Management principles: a contemporary edition for SAPS*. Cape Town: Juta, p. 148.
7. Drucker, P. 1954. "The practice of management". New York: Harper & Row, pp. 14–24.
8. SABMiller. 2009. "SABMiller 2009 – Business Overview". [Online] Available: http://www.sabmiller.com/files/pdf/corporate_presentation.pdf Accessed 2 December 2009.
9. SABMiller. 2009. "SABMiller 2009 – Business Overview". [Online] Available: http://www.sabmiller.com/files/pdf/corporate_presentation.pdf Accessed 2 December 2009.

CHAPTER

7

ORGANISING

The purpose of this chapter

Once management has devised a plan to achieve the organisation's goals, it must deploy resources such as people, equipment, money and physical resources. In addition, it must design jobs, assign tasks, duties and responsibilities to people, co-ordinate activities, and establish lines of communication and reporting. This is called organising. This chapter examines organising as the second fundamental task of management. An overview of the importance of organising is provided, followed by an examination of the fundamentals of organising. An exposition is given of how an organisation evolves from a one-man business to a large business organisation with many departments. Authority relationships as well as reporting relationships are explained, and thereafter co-ordination is discussed. A brief overview of the informal organisation is also given. Finally, the factors influencing the design of an organisation's structure are discussed, and it is emphasised that such a structure must enable the people concerned to work effectively towards the organisation's mission and goals.

Learning outcomes

On completion of this chapter you should be able to:

- explain the concepts of organising and organisational structure
- describe the importance of organising
- discuss the fundamentals of organising
- explain how an organisation evolves from a single-entrepreneur organisation to a large one
- present viewpoints regarding the factors that influence organising.

7.1 Introduction

Planning, the first fundamental element of the management process, is defined as the setting of goals and the development of a plan of action to achieve the goals as productively as possible. Thus planning requires managers to decide where the organisation should go in future and how to get it there. Planning, however, is only one component of the management process, and it alone cannot guarantee that the goals of the business organisation will be accomplished. Once the plan to achieve certain goals has been selected, management must combine human and other resources, such as money, machines, raw materials and information or knowledge, in the best possible way to achieve the organisation's goals. The most important of these is the task of grouping people into teams, functions or departments to perform the activities that will convert the plan into accomplished goals. In the Edcon case study that follows, note the grouping of people and other resources in three divisions: the department-store division, the discount-store division and the financial-services division. The structured grouping and combining of people and other resources, and co-ordinating them to achieve organisational goals, constitute the second fundamental element of management: organising.

Organising means that management has to develop mechanisms in order to implement the strategy or plan. The organising process's point of departure is the vision, mission, goals and strategies of the organisation. Arrangements have to be made to determine what activities will be carried out, what resources will be employed, and who will perform the various activities in order to achieve the organisation's vision, mission and goals. This involves the distribution of tasks among employees, the allocation of resources to persons and departments, and giving the necessary authority to certain people to ensure that the tasks are in fact carried out. Above all, there must be communication, co-operation and **co-ordination** between the people and the departments or sections performing the tasks. Lastly, a control mechanism should be put in place to ensure that the chosen organisational structure does indeed enable the organisation to attain its vision, mission and goals.

The organising process leads to the creation of an **organisational structure**, which defines how tasks are divided and resources are deployed. Organisational structure can be defined in the following three ways:

- the set of formal tasks assigned to individuals and departments
- formal reporting relationships, which include the lines of authority, responsibility, the number of hierarchical levels and the span of management's control
- the design of systems to ensure effective co-ordination of employees across departments.

Ensuring co-ordination across departments is just as critical as defining the departments to begin with. Without effective co-ordination systems, no organisational structure is complete.

The set of formal tasks and formal reporting relationships provides a framework for the vertical control of the organisation. The characteristics of vertical structure are portrayed in the organisation chart, which is the visual representation of an organisation's structure.

In a newly established business, decisions have to be taken about equipment, supplies, processes to be followed and the people who must perform the tasks. In addition, the structure indicating the distribution of tasks among departments and individuals has to be drawn up, indicating the responsibilities and lines of authority and communication. In an existing business, organising has to be constantly reviewed and adapted to accommodate new strategies, new products and new processes or any organisational changes that affect the activities. In line with the strategy or plan, management still arranges what needs to be done so as to reach the objectives.

The case study on page 193 provides an illustration on how the principles of organising are applied to a real-life situation in South Africa.

7.2 The importance of organising

Organising, like planning, is an integral and indispensable component of the management process. Without it, the successful implementation of plans and strategies is not possible because of the absence of a systematic, effective and efficient allocation of resources and people to execute the plans. Leadership and control are not possible if the

Case study

Organising in Action: Edgars Consolidated Stores Ltd (Edcon)

Edcon (Pty) Ltd is the leading clothing, footwear and textiles (CFT) retailing group in South Africa through a range of retail formats. The first Edgars store was opened on 6 September 1929 in Joubert Street, Johannesburg. Since then, the company has grown to ten retail brands trading in over 1 000 stores in South Africa, Botswana, Namibia, Swaziland and Lesotho.

Edcon's retail business has, through recent acquisitions, added top stationery and houseware brands as well as general merchandise to its CFT portfolio. Defined by the target market served, all retail business is structured under two divisions:

- the department-stores division, including Edgars, CNA, Boardmans, Prato, Red Square and Temptations, serving middle- and upper-income markets
- the discount division, including Jet, Jet Mart, Jet Shoes, Legit and Blacksnow, serving middle- to lower-income markets.

Edcon Financial Services provides credit facilities and financial-services products to the group's cardholders (in excess of four million people).

Edcon has over 20 000 employees who, according to the Deloitte/Financial Mail "Best Company to Work For" survey, consider it the best retail company to work for.

Source: Edcon. 2008. "Welcome to Edcon" [Online] Available: http://www.edcon.co.za Accessed 1 February 2010.

activities of management and subordinates are not organised, or if the business does not clearly designate the individuals responsible for specific tasks.

The reasons for the importance of organising in an organisation include the following points:

- Organising entails a detailed analysis of work to be done and resources to be used to accomplish the aims of the business. It is through organising that tasks and resources, and methods or procedures, can be systematised. Everyone should know their duties, authority and responsibility, the procedures they must follow or the methods they have to adopt, and the resources they can use. Proper organising ensures that the joint and co-ordinated efforts of management have a much greater and more effective result than the sum of individual efforts.
- Organising divides the total workload into activities that can comfortably be performed by an individual or a group. Tasks are allocated according to the abilities or qualifications of individuals, thus ensuring that nobody in the business has either too much or too little to do. The ultimate result is higher productivity.
- Organising promotes the productive deployment and utilisation of resources.
- Related activities and tasks of individuals are grouped together rationally in specialised departments, such as marketing, personnel or finance departments, in which experts in their particular fields carry out their given duties.
- The development of an organisational structure results in a mechanism that co-ordinates the activities of the whole business into complete, uniform, harmonious units.

Successful organising, then, makes it possible for a business to achieve its goals. It co-ordinates the activities of managers and subordinates to avoid the unnecessary duplication of tasks, and it obviates possible conflicts. It also reduces the chances of doubts and misunderstandings, enabling the business to reach its goals efficiently. Against this background, an examination of the building blocks or the fundamentals of organising will follow.

7.3 The fundamentals of organising

Building an organisational structure revolves around the building blocks or the fundamentals of organising. There are five building blocks or fundamentals of organising that managers can use in constructing an organisation:

- designing jobs
- grouping jobs (departmentalisation)
- establishing reporting relationships
- establishing authority relationships
- co-ordinating activities.

7.3.1 Designing jobs

The first building block of organisational structure is **job design**. Job design is the determination of an employee's work-related responsibilities. The job design and description of a sales manager of the department-store division of Edcon, for example, would give a detailed exposition of sales objectives per week, per month and per year.

The point of departure when designing jobs for employees is to determine the level of **specialisation** or the degree to which the overall task of the organisation is broken down into smaller, more specialised tasks. Specialisation is the way in which a task is broken up into smaller units to take advantage of specialised knowledge or skills to improve productivity. **Job specialisation** is normally an extension of organisational growth. Put differently, the growing business is continually compelled to apply specialisation or the division of labour. This is illustrated in the case study about The Walt Disney Company on this page.

Job specialisation provides benefits as well as limitations to organisations. Table 7.1 on page 195 summarises the benefits and limitations of job specialisation.

Although some degree of specialisation is necessary in every organisation, it should not be carried to extremes because of the possible negative consequences. Managers should be sensitive to situations in which extreme specialisation should be avoided.

To counter the limitations or problems associated with specialisation, managers

Case study

The Walt Disney Company

The Walt Disney Company is the largest media and entertainment conglomerate in the world, known for its family-friendly products. The company was founded as an animation studio on October 16 1923 by brothers Walt and Roy Disney. In those early days, the entrepreneur Walt Disney did everything himself. He wrote cartoons, drew the pictures and then marketed his movies to theatres. As the business grew, he hired additional animators as well as other employees to perform many of these functions. As growth continued, so too, did specialisation. Today 150 000 employees work for the six divisions of the company: Walt Disney Studio Entertainment, Disney-ABC Television Group, Disney Interactive Media Group, Disney Consumer Products, Walt Disney Parks and Resorts, and Disney Interactive Studios.

Source: Wikipedia. 2010. "The Walt Disney Company". [Online] Available: http://en.wikipedia.org/wiki/The_Walt_Disney_Company Accessed 1 February 2010.

Table 7.1: The benefits and limitations of specialisation

Benefits of specialisation	Limitations of specialisation
Workers performing small and simple tasks become very proficient at each task.	Workers who perform highly specialised jobs may become bored and dissatisfied, which may lead to absenteeism and lower quality of work.
The transfer time between tasks decreases. If employees perform several different tasks, some time is lost as they stop doing a task and move to the next task.	The anticipated benefits of specialisation do not always occur. For example, the time spent on moving work in process from worker to worker can be greater than the time needed for the same individual to change from job to job.
The more narrowly defined a job is, the easier it is to develop specialised equipment to assist with that job.	
When an employee who performs a highly specialised job is absent or resigns, the manager is able to train somebody new at relatively low cost.	

Source: Griffin, R.W. 2005. *Management.* 8th ed. Boston: Houghton Mifflin Company, p. 344.

have sought other approaches to job design that achieve a better balance between organisational demands for productivity, efficiency and effectiveness on the one hand, and individual needs for creativity and autonomy on the other. Job rotation, job enlargement, job enrichment and work teams are amongst these alternative approaches.

Job rotation involves systematically moving employees from one job to another. For example, a worker in a warehouse might unload trucks on Monday, carry incoming inventory on Tuesday, verify invoices on Wednesday, pull outgoing inventory from storage on Thursday and load trucks on Friday. The jobs do not change, but instead, workers move from job to job. For this very reason, job rotation has not been very successful in enhancing employee motivation or satisfaction. Jobs that are amenable to rotation tend to be relatively standard and routine. Job rotation is most often used today as a training device to improve worker skills and flexibility.

Job enlargement was developed to increase the total number of tasks that a worker performs. As a result, all workers perform a variety of tasks. It was assumed that this would reduce the level of job dissatisfaction. Unfortunately, although job enlargement does have some positive consequences, these advantages are often offset by the disadvantages. For example, training costs may be higher, unions may argue that pay should increase because the worker is doing more tasks, and in many cases, work remains boring and routine even after job enlargement has taken place.

Job enrichment is a more comprehensive approach than job rotation and job enlargement. It involves increasing both the number of tasks the worker does and the control the worker has over the job. To implement job enrichment, managers remove some controls from the job, delegate more authority to employees and structure the work in complete units. Job enrichment may also involve continually assigning new and challenging tasks, thereby increasing employees' opportunities for growth and advancement.

Another alternative to job specialisation is work teams. Work teams allow an entire group to design the work system it will use to perform an interrelated set of tasks. For example, a work team may assign specific tasks to team members, monitor and control its own performance, and have autonomy over work-scheduling.

7.3.2 Grouping jobs: Departmentalisation

A second principle or building block of organisational structure is the formation of departments. While this is a result of specialisation, it also promotes specialisation since it is necessitated by the logical grouping of activities that belong together. By grouping financial-services activities into one division, Edcon allows its employees to specialise in this field and also to contribute to the company's overall performance. The reasons for **departmentalisation** are therefore inherent in the advantages of specialisation and the pressure in a growing business to split the total task of management into smaller units. As soon as a business has reached a given size, it becomes impossible for the owner-manager to supervise all the employees, and so it becomes necessary to create new managerial positions according to departments based on a logical grouping, in manageable sizes, of the activities that belong together.

The various departments created constitute the organisational structure of the business as they appear on the organisation chart. Depending on such factors as the size and kind of business, and the nature of its activities, various organisational structures may be developed through departmentalisation.

Some common bases for departmentalisation include the following:

- functional departmentalisation
- product departmentalisation
- location departmentalisation
- customer departmentalisation
- the matrix organisational structure.

7.3.2.1 Functional departmentalisation

Functional departmentalisation, as shown in Figure 7.1, is the most basic type of departmentalisation. Here, activities belonging to each management function are grouped together. Activities such as advertising, market research and sales, for example, belong together under the marketing function, while activities concerned with the production of goods are grouped under operations.

7.3.2.2 Product departmentalisation

Product departmentalisation is illustrated in Figure 7.2 on page 197. Departments are designed so that all activities concerned with the manufacturing of a product or group of products are grouped together in product sections, where all the specialists associated with the particular products are grouped. Edcon applied product departmentalisation by grouping all its activities and resources into three divisions. Edcon's personnel, financing and marketing needs for the various divisions will differ. For example, the personnel, marketing and financing needs for the department-store division will differ from those needs in the financial-services division. This is a logical structure for large businesses

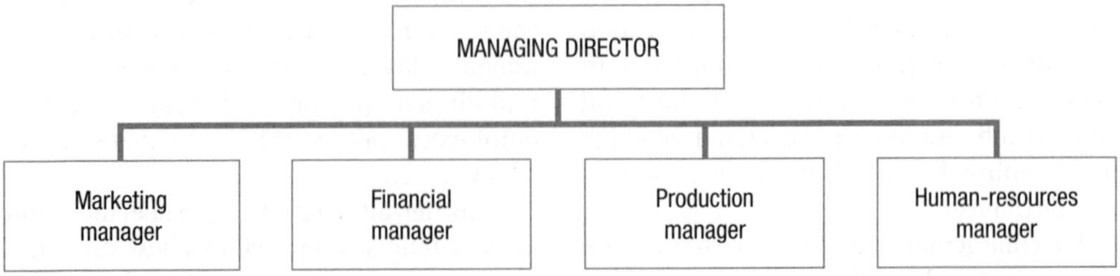

Figure 7.1: Functional departmentalisation

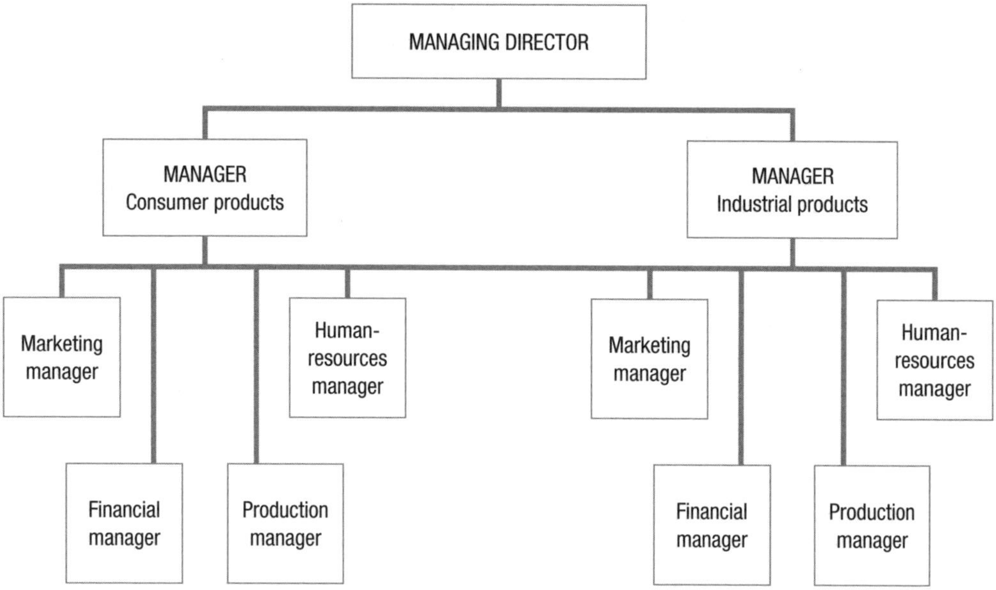

Figure 7.2: Product departmentalisation

providing a wide range of products or services. The advantages of this structure are that the specialised knowledge of employees is used to maximum effect, decisions can be made quickly within a section and the performance of each group can be measured easily. The disadvantages are that the managers in each section concentrate their attention almost exclusively on their products and tend to lose sight of the products of the rest of the business. Moreover, administrative costs increase because each section has to have its own functional specialists such as market researchers and financial experts.

7.3.2.3 Location departmentalisation

Location departmentalisation is illustrated in Figure 7.3 on page 198. This is a logical structure for a business that manufactures and sells its products in different geographical regions, for example, SABMiller, which operates and markets its range of products all over the country as well as internationally. This structure gives autonomy to area managements, which is necessary to facilitate decentralised decision-making and adjustment to local business environments. This structure is also suitable for a multi-national business.

7.3.2.4 Customer departmentalisation

Customer departmentalisation is adopted particularly where a business concentrates on some special segment of the market or group of consumers or, in the case of industrial products, where it sells its wares to a limited group of users. Figure 7.4 on page 198 illustrates this structure. The structure has the same advantages and disadvantages as departmentalisation according to product and location or geographical area. A bank, for example, can have various departments servicing private and corporate clients.

Unlike a functional structure in which activities are grouped according to knowledge, skills, experience or training, a section based on product, location or customers resembles, in some respects, a small privately owned business. It is more or less autonomous and is accountable for its profits or losses. However, unlike an independent small business, it is still subject to the goals and strategies set by top management for the business as a whole.

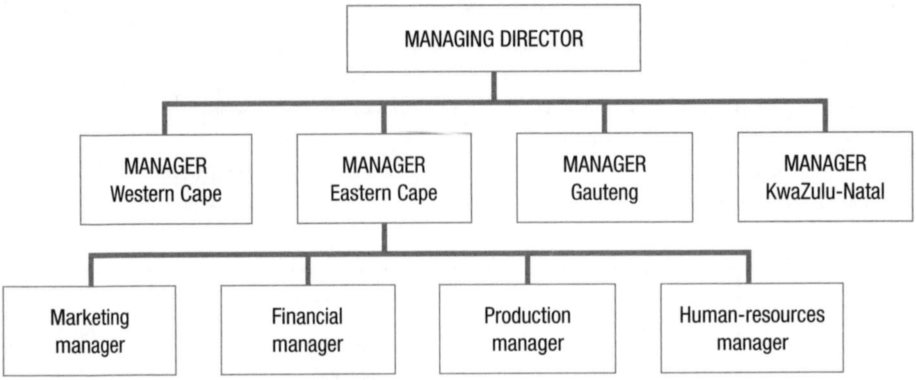

Figure 7.3: Location departmentalisation

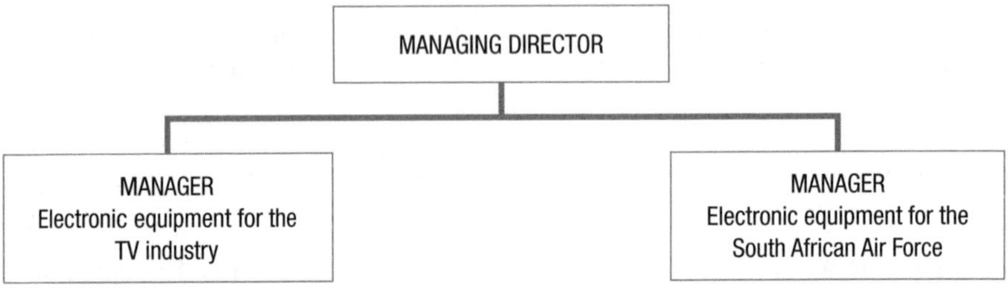

Figure 7.4: Customer departmentalisation

7.3.2.5 Matrix organisational structure

The **matrix organisational structure** is important because no organisational structure, whether designed according to function, product, location or customer, will necessarily meet all the organisational needs of a particular business. Where departments are formed according to function, there is sophisticated specialisation, but co-ordination remains a problem. If they are formed according to product, location or customer, certain products or regions may be successful, but the rest of the business will not reap the benefits of good organisation. To overcome these problems, which mainly occur in large businesses and in businesses handling specific projects, the matrix organisational structure has been created to incorporate the advantages of both structures discussed earlier. As indicated in Figure 7.5 on page 199, horizontal (staff) and vertical (line) authority lines occur in the same structure so that project managers (horizontal) and functional managers (vertical) both have authority.

This organisational structure is particularly suited to *ad hoc* and complex projects requiring specialised skills. For example, IBM created a matrix structure for the development of its personal computer and disbanded the team when the product had been launched successfully. However, in other businesses, the matrix structure may be permanent. An example is a car manufacturer that continually develops certain models as projects. The major advantage of the matrix structure is that specialist project managers can help manage complex projects while the advantages of functional specialisation are retained. The disadvantage is divided authority. Both project leader and departmental head can exercise authority over the same subordinates. The unity of command is therefore affected, and there is a serious risk of soured relations between the

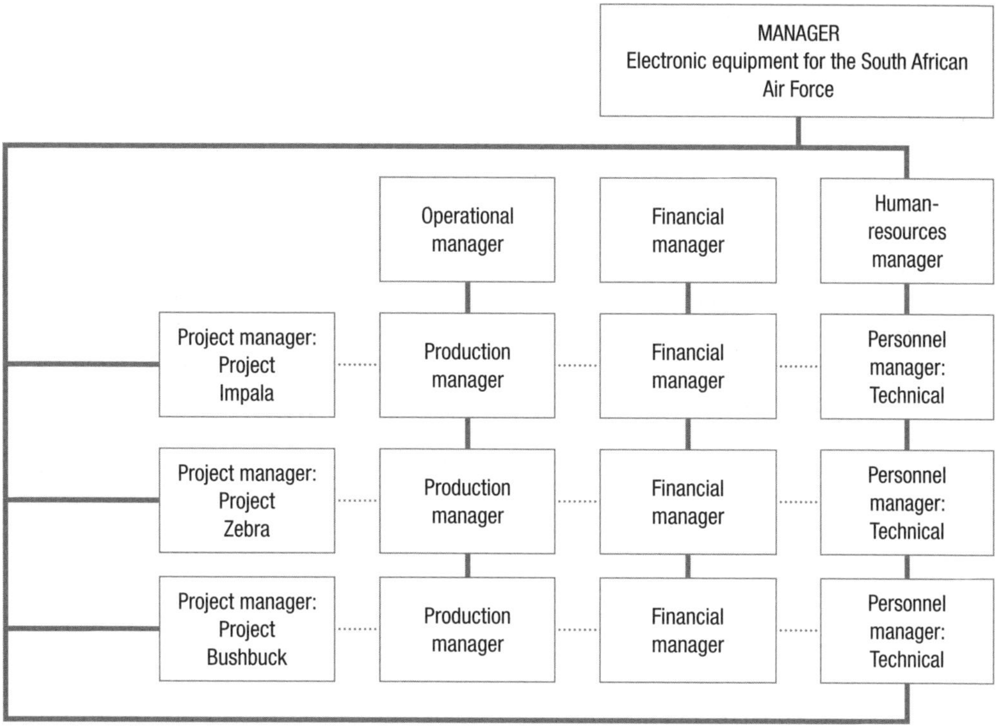

Figure 7.5: The matrix organisational structure

project and functional executives. In addition, the position of subordinates may be difficult since they have to satisfy two bosses.

The case study about ABB that follows is an illustration of a real-life matrix organisation.

Case study

Managing a matrix organisation

Perhaps the largest and most well-documented example of a matrix organisation is ABB, which was created by the merger of the Swedish firm Asea and the Swiss firm Brown Boveri, and managed by Percy Barnevik for its first decade after the merger. Barnevik's challenge was to create a streamlined entrepreneurial organisation with as few hierarchical layers as possible, starting with what was essentially a group of 1 300 companies with more than 200 000 employees in 150 countries. To do this, he introduced what came to be a highly regarded and very complex matrix organisational structure, which divided ABB into 35 business areas, more than 100 country organisations and 5 000 profit centres. Each of these 5 000 divisions was expected to show a profit. The manager of a profit centre would report to both a country manager and a business area manager.

Source: Dyck, B. & Neubert, M.J. 2010. *Principles of management.* International edition, p. 307. ©South-Western, a part of Cengage Learning, Inc. Reproduced by permission. www.cengage.com/permissions.

7.3.3 Establishing reporting relationships

The third basic principle or building block of organisational structure is the establishment of reporting relationships among positions. An organisation like Edcon needs to be able to answer questions such as: Will the marketing manager of Edcon's department store division report to the operations manager, or will the operations manager report to the marketing manager? Or should both report to the general manager? Furthermore, who should report to Edcon's chief executive officer?

The first step in establishing **reporting lines** is to determine who reports to whom. Clear and precise reporting lines are important so that everybody knows who is in charge of what activities. This is called the **chain of command**. The chain of command can formally be defined as a clear and distinct line of authority among the positions in an organisation. The chain of command has two components: the unity of command and the scalar principle. Unity of command suggests that each person within an organisation must have a clear reporting relationship to one, and only one, supervisor. The scalar principle suggests that there must be a clear and unbroken line of authority that extends from the lowest to the highest position in the organisation. The popular saying, "The buck stops here" is derived from this idea. Someone in the organisation must ultimately be accountable for every decision.

The second step in establishing reporting lines is to determine how many people will report to one manager, known as the **span of management** (also called the span of control). Figure 7.6 illustrates this concept schematically.

For years, managers and researchers sought to determine the optimal span of management. For example, should it be narrow (with few subordinates per manager) or wide (with many subordinates per manager)? A narrow span of management will result in a relatively tall organisational structure, which may mean that managers are being under-utilised and that there is excessive control over subordinates. A wide span of management will result in a flat organisational structure, in which it may be difficult to co-ordinate and control the tasks

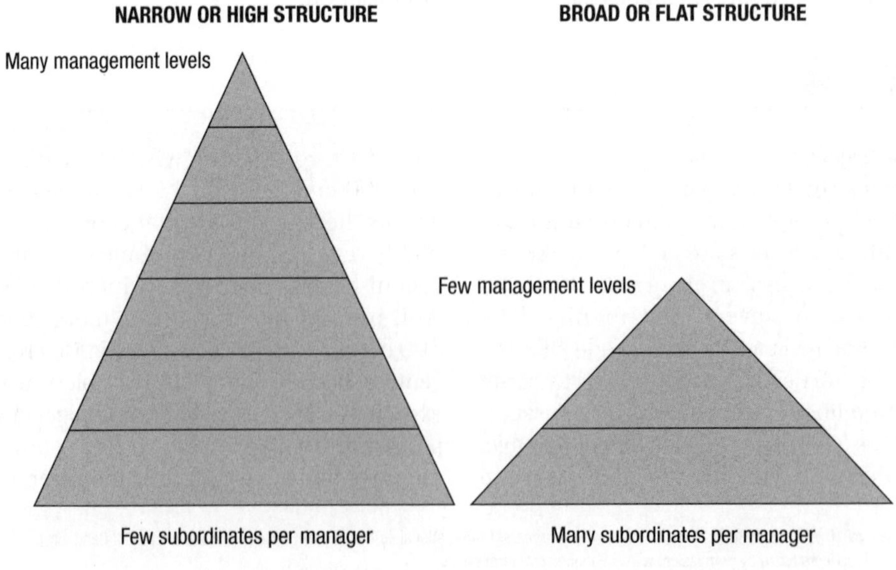

Figure 7.6: The span of management

The span of management

The following factors influence the appropriate span of management:

- the skills, competence and maturity of the supervisor and the subordinate (the greater the skills, competence and maturity are, the wider the potential span of management is)
- the physical dispersion of subordinates (the greater the dispersion is, the narrower the potential span of management is)
- the complexity of the business (the more complex the business is, the narrower the potential span of management is)
- the extent of non-supervisory work in a manager's job (the more non-supervisory work there is, the narrower the potential span of management is)
- the degree of required interaction between supervisor and subordinate (the less interaction that is required, the wider the potential span of management is)
- the extent of standardised procedures (the more standardised the procedures are, the wider the potential span of management is)
- the similarity of tasks being supervised (the more similar the tasks being supervised are, the wider the potential span of management is)
- the frequency of new problems (the more frequently new problems arise, the narrower the potential span of management is)
- the preferences of supervisors and subordinates.

Source: Adapted from Griffin, R.W. 2005. *Management*. 8th ed. Boston: Houghton Mifflin, p. 355.

of a large number of subordinates. In order to find the ideal or most appropriate span of management for an organisation, various factors should be taken into account.

In some organisations, additional factors may influence the optimal span of management. The relative importance of each factor also varies in different organisational settings. Hence, managers need to assess the relative weight of each appropriate factor or set of factors when deciding on the optimal span of management for their unique situation.

7.3.4 Establishing authority relationships

The fourth building block in structuring organisations is the determination of how authority is to be distributed among positions. The previous section discussed the process of task distribution. Here, the total task of the business is broken up into smaller specialised units that are allocated to certain departments and persons. However, this is not the end point of organising. The assignment of tasks to sections and members of staff also entails the assignment of responsibility, authority and accountability to each post in an organisational structure. This further entails the creation of organisational relations, that is, stipulating the persons from whom subordinates receive instructions, to whom they report, and to whom and for what they are responsible.

Responsibility can be defined as the duty to perform the task or activity as assigned. **Authority**, on the other hand, is the right to command or to give orders. Authority is power that has been legitimised by the organisation. It includes the right to take action to compel the performance of duties and to punish default or negligence. In the formal business structure, several examples of which have been discussed, the owners of the business possess the formal authority. They appoint directors and give them authority. These directors in turn appoint managers, who assign a certain authority to subordinates. In this way, authority flows down the line.

Formal authority is distinguished by three characteristics:

- Formal authority is vested in organisational positions, not in people. Managers have formal authority based on their position in the formal organisational hierarchy. Other people in the same position have the same authority.
- Formal authority is accepted by subordinates. Subordinates comply in an organisation because they believe that managers have a legitimate right to issue orders.
- Formal authority flows down the vertical hierarchy of an organisation. Positions at the top of the organisational hierarchy are vested with more formal authority than positions at the bottom.

An important distinction in many organisations is between line authority and staff authority, reflecting whether managers work in line or staff departments in the organisational structure.

7.3.4.1 Line authority

Line authority is authority delegated down through the line of command. In Figure 7.7, the managing director has line authority over the financial, human-resources and marketing managers, while the marketing manager has line authority over the advertising manager, and so on, down the line of command. The managers in this line are directly responsible for achieving the goals of the organisation.

7.3.4.2 Staff authority

Staff authority is an indirect and supplementary authority. Individuals or sections with staff authority, for example, the legal adviser and the marketing-research section shown in Figure 7.7, assist, advise and recommend. Their source of authority is usually their special knowledge of a particular field.

Accountability is the mechanism through which authority and responsibility are brought into alignment. Accountability means that the people with authority and

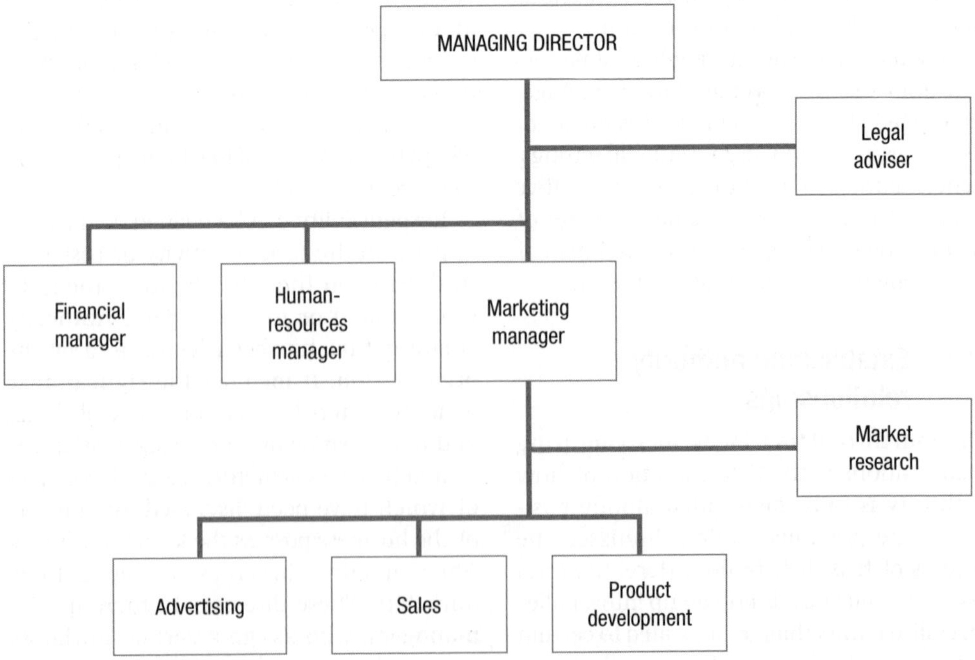

Figure 7.7: Line and staff authority in the organisational structure

responsibility are subject to reporting and justifying task outcomes to those above them in the chain of command. For an organisation to function well, every employee needs to know what he/she is accountable for, and accept the responsibility and authority for performing those tasks.

Another important concept related to authority relationships is delegation. **Delegation** is the process used by managers to transfer authority and responsibility to positions below them in the organisational hierarchy. It is important to note that managers can delegate authority and responsibility, but they will always stay accountable for the task outcomes.

Just as authority and responsibility can be delegated from one individual to another, organisations also develop patterns of authority across a wide variety of positions and departments. **Decentralisation** is the process of systematically delegating power and authority throughout the organisation to middle- and lower-level managers. It is important to note that decentralisation is actually one end of a continuum anchored at the other end by **centralisation**, the process of systematically retaining power and authority in the hands of higher-level managers. Thus, in a decentralised organisation, decision-making power and authority are delegated as far down in the chain of command as possible. In a centralised organisation, decision-making power and authority are retained at the higher levels of management.

Once authority relationships have been completed, management has to design an organisational structure that will enable the various jobs to be done in a co-ordinated fashion.

7.3.5 Co-ordinating activities

The fifth and last building block in structuring an organisation is co-ordination.

Organisation means dividing up the total task of the business into smaller units so as to take advantage of specialisation and achieve the goals of the business as productively as possible. However, this division of work into smaller jobs immediately raises the problem of co-operation, or the co-ordination of divided tasks and various departments into an integrated whole to achieve the goals of the business.

The key to keeping each department focused on the organisation's goals is co-ordination or the process of linking the activities of the various departments in the organisation into a single integrated unit. The primary reason for co-ordination is that departments and groups are interdependent. They depend on each other for resources in order to be able to perform their activities. The greater the interdependence between the departments, the more co-ordination the organisation acquires.

In the case of Edcon, the various sections in the department-store division are interdependent. Furthermore, all three divisions of Edcon are interdependent. The combined performance of the three divisions will determine the overall performance of Edgars Consolidated Stores Ltd.

Without co-ordination, individuals and departments lose sight of the organisation's primary goals and of their part in that effort. Co-ordination is the synthesis of separate parts into a unity, and as such it is the binding factor in the managerial process. It means the integration of goals and tasks at all levels, and also the integration of all departments and functions to enable the business to work as a whole. In addition, an element of timing is necessary because various smaller tasks have to be scheduled to mesh with each other.

Hence, co-ordination is an endeavour by management to develop congruence, or harmony of goals, through organising. Other mechanisms that promote co-ordination are the organisation chart, the budget, a committee, the broad policy and procedures in accordance with which tasks are carried out, and the information system of the business.

Once management has deployed all the building blocks of the organisation, it can finalise the formal structure of the organisation. Besides the formal organisation of a business, there is also an informal organisation that often supplements it and helps it to run smoothly.

7.4 The informal organisation

So far, only the formal organisation has been considered. However, relations within a particular business are not confined to those prescribed by the formal organisation chart. Alongside the formal structure there is also an informal organisation, which may be defined as the interpersonal relations between people in a business that are not defined by the formal organisational structure.

Because there is regular interaction between people, social relations are established that assume a definite form. This interaction is achieved by informal communication, also known as "the grapevine". Moreover, these relations exist not only between individuals, but also between groups, though on an informal basis. If these relations are sound, they can support the formal structure, but if not, they may include activities that are not in harmony with those activities envisaged in the formal structure. Rather than trying to suppress the informal structure, management should encourage it, for the following reasons:

- Informal communication takes place much more rapidly than formal communication, and therefore decision-making could be expedited.
- The informal organisation promotes teamwork within departments, as well as co-operation between departments.
- The informal organisation supports the formal organisation.

Having considered the basis of the task of organising, we will now examine some of the factors that may influence the organisational structure.

7.5 Factors that influence organisational structure

Organising can only be carried out effectively if the organisational structure has been developed to optimise the execution of strategies and plans. In other words, plans can only be implemented successfully if the organisational structure makes this possible. Planning, leading and control are facilitated if management has an effective and dynamic organisational structure. This raises the question: Which organisational structure is the best? There is no definite answer. Each business must choose a structure that is best suited to its particular activities or may be adapted to its strategy and requirements.

Organising is carried out in a context where many different factors need to be taken into account. Each of these factors may provide input in the designing of the organisational structure.

Some experts believe that the environment in which a business operates is a decisive factor. Others emphasise the connection between strategy and structure. Obviously, the size and complexity of the business, the competence of its employees, and the nature of the product and the market all play important parts. Moreover, the organisational climate or corporate culture should not be ignored in designing the structure, and in forming departments and distributing tasks. Above all, according to modern management theory, whatever structure is designed should be adaptable to changes in the business environment. These factors will now be examined briefly.

7.5.1 The environment in which a business operates

The environment in which a business operates may be taken as a basis for designing an organisational structure, since it is the starting point for the development of strategy, on the one hand, and because the organisational structure is the mechanism that should keep the business in touch with its environment, on the other. A business has to adapt to its environment to survive. There are various types of environment.

7.5.1.1 Stable environment

A stable environment is one that does not change much or is not subject to unexpected change. Here, product changes are the exception rather than the rule and, when a change does occur, plans can be made to cope with it in good time. Demand for the product is regular, with only slight fluctuations. New technological changes are small or unlikely. A foundry manufacturing manhole covers and a workshop making violins both operate in stable environments. In a stable environment, the functional structure is suitable because there is little in the way of innovation, and no great need for co-ordination and co-operation between departments. Similarly, businesses with fewer competing markets, which are under less pressure regarding product development to satisfy consumers' needs (for example, a manufacturer of nuts and bolts), will have a functional structure with few specialists such as market researchers and advertising experts. Decision-making takes place mainly at the top level.

7.5.1.2 Turbulent environment

A turbulent environment is one in which changes are the norm rather than the exception: competitors unexpectedly bring out new products and technological innovations cause revolutionary changes in the manufacturing process or the product itself. The pharmaceutical industry is an example of such an environment, which necessitates many specialists for market research, product development and production, and close co-ordination and communication between them. In such a business, departmentalisation according to product is especially suitable, as this speeds up decision-making. More decisions are made in the separate departments than by top management. The retail environment in which Edcon operates is a challenging environment. Edcon boasts ten retail brands with over 1 000 stores. Product departmentalisation is therefore also suitable for the company. Businesses in stable environments are less differentiated in structure than businesses in turbulent environments.

7.5.1.3 Technologically dominated environment

The organisational design for a technologically dominated environment (when a particular technology forms the basis for a business's product) will be influenced by the level of technological sophistication. Technologically complex firms tend to have more managers and more levels of management because specialised technicians work in small groups with a narrow span. Technology and especially technological innovation require an adaptable organisational structure that is based on one or other form of departmentalisation.

7.5.2 The relationship between strategy and structure

The close relationship between the strategy of a business and its organisational structure is well known. The implication is that the strategy provides a direct input in the design of the organisational structure and that the structure cannot be separated from the strategy. Structure should always follow strategy.

7.5.3 The size of the business

It is equally obvious that the structure also depends on the number of employees and managers to be co-ordinated. An increase in the size of the business also creates a need for greater specialisation, more departments and more levels of management. The danger of bureaucratic management as a result of detailed procedures, strict job demarcation and, consequently, less emphasis on initiative and regeneration, is always present in large businesses.

7.5.4 Staff employed by the business

There is also a close relationship between an organisational structure and the competence and role of staff, whether this competence is a result of training or experience, availability or attitude. Edcon has established the Edcon Academy, which provides training related to merchandising and operations to employees. In this way, Edcon improves the competence of its staff. In management, especially in top management, the structure influences both the choice of strategy and the preferences as to how things should be done. Most managers have a personal preference for a particular organisational structure, for the type of relations with subordinates, and also attitudes to formality and authority. As to the latter two, some experts maintain that the tendency is to move away from the strictly formal bureaucratic structure.

7.5.5 The organisational culture

The final factor that plays an important part in organisational design is organisational culture. This so-called culture is a concept that may be defined as the beliefs and values shared by people in a business. It is the "personality" of the business. Unless management analyses this concept correctly, it will never know why employees do, or do not do, certain things. Corporate culture comprises basic values that are reflected not only in organisational behavioural patterns, but also in aspects such as the business's architecture, office decor, dress regulations and the general way in which things are done. Edcon's culture is one of inclusiveness, built on the organisation's values of people, integrity, performance and professionalism.

The type of structure that leads to the successful implementation of tasks also depends on the culture of the business. The structure of a business with a formal culture will differ from one with a more informal culture.

These factors are some of the considerations that may influence the design of an organisational structure. They are, however, no more than guidelines for organising. It should be understood that the organising process is not only used for a new structure. Any existing organisational structure should be revised whenever the organisation's strategy or plans are changed.

7.6 Summary

The setting in motion of the planned activities is part of the organising task of management. Organising is the development of a structure or framework within which the tasks to be performed for the accomplishment of goals and the resources necessary for this are allocated to particular individuals and departments. This division of labour may be done in various ways, and must ultimately be co-ordinated to make concerted action possible. Someone, however, has to take the lead in setting in motion the activities involved in the various phases of planning, organising and control. The third fundamental element of management will be dealt with in Chapter 8.

Key terms

authority	matrix organisational structure
chain of command	organisational culture
co-ordination	organisational structure
customer departmentalisation	organising
departmentalisation	product departmentalisation
functional departmentalisation	reporting lines

job design	responsibility
job specialisation	span of management
location departmentalisation	work specialisation

Questions for discussion

Reread the case study on page 193 and answer the following questions:

1. Do you agree that departmentalisation according to product is the most suitable organisational structure for Edcon? Substantiate your answer.
2. Identify the various authority relations that could exist in the Edcon group.
3. Do you think that a narrow or high organisational structure would be appropriate for Edcon? Substantiate your answer.
4. Identify factors that could influence the organisational design of Edcon.

Multiple-choice questions

1. Look at the statements below.
   i. The transfer time between tasks may decrease.
   ii. Workers performing small and simple tasks will become very proficient at each task.
   iii. Specialisation may lead to absenteeism and lower quality of work.
   iv. When an employee who performs a highly specialised job is absent or resigns, the cost of training a replacement is high.
   v. The more narrowly defined a job is, the easier it is to develop specialised equipment to assist with that job.

   Now select the combination of statements that are all benefits of specialisation.
   a. i, ii
   b. i, ii, v
   c. iii, iv, v
   d. iv, v
2. Mrs Mabula, the operations manager of a large organisation, decides to remove some controls from the jobs that her subordinates perform, to delegate more authority to subordinates and to structure the work in complete work units. Mrs Mabula is implementing __________.
   a. work teams
   b. job enlargement
   c. job enrichment
   d. job rotation
3. In __________, horizontal and vertical authority lines occur in the same organisational structure so that project managers and functional managers both have authority.
   a. product departmentalisation
   b. customer departmentalisation
   c. a matrix organisational structure
   d. location departmentalisation
4. Which one of the following is a characteristic of formal authority in an organisation?
   a. Formal authority is vested in people.
   b. Formal authority is accepted by subordinates.
   c. Formal authority flows down the horizontal hierarchy of an organisation.
   d. Formal authority cannot be delegated to lower levels of management.
5. Read the list of factors below.
   i. The environment in which an organisation operates
   ii. The strategy of the organisation
   iii. The competence and role of staff
   iv. The organisational culture
   v. The size of the organisation

   Now select the combination of factors that influence organisational structure.
   a. i, ii
   b. i, ii, iii, iv, v
   c. ii, iv, e
   d. iii, v

Answers to multiple-choice questions

1. b
2. c
3. c
4. b
5. b

CHAPTER

8

LEADING

The purpose of this chapter

This chapter deals with the nature of the leading function. It discusses the difference between leadership and management. It examines the components of the leading function: influence, authority, power, delegation, responsibility and accountability. It also examines the major leadership theories and investigates the importance of motivation, communication, and groups and teams in leadership.

Learning outcomes

On completion of this chapter you should be able to:

- define the term "leadership"
- differentiate between leadership and management
- describe the components of leadership
- discuss the major leadership theories
- identify contemporary leadership issues
- explain why managers should understand what motivates their employees' behaviour
- differentiate between groups and teams in organisations
- describe a simple communication model.

8.1 Introduction

If organisations were comprised solely of machines that could implement plans predictably and with precision, only the planning, organising and control functions of management would be necessary to achieve an organisation's goals. However, organisations employ people to activate the financial, physical and informational resources of the organisation. In order to manage these important human resources, managers perform the management function of leading by influencing, guiding and directing the organisation's employees towards achieving its goals. This chapter examines the nature of the leading function.

8.2 The nature of leadership

Leadership is one of the most researched and most controversial topics in management. Many researchers[1] have attempted to define "leadership" during the past fifty years, using various variables such as traits, behaviour, influence, interaction patterns and role relationships, but it remains an elusive concept. A popular contemporary definition of "leadership", from a managerial point of view, describes it as "the process of influencing employees to work willingly towards the achievement of organisational objectives"[2].

Chapter 6 and Chapter 7 discussed the first two management functions: planning and organising. While planning and organising set the wheels of the management process in motion, the process is by no means complete, since the plans formulated to achieve the goals must still become a reality. Thus the third fundamental function of management comes into play: leading.

In order to influence their subordinates to achieve goals, managers should understand what motivates their employees' behaviour, and they should create working environments where their employees are motivated to work productively (as discussed in section 8.4).

In modern organisations, managers manage individuals as well as groups or teams. Groups do much of the work in organisations and may consist of task groups, command groups and informal groups. Managers manage these groups (for example, the legal section or the purchasing department) to enable them to achieve the organisation's goals and objectives. Increasingly, managers in contemporary organisations need to build teams that perform a variety of tasks. Managers should understand the dynamics of teams and know what **team leadership** entails. (This is discussed in section 8.5.)

Managers communicate their organisations' visions, missions, goals, strategies, plans, problems and expectations to employees. They also listen to the employees' problems and aspirations. The ability to communicate effectively is an important element of leading. (Section 8.6 examines a simple communication model.)

When they perform the **leading** function, managers take the lead to bridge the gap between formulating plans and reaching goals. They transform plans into reality by influencing individuals, groups and teams in the organisation, by communicating with them and by ensuring that they are motivated.

8.2.1 Leadership and management

Leadership is not the same as management. Management is broader in scope, comprising four management functions, of which leading is only one[3]. People can work as managers without being true leaders because they do not have the ability to influence others. Conversely, there are leaders in organisations who are not managers. For example, the informal leader of a group may have more influence in the group than the manager because of his/her ability to influence group members.

Influencing[4] is the process leaders follow when communicating ideas, gaining acceptance of them, and inspiring followers to support and implement the ideas through change. Influencing is also about the relationship between leaders and followers. Managers may coerce employees in order to influence their behaviour, but leaders do not.

While leadership is not the only ingredient of organisational success, it is one of the most important variables influencing this success. Indeed, in the South African business context, there are innumerable examples where the success (or failure) of organisations is attributed to a particular leader. For example, Brian Joffe built The Bidvest Group, a South African success story, from a cash shell to an international trading, services and distribution group in fewer than 20 years.

Case study

Brian Joffe, CEO of The Bidvest Group Limited

Brian Joffe was born and educated in Johannesburg. He graduated as a chartered accountant in 1971. His first independent business venture was in the animal-feed market. He built the business, sold it and "retired", aged 32, to the United States. However, he returned to South Africa and in 1988 gained control of a cash shell, from which he built The Bidvest Group into an international trading, services and distribution group.

Joffe is primarily an entrepreneur, a ground-breaker and sensible risk-taker who creates jobs while creating wealth. He believes South Africa should tap into its vast under-utilised pool of talent and empower a new generation of entrepreneurs.

Joffe built his unique business model on his own experience. He has always believed that incentivised entrepreneurs generate rapid growth and that competition between managerial peers drives top performance. He set the vision to work by building a decentralised group of companies with revenue of more than R112 billion a year. His business model is at the extreme end of decentralisation. The Bidvest Group employs more than 80 000 people, yet the head office contains only six executives and no more than a dozen people in all. Bidvest does not have systems, corporate manuals or car policies, only a few "Bidvest ways", such as a daily cash-flow report from all companies.

The annual Trust Barometer study by Ask Africa draws a link between a company head's strong leadership qualities and its ability to attract talent, customers and investors. Joffe won the 2009 title of Most Trusted CEO in South Africa's Entrepreneurial/Founder companies.

Bidvest's diversification, operationally and geographically, provided stability during the recent recession whose timing and severity were not expected. Joffe has said he does not like to talk about difficult conditions. According to him, you do well or you do not, and bad conditions create more opportunities. Certainly, it is this attitude that is helping Bidvest to position itself for the 2010 Soccer World Cup. The group's food services business has secured catering contracts, Bidpaper Plus will cash in on sales tickets and Bid Auto will offer tourists car rentals. Joffe observed that there is a lot of speculation regarding Bidvest's involvement in the World Cup and how much Bidvest will benefit from this. In his view, sporting events themselves do not necessary bring all the benefits, but the fact is that South Africa will have about 500 000 foreign visitors for the period of one month. This means that there will be an increase in the number of beds that need laundering, the number of available rental cars and the number of portable toilets. Clearly Bidvest is in safe hands.

Sources: Adapted from *Financial Mail*. 2009. "Brian Joffe". September 11. [Online] Available: http://www.brianjoffe.com/pages/aboutBJcontent.htm. Accessed 7 December 2009 & *Engineering News*. 2009. "Bidvest looking to expand automotive, food services businesses – CEO", August. [Online] Available: http://www.engineeringnews.co.za/article/bidvest-looking-to-expand-automotive-food-services-businesses-ceo-2009-08-31 Accessed 7 December 2009.

In the dynamic and fast-changing business environment of the twenty-first century, organisations need managers who are also strong leaders. Organisations worldwide use the extensive body of knowledge on leadership to improve the leadership skills of their managers. Figure 8.1 on page 212 illustrates the process of developing managers into leaders.

Figure 8.1: The integration of leadership and management

8.2.2 The components of the leading function

Chapter 7 discussed organisational structures and the authority relations they create in organisations. These authority relations relate strongly to the leading function of managers because the leading function gives managers the right to use authority, power, responsibility, delegation and accountability to influence employees to achieve the organisation's goals[5].

The **components of leadership** entail the following:

- **Authority** denotes the right of a manager to give commands to, and demand actions from, employees.
- **Power** is a manager's ability to influence his/her employees' behaviour.
- **Responsibility** is the obligation to achieve organisational goals by performing required activities. Managers are responsible for the results of their organisations, departments or sections.
- **Delegation** is the process of assigning responsibility and authority for achieving organisational goals. Managers delegate responsibility and authority down the chain of command. Delegation refers to giving employees new tasks. Such a task may become part of a redesign job or may simply be a once-off task.
- **Accountability** is the evaluation of how well individuals meet their responsibilities. Managers are accountable for all that happens in their sections or departments. Managers can delegate authority and responsibility, but they can never delegate their accountability.

Authority and power are probably the most important components of leading and therefore deserve a few further remarks.

8.2.2.1 Authority

Managers are responsible for ensuring that employees work together to achieve the organisation's goals. Without authority, managers are unable to manage, initiate or sustain the management process. Authority therefore revolves around obtaining the right to perform certain actions (within specified guidelines) to decide who does what, to demand the completion of tasks and to discipline those who fail to do what the organisation expects of them. In short, this entails the right to demand action from employees and the right to take action.

Final authority rests with the owners or shareholders of an organisation, who transfer or delegate authority to the board. The board, in turn, delegates authority to top management, top management delegates it to middle management and so on, to the lowest levels. Managers, in turn, delegate authority to employees to enable them to execute tasks. For example, certain bank officials have the authority to enter the bank's vault, certain managers have the authority to sign cheques in the organisation's name, and others have the authority to negotiate and conclude contracts on behalf of the organisation. The organisation confers this formal authority on them.

A clear manifestation of formal authority is evident in an army, wherein those with specific powers wear insignia to indicate their authority or rank: captains have authority over lieutenants, lieutenants over sergeants and so on. Although managers do not wear insignia, their organisations confer authority in the same way on a specific position or rank. The organisation confers on a manager the right to expect action from employees. Members of organisational groups also confer authority on a manager if they accept him/her as their leader. Authority and leadership are therefore closely related – the organisation grants authority to particular managers to lead individuals and groups in achieving the organisation's goals.

8.2.2.2 Power

Managers who are strong leaders influence their employees because they possess power and therefore are able to exercise their authority fully. Leadership and power go hand in hand. Without power, a manager would not be able to influence employees sufficiently towards achieving organisational goals.

Leaders have two types of power: position power and personal power. Top management delegates **position power** down the chain of command. Managers have **personal power** when their followers bestow it on them.

Figure 8.2: The power continuum

Source: Adapted from Lussier, R.N. & Achua, C.F. 2001. *Leadership: Theory, Application, Skill development.* 1st ed., p. 342. © South-Western, a part of Cengage Learning, Inc. Reproduced by permission. www.cengage.com/permissions.

As indicated in Figure 8.2, there is a power continuum from position power to personal power, on which the following types of power can be placed:

- **Coercive power** is the power to enforce compliance through fear, whether psychological, emotional or physical. Criminals often make use of such power through physical force or violence. Modern organisations do not use physical force, but employees' psychological or emotional fear that the organisation will retrench them or exclude them from a group gives managers a form of power that could be used to put pressure on employees.
- **Reward power** is based on the manager's ability to influence employees with something of value to them. It concerns the power to give or withhold rewards. Such rewards include, for example, salary raises, bonuses, praise, recognition and the allocation of interesting assignments. The more rewards a manager controls and the more important these rewards are to employees, the greater reward power a manager possesses.
- **Legitimate power** is the power an organisation grants to a particular position. Accordingly, a manager has the right to insist that employees do their work and the right to discipline or dismiss them if they fail to comply.
- **Referent power** refers to a manager's personal power or charisma. Employees obey managers with referent power simply because they like them, respect them and identify with them. In other words, the leader's personal characteristics make him/her attractive to others.
- **Expert power** is the power that a manager's expertise, knowledge and professional ability give him/her, particularly over those who need the knowledge or information. The more important the information and the fewer the people who possess it, the greater is the power of the person who commands it.

A manager who commands all five types of power is a strong leader. In organisations, managers are not the only ones to possess power. Occasionally employees possess it too, for example, when a manager is dependent on a subordinate for information or for social influence. Managers should be aware that their employees also possess power. They

Table 8.1: Uses and outcomes of power

Source of leader influence	Type of outcome		
	Commitment	Compliance	Resistance
Referent power	*Likely* If request is believed to be important to leader	*Possible* If request is perceived to be unimportant to leader	*Possible* If request is for something that will bring harm to leader
Expert power	*Likely* If request is persuasive and subordinates share leader's task goals	*Possible* If request is persuasive, but subordinates are apathetic about leader's task goals	*Possible* If leader is arrogant and insulting, or subordinates oppose task goals
Legitimate power	*Possible* If request is polite and highly appropriate	*Likely* If request or order is seen as legitimate	*Possible* If arrogant demands are made or request does not appear proper
Reward power	*Possible* If used in a subtle, very personal way	*Likely* If used in a mechanical, impersonal way	*Possible* If used in a manipulative, arrogant way
Coercive power	*Very unlikely*	*Possible* If used in a helpful, non-punitive way	*Likely* If used in a hostile or manipulative way

Source: Cartwright, D.P. (ed.) 1959. Studies in Social Power, Ann Arbor, Research Center for Group Dynamics, Institute for Social Research, University of Michigan, Research Center for Group Dynamic series, publication no. 6.

should use their own power judiciously and only to the extent necessary to accomplish the organisation's goals. Table 8.1 provides a useful perspective on how managers may wield power.

Effective managers use their power in such a way that they maintain a healthy balance between their own power and that of employees. Figure 8.3 illustrates such a balance.

8.3 Leadership theories

Researchers have studied, developed and tested a variety of leadership theories to determine the key characteristics and behaviour patterns of a good leader. The major leadership theories are trait theory, behavioural theory and contingency theory[6].

Early research into leadership involved the identification and analysis of the traits of

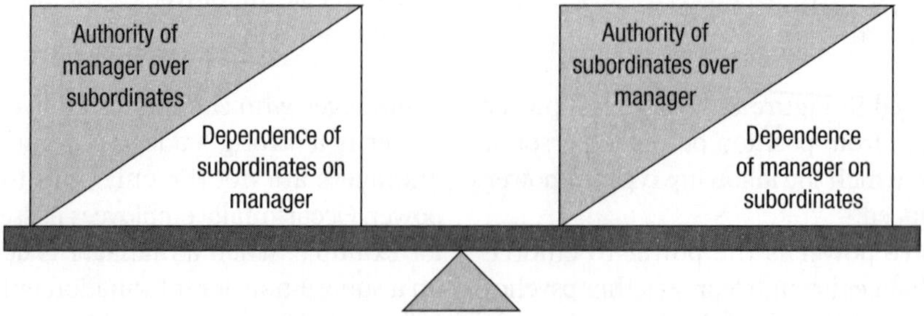

Figure 8.3: Equilibrium between the power of management and that of employees

strong leaders. The assumption of **trait theory** was that strong leaders have certain basic traits that distinguish them from followers and unsuccessful leaders. Many researchers have tried to list the distinctive characteristics of effective leaders. The results of these research efforts have been largely inconclusive because traits vary from one leader to another, and some traits develop only after a leader assumes a leadership position.

Research interest then turned towards investigating how successful leaders behave. An assumption that **behavioural theory** makes about leadership is that successful leaders behave differently from unsuccessful leaders. Researchers tried to determine what successful leaders do – how they delegate, communicate with and motivate their employees. The belief was that managers could learn the "right" behaviour. Research conducted at the University of Iowa, the Ohio State University, the University of Michigan, and the work of Blake and Mouton support the behavioural approach to leadership.

Researchers at the University of Iowa identified three basic leadership styles: autocratic, democratic and *laissez-faire* leadership styles. The researchers concluded that the *laissez-faire* style, whereby leaders leave all decisions to their employees and do not follow up, was ineffective on every performance criterion when compared to the other two styles. The researchers found that the democratic leadership style (the style of a leader who involves employees in decision-making, delegates authority, encourages participation in deciding work methods and goals, and gives feedback) was the most effective style.

Researchers at the Ohio State University also identified two leadership styles:

- **initiating structure** is the extent to which a leader defines and structures his/her role and the roles of employees to attain goals
- **consideration** is the extent to which a leader has job relationships characterised by mutual trust, respect for employees' ideas and regard for their feelings.

According to the researchers, effective leaders exhibit both dimensions strongly in their leadership style. At the University of Michigan, researchers distinguished between **production-oriented leaders**, who emphasise the technical or task aspects of a job, and **employee-oriented leaders**, who emphasise interpersonal relations. In these studies, employee-oriented leaders were associated with higher group productivity and higher job satisfaction.

Blake and Mouton developed the **"managerial grid"**, an instrument that identifies various leadership styles on a two-dimensional grid. They used a questionnaire to measure **concern for people** and **concern for production** on a scale of one to nine. The researchers identified the "ideal" leadership style as the "team-management style" where a manager is strong on both dimensions (9,9).

In general, the behavioural theories had little success in identifying consistent patterns of leadership behaviour and successful performance because results varied over different ranges of circumstances. This led researchers to investigate the effect of the situation on effective leadership styles.

The contingency (or situational) approach to leadership acknowledges that predicting leadership success is more complex than examining the traits and behaviours of successful leaders. **Contingency theory** attempts to determine the best leadership style for a given situation. In the development of contingency theories, researchers considered variables such as how structured the task is, the quality of the relationship between the leader and the employees, the leader's position power, the employees' role clarity and the employees' acceptance of the leader's decisions.

Fred Fiedler's contingency theory of leadership proposes that effective group performance depends on the proper match between a leader's style of interaction with employees, and the degree to which the situation gives control and influence to the leader. Fiedler developed an instrument to measure whether the leader is task oriented or relationship oriented, and he identified three situational criteria that organisations can manipulate to create a proper situational match with the behaviour orientation of the leader. According to Fiedler, an individual's leadership style is fixed. If, for example, a situation requires a task-oriented leader and the person in the leadership position is relationship oriented, the organisation must either change the situation or move the leader to another situation where his/her leadership style is compatible with the situation.

Robert House developed the path-goal model, asserting that it is the leader's responsibility to help employees to achieve their goals. Leaders should provide the necessary direction and support to ensure that employees' goals are in line with the organisation's goals and objectives. House identified four leadership behaviours (directive, supportive, participative and achievement-oriented behaviour), which managers can use in different situations. The majority of research evidence supports the logic of this theory: if the leader counteracts the employee's limitations in the work situation, this will probably influence the employee's performance positively.

Paul Hersey and Ken Blanchard proposed a **situational leadership model** where the premise is that the work maturity of employees determines the best leadership style for a particular situation. The employees' need for achievement, their willingness to accept responsibility, their task-related ability and their experience determine their work maturity. The manager uses one of four leadership styles (telling, selling, participating and delegating) to match the employees' maturity level in a given situation.

8.3.1 Contemporary issues in leadership

In the aftermath of the worldwide financial crisis, where many business leaders stood accused of violating the trust of their employees and other stakeholders, it is vital that the employees and stakeholders in organisations perceive their business leaders as trustworthy. In the case study, it was mentioned that Joffe of Bidvest earned the title of Most Trusted CEO in his category, which will naturally influence current and prospective shareholders and employees who are making investment or employment decisions.

The five dimensions of **trust** include the following:

- integrity (a manager's honesty and truthfulness)
- competence (a manager's technical and interpersonal knowledge and skills)
- consistency (a manager's reliability, predictability and good judgement in handling situations)
- loyalty (a manager's willingness to protect another person)
- openness (a manager's reliability when it comes to telling the whole truth)[7].

Leaders are increasingly described as "individuals who define organisational reality through the articulation of a vision"[8]. Joffe is an example of this, as he used his vision of achieving growth through incentivised entrepreneurs and of achieving top performance through competitive managers when he built a decentralised group of companies.

However, this view of leadership is not confined to top managers. Managers at all levels are stronger leaders if they can convey the vision of their section, department, group or team to their employees.

Leaders who communicate and share their vision for their organisation can be classified as visionary leaders, charismatic leaders and transformational leaders.

8.3.1.1 Charismatic leadership

The perception is that a strong positive relationship exists between **charismatic leadership** and the employees' performance and satisfaction. Charismatic leaders often have traits such as self-confidence, vision, the ability to articulate the vision, strong convictions about the vision, unconventional behaviour and environmental sensitivity. Charismatic leadership may be most appropriate when the followers' task has an ideological component, perhaps explaining why charismatic leaders most often appear in politics, religion or unusual business organisations.

8.3.1.2 Visionary leadership

Visionary leadership goes beyond charisma. Visionary leaders have the ability to create and articulate a realistic, credible, attractive vision of the future of the organisation; this vision grows out of and improves on the present. Such a vision creates enthusiasm, and brings energy and commitment to the organisation. Visionary leaders exhibit certain skills: the ability to explain the vision to others, the ability to express the vision through their behaviour and the ability to extend the vision to different leadership contexts[9].

8.3.1.3 Transactional and transformational leadership

James Burns was the first researcher to distinguish between **transactional and transformational leadership** behaviour. According to him, transactional leaders motivate followers by appealing to their self-interest, for example, corporate leaders exchanging pay and status for work effort. He contrasts transactional leadership with transformational leadership, which he describes as a process in which "leaders and followers raise one another to higher levels of morality and motivation"[10]. Bass[11] further refined the distinction between transactional and

Visionary leaders: Are they over-rated?

In recent years, studies of visionary leadership created excitement among researchers. But are visionary leaders best suited to lead their organisations through the major changes that contemporary organisations face? The excerpt below offers a controversial point of view:

> The visionary leader has become the hero of the business myth, but most organisations do better in the long term by hiring solid performers strong on consistency rather than charisma and celebrity status.
>
> The test of effective leadership is what the leader achieves with the organisation, not what was once envisioned. By emphasising the performance qualities that make a great visionary, a senior executive can neglect the development of the practical attributes that will get the job done.
>
> Often business leaders do not learn the basic functional skills that will enable them to execute the vision. If they are lucky, they work in an organisation whose culture enables them to learn the implementation basics of the job. Most organisations do not have this cultural predisposition to prompt execution. The danger is then that a leader who believes his/her job is purely the development of strategy will take the organisation precisely nowhere. Case studies cited in the book *Good to Great* by Jim Collins confirm this. Collins identified the United States organisations that had been consistently successful for the longest period. The results were heartening for the vast majority of executives who lack star quality: the case studies showed that leaders who consistently achieved their organisational goals without fanfare achieved long-running success. These uncelebrated leaders set out clear strategic ambitions, lay down a change agenda that can be implemented, put together a strong leadership team and develop a process to ensure that the job is done.

Source: Adapted from *Business Day Management Review*. 2007. "Visionary leaders: Are they over-rated?". January, p. 15.

transformational leadership by proposing a theory of transformational leadership. He describes transactional leadership as an exchange of rewards for compliance, while he views transformational leadership as the leader's effect on followers in that they feel trust, admiration, loyalty and respect for their leader, and are motivated to do more than is expected of them.

Transformational leaders display behaviour associated with four transformational styles: idealised behaviour, inspirational motivation, intellectual stimulation and individualised consideration, and a fifth characteristic, based on the other four leadership styles, idealised attributes[12].

In most organisational contexts, transformational leadership is desirable because it improves employee satisfaction, trust and commitment[13], and results in employees being motivated to do more than is expected of them. Research findings indicate that transformational leadership consistently promotes greater organisational performance[14]. Furthermore, transformational leaders are effective in organisations where major change and transformation are taking place.

> **Critical thinking**
>
> **Leadership research**
> Researchers have studied leadership in different ways, depending on their preferences and their research time line. This chapter has examined various theories of leadership, including the trait theory, behavioural theory, contingency theory and the more contemporary issues in leadership. Clearly, researchers have made some progress in probing the "mysteries"[15] surrounding leadership, but many questions remain on why some people seem to perform much better in a leadership position than others. It is for this reason that the concept of leadership still attracts vigorous research attention as researchers strive to solve the mysteries of leadership.

8.4 Motivation

Employees (the human resources) influence the organisation's productivity and profitability directly. In order to manage employees effectively, managers should understand what motivates the behaviour of their employees. This is a crucial aspect of the leading function.

"**Motivation**" is defined as "an inner desire to satisfy an unsatisfied need"[16]. It is an intrinsic process and therefore managers cannot "motivate" their employees. However, they can create a working environment where their employees will be motivated to achieve the organisation's goals. To use an example from the case study, managers at Bidvest are motivated to create rapid growth because the company allows them to take responsibility for the success of their businesses. Thus, from an organisational perspective, motivation is the willingness of an employee to achieve the organisation's goals[17].

The motivation process starts with an unsatisfied need and moves in a certain sequence[18]. For example, an employee has an unsatisfied need for higher status in the organisation. Her motive is the desire to advance to a first-line managerial position, which leads to certain behaviour, such as working over-time or enrolling for a management course. The consequence of the behaviour might be that she receives a promotion (or does not receive a promotion), which will lead to the satisfaction (or dissatisfaction) of her need. If dissatisfaction occurs, the need remains unsatisfied and the motivation process will start all over again. Satisfaction is usually short lived because people have many needs, and as soon as one need is satisfied, another need will surface. If the person in the example advances to a first-line management position, she may very soon want a further promotion to a middle-management position. This will again cause dissatisfaction and the motivation process will start all over again.

If managers understand what motivates the behaviour of their employees, they can influence the employees' work performance. Yet it is important to note that motivation is not the only factor that influences work performance. The variables that determine performance are motivation, ability (training, knowledge and skills) and the opportunity to perform (resources)[19]:

performance = ability × motivation × resources

Effective managers understand that employees must possess a high level of motivation plus the appropriate training, knowledge and skills to perform effectively in a given work situation. If employees lack the skills they need to perform, they will not be able to do their work properly, no matter how motivated they are. Employees should also have the opportunity to perform, which means that they must have adequate resources (such as tools, equipment, materials and supplies) to be able to do the work.

From the above discussion, it is clear that managers have a major role to play in terms of the work performance of their employees.

The value of theories on leadership and motivation is that they provide managers with a better understanding of how to manage their employees in order to make them perform best. At the same time, these theories ensure that the organisation creates an environment where employees can satisfy their needs. (The motivation theories are discussed in Chapter 11.)

8.5 Groups and teams in organisations

The employees of modern organisations do not work merely as individuals with individual needs and goals, but also as members of groups and teams. To achieve the organisation's goals, managers lead groups and teams as well as individual employees.

Many writers use the words "group" and "team" interchangeably, but recent management literature makes a definite distinction between them, saying that while all teams are also groups, not all groups are teams. A team is a special kind of group, and changing groups into teams is a process that requires special management skills. This section first focuses on groups in general and then discusses work teams as an integral part of successful contemporary organisations[20].

How much do South African bosses really know about what motivates employees?

Research from a *Financial Mail* "Best companies to work for" survey shows a growing gap between managers' perception of how well they treat their employees and how the employees themselves see the results of company initiatives.

The following is a list of ways to ensure that employees are motivated, based on interviews with a group of HR specialists, employees and responses to the Best Company questionnaires.

The top ten ways to turn your staff on:

1. development and career opportunities
2. fair reward and recognition
3. leadership by example and through vision
4. open two-way communication
5. treating staff as individuals and with respect
6. trusting staff
7. staff understanding how their jobs contribute to the business
8. a clear performance-management system
9. team spirit and a common goal
10. a healthy work/life balance.

Source: Adapted from *Financial Mail*. 2006. "Is that all?". 29 September, pp. 32–33.

8.5.1 Groups

A **group** comprises two or more individuals who regularly interact with each other and who work for a common purpose. People join groups for a variety of reasons, ranging from satisfying their social needs to achieving goals that are impossible for them to achieve as individuals. Some people join groups to achieve some level of prestige or status. Others feel that they enhance their self-worth by belonging to a specific group. Individual group members often feel they have more power by joining a group because group action can achieve more than individual action.

In organisations, there are informal and formal groups.

8.5.1.1 Informal groups

Informal groups can be interest groups or friendship groups:

- In **interest groups**, the group members usually share a common interest. For example, a group of employees might campaign for better cafeteria facilities at their workplace. When the organisation provides better facilities, the group will disband.
- **Friendship groups** usually exist to satisfy the social needs of their members. For example, a group of employees might play bridge once a week.

8.5.1.2 Formal groups

Formal groups can be command groups or task groups:

- **Command groups** appear on the organisational chart, which indicates their line of authority, for example, from managers to their employees. The organisation's structure defines formal groups in terms of allocated work assignments that determine tasks and the formation of work groups.
- **Task groups** are created by organisations to complete a specific task or project in the organisation. After completion of the task, the group disbands. Organisations can create task groups across hierarchical boundaries. For example, the dean of a university's College of Management Sciences might appoint a committee comprising staff members from the production department and the editorial department as well as junior and senior academics to investigate the quality of the study material produced for all departments in the college. On completion of the project, the group will disband.

8.5.2 The characteristics of groups

Every group in an organisation is different in terms of its structure or set of characteristics that shapes the behaviour of both the group and the individual group members[21] (for example, the size of the group, the composition of the group, group norms and group cohesiveness).

Group size affects the group's overall performance. If the group is too big, social loafing occurs. "Social loafing" refers to the tendency of individuals to put in less effort when working in a group than when working individually. Thus, group size has an influence on the productivity of groups.

Group composition can influence a group's performance. Heterogeneous groups (with members who are diverse in terms of, for example, gender, race and nationality) have more difficulty working together at first, but they outperform homogeneous groups over time.

Group norms are standards shared by members of a group that develop from interaction between these members. Norms can be positive or negative, and should be managed by managers. An example of a positive norm is that the group strives to outperform other groups; a negative norm is: "We only do what is asked of us – no more, no less".

Group cohesiveness is the way a group stands together as a unit rather than as individuals. There is a strong relationship between performance norms and cohesiveness, which can be either beneficial or detrimental to the organisation. If a group is very cohesive, the members' adherence to group norms will be stronger.

Status in groups can be formal or informal, meaning that groups sometimes give higher (informal) status to group members who are relatively low on the hierarchical level of the organisation. Such status derives from factors such as the age or experience of a group member or the social influence of a group member.

The formal leader in a group usually has a title such as section or department manager, supervisor, project leader, task-force head or committee chair. However, sometimes an informal leader has more influence in a group, which may influence the performance of the group positively or negatively.

In order to manage groups in an organisation effectively, managers should understand how groups are structured and how the various characteristics of specific groups influence the organisation's performance.

Managers should not under-estimate the role of groups in the overall accomplishment of organisational goals. They should understand group dynamics so as to manage the groups in their organisations effectively.

8.5.3 Teams

As stated earlier, not all groups are teams. A work group is a unit of two or more people who interact primarily to share information and make decisions that will help each group member perform within his/her own area of responsibility[22]. Individual members of work groups are accountable for their own performance and are rewarded for it. However, a **work team** "comprises a small number of employees with complementary competencies who work together on a project, are committed to a common purpose and are accountable for performing tasks that contribute to achieving an organisation's goals."[23] Work teams perform collectively and members are dependent on each other to complete their work, while work group members only share information.

An example of a work group is a pool of administrative clerks. One clerk's performance appraisal and rewards are not dependent on the performance of the other clerks. Furthermore, the group's performance is the sum of the group members' individual performances.

An example of a work team is a team tasked with developing a new product from conception to completion. All the members are dependent on each other because the output of one member becomes the input of another member.

While work groups have neutral and sometimes negative synergy, work teams have positive synergy, meaning that the performance of an effective team can be greater than the sum of the performance of individual team members. For example, the efforts of the team tasked with developing a new product can amount to more than the sum of their individual performances because they are creating something new.

Whilst group members are only accountable for their own performance, team members are individually and mutually accountable for the performance of the team. In the above example of the product-development team, the team members are mutually responsible and accountable for the new product, but are also individually accountable for their own inputs.

Lastly, while the skills of the members of work groups are random and varied, the skills of members of work teams are complementary because of the interdependent nature of their work[24].

Work teams have many strengths, but it is wrong to perceive them as a cure-all solution to organisational problems. Teams are not suitable in all organisational settings. Teams are effective only in organisations where the organisational culture is conducive to teamwork. Furthermore, the organisation's reward system must reward team performance. Top managers' commitment and support for teams must be evident throughout the organisation, and the organisation's work must be suited to being performed in a team environment.

Yet, despite these considerations, teams are gaining popularity throughout the world and complex global organisations cannot function without effective teams.

The following are the different types of teams[25]:

- Problem-solving teams comprise employees from the same department who meet regularly to discuss ways of improving quality, efficiency and the work environment.
- Self-managed work teams take on the responsibilities from their former managers, including tasks such as planning, scheduling and control. Team members address problems in the work process, sometimes, even, the selection of team members and discipline.
- Cross-functional teams comprise employees at the same hierarchical level, but from different work areas, who come together to accomplish a task. These teams are effective in allowing people from diverse areas in an organisation to exchange information, develop new ideas, solve problems and co-ordinate complex projects. Task forces and committees are common examples of cross-functional teams.

High-performance teams have a number of characteristics in common:

- a clear understanding of the team's goals, and the technical skills and abilities needed to achieve these goals
- members who are capable of adjusting their skills
- high mutual trust among members and unified commitment
- good communication and adequate negotiating skills
- team leaders who encourage team members by clarifying goals and who help members to realise their potential[26].

Using teams in an organisation is a challenging managerial task, involving the selection and training of potential and current employees to become effective team members. It is also important that the organisation's performance and reward systems should encourage team effort.

8.6 Communication

Communication is an essential element of leading. Effective leadership depends on constant communication between leaders and their employees. It is important in building and sustaining relationships in an organisation.

When are teams appropriate?

Do teams work in all organisations? The answer is: "Not always".

Teams should be used when:

- there is a clear, engaging reason or purpose
- people must work together to get the work done
- the organisation rewards teamwork and team performance
- ample resources are available
- teams will have clear authority to manage and change the work they are doing.

Teams should not be used when:

- there is no clear purpose
- people working independently can do the work
- the organisation rewards individual effort and performance
- the necessary resources are not available
- management will continue to monitor and influence the work they are doing.

Source: Wageman, R. 1997. "Critical success factors for creating superb self-managing teams" in *Organisational Dynamics*. Vol. 26, No.1, pp. 49–61.

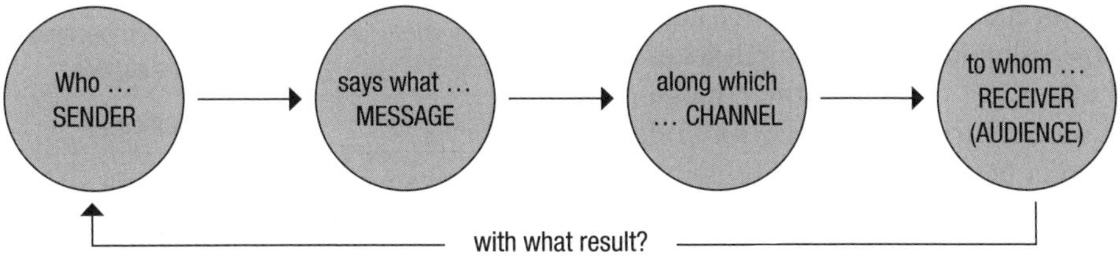

Figure 8.4: A basic communication model

Good communication is conducive to good relations between managers and individual employees, groups, teams and, ultimately, the organisation and its environment. A considerable proportion of a manager's time is devoted to communicating with the organisation's stakeholders, both inside and outside the organisation. Furthermore, the management process is dependent on effective communication.

Theoretically, communication is the transfer of information or messages from one person to another. Figure 8.4 illustrates a simple communication model, which provides a basis for understanding the key elements of interpersonal communication.

The **sender** is the source of a message. To communicate effectively, the sender should know exactly what the message is that he/she wishes to transmit. The sender should take care with his/her choice of words and their meaning, and should encourage two-way communication by showing insight into the receiver's perceptions.

The **message** may convey ideas, opinions, plans, orders or explanations. In the interests of effective communication, the message should be simple and clear.

The communications **channel** is the manner in which the message reaches the receiver. It may assume any form that can be perceived by any of the recipient's senses, as long as it is comprehensible. For example, the recipient can hear spoken language, see or feel gestures and read the written word.

The **receiver** of the message should absorb the message and show that he/she has received and understood the message (listening skills are important here).

For communication to be effective, the recipient should receive the message unimpeded, meaning that the recipient should understand the message in accordance with the sender's intentions. Because effective

Listening

Listening is an important component of effective communication. A good listener:

- stops what he/she is doing and gives his/her complete attention to the speaker
- avoids distractions such as fiddling with pens
- stays "tuned in" (not letting his/her mind wander)
- does not assume he/she knows what the speaker is going to say and does not jump to conclusions
- listens to the entire message without interrupting the speaker
- asks questions if he/she feels he/she has incomplete information
- takes notes to help him/her remember the message and to document it, if necessary
- conveys meaning, for example, uses verbal clues to let the speaker know that he/she is listening (such as nodding, making eye contact, or saying, "I see" and, "I understand")
- watches for non-verbal cues such as body language and eye expression (because sometimes people say one thing and mean something else, which may be shown in the non-verbal cues).

communication is so important in leadership, managers should remove all hindrances that may affect the clarity of their messages, such as obscurity, language differences, erroneous perceptions, doubts about the source or sender and ambiguities. Managers should promote effective communication by encouraging feedback and by using face-to-face communication wherever possible. Managers can enhance their communication by using simple language. They should contemplate any symbolic content in their communication before sending the message.

8.7 Summary

In order to be successful, organisations need managers who are also good leaders. Managers perform the leading function to manage the human resources in their organisations effectively. They use authority and power to influence their employees to strive willingly to achieve organisational goals. Leadership theories help managers understand what leadership entails. This chapter examines the most important categories of leadership models as well as contemporary issues in leadership. Effective managers should understand how their employees' behaviour is motivated. Modern organisations use work groups and work teams extensively, and managing them is an added responsibility of contemporary managers. Communication is a crucial element of the leading function without which a manager will not be a good leader.

Key terms

accountability	management versus leadership
authority	managerial grid
autocratic leadership style	path-goal model
behavioural leadership theories	power
charismatic leadership	production-oriented leadership style
coercive power	referent power
concern for people	responsibility
concern for production	reward power
democratic leadership style	team leadership
employee-oriented leadership style	trait theory
expert power	transactional leadership
Fiedler's contingency theory of leadership	transformational leadership
Hersey and Blanchard's model	trust
laissez-faire leadership style	two-dimensional leadership
leadership	visionary leadership
legitimate power	

Questions for discussion

1. How would you define the leading function of managers?
2. How does the leader in the case study on page 211 see his leadership role?
3. a. Are managers also leaders?
   b. Explain the differences between managers and leaders.
4. How would the behaviour of a manager who is a strong leader compare with that of a manager who is not a strong leader? To answer this question, draw on your observations of managers known to you, or use information from the internet or newspapers.
5. What are the components of leadership?
6. Why are managers who use power effectively strong leaders?
7. What are the shortcomings of the trait theory and the behavioural theories?

8. a. Compare work groups and work teams.
   b. Why is it not always appropriate to use work teams?

? Multiple-choice questions

1. Which statement is true?
   a. Organisations need managers more than leaders.
   b. Leadership is one of four management functions.
   c. All managers are leaders and all leaders are managers.
   d. Managers and leaders do not have the same sources of power.
2. Which statement is false?
   a. Leadership is about bridging the gap between formulating plans and achieving goals.
   b. The behavioural approach to leadership focuses on how leaders should behave in a specific situation.
   c. According to Fiedler's theory of leadership, how well a leader's style fits the situation determines his/her effectiveness.
   d. House developed the path-goal theory.
3. The variables that determine an individual's work performance are _______.
   a. motivation and ability
   b. motivation, authority and resources
   c. responsibility, motivation and resources
   d. ability, motivation and resources
4. Group _________ influences the group's adherence to group norms positively.
   a. size
   b. composition
   c. leadership
   d. cohesiveness
5. After managers had informed employees by e-mail of a new retirement policy they plan to institute, the employees demanded a question-and-answer session with management. This represents the _________ step in the communication process.
   a. encoding
   b. message
   c. feedback
   d. decoding

Answers to multiple-choice questions

1. b
2. b
3. d
4. d
5. c

References

1. Yukl, G. 1998. *Leadership in organizations*. 4th ed. Upper Saddle River, New Jersey: Prentice-Hall, p. 2.
2. Lussier, R.N. 2000. *Management fundamentals*. Cincinnati: South-Western, p. 452.
3. Lussier, R.N. 2000. *Management fundamentals*. Cincinnati: South-Western, p. 453.
4. Lussier, R.N. & Achua, C.F. 2001. *Leadership: Theory, application, skill development*. Cincinnati: South-Western, p. 7.
5. Lussier, R.N. & Achua, C.F. 2001. *Leadership: Theory, application, skill development*. Cincinnati: South-Western, p. 187.
6. This section is based on Lussier, R.N. 2000. *Management fundamentals*. Cincinnati: South-Western, pp. 453–457 & Robbins, S.P. 2003. *Organizational behavior*. 10th ed. Upper Saddle River, New Jersey: Prentice-Hall, pp. 316–328.
7. Robbins, S.P. 2003. *Organizational behavior*. 10th ed. Upper Saddle River, New Jersey: Prentice-Hall, p. 336.
8. Robbins, S.P. 2003. *Organizational behavior*. 10th ed. Upper Saddle River, New Jersey: Prentice-Hall, p. 340.
9. Robbins, S.P. 2003. *Organizational behavior*. 10th ed. Upper Saddle River, New Jersey: Prentice-Hall, p. 340.
10. Burns, J.M. 1978. *Leadership in organisations*. New York: Harper & Row, p. 20.
11. Bass, B.M. 1985. "Leadership and performance beyond expectations". In Yukl, G. 1998. *Leadership in organisations*. New York: Prentice-Hall.
12. Vrba, M. 2007. "Emotional intelligence and leadership behaviour in a sample of South African first-line managers". *Management Dynamics*. Vol. 16(2), pp. 25–35.

13. Barling, J., Slater, F. & Kelloway, E.K. 2000. "Transformational leadership and emotional intelligence" in *Leadership and Organizational Development Journal*. Vol. 21, No. 3, pp. 157–161.
14. Lowe, K.B. & Kroeck, K.G. 1996. "Effectiveness correlates of transformational and transactional leadership: A meta-analytic review". *Leadership Quarterly*, Vol. 7, pp. 385–426.
15. Yukl, G. 1998. *Leadership in organizations*. 4th ed. Upper Saddle River, New Jersey: Prentice-Hall, p.14.
16. Lussier, R.N. 2000. *Management fundamentals*. Cincinnati: South-Western, p. 420.
17. Lussier, R.N. 2000. *Management fundamentals*. Cincinnati: South-Western, p. 420.
18. Lussier, R.N. 2000. *Management fundamentals*. Cincinnati: South-Western, p. 420.
19. Robbins, S.P. 2003. *Organizational behavior*. 10th ed. Upper Saddle River, New Jersey: Prentice-Hall, pp. 173–174.
20. Robbins, S.P. 2003. *Organizational behavior*. 10th ed. Upper Saddle River, New Jersey: Prentice-Hall, p. 258.
21. Based on Robbins, S.P. 2003. *Organizational behavior*. 10th ed. Upper Saddle River, New Jersey: Prentice-Hall, pp. 226–238.
22. Robbins, S.P. 2003. *Organizational behavior*. 10th ed. Upper Saddle River, New Jersey: Prentice-Hall, p. 258.
23. Robbins, S.P. 2003. *Organizational behavior*. 10th ed. Upper Saddle River, New Jersey: Prentice-Hall, p. 258.
24. Robbins, S.P. 2003. *Organizational behavior*. 10th ed. Upper Saddle River, New Jersey: Prentice-Hall, p. 258.
25. Robbins, S.P. 2003. *Organizational behavior*. 10th ed. Upper Saddle River, New Jersey: Prentice-Hall, pp. 260–270.
26. Robbins, S.P. & Decenzo, D.A. 2001. *Fundamentals of management*. 3rd ed. Upper Saddle River, New Jersey: Prentice-Hall, p. 290.

CHAPTER

9

CONTROLLING THE MANAGEMENT PROCESS

The purpose of this chapter

Control is the last of the four fundamental tasks of management. It is the final step in the management process, where the assessment of actual performance against planned performance initiates a new cycle of planning, organising, leading and control. This chapter deals with the purpose of control and examines how the control process works. It also examines the areas of control that management should focus on, such as the control of physical resources, quality control, financial control, budgetary control, the control of information and the control of human resources. The characteristics of an effective control system are also briefly examined.

Learning outcomes

On completion of this chapter you should be able to:

- give an overview of the purpose of control
- describe how a control process should function
- explain the various types of control
- discuss the characteristics of an effective control system.

9.1 Introduction

Organisations use control procedures to ensure that they are progressing towards their goals, and that their resources are being used properly and productively. This chapter examines the final component of the management process: **controlling**. Although it is the final step in the management process, it forms the basis for a new cycle of management activities because it gives feedback to and influences the first step in the management process (planning). Without any knowledge of how successfully the plans were implemented or how effectively the goals were achieved, managers would not be able to start the next management cycle of planning, organising, leading and, ultimately, controlling.

Controlling is the final step in the management process and it is an important part of the management cycle. Brilliant plans may be formulated, impressive organisational structures may be created and good leadership may be applied, but none of this ensures that the activities will proceed according to plan or that the goals and carefully laid plans will in fact be realised.

An effective manager is therefore someone who follows up on planned activities, seeing to it that the things that need to be done are carried out and that the pre-determined goals are reached. Managers at all levels and in all departments should be involved in the process of control. Until the activities of individuals, departments or units are evaluated (in other words, until **actual performance** is compared with the standard required), management will not know whether activities have been executed according to plan and will be unable to identify weaknesses in their plans. Controlling means narrowing the gap between what was planned and the actual achievement of management, and ensuring that all activities are carried out as they should be. The management process takes place between planning and control. Successful management is often dependent on sound planning and effective control.

This chapter deals with the purpose of control and examines how the control process works. It also examines the areas of control that management should focus on. Lastly, it examines the characteristics of an effective control system.

The case study that follows provides an illustration of the importance of effective control mechanisms in an organisation.

Case study

Control in action: IBM

In 1993, Louis Gerstner undertook the monumental task of turning IBM around when the blue-chip company was in freefall. IBM had lost USD17 billion and half its market share, the media was writing its obituary and competitors laughed at the company. IBM had dominated the industry for decades with mainframe systems used by virtually every corporation and government agency. In the late 1980s, competitors were offering mainframe alternatives at lower prices and the personal computer market, which IBM did not enter at that stage, exploded. Gerstner had only a few months to set IBM on the right track.

The turnaround, Gerstner concedes, depended on actually focusing on controlling business fundamentals, such as consolidating the company's 266 bookkeeping systems, 128 chief information officers and 339 surveys for measuring customer satisfaction. He put an end to any talk of breaking IBM into several little blues, the prevailing wisdom on how to harness the company's valuable assets. Instead, Gerstner moved to transform the company into an "integrator" that would build, run and house systems for customers using its own components as well as those of competitors.

Gerstner described the IBM of that era as suffering from "success syndrome", a disorder afflicting companies that have been successful for decades. This locks them into repeating what made them successful in the past, even when the competitive environment changes and new control steps are required to remain relevant. He rebuilt company culture to focus on performance. Employees returned to fundamentals like talking to customers and actually selling products rather than simply developing them. Gerstner also changed internal processes. For example, he revamped compensation, promotion and training programs.

All these efforts paid off. Between 1993 and 2001, IBM's annual net income rose to USD7,7 billion from a loss of USD8,1 billion;

revenues rose to USD85,9 billion from USD62,7 billion, and the stock price rose to USD120,96 per share from USD14,12 per share. Gerstner says, "Changing the attitude and behaviour of thousands of people is very, very hard to accomplish ... You cannot simply give a couple of speeches or write a new credo for the company and declare that a new culture has taken hold. You can't mandate it, can't engineer it. What you can do is create the conditions for transformation and provide incentives." Gerstner seems to have done that. After his retirement, he noted that IBM was rich with creative talent that only needed to be set loose.

IBM helped pioneer information technology over the years. Today it stands at the forefront of a worldwide industry that is revolutionising the way in which enterprises, organisations and people operate and thrive.

Source: IBM Archives. Not dated. [Online] Available: http://www-03.ibm.com/ibm/history Accessed 28 March 2010.

9.2 The purpose of control

An organisation needs a control process because even the best-laid plans may go wrong. For IBM, for example, a control process was crucial in order to align the company's goals and actual performances.

A control process is necessary for the following reasons:

- Control is linked with planning, organising and leading. Planning is the first step in control. Without control, planning is pointless.
- Control helps companies adapt to environmental change. It enables management to cope with change and uncertainty. If an organisation is to reach its goals according to plan, control is necessary. The variables in the turbulent contemporary business environment mean that an organisation is seldom able to realise its goals strictly according to plan. Raw materials may not be delivered on time, labour unrest or defective machinery may delay the organisation's operations, unexpectedly high interest rates may affect the cost structure and so on. Without control, the impact of environmental change on the organisation is difficult to detect.
- Control helps limit the accumulation of error. Managers and subordinates are capable of making poor decisions and committing errors. An effective control system should detect such errors before they accumulate and become critical.
- Control helps companies cope with increasing organisational size and complexity. As a business grows, more people are employed, new products are developed, new equipment is bought, new industries are entered and branch offices are opened as the activities of the business expand into different geographical regions. Over time, the business becomes an extensive network of activities that include production, finance, administration, staff and marketing. Without an effective system of control, it would be extremely difficult to spot weak points in a highly complex network and rectify them in good time.
- Control helps minimise costs. When implemented effectively, control can help reduce costs and increase output.

An overview of the control process will clarify the importance of control.

9.3 The control process

As mentioned in the introduction, control is the process whereby management ensures that the organisation's goals are accomplished or that actual performance compares favourably with the pre-determined standards. This process comprises four steps (see Figure 9.1).

The control process includes setting standards against which actual performance can be measured, measuring actual performance, evaluating any deviations that might occur and taking steps to rectify deviations. Each of these steps is discussed below.

9.3.1 Step 1: Establish standards

The first step in control is to establish performance standards at strategic points. Because of the close relationship between planning and control, it may be said that control in fact begins at the planning stage. It is often difficult to distinguish between these two tasks of management because, in a sense, control means revised planning and the revised allocation of resources. The control system should therefore be a mirror image of planning, as the plans indicate the goals and setting of standards or norms necessary for control.

A performance or control **standard** is a planned target against which the actual performance will be compared. A building project that has to be completed on a certain date will have control standards at strategic stages, such as completion of foundations by 31 March, completion of concrete structure by 30 June, completion of roof by 15 June and so on.

To make the control process possible and worthwhile, the performance standard should be relevant, realistic, attainable and measurable, so that there can be no doubt whether the actual performance meets the standard or not. Although it is difficult to make generalisations about suitable performance standards for different businesses, it should be possible in any particular business to convert strategy into comprehensive plans and goals. From these, appropriate performance standards can be developed, for example:

- Profit standards indicate how much profit the business expects to make over a given period.
- Market-share standards indicate what share of the total market the business is aiming to conquer.
- Productivity standards are indicated by expressing inputs and outputs in relation to each other as ratios. Such ratios indicate

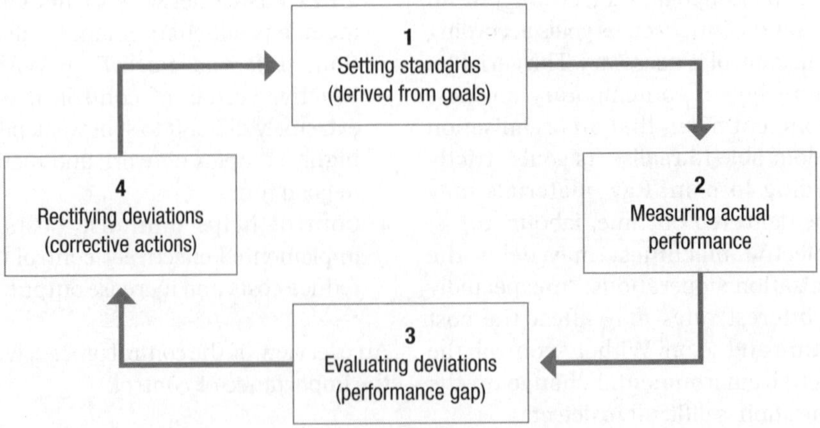

Figure 9.1: The control process

the relative productivity with which tasks are performed.
- Staff-development standards indicate the effectiveness of training programs for staff.

In the case study, IBM would certainly have formulated performance standards related to profitability, market share, productivity and staff development.

Standards are a function of the goals that are set in the planning phase. Performance standards, of which the above examples are only a few, enable management to distinguish between acceptable and unacceptable performance. They also enable management to monitor strategies and goals. To be effective, these standards should be the responsibility of a particular individual at some strategic point.

The box at the bottom of this page gives examples of performance standards for an organisation that builds medical devices.

9.3.2 Step 2: Measure actual performance

The collection of information and reporting on actual performance are continuous activities. As in the case with performance standards, it is also important for the activities to be **quantifiable** before any valid comparisons can be made. Another important requirement regarding the measurement of actual achievement is that the reports should be absolutely **reliable**. Unless they are totally accurate, control will not be effective. Moreover, observation and measurement must be carried out at the necessary strategic points and according to the standards determined by the control system.

Important considerations in the measurement and reporting of activities are **what information** and **how much** information should be fed back, and **to whom**. In a small business or at the lower-management levels of a fairly large business, operational management is more or less fully informed, and this is not of vital importance. But as a business increases in size and information about activities has to be transmitted to higher levels, the question of control becomes more important. It is at that point that the principle of **control by exception** is applied. This means that only important or exceptional disparities between real and planned achievement are reported to top management. Less important deviations are dealt with by subordinates.

Management information is presented to indicate the disparities between performance standards and actual performance, and

Establishing performance standards in practice

An organisation building medical devices, for example, needs to establish performance standards to ensure that the following criteria are met:
- Suppliers follow stringent quality controls.
- All raw materials are traceable and a recall system is in place to identify which products would need to be removed from the market in case of a problem.
- Chemicals used are stored safely and with proper documentation.
- Adequate measures are in place for cleaning the equipment.
- Staff has proper training in safety standards.
- Pest control is in place.
- Packaging materials are not contaminated.
- Shipping occurs under proper environmental conditions, including temperature and humidity.

Source: Dyck, B. & Neubert, M.J. 2010. *Principles of management*. International edition, p. 416. © South-Western, a part of Cengage Learning, Inc. Reproduced by permission. www.cengage.com/permissions.

to enable management to concentrate on deviations or problem areas. For example, management might be highly satisfied with a report indicating that sales are 10% higher than in the previous year, but they are likely to feel less complacent about the fact that sales of the company's market leader have shown a drop of 10%. The lapse of time between performance and measurement must be kept to the minimum so that deviations may be spotted as early as possible.

In the IBM case study, the company's actual performance measurement showed a loss of USD17 million and half the company's market share in 1993. Gerstner's task was to turn IBM around by concentrating on problem areas.

9.3.3 Step 3: Evaluate deviations

This step comprises the determination of the performance gap between the performance standard and actual performance. It is important to know why a standard has only been matched and not exceeded, or even why performance has been much better than the standard. This could, for example, be the result of a new trend in the business environment, which might then be exploited more effectively. The nature and scope of the **deviations** responsible for the so-called performance gap may have various causes. In some cases, the causes may be fairly obvious. In other cases, the causes may be so obscured that it becomes difficult to identify them. It is therefore impossible to make generalisations about the causes of disparities between actual performance and standards.

Firstly, it is necessary to make sure that the disparities are genuine. In other words, it must be determined whether both the performance standard and the actual performance have been set and measured objectively. If the standard is set too high, further examination of apparent deviations may be a waste of time.

Secondly, it must be determined whether the deviations are large enough to justify further investigation. Upper and lower limits should be set for each deviation, and only those deviations that exceed the limits should be subjected to further examination.

Thirdly, all the reasons and activities responsible for the deviation should be identified.

At this point, decisions about **corrective action**, the last step in control, must be taken.

9.3.4 Step 4: Take corrective action

The final step in the control process is to determine the need for **corrective action** and to ensure that deviations do not recur. If actual achievements match the standards, then of course no corrective action is needed, provided that standards have been set objectively. If actual achievements do not match the performance standards, management has a choice of three possible actions:

- Actual performance can be improved to reach the standards.
- Strategies can be revised to accomplish the standards.
- Performance standards can be lowered or raised to make them more realistic in the light of prevailing conditions.

In the IBM case study, Gerstner decided to focus on controlling business fundamentals by consolidating some of the company's organisational structures, internal processes and systems. He rebuilt company culture to focus on performance.

Step 4 completes the cycle of the control process. Corrective action is, in a sense, the point of departure for the next cycle in the management process. However, the term "control" has different meanings for different people. It often has a negative connotation for people who feel that their freedom and initiative are being restricted. It is therefore important to maintain a balance between control measures and control of people. It should also be remembered that there are limits to the time and money that can be spent on control. Moreover, control should be continually adapted to changing circumstances.

The following case study illustrates the implementation of the control process by James Burke, CEO of Johnson & Johnson in 1982.

Case study

Johnson & Johnson

James Burke's biggest career challenge came, as chairman and CEO of Johnson & Johnson (J&J), in 1982 when seven people died in the Chicago area after taking cyanide-laced extra-strength Tylenol capsules, a pain reliever sold by J&J subsidiary McNeil Consumer Products Co. The most prominent, and by now legendary, example of good crisis management remains J&J's handling of the Tylenol disaster. James Burke's actions in the weeks after the first death, which was reported on September 30 1982, have been the subject of case studies in numerous business schools and management texts, not to mention the impetus for a new subspeciality in public relations. Burke not only preserved the reputation of his highly respected consumer company, but he saved the Tylenol brand.

At no point did Burke try to back off from the company's responsibility in the incident, even though it was later proven that the tampering had occurred at the retail level. "When those people died," says Burke, "I realised there were some things we hadn't done right. Responsibility for that incident had to be, in part, ours. It wasn't easy to take responsibility ... but it was clear to us, to me especially, that whether we could be blamed for the deaths or not, we certainly could have helped to prevent them. How? Through packaging. The fact is that the package was easily invaded. You could take out the capsule, open it up, put the poison in and then put the capsule back together. It was easy to do. I felt, and still feel, that it was our responsibility to fix it."

Burke's conviction and his total commitment to the safety of the customer led the company to spend USD100 million on a recall of 31 million bottles of Tylenol, which before the tampering had been the country's best-selling over-the-counter pain reliever. The recall decision was a highly controversial one because it was so expensive. There were plenty of people within the company who felt there was no possible way to save the brand and that it was the end of Tylenol. Many press reports said the same thing. But Burke had confidence in J&J and its reputation, and also confidence in the public to respond to what was right. It helped turned Tylenol into a billion-dollar business. Within eight months of the recall, Tylenol had regained 85% of its original market share and a year later, 100%. The person who tampered with the Tylenol was never found. In 1984, J&J replaced capsules with caplets. In 1988, the company introduced gel caps, which look like capsules but cannot be taken apart. Within several years, Tylenol was once again the most popular over-the-counter analgesic in the US.

The Tylenol incident inspired the pharmaceutical-, food- and consumer-product industries to develop improved quality-control methods and tamper-resistant packaging such as induction seals. Moreover, product-tampering was made a federal crime.

Source: Wikipedia. 2010. "Chicago Tylenol murders". [Online] Available: http://en.wikipedia.org/wiki/1982_Chicago_Tylenol_murders Accessed 2 February 2010.

9.4 Types of control

In the introductory discussion of control, it was stated that organisations use control procedures to ensure that they are progressing towards organisational goals and that resources are being used properly and productively. But what exactly should be controlled to ensure that an organisation is progressing towards its goals?

This section focuses on the different areas and levels of control in an organisation.

9.4.1 Areas of control

As a rule, management should identify the key areas to be controlled. These are the areas responsible for the effectiveness of the entire organisation. For example, the production department of a manufacturing organisation is a key area, as is the purchasing department of a chain store. Generally, a small percentage of the activities, events or individuals in a given process are responsible for a large part of the process. Thus, 10% of a manufacturing organisation's products may be responsible for 60% of its sales, or 2% of an organisation's personnel may be responsible for 80% of its grievances. By concentrating on these strategic points, for example, the organisation's main activities are exposed to control. The IBM case study showed that by successfully identifying the company's strategic points, Gerstner turned IBM around.

Most organisations define areas of control in terms of the four basic types of resources they use. Generally, human, financial, physical and information resources are deployed to accomplish specific goals, especially those revolving around profitability. Control should therefore focus on the effective management of these resources. Figure 9.2 illustrates these four key areas of control:

- physical resources, which entails factors such as inventory control and quality control
- human resources, which involves orderly selection and placement of employees, control over training and personnel development, performance appraisal and remuneration levels
- information sources, which relates to accurate market forecasting, adequate environmental scanning and economic forecasting
- financial resources.

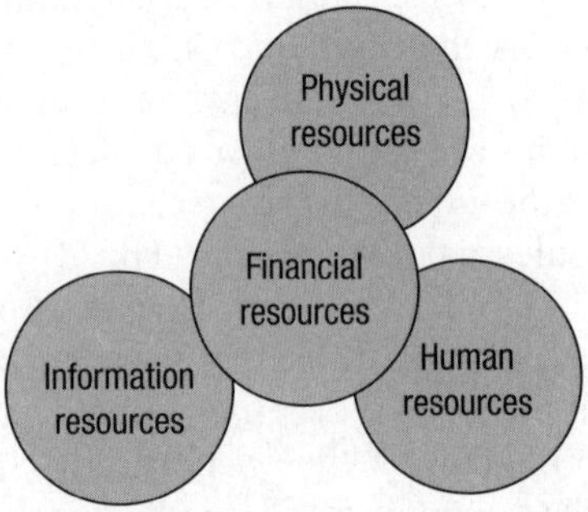

Figure 9.2: Key areas of control

Note that in Figure 9.2, financial resources are situated at the centre of the other three resources because they are controlled in their own right (for example, cash-flow or debtor control) and because most control measures or techniques (for example, budgets, sales, production costs, market share and various other magnitudes) are quantified in financial terms.

The four focal points of control are discussed in greater detail below.

9.4.1.1 The control of physical resources

An organisation's physical resources are its tangible assets, such as buildings, office equipment and furniture, vehicles, manufacturing machinery and equipment, trading stock, raw materials, work in process and finished products. Various control systems of an administrative nature can be established to **control physical resources** (in particular, office furniture, equipment and vehicles) that normally appear on an asset register. Control systems for these resources involve usage procedures, periodic inspections and stock-taking, which often fall within the ambit of the internal audit. The control systems for inventories, raw materials and finished products are inventory control and quality control. Although inventory control falls within the field of purchasing and logistics management, it is necessary to make a few remarks about it here.

Inventory control

Inventory refers to the reserves of resources held in readiness to produce products and services, as well as the end products that are kept in stock to satisfy consumers' and customers' needs. It normally refers to the four basic kinds of inventory (raw materials, work-in-process, components and finished products), but it need not only have to do with manufacturing. For an airline, a seat on an aircraft is inventory and an unsold seat on a flight is a loss. By the same token, money in a safe in a bank is inventory that can be lent to clients at a certain interest rate. Organisations keep inventories – and here the word is used in a wide sense – mainly for the following purposes:

- to satisfy the needs of customers and consumers
- in the case of raw materials and components, to keep uncertainties regarding delivery and availability to a minimum so that the manufacturing process is not interrupted
- as a hedge during times of high inflation.

The following three control systems are relevant in the control of inventory:

- **Economic-ordering quantity (EOQ)**, in use as early as 1915, is based on replenishing inventory levels by ordering the most economic quantity. The disadvantage of this control system is that inventory must be kept, regardless of the needs of the manufacturing department or customer, for particular raw materials, components or finished products. This means that items must be kept in stock for indefinite periods in spite of efforts to keep inventory costs as low as possible.
- The **materials-requirements planning (MRP)** system was developed in the 1960s to eliminate the shortcomings of the EOQ control system. With this system, an estimate is made of the demand for raw materials and the components necessary to create a finished product. Inventories are ordered only when they are needed and the costs of maintaining inventory levels over extended periods of time are thus eliminated.
- The **just-in-time (JIT)** system is a refinement of the MRP system. It originated in Japan, where it was developed by Toyota in the 1970s. The JIT philosophy is the same as MRP in the sense that organisations endeavour to manufacture products without incurring significant inventory costs. However, in contrast to MRP, where the need for raw materials and components is estimated and they are ordered according to demand, JIT is based on the premise that actual orders for finished products are converted into orders for raw materials and components, which arrive just in time for the manufacturing process. A manager applying the JIT principle orders materials and components more often in smaller quantities, thereby reducing risk and investment in both storage and actual inventory.

An element that is closely intertwined with inventory control is quality control.

Quality control

Quality has become an increasingly important issue in management. The Tylenol incident of Johnson & Johnson inspired the pharmaceutical-, food- and consumer-product industries to introduce improved quality-control methods. The management approach that emphasises the management of quality is known as **total quality management (TQM)**. Because of its importance, particularly in competitive international markets, it is necessary to give a brief overview of **quality control**.

Japanese products were once regarded as cheap goods. Today, however, the quality of Japanese products is acknowledged globally. Because of the success of Japanese products, especially in the United States, western managers are realising increasingly that access to international markets depends not only on mass production, but also on quality. Whereas quality control was formerly the responsibility of a single department or section, TQM means that quality is the responsibility of everyone in the organisation, from the chairman of the board of directors down to clerks, purchasing managers, engineers, and selling and manufacturing personnel. TQM emphasises how managers can continuously improve an organisation's work systems so that its products and/or services are better able to deliver the quality desired by customers.

Edwards Deming is known as the founding father of the quality movement. The example below illustrates Deming's approach to the implementation of control systems in organisations.

A strategic commitment on the part of top management will ensure that quality is included in the mission statement of the organisation and transmitted to operational levels. The ultimate test of product quality is in the marketplace, where it becomes evident whether or not the product satisfies consumers' needs.

The discussion of the control of the organisation's physical resources highlights the complexity of controlling physical resources

Applying the concept: W. Edwards Deming, founding father of the quality movement

Deming is well known for the "Red Bead Experiment" that he often used at his four-day seminars. In this experiment, ten volunteers are recruited to work in an "organisation": six willing workers, two inspectors, an inspector of the inspectors and one recorder. Deming pours 3 000 white beads and 750 red beads into a box, where they are mixed together. Each worker scoops beads out of the box with a scoop that holds 50 beads. Each full scoop is considered to be a day's production. White beads are acceptable; red beads are defects. Workers are asked to scoop out only white beads and no red beads.

Of course, owing to the laws of statistical variability, each worker scoops out some red beads, regardless of how motivated the worker is to get only white beads, how much the "manager" (Deming) exhorts them not to or how much he praises workers who have fewer-than-average red beads. Deming's message is simple: from a statistical point of view, it is foolish for a manager to use data about the number of red beads any particular worker produces as information for promoting or demoting workers. Rather, statistically speaking, management should acknowledge the following truths:

- There will always be variation in any process or system.
- As a result, there will always be variation in the performance of workers (some will perform well and other will perform less well).
- It is up to management to improve the system, not to reward and control the individuals within the system.

Many organisations have enjoyed improved performance when implementing control systems that are consistent with Deming's principles. For example, the Ford Motor Company found that transmissions manufactured according to these principles resulted in warranty repairs decreasing tenfold, and that "things-gone-wrong" customer reports dropped by 50% over a period of five years.

Source: Dyck, B. & Neubert, M.J. 2010. *Principles of management.* International edition, p. 140.

as well as the importance of control in the success of the organisation. Aspects of control are expressed mainly in financial magnitudes. Control of the organisation's financial resources is the next topic of discussion.

9.4.1.2 The control of financial resources

An organisation's financial resources are the second group of resources that management must control. Financial resources and abilities are vital to the success of the organisation and are at the heart of the control process, as indicated in Figure 9.2 on page 234. While financial resources are a group of resources in their own right, the control of financial resources is central to the control of other resources of the organisation. Financial control is concerned with the following aspects:

- resources as they flow into the organisation (for example, returns on investments)
- financial resources that are held by the organisation (for example, working capital and cash)
- financial resources flowing out of the organisation (for example, the payment of salaries and other expenses).

Each of these categories of financial resources is controlled so that revenues are sufficient to cover expenses and show a profit. Incoming funds, which normally represent revenue in the form of electronic transfers, cheques and cash, must be controlled rigorously because this is an area where fraud is often experienced. Funds that are held by the organisation, such as working capital, should not be tied up in areas such as outstanding debtors or slow-moving inventory. Of equal importance is the control of outgoing funds (for example, salaries and expenses), which is also an area where fraud and serious errors may be found.

Financial-management principles that deal with cash flows, cash management, investment returns and so on can also be regarded as financial-control measures, but it is beyond the scope of this chapter to deal with these issues in detail. However, since financial control is pivotal to the control process, we will examine two instruments of financial control: budgetary control and financial analysis.

The budget

As part of the planning process, management allocates financial resources to different departments of the organisation in order to enable them to accomplish certain goals. By allocating funds to specific activities, management can implement certain strategic plans. This allocation of financial resources is done by means of the **budget**. From the point of view of control, management wants to know how the financial resources are applied. The budget is therefore used as an instrument of control.

A budget is a formal plan expressed in financial terms that indicates how resources are to be allocated to different activities, departments or subdepartments of an organisation. At the same time, it forms the basis for controlling the financial resources, a process known as budgetary control. Budgets are usually expressed in financial magnitudes, but can also be expressed in other units such as sales volumes, units of production or even time. It is precisely because of the quantitative nature of budgets that they provide the foundation for control systems. They provide benchmarks or standards for measuring performance and making comparisons between departments, levels and periods. More specifically, a budget makes the following contributions to financial control:

- It supports management in co-ordinating resources, departments and projects.
- It provides guidelines on the application of the organisation's resources.
- It defines or sets standards that are vital to the control process.
- It makes the evaluation of resource allocation, departments or units possible.

Various kinds of budgets, some examples of which are provided in Table 9.1 on page 238,

Table 9.1: Types of budgets

Type of budget	Focus	Examples
Financial budgets	• Focus on cash flow • Focus on capital expenditure	• Cash-flow budget • Capital budget
Operational budgets	• Revenue • Focus on the operational aspects of the organisation	• Sales budgets and contract budgets
Non-financial budgets	• Focus on diverse aspects of the organisation that are not expressed in financial terms	• Production budgets in units • Sales volumes in units • Time projections of projects

can be used to make financial control possible across the financial spectrum.

Budgets were traditionally developed in a top-down fashion, where top management would develop the budget and impose it on the rest of the organisation. However, the way budgets are set today, especially in larger organisations, is to involve all managers of operating units, from the bottom to the top, in the budget process. A great deal of interaction takes place between heads of operating units (supervisory management), dimensional heads (middle management) and top management. The budget is usually set by a budget committee consisting of top managers. It is here that members of top management implement their strategies, which they do by allocating financial resources to the areas or divisions that must lead the organisation's strategy.

Budgets have a number of strengths as well as weaknesses. The most important advantage of a budget is that it facilitates effective control by placing a money value on operations, enabling managers to pinpoint problems. Budgets also facilitate co-ordination between departments and maintain records of organisational performance. On the negative side, however, budgets may sometimes limit flexibility.

Budgets are not the only instrument that management uses to apply financial control. To complement the budget, management can use **financial analysis**, also known as **ratio analysis**, to apply financial control. This will be discussed in Chapter 13.

9.4.1.3 The control of information resources

All the tasks of management (planning, organising, leading and controlling) are dependent on supporting information in order to function effectively. However, it is the relevant and timely information that is made available to management during the management process that is vital in monitoring how well the goals are accomplished. Accurate and timely information allows management to implement plans and determine on a continuous basis whether everything is proceeding according to plan, and whether adjustments need to be made. The faster management receives feedback on what is going smoothly or badly in the course of the management process, the more effectively the organisation's control systems function.

9.4.1.4 The control of human resources

Although the control task of management focuses mainly on financial and physical resources, this does not mean that the performance of one of the organisation's main resources, people, is exempt from control. A few remarks will be sufficient to emphasise the scope of control of human resources throughout the organisation.

The main instrument used to control an organisation's human resources is performance measurement. This entails evaluating employees and managers in the performance of the organisation. More specifically, from a control point of view, the performance of individuals and groups is assessed and compared with pre-determined standards. Tasks are subdivided into components. The importance of each subtask is determined so that criteria and measuring instruments can be developed. Performance standards must then be developed, for example, 40 production units per hour, an accuracy level of 98% in tuning machines, or a quality level of at least 93%. Actual performance can be measured against these standards for feedback to and action by management.

Other human-resources control instruments include **specific ratio analyses** that can be applied in respect of labour turnover, absenteeism and the composition of the labour force.

The preceding discussion of the control of an organisation's resources mainly emphasises the formal control systems developed by management. As far as informal control systems are concerned, however, people in the organisation play a decisive role in social-control mechanisms. This refers specifically to group behaviour. When a group of people work together on a regular basis, they develop norms that lay down guidelines for the behaviour of the group. These norms, which may include the quality of products, speed of production and reliability, are usually not written down and have nothing to do with the formal organisational structure. Nevertheless, they have a profound influence on the behaviour of groups when it comes to control or social control. Members of the group subject themselves to the norms of the group because, if they do not, they may be punished by the group in ways that range from light-hearted teasing to outright rejection. Compensation by the group for group cohesiveness and control consists of approval of action, emotional support and the assignment of a leadership role to the leader of the group.

The above discussion of the areas of control provides an overview of the control process as it applies to the organisation's different resources and of some of the instruments that enable management to control resources.

9.5 Characteristics of an effective control system

The following are characteristics of an effective control system:

- integration
- flexibility
- accuracy
- timeliness
- simplicity.

These characteristics are discussed in more detail below.

9.5.1 Integration

A control system is more effective when it is integrated with planning, and when it is flexible, accurate, objective, timely and simple. The interface between control and planning is discussed in the introduction to this chapter. Control complements planning because deviations highlight the need to review plans and even goals. In this way, control provides valuable inputs to planning. The closer the links between control and planning, the better the eventual control system will be. This is why provision should be made at the planning stage to make control possible, for example, by formulating goals in such a manner that they can be converted into or applied as control standards. This means setting quantifiable goals. Figure 9.3 on page 240 shows how planning and control should be integrated.

9.5.2 Flexibility

The second characteristic of an effective control system is flexibility. This means that

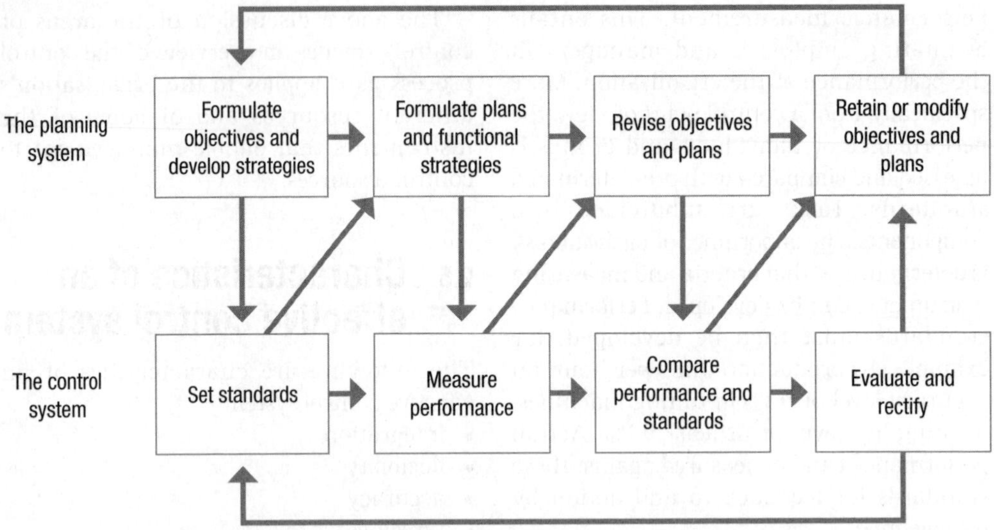

Figure 9.3: Integration of planning and control

the system should be able to accommodate change. Timeous adjustments in objectives or plans should not be regarded as deviations, but as revised objectives or plans. The control system should be able to adjust to such revisions, within limits, without management having to develop and implement an expensive new control system.

9.5.3 Accuracy

A control system should be designed in such a way that it provides an objective and accurate picture of the situation. Errors or deviations should not be concealed in the data. A total amount expressed in rand certainly does not show a profit, nor does it indicate which products sell better than others. Similarly, production management can conceal indirect costs to make production performance look good. Inaccurate information leads to incorrect modifications of new plans based on unreliable control data.

9.5.4 Timeliness

Timely control data are not obtained by means of hasty, makeshift measurement. Control data should be supplied regularly, as needed. A sensible approach is one that is based on the principle of timeliness.

9.5.5 Simplicity

Unnecessarily complex control systems are often an obstacle because they can have a negative influence on the sound judgment of competent managers. If managers are hampered by red tape, they may leave the system to keep things going. In so doing, they may lose their personal involvement and motivation to see to it that things proceed according to plan. Unnecessary control is equally demotivating for personnel and leads to resistance to control systems. Too much information, especially if it is irrelevant, makes great demands on the time and attention of management, which means that the control process becomes too expensive. The unwritten rule of effective control is that control should not become so complex that the implementation of the control system becomes more expensive than the benefits derived from it. At the same time, a system should not be over-simplified to the extent that the essence of control is lost.

9.6 Summary

Control is one of the four fundamental management functions. It is the final step in the management process, and the starting point for planning and strategic development. The control process narrows the gap between planned performance and actual performance by setting performance standards in the right places. The performance of management, subordinates and resources can be measured against these standards and deviations can be rectified if necessary. Control focuses on virtually every activity or group of activities in the organisation, but normally aims at physical, financial, information and human resources. Effective control systems are characterised by the extent to which planning and control are integrated, as well as the flexibility, accuracy and timeliness of the system. Management information plays an important role here.

However, too much information, especially irrelevant information, demands too much time and attention from management, which makes it too expensive. This ties in with the unwritten rule pertaining to control: the application of the control system should not become so complex that it costs more than it saves. At the same time, the system should not be over-simplified to the point of losing its significance.

This discussion of control as the final fundamental element of management completes the examination of the management process, and with it, Part 2 of this book. It should be clearly understood, however, that the general principles forming the subject of this section are also relevant in Part 3, which deals with the specialised or functional areas of management. Less detail from this section is provided when discussing, say, financial planning or marketing control, where the emphasis in the treatment of different business functions falls mainly on the activities peculiar to a particular functional area.

Key terms

accuracy	flexibility
actual performance	integration
budget	inventory
control	just-in-time system
control of financial resources	materials-requirements planning
control of human resources	quality control
control of physical resources	simplicity
corrective action	standards
deviation	timeliness
economic-ordering quantity	

Questions for discussion

Reread the case study on pages 228–229 and answer the following questions:

1. What steps did Louis Gerstner take to turn IBM around?
2. Identify the key areas of control in IBM.
3. How did the control process implemented by Louis Gerstner provide feedback for the revision of planning?
4. Explain the characteristics of an effective control system.

Multiple-choice questions

1. Which statement is false?
   a. Control helps organisations to cope with environmental change.
   b. Control systems increase costs in an organisation.
   c. Control helps an organisation to cope with increasing organisational size and complexity.
   d. Control helps limit the accumulation of error.

2. If actual achievements do not match performance standards, management can:
   a. improve actual performance to reach standards.
   b. raise standards to accomplish strategies.
   c. make strategies more realistic.
   d. none of the above.
3. Read the list of control systems given below.
   i. Economic-ordering quantity
   ii. Materials-requirements planning
   iii. Budgets
   iv. Just-in-time systems
   v. Total quality management
   Which combination of control systems is relevant in the control of inventory?
   a. i, ii
   b. i, ii, iv
   c. iii, iv
   d. iii, v
4. Financial budgets focus on ________, whereas operational budgets focus on ________.
   a. revenue, capital expenditure
   b. sales volume, time projection of projects
   c. cash flow, revenue
   d. capital expenditure, cash flow
5. An effective control system is:
   a. integrated with planning.
   b. able to accommodate change.
   c. objective.
   d. all of the above.

Answers to multiple-choice questions

1. b
2. a
3. b
4. c
5. d

PART 3

The functional AREAS OF A BUSINESS

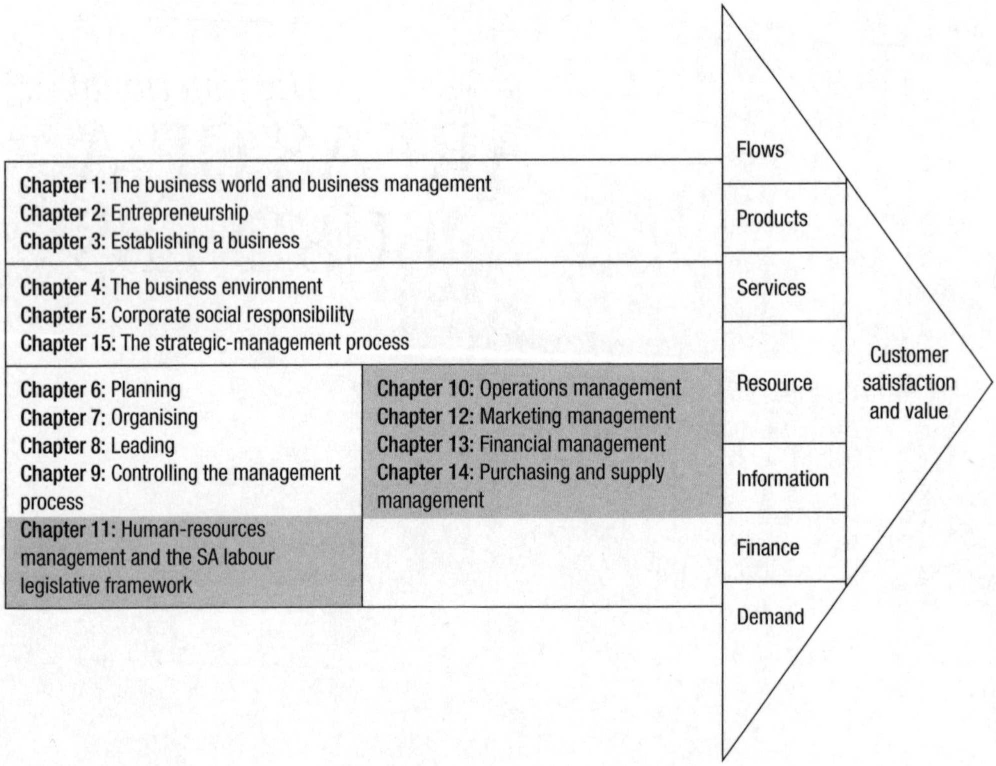

Source: Adapted from Mentzer, T. J. (ed.). 2001. *Supply Chain Management*. London: Sage, pp. 22–23.

CHAPTER

10

OPERATIONS MANAGEMENT

The purpose of this chapter

This chapter provides a broad overview of important aspects covered in the subdiscipline of operations management. It considers the nature of operations management and provides some definitions of related concepts, and it depicts an operations-management model and discusses each of its components individually. The chapter also classifies different process types for manufacturers and service providers. It then focuses on the three main activities of operations management: operations design, operations planning and control, and operations improvement. Selected tools, techniques and methods that can be used in performing these activities are also introduced.

Learning outcomes

On completion of this chapter you should be able to:

- explain why operations management is important for a business
- define what "operations management" encompasses
- identify and explain the components of an operations-management model
- distinguish between the six general operations-management performance objectives and explain what each entails
- explain how systems for classifying process types in manufacturing and services may assist operations managers
- identify the aspects involved in operations design
- explain how these aspects need to be managed in order to develop an effective design for products and services, including the processes for their manufacture or delivery
- identify the aspects involved in operations planning and control
- explain how these aspects need to be managed to manufacture or deliver products and services efficiently
- identify the aspects involved in operations improvement
- explain how these aspects need to be managed in order to provide a more effective and efficient operation for the manufacture of products and the delivery of services for competitive advantage.

10.1 Introduction

A business transforms inputs from the environment into outputs to the environment. The **operations function** is that function of the business aimed at executing the transformation process. The operations function and the management thereof (operations management) are therefore directly concerned with creating products and providing services in order to realise the objectives of the business.

10.1.1 The importance of operations management

An effective and efficient operation can give a business four types of advantages[1]:

- Firstly, it can **reduce the costs** of making the products or offering the services. (As profit equals revenue minus costs, reducing the costs of production by being more efficient and having less waste, rework, scrap, spillage and so on will directly contribute towards the profitability of production.)
- Secondly, it can **increase the revenue** the business receives for offering its products and services to its customers/clients. (According to the profit equation given above, increasing sales through superior-quality products and service excellence, or just by offering "good value for money", again directly contributes towards the profitability of a business.)
- Thirdly, it can **reduce the amount of investment** (capital) needed to manufacture the type and quantity of products or to offer the service required. (Increasing the effective capacity of the operation by better use of facilities, machines or equipment, and seeking new ways and procedures to optimise the functioning of the operation may decrease the amount of capital required for investment in the acquisition and running of these facilities, machines or equipment.)
- Fourthly, it can **provide the impetus for new innovation** by using its solid base of operational skills and knowledge to develop new products and services. This can involve manufacturing's production capability or the offering of new products and services in accordance with international best standards and practices.

Other reasons that operations management is considered important to a business include the following:

- Operations management can improve productivity. Productivity, measured as the ratio of output to input, is a yardstick for the efficacy with which operations management transforms (or converts) the resources of a business into products or services. If a business produces more error-free outputs with less wastage of material inputs, or puts its manufacturing staff to better use, its overall productivity will improve. Higher productivity, in turn, is directly related to increased profitability for businesses, which benefits the country in which the business operates.
- Operations management can help a business to satisfy the needs of its customers/clients more effectively. The customer/client is an important focal point in operations management, and the operations manager should see to it that quality products or services are provided for the consumer at a reasonable price. Satisfied customers/clients are of crucial importance to any business since its long-term survival or existence is dependent on them. Businesses will endeavour, by means of their particular operations skills, to satisfy the needs of their customers/clients more effectively than their competitors do.
- Operations management can be decisive for the general reputation of the business. Some businesses have, through their particular operations skills, built up outstanding reputations as far as high-quality products or services, low costs, or simply "good value for money" are concerned. The operations skills of a business make (and also break) such reputations. Businesses

Critical thinking

Why is operations management deemed to be important?

The importance of operations management

While an effective and efficient operation can give a business several types of advantages, how important is operations management really? Is it more important than marketing, finance and other management functions?

Some people argue that nothing is possible without a good idea, while others say that without money, nothing is possible. Some see operations management as a dynamic and creative discipline: if human beings are seen as the rulers of creation, then operations management brings humans as close as they can be to the act of creation and creating value.

Business life is primarily concerned with creating products and services, putting operations management at the heart of its existence. All managers directly and indirectly create products or services, be they through micro- or macro-processes, for internal or external customers. In this sense, all managers can be viewed as operations managers. Every manufactured thing people see around them, sit on, eat, read, wear, buy and enjoy comes to them courtesy of operations managers who planned and controlled the production system involved.

such as Woolworths and Panasonic have built up exceptionally good reputations for high quality, and for such businesses quality is a competitive advantage that can be used to protect and further expand their market position.

10.1.2 Defining terms used in operations management

There are many definitions of "**operations management**". A common characteristic of all these definitions is that operations management is concerned with the management of the transformation process (the operations process) whereby products are manufactured or services rendered. To clarify further what is meant by operations management, the following concepts are defined[2]:

- The operations function is that function in the business primarily aimed at the utilisation of resources to manufacture products or render services.
- Operations managers are the personnel in the business who are directly responsible for managing the operations function.
- Operations management (the operations-management function) involves operations managers' activities, decisions and responsibilities that tie in with the execution of the operations function. The operations-management process includes operations planning, operations organising, operations scheduling and operations control.

Case study

BMW South Africa (Pty) Ltd: A world-class operation in action

BMW South Africa was established in 1975 when it acquired a full shareholding in Praetor Monteerders, which, at the time, assembled BMWs at its factory in Rosslyn, Pretoria. It was the first BMW plant to be established outside Germany.

Over the past 35 years, BMW South Africa has moved from operating a limited vehicle-production plant that merely assembled vehicles with a few customisation possibilities for the local market to a world-class plant capable of producing highly customised cars for customers across the globe. BMW's R1 billion investment in the Rosslyn plant during 1996 paved the way for the upgrade of the production facility into one of the most modern in the world, bringing it in line with other BMW plants worldwide. This earned the local plant the right to be known, since 1996, as "BMW World Plant Rosslyn".

BMW Plant Rosslyn produces an average of 50 000 BMW 3 Series sedans per annum, of which 75% are directly destined for export markets – going to countries such as the United States, Canada, Japan, Australia, New Zealand, Taiwan, Singapore, Hong Kong, the Phillipines and Korea.

BMW process technology

The production of the BMW 3 Series takes a car through different "shops" where specific technology is applied to ensure that a quality car is delivered to the customer. The process starts at the "Body Shop", where different steel pressings are assembled into a body shell. From here, the process moves to the "Paint Shop", where the body shell is painted according to the customer's order. This is done in a facility called the Vario-Shuttle. This extremely efficient way of dipping bodies produces paintwork of a superior quality. Cavity wax is then injected into cavities using purpose-built nozzles to prevent corrosion. Next, the bodies are taken on conveyer belts to the Assembly Plant. They are stored in an area called Selectivity where they are randomly engraved with the VIN (Vehicle Identification Number), which automatically activates the body number of the vehicle in question. The bodies are then lowered onto the production line. The doors are removed and loaded onto the door hangers that ferry them to the Door Assembly area. On the production line, the vehicle is fitted with different parts in tandem with the information on the Vehicle Verification Card. The completed engine is hoisted up underneath the vehicle and tightened to the vehicle via a sophisticated torque ranch with inbuilt programmed tightening mechanism. On arrival at the Final Line, the vehicle lands for the first time on its four wheels and thus is said to be "on rubber". The various liquids (for example, transmission oil, air-conditioner gas and fuel) are filled up while the control units within the vehicle are also adjusted prior to the vehicle being started for the first time. At this point, various tests are done. These include wheel alignment, wheel camber, and testing of the handbrake and the foot brakes. The fog lights and the headlights are aligned and adjusted. The vehicle is tested on the rattle track. Once the vehicle has passed all the tests, it is bought off, gets a buy-pack and is ready for shipment.

BMW quality

BMW aims to deliver world-class quality products to customers across the globe. All production operations are managed so that optimum quality is delivered. Each and every process involved in manufacturing the car must be checked for process capability, and inspections are implemented where required. Parts fitted into the car are assessed every step of the way from supplier to plant and the supplier's production facilities are audited against process conformity at pre-determined intervals. In 1994, BMW South Africa was the only local motor manufacturer to achieve the ISO 9002 certification. This certification proves the company is capable of producing cars and components within a quality management system that meets the highest international standards.

In recognition of its commitment to quality, BMW Plant Rosslyn has won numerous awards, including, in 2002, the coveted and prestigious J.D. Power and Associates' European Gold Plant Award for best car from a European plant (BMW Plant Rosslyn is included in this section for evaluation purposes), and in 2004 and 2005, the J.D. Power Award for Best South African Manufacturing Plant.

BMW South Africa embraces skills development and acts decisively in stimulating learning within the workforce. Following the decision to manufacture the BMW 3 Series at BMW Plant Rosslyn, the intensity of the training provided both locally and abroad contributed to the acquisition of the necessary skills required to build a quality product.

The J.D. Power Gold Award of 2002 referred to above is testimony to how committed all members of staff at BMW South Africa are. Yet the demand for higher skills in the future will increase as the manufacturing processes of BMW products become more and more complex. Training interventions must thus continually increase in order to play an even greater role in meeting these demands for higher and more sophisticated skills. BMW South Africa was one of the first companies in South Africa to receive accreditation as an "Investor in People", which is an International Standard for a level of good practice in training and development.

BMW's approach to its employees (who are referred to as "associates" within the company) tries to ensure that everyone has a strong sense of purpose. This builds organisational alignment so that everybody pursues common goals. High-level commitment is ensured by means of the performance-management system (called Portfolio), which allows for real responsibility and choice, helps build self-esteem and identity, and encourages employees to have a sense that they are making a real contribution. Remuneration and rewards (salaries and bonuses) are based on individual and team performance, which ensures that the best individuals are attracted and retained.

In addition, a wellness culture is promoted under the motto "BMW Caring Together". This culture aims to create an environment where all employees and the community readily take responsibility for their own physical, mental and spiritual wellness. Employees can choose from an array of confidential services ranging from physiotherapy to financial counselling. Most of these services are completely free or covered by the BMW employees' medical-aid society. In addition, BMW South Africa has implemented an HIV/Aids program designed by the workforce that strives to minimise the effect of the epidemic on employees and their families.

This HIV/AIDS program is an international best-practice for the BMW Group. It has been "exported" to other countries, including China, Russia and India.

BMW South Africa's commitment to its diverse culture is also entrenched in support of transformation through employment equity practices that aim for a truly inclusive and empowered culture. BMW South Africa has a commitment to corporate social responsibility that is based on developing partnerships with local communities through empowerment, developing sustainable skills and contributing in the long term to a better quality of life. These CSR initiatives support the development of the community at large as well as the requirements of BMW by concentrating on education in the fields of Maths, Science and Technology, and the Environment.

Finally, BMW South Africa believes its competitive edge is a result of its drive to become a learning organisation in which training and development are completely integrated with organisational objectives, the managers have the tools and incentives to actively develop staff, and everyone has access to development. To this end, the company aimed to have all its training initiatives accredited as either externally recognised or contributing towards these qualifications by the year 2009.

The BMWs that are currently being designed in the development departments will be on the market in three or four years' time and will continue to be manufactured for a further seven or eight years. These cars will continue to be used for a further eleven to twelve years. Therefore decisions made today have an effect over almost 25 years (without even taking into consideration the long-term repercussions of irresponsible waste disposal). Therefore, BMW South Africa has to consider its environment and sustainability commitment carefully.

BMW's commitment to the environment and sustainability

BMW South Africa communicates its safety, health and environmental practices to the public via its SHE Status Report. In the 2004/2005 report, the company stated that it believes it must act responsibly in the use of technology, which encompasses the use of raw materials, the sources of energy and the entire question of mobility as relevant to a car manufacturer (including the demands for the protection of the environment, safety and health). The company feels it should be possible for humankind to enjoy mobility, expand knowledge by providing new insights on underlying considerations, and safeguard health and improve quality of life without damaging or impairing the planet.

The authors of this chapter gave a six-month course in the basics of total quality management at the BMW World Plant Rosslyn at the time the J.D. Power Gold Award was bestowed. After this momentous event, when a South African plant was ranked first above its parent company in Munich, Germany, the authors felt that the following stood out:

- the commitment of the management of BMW South Africa to quality training
- dedicated individuals at the plant who encouraged all to be part of the quality drive
- the emergence of a quality culture through the combined efforts of management and staff
- the enthusiasm of the employees on the assembly lines, who wanted to learn more about quality management in general and apply it in their specific work practices.

Source: Information based on BMW South Africa. 2009. The BMW South Africa website. [Online] Available: http://www.bmw.co.za Accessed 12 August 2009.

10.2 An operations-management model

An **operations-management model**[3] that can be used to illustrate the management of the operations function is depicted in Figure 10.1 on page 251. The most notable elements of this operations-management model are the operations-management strategies and objectives, and the management activities that influence the transformation process that produces outputs.

10.2.1 Operations-management strategies and performance objectives

All businesses formulate business objectives, and if a business intends surviving in the long term, consumers who are satisfied with the business's products or services should be a top-priority objective. The operations-management function should take cognisance of customers'/clients' needs and continually formulate its management strategies and objectives in such a way that the competitive position and customer/client base not only

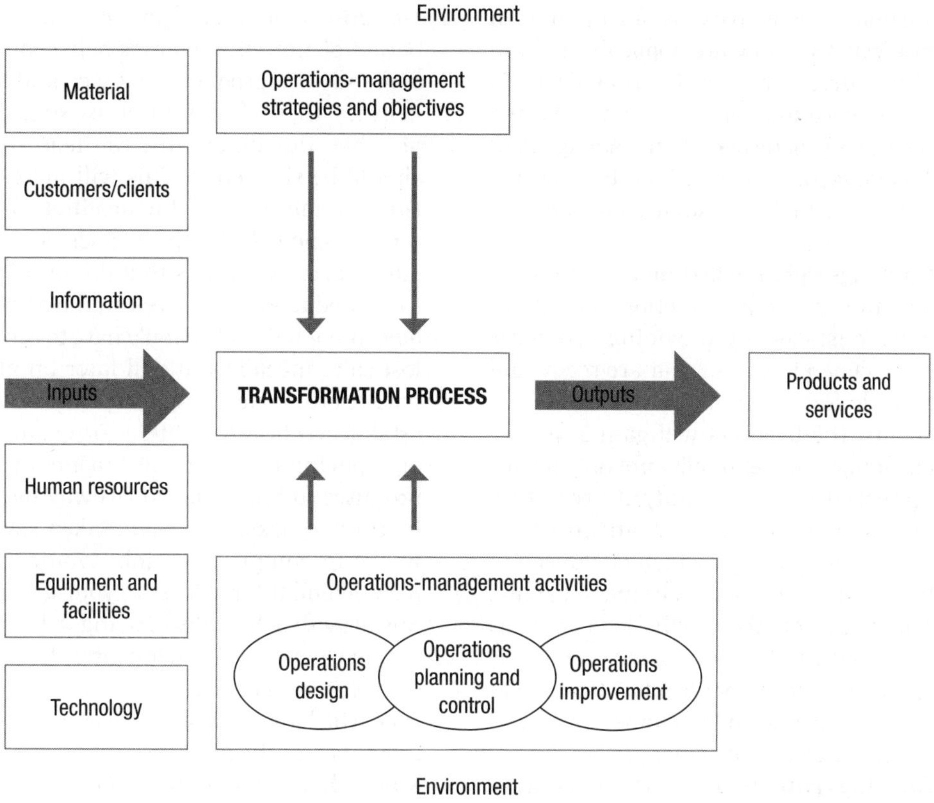

Figure 10.1: A general model of operations management

Source: Adapted from Slack, N., Chambers, S. & Johnston, R. 2004. *Operations management.* 4th ed. Harlow: Financial Times Prentice Hall, p. 5. Reprinted by permission of Pearson Education Ltd.

remain intact, but, where necessary, are also strengthened and expanded.

Although **customer/client needs** are numerous, they can be reduced to six main elements[4]:

- higher **quality**
- lower costs
- shorter **lead time** (quicker manufacturing or provision of services)
- greater adaptability (**flexibility**)
- lower variability with regard to specifications (reliability)
- high level of service (better overall service).

With these six customer/client requirements as a basis, operations-management performance objectives can be formulated to give the business an "operations-based advantage" over other businesses. Managing operations for competitive advantage or as a "competitive weapon" is an imperative for modern businesses in the face of increased global competition, rapid technological change, and the higher visibility and importance of ethical business practices, workforce-diversity issues and environmental-protection concerns.

Operations-management performance objectives must therefore indicate the specific areas within the domain of the operations function that will be emphasised when products and/or services are produced or provided. The operations-management performance objectives are formulated in such a way that they are applicable to both manufacturers and service providers. To acquire operations-based advantages, the following six general operations-management performance objectives (which incorporate the above-mentioned customer/client needs) can be followed:

- **Do things right the first time.** This means that the operations function should not make mistakes. By providing error-free products and services that are ready and suitable for consumption by customers/clients, the business will gain a quality advantage. Higher quality not only means increased error-free outputs resulting in lower costs, but also an improved competitive position, which could lead to higher prices and a greater market share. Think again of Woolworths' food products in this regard. This business is certainly one of the best known for providing top-quality food products, for which some consumers are prepared to pay higher prices.
- **Do things cost effectively.** It is imperative that products and services be produced or provided at a cost that will enable the business to place them on the market at a price that will ensure an acceptable profit for the business. This also applies to non-profit organisations because taxpayers and funders insist on good value, which they will receive only if institutions function cost effectively. Hence, when the operations-management function operates cost effectively, it can provide the business with a cost advantage. However, when this does not happen, for example, in the case of a gold mine where the cost per metric ton of mined gold-bearing ore is too high to run the mine profitably, drastic cost-saving measures, such as the large-scale retrenchment of miners, are necessary. In the case of PetroSA, for example, where the high procurement cost of the gas and oil made the project uneconomical, the state had to subsidise the project continuously at the expense of the taxpayer.
- **Do things fast.** This means that the period of time that elapses between the demand for a product or service and the delivery thereof should be as short as possible. Put differently, the lead time should be shortened. This will increase the availability of the products and services and will give the business a speed advantage. Businesses that do not place their products and services on the market quickly enough will not only have to accept lost sales initially, but will later on also have to overcome strong competition from established brands. Think, for example, of a paving construction business that promises to have a new driveway paved in three weeks, but then takes seven weeks to complete the job. Would you recommend this business to your friends? Businesses such as Boss Paving, which is reputed to complete paving faster than its competitors, acquire a speed advantage from which they will later build up a sound reputation in the market.
- **Make changes quickly.** The operations-management function should be able to adapt or change activities if unforeseen circumstances make it necessary to do so. This applies, for example, when more customers/clients demand a product or service, or if a customer/client requires the delivery of a wider variety of products or services within the agreed time. If the operations-management function can change activities in this way to satisfy customer/client demands both quickly and adequately, the business will have an adaptability advantage. During the 2002 World Summit on Sustainable Development in Johannesburg, South African businesses reacted quickly to the sharp increase in overseas visitors, and car rental companies such as Avis, for example, were able to cope with the sudden increased demand for rental cars. Businesses such as Toyota, in turn, are known for their ability to adapt their product line quickly to changing customer

needs, as in the case of the Toyota Tazz, which met the need for a more economical car.

- **Do things right every time.** Error-free products and services that satisfy set specifications should regularly and continuously be provided to customers/clients. This gives the business a high-reliability or low-variability advantage. This guideline ties in with the customer/client requirement of high quality. However, it emphasises the ability of the business to meet specifications continuously in the long term. This is of particular importance to businesses that produce or provide products or services on a continuous (or mass) basis. Take the example of McDonald's Big Mac hamburgers. McDonald's is an international business that claims that a Big Mac will taste the same in any place in the world where business is conducted. Thus, when people buy their second Big Mac, they will know exactly what they are getting. South African Airways (SAA) also strives for low variability in respect of times of scheduled departures to various destinations. If SAA's flights over a period of a year, for example, depart on schedule and reach their destinations 90% of the time, one could say that the airline renders a reliable service.
- **Do things better.** With due regard to all the preceding operations-management guidelines, a business will also endeavour to provide a better total product or service package compared to that of its competitors. This gives the business a service advantage. Think of businesses such as M-Net and BMW, which have gained reputations because they stand out above their rivals as far as service is concerned. This guideline is closely intertwined with the concept of total quality management (TQM), which is today the focal point of many top businesses internationally. TQM's point of departure is that quality products or services cannot be produced or provided unless the whole business (all the different functional-management areas) work together to achieve this goal. TQM will be discussed in more detail in section 10.6.3.

Figure 10.2 illustrates the positive results that can be obtained by each of the above-mentioned operations-management performance guidelines.

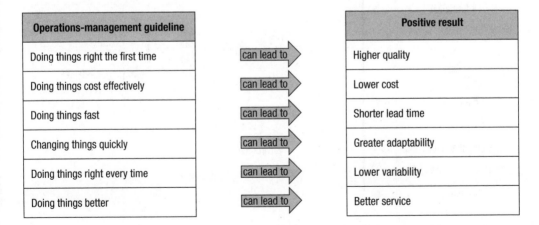

Operations-management guideline		Positive result
Doing things right the first time	can lead to	Higher quality
Doing things cost effectively	can lead to	Lower cost
Doing things fast	can lead to	Shorter lead time
Changing things quickly	can lead to	Greater adaptability
Doing things right every time	can lead to	Lower variability
Doing things better	can lead to	Better service

Figure 10.2: Positive results obtained by the application of operations-management guidelines

Source: Adapted from Slack, N., Chambers, S. & Johnston, R. 1995. *Operations management.* London: Pitman, p. 54. Reprinted by permission of Pearson Education Ltd.

10.2.2 The transformation model

The operations function is primarily concerned with using resources (inputs) to provide outputs by means of a transformation process. Therefore the **transformation model** comprises three main components: inputs, the transformation process itself and outputs.

A basic transformation model (also referred to as an input-transformation-output model) is depicted in Figure 10.3. This model can apply to both manufacturers and service providers.

10.2.2.1 Inputs

Inputs used in the transformation process comprise both the resources that are to be transformed (processed, changed or converted) and the resources required to make the transformation possible.

The resources to be transformed include the following:

- **Material.** A wide variety of material, both processed and unprocessed, can be used as inputs in the transformation process. For example, a motor manufacturer will use mainly processed material such as steel, glass and plastic, while a gold mine will use primarily unprocessed material (gold ore). For a service provider such as a hairdresser, different hair products, for example, shampoo and tinting agents, represent the material inputs.
- **Customers/clients.** Clients can serve as the inputs in the transformation process when the client is the subject being transformed

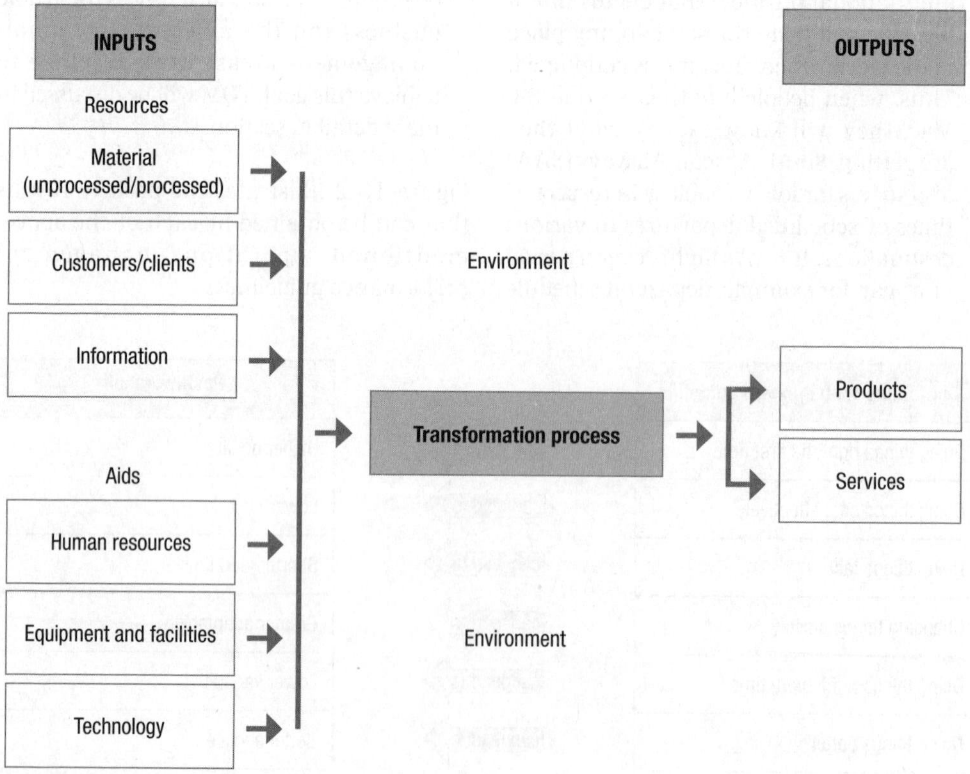

Figure 10.3: A basic transformation model

Source: Adapted from Schonberger, R.J. & Knod, E.M. 1991. *Operation management: Improving customer service.* 4th ed. Homewood, Illinois: Irwin, p. 3. Reproduced with permission of The McGraw-Hill Companies.

or "processed". For example, the client who receives dental treatment is the primary input in the transformation process. The same applies to recreational facilities such as gymnasiums and recreational events such as rock concerts because the client is the most important input who is transformed through being exercised or entertained.

- **Information.** Information can either be the primary input that is transformed, as when information is processed into news for a newspaper, or it can be used as the secondary input in a transformation process, as when information about consumer preferences regarding vehicle colours is used when a vehicle is processed.

The resources required to make transformation possible include the following:

- **Human resources.** In most transformation processes, some or other form of human involvement is necessary. This includes both workers who are physically involved in the transformation process and the people involved in a supervisory capacity. Some manufacturing processes are more labour intensive than others. A gold mine, for example, is more labour intensive than a motor-vehicle manufacturing plant, where many of the processes have been automated. Service providers such as hotels are normally also labour intensive, and the service sector is therefore seen as the sector with the most potential for job creation.
- **Equipment and facilities.** Equipment and facilities can assume many different forms. For example, manufacturers uses factories, machinery and equipment; hospitals use wards, examination rooms and operating theatres; banks use offices, computers and telephones; restaurants use eating areas, tables, chairs, gridirons, serving counters and take-away counters; universities use lecture halls, laboratories, theatres and sports fields; supermarkets use shopping areas, storage rooms, display areas, shelves, aisles and cash registers.
- **Technology.** The role of technology as an input in the transformation process is becoming increasingly important. Technology is generally used to enable the transformation process to function more efficiently. Thus, new knowledge and techniques (automation) can help a manufacturer to manufacture better products of higher quality more quickly. Service providers can also apply technology (for example, satellite communication) to render better services more quickly.

10.2.2.2 The transformation process

The **transformation process** converts inputs into outputs. The nature of the process is determined by what type of input is predominantly being processed.

When materials are transformed, the transformation process is primarily geared towards changing their physical characteristics (shape or composition). Most manufacturers, such as motor-vehicle or furniture manufacturers, employ such transformation processes. Service providers that also fall into this category include those that involve materials changing location (a delivery business), changing ownership (wholesalers and retailers) or primarily being stored (warehouses).

When information is transformed, the primary input is being processed. This occurs when information changes in composition or shape (for example, an auditor's report), changes ownership (for example, a market-research publication), is disseminated and changes location (for example, telecommunication) or is merely stored (for example, a library).

When customers/clients are transformed, this may also occur in a variety of ways. Some processes change the physical characteristics of clients (for example, hairdressing), while others change their physiological condition (for example, medical treatments at hospitals) or emotional condition (for example, entertainment at cinemas). The location of clients can also be changed (for example, by airlines) or they can merely be "stored" or accommodated (for example, in hotels).

10.2.2.3 Outputs

The ultimate goal of any transformation process is to transform inputs into outputs. **Outputs** assume the form of products or services. Manufacturers normally produce certain products (for example, motor vehicles or furniture), while service providers render certain services (for example, haircuts or transport).

The characteristics of products and services differ in ways that have specific implications for the management of the various operations processes. Important differences between products and services are represented in Table 10.1.

The differences listed in the table represent two extreme positions on a continuum between pure products manufacturers and pure service providers. In practice, however, businesses are, to a greater or lesser degree, involved in both the manufacture of products and the provision of services.

The transformation process, which comprises three main components of inputs, the transformation process and outputs, has already been explained. Table 10.2 on page 257 provides examples of the inputs, the nature of the transformation process and the outputs of a variety of businesses.

10.2.2.4 Different operations have different characteristics

While the basic purpose of all operations is similar in that they transform inputs into outputs, the processes may differ fundamentally in four ways (the four Vs)[5]:

- The **volume of output** may differ. This refers to the number of items produced by the operation over a given period of time. The more of one type of product that is made, the greater the benefit that may be obtained through standardisation and repeatability of the tasks and procedures. The most important implication of this characteristic with regard to the operational process is its influence over the cost of making a product or delivering a service: a lower production cost per unit is possible as fixed costs are spread over a larger number of units. The volume of output may range from high (for example, 220 motor vehicles per day) to low (for example, 20 aeroplanes per year).
- The **variety of output** may differ. This refers to the range of different items produced by the operation over a given period of time. The more types of products made by the same operation, the greater will be its flexibility and ability to provide non-standardised products or services – though these will inevitably come at the price of a higher cost per unit of manufacture or delivery. The most important implication of this characteristic with regard to

Table 10.1: Characteristics of products and services

Products produced by manufacturer	Services produced by service provider
• Physically tangible and durable	• Intangible and perishable
• Output kept in stock	• Output not kept in stock
• Little customer contact	• Plenty of client contact
• Manufactured before use	• Provision and consumption simultaneous
• Long response time	• Short response time
• Local and international markets	• Mainly local markets
• Large production facilities	• Small service-provision facility
• Capital-intensive production	• Labour intensive
• Quality easily measurable	• Quality difficult to measure

Source: Krajewski, L.J. & Ritzman, L.P. 1993. *Operations management.* 3rd ed. New Jersey: Pearson, p. 5.

Table 10.2: Inputs, transformation processes and outputs of various businesses

Type of business	Inputs	Transformation process	Outputs
Rail transport	• Locomotives • Passenger coaches and trucks • Locomotive drivers and personnel • Railway tracks and sleepers • Passengers and freight	• Change location of passengers and freight	• Passengers and rail freight at new destinations
Banks	• Bank tellers and financial advisers • Safes and computers • Bank notes and coins • Clients	• Receipt and payment of money (cash) • Record-keeping of accounts • Safekeeping of valuable articles	• Clients with financial peace of mind • Accurate bank statements • Financial earnings (interest)
Hairdressing salon	• Hairdresser and assistants • Combs, brushes and scissors • Treatment agents • Clients	• Shampooing, tinting, treating, drying and cutting of hair	• Clients with neat appearances
Gold mine	• Gold-bearing ore • Pneumatic drills and explosives • Lifts and conveyor belts • Miners and engineers	• Mine gold-bearing ore and transport to processing plant • Process ore and melt gold concentrates	• Gold bars
Furniture manufacturer	• Wood, steel and other materials • Saw and planing equipment • Factory workers	• Design furniture • Make furniture • Sell furniture to wholesalers	• Completed furniture such as lounge and dining-room suites
Printing works	• Printing and binding machines • Paper, cardboard and ink • Design and printing personnel	• Design, print and bind books, periodicals and reports	• Designed and printed material
Construction firm	• Sand, cement and other building material • Construction equipment • Construction workers • Building plans	• Plan and construct buildings according to plans	• Residential and commercial buildings
Missile manufacturer	• Electronic component • Rocket launchers • Engineers and technicians • Computers	• Design, assemble and test missiles	• Air-to-air or ground-to-ground missiles

the operational process is its capability of matching its products and services to the exact needs of customers/clients. Variety of output may range from high (for example, a taxi service to and from any location in and around Johannesburg) to low (for example, a fixed route and time schedule for a metropolitan bus service).

- The **variation of output** may differ. This refers to the particular demand pattern for the output of the operation, which may be constant or may be highly irregular, non-routine and unpredictable. The most important implication of this characteristic with regard to the operational process is the possibility of a sudden and dramatic change in the operations capacity required to supply products and services in order to meet the needs of customers/clients. Operations likely to experience seasonal variations (for example, hotel resorts in coastal locations) must be able to deal with marked variation in demand levels, from full occupancy during peak season to under-utilisation for the remainder of the year. Other hotels located in city centres may have constant patronage from business guests during most of the week and utilise special tariffs over weekends to level the demand. In the latter case, the unit costs will be lower than those of a comparable hotel with a highly variable demand pattern.
- The **visibility of output** may differ. This refers to how much of the operation's activities the customers/clients experience themselves or are exposed to. In high-visibility operations, the customers/clients experience most of the value-adding activities firsthand or directly, for example, in a designer's wedding-dress shop. This type of operation must be able to deal with a short waiting tolerance compared to low- or zero-visibility operations, with which the customer/client does not have much contact, as in the case of a larger departmental clothes store, or no contact at all, as in the case of a catalogue clothing retailer.

The implications of these four Vs of operations can be quite significant in terms of the cost of creating the products and services. While high-volume, low-variety, low-variation and low-visibility operational processes keep processing costs down, low-volume, high-variety, high-variation and high-visibility operational processes generally have a "cost penalty" (as explored in the box below).

Two service providers with very different models

The University of Pretoria (UP) is the largest contact residential university in South Africa's tertiary education sector, with approximately 38 500 residential students. The University of South Africa (Unisa) is the largest distance non-residential university, with approximately 280 000 students.

For UP, the tuition cost and fees per student will be markedly higher than in the case of Unisa because of on-campus class attendance with lecturers for all courses, limits on class sizes, and other more customised learning assistance found in laboratories and practical class sessions. However, Unisa offers distance education with hard-copy study materials with no or minimal lecturer contact. It accepts students from across South Africa and even worldwide. Unisa can therefore offer a quality tertiary-education package to students far afield at much lower tuition fees per student.

UP is good at what it does through its particular tuition model. Unisa, similarly, has been exceptionally good for over 130 years at non-contact distance education, and should not try to emulate residential universities in offering high-cost customised tuition activities, since, inherently, its operational processes are not designed for these and cannot be modified superficially for such a different tuition model.

A manufacturer versus a service provider

A motor-car manufacturer produces products that are physically tangible (the vehicle itself), durable (not used up in one period) and can be kept in stock (when more vehicles are manufactured than the number demanded immediately). There is no customer contact while the vehicle is being manufactured, and unless there are already a few vehicles in stock, it may take a while to deliver the vehicle to the customer. Motor-car manufacturers usually have large production facilities and expensive equipment, which make this a capital-intensive industry. Because of the tangible nature of vehicles, it is possible to set, monitor and ensure objective standards as far as quality is concerned.

A dentist renders a professional service. The service itself is intangible (it cannot be held or touched) and can also not be kept in stock if it is not used immediately. The presence of the user of the service (the patient) is necessary while the service is being rendered and the response time is usually short. Provision of the service takes place in a small service facility (a dental surgery), the service itself is labour intensive (the dentist is involved) and because the service is intangible, it is more difficult to set and maintain objective standards.

10.3 The classification of process types for manufacturers and service providers

Section 10.2 described an operations-management model that is applicable to both manufacturers and service providers, yet the exact nature of the transformation processes does differ. Such differences are important when the management of a particular operation is considered because certain management techniques and methods are suitable for application only in certain types of operation. Therefore it is useful to classify the process types that manufacturers and service providers use.

10.3.1 The classification of process types for manufacturers

In manufacturing, the most common **classification system** classifies different operations processes according to the **volume of output** (scope) and the **variety of products**. Thus, a business that produces a product in large volumes with little variety (for example, a manufacturer of bricks) will be placed in a different category from a business that manufactures small volumes of a large variety of products (for example, a clothing manufacturer). According to such a classification system (see Figure 10.4 on page 260), five main categories are identified. Each is discussed below with the aid of practical examples[6]:

- **Project processes.** Projects represent operational processes that are highly individual and unique, but that are normally tackled on a large scale. It can take a project team months or even years to complete such projects. Examples are construction projects (such as the building or upgrading of an airport, bridge, highway or shopping complex), the development program for a new car or the upgrading of an assembly line. Each project produces an output volume of one (the volume is therefore low), but a wide variety of project types can be undertaken (variety is therefore high). Two such large projects currently being planned in South Africa are the 2010 FIFA World Cup and the construction of the Gautrain (a high-speed commuter railway line between Johannesburg, Midrand and Pretoria).

- **Jobbing processes.** Jobbing normally represents operational processes conducted on a small scale with a low volume of output. The nature of the work is the same throughout, but the specific requirements differ from one task to the next. Examples are the process whereby a goldsmith manufactures jewellery (each piece of jewellery is usually unique and takes the unique design preferences of the client into consideration) and the printing of wedding invitations at a printing works (two wedding invitations for two different couples are usually not exactly the same in all respects). Thus, an important feature of these types of processes is that they combine a wide variety of products with a small volume of products.
- **Batch processes (job lots).** In batch production (lot production), a limited range of products is manufactured by the business and production occurs in batches (or lots). Batch production appears to be nearly the same as jobbing, but it does not have the same degree of variety. Examples of batch production are the manufacture of domestic appliances such as toasters, grills, irons and fridges by Defy, or the manufacture of televisions, DVD players and sound equipment by Samsung.
- **Mass processes.** Mass production is a well-known term for the production of products in high volumes, but with relatively little variety. While there may be some variants of the product itself (for example, the colour, engine size and installation of optional equipment offered by motor-car manufacturers), the basic process of production is the same, repetitive in nature, largely predictable and easier to manage than both jobbing and batch processes.

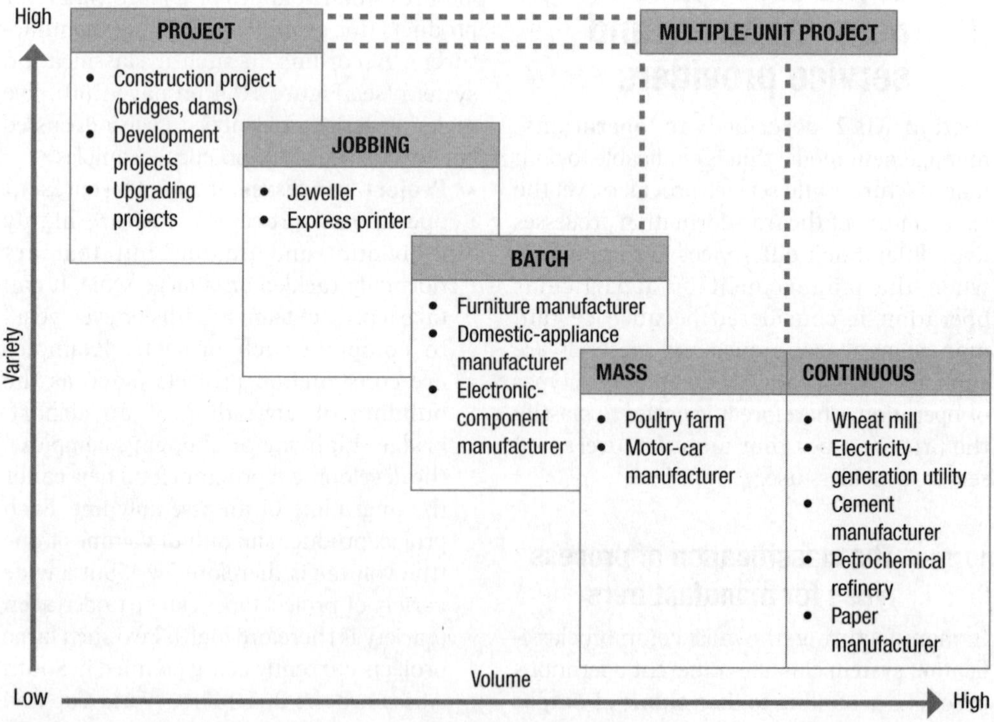

Figure 10.4: The classification of manufacturers' operational processes

Source: Adapted from Slack, N., Chambers, S., Harland, C., Harrison, A. & Johnston, R. 1995. *Operations management*. London: Pitman, p. 141.

- **Continuous processes.** Continuous production is a step beyond mass production because the volumes are even greater, but there is very little variety in the type of product. Such processes provide the same product on a continuous basis without a break, other than the occasional need for maintenance or plant upgrading. Examples are a wheat mill (Sasko), an electricity generation utility (Eskom), a cement manufacturer (PPS cement), a petrochemical refinery (Sasol) and a paper manufacturer (Sappi).

10.3.2 The classification of process types for service providers

The same classification criteria used for manufacturers can be used for service providers (one based on output volume and output variety). According to such a classification system (see Figure 10.5), three main categories can be identified. Each is discussed below with the aid of practical examples[7]:

- **Professional services.** Professional services represent operational processes provided on a high client-contact basis, where the client is usually present within the service process for a considerable period of time. Contact often occurs on a one-to-one basis. The nature of the service provided takes the specific needs of clients into consideration and is therefore more people oriented than equipment oriented. Because of the client-focused nature of these services, the extent (volume) of presentation is low, while the variety of services that can be provided is high. Examples of professional services (referred to as such because of the formal academic qualifications and registration that such professional practitioners need to obtain) include the services of dentists, doctors, attorneys, auditors and management consultants.
- **Service shops.** Service shops represent operational processes where the characteristics of service provision fall between those of professional services and those of mass services. There is a fair amount of client contact and services are standardised to a certain extent, but the services are also adapted to accommodate the unique needs of clients (there is more variety than there is in mass services). The number of

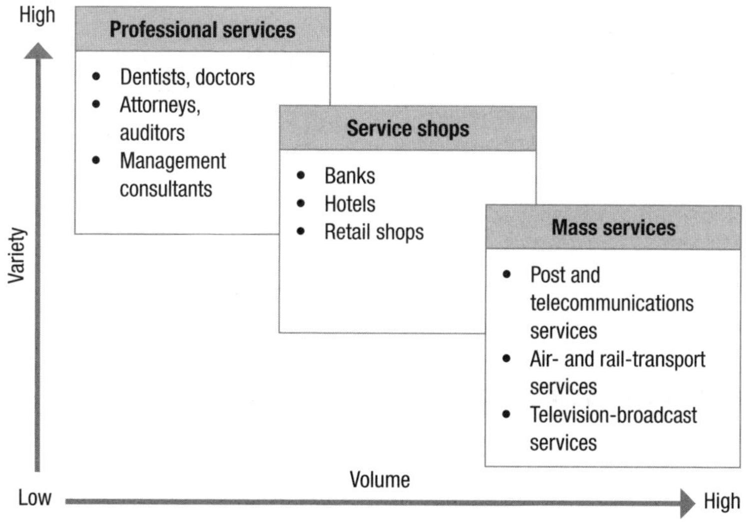

Figure 10.5: The classification of service providers' operational processes

Source: Adapted from Slack, N., Chambers, S., Harland, C., Harrison, A. & Johnston, R. 1995. *Operations management.* London: Pitman, p. 143.

clients served is also greater (the volume processed is usually more than with professional services). Examples of service shops are banks, hotels and retail stores.

- **Mass services.** Mass services represent operational processes where many client transactions take place with limited client contact and in which the nature of the services provided is largely standardised (variety is therefore low). These services are usually equipment oriented and are provided on a larger scale (volume is therefore high). Examples of mass services include post and telecommunication services, air- and rail-transport services, and television-broadcast services.

Classifying a restaurant

Sometimes it is difficult to place a specific operation in one of the above categories, or even to decide whether it is a manufacturer or service provider.

For example, is a restaurant that serves *à la carte* meals a manufacturer or a service provider (see Table 10.1 on page 256)? Obviously food is prepared, but clients are also served. The nature of the activities that have to be undertaken corresponds to that of a service provider (for example, the labour intensity required and the need for the client to be present). On the strength of this, the restaurant is classified as a service provider. However, since there is a certain amount of standardisation (a fixed menu is normally used), it can also be placed in the category of a service shop.

10.4 Operations design

10.4.1 The nature of operations design

The design of a product, for example, a motor car, entails far more than merely determining its physical appearance in terms of shape, colour and finish. It also includes the design of the operational processes for manufacturing the different components of the motor car, such as the body assembly, paintwork and composition of the chassis and engine. Similarly, in the design of a service, for example a 24-hour security monitoring and reaction service, the processes (or systems) should be designed to execute the particular service as specified. This may involve an alarm system, a control room, security personnel and reaction vehicles.

Thus it is clear that **operations design** entails two interdependent aspects:

- the design of products and services (also referred to as "product design")
- the design of operations product or service processes to manufacture or provide these products or services (also referred to as "process design").

The primary aim of operations design is to provide products and/or services and processes that satisfy the needs of customers/clients in the best possible way.

Figure 10.6 on page 263 provides a broad framework of the different activities involved in operations design.

Obviously, design, as an operations activity, helps to achieve the operations-management objectives with regard to quality, cost, lead time, adaptability, variability and service. The designers of a product such as a fridge, for example, will endeavour to design an aesthetically acceptable product that will satisfy customers' expectations regarding functionality and reliability, as well as be quick and easy to manufacture. The design should also be such that errors in the manufacturing process are kept to a minimum so that manufacturing costs can be kept at a reasonable level.

Designers of services (for example, a telephone service) are also expected to construct the service in such a way that clients' expectations are met and the service can be rendered affordably and within the operational ability of the business. Most, if not all, products and services encountered in the market today first have their origin

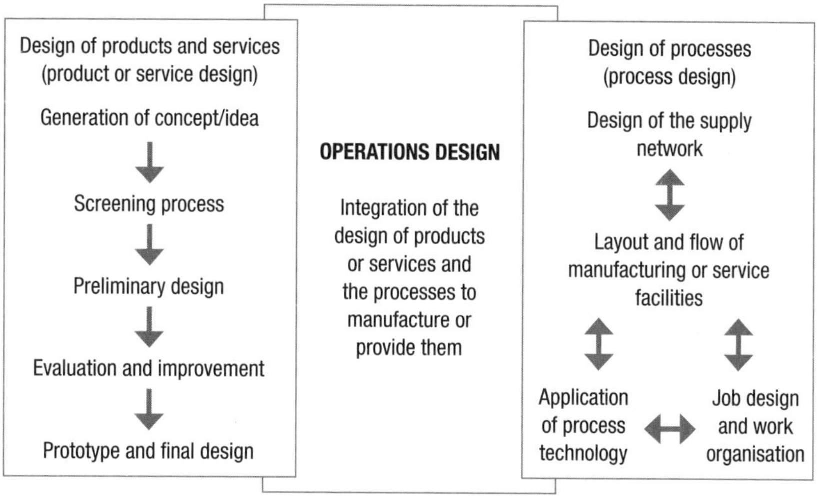

Figure 10.6: The nature of operations design

Source: Slack, N., Chambers, S. & Johnston, R. 2004. *Operations management.* 4th ed. Essex: Pearson, p. 95.

as a vague idea or concept put forward as a suitable solution to a perceived need of a customer/client. The idea or concept is refined over a period of time and, in the process, more and more detailed information is attached to the idea or concept. Ultimately, there is sufficient information to put together a specification for the product or service, and the process for its manufacture or provision.

10.4.2 The design of products and services

Although the operations manager is usually not solely and directly responsible for the design of a product or service, he/she is indirectly responsible for providing the information and advice on which the ultimate success of the development, manufacturing or delivery of the product or service depends.

10.4.2.1 The competitive advantage of good design

The design of a product or service begins and ends with the customer/client. Initially, products and services are designed with a view to satisfying the needs of the customer/client in the best possible way. If they are well designed, produced and provided so that the expectations of customers/clients are realised or even exceeded, the business's competitive position will be reinforced through the increased sales of these products and services. For example, the design and production of the well-known Venter trailer is a good example of how a competitive advantage can be gained in the market. Other manufacturers have since entered the market with similar products, but Venter is still the market leader.

10.4.2.2 The components of products and services

All products and services consist of three interdependent components[8]: a concept, a package and a process.

The **concept** (or idea) is the set of expected benefits that the customer/client purchases when purchasing a product or service in response to his/her needs. Because customers/clients are not just buying the product or service, but also this set of expected benefits, the product or service should meet all their expectations. For example, when someone buys a new car, not only the car itself is bought, but also all the expected benefits that go with it, such as safety, reliability, outstanding road-holding ability and, possibly, a high value at resale. The same applies when a service, for example, medical treatment at a hospital, is purchased. The patient expects a set of benefits such as good medical care, the timeous receipt of prescribed medication, and a secure and peaceful environment so that he/she can recover from the illness.

The set of expected benefits that a customer has is referred to as the "product concept", while the set of expected benefits that the client has is referred to as the "service concept". When the product or service is designed, the operations manager should understand exactly what the customer/client expects from the business. This knowledge and insight is of vital importance to ensure that the transformation process provides the "right" product or service concept.

Concepts involve a **package** of products and services. The concept of a product usually refers to a tangible physical object such as a car, dishwasher or article of clothing, while the concept of a service indicates an intangible object such as a visit to a theatre, a hairdressing salon or a night club. However, as mentioned above, it is often difficult to make a clear distinction between these two concepts. Take, for example, a new car. The physical vehicle is clearly a tangible object, but the other benefits – such as the guarantee and the regular repairs at scheduled times – are an intangible service. A meal in a restaurant comprises physical products such as food and drink, but also service in that the food is prepared and served, and even the atmosphere in the restaurant plays a role. Thus, regardless of whether it is a product or service that has been designed, the package comprises a combination or "bundle" of products and services. It is this package that the customer/client in fact purchases.

Two further aspects should be kept in mind in the composition of a service package:

- Firstly, services cannot be inventoried. For example, if an appointment or flight ticket is not used, then the opportunity "lapses" and is wasted.
- Secondly, services usually involve direct interaction between the customer/client and the process[9]. They can involve high contact (seeing a psychotherapist) or low contact (posting a letter).

A **process** is necessary to create the package of products and services. The design of the products or services takes place in conjunction with the design of the processes required to manufacture or provide them. (The stages of the design of products and services are discussed in section 10.4.2.3, and the design of the processes is discussed in section 10.4.3.)

10.4.2.3 The stages in the design of products and services

The design of a product or service ultimately results in a **full detailed specification** of the product or service. To compile this specification, detailed information must be obtained about the concept (the form, function, aim and benefits of the design), the package (the composition of products and services required to support the concept) and the process of creating the package (which determines the way in which the individual products and services of the package will be manufactured or provided).

To obtain this full detailed specification, it is necessary to first follow certain **consecutive steps**. Although not all businesses necessarily follow the same steps, the typical sequence of steps is as follows:

- **Concept generation.** The first step in designing a product or service starts when different ideas for new product concepts or service concepts are generated. New ideas for products or services can come from within the business itself (for example, the ideas of personnel or those from formal research and development programs) or from outside the business (for example, the ideas of customers/clients or competitors).

- **The screening process.** Not all concepts that are generated will necessarily develop into new products and services. Concepts are evaluated by means of a screening process based on certain design criteria, such as feasibility (how difficult is it and what investment is needed?), acceptability (how worthwhile is it and what return is possible?) and vulnerability (what could go wrong and what risks are there?). Each of the stages that follows progressively refines the original concept up to the point where there is sufficient information and clarity for it to be turned into an actual product or service with an operational process to produce or deliver it. Such progressive reduction of the multitude of design options for a new product and service occurs through a process of elimination that is referred to as the "design funnel"[10]. Overall, the purpose is to determine whether the new concept will make a significant contribution to the product or service range of the business. Several functional management areas – such as marketing, operations and finance – are involved in the screening process of new concepts, and each may use different criteria in this process. The operations manager is responsible for operations-focused screening to determine whether the business has both the ability (people, skills and technology) and the capacity to produce or provide the concepts.
- **Preliminary design.** Once the ideas and the concepts generated by the particular functional-management areas in the business are reduced to one or two potentially acceptable product or service concepts, the next step is the preliminary design of the product or service. The preliminary design is the first attempt to specify the composition of the components of the product or service to be included in the package and to identify the processes that will be necessary to produce or provide the product or service package.
- **Evaluation and improvement.** The aim of this step is to evaluate the preliminary design with a view to improving it, and making the process of manufacture and provision less expensive and easier. Various techniques and methods can be used as aids in this step.
- **Prototype and final design.** The last step in the design of products or services is the development of a prototype of the product, or a simulation of the service, in order to test it in the market. If the prototype, which is based on the improved preliminary design, is favourably received in the market, the final design and specifications of the product or service can be compiled.

10.4.3 The design of operations processes

The design of operations processes to manufacture products or provide services is just as important as the design of the products or services themselves. Without both competent product design and competent process design, it is impossible to develop, manufacture or provide a successful product or service.

10.4.3.1 The design of supply networks

No operations process exists in isolation; it is always part of a greater, integrated **supply network**[11]. Besides the specific operations process itself, the supply network also includes the suppliers of materials or services, as well as intermediaries and final customers/clients.

In the design of a particular operations process, it is important for the entire supply network to be taken into consideration. This enables the operations manager to determine precisely what the inputs for the specific operations process are and the customer/client needs that have to be satisfied. Such a study also helps the business to determine its competitive position in the supply network, identify significant interfaces in the supply network and reflect on its long-term involvement in the supply network.

10.4.3.2 The layout and flow of manufacturing and service-provision facilities

The **layout** of the operations facility determines the physical arrangement of the resources (such as machines, equipment and personnel) used in a particular transformation process. The layout of a manufacturing or service-provision facility is usually the first characteristic of an operational process to be observed because it determines the physical form and appearance of the facility. At the same time, the layout determines the way in which resources such as materials, information and customers/clients **flow** through the transformation process. Both the layout and flow of an operations facility are of particular importance since small changes in the placement of machines and the flow of material and people can greatly influence the operational process in terms of cost and efficiency.

The layout of a manufacturing or service-provision facility entails three steps: selecting the process type, selecting the basic layout type and making a detailed design of the layout.

The first step is **selecting the process type**. The different process types for both manufacturers and service providers were discussed in section 10.3. The process types for manufacturers are project, jobbing, batch, mass and continuous processes. For service providers, they are professional services, mass services and service shops.

The second step is **selecting the basic layout type**. Four basic layout types[12], which depict the general form and arrangement of operations facilities, can be identified (see the box on page 267). The four basic layout types are as follows:

- **The fixed-position layout.** In this layout, the product cannot be shifted on account of its size, shape or location. The resources for transformation (equipment, machinery and people) are taken to the receiver of the processing, which is static, for example, a construction site or a shipyard.
- **The process layout (flexible-flow layout).** In this layout, similar processes (operations) are grouped together into sections. For example, if a business manufactures not only basic office chairs, but also tables and desks, these can be grouped together for the tasks (sawing, planing, turning and attaching).
- **The product layout (line-flow layout).** In this layout, the different processes (operations) required to manufacture a product or provide a service are arranged in consecutive order. Thus the layout is adapted to the product, as in the case of an assembly line for motor vehicles or the service counters in a self-service cafeteria.
- **The cellular layout (hybrid layout).** In this layout, specific processes are placed in a cell, which is then arranged according to either a process or a product layout. A good example here is a department store selling men's, ladies' and children's clothing. The men's department functions as an independent cell with its own layout, and the same applies to the ladies' and children's departments.

However, the selection of a basic layout type merely provides an indication of the broad layout of the operations facility. It does not determine the precise placement of the various machines and equipment. The final step in the layout of a manufacturing or service facility therefore entails making a **detailed design** of the layout.

10.4.3.3 The application of process technology

All operations processes use some or other form of process technology. "**Process technology**" refers to the machines, equipment and apparatus used in the transformation process to transform materials, information and clients so that products can be manufactured or services provided. Process technology may range from relatively simple processes

Applying the concept: Four basic layout types

Fixed-position layout

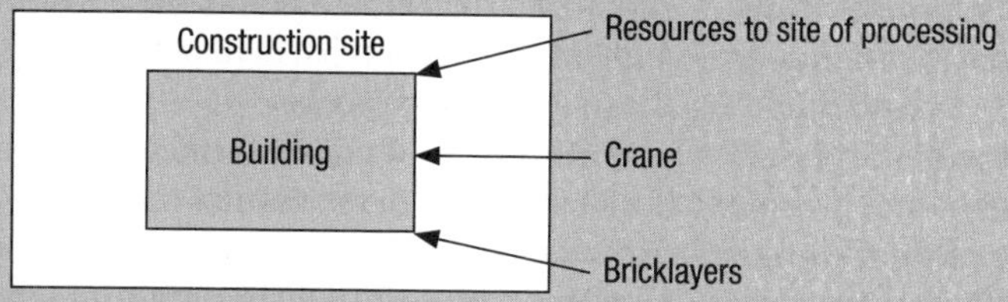

Process layout or flexible-flow layout

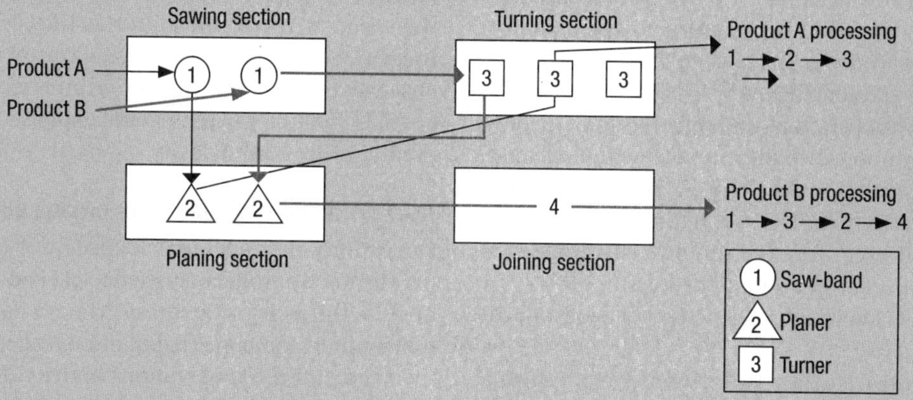

Product layout or line-flow layout

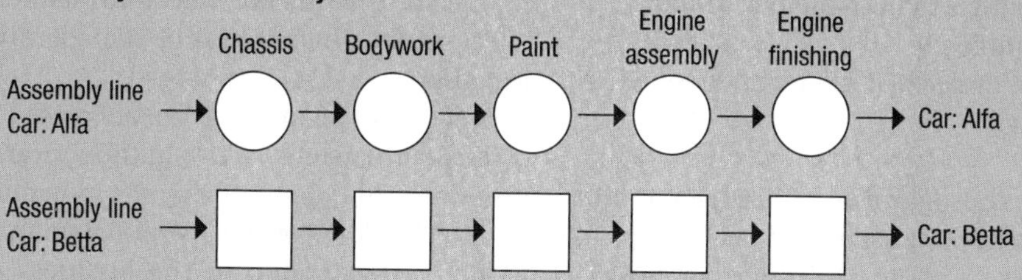

Cellular layout or hybrid layout

Department-store floor plan

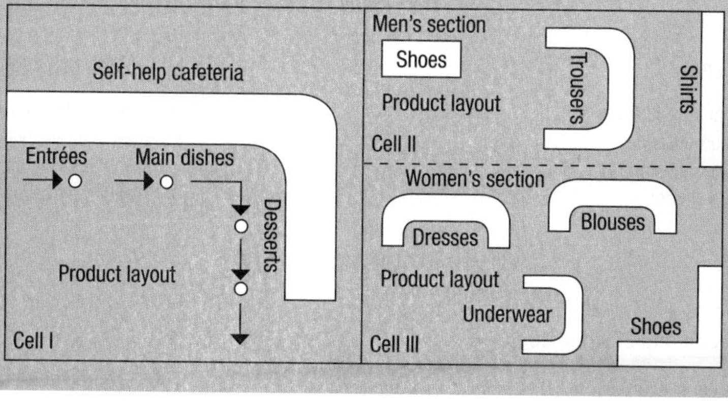

(for example, a basic extraction process such as using a machine to dig a hole for a new pipeline) to highly complex and sophisticated systems (such as automated manufacturing, which uses robots). Automated manufacturing represents the future of "overall better" manufacturing and service provision. This will involve less human involvement and greater use of robotics to develop the "ultimate machine" that will be able to deliver extraordinarily high levels of error-free products and services (quality), nearly instantaneously (speed), whenever required (dependability), cheaply (cost) and with much-reduced waste and greater efficiency[13].

The operations manager has to be involved continuously in the management of all facets of process technology. To perform this task effectively, he/she needs to:

- foresee how technology can improve a specific operational process
- decide which technology or technologies to use
- integrate the new technology with existing operations activities
- continually monitor the performance of the technology
- upgrade or replace the technology when necessary.

Although the operations manager is not necessarily a specialist in each technological field, he/she should still have an understanding of what a particular technology essentially entails and how the technology performs the particular function. He/she should also be able to identify the advantages and limitations of a particular technology in the operational process.

For example, a cotton farmer will have to decide whether to mechanise the harvesting process by using a cotton harvester or whether to continue using manual labour. The advantages of mechanising the operational process would be likely to include the speed at which the cotton is harvested, the better quality of the collected cotton and cost savings over time. Limitations would possibly include greater capital expense and greater process complexity.

10.4.3.4 Job design and work organisation

Operations management focuses not only on the technologies, systems, procedures and facilities in a business (the so-called non-human component), but also on people's involvement in the operations activity itself. The way in which human resources are managed in a business has a fundamental effect on the effectiveness of the operations function.

Since most people who are appointed in a business are usually active in the operations function, this places a huge responsibility on the shoulders of the operations manager as far as leadership in the business and

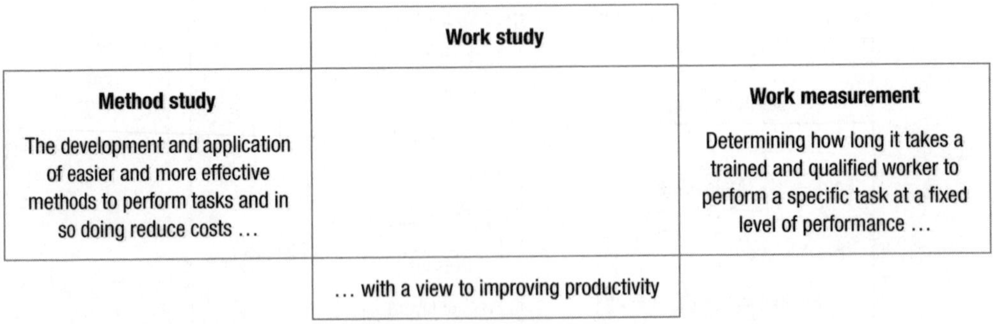
Work study
Method study
The development and application of easier and more effective methods to perform tasks and in so doing reduce costs ...
Work measurement
Determining how long it takes a trained and qualified worker to perform a specific task at a fixed level of performance ...
... with a view to improving productivity

Figure 10.7: Components of work study

Source: Slack, N., Chambers, S. & Johnston, R. 2007. *Operations management.* 5th ed. Essex: Pearson, p. 261.

Critical thinking

Which products and/or services were originally developed in South Africa?

Some true South African innovations

New products and services are important for the emergence of new businesses. Consider, for example, the relatively new product now known as a cellphone or mobile. Some new businesses (for example, Nokia) came into being as manufacturers of cellphones, although other existing businesses (for example, Sony, Motorola and Samsung) merely expanded their product ranges. In South Africa, no service providers existed at the time when cellphones first made their appearance, but some new businesses were subsequently started (for example, Vodacom, MTN and later Cell C).

Not only can new products and services be seen as catalysts for the emergence of new businesses, but they can also be considered as vital for the continued success of other businesses. Some countries (such as the United States and Germany) are known for regularly offering new product ideas or new technologies and innovations, while others (such as Japan and China) are said to prefer, in the main, to copy others or apply technology already discovered. Some innovative new products and services are accredited to South Africans. The following new ideas for products or services received recognition from the MTN ScienCentre in Cape Town as the top ten inventions or discoveries by South Africans:

1. Dolosse. These concrete blocks, shaped like interlocking bones, are used on breakwaters to withstand wave action. First used in East London and later around the world, they were invented by harbour engineer Eric Merrifield and his team.
2. Kreepy Krauly. This automatic pool-cleaning device was originally a South African invention, but it is now owned by an American company. Other pool-cleaning devices that originated from South Africa include brand names such as Aquanaut, Baracuda and Pool Ranger.
3. Tellurometer. This pioneering distance-measuring device was invented by Trevor Wadley.
4. Pratley Putty. This is a two-part clay-like mixture that bonds into a very hard and strong compound. It is the only South African invention to have gone to the moon. It was invented by K.G.M. Pratley.
5. Lunar stick. This is the oldest mathematical artefact in the world (35 000 years old), and was found in a cave in northern Zululand.
6. Scheffel bogey. This revolutionary train-carriage wheel assembly is used in Austria and South Africa.
7. Disa telephone. This was the first push-button telephone in the world. It was invented by Telkom technicians.
8. Appletiser and Grapetiser. These sparkling drinks use a pure fruit-juice recipe.
9. Computicket. This was the first computerised ticket-sales system in the world.
10. Vibol fuel-saving exhaust system. This is used all over the world.

Source: *South Africa at a glance 2005–2006.* 2006. Greenside: Editors Inc., pp. 268–269.

development of employees are concerned. **Job design** is of vital importance in operations management because it determines how workers perform their various daily tasks.

Work study is a scientific approach that can be used to great effect in job design and **work organisation**. It refers to the application of different techniques to study all the factors influencing the people in the work environment systematically in order to improve the execution of tasks in terms of efficiency and effectiveness. Two work-study techniques often encountered in the literature are method study and work measurement[14].

Method study entails the systematic recording and critical investigation of present and proposed work methods, with a view to the development and application of easier and more effective methods in an effort to reduce costs. **Work measurement** entails the application of techniques designed to determine how long it takes a trained and qualified worker to do a specific job at a fixed level of performance. The components of work study are illustrated diagrammatically in Figure10.7 on page 268.

10.5 Operations planning and control

10.5.1 The nature of operations planning and control

In section 10.4, design was examined as one of the activities of operations management. This design activity determines the physical form and structure of the operations process, and it has to be activated within the limits imposed by the design of the operations process. This is done by means of operations planning and control. Operations planning and control focuses on all the activities required to put the operations process into action efficiently on a continuous basis so that products can be manufactured or services can be provided to meet the needs of customers/clients.

In contrast to operations design, which may be regarded as a "passive" activity primarily aimed at determining the broad limits of the operational process, operations planning and control is an activating activity that starts the operational process "physically" so that products can be manufactured or services can be rendered. In the activation of the operational process, the operations manager is responsible for ensuring that the operations-management performance objectives of quality, cost, lead time, adaptability, variability and service (see section 10.2.1) are pursued and achieved.

Operations planning and control activities broadly endeavour to reconcile two entities. On the supply side, there are the products manufactured or services provided in the operational process. On the demand side, there are the specific needs of actual and potential customers/clients for products or services. Planning and control activities are aimed at reconciling the provision ability of the operations facility with the demand for specific products or services. Figure 10.8 illustrates the nature of operations planning and control in this process of reconciliation.

Reconciling the supply of products or services with the demand for them by means of planning and control activities occurs in terms of three dimensions:

- volume (the quantity of products or services)
- timing (when the products or services have to be manufactured or provided)

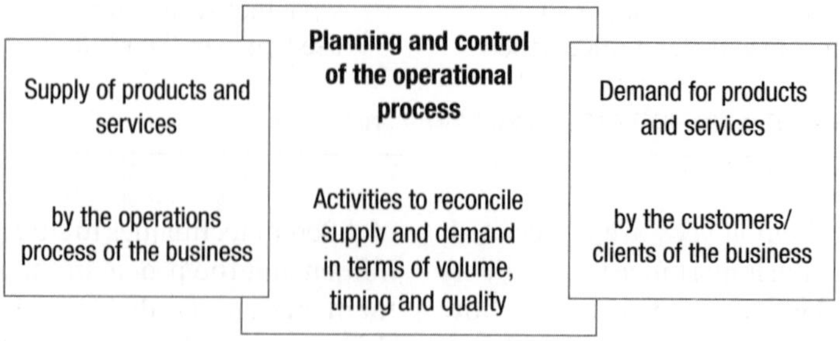

Figure 10.8: The nature of operations planning and control

Source: Adapted from Slack, N., Chambers, S. & Johnston, R. 2004. *Operations management.* 4th ed. Essex: Pearson, p. 323.

- quality (whether products or services consistently conform to customers'/clients' expectations)[15].

To reconcile the volume and timing dimensions with each other, three different but integrated activities are performed: the loading of tasks, the sequencing of tasks and the scheduling of tasks.

The "**loading of tasks**" refers to the volume or quantity of work allocated to a particular work centre. The available capacity of the operations process needs to be taken into consideration in the loading of work centres. For example, a medical practitioner will examine only one patient at a time in his/her consulting rooms, while the other patients wait in the waiting room.

The "**sequencing of tasks**" refers to the sequence in which the tasks are performed. The sequence in which tasks are performed can be determined beforehand by the use of certain priority rules, such as dealing with the job with the earliest deadline first, or following a first-in first-out approach. A commercial bank, for example, will serve the client who is at the front of the queue first.

The "**scheduling of tasks**" refers to the use of a detailed roster that indicates when a specific task should start and when it should be completed. Gantt charts are especially popular for planning and scheduling projects, and also give an indication of which tasks are late and which tasks are at a more advanced stage than anticipated.

After having viewed operation planning and control from a general perspective, the focus moves to specific operations activities: capacity, inventory and supply chain, and quality.

10.5.2 Capacity planning and control

The focus of capacity planning and control is on the provision of the manufacturing or service capacity of a particular operations process. When a suitable balance is found between the available capacity and the expected demand, it is possible that the business will have both satisfied customers/clients and acceptable profits. However, if the balance is "wrong" – that is, too much capacity with too little demand, or too little capacity with too much demand – the business is faced with a potentially disastrous situation. Businesses in this position may sit with either costly surplus capacity or possible lost sales opportunities. Because of the far-reaching impact that capacity decisions may have on the business as a whole, capacity planning and control are of vital importance in operations management.

10.5.2.1 Defining "capacity"

The term "**capacity**", as it is used in everyday parlance, usually refers to the fixed volume of, for example, a fuel tank (50 litres) or the space, for example, in a parking garage (bays for 500 vehicles). However, from an operations point of view, these scale or size dimensions are not sufficient, since capacity also has a time dimension (as illustrated in the box below).

> **Applying the concept: Calculation of the total capacity of a parking garage**
>
> If there are 500 parking bays in a parking garage at a supermarket, 500 vehicles can park there at a given time. However, this is not the total capacity. If the parking garage and supermarket are open ten hours a day and customers take on average an hour to do their shopping, the total capacity of the parking garage is actually 5 000 motor vehicles (number of parking bays × number of hours the parking garage is open ÷ average time a car is parked).

In an operations process, "capacity" is defined as "the maximum level of value-added activity over a period of time that the process can achieve under normal operating circumstances"[16].

10.5.2.2 The nature of capacity planning and control

While long-term capacity is already determined during the design of the operations process in the medium and short terms, there is the possibility of adapting or varying the capacity of the operations process in accordance with changes in the demand for particular products or services. Thus, particular machinery or equipment can be used for longer periods each day, or workers can be asked to work over-time during peak periods.

Operations managers generally have to work with a demand forecast that is by no means completely accurate and, moreover, is sometimes subject to regular fluctuation. **Quantitative data** on the expected demand and the **required capacity** to satisfy this expected demand must be obtained by applying the three steps described below.

Firstly, the total demand and required capacity must be determined. As a rule, the marketing function is responsible for determining the total demand by means of demand forecasting. Since this forecasting is an important input in determining the required capacity, the operations manager must at least have some knowledge of the basis for and rationale behind the demand forecasts. The way in which the required capacity will be determined depends on the nature of the products manufactured or services provided. With standardised products and services (where there is high volume with little variety), capacity will be measured in terms of output (for example, the number of television sets to be produced per week or the number of flights to be provided to Cape Town each day). In the case of less standardised products and services (where there is lower volume and more variety), capacity will instead be measured in terms of input. (Examples here are the number of working hours per week of a goldsmith making items of jewellery or the number of beds available in a hospital per day.)

Secondly, alternative capacity plans must be identified. The operations manager is expected to have alternative capacity plans in order to accommodate possible changes in demand. Three options are available[17]:

- a level-capacity plan in which the capacity levels are kept constant and demand fluctuations are ignored
- a chase-demand plan in which capacity levels are adjusted according to fluctuations in demand
- a demand-management plan in which demand is adjusted to tie in with available capacity.

In practice, operations managers usually use a mixture of the three alternative capacity plans, although one of them may be more dominant than the others.

Thirdly, the most suitable approach to capacity planning and control must be chosen. Here an endeavour is made to choose an approach that will best reflect the business's specific circumstances. For example, a fruit-packing plant will employ more temporary workers during the harvesting season to help with the packing of the fruit.

10.5.2.3 Techniques and methods used during capacity planning and control

Various techniques and methods can be applied during capacity planning and control to execute this activity better. Two of these methods are the moving-average demand-forecasting technique and the cumulative representations of demand and capacity. (Other techniques and methods, such as exponential levelling, demand-forecasting accuracy measures and the application of the queuing theory, are regarded as advanced topics and are therefore not included in this text.)

The **moving-average demand-forecasting technique** is based on the availability of actual demand data over preceding periods. This technique can be used to forecast the demand for the following period and is especially suitable for applying to the demand for products where the demand pattern is stable over the short term.

Applying the concept: The moving-average demand-forecasting technique

Table 10.3 shows how the moving-average demand-forecasting technique is applied to forecast the demand for washing machines for May 2010.

Table 10.3: Three-month moving-average demand forecast for washing machines

Month	Demand (actual)	Demand (forecast)	Three-month moving average (calculation)
December 2009	480		
January 2010	530		
February 2010	520		
March 2010	540	510	480 + 530 + 520 = 1 530 ÷ 3 = 510
April 2010	590	530	530 + 520 + 540 = 1 590 ÷ 3 = 530
May 2010	–	550	520 + 540 + 590 = 1 650 ÷ 3 = 550

Based on a three-month moving average, the demand forecast for May 2010 is therefore 550 units of washing machines.

However, the disadvantage of this approach is that if the demand continues to grow, the predicted demand is always going to be too low. In this example, the actual demand may be 610 but, according to the moving average, only 550 washing machines will be manufactured and there will therefore be a shortage.

Cumulative representations of demand and capacity is a method that can be used to evaluate the effect of different capacity plans graphically.

10.5.3 Inventory and supply-chain planning and control

These days, inventory and supply-chain planning and control are regarded as activities executed by a separate functional management area called purchasing management. However, since the inventory of materials and the purchase thereof have significant implications for the smooth functioning of the transformation process, for which the operations manager is mainly responsible, "**inventory**" is usually defined (from an operations-management perspective) as all stored resources (material, information and clients) required for the smooth functioning of the operations process. The operations manager should therefore liaise closely with the purchasing manager in order to manage inventory levels optimally.

Inventory and purchasing planning and control are discussed in Chapter 14.

10.5.4 Quality planning and control

Nowadays, quality is regarded as being so important in many businesses that responsibility for it is not confined to the operations-management function only. The basic premise of concepts such as total quality management (TQM) is that quality products and services can be manufactured only if the entire business contributes to the achievement of such an objective.

Quality is one of the main methods of adding value to products and services, and thereby obtaining a long-term competitive advantage. Better quality influences both factors that contribute to the business's

Applying the concept: Cumulative representations of demand and capacity

This method can be applied to evaluate a capacity plan for a coal mine. It would appear from the example that the production of coal during the months January to April was greater than the demand for it, and that there was "surplus" production during this period. From April to July (autumn and winter), the demand for coal was greater than production – hence there was a period of "under-production".

Cumulative representation of demand and capacity for a coal mine

	Jan	Feb	Mar	Apr	May	Jun	Jul	Aug
Demand (in thousands of cubic metres of coal)	50	75	75	200	200	100	100	100
Cumulative demand	50	125	200	400	600	700	800	900
Production (in thousands of cubic metres of coal)	100	100	100	100	100	100	200	200
Cumulative production	100	200	300	400	500	600	800	1 000
Production surplus/shortfall	50	75	100	0	–100	–100	0	100

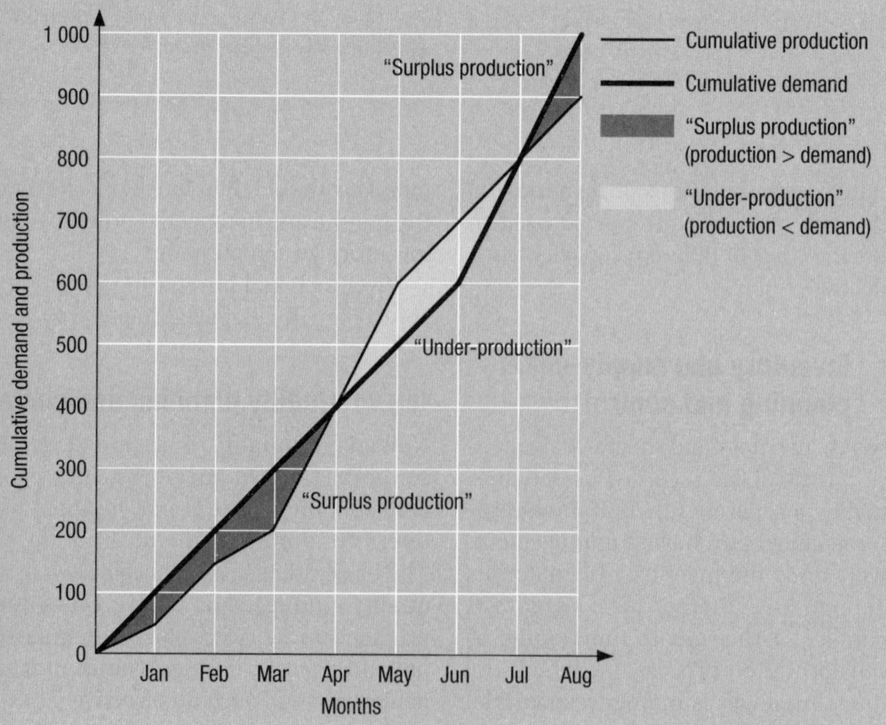

profitability: income and cost. Income can be increased by more sales and greater market share, while costs can be reduced by lower repair and inspection costs, and reduced wastage, inventory and processing time.

10.5.4.1 Defining "quality"

Different definitions of quality are often advanced. Each of them stems from a different approach to or view of quality. Thus, "**quality**" has been defined as "the absolute best", "something flawless", "suitable for the purpose for which it was designed", "meeting a set of measurable characteristics" or "good value for money". From an operations-management perspective, quality is defined as "consistent conformance to customers'/clients' expectations"[18].

Operations management therefore defines quality in terms of what a customer/client expects of a particular product or service, while the customer/client sees quality in terms of his/her own perception of the product or service. This difference between expected quality (by operations management) and perceived quality (by customers/clients) is known as the quality gap. Operations management, in conjunction with the other functional management areas, should endeavour to eliminate any quality gaps.

10.5.4.2 The nature of quality planning and control

The aim of quality planning and control is to ensure that the products or services that are manufactured or provided conform to or satisfy design specifications. The discussion of the design of products and services stated that the ultimate goal of this activity is to establish specifications for products or services that will satisfy the needs of customers/clients. Hence, what exists here is a customer/client–marketing–design–operations cycle. This design cycle (see Figure 10.9) can be further extended to include quality planning and control activities to ensure that products or services do in fact meet design specifications.

10.5.4.3 The steps in quality planning and control

Quality planning and control can be divided into six steps.

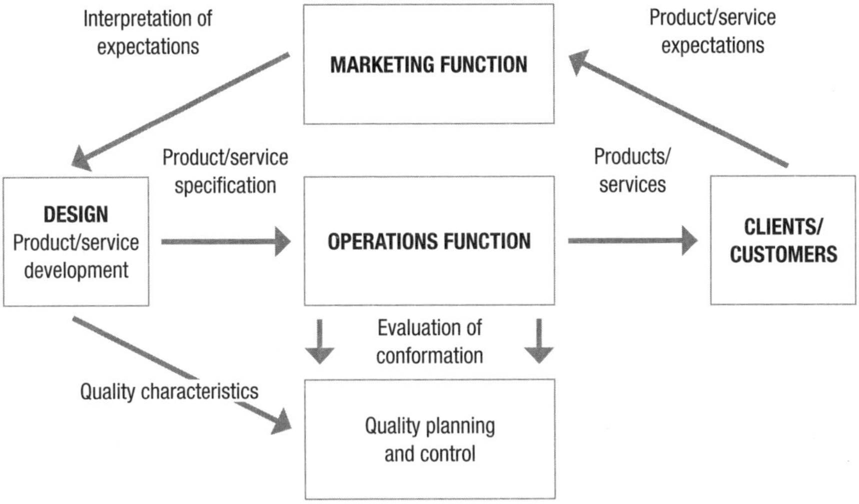

Figure 10.9: Extending the product/service design cycle for quality planning and control

Source: Slack, N., Chambers, S. & Johnston, R. 2004. *Operations management*. 4th ed. Essex: Pearson, p. 601.

The first step is defining the quality characteristics of the product or service. The design specifications for products or services are determined in the design activity. The design specifications as such are not monitored by quality planning and control, but rather by the operations process that manufactures the products or provides the services. This is to ensure that the specifications are met. For the purposes of **quality planning and control**, it is necessary to define certain quality characteristics that relate directly to the design specifications for products or services. **Quality characteristics** that are often used include:

- functionality (performance ability)
- appearance (aesthetic attractiveness)
- reliability (continuous performance capability)
- durability (total life expectancy)
- serviceability (reparability)
- contact (convenience of interaction).

Thus, for example, a customer will expect an expensive video recorder to record and replay TV programmes clearly, to be aesthetically pleasing, and to have a long and reliable lifespan and problem-free maintenance and repair.

The second step is measuring the quality characteristics of the product or service. For each individual product or service, the quality characteristics should be defined in such a way that they can be **measured and controlled**. The different quality characteristics should thus be further broken down to make such measurement possible.

For example, if the quality characteristic of functionality is measured in relation to a motor car, it can be broken down into the measurable dimensions of speed, acceleration, fuel consumption and road-holding ability. However, it is sometimes difficult to measure specific quality characteristics, such as the "friendliness" of the cabin crew of an airline. Here, an effort will instead be made to gauge passengers' perceptions of the friendliness of staff, in order to measure this. Indeed, every few months, SAA conducts such a survey among its regular passengers (SAA Voyager members).

The third step is setting **standards** for each quality characteristic of the product or service. Once the operations manager has ascertained which quality characteristics are going to be measured and how, the next step is to set specific quality standards against which the achievement of, and conformance with, the quality characteristic can be measured. Although most businesses strive for "absolutely perfect" standards (for example, "the quest for zero defect"), it is generally too expensive or unrealistic to expect a motor vehicle, for example, to last forever. Instead, realistic achievable standards are set, for example, that the motor vehicle will have an effective lifespan of ten years.

The fourth step is **controlling quality** against the set standards. Once realistic standards for measuring the output of the operations process have been laid down, the next step is to determine whether or not the product or service does in fact measure up to them. Three questions in particular are of importance to the operations manager here:

- Where in the operations process should one check to see if the standards have been satisfied? There are three possible positions: at the beginning of the process (preventive control), during the process (in-time control) or after the process (reactive control).
- Should each individual product or service provided be checked to determine whether the standards have been met? It is not always possible or desirable to inspect all products or services fully, and managers could instead use samples to determine whether the products or services do in fact meet the standards.
- How should the inspection be conducted? In practice, most businesses use sampling to ascertain whether their products or services measure up to standards. Two methods used here are statistical process control (SPC), whereby the inspection of

a quality characteristic takes place during the process of manufacturing or service rendering, and acceptance sampling (AS), whereby inspection occurs after the process of manufacture or service rendering.

The fifth step is identifying and rectifying the **causes of poor quality**. An important goal in quality planning and control is to identify the presence of poor quality and the reasons for it, and then rectify the poor quality.

The sixth step is continuously improving quality. As was mentioned earlier, quality is one of the most important ways of adding value to products or services in order to obtain a long-term competitive advantage – hence the importance of **improving quality** on a continuous basis. (This aspect will be discussed further in section 10.6.)

Critical thinking

What constitutes a good-quality product or service?

Good-quality products and/or services

Much attention is paid in the business world to the concept of good-quality products and services. However, some businesses view "quality" as important, but not necessarily critical for business success, while other businesses stake their reputations on quality and are known for providing their customers/clients with the best possible quality products and services. Think of Woolworths foods and Avis car rentals in this regard.

This leads to the question: Is quality really so important? To help answer this question, it is worth asking another question: Who wants a product that is broken or performs below expectations, or wants poor service delivery? Undoubtedly the answer to this is: "No-one".

If good-quality products and services are considered important for customers and clients alike, it logically follows that businesses that want to be successful over the long term should pay attention to these requirements. Thus better-quality products and services have definite advantages for a business.

Firstly, better-quality products and services improve the competitive position of the business by:

- enabling it to sell its products or services at a premium or a higher price in the marketplace
- creating the possibility of increasing the business's market share.

Both of these aspects lead to increased revenue for the business through market-route benefits and, in the end, increased profitability.

Secondly, better-quality products or services increase the defect-free output of the business by:

- lowering the costs of operations (through reductions in waste, rework, scrap and so on)
- increasing the level of overall productivity.

Both of these aspects lead to increased revenue for the business through cost-route benefits and once again, in the end, increased profitability.

Clearly, better-quality products and services have the possibility of not only increasing the revenue of the business through the market and cost routes, but, more importantly, they have the possibility of improving its long-term profitability.

To conclude, good or better-quality products and services are important for customers/clients, and businesses can only profit from improving their total quality initiatives.

Source: Based on an illustration of the benefits of TQM as contained in Schonberger, R.J. & Knod, E.M. (Jr). 1991. *Operations management: Improving customer service.* 4th ed. Homewood, Illinois: Irwin, p. 139. Reproduced with permission of The McGraw-Hill Companies.

10.6 Operations improvement

10.6.1 The nature of operations improvement

Sections 10.4 and 10.5 examined the design of the operational process, and the planning and control of the operational process. Yet even if both of these activities are successfully executed, the task of the operations manager is still not complete. Any operational process, regardless of how well it is initially designed or how well it is planned and controlled, can certainly be improved. Nowadays, the **improvement of the operational process** of a business is seen as a further (and probably even more important) activity of the operations manager.

Figure 10.10 provides a broad framework of the various activities that are pertinent in operations improvement.

Before any operations process can be improved, it is necessary to determine what its current performance is. Performance measurement is therefore a prerequisite for any improvement. In measuring performance, managers ascertain the extent to which the present operations process satisfies the formulated operations-management objectives as far as quality, service, adaptability, lead time, cost and variability are concerned.

10.6.1.1 Different types of performance standards

Once managers have determined by means of performance measurement the extent to which the present operations process satisfies the set operations-management objectives, the overall performance of the process should be evaluated. This is done by comparing the present performance level with certain standards. Four kinds of **performance standards** are generally used:

- **historical performance standards** (whereby present performance is compared to the particular business's own performance in previous years)
- **target performance standards** (whereby present performance is compared to pre-determined standards, which indicate an acceptable or reasonable level of performance)
- **competitors' performance standards** (whereby present performance is compared to that of one or more similar competitors – as in the case of benchmarking, where businesses evaluate their own operations function by comparing their product or service package with that of their competitors)
- **absolute performance standards** (whereby current performance is compared to the theoretical maximum achievable performance standards).

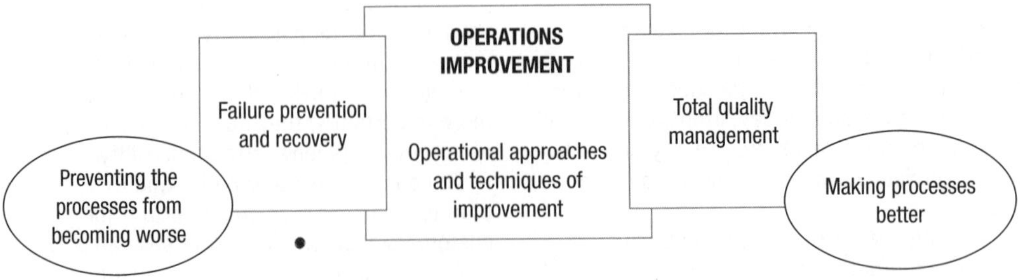

Figure 10.10: The nature of operations improvement

Source: Adapted from Slack, N., Chambers, S. & Johnston, R. 2004. *Operations management.* 4th ed. Essex: Pearson, p. 639.

10.6.1.2 Priorities for improvement

Once the performance of the present operations process has been measured and compared with one or more of the performance standards, the areas that need improvement should be clear. However, not all areas earmarked for improvement are equally important. **Priorities for improvement** therefore need to be determined. This is done by taking into consideration the needs and preferences of customers/clients, and the performance and activities of competitors.

The **needs of customers/clients** provide an indication of those performance areas of particular importance to them. Operations-management objectives should reflect the preferences of clients/customers, such as high quality or low costs. The internal operation or functioning of a specific operations process should be focused on achieving these preferences.

However, the competitors' performance and activities play a different role in establishing priorities for improvement. The performance of the business's operations process in relation to the performance of its so-called competitors enables the business to identify its operations-based advantages.

10.6.1.3 Approaches to improvement

Once the priority areas for improvement have been determined, a specific approach or strategy for improvement must be decided upon. Two divergent **approaches to improvement** can be followed: breakthrough improvement or continuous improvement.

In **breakthrough improvement**, dramatic and large-scale changes occur in the functioning of an operations process, but not very regularly. The major changes in respect of products or services, process technology, or methods of work will, it is hoped, lead to improved performance. Business process re-engineering (BPR) is an example of a radical breakthrough-improvement approach that is today encountered in practice.

In **continuous improvement**, also known as Kaizen improvement, more regular, but smaller, incremental changes take place in the functioning of the operations process. The aim is to improve the process on a continuous basis. The plan–do–check–act (PDCA) cycle is an example of a continuous improvement approach that is used in practice. South African motor manufacturers make frequent use of this approach. Their staff are, accordingly, strongly encouraged to suggest continuous small changes in the work process.

10.6.2 Failure prevention and recovery

Regardless of how well a particular operations process is designed, and thereafter put into operation by means of planning and control, there remains the chance of failures or breakdowns occurring. No operations process is always perfect. However, acceptance of the fact that failures will occur does not mean that such events should be ignored. Some failures may have less serious consequences than others, while other failures may be critical for the functioning of the operations process itself. Hence, a continuous endeavour should be made to limit the occurrence of failures. Operations managers have a particular responsibility to improve the reliability of the operations processes that manufacture products or provide services on a continuous basis.

10.6.2.1 Types of failures

Failures in operations processes may occur for one or more of the following reasons:

- **design failures** (these occur when the design of the process is found to be wrong or inadequate, for example, all Pentium personal computers were withdrawn after it was established that there was a design error in the processors)
- **facility failures** (these happen when one or more components of the facility itself, such as machines or equipment, breaks and causes parts of, or the whole facility, to grind to a halt; an example of this failure

is the failure resulting from lightning striking out all the computers of a service provider)

- **staff failures** (these happen when mistakes are made or set procedures are not followed, for example, when workers are not properly trained or where job performance comes to a standstill because of strikes)
- **supplier failures** (these happen when suppliers do not provide products or services according to the agreement, for example, when supermarkets place advertisements for special offers and the suppliers do not deliver the order on time)
- **customer/client failures** (these occur when customers/clients use a product or service incorrectly or do not use it for the purpose for which it was designed; an example of this failure is the failure resulting from a customer using a 1 300 cc car to tow a caravan that requires a car engine of at least 3 000 cc for towing).

10.6.2.2 Failure detection and analysis

As failures will unfortunately and inevitably occur, operations managers should have mechanisms in place to detect such failures, and then be able to put procedures into operation to determine the causes of the failures. **Mechanisms to detect failures** include process-monitoring, complaints and feedback questionnaires from customers/clients. In failure analysis, techniques such as cause-effect diagrams and analysis of customer/client complaints are used. Feedback questionnaires from clients are especially important to detect shortcomings in the rendering of services. This is one of the principal reasons for hotels asking their guests to fill in forms on the quality of their service.

10.6.2.3 Systems-reliability improvement

When there is clarity about the causes and consequences of failures, operations managers should endeavour to prevent them in the first place. This will increase the reliability of the entire operations process. This can be done by redesigning the products and services, or the processes that manufacture or provide them, or by implementing regular maintenance and repairs. In the case of failures that still do occur, additional back-up systems or components can be used. It may also be necessary to launch a training or motivation program for the staff.

10.6.2.4 Recovery of failures

Operations managers attempt to reduce the occurrence of failures and the results thereof by means of failure detection and analysis, and systems-reliability improvement. However, when failures still occur, **recovery procedures and contingency plans** should already have been devised and put in place to minimise the potential detrimental effects on customers/clients.

10.6.3 Total quality management

The concept of total quality management (TQM) appears above in the discussion of the quality-planning and control activities of operations management (section 10.5.4). It was also stated that these days, the quality of products or services is not regarded as the responsibility of the operations manager alone. The concept of TQM is far wider, hence the entire business is responsible.

10.6.3.1 Defining "total quality management"

"**Total quality management**" (TQM) may be defined as a management philosophy that primarily aims to satisfy the needs and expectations of customers/clients by means of high-quality products or services, and that endeavours to shift the responsibility for quality from the operations-management function to the entire business (that is, all other functional management areas and the employees therein). TQM is further primarily aimed at[19]:

- meeting the needs and expectations of customers/clients

- covering all parts of the business regardless of how small or seemingly insignificant they are
- making each and every employee in the business quality conscious, and holding him/her responsible for his/her contribution to the achievement of TQM
- identifying and accounting for all costs of quality (both prevention and failure costs)
- doing things right the first time (proactive rather than reactive action)
- developing and implementing systems and procedures for quality and the improvement thereof
- establishing a continuous process for improvement.

The concept of TQM did not develop overnight. Many so-called "quality gurus", such as A. Feigenbaum, W.E. Deming, J.M. Juran, K. Ishikawa, G. Taguchi and P.B. Crosby, contributed to what has today become known as TQM.

According to J.S. Oakland's TQM model (see Figure 10.11), the focal point of total quality is the underlying processes that occur at each customer/client and supplier interface. To this should be added specific hard-management components (quality systems, techniques and methods, and teams) and soft-management (or human) components (commitment, communication and culture).

10.6.3.2 The ISO 9000 quality standard for quality systems

Improving quality within a business requires a great deal more than good intentions. It demands concrete action. One such action should be the development of a quality system. Such a system includes the organisational structure, responsibilities, procedures, processes and resources for implementing quality.

A standard for quality management that is used throughout the world to lay down the requirements for a quality-management system is the **ISO 9000 series**. This series provides comprehensive recommendations as to how a quality-management system should be compiled for a particular type of business.

The ISO 9001:2000 document[20] includes guidelines under five headings: documentation requirements, management responsibility, resource management, product realisation, and measurement, analysis and improvement.

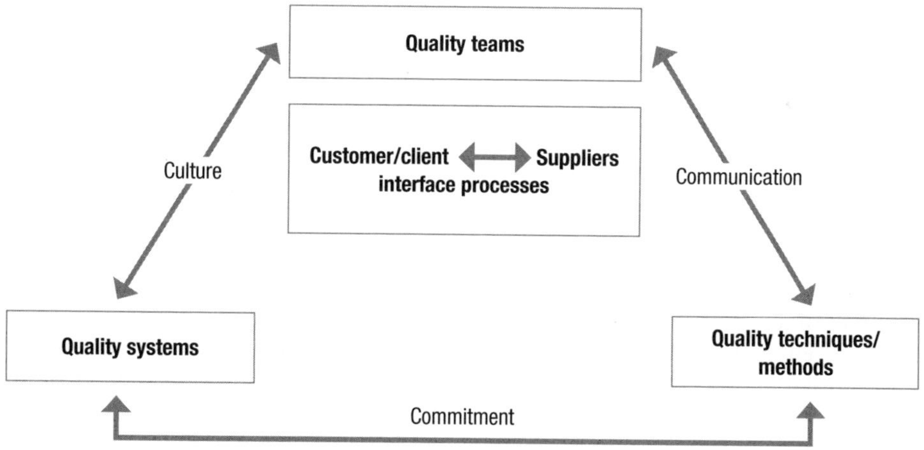

Figure 10.11: Total-quality-management model

Source: Oakland, J.S. 2003. *Total quality management.* 3rd ed. Oxford: Butterworth-Heinemann, p. 21. © Elsevier.

The section on documentation requirements deals with what documents are required for establishing, implementing and maintaining the quality management system (QMS), as well as compiling the quality manual. This section also sets procedures for the control of quality documents and records.

The section on management responsibility deals with management commitment to the QMS's customer focus through the use of the quality policy and through setting quality objectives. This section also covers management responsibility, authority and communication of quality matters, and conducting management reviews of the whole QMS.

The section on **resource management** deals with using resources to implement the QMS, developing human resources, satisfying infrastructure requirements and creating a working environment that enhances performance.

The section on **product realisation** deals with planning the operation and supporting processes for the realisation of the required outputs. It also deals with defining customer-related communication processes, designing and developing the organisation's products and services, setting purchasing procedures and supplier evaluations, controlling production and service provision, and controlling the monitoring and measuring devices to inspire confidence in the QMS.

The section on **measurement, analysis and improvement** deals with monitoring and measuring through customer satisfaction, internal audits and process achievement. It discusses the control of non-conforming products, the analysis of data (including the use of statistical techniques), and the creation of a continuous improvement culture and environment with corrective and preventive action. It also deals with establishing methods for the improvement of the QMS.

10.6.3.3 The implementation of total quality management

The way in which TQM is implemented in a business determines how successful this application will be. Factors that should be taken into account are listed below[21], along with bracketed terms referring to management components of Oakland's TQM model[22] (see Figure 10.11 on page 281):

- integration of TQM in the overall business strategy (systems)
- top management's and employees' support and involvement (commitment)
- teamwork in the improvement initiatives (teams)
- feedback on quality successes that have in fact been achieved (communication)
- creation of quality awareness (culture)
- training of employees in quality techniques and methods (techniques/methods).

Oakland revised his model in 2003. In this revised model, he referred to the four Ps (hard components) and three Cs (soft components) of TQM[23]. While the "soft" components of the earlier model remain the same, the new "hard" components are processes (systems), people (teamwork) and planning (techniques/methods), which are all linked to performance.

10.7 Summary

This chapter provided a broad overview of the important aspects covered in the subdiscipline of operations management. It examined the nature of operations management and introduced a general model of which all components were discussed in more detail. The classification of different process types for manufacturers (goods or product producers) and service providers was also illustrated.

Hereafter, the chapter examined in more detail three of the activities of operations managers: design, planning and control, and improvement. Operations design is concerned with the design of products or services that will satisfy the needs of customers/clients and the design of operational processes to manufacture or provide them. Once the design activities have been completed, the operations process must be put into action by means of operations planning and control. Specific responsibilities in this regard include capacity planning and control, inventory and purchasing planning and control, and quality planning and control. Once these activities have been executed, the operations manager should consider how to improve the operation. Operations improvement involves both improving the reliability of the entire operations process on a continuous basis by failure prevention and recovery, and improving the entire business by applying the concept of TQM so that quality products or services can be manufactured or provided to satisfy customers'/clients' needs optimally.

Key terms

approaches to improvement	operations design (process design)
batch operation/process	operations improvement
capacity planning and control	operations objectives
competitive advantage of good design	operations planning and control
composition of products and services	operations processes
continuous operation/ process	operations strategy
customers/clients	outputs
design of products/ services (product or service design)	performance standards
design of supply network	priorities for improvement
failure prevention and recovery	process technology
flexibility	process types
inputs	productivity
inventory and supply-chain planning and control	project operation/process
ISO 9000 quality standard for quality systems	quality
jobbing operation/ process	quality planning and control
job design and work organisation	reliability
layout and flow	stages of products or service design
lead time	total quality management (TQM)
mass operation/process	transformation

Questions for discussion

Reread the case study on pages 247–250. Then visit the BMW South Africa and BMW AG websites if you have access to the internet, and conduct your own further research and investigation of aspects you are not familiar with. Answer the following questions:

1. Do you agree with the argument that BMW South Africa winning the J.D. Power and Associates Gold Award in 2002 is testimony to the fact that its operational process was well designed, planned and controlled, and improved on a continuous basis? Give reasons for your answer by explaining why you agree or disagree.
2. In 1999, BMW South Africa was the first motor-vehicle manufacturer in the world to achieve certification for its integrated SHEQ (Safety, Health, Environmental and Quality) Management System. It received the ISO 9001:2000, ISO 14001 and BS 8800 certifications. What is the importance of such certifications for the company and its customers?

3. BMW South Africa was the first BMW plant to be located outside the country of its parent company, BMW AG, which is situated in Munich, Germany. It was opened in 1973, and today it is still one of only three complete BMW manufacturing plants where cars are produced to end items. The other such plants are the Spartenburg plant in the United States and the original BMW plant in Germany. Why is this significant for South Africa and its people?
4. At the end of the 1970s, BMW South Africa was the only South African car manufacturer to export cars on a regular basis and in significant numbers. This export drive has steadily continued over the years with BMW South Africa's full integration into BMW's worldwide supply network, and the production of both left-hand and right-hand drive vehicles for the South African and overseas markets. Why are such continued exports so important for South Africa, and what positive effects could one expect for the South African economy at large?
5. To ensure optimum customer satisfaction, the "build quality" of the vehicles produced at BMW Plant Rosslyn is measured through a process of complete product audit.
   a. What does this audit entail?
   b. When are such audits performed?
   c. Are different standards applied at the various BMW plants to make provision for local circumstances?

? Multiple-choice questions

1. An effective and efficient operation can give a business many advantages. Which of the following is not one of these advantages?
   a. It can reduce the costs of making the products or offering the services.
   b. It can reduce the amount of investment (capital employed) needed to manufacture the type and quantity of products or offer the service required.
   c. It can be decisive for the general reputation of the business unless the customer/client is not regarded as the focal point in operations management.
   d. It can improve productivity and it can help a business to satisfy the needs of its customers/clients more effectively.
2. The performance objectives of an operation are related to the numerous customer/client needs. Which of the following is not one of these performance objectives?
   a. Higher quality and lower costs
   b. Shorter lead time (quicker manufacturing or provision of services)
   c. Low variability and low adaptability (flexibility)
   d. Lower variability with regard to specifications (reliability)
3. Reconciling the supply of products or services with the demand for them by means of planning and control activities does not entail:
   a. the loading of tasks (this refers to the volume or quantity of work allocated to a particular work centre).
   b. the maintaining of tasks (this refers to the revision, rectification and improvement of task design).
   c. the sequencing of tasks (this refers to the sequence in which the tasks are performed, which can be determined beforehand by the use of certain priority rules such as earliest deadline first, or first-in first-out).
   d. the scheduling of tasks (this refers to the use of a detailed roster that indicates when a specific task should start and when it should be completed; Gantt charts are

especially popular for planning and scheduling projects, and also give an indication of which tasks are late and which are at a more advanced stage than anticipated).

4. For the purposes of quality planning and control, it is necessary to define certain quality characteristics that relate directly to the design specifications for products or services. Which quality characteristic is not often used?
   a. Performance ability
   b. Reliability (continuous performance capability)
   c. Durability (total life expectancy)
   d. Limited customer contact (for the convenience of privacy)
5. Operations improvement entails several functions, such as comparing the present performance level with certain standards. Which of the following kinds of performance standards are not generally used?
   a. Hypothetical unpublished international benchmarks
   b. Absolute performance standards, whereby current performance is compared to the theoretical maximum achievable performance standards
   c. Historical standards, whereby present performance is compared to the particular business's own performance in previous years
   d. Target performance standards, whereby present performance is compared to pre-determined standards, which indicate an acceptable or reasonable level of performance

Answers to multiple-choice questions

1. c
2. c
3. b
4. d
5. a

References

1. Slack, N., Chambers, S. & Johnston, R. 2007. *Operations management*. 5th ed. London: Pitman, p. 22.
2. Slack, N., Chambers, S. & Johnston, R. 2007. *Operations management*. 5th ed. London: Pitman, p. 4.
3. Slack, N., Chambers, S. & Johnston, R. 2007. *Operations management*. 5th ed. London: Pitman, p. 25.
4. Schonberger, R.J. & Knod, E.M. (Jr). 2001. *Meeting customers' demands*. 7th ed. New York: McGraw-Hill, pp. 17–18.
5. Slack, N., Chambers, S. & Johnston, R. 2007. *Operations management*. 5th ed. London: Pitman, pp. 16–21.
6. Slack, N., Chambers, S. & Johnston, R. 2007. *Operations management*. 5th ed. London: Pitman, pp. 94–97.
7. Slack, N., Chambers, S. & Johnston, R. 2007. *Operations management*. 5th ed. London: Pitman, pp. 98–100.
8. Slack, N., Chambers, S. & Johnston, R. 2007. *Operations management*. 5th ed. London: Pitman, pp.121–122.
9. Davis, M.M. & Heineke, J. 2005. *Operations management: Integrating manufacturing and services*. 5th ed. New York: McGraw-Hill, p. 11.
10. Slack, N., Chambers, S. & Johnston, R. 2007. *Operations management*. 5th ed. London: Pitman, pp. 127–128.
11. Slack, N., Chambers, S. & Johnston, R. 2007. *Operations management*. 5th ed. London: Pitman, pp. 148–151.
12. Krajewski, L.J. & Ritzman, L.P. 2005. *Operations management: Processes and value chains*. 7th ed. Upper Saddle River, New Jersey: Pearson, pp. 302–303.
13. Krüger, L.P. 2000. "The changing role of production and operations management: Moving towards the ultimate in robotic manufacturing and service provision". Pretoria: University of South Africa, Unpublished inaugural lecture, p. 21.
14. Slack, N., Chambers, S. & Johnston, R. 2007. *Operations management*. 5th ed. London: Pitman, p. 261.
15. Slack, N., Chambers, S. & Johnston, R. 2007. *Operations management*. 5th ed. London: Pitman, p. 539.
16. Slack, N., Chambers, S. & Johnston, R. 2007. *Operations management*. 5th ed. London: Pitman, p. 322.

17. Knod, E.M. (Jr) & Schonberger, R.J. 2001. *Operations management: Meeting customers' demands*. 7th ed. New York: McGraw-Hill, pp. 138–140.
18. Slack, N., Chambers, S. & Johnston, R. 2007. *Operations management*. 5th ed. London: Pitman, p. 539.
19. Slack, N., Chambers, S. & Johnston, R. 2007. *Operations management*. 5th ed. London: Pitman, p. 653.
20. South African National Standard. 2000. *ISO 9001:2000 South African Standard, Code of practice, Quality management systems – Requirements*. Pretoria: Standards South Africa.
21. Slack, N., Chambers, S. & Johnston, R. 2007. *Operations management*. 5th ed. London: Pitman, pp. 663–665.
22. Oakland, J.S. 2000. *Total quality management: Text with cases*. 2nd ed. Oxford: Butterworth-Heinemann, pp. 81–91.
23. Oakland, J.S. 2003. *Total quality management: Text with cases*. 3rd ed. Oxford: Butterworth-Heinemann, pp. 26–27.

CHAPTER

11

HUMAN-RESOURCES MANAGEMENT AND THE SA LABOUR LEGISLATIVE FRAMEWORK

The purpose of this chapter

The purpose of this chapter is to introduce the issues relating to the management of human resources within an organisation, to explain the theories on the motivation of human resources and to provide an overview of the most important labour legislation that has an impact on the workplace.

Learning outcomes

On completion of this chapter you should be able to:

- describe the basic steps involved in human-resources planning
- explain how companies use recruiting to find qualified job applicants
- describe the selection techniques and procedures that companies use when deciding which applicants should receive job offers
- describe how to determine training needs and select the appropriate training methods
- discuss how to use performance appraisal to give meaningful performance feedback
- describe basic compensation strategies and how they affect human-resources practice
- describe the role of the human-resources function in organisations
- explain the contribution human-resources management can make to the effectiveness of an organisation
- provide an outline of who is responsible for human-resources management
- list and explain the different content theories of motivation
- discuss the process theories of motivation
- evaluate the different motivation strategies
- understand the importance of the Constitution of the Republic of South Africa, 1996
- describe and analyse the impact of the following acts on the management of human resources in organisations:
  - The Labour Relations Act (No. 66 of 1995)
  - The Basic Conditions of Employment Act (No. 75 of 1997)
  - The Skills Development Act (No. 97 of 1998)

- The Skills Development Levies Act (No. 9 of 1999)
- The National Qualifications Act (No. 67 of 2008)
- The Employment Equity Act (No. 55 of 1998)
- The Occupational Health and Safety Act (No. 85 of 1993)
- The Compensation for Occupational Injuries and Diseases Act (No. 130 of 1993)
- The Unemployment Insurance Act (No. 63 of 2001).

Case study

Coca-Cola South Africa

Established in 1886, the Coca-Cola Company is the world's largest beverage company. Its product portfolio numbers nearly 500 brands, including Coca-Cola (the world's most valuable brand), Diet Coke, Fanta, Sprite, Coca-Cola Zero, vitaminwater, Powerade and Minute Maid. Coca-Cola South Africa has been ranked number one as small-sized employer in a 2009/2010 survey on the best employers to work for.

The Coca-Cola Company products are consumed in more than 200 countries at a rate of nearly 1,6 billion servings a day. With an enduring commitment to building sustainable communities, the company focuses on initiatives that protect the environment, conserve resources and enhance the economic development of the communities in which it operates.

Coca-Cola South Africa has two invaluable assets – its brands and its people – and that's where the magic lies. The two are closely intertwined. For example, the people who work at Coca-Cola take pride in their work and in building brands others love.

Like most other companies, the impact of the economy on employees and their morale is a challenge. Stress levels are constantly increasing, especially as some employees begin to witness the impact of job losses affecting other family members or relatives. Inevitably this has an impact on those who remain employed.

The business

The origins of the Coca-Cola Company can be traced back to 8 May 1886, when a pharmacist by the name of Dr John Stith Pemberton produced the syrup for Coca-Cola in Atlanta, Georgia. The reaction from those who tasted it was universally positive – it was pronounced "excellent". Based on this feedback, the syrup was combined with carbonated water and sold for five cents a glass as a soda-fountain drink. The Coca-Cola name and trademark were the brainchild of Dr Pemberton's partner and bookkeeper, Frank M Robinson, who thought that the two Cs would look good in advertisements. Today the company is the world's number one producer of sparkling beverages, juices and juice drinks.

Differentiating factors

The first differentiating factor is fairly obvious: the Coca-Cola Company is the custodian of the world's most-loved brands. This is a significant differentiator that also imposes a huge sense of responsibility. Secondly, the company's ability to innovate is a key differentiating factor. Its Glaceau vitaminwater, the first enhanced water on the market, is a case in point. The third key differentiating factor is its strong partnership with its bottlers.

Talent management and development

According to Jonathan Muthige, Human Resources and Transformation Director, particular emphasis is being placed on talent management and succession planning at Coca-Cola South Africa. "It's all about securing the right capabilities for the future. We are launching a new management-development program this year. The candidates for this development program will be drawn both from within and outside the company. The 24-month program is designed to offer an in-depth development and understanding of our business in South Africa. Our philosophy is that if you can develop your leaders and managers to nurture your talent effectively, half the battle is won," he reports.

Emphasis is also being placed on nurturing female talent. "All up-and-coming key female staff members have been tagged to a senior mentor, to ensure that we succeed and get traction on this very important strategy that underpins our diversity agenda," says Muthige.

There are a number of interesting and unusual jobs available at Coca-Cola South Africa. Just one is that of innovations manager. "This person spends time thinking about issues such as packaging, considering research concerning flavours and focusing on new product development. We look for someone who has worked in a creative space, someone who has been in branding or marketing," explains Multhige.

Yet another interesting job is that of integrated marketing and communications manager. This person considers the brands and the media channels available, and looks at how best to marry the two. Ideally an integrated marketing and communications manager should have a marketing background and some media experience.

Salaries, rewards and benefits

There is no formal flexitime policy in place at Coca-Cola South Africa, although flexitime is available on a global basis. Having said this, managers often allow staff members to work from home. "We are, however, looking to formalise a policy in this regard. Our employees are asking for it and we are hearing them," says Muthige.

Staff members receive four months' paid maternity leave, study assistance, a provident fund and medical aid. Health-club fees are paid to encourage healthy lifestyles, meals in the canteen are subsidised (the canteen is open for breakfast and lunch), cellphones are provided as a tool of trade and 3G cards are given to staff members who travel. Every month employees are offered four cases of beverages free of charge. A donation of R20 000 is made to the family on the death of a staff member and the family also receives 15 cases of beverages.

Some staff members have the opportunity to travel globally and work overseas. There are six South Africans in Turkey at present, for example. Coca-Cola South Africa also invites staff members to sporting events such as the Confederations Cup, and their children have been given the opportunity to be flag bearers.

Salaries are extremely competitive. "We target the top quartile companies and pay competitive packages; the logic is that we are looking to attract premium talent," says Muthige. "Furthermore, in the spirit of being an innovative and creative company, we are creating flexbility in some of our benefits, like the company car policy, which offers employees wide choices."

Black economic empowerment

Coca-Cola South Africa is currently going through the BEE rating process. "However, the reality in the BEE space is that we have invested a lot of time and money in the development of spaza shops, taxi ranks and car washes in the townships, where we are providing training and support. We have made a huge investment in terms of economic development. We have a dedicated team that focuses on this market and develops sustainable small businesses," says Muthige.

Responsible citizenship

The Coca-Cola Company has a clear corporate social investment (CSI) strategy that focuses on four key areas: health, education, environment and entrepreneurship. The Coca-Cola Africa Foundation sets strategy for the continent, while each company has a community affairs department that implements its own programs. Multhige explains that companies typically address problems pertinent to their areas of operation. "For example, in Mozambique, malaria is the biggest problem – so that's the focus there. In South Africa, HIV/Aids is of greater concern, so we focus on this pandemic instead."

One of the continent's greatest challenges is an ongoing supply of clean water and so Coca-Cola South Africa invests heavily in this area. "We work with our bottling partners at schools, fixing leaks and plumbing problems. Within communities, we drill boreholes, which are often located next to schools. We also teach community members to maintain the boreholes," explains Muthige.

Coca-Cola South Africa is committed to recycling both water and packaging. In terms of the latter, it works closely with Collect-a-Can and PETCO, recycling cans and plastic bottles. "We are involved in a school's collection program whereby we encourage learners to collect cans. The school that collects the most cans gets a monetary reward; last year a Pietermaritzburg school received R110 000," says Muthige.

Additional CSI projects supported by Coca-Cola South Africa include the Nurisha School Feeding Project (nutritional drinks for scholars), Discovery Channel Global Education Partnership (educational DVDs), entrepreneurship programs (junior achievers), the Men-as-Partners Program (aims to reduce gender-based violence), and it works with orphaned and vulnerable children who have been affected by HIV/Aids.

International stance

The Coca-Cola Company is a global business operating in more than 200 countries. It employs 92 400 people across the globe, of whom 280 work in South Africa. Working with its bottling partners, the company produces beverages in more than 800 plants around the world. In addition, the bottling partners employ hundreds of thousands of people around the world and are committeed to supporting community investment programs. The economic impact of the company is immense. A recent study showed that, in South Africa, one job in the Coca-Cola system indirectly supports 16 additional jobs throughout the value cycle.

The people

Muhtar Kent, Chairman of the Board and Chief Executive Officer at the Coca-Cola Company, is the leader of the business. He is known to have a firm commitment to the values and spirit of the world's greatest brand. On the local front, William (Bill) Egbe is the South African business unit leader.

Muthige says recruitment is relatively easy. "The nature of our brand is such that most people are curious about it and willing to talk about it. We typically find talent through employee referrals, and we are also inundated with calls and CVs from potential employees. We also work with agencies that have grown to understand our needs in specific areas. In certain cases, we commission those agencies to do talent mapping," he notes.

Individuals who thrive in a challenging environment flourish at the company. "Staff members need to be able to deal with ambiguity and constant change. Furthermore, they need to be creative and be able to build relationships with fellow employees."

Company culture and style

According to Muthige, the culture is very performance orientated. "We need to ensure that we continue to deliver on our brands' promises. It is a fun, relaxed culture, but the focus is also on performance. Accordingly, we constantly reward top performers. The connection between performance and reward is more pronounced now than in the past."

Employee relations are boosted by the weekly "Briefcase" newsletter, which contains pertinent announcements, acknowledges birthdays and features other staff news. In addition, staff members receive a glossy quarterly magazine, have access to a local website and are also encouraged to consult the revamped global site. "Ask Bill" is a facility whereby staff are encouraged to pose questions to the CEO, while quarterly briefing sessions are conducted to inform staff members about the performance of the business. This is supplemented by the "Kick off" strategy meeting at the start of each year. The CEO also leaves a voice-mail for all staff members every month, updating them on developments at the company.

The future

Muthige says that the Coca-Cola Company will remain committed to the country and the continent. "Furthermore, consumers can look forward to great innovations and they can expect us to remain responsible custodians of their much-loved brands," he adds. The various soccer events the company sponsors represent meaningful opportunities for the company and its brands. At the time of writing, the Confederations Cup was in full swing while the company was planning the FIFA World Cup Trophy Tour by Coca-Cola. "This involves an unprecidented journey across the continent in anticipation of the 2010 FIFA World Cup™,"explains Muthige. "We are planning a tour that will allow thousands of Africans from more than 50 countries the opportunity to see the real solid-gold trophy in person." This joint project between the Coca-Cola Company and FIFA, football's world governing body, gives fans the chance to enjoy a rare close-up view of the authentic FIFA World Cup Trophy. "We are also doing a considerable amount of work at grassroots soccer development level to energise the continent," reveals Muthige.

Source: Adapted from an article by Best employers™ South Africa 2009/10. "South Africa's BEST Employers™ Top 10 and A–Z listing". [Online] Available: http://www.bestcompaniestoworkfor.co.za/employers.html.2009 Accessed 7 December 2009.

11.1 Introduction

Internationally renowned HR consultant Jeffrey Pfeffer contends in *Competitive advantage through people*[1] that what separates top-performing companies from their competitors is the way they treat their workforces. He goes on to argue that companies that invest in their employees create long-lasting competitive advantages that are difficult for other companies to duplicate. However, the process of finding, developing and keeping the right people to form a qualified workforce remains one of the most difficult and important of all management tasks[2]. To assist in this regard, this chapter is structured around the various parts of the human-resources management process: determining human-resources needs, and attracting, developing, motivating and keeping a qualified workforce within the South African labour legislation framework.

Accordingly, the chapter begins by reviewing how human-resources planning determines human-resources needs, such as the kind and number of employees a organisation requires to meet its strategic plans and objectives. Next, the chapter explores how organisations use recruiting and selection techniques to find and hire qualified employees to fulfil those needs. The section that follows examines how training and performance appraisal can develop the knowledge, skills and abilities of the workforce. The chapter continues with a review of compensation, that is, how organisations can keep their best workers through effective compensation practices[3]. The chapter then addresses the important aspect of motivation. The last part of the chapter focuses on the influence of related labour legislation on the employment relationship.

11.2 The relationship between line management and the human-resources department

11.2.1 The role of human-resources management in the organisation

The **human-resources function** is a crucial element in organisational success. This section considers certain aspects of human-resources management in organisations, such as the role of the human-resources function, human-resources management and **organisational effectiveness**. It then looks at the person who performs the human-resources function in organisations.

11.2.1.1 The human-resources function

Today, human-resources management strategies should be integrated with organisational plans and should be in line with the broad organisational strategy. The human-resources function is concerned with much more than filing, routine administration actions and record-keeping activities. Its main role should be that of strategic partner, and human-resources strategies should clearly demonstrate the organisational strategy regarding people, profit and overall effectiveness. (The Coca-Cola case study at the beginning of the chapter illustrates the link between brand value and strategy with people investment.) Various international competitive studies have indicated that labour productivity is a factor that must be addressed in order for South Africa to be competitive in a global market. In the South African context, a crucial role of the human-resources (HR) manager is to improve the skills base of employees and to contribute to the profitability of the organisation. The human-resources function must be accountable for its actions and it should operate as a "profit centre".

The emphasis on accountability is even more important if one considers the legal environment in which decisions related to human resources have to be taken and the very negative consequences for the organisation if the right decisions are not made. If, for example, the correct procedures as prescribed by the Labour Relations Act (No. 66 of 1995) are not followed in the event of a retrenchment, the consequences for the organisation can be dire.

Every manager in the organisation should realise the importance of recruiting, selecting, training, developing, rewarding, assisting and motivating employees. However, to achieve organisational success both locally and internationally, the focus should be on integration and teamwork among employees.

11.2.2 Human-resources management and organisational effectiveness

An effective organisation must have a vision, a mission and strategy, an organisational structure and human resources. It is people in organisations who create the ideas and allow organisations to prosper. Even the most capital-intensive organisation needs people to run it. Studies have shown that successful organisations all share the following human-resources management attributes:

- a participative style of management
- communication with all levels of employees
- promotion from within
- training of employees
- rewarding of good work[4].

These findings are also in line with the profile of the most promising organisations in South Africa. Human resources in organisations thus either limit or enhance the strengths or weaknesses of organisations. While it is easy to evaluate other resources such as machines and equipment in terms of their monetary value, it is very difficult to put a monetary value on people. Various research projects, for example, human-resources accounting practices, have been launched to do this, but a conclusive methodology and process have not yet been established.

For organisations to be really effective, top managers should treat human resources as the key element of effectiveness. The contribution of human resources to organisational effectiveness includes the following[5]:

- assisting everybody in the organisation to reach stated goals
- making efficient use of the skills and abilities of the workforce
- providing the organisation with well-trained and motivated employees
- assisting in the attainment of the employees' job satisfaction and self-actualisation
- developing a quality of work life that makes employment in the organisation desirable
- assisting with the maintenance of ethical policies and socially responsible behaviour
- managing change to the mutual advantage of individuals, groups, the organisation and the public
- executing human-resources functional activities in a professional manner.

11.2.3 Who performs the human-resources function?

As soon as a new person (employee) is recruited and appointed in an organisation, management's main concern must be to get that person to do his/her work as well as possible. In this process, certain functions have to be performed by the human-resources specialist, who would normally be situated in a human-resources department, as well as by line managers and direct supervisors. Line managers are those people in other departments, such as operations, marketing and finances, who have the responsibility to make optimal use of all the resources at their disposal.

The human resource is a unique resource because if it is not properly managed, effectiveness can decline drastically. For this reason, it is essential to understand why people work in organisations and why some people want to perform better than other people. In South Africa, where there is high unemployment, having a job has become an important goal and people compete fiercely for jobs. It is thus important for managers to take note of the complex issues motivating employees and to manage these. In most organisations – apart from capital-intensive organisations – the investment in people has more effect on organisational success than investment in other resources such as materials, equipment or capital.

In large organisations, the human-resources function is mainly co-ordinated by the human-resources department. In smaller organisations that do not have human-resources departments, the main human-resources functions (for example, recruitment and selection, scheduling of work, training and development, performance management, compensation and labour relations) are performed by line managers over and above their normal duties. As the organisation grows and increases in size, the line manager's job is divided up, and some aspects, such as recruitment and selection, become more specialised. These duties are then dealt with by a human-resources specialist.

Depending on the nature of the organisation, a human-resources specialist is normally employed in organisations with approximately 50 to 150 employees[6]. In South Africa, the ratio of full-time human-resources specialists to employees is 50, while the global average is about 62[7]. A human-resources department or section is typically created when the number of employees in an organisation reaches a figure of between 200 and 500.

This discussion on the role of the HR manager makes it clear that organisations cannot be successful without well-trained and motivated workforces. Both human-resources specialists and line managers are responsible for managing the people talent in organisations. One aspect that can make a difference in achieving organisational success is the level of employee motivation, which is dealt with later in this chapter.

11.3 Human-resources planning

Human-resources planning is the process of using an organisation's goals and strategy to forecast the organisation's human-resources needs in terms of finding, developing and keeping a qualified workforce. Human-resources planning can be divided into three specific steps:

- Step 1: Identify the work being done in the business at present (job analysis and job description).
- Step 2: Identify the type of employees needed to do the work (job specification).
- Step 3: Identify the number of employees who will be needed in the future (human-resources forecasting and planning).

11.3.1 Job analysis

The first step in human-resources planning is to determine the nature of the work being done. **Job analysis** is the process of describing and recording information about job behaviours and activities[8].

The following questions might be asked when undertaking a job analysis:

- What is the employee responsible for?
- What tasks are performed?
- What decisions are made?
- What information is needed to enable the work to be done?
- Under what conditions is the job performed?

There are various ways in which this information can be collected. One method is observation by a qualified job analyst. The job analyst observes the employee working and records all the relevant information. Observation may also include videotaping, audiotaping and electronic monitoring. This method is especially suited to manual labour, where it is easy to see exactly what the employee is doing. However, administrative work is more difficult to observe.

The method generally followed for administrative work is interviewing, where the job analyst interviews an employee and asks for a description of responsibilities and tasks.

Questionnaires may also be used. Here the employee (and sometimes his/her immediate superior) answers a number of specific questions about the tasks and responsibilities of the job. Questionnaires may be developed for specific circumstances, or standardised questionnaires (which are more economical) may be purchased from external vendors. (Take note of the different jobs as illustrated in the Coca-Cola case study.)

11.3.2 Job description

Whatever method of data collection is used for job analysis, the information is put in writing in a certain format – a **job description** – so that other people who are not involved in the job analysis can gain thorough insight into the contents of the job.

A job description does not merely list a number of facts. It is usually prepared in a pre-determined format so that it is easily readable. It generally starts with a summary of the job, followed by a brief description of each main task, with more detail and practical examples as subdivisions. A description of the kind of decisions that need to be taken by the employee may follow[9].

The format of the job description differs from business to business. The important point, however, is that the content of jobs must be put on record in an understandable way.

11.3.3 Job specification

The personal qualifications an employee must possess in order to perform the duties and responsibilities depicted in the job description are contained in the **job specification**[10]. Typically, job specifications detail the knowledge, skills and abilities relevant to a job, including the education, experience, specialised training, personal traits and manual dexterity of the person doing the job. At times, an organisation may also include the physical demands the job places on an employee. These might include the amount of walking, standing, reaching or lifting required of the employee[11].

11.3.4 Human-resources forecasting

A further step in human-resources planning is to conduct regular forecasts of the quantity and quality of employees the business is going to need in the future. As indicated in Figure 11.1 on page 296, the purpose of **human-resources forecasting** is to balance **human-resources supply** and **human-resources demand.** Demand is affected by business objectives because these objectives determine the number of people needed to attain them. Supply is affected by the human-resources programs providing the human resources. The following factors should be considered during forecasting:

- **Economic growth.** This involves forecasting the expected growth (or shrinkage) of the business in view of probable economic developments. For example, will there be a recession or growth in the near or distant future?
- **New developments in the business.** These include planned physical extensions, the establishment of new branches and technological changes (especially those that will affect staff, for computerised machinery might create a greater need for technically skilled employees).
- **The labour market.** Important questions in this regard include: Are there sufficient opportunities in the labour market, or is there a high level of unemployment? What will be the nature and scope of labour turnover in the future? Will there be a shortage of a certain type of skilled employee? Will employees be readily available?

11.3.5 The human-resources plan

Using the information obtained thus far, the HR manager can compile a human-resources plan, the final step in the process. The purpose of this plan is to provide concrete guidelines and steps that indicate how the business's short-, medium- and long-term human-resources requirements can be provided for. In other words, it answers the question: What must we do today to be prepared for tomorrow? The human-resources plan should dovetail with the strategic plan of the business, as mentioned earlier. In the case study earlier in this chapter, it became obvious that the success of the Coca-Cola Company is dependent on future human-resources needs.

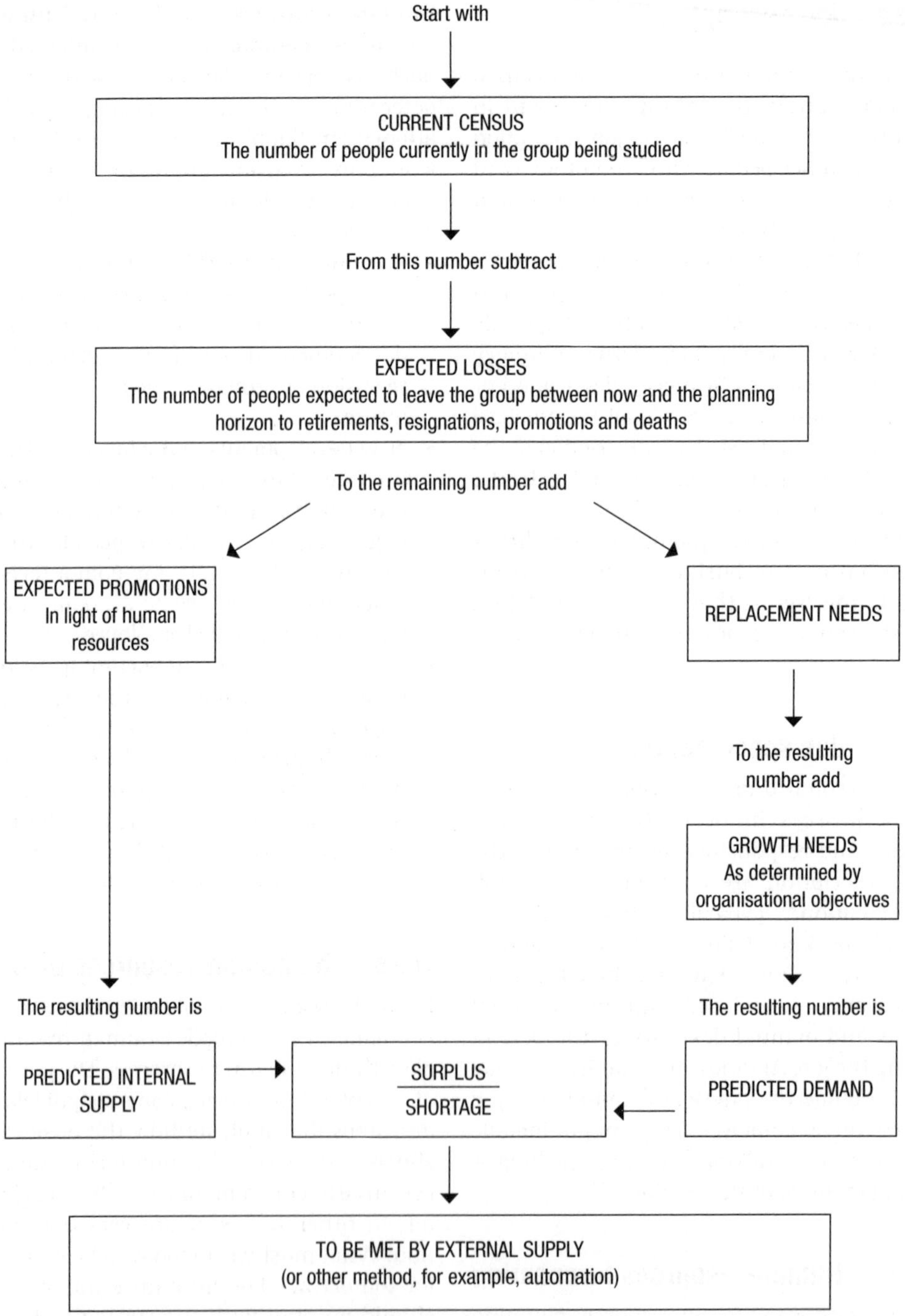

Figure 11.1: A procedure for estimating the human-resources shortage or surplus for a job or occupational category

Source: Anthony, W.P., Kacmar, K.M. & Perrewé, P.L. 2002. *Human resource management: A strategic approach.* 4th ed. South-Western, p. 127. Reprinted by permission of Dr W.P. Anthony.

Such a human-resources plan might, for example, make provision for an active recruiting campaign, emphasise the need for intensive training programs or even make a strong recommendation to automate because of a possible shortage of human resources.

This stage concludes the process of human-resources planning. The next activity in the process is finding qualified workers.

11.4 Finding qualified workers

11.4.1 Recruiting

The express purpose of **recruiting** is to ensure that a sufficient number of applicants apply for the various jobs in the business as and when required. Therefore, as soon as vacancies occur, the HR manager must decide from where suitable candidates for the job will be obtained. There are two basic sources: recruitment from inside the organisation and recruitment from outside the organisation.

11.4.1.1 Recruitment from inside

Recruitment from inside (**internal recruiting**) means trying as far as possible to fill vacant positions with existing staff members, except for jobs on the lowest levels. In practice, it means that people from outside are appointed only at the lowest level and that all more senior jobs in the hierarchy are filled by means of promotion (or sometimes lateral transfers) of existing staff. When a job at a very senior level becomes vacant, the result is a whole series of promotions. Whatever a business decides, it also has to take into account labour legislation such as the **Employment Equity Act (No. 55 of 1998)** and the **Labour Relations Act (No. 66 of 1995) (as amended)**[12].

The advantages of a policy of recruiting from inside are the following:

- Career planning becomes possible, in that individual employees see a future for themselves in the business. This has a positive effect on morale.
- Assessment of applicants is easier because the business already has considerable information on the possible candidates' abilities, work performance and potential.
- The cost of recruitment is low because advertising, travel and board-and-lodging expenses are largely eliminated.

However, there are also three disadvantages connected with such a policy:

- The business tends to stagnate because staff members often think like their predecessors. There are therefore no new ideas.
- Staff appointed at lower levels do not necessarily have the potential to fill senior management posts. If people with high potential are appointed at the lowest levels, they might not be prepared to wait long for promotion opportunities.
- There can be a lot of personal competition among colleagues, to the detriment of co-operation between them.

11.4.1.2 Recruitment from outside

Recruitment from outside means looking for suitable applicants outside the business when a post becomes vacant (**external recruiting**).

Recruitment from outside has the following two advantages:

- An active effort is made to obtain the right person for the job, that is, someone with the most suitable qualifications and experience.
- The opportunity is created for bringing in new ideas, schools of thought and approaches, which considerably increase the possibility for innovation in the business.

However, the disadvantages must also be taken into consideration:

- Recruiting costs are considerably higher for items such as advertising and travelling expenses to enable applicants to come from elsewhere for the interview, and the reimbursement of successful applicants' moving costs.

- It is risky because the assessment of applicants can never be perfect. The possibility therefore exists that the successful applicant will not be successful in the job.
- The morale of existing personnel can be negatively influenced. Employees with high potential will not be prepared to stay indefinitely at the same level and might consider resigning.

This last disadvantage is why most businesses do not follow a policy of recruitment only from outside. Most businesses apply both approaches in one of two ways:

- Some businesses first look inside. They only recruit outside if they cannot find a suitable candidate.
- Some businesses advertise all jobs above a certain level, but encourage existing personnel to apply. In this way, management tries to find the most suitable candidate, regardless of whether the person comes from inside or outside.

The Coca-Cola case study emphasises the importance of recruiting the right talent with the required capabilities.

11.4.1.3 The recruiting procedure

If a business recruits from inside, the HR manager must ensure that an efficient human-resources record system exists. Such a record system, which is now available in a computerised form known as a **human-resources information system (HRIS)**[13], should contain information on each employee's qualifications, training and experience, as well as an assessment of achievements and interests. When a job becomes vacant, the HR manager should be in a position to identify the most suitable candidates.

Recruitment from outside the organisation is much more complex. The HR manager must know exactly whom to recruit, where to recruit from and how the people should be recruited. Successful recruitment does not only mean that enough people apply for a job. If too many applicants apply for a job, selection will be a very time-consuming process. The ideal is therefore that only those people who are suitable for the job apply.

To begin with, recruitment from outside requires a thorough analysis of the labour market. A **labour market** can be defined as the social or geographical area from which a business draws its employees. Certain mines in South Africa draw most of their staff from neighbouring countries. Their labour market is, for example, Lesotho or Malawi (that is, a geographical area). Other businesses, again, might employ mainly women who want to work half-days. This market can be regarded as a social area.

Every labour market has unique characteristics. A characteristic of the South African labour market is that the relationship between skilled and unskilled workers is relatively unbalanced. Obtaining unskilled labour does not appear to be a big problem, while skilled and professional people are exceptionally scarce. HR managers must therefore know the composition of their company's labour market as well as that of the South African labour market as a whole, if they are to recruit effectively.

11.4.1.4 Recruiting techniques

The HR manager can employ various **recruiting techniques**[14]:

- **Recruitment through advertisements.** This is probably the most common form of recruiting, in spite of its high cost. The compilation and placement of an advertisement is a specialised task, and because it can cost thousands of rands, some companies use professional advertisement compilers. With the implementation of the Labour Relations Act (No. 66 of 1995) (as amended), as well as the Employment Equity Act (No. 55 of 1998), it is crucial that the advertisement be worded neutrally. If a requirement that may preclude one of the disadvantaged groups is set, then it must be a genuine prerequisite for the performance of the job. It has been found that the more specifically the responsibilities for the job are defined, the better are the chances of drawing the "right" applicants. Qualifying requirements, such as a certain academic qualification or language ability, must be included to limit unsuitable applications to a minimum. An indication of the remuneration offered is also important, firstly to draw the right applicants and secondly to eliminate potential applicants who already earn more. Specifying general requirements such as loyalty, initiative, sense of responsibility and drive in the advertisement is superfluous, because it never deters an unsuitable person from applying for a job. Advertisements may be placed in journals and newspapers or on bulletin boards.

- **Recruitment through consultants and labour agencies.** This approach is becoming increasingly prevalent in South Africa. The use of human-resources consultants is especially suitable for smaller businesses for which the services of a full-time HR manager cannot be justified. Such businesses inform a consulting firm of their needs, and the latter undertakes all the recruitment, including preliminary selection and recruitment administration for the business. In most cases (depending on the job level), the consultant recommends two or three applicants to the business, which must make the final choice.
- **Recruitment through existing employees.** Existing employees are asked to recruit friends or acquaintances for the business. The rationale of this approach is that if members of staff feel positively about their work, they will more easily persuade others to apply. This method obviates the necessity for advertisements.
- **Recruitment through personal approach.** This method is often called head-hunting. An individual known personally to the management of a business or consulting firm is approached and offered a job. This method saves a lot of recruiting costs, but has the disadvantage that the person cannot be weighed objectively against other applicants. The selection process takes place before the recruitment process, in that the business first decides to appoint an individual to a specific job and then asks him/her to consider the appointment.
- **Recruitment through radio, TV and the internet.** Using the TV is costly and still in its infancy in South Africa. However, following international trends, such approaches should become more popular in the future, especially recruitment via the internet.
- **Sundry recruiting strategies.** Businesses often use visits to schools and universities to draw students' attention to employment opportunities. The intention is not so much to recruit for specific jobs, but with long-term objectives in mind. The allocation of study bursaries with a compulsory period of service linked to them is another method of drawing candidates with high academic potential. Other techniques available to the HR manager to ensure a sufficient flow of suitable applicants from whom appointments to the business can be made include participation in career exhibitions and the distribution of general recruitment brochures.

Once applicants have been recruited, the next step is to select the best candidates.

11.4.2 Selection

The **selection** process can vary from a very short interview to obtain a general impression of the applicant to an intensive assessment process. However, the process differs from business to business and depends especially on the level of the appointment[15]. Figure 11.2 on page 300 depicts nine steps in a typical selection process.

The process described below, however, is the more intensive approach followed in the selection of applicants for senior management posts. For this reason, not all the steps indicated in Figure 11.2 are followed in this discussion. The selection process to be used for senior management posts can be divided into the following three phases:

- preliminary screening
- intensive assessment
- final selection.

With the implementation of the Labour Relations Act (No. 66 of 1995) and the Employment Equity Act (No. 55 of 1998), a number of important components of the selection process (including the application form, the interview and the tests used) have been affected. For example, the application form must not contain discriminatory questions such as: Are you married, divorced or single? Moreover, these types of question may not be asked during the interview, and the various tests used must not be culturally biased (see section 11.8).

11.4.2.1 Preliminary screening

The most efficient method for separating undesirable candidates from potential applicants is to compare the application with the job specification (step 1 in Figure 11.2).

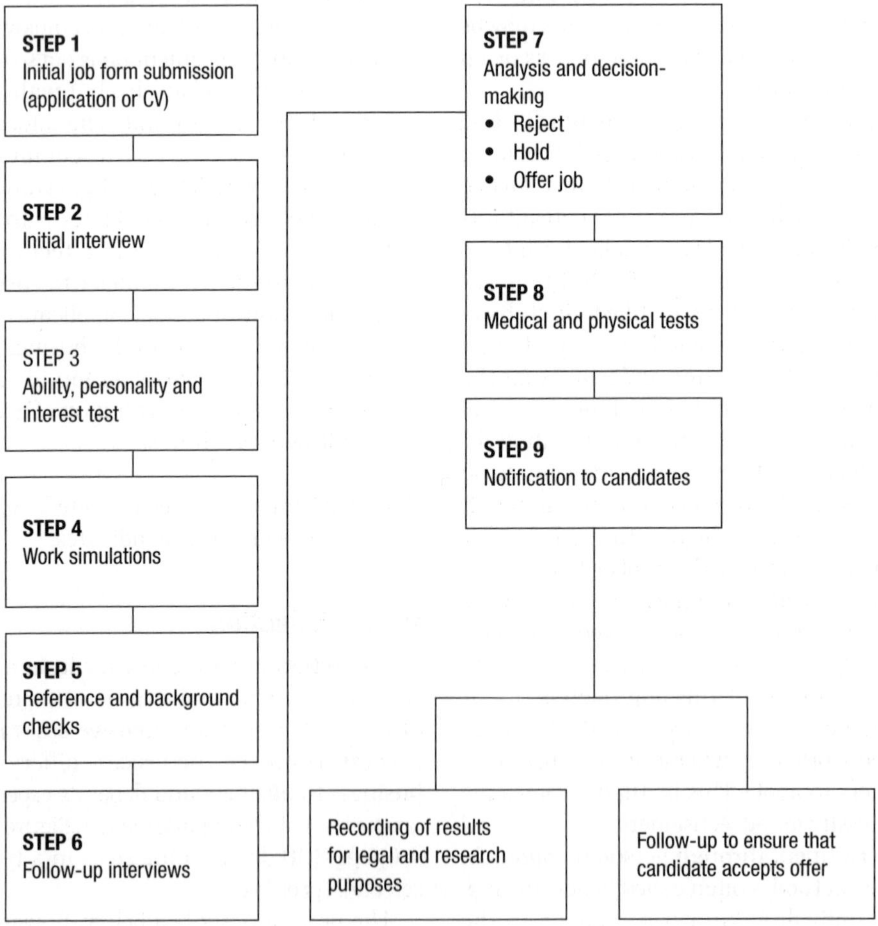

Figure 11.2: Steps in a typical selection process

Source: Adapted from Jackson, S.E. & Schuler, R.S. 2000. *Managing Human Resources: A Partnership Perspective.* 7th ed., p. 315.

A great deal of information can be included on the application form. What is asked depends largely on the needs of the specific business and the nature of the selection process. An application form usually requests the **personal details** (for example, name, address and educational qualifications) and **work history** (for example, jobs held in the past, reasons for resignation and salary progress) of the applicant. References are usually requested, that is, persons or institutions who can be approached to support the information given on the form (step 5 in Figure 11.2).

Questions can also be asked about the applicant's significant achievements, disappointments, career expectations, and communal and leisure-time activities. What is important is that the application form serves as a preliminary selection instrument. In this preliminary selection, the HR manager should learn answers to the following questions:

- Does the applicant comply with the minimum requirements as given in the job specification?
- What type of jobs did the applicant hold in the past?
- How quickly did he/she progress?
- How often has he/she changed jobs?

After these activities have been completed, the next step is to have a short interview with the applicants who, according to information in the application form, are suitable candidates (step 2 in Figure 11.2). This interview provides the HR manager with the opportunity to form a general opinion of the applicant based on appearance, articulateness and self-confidence. It also gives the applicant the opportunity to obtain more information about the business and the specific job.

A preliminary interview is usually not practical for applicants who would have to travel far. They would instead be invited to report for a more intensive assessment.

11.4.2.2 Intensive assessment

Intensive assessment basically involves two steps: **psychological testing** and **diagnostic interviewing**. Although medical selection usually forms part of the final selection process (step 8 in Figure 11.2), it is advisable to have the applicant assessed medically first if the job has stringent physical requirements, for example, in the case of an airline pilot. However, the use of general medical tests in South Africa could have legal implications for the business, depending on the results of the medical examination. Businesses must avoid any hint of discrimination in their interpretation or use of these results.

- Psychological testing can provide valuable information about an applicant. Tests usually involve a measurement of the applicant's personality, abilities and management skills (steps 3 and 4 in Figure 11.2). An important aspect here is to ensure that the tests used are not culturally biased, as mentioned earlier. Some HR managers have the qualifications required for doing testing themselves, while others have the testing done by professionals. However, it is important to remember that a test can never predict accurately whether an applicant will be successful or unsuccessful. Test results only give a general indication that must be considered together with other factors.
- A diagnostic interview is used to obtain information that was not highlighted in the tests or on the application form (step 6 in Figure 11.2). A good interviewer looks for certain characteristics by asking specific questions about the applicant's past performance. For example, an applicant's initiative can be assessed by asking about new projects that he/she may have initiated in previous jobs. The interview also gives the HR manager a chance to delve deeper into possible shortcomings indicated by tests. If, for example, the interviewer suspects that the applicant does not always have good relationships with other people, questions can be asked about interpersonal

relationships. However, as mentioned previously, questions of a discriminatory nature must be avoided. The interviewer may not ask any questions about the person's religious convictions or sexual preferences, for example. The key to good interviewing is to ask questions that give no indication of what answer is expected. Some HR managers prefer to do diagnostic interviews alone, without involving the line functionaries under whom the applicant will work. Others, however, find it useful to include line functionaries at this stage. They may even ask these functionaries to be involved in the interview.

11.4.2.3 Final selection

At the stage of **final selection**, there is usually enough information available about the applicants to compile a **shortlist** of, at most, three persons.

Before the applicants on the shortlist are weighed against each other, the HR manager must consult their **references** to confirm the information they have provided. (In Figure 11.2, this was done before the diagnostic interview. However, there is no right or wrong stage at which to consult references.) Some HR managers do not attach much value to references because applicants would not refer HR managers to people who did not have a high regard for them. Therefore it is not, in fact, worth very much simply to ask referees for an opinion about the applicant's suitability. However, if referees are asked to confirm information (whether positive or negative) obtained in the intensive assessment phase, they can make a very valuable contribution to the selection process.

In the final **comparison of applicants**, it may be useful to interview all three (or two) again briefly. What is essential, however, is to record the strengths and weaknesses of each of the final applicants in writing before the final decision is made (step 7 in Figure 11.2). These documents must be kept for record purposes should a problem arise in the future.

After the most suitable applicant has been decided on, the person concerned is offered the job (step 9 in Figure 11.2). This is the time to explain what is expected of the person in the job and to advise what the conditions of employment are. The applicant can then decide whether to accept the job or not.

If the job is accepted, the applicant usually has to undergo a **medical examination** to ensure that there are no serious health problems.

11.4.2.4 Placement and induction

Once the job offer has been accepted, the new employee must report for duty as soon as possible. With the placement of the person in the job, a number of outstanding matters can be finalised. The business might need to make arrangements for the transportortation of the new employee's furniture and organise temporary housing for him/her. Missing information and documents such as copies of education certificates must be collected, and the forms authorising tax and medical-aid contribution deductions must be completed.

The new employee must go through a process of **induction** (also known as **orientation** or **socialisation**). Experience has shown that when employees do not do this, it takes much longer for them to start working productively.

An induction program will achieve the following[16]:

- introduce new employees to their colleagues, and facilitate and expedite the socialising process
- explain the business's policy, procedures and rules to new employees so that they are aware of the environment in which they will work
- inform new employees about the business's history, products and services, as well as its reputation in the market (this serves to fix the new employees' attention on their futures and to make them aware of the contribution they might make to the realisation of the business's objectives)

- inform employees about practical arrangements, for example, payment procedures, over-time payment, incentive systems, eating arrangements and leave benefits
- inform them about the organisational structure of the business, and show them where they fit in and which communication channels are available to them.

Once employees have been recruited, selected and placed in their jobs, the next step is training. This involves providing them with the skills, knowledge and abilities necessary to perform their jobs successfully.

Critical thinking

Employee selection seems simple enough, but as the discussion in section 11.4 shows, the HR manager faces enormous challenges in choosing the right person for a specific job. The question that must be asked is: What other issues can assist in this regard? The excerpt below provides some answers.

What people tend to forget during selection

Why is it that the highly skilled and competent employee that you've hired is not performing well or, worse, seems unable to work with others?

Many of the human-capital problems that organisations are facing could have been prevented, directly or indirectly, if only more time and energy had been invested in selecting the "right" person. In this context, the word "right" means not only the person with the job-related knowledge, skills and abilities derived from education, experience and specific identifiable skills, but also the person with the right set of character attributes. Research studies by Hunter and Schmidt indicate that, on average, education has a predictive validity of only ,10, while experience has an unimpressive predictive validity of ,18 when linked to job performance.

The importance of selecting the right person (in the sense just outlined) for your company is reinforced by Jim Collins in his book, *Good to Great*, when he states that leaders of companies who have really made a success did not begin by setting a new vision and strategy; they first got the right people on the bus, the wrong people off the bus and ensured that the right people were in the right seats. Only then did they figure out where to drive. Collins emphasises that people are not your most important asset, but that the right people are.

Getting the right people on the bus places more emphasis on identifying the "right" character attributes of individuals and less emphasis on the specialised knowledge they possess. Given time, most people can learn the skills you may require them to have or acquire the knowledge you need them to acquire over time, but they may not possess the essential character traits that make them right for your team or organisation. In other words, they do not have the potential embedded in their character that you're looking for in order to make your department, team or organisation successful.

Character attributes that may be considered when selecting prospective employees are self-efficacy, hope, optimism, resilience and an internal locus of control.

Source: Adapted from Pienaar, C. & Bester, C. 2006. "What people tend to forget during selection". People Dynamics, Vol. 24, No. 5, pp. 3–4. Used with permission.

11.5 Developing qualified workers

11.5.1 Human-resources development (HRD)

The HR manager has the dual responsibility of ensuring that the company employs sufficient staff and of creating opportunities for employees to make themselves more valuable to the company. This activity can be subdivided in several ways, but a good method is to distinguish firstly between **training** and **development**, and secondly between **technical** training and **management** training.

Training typically involves providing employees with the knowledge and skills needed to do a particular task or job, although attitude change may also be attempted (for example, in training to create awareness of sexual harassment). **Developmental** activities, in contrast, have a longer-term focus on preparing for future work responsibilities, while at the same time increasing the capacities of employees to perform their current jobs[17].

While the methods used for training and development are basically the same, the purpose differs. Thus, one person may attend a course on marketing because he/she currently fills a marketing post, whereas another person may be sent on the same course because management wants him/her to fill a marketing post at some future point. Similarly, a superior may spend time teaching a subordinate how to do his/her work correctly, but may also spend time teaching the subordinate to do the superior's work with a view to future promotion.

For our purposes, we will speak of **development** as the overall concept, with the understanding that it includes both training and development in the narrower sense of the word. We can thus define **human-resources development** as a set of systematic and planned activities designed by an organisation to provide its members with the opportunities to learn necessary skills to meet current and future job demands. Consequently, learning is at the core of all HRD activities[18].

The word "technical" means not so much tasks performed in a workshop, but any task that has to be performed physically. Accordingly, the keeping of journals is just as technical as the repair of a machine. In its wider sense, we use the word "technical" to refer to all non-management tasks. By "management work", we mean tasks such as planning for, organising, controlling and, especially, managing people.

HRD activities should begin when an employee joins an organisation and continue throughout his/her career, regardless of whether that employee is an executive or a worker on an assembly line. HRD programs must respond to job changes, and must integrate the long-term plans and strategies of the organisation to ensure the efficient and effective use of resources.

The HR manager does not have to train other employees personally (usually there are HRD professionals to do this), but he/she is primarily responsible for providing development facilities and courses. The HR manager must ensure that the employees are given an opportunity for training and development, and that they are encouraged to develop to higher levels of competence.

11.5.2 Development methods

The development activities can be executed in four basic ways[19]:

- informally within the work situation
- formally within the work situation
- informally outside the work situation
- formally outside the work situation.

11.5.2.1 Informal development inside the work situation

In this situation, the employee does not follow an official training program. He/she is put to work immediately and expected to learn in due course. It might also happen that a newcomer works with an experienced employee for a while to give the new employee time to "find his/her feet".

Informal development within the work situation can also occur through coaching by the employee's immediate superior. The superior may, for example, give his/her subordinate certain responsibilities and show the employee how to perform certain tasks.

Another common form of informal internal development is job rotation. This means that a staff member is moved to a new job as soon as he/she knows the current job well. The rotation could be short term, for example, two weeks in every job, or long term, for example, one year in every job. The latter usually applies to more senior management jobs and is often preparation for a general management position. What is important, however, is that the development does not take place at random. The HR manager can make an important contribution in this regard by:

- keeping a careful record of each employee's development progress
- encouraging line managers to establish this type of development (the HR manager does not usually have the official authority to enforce the development described)
- discussing the progress and prospects of individual staff members with those individuals themselves.

Often, when an employee resigns, he/she is informed for the first time of all the development plans that the company had for him/her. In most cases, however, it is then too late. The HR manager can prevent many resignations by ensuring that individuals are kept informed of the career path planned for them in the enterprise. The Coca-Cola case study illustrates the importance of mentoring and talent development as key drivers for success.

11.5.2.2 Formal development inside the work situation

"Formal development"refers to a training process in which the employee receives a formal qualification. The most common form of this type of development is a **learnership**. The subordinate is allocated to a qualified artisan and so is provided with the necessary practical training. From time to time, the subordinate must attend a few block courses, usually at a technical institution. After a certain period (the time varies according to the nature of the training), the subordinate receives a certificate if he/she has passed the compulsory examination. Other examples of this type of training are the qualifying exams for promotion in the South African National Defence Force and banking exams. The purpose of this type of training is not only to equip employees for their present jobs, but also to give them a wider perspective and background on the work situation in which they find themselves.

11.5.2.3 Informal development outside the work situation

In this sort of training, an employee does not receive a qualification, although a certificate is sometimes issued to indicate that he/she has attended a particular training program.

Probably the most common form of this type of development is a **training course** offered inside the company. Many companies (especially larger ones) have training centres where staff members receive training in a variety of subjects, for example, interpersonal relationships, sales techniques, secretarial skills, supervision techniques, communication techniques and planning techniques.

An **induction course** would also fall into this category. These courses are sometimes presented by the HR manager or by an HRD manager specially appointed for the job. The courses can also be presented by outsiders who specialise in presenting this type of course.

The advantage of courses presented within a company is that the training material is aimed specifically at the circumstances and operations of that particular company. This type of course is not meant only for workers at the lowest level of the company, but also for managers.

There are many courses in which managers can learn skills for handling and motivating subordinates. By arranging for managers in the company to attend such training programs, the HR manager can make a big contribution towards line managers' optimal utilisation of employees.

Another form of informal development outside the work situation is the public seminar presented by an outside institution (for example, a consultant or professional institution). Such courses are normally attended by a variety of employees from various companies. This type of course is especially valuable to smaller companies that want to expose only a few staff members to this type of training and can therefore not present the course within the organisation. The disadvantage here is that training material becomes generalised because it must apply to a number of widely divergent companies.

The above-mentioned courses normally last a few days or weeks, full-time. However, staff members might also attend a training session one morning a week, for example, and such a program could last for a number of months.

Some companies use **programmed instruction** (PI) as a training method. Here, the instructional material is broken down into frames and programmed for the computer. Each frame represents a small component of the entire subject to be learnt, and each frame must be completed successfully before the next one can be tackled. An advantage of PI is that large numbers of employees can be trained simultaneously, with each learner free to explore the material at his/her own pace. In addition, PI includes immediate and individualised feedback. A disadvantage is that development costs are high, especially for computerised PI[20].

Another form of informal development is a fixed **reading program**. For example, an employee may undertake to study certain books before a certain date, or to become a regular subscriber to a professional journal. If such a program is agreed on, the HR manager must follow it up regularly, otherwise it is likely to peter out over time.

11.5.2.4 Formal development outside the work situation

This refers to formal study programs presented by educational institutions, for example, universities and colleges. This kind of extensive and general training contributes to the employee's general development, rather than equipping him/her for the specific job he/she is currently doing. Many companies encourage their employees to attempt this type of development and even offer to pay the fees if the employee is successful in his/her studies.

11.5.3 The danger of the "shotgun" approach to development

The descriptions of the various kinds of development activity given above emphasise the variety of development possibilities that are available to the HR manager. However, a problem is that many HR managers believe that "any training is valuable". They therefore encourage employees to attempt extramural studies and they arrange for a certain number of employees to attend some training programs every year. They aim, as if with a shotgun, in a general direction and hope to hit something[21].

The successful HR manager, however, attempts to obtain as much value as possible from development programs. Firstly, he/she makes a thorough analysis of the development needs that exist within the company and then chooses training programs on the basis of how specific programs comply with these needs. Secondly, he/she ensures that training money is spent only on members of staff who show a potential for further development. Thirdly, the HR manager makes plans with the immediate superior of the employee concerned to utilise his/her new skills or

Critical thinking

Organisations spend a substantial amount of their human-resources budgets on the training and development of their employees. In order to convince top management that this amount is being well invested, the HR manager has to convince management of the contribution that proper training and development can make to organisational goal achievement. The question thus is: What focus should the training have to achieve this goal? The excerpt below provides some answers.

Real-time training for real-time issues

Gone are the days of training being an unnecessary expense – a great idea with the hope of making participants better at what they do that fails to become real beyond the four walls of the training room. The new business reality involves concepts, products and solutions that need to be taken to market swiftly under greater pressure and with greater risk than ever before. The call is for training that facilitates this process. Individuals and teams need training that gives them the skill and confidence to deal positively and successfully with their company's real-time issues. They need practical training that has a lasting and tangible effect, and is not forgotten as soon as the training manual has been filed away in the cabinet with the comment: "It was thought provoking while it lasted."

It's the Cinderella complex: everything seems value-adding until the training clock strikes twelve, and what initially seemed like a worthwhile training investment leaves the business feeling disenchanted soon after, pumpkin-style. Companies determined to find the right "fit" are therefore having to look beyond what training providers can do WITHIN training time at how they can assist individuals and teams in effecting business change AFTER training.

The reality is that employees already HAVE the knowledge. If you take the average sales team, chances are they would score 100% in a multiple-choice test on their product knowledge, so to what degree would booking 30 of them on to a generic "sales-impact" course assist them when they have to present a new product to a challenging client the next day? No-one wants a walking brochure, they want an indispensable business partner and trusted advisor.

The issue is that most training initiatives focus on telling people what they already know instead of addressing the implementation gap between what we know versus what we do.

The new ... interventions that are making an impact are those that don't undermine participants by assuming that their know-how isn't in place. Instead, they focus on using training sessions as realistic problem-solving sessions with a bias to action. Knowledge is base camp. The summit lies in creating a discipline of execution. This could be where the company's brand and service promise is proactively taken from the "walls to the halls" internally, or when a product is taken to market by participants who have learnt to communicate solutions to clients in a way that gets their buy-in.

Be practical

Powerful business outcomes-based training therefore starts with a strong practical component. It doesn't matter whether participants staple themselves to their process in service initiatives, track their service processes through the eyes of the client or ensure a benchmark level of service excellence and value-driven actions at all critical touch points. They must learn to bring brand values to life through concrete behaviours at critical touch points in values initiatives or "real-play" how to leverage their technical and product knowledge – translating it into marketing and sales opportunities to grow the profitability of their existing client base and acquire new clients in solutions-based selling and presentation workshops – the experiential opportunity to rehearse for business-relevant realities is key.

It's essential that whatever the nature of the training, participants take the initiative as they leave the session, having committed to a gutsy personal and business-unit action plan, which translates training into tangible results around the desired outcomes set by the client. This challenges the dominant logic of feel-good inspirational sessions, which may leave you with a short-term high, but a famously low impact in the long term.

So think twice before you "okay" the next training day. Your training spend should be value-adding enough that your end clients feel its resonance. Ask yourself: Am I training merely for training's sake? Or am I unleashing a new energy and imagination in my team, with training as a powerful vehicle to establish momentum, to plan participatively and translate the way forward into a high-impact reality?

It's not about filling out definitions in a training manual, or about exploring the five new sales techniques to close the deal. It's about a customised process that aligns strongly with business objectives. It's an investment that can give birth to sustained and measurable confidence and competence in teams to impact the bottom line.

Source: © Bluen V. from HR Future, Osgard Media through DALRO 2008.

insight in the work situation. Lastly, the HR manager undertakes follow-up studies to determine whether the training programs have had the desired results.

Thus far, this chapter has focused on some of the most effective methods available to managers for finding and developing top-notch employees. However, having talented employees is not enough. Successful organisations are particularly adept at engaging their workforces to achieve goals that benefit the organisation as well as the individual. One of the most helpful tools a company can use to maintain and enhance productivity and facilitate progress towards strategic goals is performance-appraisal programs[22]. It is clear from the Coca-Cola case study that human-resources development is a priority. The company focuses on management development and succession planning.

11.5.4 Performance appraisal

The purpose of a **performance appraisal** is to determine in which aspects the employee has:

- performed exceptionally well (that is, surpassed the requirements for the job)
- complied with the requirements for the job
- not complied with the requirements for the job.

Performance appraisal is also called **employee rating**, **employee evaluation**, **performance review**, **performance evaluation** and **results appraisal**[23]. Performance appraisal can be done by anyone who is familiar with the performance of individual employees, including supervisors who rate their employees, employees who rate their superiors, team members who rate each other, employees who do self-appraisal or outside sources.

The more **objective** this appraisal is, the more successful it is likely to be. It is therefore important for the HR manager to ensure that there are objective criteria against which the performance of the individual or team can be measured. Thus, an ideal performance appraisal involves the comparison of work results with quantitative objectives[24]. For example, a salesperson's actual sales are compared with a sales target, a truck driver can be appraised against, amongst other things, the maintenance costs of his/her truck and a teller's performance may be measured against the number of times he/she did not achieve a balance.

Some performance-appraisal methods also provide for the assessment of an employee's **characteristics**, such as attitude, enthusiasm, initiative and neatness. However, this type of assessment is much more subjective than the comparison of results with objectives because it depends mainly on the opinion of the immediate superior.

The least-effective form of performance appraisal is that whereby employees are compared with each other in general. In this approach, the employee is assessed mainly on the basis of the **impression** the superior has of him/her, and the risk of prejudice (positive or negative) is much greater.

As a result of the numerous problems that arise out of traditional performance-appraisal methods, a new approach called the **360° system** was developed some years ago. This multi-source rating recognises that the manager is no longer the sole source of performance-appraisal information. Instead, feedback from various colleagues and constituencies is obtained and given to the manager, who then interprets the feedback from the various sources[25].

In practice, and for a number of reasons, formal performance-appraisal programs sometimes yield disappointing results.

Primary causes include a lack of top-management information and support, unclear performance standards, rater bias, too many forms to complete and the use of the programs for conflicting purposes[26]. The **results** of a performance appraisal can be used for three basic purposes:

- to provide a basis for financial rewards
- to determine whether the employee should be promoted to a higher level of work
- to provide the employee with feedback on how well he/she is doing.

It is not possible for the HR manager to do the performance appraisal him-/herself (except where employees – that is, the HR officers – fall directly under his/her control). Therefore the HR manager must ensure that performance appraisal is done by the line managers and must help them to do it, especially by providing them with suitable instruments for doing appraisals.

A critical aspect in performance appraisal is **feedback** to the individual or team concerned. In order to be effective, feedback should possess characteristics other than timeliness. For example, it must be concise (not too lengthy), specific (examples must be provided), relevant (it must be job related) and supportive (it must offer suggestions for positive change)[27].

It is important and necessary to reward employees whose performance appraisals are excellent. From the Coca-Cola case study, it is clear that "performance" is integrated in organisational values. However, organisations also use compensation to attract the quality and quantity of employees needed, retain those employees and motivate them towards organisational goal achievement. The following section discusses the important role played by compensation within an organisation.

11.6 Keeping qualified workers

11.6.1 Compensation of employees

Compensation refers to all forms of financial returns, tangible services and benefits employees receive as part of an employment relationship[28]. It is one of the most important factors that motivates an individual to seek employment with a specific company. The other is the nature of the work. If an employee is dissatisfied with his/her compensation, there is a good chance that the employee will not remain with the company for long. The HR manager must therefore ensure that the compensation policy does not lead to a high staff turnover. From the case study earlier in this chapter, it is clear that above-average salaries are paid to employees at Coca-Cola.

Thus, the establishment of a compensation policy is an absolute necessity[29]. Although the HR manager, in most companies, does not have the final say in the compensation policy, it must nevertheless be initiated by him/her. Here are some important points to note when drawing up this policy:

- Firstly, a decision must be made about how the company's compensation in general should compare with that of the labour market. Will it be the same? A little higher? Considerably higher? Or a little lower? What form should the compensation take? How much will be in the form of direct financial compensation? And how much in the form of fringe benefits? The fringe benefits of some companies do not involve more than 30–40% of the total compensation, while those of other companies are as high as 50%.
- Secondly, a policy must be determined on a cost-of-living adjustment. Does every employee automatically receive an increase that corresponds with the Consumer Price Index (CPI), or does each person receive a larger or smaller increase?
- Thirdly, the compensation policy must determine what form rewards will take. Most companies reward by means of salary increases. Other companies, however, only give salary increases in accordance with the rise in the cost of living, and then give cash bonuses to reward good work performance.

11.6.2 Types of compensation

Compensation can be regarded as the output an employee receives for the input (work) he/she produces. **Direct compensation** is the basic salary or wage an employee receives, while **indirect compensation** refers to the fringe benefits an employee receives, such as leave, medical aid and a pension scheme[30]. The other aspect of compensation is **reward**, that is, the recognition of good work performance.

11.6.2.1 Direct compensation

A person who is paid monthly receives a **salary**, whereas someone who is paid daily or weekly receives a **wage**. Most employees' salaries or wages are based on the period of time they have worked for the company, measured in days, weeks or months. Thus, there is no direct relationship between the compensation employees receive and the amount of work that they perform. Such a system is simple to administer, but has the disadvantage that, for remuneration purposes (in the short term, at any rate) there is no distinction between productive and unproductive workers. To overcome this problem, some companies use a **piece-wage** system. Here, the employee is compensated for the amount of work he/she performs, regardless of the time taken to perform the work.

Example:
Time wages and piece wages

A vegetable farmer in KwaZulu-Natal pays the labourers R30 per day (that is, time wages), but at harvesting time the farmer pays them R6,00 for every bag of peas they pick (that is, piece wages). If they only pick three bags a day, they receive R18,00 for the day's work. If they pick eight bags, they receive R48,00 for the day's work.

11.6.2.2 Indirect compensation

The **benefits** an employee receives from his/her membership of an organisation are called **fringe benefits**. These benefits increase in size and scope as the employee moves to higher levels in the organisation.

Fringe benefits generally provided are:

- **leave benefits**, for holidays, illness, studies and so on
- **insurance benefits**, for example, against medical costs, injury and unemployment; these also include life cover and pension benefits
- **housing benefits**, in the form of free housing, housing at a low rental or loan subsidies for buying a house
- **car benefits**, which can vary from a free car with all expenses paid to financial assistance in buying a car.

There are also other types of fringe benefits. These differ from company to company. The important point, however, is that fringe benefits are a form of compensation linked to the hierarchical level of the employee. For example, only staff members above a certain status level enjoy cars as a fringe benefit, and the higher the status level, the more expensive the car.

11.6.2.3 Reward

In most cases, neither direct nor indirect compensation is linked to an individual's work performance, and both forms of compensation are therefore regarded as "rights" by most employees. Both forms of compensation therefore have very little influence on the motivation of employees. The fact that an employee receives an end-of-year bonus (often equivalent to a month's salary) will not cause him/her to work twice as hard to merit this in future.

The HR manager must therefore ensure that there are other ways of rewarding an individual's work performance. Such rewards can take various forms, some of which include the following:

- The most common form of reward is a **salary increase** based on the individual's work performance (that is, a merit award). A distinction must be made here between the **cost-of-living adjustment** (given to all employees to adjust to the inflation rate) and **merit increases** given in recognition of the individual's achievement.
- Some companies give **financial bonuses** to those employees who have performed exceptionally well.
- Other companies reward outstanding employees with a **paid holiday** or an **overseas trip** with all expenses paid.

To summarise: **compensation** is part of an agreement and is given to the employee for satisfactory performance. It can therefore correctly be regarded as a **right** because the company is **committed** to paying it. A **reward**, however, is not a commitment on the part of the company. It is the company's **voluntary** acknowledgement of an individual's good work performance.

11.6.3 The amount of compensation

The question that now arises is: How much should a specific staff member be paid by way of compensation (salary and fringe benefits)? We know that a factory manager will probably earn more than a machine operator, but how large ought the difference to be and how much should each person receive?

The first step in deciding on compensation is to make an **external comparison.** How much do factory managers at other companies earn? What is the nature and scope of their fringe benefits? The HR manager must do a **salary survey** to obtain this information.

Salary surveys are undertaken country-wide by different institutions. The HR manager may choose to use such surveys rather than do his/her own survey. However, it is important in such a survey that equivalent jobs are compared with each other. The mere fact that two people have the job title "factory manager" does not necessarily mean that they do the same type of work. So, for example, a person in control of a small workshop where hand-made chairs are manufactured by three artisans might carry the title "factory manager", but it is obvious that this job is not equivalent to that of a factory manager in a large motor-manufacturing plant.

The second step is to make an **internal comparison**[31]. This means that the value of jobs must be compared with each other in terms of the demands they make on the employee. Accordingly, it may be said that the demands made on an accountant are higher than the demands made on an accounting clerk.

This internal comparison is known as **job evaluation**[32], and there are various methods of undertaking it. One method is to rank all jobs in the company in terms of their "value". This ranking system is usually used in small- to medium-sized companies, and the assessment is made by a panel of senior managers.

A second general method of job evaluation is the **factor-comparison** method. According to this method, jobs are compared according to the demands they make on the employee in terms of factors such as knowledge, communication skills, level of responsibility and, especially, decision-making skills. Points are awarded to each factor (also known as **compensable factors**), and the total points indicate into which job grade a specific job falls. The information about the jobs can be obtained from the **job description**. Job descriptions therefore have a twofold purpose:

- Firstly, they form the basis for a **job specification**, with a view to recruitment, selection and training.
- Secondly, they provide a basis for job comparison, with a view to job evaluation.

It is important to remember that in job evaluation, only the job is assessed and not the job incumbent. The value of the job has nothing to do with how well or how badly the present incumbent carries it out.

Job evaluation in itself cannot indicate exactly how much a specific staff member ought to earn. The HR manager can only determine, in the light of the findings of the external comparison, what the broad salary range of an accountant, for instance, ought to be.

The decision as to what a specific employee ought to earn once he/she is employed will depend on years of experience, qualifications, what other employees on the same level earn and other similar considerations. The question can be decided by the HR manager in conjunction with the line manager. However, the HR manager cannot decide

Critical thinking

One of the most significant tasks confronting HR managers is the design and implementation of compensation systems. The primary goal of these systems, which are designed to serve many purposes, is to provide fair and equitable remuneration for all employees. What approach should the HR manager follow to achieve success in this regard? Some answers to this question are provided in the excerpt below.

Trends in remuneration philosophy

Firms, like other economic organisations, serve to co-ordinate the actions of groups of people and to motivate them to carry out needed activities. The difficulty in motivating people in organisations comes from the fact that their own self-interest may not automatically lead them to act in ways that the organisation would want. This divergence of interest arises because the individual members of an organisation typically do not bear all of the costs and benefits of actions they take and decisions they make within the organisation. Consequently, when they make decisions – about how to spend their time, how hard to work and on what, what risks to take and so on – the choices that appear best from their personal point of view may not maximise the total value generated for the organisation. Even if they are cognisant of the larger interests, they may not automatically take these fully into account. Companies try to manage this through five primary mechanisms:

- developing and providing clear strategic direction
- implementing good organisational design
- creating a sense of shared purpose
- effective performance management
- appropriate remuneration and reward systems.

Source: Adapted from Olivier, M. "Trends in remuneration philosophy". *People Dynamics*. Vol. 24, No. 9, 2006, pp. 47–48. Used with permission.

on an individual staff member's reward. That decision can be made only by the staff member's immediate superior. Nevertheless, the HR manager can make an important contribution by ensuring that line managers have suitable instruments for assessing their subordinates' performances.

11.7 Motivating employees

11.7.1 Introduction

In today's society, notions such as "people make up a business", "people are an organisation's greatest assets", "managing human resources is fundamental to organisational success" and "motivated employees make a difference" are in general use and are crucial to organisational success. The emphasis has shifted from endeavouring to solve people-related problems in organisations in an *ad hoc* fashion to a more professional approach where the overall organisational philosophy, culture and tone reflect this belief.

The case study on this page provides an illustration of how theories of motivation are applied in the strategies of South African companies.

11.7.2 Employee motivation

The importance and uniqueness of the human resource in the effective functioning of organisations was discussed in section 11.2.1. Part of the responsibility of the human-resources department and line managers is to turn the potential of employees into performance.

Case study

The most promising companies in South Africa: Their competitive advantage

The Corporate Research Foundation (CRF) profiles and publishes information about companies that are selected as South Africa's most promising companies. The following common features that gave the companies their competitive advantage were identified in the fourth edition of *South Africa's most promising companies*[33]:

- These companies are not only obtaining the right talent, but they are also nurturing that talent by means of skills development, transfer of knowledge, and the creation of an open and sharing environment. Flatter organisational structures are implemented, allowing for a more flexible working environment. Creativity and innovation are encouraged, and lots of opportunities are provided for challenges, as long as the end result is added value to the clients and the business. These companies also give their employees more responsibility to the point where they feel they are part-owner of the firm.
- Major emphasis is placed on good working relationships with employees, clients, suppliers and other stakeholders. The employees get recognition for their loyalty, excellent client service and performance by means of excellent remuneration, share options and other forms of incentive schemes.
- Other strategies employed by these companies include building and maintaining a strong brand in the market, an emphasis on excellent client service, and holding values such as honesty, integrity, open communication and transparency.

Some of the relevant strategies of four of these companies will be elaborated on later in this chapter.

11.7.2.1 Motivation in the workplace: A basic understanding

Employee performance in organisations is mainly determined by three things: a desire to do the job (motivation), the capability to do the job (ability) and the resources to do the job (work environment). If an employee cannot do the job, he/she can be trained or replaced (see section 11.8.4 for more information on the requirements laid down by the Labour Relations Act) and if more resources are required, the manager can rectify the problem. The problem becomes more challenging if the employee is not motivated to do the job[34]. Because of the complex nature of human beings, managers may not fully

Different approaches to motivation by different companies

The word "motivation" is not always used in companies to explain the critical role of motivation in the performance of their employees. What employers do to motivate their employees is, however, often implied by the strategies of the companies and can therefore only be deduced.

Four of the companies identified by the Corporate Research Foundation (CFR) as South Africa's most promising companies were eBucks, Fireworkx Internet, Sandvik Mining and Construction RSA, and MWEB. Here are some of the strategies that gave these companies this elevated position.

eBucks

eBucks is South Africa's leading multi-partner rewards program. It is driven by a hard-working creative team. The company has a flat structure, providing many employees with the opportunity to head a division. The company also believes in an open-door policy and employees take pride in teamwork. This creates an environment where people enjoy working together. The environment is, however, also challenging and develops employees. Employees are constantly seeking new ways of doing things better.

Fireworkx Internet

This small software company regards its very high level of staff expertise and a strong focus on product excellence as its competitive advantage. The company works on a project-by-project basis, with employees being largely responsible and independent, and encouraged to be innovative. They are paid what they are worth, and incentive bonuses and a staff share scheme are implemented.

Sandvik Mining and Construction RSA

This international company in the mining industry focuses its strategy on removing people from danger. Continuous training and skills transfer are regarded as essential to the success of the organisation. In addition, the health and safety of employees are critical and everything is done to protect them and their clients.

MWEB

MWEB's focus on human resources and customer relationships resulted in its being one of South Africa's leading internet service providers. The company fosters an open and progressive environment with a relatively flat management structure. Human resources and strategies play a pivotal role, both in terms of business-focused development of human capital and general employee satisfaction and well-being. The employees function as a results-oriented and outcomes-based team. The company follows the principles of being open, straightforward, truthful and transparent, while delivering promises. Its primary values are to be customer focused, be innovative, have mutual respect, promote a culture of learning, perform and meet goals, and participate. Internally there is a drive to be experimental in terms of new technology in order to remain ahead in the market.

Source: Brevis, T. "Most promising companies: What gives them a competitive advantage", *Management Today*, February 2005, pp. 8–12.

understand the problems experienced by employees and the effect of these problems on individual performance. The level of **motivation** thus has a direct influence on performance and it is important to understand how motivation takes place. However, motivation is not simply about performance. Deviant behaviour such as sabotage and absenteeism are also motivated behaviours!

Motivation refers to those forces within a person that affect his/her direction, intensity and persistence of behaviour that is within the control of the person. A motivated employee is willing to exert a particular level of effort (intensity) for a certain amount of time (persistence) toward a particular goal (direction)[35]. Whereas the emphasis in the past was on "effort" and subsequently on ways to energise employees, the concept of **direction** is currently emphasised. It is reasoned that all normal people will expend energy in one way or another. In a sense, employers are always competing with other forces for the time and effort of their employees. Work motivation must therefore always be looked at in the context of a rich and complex life of employees who often strive to find a work–life balance[36].

In order to distinguish between the different approaches to motivation, the theories can be classified in terms of **content approaches** versus **process approaches**:

- **Content approaches** try to determine those things that actually motivate people to do their jobs, or the "what" of motivation. These theories focus on the factors within a person that direct, energise, maintain or stop behaviour, and are therefore also known as **need theories**. Consequently, these theories try to identify employees' needs and the goals they want to attain in order to satisfy these needs[37].
- **Process theories**, in contrast, try to explain the actual process, or the "how" of motivation. According to the process theories, employees have a cognitive decision-making role in selecting their goals and the means to achieve them. These approaches are therefore concerned with trying to establish how employee behaviour is energised, directed, maintained and stopped[38].

11.7.2.2 Content approaches to motivation

The content approaches include Abraham **Maslow**'s hierarchy of needs, Clayton **Alderfer**'s ERG theory, Frederick **Herzberg**'s two-factor theory and David **McClelland**'s learnt-needs theory. While the first three theories are based on primary instinctive needs, McClelland maintains that needs are learnt and reinforced. The different theories will now be discussed in more detail.

Maslow's hierarchy of needs

Maslow's theory of a **hierarchy of needs** is one of the best-known theories of motivation. The crux of Maslow's theory is that needs are arranged in a hierarchy where the lowest-level needs are physiological needs and the highest-level needs are self-actualisation needs (see Figure 11.3).

At the bottom of the hierarchy are the **physiological needs**, which include food, drink, sex and air. These are the basic ingredients for survival and for biological functioning. In an organisation, these needs of employees are satisfied by the provision

Figure 11.3: Maslow's hierarchy of needs

Source: Maslow, A.H. et al. 1954. *A theory of human motivation.* New York: Harper, pp.35–47. Reprinted by permission of Ann Maslow Kaplan.

of things such as a salary, rest rooms, a cafeteria, heating and adequate lighting.

Safety and security needs, which include protection from physical and emotional harm, are on the next level in the hierarchy. They also include the desire for clothing, job security, pension plans, structures in the organisation to deal with grievances and employee-assistance programs. Affiliation needs include the need for friendships, love and affection, and the need to be accepted by peers. Family and, to some extent, office parties, for example, in the workplace, satisfy this level of need.

Esteem needs include the need for a positive self-image and self-respect, and the need for recognition from others. In organisations, this need can be satisfied by means of compliments to employees, access to information, job titles and challenging job assignments.

Self-actualisation needs, which involve realising one's potential through growth and development, are at the top of the hierarchy. In an organisational context, the focus should be on providing employees with development opportunities, challenging assignments and decision-making opportunities. The focus on skills development, creativity, innovation and opportunities for challenges, for example, are regarded as part of the strategies that give South Africa's most promising companies their competitive edge.

Maslow's theory assumes that a person attempts to satisfy the more basic needs before progressing to satisfying higher-level needs. A further assumption is that people strive to move up the hierarchy in terms of need satisfaction, and that a specific need ceases to motivate an employee once it has been satisfied. Unsatisfied needs cause stress, frustration and conflict within an individual, and also between individuals. Management can help employees to satisfy needs at various levels by promoting a culture wherein, for example, self-esteem and self-actualisation needs can be satisfied. The opportunity of participation in decision-making about work and the provision of learning opportunities are examples of self-actualisation opportunities.

Although it is a very popular and convenient theory to apply, Maslow's theory has many shortcomings for use in the workplace as it oversimplifies matters. The idea that all needs originate intrinsically, for example, is questionable. Needs are often learnt and develop because of social influences (see McClelland's theory) and different life experiences. Esteem needs, for example, might be desirable because we see the positive effects esteem has on others. Research has shown that not all levels of needs as identified by Maslow are always present, and certain cultures may have different need categories and hierarchies. Some people, for example, are motivated mainly by money, while others mainly want to satisfy their social needs at work. In the case of Sandvik Mining and Construction RSA (see page 314), the safety needs of the employees are of the utmost importance. Furthermore, employees may also satisfy their needs outside the workplace, making it difficult for managers to determine the genuine levels of motivation at work. Finally, it is also not the case that highly satisfied employees are always highly productive[39].

Alderfer's ERG theory

Alderfer's theory represents a refinement of Maslow's five-level hierarchy in that, according to Alderfer, there are three core needs: existence, relatedness and growth (ERG). These needs can be summarised as follows[40]:

- **Existence needs.** These needs relate to a person's basic, material, existence needs. These needs correspond to Maslow's physiological and safety needs.
- **Relatedness needs.** These needs concern a person's desire for interpersonal relationships and interaction. They are similar to Maslow's affiliation/social needs and the external aspect of Maslow's esteem needs.

- **Growth needs.** These relate to the desire of an individual to make a creative or productive contribution. They are similar to Maslow's esteem and self-actualisation needs.

The ERG theory does not subscribe to a rigid hierarchy of needs, whereas Maslow maintained that a lower-level need must first be satisfied before a higher-level need will be entertained. According to the ERG theory, two or even all three need categories can influence behaviour simultaneously. The ERG theory also suggests that if a person is continually frustrated in his/her attempts to satisfy growth needs, relatedness needs re-emerge as a major motivating force, and this may force the person to redirect efforts towards satisfying a lower-order need category. The implication is that, for example, employees' demands for higher pay or better benefits may occur because of a stifling work environment.

Herzberg's two-factor theory and job enrichment

Frederick Herzberg proposed a motivational model called the **two-factor model**, which consists of maintenance and motivational factors:

- The **maintenance (hygiene) factors** do not act as motivational factors, but if they are absent in an organisation, this could have a negative affect on employee morale. The maintenance factors are those aspects that people consider essential to do any job, for example, organisational policy and administration, equipment, supervision, interpersonal relationships with colleagues and supervisors, salary, status, working conditions and work security[41].
- **Motivational factors**, also called **growth factors**, are focused on the content of the job. They include aspects such as achievement (successful completion of tasks), recognition for what has been achieved, the job itself (meaningfulness and challenge), progress and growth, responsibility and feedback. Motivational factors are benefits over and above the normal job to be done, which tend to increase employee satisfaction because employees get more out of the normal job they do. When motivational factors are present, these are likely to motivate employees to achieve higher productivity, to be more committed to their jobs, and to find creative ways of accomplishing both personal and organisational goals[42].

As shown in Table 11.1, Herzberg's theory can be linked to Maslow's hierarchy of needs. The maintenance (hygiene) factors are similar to the lower-level needs in the

Table 11.1: Comparison of the theories of Herzberg and Maslow

	Herzberg	Maslow
Motivational factors	• Recognition • Status • Advancement	• Esteem needs
	• Work itself • Responsibility	• Self-actualisation
Maintenance factors	• Social network • Supervision	• Social/belongingness
	• Policy/administrative	• Safety and security
	• Job security • Salary • Working conditions	• Physiological

Critical thinking

Do you think that singing the song *Shosholoza* motivates employees? If so, which needs are probably satisfied by singing the song?

Shosholoza: Does this song motivate?

Shosholoza is the song that black South Africans, especially long-term convicts engaged in hard labour, traditionally sang in conditions of hardship. *Shosholoza* is like a child with no parents, however. Nobody knows when or from where it originated, but what everyone does know is that when there is some kind of deep-rooted ache in the heart, the first sound to rise from the lips will be *Shosholoza*. It is a song with no beginning and no end, as old as misery itself.

Shosholoza
Ku lezontaba
Stimela si qhamuka e South Africa

Wen u ya baleka
Wen u ya baleka
Ku lezontaba
Stimela si qhamuka South Africa

Shosholoza
You are meandering on those mountains
The train is from South Africa

You accelerate
You accelerate
On those mountains
The train is from South Africa

Here are the lyrics as recorded by Ladysmith Black Mambazo:

Chorus
Shosholoza
Ku lezontaba
Stimela si qhamuka e South Africa Shosholoza
Stimela si qhamuka e South Africa
Wen u ya baleka
Wen u ya baleka
Ku lezontaba
Stimela si qhamuka South Africa

Verse 1
Shosholoza
Work, work, working in the sun
We will work as one
Shosholoza
Work, work, working in the rain
'Til there's sun again

Verse 2
Shosholoza
Push, push, pushing on and on
There's much to be done
Shosholoza
Push, push, pushing in the sun
We will push as one

Sithwele kanzima, sithwele kanzima (ooh, aah!)
Sithwele kanzima, sithwele kanzima (ooh, aah!)
Sithwele kanzima, sithwele kanzima (ooh, aah!)
Sithwele kanzima, sithwele kanzima (ooh, aah!)
Sithwele kanzima, sithwele kanzima (ooh, aah!)

Etshe!
Shosholoza
Repeat chorus
Repeat verse
Repeat chorus

hierarchy, while the motivators are the same as the higher-level needs.

According to the theory of Herzberg, a distinction can be made between internal motivation (based on motivators) and external motivation (based on maintenance factors):

- **Internal motivation.** This motivation originates from the satisfaction that occurs when a task is executed or a duty is performed. For example, if a teacher enjoys teaching children, the activity is in itself rewarding and the teacher will be self-motivated. The intrinsic rewards of the job motivate some people more than external influences such as money and trophies do. Herzberg's theory of motivation emphasises that jobs should be enriched to provide opportunities for growth and more responsibility. Compare the strategies of the most promising companies we have mentioned regarding the use of internal motivation.
- **External motivation.** In contrast to internal motivation, external motivation usually involves action taken by a third party. Here, a person is motivated because he/she anticipates that a reward of some kind (for example, money, awards or feedback about performance) will be given. Incentives such as profit-sharing, bonuses and awards are used by organisations to instil certain work habits that are beneficial both for the organisation and the individual. Unfortunately, external rewards are not enough to motivate people in the long term. Organisations should therefore focus on a combination of both internal and external rewards. They should keep employees motivated by ensuring that they experience job satisfaction (because they find their work challenging) and have an appropriate number of external awards.

Fireworkx Internet can be regarded as an example of an organisation in which both internal motivators (responsibility, independence and innovation) are encouraged and external factors (bonuses) are applied.

An important contribution of Herzberg's theory is his emphasis on the task itself as the source of job satisfaction. **Job enrichment** as a way to design jobs is therefore a valuable practical application of his theory. It entails incorporating, by means of vertical loading (giving employees responsibilities that are usually allocated to senior employees to give them more control over aspects such as work-scheduling, cost control and work methods), the opportunity to experience achievement, recognition, stimulating work, responsibility and advancement in a job.

Most of the critiques of Herzberg's theory centre on the motivational role of lower-order needs, especially the role of money. Although money can be useful for facilitating acceptance of organisational change, research suggests that manual workers are more likely to be motivated by money than more professional or managerial groups are. More recent research however, indicates that lower-order factors such as pay and job security are not mentioned as either satisfying or dissatisfying by participants. The role of money is therefore still uncertain, though it may seem that the different needs for money by different employees or groups of employees are not taken into account by Herzberg's theory[43]. It is, however, interesting to note that although neither Maslow nor Herzberg cites money as a significant motivator, many organisations still use financial incentives as their primary motivational tool.

McClelland's theory of needs

The theories we have mentioned above focus on primary instinctive needs. According to McClelland's theory, however, needs are learnt and reinforced. This theory focuses on three needs that explain motivation[44]:

- **Need for achievement (nAch).** This is a need to excel, to be successful or to exceed a set standard.
- **Need for power (nPow).** This is a need to be influential, to control others or to make

others behave in a way they would not otherwise behave.

- **Need for affiliation (nAff).** This is the need for warm and close interpersonal relationships, and to be liked and accepted by others.

Given the many needs of employees listed above, managers have the challenge of determining the dominant need of their subordinates and of offering opportunities whereby these needs can be met. Knowledge about the motivational role of needs can be useful during the selection and placement process. For example, research has found that employees with a high need for power (nPow) and a low need for affiliation (nAff) make good managers, and that people with a high need for achievement (nAch) generally make successful entrepreneurs.

As needs can be learnt, according to this theory, employees can also be trained to increase their achievement motivation. Managers should also create challenging goals or tasks because the need for achievement is positively correlated with goal attainment, which, in turn, influences performance.

eBucks is a good example of a company that makes provision for the affiliation, power and achievement needs of its employees.

> **Critical thinking**
>
> **Motivators and maintenance factors**
> If we compare the most prominent content-based approaches to motivation, it becomes clear that a distinction can be made between motivators and maintenance factors. In your view, what are the chances that employees will be motivated if managers take care of the maintenance factors only?

Although maintenance factors are not regarded as unimportant (see for instance Sandvik Mining and Construction RSA's emphasis on safety), a critical evaluation of the most promising companies will highlight the importance of motivators such as providing recognition, challenges, opportunities for development and growth, and responsibility. Managers have to take care of maintenance factors, but if they really want motivated employees, they should create opportunities for their employees to experience internal motivation. Managers should thus be careful not to rely too much on maintenance factors or external forms of motivation.

11.7.2.3 Implications of content-based approaches

The four content theories discussed above attempt to explain behaviour[45] based on the needs of employees. Firstly, these theories suggest that needs change. Different employees have different needs at different times. For example, a job with a high salary but without security might motivate a young person, but be unacceptable to someone in his/her forties for whom job security is more important. Similarly, more vacation time may be desired near retirement age than earlier in life. The recommendation for management is to offer employees a choice of rewards in order to fulfil the different needs.

Secondly, managers need to balance the power need (competition) with the affiliation need (co-operation). It is possible to offer rewards that support both individual achievement and teamwork, for example. Managers also need to support achievement needs by providing opportunities for growth, for example, by providing novel tasks or experiences. Lower-order needs should also be taken care of by minimising unnecessary threats to personal safety, well-being and social relationships.

Thirdly, needs may be unconscious. Most people are not fully aware of the inner needs and drives that influence their behaviour. The desire of an employee to win the "salesperson of the month" trophy, for example, may be due to an unconscious feeling of inadequacy, and this would be a way of proving him-/

herself. Needs are therefore often inferred. However closely one may observe the behaviour of a colleague, it is possible only to draw conclusions (inferences) about what motives have actually caused the behaviour. It is sometimes very difficult to understand the real motives underlying certain behaviour. For this reason, it is important that managers discuss with employees the things that motivate them. This allows managers to make suggestions of changes that can be made in order to meet the needs of employees more adequately.

Lastly, content-based approaches warn managers against relying too much on financial reward as a source of employee motivation[46].

11.7.2.4 Process approaches to motivation

The difference between content and process theories has already been discussed. Process approaches try to identify the process by which factors influence motivation. The three most common process theories are the expectancy theory, equity theory and goal-setting theory. These three theories are discussed below.

Expectancy theory

According to Victor Vroom's **expectancy theory**, motivation depends on two aspects: how much we want something and how likely we think we are to get it. There are four assumptions upon which the expectancy theory rests:

- Firstly, behaviour is a combination of forces controlled by the individual and the environment.
- Secondly, people make decisions about their own behaviour in organisations.
- Thirdly, different people have different needs, goals and desires.
- Fourthly, people will act in a certain way, and the tendency to act in a certain way depends on the strength of the expectation that the action will be followed by a given outcome and the degree to which the person desires the outcome.

Three key concepts in the theory are expectancy, instrumentality and valence:

- **Expectancy** refers to a person's belief that a certain level of effort will lead to a particular level of performance (effort → performance expectancy). Factors such as a person's self-esteem, previous success, support from others, access to information and **self-efficacy** (see the section entitled "Goal-setting theory and feedback" on page 323) will influence his/her expectancy perceptions.
- **Instrumentality** refers to the strength of a person's belief that a certain performance will lead to a specific outcome (performance → outcome expectancy).
- **Valence** (desirability) refers to the attractiveness or anticipated satisfaction or dissatisfaction that the individual feels toward the outcome. It is determined by the person's perceptions about how much the outcome will fulfil or interfere with his/her needs.

The example in the box on page 322 illustrates this process.

Research indicates that the expectancy theory is able to predict employee motivation in different cultures[47]. Critics of the theory, however, argue that, as a rational theory, it does not fully acknowledge the role of emotions in employee effort and behaviour.

Some of the most important implications of the expectancy theory for management are as follows:

- Managers are advised to enhance effort → performance expectancies by assisting employees to accomplish their personal goals. They can do this by providing support, coaching, training and development, and also by increasing employees' self-efficacy. Self-efficacy refers to a person's belief that he/she has the ability to complete a task successfully. Managers should focus on linking performance to rewards that are valued by employees.
- Attempts should also be made to link personal goals to organisational goals.

Expectancy theory: An example

Imagine that a company wants to use the expectancy theory to determine if John, a sales representative, will be motivated to promote the products of that company.

- **Expectancy** refers to John's belief that a certain level of effort will lead to a particular level of performance (effort → performance expectancy). John may have the expectancy that if he works hard on promoting products, sales targets will be met (performance). If he has a zero expectancy that the effort will lead to performance (in terms of meeting the sales targets), he will most probably not promote the products. Factors such as John's self-esteem, previous success, support from others, access to information and self-efficacy will influence his expectancy perceptions. We assume John is of the opinion that his effort will most probably lead to performance.
- **Instrumentality** refers to the strength of John's belief that a certain performance will lead to a specific outcome (performance → outcome expectancy). This belief is probably based on learning from previous experiences, and the outcome refers to outcomes that are important at a specific time. John believes that meeting the sales target will lead to promotion to a managerial role. His belief is based on, among other things, the current practice in his company.
- **Valence** (desirability) refers to the attractiveness or anticipated satisfaction or dissatisfaction that John feels towards the outcome. It is determined by his perceptions about how much the outcome will fulfil or interfere with his needs. John has strong power needs that can be fulfilled in a managerial role, making promotion to a managerial role very attractive.

Based on this discussion, it seems clear that John will most probably put in a big effort to promote the products of the company, as this may fulfil his needs.

South Africa's most promising companies, for example, encourage creativity and innovation, and provide many opportunities for challenges, as long as the end result is added value to the clients and the business.

Equity theory and organisational justice

The crux of the equity theory advanced by Stacey Adams is that employees compare their efforts and rewards with those of other employees in similar situations. This theory is based on the assumption that people are motivated by the desire to be **treated equitably** in the workplace. A state of equity exists when one employee's input–outcome ratio compared with that of another employee in a similar position is equal. In contrast, if input–outcome ratios are unequal, inequity is said to exist, with the result that the person will perceive the situation as unfair and therefore be motivated to do something else. Various means can be used to restore equity after equity tension has been experienced[48]:

- The employee may change inputs.
- The employee may change outputs.
- The employee may change his/her attitude.
- The employee may change the person he/she compares him-/herself with.
- The employee may leave the job.

Despite the research that supports this theory, certain aspects remain unclear, for example, how employees deal with conflicting equity signals, and how inputs and outputs are defined. Motivation is also not only influenced by direct monetary rewards, but by indirect monetary rewards as well. (See section 11.6.2.) Another problem is that the theory incorrectly assumes that people are only rational, individualistic and selfish.

Equity theory does, however, provide an important insight into employee motivation, and every manager should take note of its implications.

The role of equity theory has been expanded to develop the concept of **organisational justice**. One of the lessons learnt from the equity theory is that employers continually have to treat their employees fairly in the distribution of rewards[49]. Organisational justice reflects the extent to which employees perceive that they are treated fairly at work. It consists of three components:

- **distributive justice**, referring to the perceived fairness of how resources and rewards are distributed or allocated
- **procedural justice**, defined as the perceived fairness of the process and procedures used to make allocation decisions
- **interactional justice**, referring to the quality of the interpersonal treatment people receive when procedures are implemented[50].

Equity theory has many practical implications for management, including the following[51]:

- Employees are powerfully motivated to correct the situation when their perception of fairness is offended. Accordingly, the best way to manage job behaviour is to understand underlying processes.
- The theory emphasises the need to pay attention to the perceptions of the employees of what is fair and equitable, and not to how fair management think its policies, procedures and reward systems are. Managers are thus encouraged to make hiring and promotion decisions on merit-based job-related information.
- Because justice perceptions are influenced by the extent to which management explains its decisions, it is important that management communicates the rationale behind decisions.
- Employees should participate in making decisions about important work outcomes. Research indicates that employees are more satisfied with their performance appraisals and resultant outcomes if they have a say.
- Employees believe that they are treated fairly if they have the opportunity to appeal against decisions that affect their welfare.
- Employees are more likely to accept and support change when they believe it is implemented fairly and when it produces equitable outcomes.
- Teamwork can be promoted by treating employees fairly.
- Employees who are denied justice are more likely to turn to litigation than employees who are given access to justice.
- Managers need to entrench values such as honesty, integrity, open communication and transparency as part of corporate governance.

Goal-setting theory and feedback

Goal-setting theory is built on the assumption that, all things being equal, the performance of employees will improve if they strive towards a definite goal. MWEB is a good example of a company that focuses on the setting and meeting of goals. Goal-setting has motivational value because goals not only direct attention, but also regulate effort (motivate employees to act), increase persistence and foster the development and application of task strategies and action plans[52].

The thrust of goal-setting theory is that the more difficult the goal is, the higher the level of performance is if employees are committed to the goals. Obviously, when goals are set, the person concerned must be capable of achieving those goals. Furthermore, research has shown that setting specific goals leads to higher performance for simple tasks than for complex tasks. This theory also pre-supposes that an employee will be committed to a goal if the goal has been negotiated between the employee and the organisation.

Another important factor is feedback. Providing feedback to employees most probably leads to the improvement of their performance. Goals inform employees about performance standards and expectations so that they can channel their energies accordingly. In turn, feedback provides information needed to adjust effort, direction and strategies for goal accomplishment. Management can give effective feedback by utilising the following principles[53]:

- Give feedback immediately.
- Evaluations should be descriptive. They should describe what was done well and why.
- The focus should be on behaviour and not on personality.
- Feedback should be specific and not general (components of performance and not performance as a whole).
- Feedback should be directed at behaviour that can be changed.
- Development activities should be agreed upon.

The concept of **self-efficacy** is also central to the goal-setting theory. It refers to the belief in one's capacity to perform a specific task to reach a specific goal. The concept is based on the work of Albert Bandura, who proposed that motivated behaviour involves a cycle of setting challenging goals, monitoring success at meeting these goals, taking actions to reduce any discrepancies between the goal and the outcome, then setting new and more challenging goals, starting the cycle all over again. Self-efficacy can be increased by applying the following approaches[54]:

- Provide guidance and support to the employee, increasing the likelihood that he/she will experience success when performing a challenging task.
- Provide successful role models (mentors) who have already mastered a similar task.
- Be a targeted "cheerleader" emphasising the employee's knowledge and ability.
- Reduce stress in the environment that is unrelated to the challenging task.

11.7.2.5 Implications of process-based approaches

Most modern approaches to work motivation are based on process theories. Process-based theories have some pre-dominant themes that are important for our understanding of work motivation:

- Firstly, intention plays a key role in motivated behaviour, with a goal as the most common form of that intention (see the example of MWEB on page 314). These goals are associated with anticipated happiness or unhappiness.
- Secondly, the concept of feedback is of critical importance.
- Thirdly, process-based theories all have a rational element, with employees critically gathering and analysing information.
- Fourthly, the theories also include some form of self-assessment. Employees tend to take stock of where they are, compared to where they want to be.
- Lastly, a non-rational component is also important in some of the most recent approaches. This element may be values, culture or the feeling that arises from the self-efficacy belief[55].

11.7.3 Employee motivational strategies

Employees need to be better motivated, not only to improve organisational effectiveness, but also to provide a better quality of life for all employees. Possible broad motivational strategies to improve employee motivation are briefly discussed below. Whereas the implications for management of the different theories have already been discussed, most of the following strategies are applied on macro- or organisational level[56]:

- **Job design.** Employees place a high value on jobs that provide satisfaction, are challenging, provide growth and allow adequate achievement opportunities. Jobs can be redesigned to make them more challenging by using job rotation, job enlargement or job enrichment. **Job**

Critical thinking

What is your level of motivation?

A motivated employee has been described as someone who is willing to exert a particular level of effort (intensity) for a certain amount of time (persistence) toward a particular goal (direction). Now, reflect on a personal experience (or that of somebody known to you) that had a positive or a negative impact on your level of motivation (not a specific need that was satisfied or not). Try to remember the process that influenced your (or the person's) level of motivation. What happened? Who was involved? What were the outcomes? How did you/the person feel? How did the experience influence your/the person's behaviour?

The following questions may help you to reflect on the experience:

1. Was it related to effort you or the person put in, but that did or did not materialise in worthwhile results?
2. Was it an experience of fairness or unfair treatment in comparison with that of other employees/people?
3. Was the experience related to the setting of and accomplishment of very clear goals?

Now that you have reflected on the experience, identify the motivational theory most relevant to that experience.

All three questions represent different process approaches to motivation discussed in this section: the expectancy theory (1), the equity theory (2) and the goal-setting theory (3). They are all based on a specific process, or the "how" of motivation. The relevance of the different theories for different people under different circumstances is clear. Can you summarise the relevance of applying these theories in the workplace?

rotation allows employees to move through a variety of jobs, functions or departments. Job enlargement focuses on expanding an employee's duties and/or responsibilities, and **job enrichment** allows jobs to become more desirable and challenging by including new and more difficult tasks and granting an employee more accountability. Other aspects to consider are variable work schedules, flexible work schedules, job sharing and telecommuting.

- **Employee involvement programs such as participative management and quality circles.** Employee involvement is a participative process that uses the entire capacity of employees to encourage commitment to the organisation's success. Employees are given autonomy and control in making decisions about their own work (see the influence of content theories, especially the theory of Herzberg and expectancy theory). Quality circles are work groups that take over the responsibility from management for solving quality problems. They generate and evaluate their own feedback, while management retains final control regarding the implementation of recommendations.
- **Management-by-objectives (MBO) strategies.** MBO strategies are closely related to the goal-setting theory and comprise cascading of organisational objectives down to individual objectives. Goals and ways of measurement, as well as specific time frames for completion, are jointly determined and feedback on performance is given.
- **Intrapreneurial incentives.** New ideas from employees can be developed within organisations with the financial support of the organisation. Such programs are known as **intrapreneurship**, which encourages employees to come up with new suggestions and ideas (see the examples of MWEB, which allows for experimentation, and South Africa's most promising companies in general).

- **Training and education.** Learning opportunities can be a strong motivational force since they are critical to individual growth and opportunity. Organisations that invest in the training and development of employees are generally more successful (see the example of Sandvik Mining and Construction RSA on page 314). In South Africa, opportunities to invest in the training and development of employees have been created by means of the Skills Development Act (No. 97 of 1998) and the Skills Development Levies Act (No. 9 of 1999). Providing opportunities for skills development and transfer of knowledge, for example, is regarded as an important strategy that contributes to South Africa's most promising companies' competitive edge.
- **Employee-recognition programs.** Recognition for above-average work performance is widely used to drive results in organisations. Employee recognition programs vary from cash, shares, profit-sharing, overseas visits and bonuses to trophies and certificates (see the example of Fireworkx Internet on page 314).
- **Empowerment programs.** Empowerment is an important method of enhancing employee motivation. Empowerment is the process of enabling employees to set their own goals, make decisions and solve problems within their sphere of responsibility and authority.
- **Reward systems.** A basic management tool to motivate employees is the organisation's reward system. A reward system is directly related to the expectancy theory of motivation, and the effect of the reward system on attitudes and employee behaviour should be fully investigated (see the examples of South Africa's most promising companies, more specifically the example of Fireworkx Internet).
- **Career management.** Career management and development is the path that an employee identifies and follows in order to achieve his/her aspirations. Employees will be better motivated if they are personally involved in decision-making about possible career options open to them than if they are not involved. This personal involvement therefore leads to a better-motivated workforce. Employees will have been empowered in being assisted by an organisational career management team to face challenges and make decisions that benefit both the individual and the organisation (see McClelland's theory of needs).

11.8 Labour legislation that has an impact on the workplace

11.8.1 Introduction

Several different environmental factors influence the way an organisation's human resources are managed. One such factor is the legal environment and, in particular, those laws that are applicable to people in organisations. Legal issues affect almost all aspects of human-resources management, including dismissal, retrenchment and retirement. The impact of legal rules is so complex that line managers and human-resources professionals should have a good working knowledge and understanding of these laws. At times, legal expertise is required to solve workplace problems or to take legal aspects further, but in most cases, legal matters can be solved independently by line managers and/or human-resources professionals. The management of human resources is a more complex matter than the simple application of various laws, but without a basic knowledge of the most important labour laws, organisations may find themselves with more people problems than anticipated.

The case study on page 327 provides an illustration of labour-law issues in the workplace.

Case study

Labour-law issues in the workplace

Steelco (Pty) Ltd produces parts for motor vehicles. It has a large factory in Gauteng with more than 300 employees. These employees work in three separate shifts because Steelco is a 24-hour operation. However, things have been going wrong in the workplace in the past few months. Three employees approached their trade-union representative and claimed that their supervisor had made racist remarks to them. After these allegations were discussed at a meeting of all four trade-union representatives in a regular meeting, the union representatives wrote a letter to the employer demanding that the racist manager be dismissed immediately and without a hearing.

But this is not the only problem in Steelco's operation, it seems. A large number of employees claim that they are regularly expected to work up to 18 hours over-time a week, but that they receive only their normal hourly remuneration for this over-time. The union and Steelco are preparing to negotiate about wages in three weeks' time, and the Steelco managers are convinced that a collective agreement can be concluded between Steelco and the union. The union is not so sure about that, as it not only wants an 11% wage increase, but also an improvement of medical-aid benefits and four extra days' sick leave during each leave cycle. The union also wants to hold monthly meetings with all union members working in the factory during a lunch break.

The union knows that management is facing a number of other problems as well. Three dismissal disputes have been referred to the **CCMA** and a number of allegations relating to **sexual harassment** have been made against one of the executive managers. This manager also tried to have his secretary dismissed when he discovered that she was **pregnant**.

Both the union and the employer hope, however, that this year's round of wage negotiations goes better than those they engaged in two years ago. Two years ago, the negotiations between the parties broke down and the union called for a strike. The employer claimed that the strike was not protected and the employees were dismissed because of their participation in the unprotected strike. Some of these employees were eventually reinstated, but 14 employees were not reinstated after the strike had come to an end. The union has approached the **Labour Court** claiming that the dismissal of these employees constituted an **automatically unfair dismissal**. Steelco's view on this point is that the dismissals were fair because the employees were engaged in an unprotected strike and because individual **disciplinary enquiries** giving each employee an opportunity to say why he/she should not be dismissed were held before the employees were dismissed.

11.8.2 The Constitution of the Republic of South Africa Act (No. 108 of 1996)

The Constitution of 1996 is the single most important piece of **legislation** in South Africa. As its name implies, it sets out the structure of the state. It provides for national government, the legislature, the judiciary (the courts of law) and the executive arm of government. When it comes to the courts, the Constitution of 1996 provides that the Constitutional Court is the highest court in respect of constitutional matters (this means that the Constitutional Court is the highest court that can hear a matter relating to, for instance, an infringement of fundamental rights). But when it comes to human-resources management, the most important part of the Constitution of 1996 is the Bill of Rights (Chapter II). The Bill of Rights protects a number of important fundamental rights. Section 23 of the Constitution of 1996 relates specifically to **labour** rights. Everyone has the right to fair labour practices, for example, and employers and trade unions have the right to organise and bargain collectively. Employees have the right to join a trade union of their choice (this is called freedom of association) and provision is made for the right to strike.

But it is not only these fundamental labour rights that have a direct impact on the workplace: other rights are as important. Section 9 of the Constitution of 1996 provides that no-one may be discriminated against unfairly and section 22 protects the right to choose a trade, occupation or profession freely.

The fundamental human rights contained in the Bill of Rights are formulated in a wide and general way. In most cases, specific pieces of legislation give further effect to these rights. In this way, the Labour Relations Act (No. 66 of 1995) gives effect to the fundamental labour rights contained in section 23 of the Constitution of 1996 and the Employment Equity Act gives further effect to the right not to be unfairly discriminated against in the workplace.

The most important recent development relates to the right to fair administrative action, enshrined in section 33 of the Constitution of 1996. Again this fundamental right has its own specific piece of legislation: the Promotion of Administrative Justice Act (No. 3 of 2000). One of the important questions that has arisen is whether employees in the public service (where the state is the employer) have additional rights and remedies in terms of the Promotion of Administrative Justice Act. It seems that South Africa's courts are now tending towards the view that workplace issues in the public service, especially dismissal of a public-service employee, must also comply with the provisions of section 33 of the Constitution of 1996 as given effect to by the Promotion of Administrative Justice Act.

Another important point in respect of fundamental rights is that none of these rights are absolutely unlimited. Section 23 of the Constitution of 1996 provides for a right to strike, but the Labour Relations Act places certain limitations on this right. Employees engaged in essential services, for example, may not strike. Furthermore, the Labour Relations Act also imposes a number of procedural requirements on strikes.

Constitutional rights

Section 23 of the Constitution of 1996 provides that every employee has the right of freedom of association. This right is further given effect to in the Labour Relations Act. But this does not mean that an employee engaged in mining activities can choose to join a union representing workers in the chemical industry. The employee's right of freedom of association is limited by the union's constitution: the union's constitution will set out which employees are eligible to join that union.

11.8.3 Laws affecting business activities

Many laws affect business activities in South Africa. Laws of this nature are found in most countries. There are laws to regulate the form and functioning of businesses, such as the Companies Act (No. 71 of 2008). There are laws that provide for various forms of tax, ranging from value-added tax and income tax to company tax. There are laws dealing with intellectual property (copyright and trademarks), laws dealing with insolvency and even some laws dealing with specific forms of contracts. This means that the labour laws are just one set of laws a business has to take into account. Many other laws impose direct or indirect duties or obligations on a business.

When it comes to the management of people in organisations, the most important pieces of legislation are the Labour Relations Act (No. 66 of 1995) (usually simply referred to as the LRA) and the Basic Conditions of Employment Act (No. 75 of 1997) (the BCEA). Other important laws include the Employment Equity Act (No. 55 of 1998) and other laws relating to skills development and workplace health and safety. The sections that follow look briefly at the most important of these laws.

In some cases, it may be necessary to look at the entire piece of legislation. Most human-resources managers have a copy of the LRA on their desks. Because the labour laws are changed (amended) from time to time, it is important to ensure that a manager refers to the correct version of the legislation. A number of important changes were made to the LRA in 2002 and some new provisions were included. A manager must therefore make sure that the version of the LRA he/she refers to contains all the amendments. The BCEA was also amended in 2002. Similar considerations therefore apply: a manager must ensure that the version of the legislation consulted is up to date.

The discussion of the acts given in this chapter is brief. If further information about these acts is required, it is probably better to study the specific act in its entirety. Copies may be obtained from the Government Printer[57].

11.8.4 The Labour Relations Act (No. 66 of 1995) (the LRA)

11.8.4.1 Background

Since the first democratic election in South Africa in 1994, the labour dispensation has changed significantly. Organised labour has played an important role in South Africa's transformation process. Not only do workers, through their trade unions, play a key role in the redistribution of wealth through collective bargaining over wages, but they are also instrumental in the broader socio-political process of transforming South African society. Consequently, the system of labour relations in South Africa has seen tremendous changes. For example, a new Labour Relations Act was introduced in 1995. A new Basic Conditions of Employment Act and a new Employment Equity Act were introduced in 1997 and 1998 respectively. Before 1994, labour legislation was made and brought into effect by government alone. The process leading up to the passing of the LRA was therefore unique. For the first time, labour legislation represented basic consensus or agreement between organised labour, organised business and the state.

The implementation of sound labour relations in businesses not only ensures fair labour practices, but also contributes to organisational success. **Labour relations**, from a business-management point of view, may be described as a complex system of individual and collective actions as well as formal and informal relationships that exist between the state, employers, employees and related institutions concerning all aspects of the employment relationship.

Relationships in a business are considered to be a crucial element in labour relations. More attention is given to the different parties in the labour relationship in the next section.

The parties involved in the labour relationship are the employer and employee as primary parties, and the state as a secondary role-player. The state's role is to provide, by means of legislation, a framework within which the primary parties can conduct their relationship. Figure 11.4 on page 330 illustrates this tripartite relationship. Basically, employees in managerial positions represent the interests of the owners of businesses in the workplace. In the private sector, this essentially means safeguarding and improving the profitability of businesses. The state's primary role is, as stated, to provide the framework or infrastructure within which labour and management can conduct their relationship.

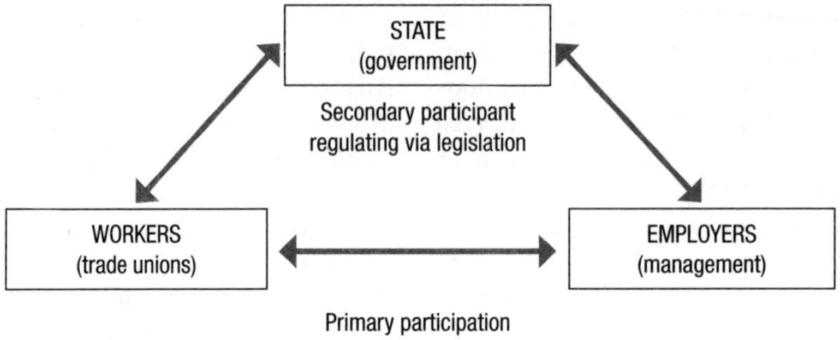

Figure 11.4: Participants in labour relations

A trade union is a permanent organisation created by workers to protect themselves at work, to improve their working conditions through collective bargaining, to better their quality of life and to provide a means of expressing their views on issues in society.

11.8.4.2 The contents of the LRA[58]

In day-to-day human-resources management, the LRA is the single most important piece of legislation, especially because it contains the rules relating to dismissal of employees. But it is worth repeating that the LRA gives effect to all the fundamental rights contained in section 23 of the Constitution of 1996 and it therefore deals with a large number of issues. It is wide in scope, which explains why the LRA is so long (there are 213 sections in the LRA and numerous schedules). The purpose of the LRA is set out in section 1, including giving effect to and regulating the fundamental rights contained in the Bill of Rights and providing a framework within which employees, their trade unions, employers and employers' organisations can engage in collective bargaining and formulate industrial policy. The purposes of the LRA also include the promotion of orderly collective bargaining and the effective resolution of labour disputes.

The LRA applies to all employees and employers, but members of the South African National Defence Force, the National Intelligence Agency, the South African Secret Service, the South African National Academy of Intelligence and Comsec are excluded from the operation of the LRA. Comsec, or Electronic Communications Security (Pty) Ltd, was established by the Electronic Communications Security (Pty) Ltd Act (No. 68 of 2002).

Freedom of association

Freedom of association means that employees have the right to form a trade union or to join a trade union of their choice. They also have the right to participate in the lawful activities of a trade union. The protection of freedom of association in the LRA must be seen within the context of the fundamental right of freedom of association contained in section 23 of the Constitution of 1996. Employers have a similar right: to form or to join an employers' organisation. These rights of association (the foundation of the notion of collectivism) are recognised in most modern labour-relations systems and they are also enshrined in the international labour standards of the International Labour Organisation (ILO).

Organisational rights

Trade unions may apply for and exercise certain **organisational rights** in respect of the employer's premises or the employer's operations. Provision is made for the trade union to gain access to the employer's premises to recruit members, to communicate with members or to represent members' interests. Unions may hold meetings at the employer's premises after hours. This organisational right is not unlimited, of course: the union's right to gain access to the employer's premises may be subject to conditions regarding time and place that may be necessary "to safeguard life or property or to prevent the undue disruption of work". The right of access to the employer's premises is just one of a number of organisational rights provided for in the LRA. Other organisational rights include time off for trade union activities, the right of a trade union to have trade union dues or subscriptions deducted from employees' wages or salaries, and the right of a trade union to information it needs when consulting or negotiating with the employer.

Organisational rights

An employer and a trade union are engaged in wage negotiations. In response to the union's demand for an 8% wage increase for all employees who are paid on a weekly basis, the employer responds that it cannot afford an 8% increase because business has not been as good as it expected. The union challenges this statement, saying that productivity and sales have increased. The union then demands to see the employer's financial statements, but the employer responds by saying that this information is for the employer only. Section 16 of the Labour Relations Act provides that in this kind of situation, a trade union representing the majority of employees in a workplace has the right of access to certain kinds of information that are relevant to the negotiations. If, however, the union were to demand to see details of the remuneration of senior executives, the employer may respond that this information is private and personal information (one of the exceptions to the union's right of access to information in terms of section 16 of the LRA).

Bargaining and statutory councils

Large parts of the LRA focus on collective bargaining. Bargaining councils are bargaining and dispute-resolution structures introduced by the Act. They are centralised at sectoral level. One or more registered trade unions and one or more employers' organisations may form a bargaining council. The union and the employers' organisation agree to the council's constitution and the council is then registered.

The powers and functions of bargaining councils include the following:

- the conclusion of collective agreements
- the enforcement of collective agreements
- the prevention and resolution of labour disputes
- the performance of dispute functions set out in the Act
- the establishment and administration of a fund to be used for resolving disputes
- the promotion and establishment of training and education schemes
- the establishment and administration of funds related to pension, provident, medical aid, sick pay, holiday, unemployment schemes, or other schemes or funds for the benefit of one or more of the parties to the bargaining council or their members
- the determination, by collective agreement, of the matters that may not be an issue in dispute for the purpose of a strike or lock-out at the workplace
- the consideration of workplace forums or additional matters for consultation.

A representative trade union (or more than one, combining forces) with members who constitute at least 30% of the employees in a sector, or one or more employers' organisations, may apply to the Registrar (Department of Labour) for the establishment of a statutory council in a sector or area in which no bargaining council is registered. The difference between a **bargaining council** and a **statutory council** lies in the fact that a bargaining council is established by agreement between unions and employers, while a statutory council is established by the state after receiving a request from either unions or employers.

The Commission for Conciliation, Mediation and Arbitration (the CCMA)

The CCMA is the best-known and most important institution for the resolution of labour disputes established by the LRA. The CCMA deals with certain types of unfair-dismissal disputes. These dismissal disputes constitute the bulk of the CCMA's workload. The CCMA has a director and commissioners who carry out its dispute-resolution functions. It is independent of the state and of any political party or other organisation. Its functions are to attempt to resolve, through conciliation, any dispute referred to it in terms of the LRA and then to arbitrate any dispute that remains unresolved by these means, if the LRA requires arbitration. Most labour disputes are referred to either a bargaining council (if there is a bargaining council registered for the sector and area in which the dispute arises) or the CCMA (if there is no council) for conciliation. This is where a commissioner tries to get the parties to agree to a settlement of the dispute. If conciliation fails, the LRA prescribes that certain disputes return to the council or the CCMA for arbitration. Here a commissioner or arbitrator hears both parties to the dispute and then makes a final and binding ruling or award.

Other types of dispute are referred to the Labour Court if conciliation fails. The CCMA also has other functions. It assists in the establishment of workplace forums, and compiles and publishes statistics concerning its activities. The Commission may also:

- advise a party to a dispute about the appropriate dispute-resolution process
- advise a party to a dispute to obtain legal advice
- accredit councils or agencies to perform dispute-resolution functions
- oversee or scrutinise any election or ballot of a registered trade union or registered employers' organisation
- issue guidelines in relation to any matter dealt with in the Act
- publish research.

Dispute-resolution processes

In the course of one year, an employer has dismissed four employees for misconduct (allegations of fraud) and another two employees for poor work performance (the employees did not succeed in meeting their production targets). But the employer also retrenched more than 100 employees in the course of that year. In all cases, the employees challenge their dismissals as being unfair. Different dispute-resolution procedures apply in respect of these dismissal disputes in terms of the LRA. Dismissal disputes relating to misconduct or incapacity (poor work performance, for example) are referred to the CCMA (if there is no bargaining council with jurisdiction) for conciliation followed by arbitration if conciliation fails to settle the matter. Dismissal relating to the employer's operational requirements (such as a large-scale retrenchment) are referred to the CCMA for conciliation and, if conciliation fails, to the Labour Court.

The Labour Court and the Labour Appeal Court

The LRA establishes two courts of law to deal specifically with labour disputes. The Labour Court is similar to a provincial division of the High Court. It consists of a Judge President, a Deputy Judge President and as many judges as the President may consider necessary. The Court is constituted before a single judge and may sit in as many courts as the available judges allow. The Court has various functions, which are stipulated in the Act. But unlike the High Court, the Labour Court's jurisdiction is limited. It can only hear and decide disputes as provided by the LRA. For some time now, drawing the line between the jurisdiction of the Labour Court (in other words, the matters the Labour Court can or cannot decide) and other courts has become very difficult.

The Labour Appeal Court can hear and rule on all appeals against final judgments or final orders of the Labour Court. It may rule on any questions arising from proceedings in the Labour Court.

Strikes and lock-outs

The LRA defines a **strike** as "the partial or complete concerted refusal to work, or the retardation or obstruction of work, by persons who are or have been employed by the same employer or by different employers, for the purpose of remedying a grievance or resolving a dispute in respect of any matter of mutual interest between employer and employee, and every reference to 'work' in this definition includes over-time work, whether it is voluntary or compulsory". This definition is broad, in that it also covers any refusal to work overtime, irrespective of whether the overtime is compulsory or voluntary.

If a strike or lock-out does not comply with the provisions of the LRA, the Labour Court has exclusive jurisdiction to grant an interdict or order to restrain any person from participating in or furthering such action, and also to order the payment of just and equitable remuneration of any loss attributable to the strike or lock-out.

The LRA also makes provision for protest action and includes stipulations regarding replacement labour during strikes, picketing, essential and maintenance services, and lock-outs.

Collective agreements

The aim of collective bargaining is to reach an agreement. The LRA provides mechanisms through which the parties can achieve this. Although disputes or industrial action may form part of the process of negotiation, the ultimate goal is to conclude collective agreements. The primary forum for collective bargaining is a bargaining council and the LRA contains a number of important provisions relating to bargaining-council agreements. Other collective agreements concluded between a trade union and an employer outside a bargaining council are also provided for.

There are two types of collective agreements: **procedural agreements** and **substantive agreements**. Recognition agreements (procedural) regulate how the parties will conduct the relationship. Substantive agreements deal with the content of the relationship and conditions of service.

Agency shop agreements and closed shop agreements

A representative trade union whose members are in a majority in a workplace may conclude with the employer an agency shop agreement requiring the employer to deduct an agreed agency shop fee from the wages of its employees who are not members of the trade union and to whom the agreement applies.

Alternatively, a representative trade union whose members are a majority in a workplace may conclude with the employer a closed shop agreement requiring all employees in respect of whom the agreement applies to be members of the trade union.

Workplace forums

Workplace forums are designed to facilitate a shift at the workplace from an adversarial relationship between trade unions and employers to a joint problem-solving and participatory relationship on certain issues. These forums are also designed to foster co-operative relations through dialogue, information-sharing, consultation and joint decision-making, which is not possible through collective-bargaining processes. The focus is on non-wage matters, such as restructuring, the introduction of new technologies, changes in work-scheduling, physical conditions of work, health and safety, and those issues that can best be resolved at workplace level.

The **functions** of a workplace forum are to promote the interests of all employees in the workplace, irrespective of whether or not they are union members, and to enhance efficiency in the workplace.

A workplace forum may be established in the workplace of any employer with more than 100 employees. Only representative trade unions may apply to the CCMA for the establishment of a workplace forum. Workplace forums employ a consultative approach and a joint decision-making approach.

Unfair dismissals

Section 185 of the LRA provides that every employee has the right not to be dismissed unfairly. This protection applies only in respect of employees (and not, for instance, independent contractors). The term "dismissal" is also defined in the LRA and specific provision is made for a special category of dismissals called **automatically unfair dismissals**. In the case of an automatically unfair dismissal, it is the reason for the dismissal that makes it automatically unfair. If an employee exercises a right conferred by the LRA (such as the right to freedom of association or the right to participate in a protected strike) and he/she is dismissed, the dismissal would automatically be unfair. If the dismissal relates to unfair discrimination (for example, if the employee is dismissed for reasons relating to his/her age, gender, language or political beliefs), the dismissal would be automatically unfair because the employee's right not to be unfairly discriminated against would be at stake. Other forms of automatically unfair dismissals include the following:

- dismissal when the employee refuses to do the work of another employee who is participating in protected strike action, unless that work is necessary to prevent actual danger to life, personal safety or health
- dismissal in order to compel the employee to accept a demand in respect of any matter of mutual interest between the employer and employee
- dismissal related to the employee's pregnancy
- dismissal as a result of unfair discrimination, whether directly or indirectly, on any arbitrary ground.

Even if a dismissal is not automatically unfair, it must still comply with certain requirements. A dismissal must be for a valid and fair reason (substantive fairness), and this reason must relate either to the employee's misconduct or incapacity, or to the employer's operational requirements. But a dismissal must also be done in a fair manner. Schedule 8 of the LRA sets out the procedural steps the employer must take in order to ensure that a dismissal is not only substantively fair, but also procedurally fair. The essence of procedural fairness is that an employee must be given an opportunity to be heard. He/she must have the chance to respond to the charges or allegations made by the employer and to say why he/she should not be dismissed.

Unfair dismissal

An employee has had ten years' service with an employer, occupying a relatively senior position. The employee has been very active in the activities of the trade union to which he belongs, being a shop steward (a trade-union representative). He has been involved in drawing up strategies for negotiations, and he often represents other employees in disciplinary hearings and grievances. When the employer and the union were in dispute two years previously, the same employee was involved in preparing various documents for the purposes of proceedings in the Labour Court. The employer then dismissed the employee, stating that he had been insubordinate (refusing to comply with lawful and reasonable instructions) and that he had become "obstructive". The employee's response was that he had not been dismissed because of alleged misconduct, but because of his trade-union activities. The Court found that the real reason for his dismissal was not the misconduct, as the employer alleged, but the employee's trade-union role and activities. The dismissal was therefore automatically unfair. See *Kroukam v SA Airlink (Pty) Ltd* (2005) 26 ILJ 2153 (LAC).

An employee who feels that he/she has been unfairly dismissed may refer an unfair-dismissal dispute to either a bargaining council or the CCMA for conciliation. If the dismissal is for a reason relating to the employee's misconduct or incapacity, the dispute can then be referred to arbitration if conciliation fails. In the case of most dismissal disputes relating to the employer's operational requirements (including retrenchment), the dispute must be referred to the Labour Court for adjudication if conciliation has failed.

11.8.5 Communication: Grievances and disciplinary aspects

Communication has a tremendous influence on the quality of labour relations in any organisation. Structures, procedures and policies should be put in place to ensure constructive relations between management and workers. There are various ways of enhancing the quality of communication between the parties in the employment relationship, including one-on-one "chat sessions", performance appraisals, departmental meetings, safety-and-health committees, briefing sessions, workplace forums and coaching sessions.

11.8.5.1 The grievance procedure

In the context of labour relations, a **grievance** is an employee's response to a real, perceived or alleged breach of the terms of the employment contract. Possible examples include one-sided changes to the employee's conditions of employment or an employee being insulted by a supervisor. An effective grievance-handling procedure has many advantages:

- It is a safety valve that will release the tension and dissipate the latent aggression inherent in all businesses.
- It allows the raising and settlement of a grievance by a worker without fear of retribution or victimisation.
- It makes for an open and honest relationship between manager and worker.
- It allows managers to identify and remove legitimate causes of dissatisfaction or conflict.

The LRA is silent on grievance procedures and what a grievance procedure should contain.

11.8.5.2 The disciplinary procedure

Discipline can be described as any action or behaviour on the part of authority (the employer) in a social system that is aimed at stopping member behaviour that threatens to disrupt the functioning of the system. It is therefore a normal and inherent part of any business's actions and responsibilities. Discipline should not be aimed at punishment for the transgression of rules, but rather at rectifying unacceptable behaviour. This is called a **corrective approach** to discipline.

The principles underlying the disciplinary procedure are:

- the employer's right to take disciplinary action against an employee who breaches a rule or standard governing conduct in the workplace (see box on page 336)
- the employee's right to a fair procedure.

Schedule 8 of the LRA (the Code of Good Practice: Dismissal) contains numerous provisions that are important in the context of workplace discipline. The Code of Good Practice confirms that discipline in the workplace must be corrective. It also provides that discipline must be progressive. **Progressive discipline** means that dismissal is the last resort (except in the case of serious misconduct). Counselling and warnings (ranging from verbal warnings to final written warnings) may be more appropriate. Discipline should be applied consistently by the employer (similar cases should be treated similarly) and disciplinary standards must be communicated to employees. The most common way of communicating disciplinary standards is through the employer's disciplinary code and procedure. This code and procedure is often handed to an employee at the beginning of his/her employment.

Critical thinking

Dismissal for misconduct

Imagine two people, John and his supervisor, Peter. They have had some misunderstandings in the workplace about the way in which a certain piece of work is done. One Friday evening after work, both John and Peter were having a meal at a local restaurant. Words were exchanged and John attacked Peter physically outside the restaurant. Peter was not seriously injured. Would John's actions constitute grounds for dismissal?

11.8.6 The Basic Conditions of Employment Act (No. 75 of 1997) (the BCEA)

11.8.6.1 Introduction and application

The overall purpose of the **Basic Conditions of Employment Act** (No. 75 of 1997) is to advance economic development and social justice in South Africa. One of the objects of the BCEA is to give effect to and regulate the right to fair labour practices conferred by section 23 of the Constitution of 1996. Other objectives include establishing and enforcing basic conditions of employment and regulating the variation of basic conditions of employment. The BCEA applies to all employers and employees, except members of the National Intelligence Agency, the South African Secret Service, the South African National Academy of Intelligence and the directors and staff of Comsec.

Section 4 of the BCEA sets out the way the minimum standards contained in the BCEA interact with employment contracts. A minimum BCEA standard will, for instance, constitute a term of any employment contract unless the existing term in the contract is more favourable to the employee than the one contained in the BCEA. If the contract provides for more days' annual leave than the 21 days' annual leave provided for in the BCEA, the contract will apply.

The BCEA[59] covers a wide range of issues. Only a few of these issues will be discussed below.

11.8.6.2 Working time

Chapter 2 of the BCEA, which regulates working hours, does not apply to senior managerial employees, to employees engaged as sales staff who travel to the premises of customers and who regulate their own hours of work, or to employees who work fewer than 24 hours a month for an employer. As a general rule, working hours must be arranged with due regard for the health and safety of employees and with reference to the Code of Good Practice on the Regulation of Working Time.

Ordinary hours of work are limited to a maximum of 45 hours in any week: nine hours if the employee works five days a week or eight hours if the employee works more than five days a week. **Over-time** may only be worked if the employee has agreed to work over-time. No more than ten hours' over-time may be worked in a week. Over-time is expensive: the employer must pay an employee one-and-a-half times the employee's normal wage. As an alternative to over-time pay, the employee may be granted time off.

The BCEA also provides for a **meal interval** (at least 60 minutes long after five hours of continuous work), which may be reduced to 30 minutes by agreement. An employee must have a daily rest period of at least 12 consecutive hours between ending work and commencing work the following day. Every employee must have a rest period of at least 36 consecutive hours each week. The rest period must include a Sunday, unless otherwise agreed. An employee may agree in writing to rather have a longer rest period of 60 consecutive hours every two weeks.

Night work is defined as work performed between 18:00 and 06:00. Employees must be compensated by the payment of an allowance or by a reduction in working hours. Transport must be available for employees who work at night. Employers must also inform employees who work between 23:00 and 06:00 of the health-and-safety hazards of night work, and, on request, provide employees with a free medical assessment. The limits on ordinary and over-time working hours, and the requirements for meal intervals and rest periods, do not prevent the performance of emergency work.

The Minister of Labour may exclude or vary the provisions in respect of limits on hours of work and over-time to employees earning more than a certain amount.

11.8.6.3 Leave

Employees are entitled to 21 **consecutive** days' fully paid **annual leave** after every twelve months of continuous employment. An employer may not pay an employee instead of granting annual leave. However, an employee whose employment is terminated must be paid out leave pay due for leave that he/she has not taken. An employee is entitled to six weeks' paid **sick leave** for every 36 months of continuous employment. However, during the first six months of employment, an employee is entitled to only one day's paid sick leave for every 26 days worked. An employer may require a medical certificate for absence of more than two consecutive days from an employee who is regularly away from work before paying the employee for sick leave. Sick leave may not run concurrently with annual leave or notice to terminate services.

A pregnant employee is entitled to four consecutive months' **maternity leave**. This leave may begin up to four weeks before the expected date of birth, unless otherwise agreed or if the employee is required to take the leave earlier for medical reasons. An employer may not require an employee to return to work for six weeks after the birth of a child. An employee may, however, elect to do so if a medical doctor or midwife certifies that she is fit to return to work. Maternity leave is unpaid leave, although an employee is entitled to claim maternity benefits in terms of the Unemployment Insurance Act. It is also possible that the employer may pay maternity leave.

An employee who has worked for at least four months is entitled to three days' paid **family-responsibility leave** per leave cycle. This applies only to employees who work on four or more days in a week. The employee may take this leave in the event of the birth of a child, if the child is sick or if a member of the employee's immediate family dies. An employer may require reasonable proof of the purpose for which this leave is taken before paying the employee. Unused days do not accrue.

Leave

D has signed a written contract of employment with FGH CC in terms of which D works Monday to Friday from 09:00 until 16:30. This contract also states that D is entitled to 20 working days' paid annual leave per year. After listening to a radio talkshow dealing with the issue of working hours, leave and the BCEA, D believes that his employer is contravening the Act by not giving him 21 days' leave. But D would be wrong in this case: the BCEA provides for 21 consecutive days' leave (in other words, 3 weeks). The BCEA refers to calendar days, not working days. If D is entitled to 20 working days, it means, in effect, that he is entitled to four weeks' leave. This in turn means that D's leave is more favourable to him than the provision in the BCEA. This contractually arranged leave benefit would apply because nothing in the BCEA prevents an employer and an employee from agreeing to terms and conditions of employment that are more favourable to the employee.

11.8.6.4 Remuneration, deductions and notice of termination

An employer must pay an employee according to arrangements made between them. An employer may deduct money from an employee's pay only if permitted or required to do so by law, collective agreement, court order or arbitration award. A deduction for loss or damage caused by the employee in the course of employment may be made only by agreement and after the employer has established by a fair procedure that the employee was at fault. An employee may agree in writing to an employer deducting a debt specified in the agreement.

During the first six months of employment, an employment contract may be terminated on one week's notice. The notice period during the remainder of the first year of employment is two weeks, while for employees with more than a year's service, it is four weeks.

The notice period for a farm worker or domestic worker who has worked for more than four weeks is one month. The notice period may be altered (varied) by a collective agreement between the employer and a union. However, even a collective agreement may not reduce a four-week notice period to less than two weeks.

Notice must be given in writing. If the recipient cannot understand the notice, it must be explained to the employee in a language he/she can understand. An employer may pay the employee the remuneration for the notice period instead of giving notice.

An employee who occupies accommodation situated on the employer's premises or supplied by the employer may elect to remain in the accommodation for the duration of the notice period.

Termination of employment by an employer on notice in terms of the BCEA does not prevent the employee from challenging the **fairness** of the dismissal in terms of the LRA.

On termination of employment, an employee must be paid:

- for any paid time off to which he/she is entitled that he/she has not taken, for example, time off for over-time or Sunday work
- for any period of annual leave due and not taken
- in respect of annual leave entitlement during an incomplete annual leave cycle, either one day's remuneration in respect of every 17 days on which the employee worked or was entitled to be paid, or remuneration calculated on any other basis, whichever is the most favourable to the employee (this applies only if the employee has been in employment longer than four months).

When an employee's services are terminated because of the operational requirements of the employer (such as retrenchment), **severance pay** has to be paid in addition to other payments due to the employee. The minimum amount of severance pay required by the BCEA is the equivalent of one week's remuneration for each completed year of continuous service. Employees who unreasonably refuse to accept an offer of alternative employment with the same or any other employer forfeit the entitlement to severance pay.

11.8.6.5 Administrative obligations

The employer must:

- issue the employee with written particulars of employment when the employee starts employment (these particulars include the employee's ordinary hours of work, and details of the employee's wage, rate of pay for over-time work and leave)
- retain these particulars of employment for three years after the end of the contract of employment
- provide an employee with information concerning remuneration, deductions and time worked with regard to his/her pay
- keep a record of the time worked by each employee, as well as of each employee's remuneration
- display, at the workplace, a statement of employees' rights under the Act.

Upon termination of employment, an employee is entitled to a certificate of service.

Simplified provisions apply to employers who have fewer than five employees and to employers of domestic workers.

11.8.6.6 Prohibition of the employment of children and forced labour

No person may employ a child under 15 years of age. The Minister of Labour may make regulations prohibiting or placing conditions on the employment of children over fifteen years of age.

11.8.6.7 Variation of basic conditions of employment

Basic conditions of employment may be varied by bargaining council agreements, collective agreements concluded outside a bargaining council and individual agreements concluded by the employer and the employee. The Minister of Labour may also make determinations or issue sectoral determinations.

The Minister of Labour may make sectoral determinations establishing basic conditions of employment for employees in unorganised sectors. A number of important determinations have been made, the best-known relating to domestic workers and to farm workers. These sectoral determinations set out minimum wages and other conditions of employment. The BCEA prescribes the procedure that must be followed before a sectoral determination can be made. The Minister must direct a person in the public service to investigate conditions of employment in any sector or area in which it is proposed to make a sectoral determination. On completion of the investigation and after considering any representations made by members of the public, the Director General of the Department of Labour must prepare a report that must be submitted to the Employment Conditions Commission. Only once the Minister has considered the report and the recommendations made by the Commission may a sectoral determination for one or more sectors and areas be made.

Sectoral determination

Sectoral Determination 7 (15 August 2002, amended in November 2005) applies to the Domestic-Worker Sector in the whole of South Africa. This sectoral determination contains provisions relating to wages, annual wage increases and the way wages are to be paid, to name just a few issues. Provision is also made for annual leave and sick leave. Item 8(b) of this sectoral determination, for example, provides that an employer may deduct up to 10% of the employee's wage for a room or other accommodation, but only if the room or accommodation is weatherproof and kept in a good condition, if it has at least one window and a door that can be locked, and if it has a toilet and a bath or shower (if the domestic worker does not have access to any other bathroom).

Critical thinking

Basic Conditions of Employment

There are two fundamental aspects to the Basic Conditions of Employment Act. The first is to provide protection for employees in respect of minimum terms and conditions of employment. The second is to provide the employer with some degree of flexibility as to how to arrange work and when it is to be done. Which principle weighs the heaviest and why?

11.8.6.8 Employment Conditions Commission and inspectors

The Employment Conditions Commission was established to advise the Minister of Labour on the making of sectoral determinations, the effect of government policies on employment and any matters arising out of the application of the Act.

The Minister of Labour may appoint labour inspectors who perform functions such as promoting, monitoring and enforcing compliance with employment laws. Labour inspectors must advise employees and employers on their rights and obligations in terms of employment laws. They may also conduct inspections, investigate complaints and secure compliance with an employment law.

11.8.7 The Employment Equity Act (No. 55 of 1998) (the EEA)[60]

11.8.7.1 Overview

The main aim of the EEA is to do away with all forms of discrimination in employment in South Africa by promoting equity and non-discrimination in the employment sector. The overall purpose of the Act is to achieve equity in the workplace, chiefly through the following two main elements:

- the prohibition of unfair discrimination, which applies to all employers
- affirmative-action measures, which apply only to "designated" employers.

The most important provisions of the Act are as follows:

- Employers are required to take steps to end unfair discrimination in their employment policies and practices.
- Discrimination against employees or job applicants on the grounds of race, gender, sex, pregnancy, marital status, family responsibility, ethnic or social origin, colour, sexual orientation, age, disability, HIV status, religion, conscience, belief, political opinion, culture, language and birth is prohibited.
- Medical and psychometric testing of employees is prohibited unless properly justified.
- Employers must prepare and implement employment equity plans after conducting a workforce analysis and consulting with unions and employees.
- Equity plans must contain specific affirmative-action measures to achieve the equitable representation of people from designated groups in all occupational categories and levels in the workforce.
- Employers must take measures to reduce disproportionate income differentials progressively.
- Employers must report to the Department of Labour on their implementation of employment equity.
- The EEA has established a Commission of Employment Equity.
- The labour inspectors and the Director-General of the Department of Labour are responsible for enforcing equity obligations.
- Any employer who intends to contract with the state must comply with its employment-equity obligations.
- Employees are protected from victimisation for exercising rights conferred by the Act.

Inherent requirements of a job

A professional couple employed a childminder. The employer (the husband) believed that the childminder should not have children of her own because this would have a negative impact on the attention she would devote to his children. The issue was raised during the initial interview when the childminder indicated that she was single and that she had no immediate plans to have children. Two years later, however, after having established a sound working relationship with the family, the childminder fell pregnant. The employer congratulated her and terminated her employment. One of the employer's arguments was that it was an inherent requirement of her job as childminder that she not have children of her own so that she could devote all her attention to her employer's children. The Labour Court concluded that it was not an inherent requirement of the job of a child minder that she not be pregnant or a parent. *See Wallace v Du Toit* (2006) 27 ILJ 1754 (LC).

11.8.7.2 Scope of application of the EEA

Chapter 2 of the EEA, which deals with unfair discrimination, applies to all employees and employers. Chapter 3 of the EEA, which covers **affirmative action**, applies to "designated employers" and people from "designated groups" only.

A designated employer is:

- an employer who employs 50 or more employees
- an employer who employs fewer than 50 employees, but with a total annual turnover that is equal to or above the applicable annual turnover of a small business in terms of Schedule 4 of the Act
- a municipality
- an organ of state, but excluding local spheres of government, the National Defence Force, the National Intelligence Agency and the South African Secret Service
- an employer that, in terms of a collective agreement, becomes a designated employer to the extent provided for in the collective agreement.

Designated groups are:

- Black people (a general term meaning African people, Coloured people and Indian people)
- women
- people with disabilities.

11.8.7.3 Prohibition and elimination of unfair discrimination

In Chapter 2 of the EEA, the emphasis is on the prohibition of unfair discrimination. Every employer (not just designated employers) must take steps to promote equal opportunity in the workplace by eliminating unfair discrimination in any employment policy or practice. Section 6 provides that no person may unfairly discriminate (directly or indirectly) against an employee in any employment policy or practice on one or more grounds, including race, gender, sex, pregnancy, marital status, ethnic or social origin, colour, sexual orientation, disability, HIV status, culture or birth. But it is not unfair discrimination to take affirmative-action measures in terms of the EEA or to distinguish, exclude or prefer any person on the basis of an inherent requirement of a job. Sexual harassment constitutes a form of unfair discrimination.

Medical testing as part of the employment process is also prohibited, unless it is justifiable in the light of medical facts, employment conditions, fair distribution of employee benefits or the inherent requirements of the job.

Unfair discrimination

Mr Video has opened up a new store and has placed an advertisement for shop assistants under the age of 25. S applied for the post even though she was 28 years of age. To justify its policy of employing only people under the age of 25, the employer said that the salary paid to shop assistants was not high, that there was a certain youthful approach and culture in the workplace in which an older person may not feel comfortable and that older people might be reluctant to take instructions from a younger person. The employer was also reluctant to appoint S because she was married and had children. The employee's argument was that this constituted unfair discrimination on the basis of her age. In subsequent arbitration proceedings, the CCMA commissioner stated that age should not be taken into consideration when determining whether a group of employees would be compatible. If a person was prepared to work for the salary offered and prepared to accept instructions from a younger person, there was no reason why that person should not perform the work. The CCMA commissioner said the employer had unfairly discriminated against the employee, not only on the basis of her age, but also on the basis of her marital status and family responsibilities. See *Swart v Mr Video (Pty) Ltd* (1998) 19 ILJ 1315 (CCMA).

11.8.7.4 Affirmative action

The EEA introduces a duty on designated employers to take **affirmative-action measures** and to engage in a process of ensuring that, over time, progress is made towards employment equity. The main focus of the EEA is on getting employers to prepare plans to achieve progress towards employment equity and on the assessment of the plans by the Department of Labour. However, the eventual burden of the EEA on employers will, to a large extent, depend on how the Department of Labour applies the EEA and its approach to the employment equity plans submitted by employers.

In the context of affirmative action, a designated employer has the following obligations in terms of section 13 of the EEA:

- to consult with its employees
- to conduct an analysis
- to prepare an employment equity plan
- to report to the Director-General on progress made in implementing the employment equity plan.

The enforcement of the affirmative-action provisions is part of a process that starts with a labour inspector and might end up in the Labour Court. The labour inspector may, for instance, issue a compliance order to an employer who refuses to give a written undertaking to comply with the Act, or an employer who fails to comply with such an undertaking.

If an employer fails to comply with the administrative duties in the Act, the Labour Court may impose a hefty fine, ranging from R500 000 for the first offence to R900 000 for four offences. Fines cannot be imposed for not achieving targets, although the Labour Court may make any appropriate order to ensure compliance with the Act if an employer makes no *bona fide* effort to achieve the targets. However, given South Africa's history, employers should be extremely sensitive as to how they manage employment relationships, particularly because there are so many possible discrimination traps that employers could fall into.

11.8.8 The Skills Development Act (No. 97 of 1998) (the SDA)[61]

To improve the low skills base of people in South Africa, the government has promulgated three important pieces of legislation: the Skills Development Act, the Skills Development Levies Act and the National Qualifications Framework Act (NQF). These acts form part of the national skills-development strategy, a new approach that aims, among other things, to link learning to the demands of the world of work, to develop the skills of existing workers, and to enable employers to become more productive and competitive.

It must be noted, however, that there is a clear link between the different pieces of training legislation and the Employment Equity Act. The principles of equity, access and redress underpin the transformation of the legislation. The links between the various pieces of legislation may be explained as follows: The NQF Act makes provision for the National Qualifications Framework (NQF), an integrated framework where all knowledge and skills outcomes can be registered as unit standards. The SDA introduces a strategic approach to skills development by creating Sector Educational and Training Authorities (SETAs), learnerships and skills programs that are to be assessed against standards and qualifications. The Skills Development Levies Act imposes a skills-development levy on employers, and the Employment Equity Act requires all employers to eliminate unfair discrimination and promote greater representation of Black people (that is, African people, Coloured people and Indian people), women and people with disabilities.

11.8.8.1 Objectives of the Skills Development Act

Section 2 of the SDA sets out the various purposes of the Act:

- to develop the skills of the South African workforce

- to increase the levels of investment in education and training in the labour market and to improve the return on investment
- to use the workplace as an active learning environment, to provide employees with the opportunities to acquire new skills and to provide opportunities for new entrants to the labour market to gain work experience
- to employ persons who find it difficult to be employed
- to encourage workers to participate in learning and other training programs
- to improve the employment prospects of persons previously disadvantaged by unfair discrimination, and to redress those disadvantages through training and education
- to ensure the quality of education and training in and for the workplace
- to help work-seekers to find work, retrenched workers to re-enter the labour market and employers to find qualified employees
- to provide and regulate employment services.

The following institutions are established by the Act:

- the National Skills Authority
- the National Skills Fund and the skills-development levy grant scheme as stipulated in the Skills Development Levies Act (No. 9 of 1999)
- the SETAs
- labour centres
- the Quality Council for Trades and Occupations (QCTO)
- Department of Labour provincial offices
- National Artisan Moderating Body.

11.8.8.2 The National Skills Authority

The main functions of the National Skills Authority are as follows (section 5 of the Act):

- to advise the Minister of Labour on a national skills-development policy and strategy
- to liaise with SETAs, the national skills-development policy and the national skills-development strategy
- to report to the Minister on the progress made in the implementation of the national skills-development strategy
- to conduct investigations on any matter arising out of the application of the SDA and to liaise with the QCTO.

11.8.8.3 Sector education and training authorities (SETAs)

The establishment of SETAs is described in Chapter 3 of the Act. The Minister of Labour may establish a SETA with a constitution for any national economic sector.

The Minister of Labour must, however, take the following into account:

- the education and training needs of employers and employees
- the potential of the proposed sector for coherent occupational structures and career pathing
- the scope of any national strategies for economic growth and development
- the organisational structures of the trade unions, employer organisations and government in closely related sectors
- any consensus there may be between organised labour, organised employers and relevant government departments as to the definition of any sector, and the financial and organisational ability of the proposed sector to support a SETA.

SETAs have various functions, of which the most important are:

- to develop a sector-skills plan within the framework of the national skills-development strategy
- to implement its sector-skills plan by establishing learning programs, approving annual training reports, allocating grants in the prescribed manner to employers, education providers, training providers and workers, and monitoring education and training in the sector

- to promote learning programs by identifying workplaces for practical work experience, supporting the development of learning materials, improving the facilitation of learning and assisting in the conclusion of learning programs
- to register learning programs
- to liaise with the National Skills Authority on the allocation of grants, skills-development policy or strategy, and a sector-skills plan.

11.8.8.4 Learnerships and apprenticeships

Learnerships are described in Chapter 4 of the Act. A SETA may establish a learnership if it:

- consists of a structured learning component
- includes practical work experience of a specified nature and duration
- leads to a qualification registered by the South African Qualification Authority associated with a trade or occupation
- is registered with the Director-General.

Any reference to a learnership in this Act includes an apprenticeship and any reference to a learner includes an apprentice.

Learnership agreements are agreements entered into for a specified period between a learner, an employer or a group of employers, and a training provider. The employer has the responsibility to:

- employ the learner for the period specified in the agreement
- provide the learner with specified practical work experience
- give the learner time to attend the education and training specified in the agreement.

The learner has the responsibility to work for the employer, and to attend the specified education and training. The training provider must provide the education and training specified in the agreement, as well as the learner support specified in the agreement.

The Act also makes provision (in Chapter 6) for the establishment of the Skills Development Planning Unit. Labour centres are to provide employment services for workers, employers and training providers.

11.8.8.5 Financing skills development

The National Skills Fund (Chapter 7 of the SDA) must be credited with:

- 20% of the skills-development levies as stipulated in the Skills Development Levies Act
- the skills-development levies collected and transferred to the Fund
- money appropriated by parliament for the Fund
- donations to the Fund
- money received from any other source.

11.8.8.6 Artisan Development and Quality Council for Trades and Occupations

The Act makes provision for artisan development by establishing a National Artisan Moderating Body. It makes provision for the "listing of trades" and a "national register of artisans". It further requires that no person may obtain an artisan qualification unless he/she has passed a trade test offered by an accredited trade centre.

The Quality Council for Trades and Occupations (QCTO) is established by this Act. The Council consists of 16 members and must, *inter alia*, advise the Minister on all matters related to policy about occupations standards and qualifications. An employer must pay the levy to the Commissioner of Inland Revenue Services.

11.8.9 The Skills Development Levies Act (No. 9 of 1999)[62]

The purpose of the Skills Development Levies Act is to provide for the imposition of a skills-development levy. The most important aspects of the Act are outlined below.

11.8.9.1 Levy to be paid

According to section 3 of the Act, every employer must pay a skills-development levy. The South African Revenue Services is the national collection agency. Every employer must pay a levy at a rate of 1% of an employee's total remuneration. Pensions, superannuations or retiring allowances are, for example, excluded according to section 2(5) of the Act.

Employers who are liable to pay the levy must apply to the commissioner of the South African Revenue Services to be registered. Employers must indicate the jurisdiction of the SETA within which they belong. They must also register with the relevant SETA.

An employer must pay the levy to the Commissioner of Inland Revenue Services

11.8.9.2 Payment of levy to Commissioner and refund

An employer must pay the levy to the Commissioner of Inland Revenue Services not later than seven days after the end of each month. The National Skills Fund will receive 20% of the levy. Organisations will be able to claim for financing for up to 80% of the levy, less the set-up and running costs of the SETA.

11.8.9.3 Exemptions from the Act

The following categories of employers are exempted:

- any public-service employer in the national or provincial government
- any employer whose remuneration to all of its employees during the following 12-month period will not exceed R500 000 and who is not required to apply for registration in terms of the Fourth Schedule to the Income Tax Act (No. 32 of 1944)
- any religious or charitable institution that is exempt from income tax
- any national or provincial public entity that receives 80% or more of its funds from parliament.

11.8.10 The National Qualifications Framework Act (No. 67 of 2008) (the NQF)[63]

11.8.10.1 Introduction to SAQA

After the publication in 1994 of the National Training Strategy Initiative document and the debate on it, the government's White Paper on Education and Training was published in 1995. The South African Qualifications Authority Act (No. 58 of 1995) (SAQA) was passed on 4 October 1995. The objective of SAQA is to provide for the development and implementation of the NQF, and to establish the South African Qualifications Authority.

The NQF Bill was published in the *Government Gazette* No. 31039 of 9 May 2008 and the NQF Act (No. 67 of 2008) was promulgated on 17 March 2009. The NQF Act mainly provides for the NQF, the responsibilities of the Ministers of Education (the Department of Education has been abolished and two new departments have been created: the Department of Higher Education and Training and the Department of Basic Education) and Labour, the South African Qualifications Authority, quality councils and the repeal of the SAQA Act of 1995.

11.8.10.2 The South African National Qualifications Framework (NQF)

The NQF is based on a credit system for achieving learning outcomes. A **learning outcome** is, in essence, an ability developed by the learner that reflects an integration of knowledge and skill that can be transferred to different contexts. Qualifications can be obtained by means of full-time study, part-time study, distance education, work-based learning or a combination of these, together with an assessment of previous learning experiences and general experience.

The objectives of the NQF as described in Chapter 2 of the Act are the following:

- to create an integrated national framework of learning achievements

- to facilitate access to, and mobility and progression within, education, training and career paths
- to accelerate the redress of past certain discrimination in education, training and employment opportunities
- to contribute to the full development of learners
- to enhance the quality of education and training.

The NQF (see Table 11.2) is a new approach to education and training in South Africa. The NQF consists of a framework with ten levels. Each level is described by a statement of learning achievement known as a level description. This description provides a broad indication of learning achievements or outcomes for a qualification at that level.

The first subframework is the Higher Education band (contemplated in the Higher Education Act). It comprises Levels 5 to 10. The previous Higher Education Band comprised Levels 5 to 8, where Level 7 included higher degrees (honours and professional qualifications) and Level 8 referred to masters and doctoral qualifications.

The second subframework is the General and Further Education and Training band (GFET), which concerns formal schooling and Adult Basic Education (contemplated in the GENFETQA or General and Further Education and Training Quality Assurance Act). This subframework comprises Levels 2 to 4. Here a large number of providers can provide education and training. Level 4 is equivalent to Grade 12 of schooling.

The third subframework is the Trade and Occupations band (contemplated in the Skills Development Act). Note that this band is not reflected on Table 11.2.

At the time of writing, clarity on the various levels and how they relate to the different subframeworks could not be obtained. According to the framework draft policy (dated 26 July 2008) drawn up by the Department of Labour Quality Assurance for the Quality Council for Trades and Occupations, two types of occupational qualification can be obtained: a National

Table 11.2: Structure of the NQF

NQF level	Framework	Types of qualifications and certificates	Locations of learning for units and qualifications		
10	Higher Education	Doctoral degrees	Universities		
9		Master's degrees	Universities		
8		Honours/post-graduate diplomas	Universities		
7		First degrees/advanced diplomas	Universities		
6		Diploma/higher certificates	Universities		
5		Occupational certificates	Universities		
4	General and Further Education and Training	School/college/training certificates Mix of units from all	Formal high schools/ private schools/ state schools	Technical colleges/ community colleges/ police colleges/ nursing colleges/ private colleges	RDP and labour-market schemes/ SETAs/ Union/ workplace
3		School/college/training certificates Mix of units from all			
2		School/college/training certificates Mix of units from all			

Source: South Africa. Department of Education. Discussion document on lifelong learning through a National Qualifications Framework: Report of the ministerial committee for the development work on the NQF. Pretoria 1996. (Note: This version is subject to change.)

Occupational Award and a National Skills Certificate.

11.8.10.3 The South African Qualifications Authority

The South African Qualifications Authority continues to exist as a juristic person despite the repeal of the SAQA Act contemplated in Chapter 7. The purposes of the Authority are to:

- oversee the further development and implementation of the NQF
- advance the objectives of the NQF contemplated in Chapter 2.

The South African Qualifications Authority is accountable to the Minister. It has various functions, such as overseeing the implementation of the NQF, recommending level descriptors to the Minister of Labour, recognising a professional body and registering its professional designation.

11.8.11 The Occupational Health and Safety Act (No. 85 of 1993) (OHSA)[64]

11.8.11.1 Introduction to OHSA

The main purpose of this Act is to protect employees by ensuring a healthy and safe work environment. The origin of the Act can be found in the late 1800s and early 1900s, when mining operations presented many dangers to workers, and poor working conditions led to various illnesses and sometimes to death.

The Act has a wide application and covers all workers, although there are the following exceptions:

- a mining area or any works as defined in the Minerals Act (No. 50 of 1991), except insofar as the Act provides otherwise
- vessels as defined in the Merchant Shipping Act (No. 57 of 1957).

Note that the Minister may grant exemptions from any or all of the provisions of the Act and that labour brokers are not considered to be employers in terms of this Act.

OHSA provides for an Advisory Council for Occupational Health and Safety, with certain functions as stipulated in the Act.

11.8.11.2 Duties of employers and employees

According to this Act, employers have the following general duties to their employees:

- to provide and maintain a working environment that is safe and without risk to the health of employees
- to take whatever steps are necessary to eliminate any hazard or potential hazard to the safety or health of employees
- to provide any information, instructions, training and supervision as may be necessary to ensure the health and safety of all employees
- to take all necessary steps to ensure that the requirements of this Act are complied with
- to take any measures that may be necessary in the interests of health and safety
- to ensure that the work is performed and that this is done under the general supervision of a trained person
- to keep employees informed at all times.

Employees have the following general duties at work:

- to take reasonable care for their own health and safety, and also that of others
- to co-operate with their employer regarding this Act and its provisions
- to carry out lawful orders, and obey health-and-safety rules and procedures
- to report any situation that is unsafe or unhealthy
- to report any accident they may have been involved in.

11.8.11.3 Representatives and committees

Any employer with more than 20 employees must appoint one or more **safety representatives** after consultation with the workers. Health-and-safety representatives may perform certain functions and must perform other functions.

Health-and-safety representatives may:

- review the effectiveness of health-and-safety measures
- identify potential hazards
- examine causes of incidents in collaboration with the employer
- investigate complaints by employees
- make representations to the employer and inspector
- inspect the workplace
- participate in consultations with inspectors
- receive information from inspectors
- attend meetings of the health-and-safety committee.

Health-and-safety representatives must perform the following functions:

- visit the site of an accident at all reasonable times and attend any inspection *in loco*
- attend any investigation or formal inquiry in terms of this Act
- inspect any document that the employer is required to keep
- accompany an inspector on any inspection
- with the approval of the employer, be accompanied by a technical adviser
- participate in any internal health-and-safety audit.

The employer must provide such facilities, assistance and training as the representative may require. A health-and-safety representative shall not incur any civil liability by reason of the fact that he/she failed to do anything the representative was required to do in terms of this Act.

If two or more health-and-safety representatives have been designated in a workplace, the employer must establish one or more health-and-safety committees. The employer must also consult with the committee at each of its meetings to initiate, develop, promote, maintain and review measures to ensure the health and safety of employees at work.

Health-and-safety committees have the following functions:

- making recommendations to the employer or inspector
- discussing any incident that has led to a person's death or illness and reporting the incident to an inspector in writing.

Inspectors are appointed by the minister and a certificate is issued as proof of their appointment. Their duties include general functions to ensure that the provisions of the Act are complied with – and here they have special powers relating to health and safety – and also functions with regard to incidents at the workplace.

Light in the workplace

OHSA imposes general duties on employers and employees, but the detailed regulations made in terms of OHSA contain numerous detailed duties. There are, for example, Environmental Regulations for Workplaces (October 1987, amended in 1989, 1994 and 2003). This document contains specifications concerning the lighting in the workplace, ventilation, noise, precautions against flooding and fire precautions. The Facilities Regulations (August 2004, amended in September 2004) deal with issues such as changing rooms, dining rooms, drinking water and seating of employees.

11.8.12 The Compensation for Occupational Injuries and Diseases Act (No. 130 of 1993)[65]

11.8.12.1 Introduction to the Compensation for Occupational Injuries and Diseases Act

In terms of the common law, an employee had no recourse if injured in the course of performing his/her duties. The only way to claim compensation was if intent or negligence on the side of his/her employer could be proved.

The first Act to give some form of protection to the employee was the Workmen's Compensation Act of 1941, which provided for payment of compensation even if intent or negligence on the side of an employer could not be proved. The basic principle has remained the same: compensation will be paid to an employee (or his/her dependants) if an injury has been caused by an accident "arising out of and in the course of the employee's employment". It is not necessary for the employee to prove negligence or fault on the part of the employer to qualify for compensation.

The following categories of persons are excluded from the operation of this Act:

- persons performing military service or undergoing military training who are not Permanent Force members
- members of the South African National Defence Force and South African Police Services while acting in defence of the country (note that members of the South African Police Service are covered by this Act while they are performing their normal duties)
- domestic employees employed as such in a private household
- persons who contract for the carrying out of work and themselves engage other persons to perform the work (in other words, contractors).

The Act provides for the establishment of a Compensation Board, whose main function is to advise the Minister of Labour on various matters concerning the application of this Act and its provisions.

11.8.12.2 Duties of employers

Employers must register and furnish the Commissioner with details about their businesses. They must keep records of all employees, wages paid and time worked for a period of four years. The record must be sent to the Commissioner each year. The Commissioner will then determine the amount of money that has to be paid by the employer to the Compensation Fund and the employer must comply within 30 days. The state, parliament, provincial governments, exempted local authorities and employers who have obtained an insurance policy for the extent of their potential liability are exempted from giving the required details and paying the determined sum of money.

11.8.12.3 Procedure to claim compensation

The employee must, as soon as is reasonably possible, notify his/her employer of the accident, as well as his/her intention to instigate a claim. The employer must then notify the Commissioner within seven days. A claim for compensation must be lodged within 12 months of the date of the accident or the date of death.

There are, however, certain requirements that must be met before an employee qualifies for compensation:

- An employer–employee relationship must exist, and the employee must be an employee as defined in this Act.
- Injury or death must have been caused by an accident.
- The accident must have happened in the scope of the employee's employment. This means that the accident happened in the nature of the employee's duties and in the course of his/her service.

11.8.13 The Unemployment Insurance Act (No. 63 of 2001) (UIA)[66]

This Act provides for the payment of benefits for a limited period to people who are ready and willing to work, but are unable to get work for whatever reason. In terms of the UIA, some employees (those who qualify as contributors in terms of section 3 of the UIA) contribute monthly to the Unemployment Insurance Fund (UIF), which is administered by the Department of Labour. Employers also pay in a certain amount for every contributor (employee) that they employ. An employee who is out of work can claim benefits from the Fund. The UIA also provides for sickness benefits, benefits to dependants if an employee – referred to as a contributor – dies, and for maternity and adoption benefits.

The UIA should be read in conjunction with the regulations in terms of section 54 of the Act (*Government Gazette*, No. 23283, 28 March 2002) and the Unemployment Insurance Contributions Act (No. 4 of 2002).

11.8.13.1 The scope of the Act

Most employees are covered by the Act. Section 3 of the UIA excludes the following categories of employees:

- employees employed for fewer than 24 hours a month with a particular employer, and their employers
- employees employed in terms of a learnership agreement registered in terms of the Skills Development Act (No. 97 of 1998), and their employers
- employees in the national and provincial spheres of government
- persons in the Republic on a contract, apprenticeship or learnership, if the employer is required to repatriate the employee, or if the employee is required to leave the Republic at the end of the contract.

The Act provides for the institution of an Unemployment Insurance Board to assist the Minister of Labour.

11.8.13.2 Duties of employers

In terms of the Act, employers have certain duties. Every employer has the following obligations:

- As soon as a business commences activities as an employer, the business must provide the following information about its employees to the Commissioner, irrespective of the earnings of such employees:
  - the street address of the business and of its branches
  - the particulars of the authorised person who is required to carry out the duties of the employer in terms of this Act if the employer is not resident in the Republic, or is a body corporate not registered in the Republic
  - the names, identification numbers and monthly remuneration of each of its employees, and the address at which the employee is employed.
- The business must inform the Commissioner of any change to any information furnished during the previous month before the seventh day of each month.
- The business must pay into the Fund the required amount from the employer and every contributor in his/her employ. (Both the employer and the contributor must pay in an amount equivalent to 1% of the contributor's earnings, thus a total contribution of 2%. The employee's contribution can be deducted from his/her wages. Employers must make monthly payments into the Fund within seven days of the end of the month.)

11.8.13.3 Benefits and allowances

Contributors who lose their jobs are entitled (as are their dependants) to the following benefits:

- **Unemployment benefits.** These are payable for any period of unemployment lasting more than 14 days if the reason for the unemployment is the termination of a contract, dismissal or insolvency. The contributor must be registered as a work-seeker with a labour centre established under the Skills Development Act, and must be capable of and available for work.
- **Illness benefits.** These are payable if the contributor is unable to perform work on account of illness and fulfils any prescribed requirements in respect of any specified illness. The period of illness should be 14 days or more.
- **Maternity or adoption benefits.** The contributor will be paid the difference

between any maternity or adoption benefit received in terms of any other law or any collective agreement or contract of employment, and the maximum benefit payable in terms of this Act.

- **Dependant's benefits.** These are payable to a surviving spouse, life partner or dependent child if an application is made within six months after the contributor's death.

In all instances, application should be made in accordance with the prescribed requirements.

> **Critical thinking**
>
> **A safe environment**
> Section 24(a) of the Constitution of 1996 provides that everyone has the right to an environment that is not harmful to his/her health or well-being. How does labour legislation seek to promote this right? Is it only the employer's responsibility to ensure this right?

11.9 Summary

This chapter provided a brief overview of the activities associated with the human-resources function in an organisation. The first part dealt with the recruitment and selection of talent to organisations, the human-resources planning and job-analysis process, and the development of employees. The second part dealt with the importance of motivation in the workplace and considered various theories concerning ways to motivate employees. The last part discussed the legal environment that influences human-resources managers in an organisation, highlighting the importance of the Constitution as the supreme law of South Africa and giving a brief overview of the most important labour laws that line managers and human-resources practitioners should take note of in the workplace.

Key terms

affirmative action	learnerships
compensation	legislation
employee development	management by objectives
expectancy theory	motivation
external recruiting	organisational effectiveness
human-resources function	performance
human-resources planning	performance appraisal
internal recruiting	recruiting
job analysis	rewards
job description	selection
job enrichment	self-efficacy
job specification	strategic partner
labour	

Questions for discussion

Reread the case study at the beginning of the chapter and answer the following questions:

1. What are the most important human-resources initiatives that Coca-Cola South Africa embarked upon to maintain and grow its brand?
2. What is the relationship between human-resources planning and the recruitment of qualified workers in an organisation? Motivate your answer.
3. Describe human-resources development as a subfunction in human-resources management and indicate its value in improving organisational success.
4. Performance management and compensation management in organisations are inseparable components. Provide reasons why you agree or disagree with this statement.

5. Who is responsible for motivating discipline and rewarding employees in the organisation? What is the role of the human-resources department?
6. The Labour Relations Act (No. 66 of 1995) does not impose a duty to bargain on an employer. This means that there is no provision in the LRA that states that an employer must bargain or negotiate with a trade union. An employer may be reluctant to engage with a trade union, taking the view that it knows what is best for the employees. This is called a refusal to bargain. What can a trade union do to force an employer to the bargaining table? Hint: See section 64(2) of the LRA.
7. What is the role of the Constitution of the Republic of South Africa, 1996 in the labour environment of South Africa? Describe this role.
8. What are the main features of the LRA and the BCEA? Describe them.
9. How is "affirmative action" part of an employer's responsibility? Explain.
10. How effective is training legislation in South Africa?
11. Do you think that justice is done to the role of the human-resources function in South African organisations? Give reasons for your answer.
12. Which theories address content approaches to motivation? Describe them.
13. Why are the principles of equity theory important for organisational success?
14. What are the differences between the content approach to motivation and the process approach to motivation?
15. Which different motivating principles or strategies have contributed to the successes of South Africa's most promising companies? Give reasons for your answer.

? Multiple-choice questions

1. Look at the list of activities below.
   i. Human-resources planning
   ii. Recruitment of employees
   iii. Selection of employees
   iv. Development of employees
   v. Compensation of employees

   Now select the combination of activities that is important to the human-resources functions in organisations.
   a. i, ii, iv, v
   b. i, ii, iv, v
   c. i, ii, iii, iv
   d. i, ii, iii, iv, v
2. Look at the list of activities below.
   i. Training and development opportunities
   ii. Recognition for work done
   iii. Good client service
   iv. Limited communications
   v. Limited promotions

   Now select the combination of activities that will contribute to improved employee motivation in organisations.
   a. i, iii, v
   b. i, ii, v
   c. ii, iii, iv
   d. i, ii, ii
3. Choose one of the options to complete the sentence that follows:
   Based on __________, needs are learnt and enforced.
   a. expectancy theory
   b. goal-setting theory
   c. equity theory
   d. McClelland's theory
4. Which one of the following is not addressed by the Labour Relations Act (No. 66 of 1994)?
   a. Organisational rights
   b. Affirmative action
   c. CCMA
   d. Workplace forums

5 Choose one of the options to complete the sentence that follows:
According to the __________,
minimum standards are set in the workplace that will regulate conditions of service in the absence of more favourable conditions.
a. Labour Relations Act
b. Employment Equity Act
c. Occupational Health and Safety Act
d. Basic Conditions of Employment Act

Answers to multiple-choice questions

1. d
2. d
3. d
4. b
5. d

References

1. Pfeffer, J. 1994. *Competitive advantage through people*. Boston: Harvard Business School Press.
2. Williams, C. 2000. *Management*. Cincinnati: South-Western, p. 546.
3. Williams, C. 2000. *Management*. Cincinnati: South-Western, p. 546.
4. Price Waterhouse Coopers. Global Human Capital Benchmark Survey. 2002/2003 South African Survey. p. 5.
5. Reece, B.L. & Brandt, R. 1996. *Effective human relations*. 6th ed. New York: Houghton Mifflin Company, p. 152.
6. Price Waterhouse Coopers. Global Human Capital Benchmark Survey. 2002/2003 South African Survey, pp. 10–12.
7. Price Waterhouse Coopers. Global Human Capital Benchmark Survey. 2002/2003 South African Survey, pp. 10–12.
8. Jackson, S.E. & Schuler, R.S. 2000. *Managing human resources: A partnership perspective*. 7th ed. Cincinnati: South-Western, p. 220.
9. Swanepoel, B.J. (ed), Erasmus, B.J. & Schenk, H.W. 2008. *South African Human resource management in theory and practice*. 4th ed. Cape Town: Juta, p. 229.
10. Swanepoel, B.J. (ed), Erasmus, B.J. & Schenk, H.W. 2008. *South African Human resource management in theory and practice*. 4th ed. Cape Town: Juta, p. 229.
11. Swanepoel, B.J. (ed), Erasmus, B.J. & Schenk, H.W. 2008. *South African Human resource management in theory and practice*. 4th ed. Cape Town: Juta, p. 229.
12. Swanepoel, B.J. (ed), Erasmus, B.J. & Schenk, H.W. 2008. *South African Human resource management in theory and practice*. 4th ed. Cape Town: Juta, p. 258.
13. Dessler, G. 2000. *Human resource management*. 8th ed. Upper Saddle River, New Jersey: Prentice Hall, p. 645.
14. Mello, J.A. 2002. *Strategic human resource management*. Cincinnati: South-Western, pp. 242–245.
15. Williams, C. 2000. *Management*. Cincinnati: South-Western, p. 565.
16. Swanepoel, B.J. (ed), Erasmus, B.J. & Schenk, H.W. 2008. *South African Human resource management in theory and practice*. 4th ed. Cape Town: Juta, p. 297–302.
17. Desimone, R.L., Werner, J.M. & Harris, D.M. 2002. *Human resource development*. 3rd ed. Orlando: Harcourt College Publishers, p. 10.
18. Desimone, R.L., Werner, J.M. & Harris, D.M. 2002. *Human resource development*. 3rd ed. Orlando: Harcourt College Publishers, p. 3.
19. Jackson, S.E. & Schuler, R.S. 2000. *Managing human resources: A partnership perspective*. 7th ed. Cincinnati: South-Western, p. 367.
20. Jackson, S.E. & Schuler, R.S. 2000. *Managing human resources: A partnership perspective*. 7th ed. Cincinnati: South-Western, p. 371.
21. Livingston, S., Gerdel, T.W., Hill, M., Yerak, B., Melvin, C. & Lubinger, B. 1997. "Ohio's strongest companies all agree that training is vital to their success". *Plain Dealer*, Vol. 21, p. 305.
22. Bohlander, G., Snell, S. & Sherman, A. 2001. *Managing human resources*. 12th ed. Cincinnati: South-Western, p. 318.
23. Mathis, R.L. & Jackson, J.H. 2002. *Human resource management: Essential perspectives*. 2nd ed. Cincinnati: South-Western, p. 93.
24. Williams, R.S. 1998. *Performance management: Perspectives on employee performance*. Filey, North Yorkshire: International Thomson Business Press, pp. 84–85.
25. Mathis, R.L. & Jackson, J.H. 2002. *Human resource management: Essential perspectives*. 2nd ed. Cincinnati: South-Western, p. 96.
26. Bohlander, G., Snell, S. & Sherman, A. 2001. *Managing human resources*. 12th ed. Cincinnati: South-Western, p. 320.

27. Williams, R.S. 1998. *Performance management: Perspectives on employee performance*. Filey, North Yorkshire: International Thomson Business Press, p. 152.
28. Milkovich, G.T. & Newman, J.M. 2002. *Compensation*. 7th ed. New York: McGraw-Hill, p. 7.
29. Dessler, G. 2000. *Human resource management*. 8th ed. Upper Saddle River, New Jersey: Prentice Hall, p. 399.
30. Mathis, R.L. & Jackson, J.H. 2002. *Human resource management: Essential perspectives*. 2nd ed. Cincinnati: South-Western, p. 104.
31. Milkovich, G.T. & Newman, J.M. 2002. *Compensation*. 7th ed. New York: McGraw-Hill, p. 89.
32. Bohlander, G., Snell, S. & Sherman, A. 2001. *Managing human resources*. 12th ed. Cincinnati: South-Western, p. 372.
33. Brevis, T. "Most promising companies: What gives them a competitive advantage". *Management Today*, February 2005, pp. 8–12.
34. Buelens, M., Van den Broeck, H., Vanderheyden, K., Kreitner, R. & Kinicki, A. 2006. *Organisational behaviour*. 3rd ed. Berkshire: McGraw-Hill, p. 172.
35. McShane, S. & Von Glinow, M.A. 2005. *Organizational behaviour*. 3rd ed. Boston, Illinois: McGraw-Hill, p. 140.
36. Landy, F.L. & Conte, J.M. 2004. *Work in the 21st century: An introduction to industrial and organizational psychology*. Boston, Illinois: McGraw-Hill, Boston, pp. 405–408.
37. Buelens, M., Van den Broeck, H., Vanderheyden, K., Kreitner, R. & Kinicki, A. 2006. *Organisational behaviour*. 3rd ed. Berkshire: McGraw-Hill, p. 176.
38. Buelens, M., Van den Broeck, H., Vanderheyden, K., Kreitner, R. & Kinicki, A. 2006. *Organisational behaviour*. 3rd ed. Berkshire: McGraw-Hill, p. 177.
39. Dick, P. & Ellis, S. 2006. *Introduction to organizational behaviour*. 3rd ed. London: McGraw-Hill, pp. 84–85.
40. Swanepoel, B., Erasmus, B., Van Wyk, M. & Schenk, H. 2003. *South African human resource management: Theory and practice*. 3rd ed. Cape Town: Oxford University Press, p. 357.
41. Nel, P.S., Gerber, P.D., Van Dyk, P.S., Haasbroek, G.D., Schultz, H.B., Seno, T. & Werner, A. 2001. *Human resource management*. 5th ed. Cape Town: Oxford University Press, p. 331.
42. Reece, B.L. & Brandt, R. 1996. *Effective human relations*. 6th ed. New York: Houghton Mifflin Company, p. 162.
43. Dick, P. & Ellis, S. 2006. *Introduction to organizational behaviour*. 3rd ed. London: McGraw-Hill, pp. 86–87.
44. Robbins, S.P. 1998. *Organisational behaviour: Concepts, controversies, application*. 8th ed. Upper Saddle River, New Jersey: Prentice Hall, p. 134.
45. Kreitner, R. & Kinicki, A. 2007. *Organizational behaviour*. 7th ed. Boston: McGraw-Hill, pp. 253–254.
46. McShane, S. & Von Glinow, M.A. 2005. *Organizational behaviour*. 3rd ed. Boston, Illinois: McGraw-Hill, p. 147.
47. McShane, S. & Von Glinow, M.A. 2005. *Organizational behaviour*. 3rd ed. Boston, Illinois: McGraw-Hill, p. 151.
48. Moorhead, G. & Griffin, R.W. 2000. *Organisational behaviour: Managing people and organisations*. 6th ed. Boston: Houghton Mifflin, p. 492.
49. McShane, S. & Von Glinow, M.A. 2005. *Organizational behaviour*. 3rd ed. Boston, Illinois: McGraw-Hill, p. 163.
50. Kreitner, R. & Kinicki, A. 2007. *Organizational behaviour*. 7th ed. Boston: McGraw-Hill, pp. 244–245.
51. Kreitner, R. & Kinicki, A. 2007. *Organizational behaviour*. 7th ed. Boston: McGraw-Hill, pp. 252–253.
52. Kreitner, R. & Kinicki, A. 2007. *Organizational behaviour*. 7th ed. Boston: McGraw-Hill, pp. 244–245.
53. Dick, P. & Ellis, S. 2006. *Introduction to organizational behaviour*. 3rd ed. London: McGraw-Hill, p. 95.
54. Landy, F.L. & Conte, J.M. 2004. *Work in the 21st century: An introduction to industrial and organizational psychology*. Boston, Illinois: McGraw-Hill, p. 362.
55. Landy, F.L. & Conte, J.M. 2004. *Work in the 21st century: An introduction to industrial and organizational psychology*. Boston, Illinois: McGraw-Hill, p. 364.
56. Robbins, S.P., Odendaal, A. & Roodt, G. 2003. *Organisational behaviour: Global and Southern African perspectives*. Cape Town: Pearson Education, pp. 151–153.
57. While effort has been made to provide an accurate summary of the various acts in this

chapter, the editors, publishers and printers take no responsibility for any loss or damage suffered by any person as a result of reliance upon the information contained therein.

58. Based on the Labour Relations Act (No. 66 of 1995), *Government Gazette*, Vol. 366, No. 17516, Pretoria: Government Printer.
59. Based on the Basic Conditions of Employment Act (No. 75 of 1997), *Government Gazette*, Vol. 390, No. 18491, December, Pretoria: Government Printer.
60. Based on the Employment Equity Act (No. 55 of 1998), *Government Gazette*, Vol. 400, No. 19370, Pretoria: Government Printer.
61. Based on the Skills Development Act (No. 97 of 1998), *Government Gazette*, Vol. 401, No. 19420, November, Pretoria: Government Printer.
62. Based on the Skills Development Levies Act (No. 9 of 1999), *Government Gazette*, Vol. 406, No. 19984, April, Pretoria: Government Printer.
63. Based on the National Qualifications Framework Act (No. 58 of 1995), *Government Gazette*, Vol. 364, No. 1521 Pretoria: Government Printer.
64. Based on the Occupational Health and Safety Act (No. 85 of 1993), *Government Gazette*, Vol. 337, No. 14918, July, Pretoria: Government Printer.
65. Based on the Compensation for Occupational Injuries and Diseases Act (No. 130 of 1993), *Government Gazette*, Vol. 340, No. 15158, October, Pretoria: Government Printer.
66. Based on the Unemployment Insurance Act (No. 63 of 2001), *Government Gazette*, Vol. 439, No. 23064, January, Pretoria: Government Printer.

Websites: www.acts.co.za
www.labour.gov.za
www.gov.za
www.ccma.org.za

CHAPTER

12

MARKETING MANAGEMENT

The purpose of this chapter

It is important to be aware of the role of marketing as a central part of any business's activities. Initially, this chapter considers the evolution of marketing thought, the marketing concept and the definition of marketing. Then it discusses the components of the marketing process and how these elements are linked. Market research forms part of the whole marketing process. The collection, analysis and interpretation of information are used to understand the behaviour of consumers and to segment the market, as well as to position an organisation's products. The chapter concludes with a discussion of the elements of the marketing mix: the product, price, promotion and distribution.

Learning outcomes

On completion of this chapter you should be able to:
- define marketing as a part of the management process
- describe the evolution of marketing thought
- describe the marketing concept
- describe the market offering
- indicate how to use market research to know the environment
- describe the behaviour patterns of consumers
- explain how to segment the consumer market and how objectives are chosen in the market
- define the marketing mix
- describe the product, price, promotion and distribution decisions.

12.1 Introduction

A business organisation can be described as an institution of the free-market system that attempts to satisfy the needs and wants of the community while making a **profit**. A business can also be described as a system that converts inputs (for example, raw material and labour) into outputs (**products** and **services**) for society. The marketing function is that aspect of the business involved in the **marketing process**, which is the transfer of products (or services) to the market.

The marketing process consists of the following:
- environmental scanning (by means of **market research**) in order to collect information on which marketing management can base sound decisions

- the development of a market offering, which consists of tangible products and intangible services, offered at a specific price and convenient place, and about which the consumer has received adequate information.

During this process, marketing management, which is also responsible for the marketing process, needs to monitor competitors, develop strategies to exploit opportunities in the business environment and counter threats, bearing in mind the organisation's strengths and weaknesses. The basis for these activities is the primary objective of ensuring the maximisation of profit over the long term.

Marketing is central: it is the bridge between a business and its environment, bringing into contact the business and its market and consumers, providing an important input in the development of the organisation's mission and strategy, and helping to correlate the resources of the market with the demands of the market. The instruments of the marketing mix are combined with the market offering, which helps consumers to decide whether they want to purchase the product or make use of the service delivered to satisfy their needs and wants. The marketing function is the starting point for the organisation's management functions, because top management needs to determine what can be achieved in the market before making any decisions about production facilities, employing labour, purchasing raw materials and financing all these activities.

The case study below provides an insight into the marketing process.

Case study

New Balance: The new kid on the block

The Comrades Marathon is one of South Africa's premier sporting events, watched by millions of South Africans every year. What is less well known about the Comrades event is the importance that marketers of running shoes attach to it to determine their success in South Africa. Participants enter their preferred brand of shoe on their application form, which is then forwarded to the marketers of running shoes in South Africa. For the last decade of the last millennium, the top brands were Asics, followed by Nike, Adidas and Reebok, with Saucony, Brooks and Mizuno being the laggards in this brand race. By 2000, a century-old American sport-shoe brand had entered the South African market: New Balance opened a head office in Cape Town and branches in Johannesburg, Durban and Port Elizabeth. It did not follow the traditional marketing communication approach, which is to get endorsement from high-profile athletes. The family-owned business believes it has the best high-performance athletic shoes and it sees its target market as ordinary people (in other words, people with jobs and children and bonds and overdrafts) who are running, walking and playing. The company invests heavily in local events, club runners and the youth, especially at schools. It believes that this bottom-up approach generates loyalty that is sustainable over the long term. The product range is wide, with different lengths as well as different widths for running shoes. This factor is appreciated by South Africans, who have wider feet than the global average user of these shoes. New Balance's prices are about 10% cheaper than those of the established brand names such as Asics and Addidas. The company is happy being tagged "affordable" in the eyes of the customer. The company has good relationships with distributors and with final consumers, where consumer loyalty is quite high. In a recently released study from the USA, New Balance was rated the best, with a 60% customer-loyalty rating. This also works in favour of New Balance in South Africa.

By 2005, New Balance was the third most popular brand in the Comrades (after Asics and Nike) with 11,37% of runners using this brand. New Balance is now aiming to dominate the running-shoe market. It also aims to be number one in the walking and netball-shoes segments and to be one of the top three brands in trail running, tennis, training, athletic performance and children's sport shoes. In a market that has a year-on-year growth of 20% and an estimated rand-value turnover of R4,3 billion, New Balance is surely sending shock waves through the market with a fresh approach to the marketing instruments being used.

Source: Business Day, 12 June 2006 [Online] Available: http://www.businessday.co.za Accessed 19 June 2006.

12.2 The evolution of marketing thought

Over time, managers have realised the importance of marketing. Initially, management believed that contact with consumers was unimportant. However, this approach has changed over the years, mostly because of pressure from consumers and an increase in competition.

Before the Industrial Revolution, households were mainly self-sufficient. Many cottage industries produced goods that were made available for barter or sale. The concept of the intermediary originated when the distances between producers and the market increased. Intermediaries were needed to provide services to facilitate the bartering of products, which were then offered for sale. During the seventeenth and eighteenth centuries in South Africa, hawkers visited farms in donkey carts and traded their goods for the farmers' products.

The technical advances of the Industrial Revolution created machinery capable of mass-manufacturing consumer products in a relatively short time. Large factories were built to house the new machines. These factories necessitated some form of management. Over the years, management approaches to the marketing function changed, with different aspects being emphasised.

The evolution of these management approaches is described below.

12.2.1 Operation-oriented management

Initially, instead of focusing on the needs of the market, management focused on the capabilities of the organisation. Operation-oriented organisations tried to increase the number and variety of products they produced. According to this approach, management asked questions such as: "What can we do best?", "What can our engineers design?" and "What is easy to produce, given our equipment?" In the case of service organisations, management asked: "What services are most convenient for us to offer?" and "Where do our talents lie?" Organisations that engaged in this approach were organised around product lines.

A major disadvantage of operation-oriented management was that management concentrated mainly on encouraging production in order to solve operation problems. The marketing of manufactured products did not cause many problems because consumers were largely unsophisticated and not accustomed to the consumer products that factories and newly developed modern machinery produced in mass. Moreover, it was hardly necessary to encourage these unsophisticated consumers to buy the new products because they found them extremely desirable. Thus, marketing as a management function was under-valued.

12.2.2 Sales-oriented management

The situation gradually changed and top management succeeded in solving the most pressing operation problems. The new machinery worked steadily and stocks began to accumulate, which became a problem. During the period 1930–1950, management became more sales oriented in an attempt to sell these mass-produced consumer products. Misleading advertisements and unethical sales methods were employed. The objective was to sell the products at any cost. Management had to get rid of over-produced stock and did not care if consumers were exploited in the process. This led to excessive promotion, and hence high advertising and sales costs. Management was compelled, in the face of increasing competition, to look for more productive marketing methods. This gave rise to the idea that products needed to be marketed instead of merely sold.

12.2.3 Marketing-oriented management

Market-oriented management means that not only the sales message and price of the product need to be considered, but also the quality of the product, the packaging, the choice of distribution channels and the methods of informing potential consumers about the market offering. After 1950, the use of advertising became increasingly important. Management realised that advertising was an effective way of transmitting information to a mass market. Top management focused its attention on the internal organisation of the marketing function. Management also realised that all functional departments of an organisation need to work closely together to ensure the successful marketing of the organisation's products.

12.2.4 Consumer-oriented management

As increasingly competitive consumer products became available and the financial position of consumers improved, consumer demands also started changing. Management began to understand the importance of the consumer demand and the marketing component. It became clear that consumers' needs, demands and preferences needed to be considered when product-related decisions were made. These decisions included choices about the quality and packaging of a product, its brand name, the type of distribution channel used, the price and the marketing communication methods used to inform potential consumers. Management realised that there was no sense in producing a product if there was no demand for it. An organisation that is market driven must also be consumer oriented and must apply a strategic approach to marketing.

12.2.5 The strategic approach to marketing

This is a more recent development in marketing thought. Continual changes in the marketing environment, and the need to ensure the survival and growth of the organisation, meant that management had to concentrate on scanning the environment and on long-term issues. Scanning allowed management to identify environmental changes such as technological innovation, economic influences, political factors, changing consumer preferences, demographic aspects and increasing competition. It became clear that maintaining close relationships, both internally and externally, was of increasing importance in a changing environment. This led to relationship marketing.

12.2.6 Relationship marketing

In order to survive in the changing environment, marketing management needed to establish long-term relationships with people and institutions in the environment in which the marketing task was to be performed. A long-term relationship with customers leads to loyalty and the repeated purchase of need-satisfying products. A long-term relationship with a supplier ensures the availability of the raw materials and the inventory. This is especially important in retailing, where out-of-stock situations can inconvenience customers.

The primary objective of relationship marketing is to establish and maintain relationships with loyal, profitable clients. In order to achieve this goal, management needs to focus on the attraction, retention and enhancement of its customer relationships. Loyalty is of particular importance in clients who buy the products or services of the organisation most often. Loyal consumers are not only a basis for an organisation's existing operations, but are also important for the potential growth of the organisation. Marketing management is not responsible for negotiations with suppliers, but in the light of the close relationship between **buyers** and **sellers**, marketing management should help to establish long-term relationships through mutual co-operation. Both buyers and sellers need to strive towards the same objectives. These objectives can be achieved through understanding the needs of the consumer, treating consumers as partners, ensuring that employees satisfy the needs of consumers and providing consumers with the best quality relevant to their needs. The establishment of long-term relationships between producers and intermediaries such as retailers can ensure the availability of products at the right time and in the right place.

The goodwill of society towards the organisation and its products must be fostered in order to establish a favourable corporate image. Here, marketing management can make a considerable contribution because of its close contact with the general public. Internal marketing can be used to involve all personnel (not only those in the marketing department) in marketing objectives and plans. Everyone needs to realise that consumer satisfaction and marketing success will be reflected in their own career opportunities and remuneration. Relationship marketing is used to good effect by market-driven organisations.

This historical review of the evolution of marketing does not refer only to historical developments in marketing thought. Even today, many organisations are still operation or sales oriented. They are not market driven at all, and cannot hope to achieve sustainable success.

The marketing task in a market-driven organisation needs to be performed according to an ethical code or philosophy. This is closely connected to the long-term objective of corporate management. The marketing process itself often provides many opportunities for exploitation, with one participant in a transaction being enriched by taking unfair advantage of another. Many such incidents occur daily. Salespeople often make promises they cannot keep, persuading naïve people to buy their products or to invest money in dubious schemes. Soon afterwards, these salespeople (or organisations) disappear with the money, without delivering the promised product. In such cases, the marketing task is not performed according to an ethical code. In fact, these examples are not marketing at all, but rather fraud. A swindle has only a short-term objective, is mainly sales oriented and has no chance of long-term survival.

An ethical code according to which the marketing task ought to be performed is regarded as the basis of all marketing activities and decisions. It is thus necessary to describe it in more detail. The ethical code is known as the marketing concept. It is discussed in section 12.3.

12.3 The marketing concept

The marketing concept is the ethical code according to which the marketing task is performed. Four principles are contained in the marketing concept. All four principles are equally important and each one invariably influences the application of the other principles. The marketing concept directs all marketing decisions about products, distribution methods, marketing communication and price determination.

The evolution in marketing thought discussed earlier in this chapter has led to the development of the following four principles of the marketing concept:

- profitability
- consumer orientation
- social responsibility
- organisational integration.

As illustrated in the case study on this page, Pick n Pay incorporates these four principles in its day-to-day operations.

12.3.1 The principle of profitability

The first principle of the marketing concept in a profit-seeking business is the long-term maximisation of profitability. This is the primary objective of the business in a free-market system. It is therefore also the main

Case study

Pick n Pay: A retail giant

Pick n Pay is the largest grocery retail chain in South Africa. It has stores throughout the country, from hypermarkets to supermarkets to clothing stores to family stores and mini-markets. Its annual report highlighted the opening of 49 new stores in 2006, with 59 confirmed for 2007. All these stores must be managed continually as an integrated whole.

Pick n Pay's headline earnings increased by 15,2% at R705,6 million for the year. As a result of the concentration effect of share repurchases, mainly towards the end of the year, headline earnings per share were up 17,1% at 153,02 cents. It had an increase in trading profit of 16,9%, with trading margin increasing from 2,8% to 3%.

Pick n Pay's founder and past chairman, Raymond Ackerman, is known to be the homemaker's friend and his motto of "The customer is queen" is well known throughout the country. Pick n Pay's quick reaction to matters that affect the consumer shows its consumer orientation. Its reaction to increases in the bread price has positioned it as a fighter for the interests of the consumer. Raymond Ackerman is also known for his fight against the high petrol price in South Africa. He is agitated by the continued system of regulation in the industry, which he says is designed to protect the oil companies at the expense of consumers.

Pick n Pay demonstrates its responsibility towards society by sponsoring various educational and charitable events. It is very visible in athletics, sponsoring the Comrades Marathon. It also sponsors cycling events such as the Pick n Pay Cycle Challenge and the Argus Pick n Pay Cycle Tour. Its ongoing focus is promoting black economic empowerment (BEE). The group is active in supporting the development of small entrepreneurial BEE suppliers and Family Store Franchises. It also gave R8,72 million to the Kids in the Park program through the sale of green bags.

Source: "Pick n Pay to roll out 59 new stores", *Business Report*, 7 June 2006. [Online] Available http://wwwbusrep.co.za/index.php?fSectionID=563&fArticleId=3281045 Accessed 7 November 2006.

objective of marketing management. The principle of profitability is fundamental to the marketing concept. It emphasises profitability instead of sales, which do not necessarily maximise profits.

12.3.2 The principle of consumer orientation

The satisfaction of consumer needs, demands and preferences constitutes a consumer-oriented approach to marketing where emphasis is placed on what the consumer needs. Marketing decision-making is based on what the consumer wants, but even though the consumer is regarded as "the king/queen", complete satisfaction of consumer needs can never be achieved.

Satisfaction can only be given within the constraints of the profit objective and the resources of a business. If the consumer is neglected and his/her wishes are ignored, this can have serious financial implications for the enterprise. Competitors are especially keen to note and turn such opportunities to their own advantage. Consumer orientation also means that the consumer has to be supplied with adequate and correct information about the business's market offering. This information is usually incorporated into marketing communication messages. An example of this is the way in which Pick n Pay prioritises and publicises its commitment to the consumer, as illustrated in the case study on page 362.

12.3.3 The principle of social responsibility

Besides its responsibility towards the consumers of its products, marketing management also has a responsibility towards the community in which the marketing task is performed. Business often discharges this responsibility by spending money on projects such as housing, education, job creation and health. The objective of these projects is to create a stable economic, social and political environment in which future profits can be optimised. Responsibility in this regard enhances the corporate image in the eyes of employees, consumers and the general public. It has long-term dimensions that might well have a positive influence on the profit position in future. Sporting events and educational institutions such as schools are also often sponsored by large businesses. For example, Pick n Pay sponsors various sports events, as illustrated in the case study on page 362.

The other dimension of social responsibility hinges on the authority (legislation) under which the business operates. Should the business act irresponsibly or fail to abide by the laws of the land, reaction in terms of punitive legislation or, even, prosecution could result, as in the case of Leisurenet.

If a business were to disregard the norms of society, consumer resistance could result, thereby harming the primary objective of the business. Nothing should be done to violate the current norms or general moral and ethical standards of the community.

A sponsorship or a social-responsibility project must have a certain marketing benefit for the sponsor. Usually top management weighs up the merits of potential projects and decides which one to support because of its close relationship with the public and its ability to evaluate projects in terms of marketing benefits. However, it is the responsibility of marketing management to initiate projects.

A sponsorship must be supported by marketing communication to ensure a large audience. A sponsored event must also be well organised and managed. This usually requires the help of the public-relations department. An imaginative and successful social-responsibility project may mean publicity value for the business enterprise. Such projects are usually newsworthy, which ensures coverage in the mass media (newspapers, radio and television). In the case of sporting events, players usually display the name of the sponsor on equipment and clothing, while the sporting event itself offers opportunities to display brand names and marketing messages on billboards, flags and so on.

Marketing management should ensure that nothing is done that could be detrimental to the community. A case in point is the trouble taken to ensure that containers of harmful substances cannot easily be opened by children because of their tamper-proof packaging. Also, an advertisement that mocks religion, for example, offends the prevalent moral or ethical values of the community. This may provoke consumer resistance. Consumers may decide to avoid the product in future.

12.3.4 The principle of organisational integration

This principle expresses the need for close co-operation between all the functions of the business. All the functional decision-making activities should be co-ordinated in a way that will eventually lead to the successful marketing of the products of the business. Organisational integration entails close co-operation between the marketing, operational, purchasing and all other functions of the business in pursuit of the business's mission and objectives. Organisational integration is a prerequisite for success. The primary objective can never be achieved without it.

12.3.5 Merits of the marketing concept

The criticism often levelled at marketing – that it purposely exploits consumers, "robbing" them of hard-earned money to be wasted on useless articles – is refuted by the principles of the marketing concept. The true marketer is proud of his/her product and of the way it satisfies the needs of consumers. The marketer jealously guards the product's name, paying meticulous attention to complaints and criticism, even though his/her main purpose is continually to improve the profit position.

Edgars' responsibility towards society

Since 1997, Edgars has contributed more than R25 million towards community development and upliftment. The main focus has been on vulnerable children, women and families.

SOS Children's Villages have been raising orphaned and abandoned children in South Africa since 1982, and their cause has always been dear to Edgars, which has been actively involved in the project since 1997. The mission of SOS is to provide families for children who don't have their own, shape these children's futures and contribute to the development of their communities of origin. In the past three years, R5,5 million was donated to SOS.

Edgars has been involved in breast-cancer awareness campaigns since 2004. Around 4 000 South African women are diagnosed with breast cancer every year. To date, Edgars has contributed about R1,6 million to breast-cancer charities. It has also worked closely with organisations such as CANSA, Reach for Recovery and Journey of Hope.

In recognition of their customers' support throughout the years, Edgars contributed R2 million towards building a new operating theatre at the Red Cross Memorial Children's Hospital in Cape Town.

To mark its 80th anniversary, Edgars will also be sponsoring 80 students from disadvantaged communities as they study towards a qualification relevant to CFTA (clothing, footwear, textiles and accessories).

Sources: "Making a difference". *Edgars Magazine.* Special collector's edition, September 2009, p. 87 & "Scoring big with people". *Sunday Times* supplement, September 2009, p. 10.

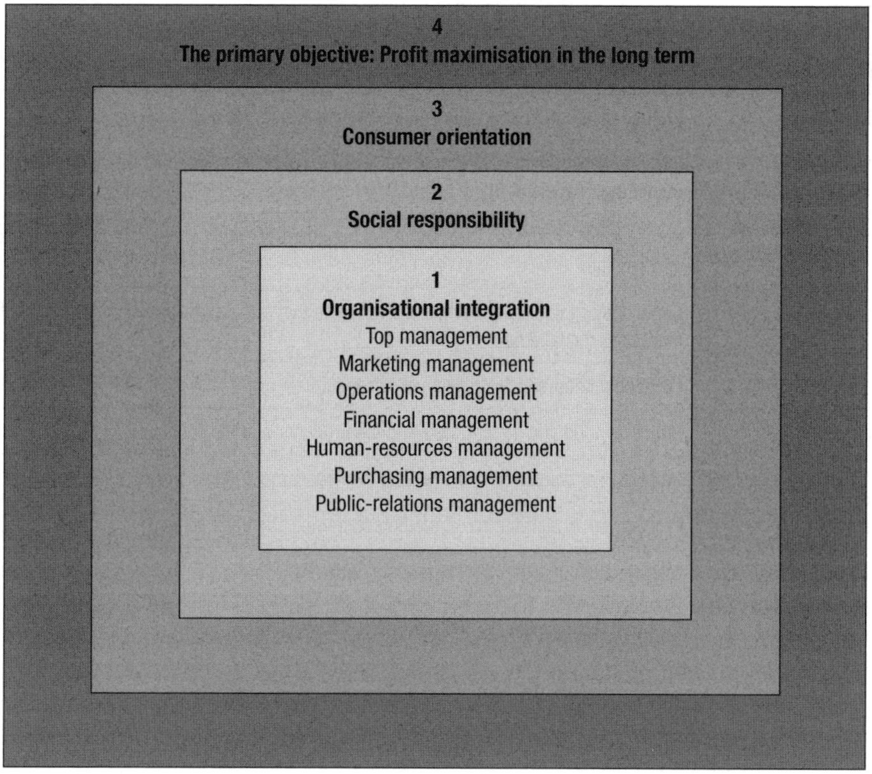

Figure 12.1: The marketing concept

According to the first principle of the marketing concept, long-term maximisation of profitability is the primary objective of the business and also that of marketing management. The business is entitled to this profit to offset the risks involved in developing products for the market. Figure 12.1 illustrates the four principles of the marketing concept, the philosophy according to which all marketing tasks are performed.

This concept provides the background for a full definition of marketing.

12.4 Defining marketing

Many people, including managers, see marketing as sales or as advertising. However, these are only aspects of marketing. **Marketing** consists of management tasks and decisions directed at successfully meeting opportunities and threats in a dynamic environment, by effectively developing and transferring a need-satisfying market offering to consumers in such a way that the objectives of the business, the consumer and society will be achieved[1].

Table 12.1 on page 366 gives an explanation of the key concepts.

12.5 The components of the marketing process[2]

In its simplest form, the marketing process entails the transfer of a product or service from one person to another. It is as old as humankind itself. Even in the earliest societies, people performed marketing activities of one kind or another. One primitive marketing process involved

Table 12.1: Key words in the definition of marketing

Management tasks	Planning, organising, leading, control
Decisions	Product distribution, marketing communication methods and price
Opportunities	Favourable circumstances in the marketing environment that must be utilised by marketing management
Threats	Unfavourable conditions that marketing management must endeavour to change into opportunities
Dynamic environment	Continually changing environmental variables that necessitate appropriate reaction from marketing management
Development	Creating a need-satisfying product or service
Transferring	Effectively bridging the gap between the producer and the consumer
Need-satisfying	Properties of a product based on what the consumer wants
Market offering	Product, price, distribution, marketing communication and service
Attainment of objectives: • The organisation • The consumer • Society	Maximisation of profitability in the long term Need satisfaction within the limits of the resources and capacities of the enterprise Ensuring the well-being of society in the longer term

bartering, where, for example, people would barter meat, of which they had a surplus, for grain that another person could spare. Initially, only useful products were bartered. Occasionally, however, one participant in a bartering transaction would use force to compel another person to participate in the exchange process.

In business management, marketing entails the transfer of a product from a business to a consumer. The fundamentals of the marketing process can be described as needs, and a transaction or exchange that leads to the satisfaction of these needs. Every time people attempt to satisfy their needs by means of an exchange, marketing is involved. However, in contrast to primitive bartering, consumers in today's free-market society are free to decide which products or services best satisfy their needs and also how much money they are willing to pay for them.

Consumers cannot be compelled to sacrifice money for a product offered by a marketer. They are free to decide for themselves what they want. However, marketers use marketing strategies to persuade consumers to accept their products. Hence, in its simplest form, the marketing process involves a transaction between at least two separate parties: a marketer (or organisation) attempting to achieve a specific objective and a consumer who wants to satisfy his/her needs. Figure 12.2 on page 367 illustrates this process. Work through the discussion that follows while referring to the figure.

In marketing management, four variables (the four Ps) are used for decision-making:

- the product itself
- the place where it is offered for sale (distribution of the product)
- the marketing communication methods used to inform consumers about the product
- the price, which reflects the product's value to consumers.

These four decision-making variables will be discussed in more detail in section 12.10. The four variables, which are known as the marketing mix, combine to form the

market offering that consumers purchase to satisfy their needs. Since the 1960s, these variables have been known as the 4 Ps of the **marketing mix** (product, place, promotion and price). Decisions about the use of the four Ps result in the **marketing strategy**, which is directed at specific consumers in a specific environment.

The market offering to consumers comprises a basic product with need-satisfying attributes. The price of this product, its easy availability and the information in the marketing communication message (advertisements) all contribute to the product's value or utility. A specific market offering is not supposed to satisfy the needs of one individual only, but rather a whole group of consumers or a **market segment**.

The larger the market segment, the more the organisation will benefit. In the total consumer market, there are various different groups of people or market segments. The people in each market segment share common characteristics and preferences. They also have similar consumption patterns and make similar product choices. From all the different market segments, the marketer selects a **target market** or several target markets. The market offering is often modified very slightly to meet the demands of the different target markets. It seldom happens that an organisation has only one target market.

As stated in Chapter 1, it is not possible for people to satisfy all their needs completely because needs are unlimited (even though resources for satisfying them are not). This means that the marketer can never fully meet consumer needs, especially those needs that are unrealistic. An example of an

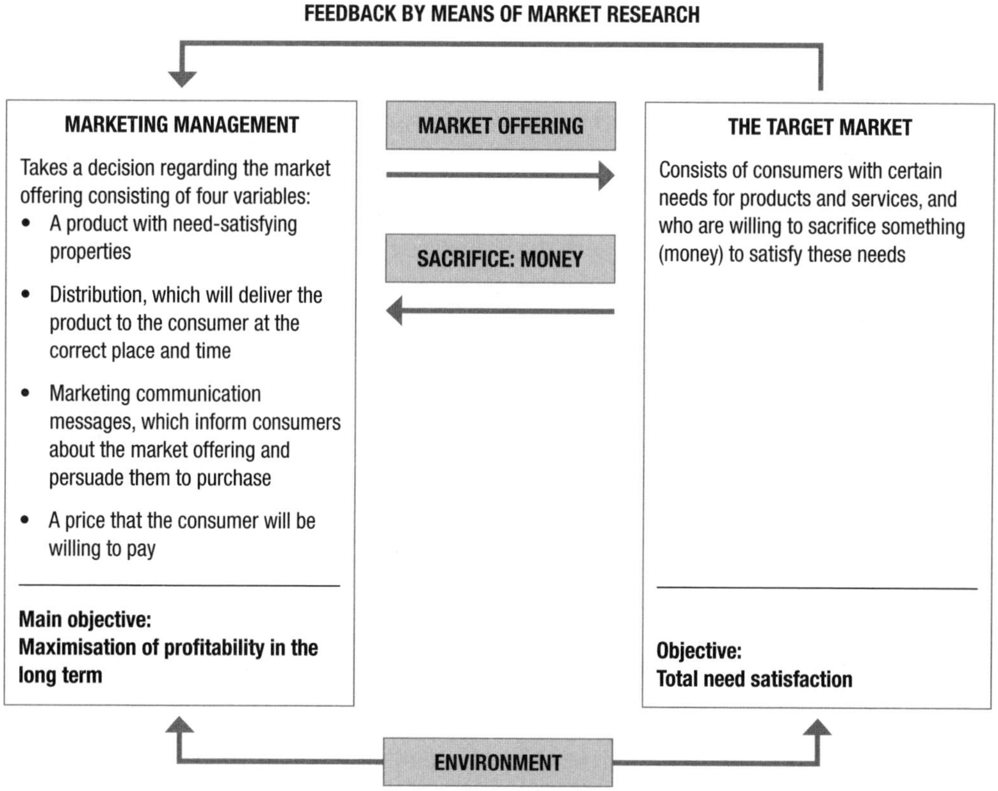

Figure 12.2: The marketing process

unrealistic need is a consumer demanding a Mercedes-Benz for the price of a Golf. Section 12.7 considers the **behaviour patterns of consumers** when they are attempting to satisfy unique needs, demands and preferences.

Profit-seeking has already been mentioned. Profit is the reason for the existence of any profit-seeking business. The marketing management of such an organisation therefore needs to strive towards this objective. This can be done by combining the four marketing instruments in an integrated marketing plan so as to maximise profits. Profitability should not only be achieved in the short term. Profitability in the long term is necessary for the organisation's survival and growth. Organisations that focus on short-term profit maximisation have a tendency to mislead or exploit consumers. To show any degree of long-term profitable growth, marketing management needs to maintain close contact with the market and to conduct market research regularly. Sometimes consumer preferences in the target market change or new competitors enter the market. Marketing management should be aware of every change that occurs, consider it carefully and then decide what to do about it.

There are often opportunities in the business environment that can be used to an organisation's benefit. There are also threats that have to be countered. By making timely changes in the four marketing instruments, marketing management can respond appropriately to these opportunities and threats. **Market research** (see section 12.6) is used to gain relevant information about the market, competitors and other environmental changes. Marketing management receives feedback on the market and the environment by conducting market research.

Look again at Figure 12.2 on page 367 and see the relationship between the **various components** of the marketing process. Note the direction of the arrows from the environment to marketing management and the target market. Both are influenced by environmental changes. In order to take effective decisions, marketing management needs feedback about the target market and the ever-changing environment.

The marketing process indicates a market-driven approach to marketing management. This approach is a distinctive characteristic of successful modern businesses. All the activities and decisions of marketing management are focused on the demands of the market. This is why market research is important.

12.6 Market research

12.6.1 The need for information

In order to manage a business effectively, a manager needs information. All businesses operate in an environment that is constantly changing. The components of the marketing environment were discussed in Chapter 4, where it was shown that continuous scanning of the micro-environment, market environment and macro-environment is necessary to identify the strong and weak points of the organisation. A SWOT analysis makes it possible to identify these strengths and weaknesses, as well as any opportunities and threats posed to the organisation, before managerial decisions are taken.

Information gathered by means of an environmental scan should include information on the following:

- external environmental variables and internal resources in the form of records and reports about current prices
- sales figures and market trends
- technological changes
- changes in market share
- consumer preferences
- new legislation
- production schedules
- internal financial problems.

Once it has been gathered, this information is arranged and stored so that it is easily accessible to marketing management.

Note that all marketing decisions are based on information about the micro-environment, market environment and macro-environment. If a problem occurs, existing information sources are consulted.

Sometimes, however, problems about which little or no information is available occur. In such cases, marketing management has to search for information before decisions can be taken. This is done by means of market research, which reveals distinctive information that provides solutions for problems regarding marketing decisions. To ensure that managers make good decisions, the information needs to:

- increase understanding of the relevant market segment and its consumers
- be pertinent to planning and controlling
- help in decision-making once alternative sources of information have been considered.

Figure 12.3 indicates that market research includes two broad types of research:

- problem-identification research
- problem-solving research.

12.6.2 Marketing-research methodology[3]

Market research can be defined as the systematic gathering, analysis and interpretation of information about all types of marketing problems by using recognised scientific methods for the accumulation of information to facilitate marketing management's decision-making.

This definition of market research refers to the use of recognised scientific methods for obtaining market data. One of the most common recognised scientific methods is the **survey method**. There are other research methods that can be used, but only the survey method will be described here. This method is a good example of an *ad hoc* research project where the information collected concerns a specific problem in the external or internal environment.

A **questionnaire** is used in the survey method. Questions are put to respondents by specially trained **field workers**, in person, telephonically or through the mail. The personal method of questioning is the most expensive and time-consuming method, because the field workers have to conduct a door-to-door survey, but it is still the best and most reliable method. The results of the survey can be subjected to statistical analysis to enable the researcher to draw meaningful conclusions. If the research has been conducted in a scientific manner, then the research results may point to a solution of the marketing problem.

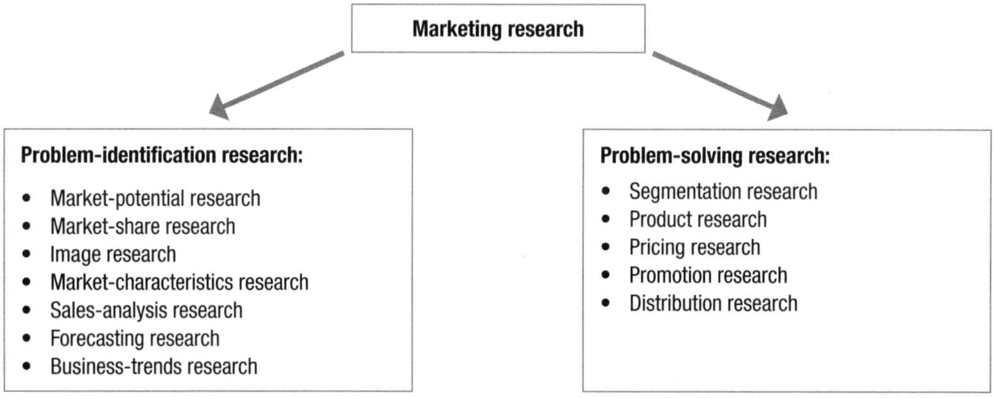

Figure 12.3: The two broad types of research in marketing research

There are 12 steps to follow when conducting a survey:

- **Step 1: Description of the problem to be investigated.** The research results will be useless unless the problem has been carefully defined.
- **Step 2: Formulation of probable explanations and causes for the defined problem.** The reasons provided are known as hypotheses. A hypothesis is a proposed explanation for the problem.
- **Step 3: Investigate all the hypotheses in order to eliminate the less likely ones and to find a solution to the problem.** Secondary information sources need to be consulted, for example, internal records and articles in trade journals, other marketing literature or the internet. The secondary data must first be evaluated in order to determine whether it can be used for the specific study. Investigation of existing secondary sources of information is known as desk research.
- **Step 4: Compilation of a questionnaire.** The compilation of a questionnaire requires skill. Each question has to be formulated carefully. The organisation's research department should be involved, and outside consultants and experts are often called in to assist. Questions on the gender, age, origin and language of the respondent should be included. Follow these steps when designing a questionnaire:
  - Specify the information needed.
  - Specify the type of interviewing method.
  - Determine the content of individual questions.
  - Design the questions to overcome the respondent's inability and unwillingness to answer.
  - Decide on the structure of the questions.
  - Determine the wording of the questions.
  - Arrange the questions in order.
  - Identify the form and layout.
  - Reproduce the questionnaire.
  - Pre-test the questionnaire.
- **Step 5: Testing of the questionnaire.** In order to ensure that all of the questions address the issue under investigation, the questions should be tested in the market before the actual research is conducted. The aim of this testing is to determine whether the questions are clear and the answers obtained are meaningful. Errors can be eliminated and mistakes rectified if the answers are ambiguous or meaningless. All aspects of the questionnaire need to be tested, including the content of the questions, the wording, the sequence, the form and layout, and the degree of difficulty of the questions and the instructions. Usually a small number of respondents (for example, ten) are used to test the questionnaire. It is, however, important that these respondents are representative of the group that will be tested.
- **Step 6: Selection of the respondents to whom the questions will be put.** The selection of respondents is known as drawing a sample. It is an important step because a biased sample leads to unreliable and invalid results. A representative sample should be selected so that every person in the target market has an equal chance of being included. For example, if homemakers are to be the respondents, then all the homemakers should have an equal chance of being selected. A list of the names and addresses of all the homemakers should be available to the marketer (researcher), who then randomly draws as many respondents as the size of the sample dictates. Only these homemakers are to be questioned and the field worker has to obtain permission to substitute one name for another name that was not included on the original list. If field workers are allowed to pick and choose, they may select only respondents who seem friendly, respondents who are about their own age or respondents whom they know personally. As a rule, it is difficult and expensive to draw a representative sample, although this is the most reliable method.

Usually a sample is drawn according to the judgement of the researcher, who decides how many respondents in each group need to be questioned.

- **Step 7: Training of the field workers.** Field work is an exacting task requiring thorough training. Training ensures that all field workers understand the questionnaire in the same way. Training should include making contact with the respondent and should cover the whole process until termination of the interview. Field workers need to know how to react to respondents who do not want to participate in the study. Field workers should ask the questions exactly as formulated in the questionnaire and should enter the responses correctly. It is important to control the execution of the field work and the completed questionnaires. The head of the marketing-research section can do this by contacting a few respondents to check whether the field workers have completed the questionnaires properly.
- **Step 8: Analysis and assimilation of information collected from the questionnaires.** A computer is usually used for this. Statistical methods facilitate the processing of information and the drawing of conclusions. Exploratory data analysis makes it possible for researchers to look at data to determine relationships and trends. Most of the research houses use more specialised programs (for example, SPSS, SAS or Statistica) for exploratory and inferential statistical analysis. These methods also include determining the mean, percentages, confidence intervals, regression and variance analysis.
- **Step 9: Interpretation of the information.** The researcher needs to decide which data to include in the research report. In the example we have been discussing, the information would show the reasons for the decline in sales. The initial hypothesis needs to be proved or disproved. The researcher interprets the reasons and draws meaningful conclusions.
- **Step 10: Writing of the research report and making of recommendations based on the conclusions.** The research report "tells the story" of the research project, gives the method used, and presents the collected information in tables, figures and graphs. It should summarise the statistical results and be presented so that it can be used as direct information for management decisions. A conclusion and possible recommendations can be made from the information. Before writing the report, the researcher needs to discuss the important results, conclusions and recommendations with the decision-makers. This will ensure that the final report satisfies the needs of the consumer. The research team's task is complete when the report is complete and has been presented to marketing management.

Example

Suppose the research shows that 70% of the respondents made a negative comparison between the organisation's product and the product of a competitor. In addition, 80% of the respondents indicated that they did not intend to purchase the product. It is easy to draw the conclusion that there is something wrong with the product compared to its competitor. However, it is more difficult to make a recommendation. Should the product be withdrawn or should it be improved? If it is improved, who is to say that the improvement will be to consumers' liking? If the questionnaire has been compiled properly, the analysis will provide answers to these questions.

- **Step 11: Management evaluation.** Management studies the report, evaluates its value and then decides either to accept or reject the recommendations.
- **Step 12: Implementation of management's decisions.** This is the final step. It will hopefully lead to a solution of the problem that was outlined in the first step.

Example

Suppose that marketing management has considered the research report and decided to accept the recommendation to improve the product. The purchasing and operation departments need to be informed about the proposed improvements. They must be told if the changes will necessitate different raw materials or methods, for example. Marketing management has to launch a campaign to inform consumers about the "new" product. Decisions need to be taken about the price, for example, the announcement of a price discount for a period of one month after the announcement occurs. Old labels will not be used any more so new labels with information about the improvements need to be designed and printed.

After a period, a further research project will have to be undertaken to determine whether or not the decisions taken and implemented were indeed correct.

The examples we have discussed entailed a survey of consumer demands and preferences. Market research can be done in more or less the same way to investigate problems with dealers, competitors and suppliers. An internal survey can also be conducted to determine the opinions of the personnel of the organisation. Sale representatives, for example, could be chosen as respondents.

12.6.3 Market forecasting

In order to be able to exploit an opportunity, the potential in terms of profit has to be established. If the potential profit is negligible, then the opportunity may be deemed to be not worth pursuing, and *vice versa* . Measuring the size of the opportunity entails the forecasting of future sales (sales forecasting) and the forecasting of the contribution to profit.

12.6.3.1 Sales forecasting

The following types of forecasting are often used:

- forecasting done by a panel of experts from within the organisation and from outside
- forecasting based on market-research results, for example, the number of potential consumers who have indicated that they want to buy the product could serve as a basis for the sales forecast for the next period
- forecasting based on the consumers' reactions in test marketing situations
- forecasting based on historical data (the previous year's sales figures could serve as the starting point)
- forecasting based on mathematical and statistical models (for example, probability models).

A combination of sales forecasting methods is often employed in practice. It is, however, extremely difficult to predict future sales as a number of factors can and will influence sales. It is nevertheless the task of marketing management to forecast not only future sales, but also to predict how uncontrollable environmental variables will influence the sales figures. In the case of new products, it becomes more difficult to predict sales as there is no history or track record to work from. Even if there is a track record, uncontrollable factors such as the recession of 2009 can seriously effect even the most carefully researched and predicted sales. Accurate sales forecasts can mean the difference between a company's survival or failure.

12.6.3.2 Forecasting of the profit contribution

The forecasting of the profit contribution of a marketing opportunity is normally done for long-term periods. It is usually done for the full payback period (the time taken to recoup capital expenses incurred in producing a product). During the payback period, the sum of money invested in utilising an opportunity has to be recovered through the earnings generated by sales. The payback amounts include the rate of return decided on at the outset by top management.

The financial aspects of forecasting the profit contribution are discussed in the chapter on financial management.

Not all consumers are the same, but all consumers are unpredictable. Thus it is important to study **consumer behaviour**.

Applying the concept: Market research

Most successful companies engage in some sort of market research before committing resources to a new product or investing in changes in existing products. When Woolworths decided to start adding other well-known brands to the Woolworths range, the step was preceded by extensive research amongst customers. The choice of which brands to add to the Woolworths brands was made in accordance with customers' preferences and levels of brand loyalty. Various methods were employed to obtain information and various reference groups were consulted.

12.7 Consumer behaviour[4]

Consumer behaviour refers to the behaviour patterns of decision-making units (individuals or families) directly involved in the purchase and use of products, including the decision-making processes preceding and determining these behaviour patterns. From this definition, it is clear that consumer behaviour consists of **overt acts** (that is, acts that can be observed by people). A consumer can be seen buying a product, enjoying it, looking at it, placing it back on the shelf or throwing it away unused. At the same time, consumer behaviour also includes **covert processes**, which cannot be seen. A consumer cannot be seen considering his/her financial position, weighing the merits of different branded products or doubting the promises made in advertising appeals, for example. Marketers need to know why consumers behave as they do because consumer behaviour can then be **explained, influenced** and **predicted**. Knowledge of the factors that determine consumer behaviour forms the basis for consumer-oriented marketing strategies.

The next section will look at the determinants of consumer behaviour, or the factors that may explain consumer behaviour. The decision-making process and the continual changes in the behaviour patterns of consumers will also be examined.

A consumer receives inputs (stimuli) from his/her environment. The outputs are what happens. The consumer's actions are observable results of the input stimuli. Between the inputs and outputs are the constructs: the processes though which the consumer goes to decide upon his/her actions.

Figure 12.4 on page 374 illustrates a model that can be used to explain consumer behaviour. **Individual factors** and **group factors** influence consumer decision-making, and may eventually lead to repeat purchasing of a specific market offering.

12.7.1 Determinants of consumer behaviour

Two main group of factors (determinants) determine consumer behaviour:

- individual factors peculiar to a particular person
- group factors.

Individual decision-making is usually straightforward. Decision-making by a buying centre requires consideration of the different roles of members of the buying centre, the differing interpretations of objectives, the interpersonal influences, the relative power and the need for some resolution of possible conflicts among members of the buying group.

12.7.1.1 Individual factors

Needs, attitudes, perception, learning abilities and personal traits are individual factors

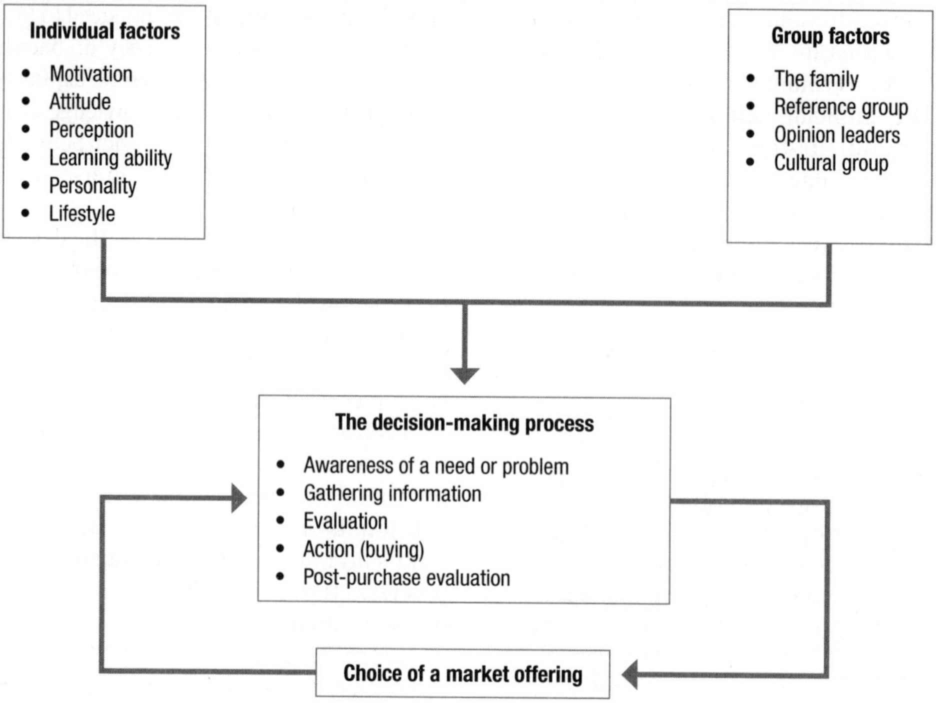

Figure 12.4: Determinants of consumer behaviour

that determine what a consumer will or will not buy. Needs (also called motives) are the driving force behind all behaviour patterns. Maslow's hierarchy of needs was discussed in Chapter 11, where it was shown that people's behaviour patterns are directed at the satisfaction of basic survival, security, social and ego needs.

Consumers buy bread, for example, to satisfy a basic **survival** need: hunger. They buy insurance to satisfy the need for **security**. They might buy flowers to fulfill their **social** need for love. They might buy expensive cars as a status symbol to provide some measure of ego satisfaction. They might focus on hobbies to satisfy the need for self-realisation. Maslow maintained that people attempt to satisfy their needs in a specific hierarchical sequence. The basic needs have to be satisfied before other needs can be attended to.

People's needs are unlimited and they never reach a point where all their needs are met. This is why consumers keep buying, even if they already have more possessions than they can use. Advertisements attempt to draw people's attention to unsatisfied needs that can be met by buying a specific product. Although the needs are universal (that is, they apply to all people), need patterns differ from person to person. An asocial person does not have as many social needs as, for example, a very social person. People's needs determine what they decide to buy and what not to buy.

Attitudes also determine purchasing patterns. A consumer with a positive attitude towards a particular product can perhaps be persuaded to buy the product, whereas a person with a negative attitude will not buy the product. For example, a mother with a positive attitude towards healthy food might be persuaded to buy margarine with extra vitamins for her children. Conversely, a teetotaler has a negative attitude towards alcoholic beverages, and therefore he/she will not react positively towards advertisements for them. It follows that marketers need to make every effort to prevent the development of negative attitudes towards their market offerings. Once a consumer has decided to avoid a particular product because it was faulty, too expensive, of bad quality or had the wrong taste, the consumer's negative attitude will not change easily. Marketers can, however, try to reinforce existing positive attitudes or turn neutral attitudes into positive attitudes through their marketing communication messages.

Consumers' **perceptions** determine what they pay attention to and what excites their interest. Consumers hear only those things that they want to hear and see only what captures their interest. This means that they subconsciously choose whether to pay attention to a marketing message or not. Furthermore, consumers' perceptions can cause them to attach their own interpretation to a message, which may not be quite what the marketer intended. Consumers seem able to defend or protect themselves against the content of communication in which they are not interested. For this reason, marketers sometimes find it difficult to convey a message in such a way that the person receiving it understands the message. Marketers should bear this in mind when creating marketing messages. Thus an advertisement needs to be simple to ensure understanding of the message, it should have some impact to attract attention and it must contain a promise of need satisfaction. If an advertisement does not meet these criteria, consumers could distort the message or ignore it completely.

The **learning ability** of consumers determines whether they are able to learn the marketer's "lesson" about the benefits of a particular product that make it worth paying for. In addition, the marketer should "teach" consumers the product's name in such a way that they remember it. Sometimes consumers forget the name of the product they intend to purchase, but they are still able to remember the characteristics of the packaging. This underlines the importance of packaging. Reminder advertising, in which only the name of the product is shown in distinctive lettering, helps to remind consumers of what they have learnt from the marketer.

Personality traits also influence consumers' purchasing patterns. People can be described by means of these traits. For example, a person could be described as cheerful, optimistic or aggressive. It is difficult to relate personal characteristics to product choice. Usually people's traits, in conjunction with other characteristics, determine what they buy and use. As a rule, a combination of people's personality traits and other characteristics determine their lifestyle. Different groups have different lifestyles. The lifestyle of students, for example, differs from that of families, and the lifestyle of farmers differs from that of people in the city. Lifestyle classification can be used to segment the consumer market. We shall discuss market segmentation in section 12.8.

12.7.1.2 Group factors

Group factors refer to the influence of various groups on consumer purchasing patterns. These groups include the following:

- the family
- reference groups
- opinion leaders
- culture group.

These groups are discussed in more detail below.

The family

Children learn their consumer function in their families. At seven, a child already understands that his/her needs can be satisfied by a process of purchase and consumption.

The family is also a decision-making unit whose members decide about purchasing products that will provide the greatest degree of need satisfaction for the family as a whole. Family members have certain roles.

One member may be the buyer (perhaps the mother), another member of the family may be the decision-maker (the father, possibly), while yet another family member (a child, for example) may be the consumer. Marketers need to know the role structure of families in their target market, because the marketing message needs to be based on such knowledge. A marketer of breakfast cereal, for example, appeals to the child who could be the decision-maker for this product. Children also play a role in family decision-making by acting as initiators and making suggestions about products of which their parents may know little. For example, boys often know more than their parents about how to use a camera or video recorder, while teenage girls are knowledgeable about the cosmetics their parents might use.

Reference groups

A reference group is any group against which people can evaluate their own behaviour and purchasing patterns. Most people want to be part of some group or other. They may imitate the habits and purchasing patterns of the group in order to gain acceptance. A circle of friends, a social club and a work group are examples of reference groups. Often, people who do not conform to group norms are ignored, held in contempt or ridiculed. For example, a teenage boy who does not own a motorbike cannot become a member of a biker group. A person who wants to become a member of a tennis club should not only be able to play tennis, but also needs to buy tennis outfits, a racquet, balls, socks and shoes.

Advertisements often portray group approval to attract the attention of those striving to gain acceptance and group membership. For example, an advertisement for a car could show friends and neighbours admiring the car, with a house in the background reflecting an upmarket neighbourhood. The implication of this is that the buyer of the car will automatically gain acceptance in a wealthy neighbourhood.

There are, however, also negative groups with which association is undesirable. Conservative, older and highly educated people, for example, often see skinheads and bikers as negative groups, and therefore disapprove of everything they do or purchase. Choosing a particular reference group to portray in an advertisement is difficult, because what one person may regard as a positive group with which to be associated may well be regarded as negative by another person.

There is a strong relationship between reference-group influence and the choice of luxury products, but the relationship is rather weak in the case of necessities. However, if the product is visible, the relationship is stronger. A good example is detergent. As many advertisements suggest, a user of detergent can easily be influenced by the "expert" advice of other, more experienced users.

Opinion leaders

They have an important function in the marketing communication process, acting as a go-between in what is known as the two-step flow of communication. Research has shown that information does not flow directly from the mass media to individual consumers in the target market, but is channeled through a person, the **opinion leader**. This person interprets and evaluates the information, and then relays acceptance or rejection of the message to other consumers in the market.

The role of the opinion leader is especially important in the purchasing of new products that have a high risk of financial loss. In the case of a new fashion, for example, a fashion-opinion leader will accept the risk of ridicule or financial loss, which ordinary consumers are usually anxious to avoid. Ordinary consumers usually only become interested after the new fashion has been vetted and approved by the opinion leader. Sports stars often act as opinion leaders in advertisements for sports equipment, reducing the risk of poor decision-making when an ordinary consumer makes the purchase.

Every consumer is a member of various reference groups. A person could be an opinion leader for a certain product while being a follower for another. One of the tasks of marketing management is to identify the opinion leader and reference group that will ensure the acceptance of its advertising message in a specific target market.

Cultural group

The cultural group to which a person belongs has a strong influence on his/her purchasing and consumption patterns. Culture comprises a complex system of values, norms and symbols, which develop in a society over time and which are shared by the society's members. Cultural values, norms and symbols are created by people and transmitted from generation to generation to ensure survival and facilitate adaptation to circumstances. Schools, churches and other social institutions also play an important role. This process is referred to as socialisation.

Each cultural group comprises several subcultures, each with its own values, norms and symbols. There are four key subcultures, categorised according to nationality, religion, race and geographical area. Besides the four main groups, smaller subcultures can also develop, perhaps according to language, age, interests or occupation.

South African society consists of many cultural groups and subgroups. Although white people are not numerically dominant, their norms, values and symbols exert great influence on the economic environment. For this reason, most advertisements reflect western culture.

12.7.2 Consumer decision-making

Every decision a consumer takes involves risks. The risks are often functional. If a product is deficient or does not work as the consumer expected it to, the consumer feels that he/she has wasted money. There are also social risks involved in decision-making. If the reference group does not approve of the purchase, the consumer may be ridiculed. To reduce the risks inherent in decision-making, consumers may wait a long time before taking a decision, thereby extending the decision-making process. During this time, and during all the phases of decision-making, marketers attempt to influence consumers to decide in favour of their market offering.

There are four influences in any organisational buying decision:

- the environment
- the organisation itself
- the buying group
- the individual buyer.

Environmental influences include the technological state of the buyer's industry, the state of the economy, government regulations, and legal and cultural factors. These factors influence the organisational climate. Group influences are broken down into task-related interactions and no-task interactions (personal motives). An individual's motives, perceptions, personality and role within the organisation influence his/her interactions within a buying centre, and thus influence the final decision process.

When making a complex decision about high-priced products, complex products and speciality goods, consumers evaluate brands in a detailed and comprehensive way. More information is sought and more brands are evaluated than is the case in other types of decision-making situation. Marketing management needs to know how consumer decisions are reached because consumer behaviour almost always entails a choice between alternatives. Marketers want to influence the decisions of the consumer. Consumer decisions are not made suddenly. The decision-making process moves systematically through various phases. Figure 12.4 on page 374 shows these five phases:

- **Phase 1: Awareness of an unsatisfied need or a problem.** A consumer experiences a difference between the current situation and the situation that he/she desires. This leads to the seeking of a solution to this problem. For example, an empty or broken container indicates a consumer need. A leaking pen may indicate a need to buy a new pen. Marketers try, by means of advertising, to make consumers aware of problems and unsatisfied needs.

- **Phase 2: Gathering of information on how best to solve the problem.** Consumers recall information or collect relevant information from external sources. They consult friends, read advertisements or visit shops to obtain more information. Marketers must make sure that the necessary information is available.
- **Phase 3: Evaluation of the possible solutions.** Consumers use criteria such as price, quality, performance standards, ethical characteristics and aesthetic qualities to gauge the contribution a product will make to need satisfaction and their lifestyle. Conflict is caused by conflicting or unsuitable criteria or criteria that cannot be compared easily. Advertisements therefore need to emphasise the benefits and utility of the product. For example, many pen advertisements reflect neatness, continuous writing and style. These characteristics are important for a consumer buying a pen. The provision of samples that can be used to test the product, a money-back guarantee or a quality mark such as the mark of the South African Bureau of Standards (SABS) can help consumers resolve conflict.
- **Phase 4: Decision on a course of action or purchase.** Although consumers might indicate intent to buy a product, this does not mean that they will in fact do so. Therefore advertisements encourage the consumer to act and purchase the product, for example by using an injunction such as: "Buy now!" When consumers act and buy the product, this entails a sacrifice (money must be paid). The transaction should therefore be concluded as painlessly as possible. If a consumer is forced to queue to pay or comes into contact with uninterested sales staff, he/she might decide to reverse the decision to buy the product. When a consumer has made the decision to buy and is ready to pay, marketers should make a special effort to ensure the consumer's goodwill. Helpful sales staff, credit facilities and point-of-purchase promotions all help to encourage the purchasing action.
- **Phase 5: Post-purchase evaluation.** In this phase, consumers evaluate purchases by using them and testing whether or not they satisfy their needs. Consumers might wonder whether they have made the right decision. If a product does not provide the satisfaction consumers expect, they may decide not to buy the product again and might influence friends to avoid it. Advertisements are often directed at people who have already purchased a product in order to reassure them that they have indeed made the right decision.

In the case of an expensive or important product such as a house, decision-making can be a long and arduous process. A person could take months to decide which type of washing machine to buy. However, in the case of impulse-buying, a consumer can move through all five phases of the decision-making process in a few seconds.

Habitual purchasing is the result of previous decisions. If a consumer is loyal to a particular brand, it may become a habit to purchase the product consistently without having to make the decision again every time.

The conclusion that can be drawn is that the theory of consumer behaviour, as it has been described briefly here, is explanatory up to a point. It provides guidelines for influencing consumers, for example, through striking advertisements. However, the many factors that can influence consumer behaviour make it virtually impossible to predict this behaviour. Marketers nevertheless attempt to do so, because market forecasting depends largely on this prediction.

Marketing management will probably never satisfy all the needs, demands and preferences of the market. Therefore the market strategy should be directed only at those groups (market segments) that are profitable and accessible.

12.8 Market segmentation

A market consists of people with different needs and wants. Not all people like the same colours or the same style of clothing. The range of diffferent cars, clothing, sweets, types of restaurant and so on that are available makes it clear that people have different preferences. It is the responsibility of the marketer to evaluate these needs and wants, and to decide which need/s or wants/s he/she would like to satisfy. No organisation can satisfy all the needs of all consumers (the market). It is therefore important that an organisation focus on some groups or segments of the market and aim to satisfy just that group's needs.

The term "market" means different things to different people. In brief, a market consists of a relatively large number of people (or organisations) who:

- have a need for a specific product
- have the money to buy the product
- are willing to spend money on it
- are legally able to buy the product.

In order for a market to exist, all of these people or organisations need to be in place. So, for example, if you have a great product and people do not have money to buy it, you do not have a market for your product. Similarly, a company cannot start marketing a new cigarette to school children as it is illegal to do so, even though many children do smoke.

Each of the different types of market has its own criteria and characteristics. The total market in a country can be subdivided into the following markets:

- The **consumer market** consists of individuals or households purchasing products for their own consumption.
- The **industrial market** consists of individuals, groups of people or organisations purchasing materials and products to be used in the production process.
- The **resale market** includes individuals, groups or organisations purchasing products in order to sell them to final consumers, for example, retailers.
- The **government market** consists of the state institutions and departments that purchase various products needed to supply services to the public.

In the discussion of the marketing function in this book, attention is focused mainly on the **consumer market**, although the principles of marketing discussed here are also applicable to the other markets. In industrial marketing, though, personal selling is more important than advertising, which is the most effective way of communicating with the consumer market. However, personal selling is seldom used in the government market.

The consumer market is very diverse with numerous markets. A person can, for example, be a part of many different markets and play different roles in these different markets. There is a market for vehicles, for food products, for clothing and so on. There are different submarkets in each of these markets. For example, the clothing market consists of markets for ladies' clothing, men's clothing, children's clothing, school clothing and so on. Consumers are members of various markets according to their needs. An elderly couple is not likely to be part of the market for children's clothes, for example. Rather, they are in the market for leisure and travel clothing. Their children have probably already left home, so they focus on their own needs and wants instead of those of their children. Each separate market for a specific product can be subdivided into segments, as not all people have exactly the same needs.

Effective market segmentation should follow these steps:

- Identify the needs of the consumers in the market.

- Group these identified needs of the consumers into homogeneous subgroups or segments that have similar characteristics.
- Select target markets on which the company will focus its marketing effort based on its resources and know-how.
- Position the product or service offering within the selected segment or segments.

12.8.1 The total-market approach (market aggregation)

Marketing management may decide to target all consumers in a similar way if they assume that all potential consumers have similar preferences and needs regarding the market offering. This uniform approach is followed in marketing staples such as salt, sugar and flour, because virtually everyone requires these products and wants them in more or less standard packaging.

Market aggregation is, however, more the exception than the rule. Even in the case of staple items, it is not always applicable. Premier Milling, for example, markets different kinds of Snowflake flour in packs with different colours. Even though it would be more cost effective to have one product, one type of packaging, one price, one distribution channel and one marketing message directed at the mass market, it is seldom possible to do so because the market is not homogeneous. People are not the same, so they have different needs.

It is therefore better for the marketer to try to satisfy the divergent needs of specific market segments rather than provide only some measure of satisfaction to everyone in the total market.

12.8.2 The market-segmentation approach

Market segmentation is the process in which the total heterogeneous market is divided into smaller, more homogeneous groups with relatively uniform needs or characteristics. Attempts are made to satisfy the needs of different homogeneous groups by developing different market offerings. Marketing management can follow a multi-segment approach, in which many different segments are served with some basic product or with small product modifications. Alternatively, it can select only one segment of the market and concentrate its marketing effort on that segment.

Figure 12.5 on page 381 illustrates the three approaches to market segmentation:

- the total-market approach (market aggregation)
- a single-segment approach
- a multi-segment approach.

The first approach in Figure 12.5 shows that marketing management concentrates on only one market offering aimed at the total market. The second approach shows that marketing management selects a specific target market and aims its market offering only at that market, paying no attention to other segments of the market. The third approach shows that three separate market offerings are made to three different target markets. Remember that any changes, however small, in the product itself (for example, in packaging), the price, the distribution channel, the marketing communication methods or the marketing communication messages mean that a different market offering is being made.

The marketer of Johnson's baby products identified women and sportspeople as separate market segments in addition to people with babies. Even though the baby powder is sold in the same packaging and at the same price to all three market segments, the marketing messages differ greatly. In reality, this means that three different market offerings are being made to three separate market segments. If the product is intended for babies, the advertisement shows a mother lovingly caring for a baby. When it is intended for sportspeople or women, the advertisements show models with whom adults can identify. In these cases, the models act as opinion leaders.

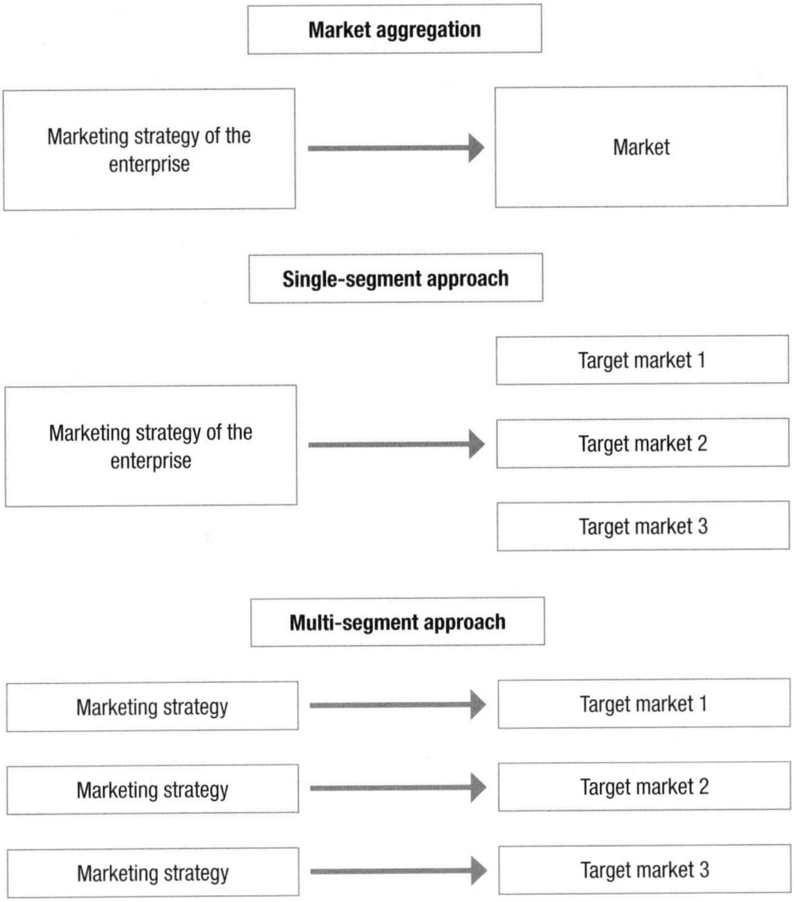

Figure 12.5: Approaches to market segmentation

Even when marketing management has succeeded in identifying a promising segment of the market, it does not necessarily follow that a market offering will be developed for that segment. Certain requirements have to be satisfied before marketing management can claim a segment as a target market.

12.8.3 Requirements for meaningful market segmentation

In order for segmentation to be meaningful, the following criteria must be met:

- **The segment must be identifiable and measurable.** In other words, it must be possible to identify the segment and measure its size. Data about provinces, sex, age and so on are readily available, but data on people who are prepared to test a new medical product are not readily available.
- **The segment must be substantial and sustainable.** In other words, the segment should be large enough to make profitable exploitation possible and it must be sustainable over a period of time. The fragmented population in South Africa makes it possible to distinguish various small market segments. Some of these segments are, however, so small that it would not be profitable to develop separate market offerings for them all.

- **The segment must be reachable.** In other words, it should be possible for marketing management to reach its chosen segment with its product and marketing communication methods.
- **The segment must be responsive.** For a segment to be cultivated, it needs to be receptive to a separate approach. If all consumers are equally conscious of a product, there is no need to offer high, medium and low prices to different segments.

When marketing management is satisfied that these requirements have been met with regard to a particular market segment, it can select this segment as a target market. A target market is a specific segment for which marketing management can develop and implement a marketing strategy. The question to be answered now is: How does marketing management isolate the factors or criteria according to which homogeneous groups in the total consumer market are to be distinguished? Several of these criteria have already been mentioned, for example, age and language.

12.8.4 Criteria for market segmentation

The total market can be **segmented** into different groups according to a variety of criteria, as shown in Table 12.2 on page 383.

Segmenting the market according to demographic and geographic criteria usually gives a good indication of the potential of particular market segments, that is, the number of consumers in each segment. Segmentation according to the psychographic and product-usage criteria gives an indication of the reasons for consumers' choice and purchase of specific products. Each of these criteria merits further scrutiny.

12.8.4.1 Geographic criteria

Geographic criteria relate to place of residence. Geographic factors result in the development of different need patterns, thereby affording marketers opportunities they can use.

12.8.4.2 Demographic criteria

Marketers often segment the market according to **demographic** criteria, as the information is easily obtainable. For example, it is easy to determine how many students are registered for this course, and therefore how large the potential market is for this book.

The other demographic variables mentioned in Table 12.2 are self-explanatory and therefore will not be discussed separately.

12.8.4.3 Psychographic criteria

Table 12.2 shows the main **psychographic** variables according to which markets can be segmented. The main variables in this group are personality factors and lifestyle.

Personality traits are difficult to quantify, but they nevertheless offer opportunities to marketing management for market segmentation.

Aggressiveness, conservatism, optimism, progressiveness and materialism are examples of personality traits of individuals. Marketers know that these traits are related to product and brand selection. Many advertisements aimed at men, for example, contain elements of aggressiveness to capture their attention because men tend to be more aggressive than women. Lifestyle segmentation comprises a group of characteristics known as the AIO classification (activities, interests and opinions of the consumers).

12.8.4.4 Behavioural criteria

Table 12.2 shows the behavioural criteria according to which the consumer market can be segmented. **Product usage** refers to the way in which products are used by different consumers. Consumers can be light, medium or heavy users of a product, and they can be

Table 12.2: Criteria (bases) for segmenting consumer markets

Bases	Possible variables
1. Geographic	
Region	Gauteng, Durban-Pinetown, Cape Peninsula, KwaZulu-Natal, Northern Province
Size of city or town	Under 10 000, 10 000–20 000, 20 000–25 000, over 25 000 inhabitants
Density	Urban, suburban, rural
Climate	Summer rainfall, winter rainfall, very hot and humid, very hot and dry
2. Demographic	
Age	Under 7, 7–13, 14–19, 20–34, 35–49, 50–65, above 65 years
Gender	Male, female
Family size	One and two, three and four, more than four members
Family life cycle	Young, married without children; young, married with children; older, married with children; married couples without children living at home; singles
Income	Under R20 000, R20 001–R50 000, R50 001–R80 000, R80 001–R110 000, R110 001–R140 000, R140 001–R170 000, over R170 000
Occupation	Professional and technical, managerial, clerical, sales and related services, farmers, students, housewives, unemployed, retired
Religion	Protestant, Catholic, Muslim, Hindu, Jewish
Race	White, Black, Coloured, Asian
Education	Grade 10, Matric, diploma, degree, postgraduate
3. Psychographic	
Lifestyle	Conservative, liberal
Personality	Gregarious, authoritarian, impulsive, ambitious
Social class	Upper class, middle class, lower class
4. Behavioural	
Purchase occasion	Regular use, special occasion
Benefits sought	Economy, convenience, prestige, speed, service
User status	Non-user, ex-user, potential user, regular user
Usage rate	Heavy user, medium user, light user
Loyalty status	None, medium, strong, absolute
Readiness stage	Unaware, aware, informed, interested, desirous, intending to buy
Attitude to product	Enthusiastic, positive, indifferent, negative, hostile

Source: Cant, M.C., Strydom, J.W., Jooste, C.J. & Du Plessis, F.J. 2006. *Marketing management.* 5th ed. Cape Town: Juta, p. 107.

existing or potential consumers. Teetotalers are non-users of liquor, and all attempts by a marketer to persuade this group to become users will be to no avail. However, marketers often attempt to persuade light and medium consumers of a specific product to purchase more of the product. A good example is potato chips, which were initially seen as a snack for consumption at social events. However, consumers are now encouraged to eat them at any time of the day, even during ordinary meals.

Brand loyalty is a behavioural criterion that is encouraged by marketers because when consumers are loyal to a particular brand, the competitive position of the marketer is strengthened. Brand-loyal consumers buy products that have provided need satisfaction previously, and they do not think twice about doing so. Black consumers tend to be more brand loyal than White consumers. The following brands enjoy considerable loyalty from many Black consumers: Super Sun, Zambuk and Black Label. Brand loyalty develops only if a product provides such complete need satisfaction that the consumer never even considers competing products.

Some consumers are extremely **price sensitive** and can be persuaded to buy a product by means of small decreases in price. These consumers are always on the look-out for discount shops and like to bargain. Most wealthy consumers are not price sensitive. They will usually purchase what they need and are averse to shopping around for bargains or sales.

Reverse price sensitivity means that consumers react negatively when a price is perceived to be too low. They immediately conclude that the cheap product lacks quality. They associate high prices with good quality and low prices with poor quality. If prices are reduced, these consumers buy less instead of more.

Consumers can also be sensitive to service, quality and advertisements. The advertisement promising: "You are Number One" is directed at consumers who are sensitive to service quality, while the "Quest for Zero Defect" points to quality excellence for quality-sensitive buyers. Other consumers are sensitive to advertising and respond immediately when an advertisement attracts their attention. They are ready to buy if they perceive the message as promising.

The total potential market for a product can also be divided into segments according to the benefits a product is thought to offer. The box that follows shows the segmentation of the toothpaste market according to benefits.

Product benefits of a toothpaste

The product benefits that a consumer might expect from a toothpaste may include:

- tingly feeling
- fresh smell
- crispy feeling
- social acceptance
- fresh breath
- ease of use
- effectiveness.

The market for margarine is also segmented according to **product benefits**. Some people use margarine for a healthier life because of its low cholesterol content, while other people are motivated by its vitamin content, the belief that it helps them to lose weight or because it is a cheap substitute for butter. Some marketers follow a multi-segment approach and promise all the benefits listed above. According to their advertisements, their margarine not only encourages weight loss, but also prevents cholesterol and tastes pleasant.

Criteria are often combined to define a **segment profile**.

12.8.5 Segment profiles

Demographic, geographic and usage criteria together provide a profile of a specific segment, as shown in the example in the box on page 385.

Profile of Rooibos tea consumer

The consumers of Rooibos tea can be divided into two groups: the primary and the secondary group. The primary group is Black people (all income groups) in the age group of 16–34 years. The secondary group is White people in the age group of 16–34 years. The reason for the grouping is because young adults have a high life time value and they teach younger people to drink tea.

Source: Cant, M.C. & Machado, R. 2002. *Marketing success stories.* 4th ed. Cape Town: Oxford University Press, p. 169.

12.9 Target-market selection and positioning

Once the heterogeneous total mass market has been subdivided into smaller homogeneous segments, the marketer has to identify a segment that looks promising as a target market. The objectives and resources of the business have to be carefully considered before a target market can be selected. When selecting target markets, the abilities and expertise of the business have to be linked to the characteristics of consumers in the different market segments. A market offering is developed for each target market chosen in this manner. It is clear that target-market selection does not necessarily involve only one target market. Numerous individual target markets can be selected.

The fact that marketing management has analysed the market and decided to target a specific market does not mean that the organisation now owns that target market. On the contrary, a survey of the market would probably have indicated the presence of competitors. Marketing management has to consider the competitive situation in the market carefully and decide if it wishes to confront competitors directly or if it should rather seek and occupy a gap (or niche) in the market. A positioning guide is often used to show the competitive position confronting marketing management. This guide makes it easier to identify gaps in the market. Figure 12.6 on page 386 is an example of such a guide.

Once marketing management has segmented the market and selected a target market or markets, a decision must be made regarding the four marketing instruments that will be aimed at the market/s. These four marketing instruments are discussed in section 12.10.

12.10 The marketing instruments

Marketing management constantly modifies decisions about the four marketing-mix instruments (that is the product, distribution, marketing communications and pricing) as circumstances change and consumers' acceptance of the product gradually increases. For instance, consumers first have to be educated to accept an innovation, that is, an original new product. At the same time, an existing product that is in a later phase of its life cycle should be actively promoted to prevent consumers from possibly buying a competing product.

12.11 Product decisions

12.11.1 The product offering

The **product offering** of a business may comprise a single product item or a number of **product items** and **product ranges**. This product offering changes according to the demands of time and the situation of the market.

Product decisions entail decision-making about the product itself (for example, the type of packaging and the brand), as well as about the composition of the product offering. Before these decisions can be discussed, the concept "product" will be described in greater detail.

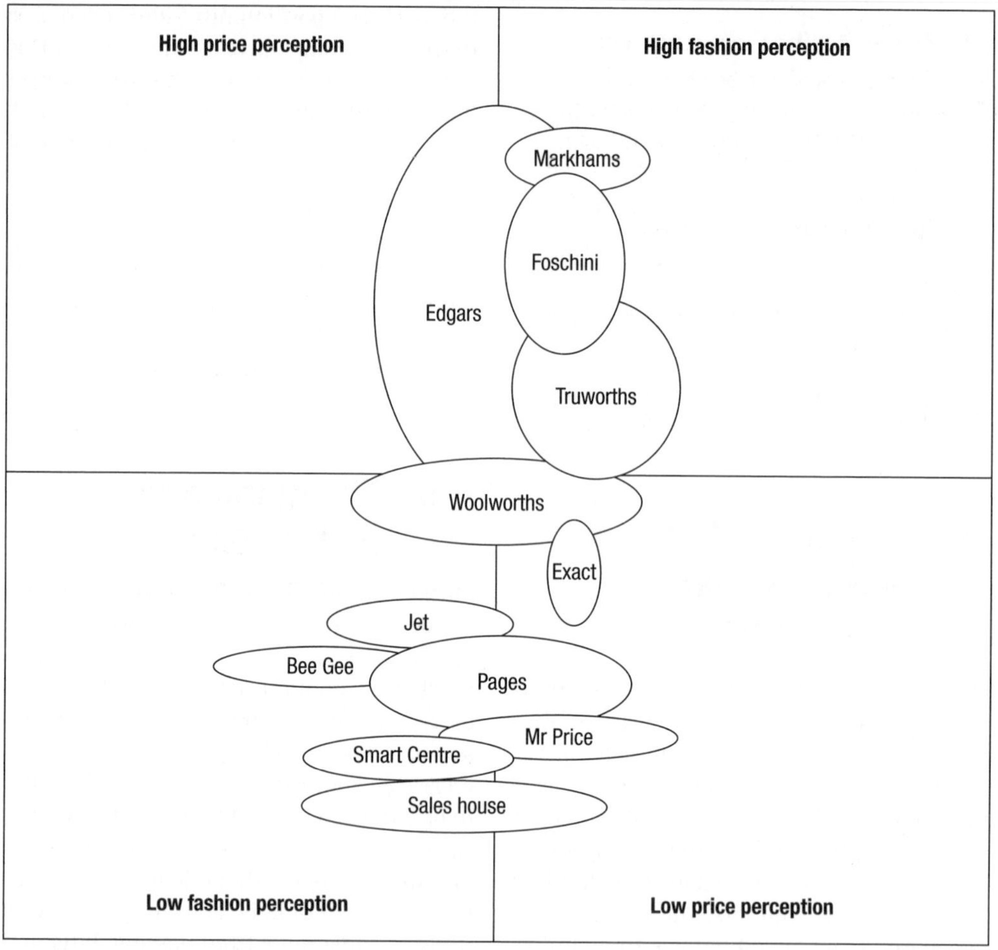

Figure 12.6: Positioning guide: Exact!

Source: Cant, M.C. & Machado, R. 2002. *Marketing success stories.* 4th ed. Cape Town: Oxford University Press, p. 48.

The differences between the concepts "product offering", "product range" and "product item"

A product offering consists of various product ranges. The product ranges of Toyota SA consist of the following:

- passenger cars
- bakkies (also called light delivery vehicles)
- SUVs (sport utility vehicles)
- heavy transport vehicles (also called lorries).

The product range consists of various product lines. The passenger-car product range consists of four product lines:

- Yaris – one of the top-selling small cars in South Africa for a number of years
- Corolla – also exported to Australia
- Avensis – fully imported from Australia
- Lexus – fully imported.

In the Yaris product line, there are a number of product items, of which the Yaris 180 is an example.

12.11.2 What is a product?

A **product** may be described as a composition of tangible and intangible need-satisfying utilities offered to consumers by a business, so that the consumers can take note of them, procure them and use them. The need-satisfying utilities may include consumer products, services (for example, services provided by a hairdresser), personalities (such as a film star), places (such as the local cinema), institutions (such as the SPCA) and ideas (such as the "Keep South Africa Clean" campaign). As indicated in a previous section of this chapter, this book focuses on consumer products. Product decisions, however, also apply to the other types of "products" or utilities mentioned above.

A consumer product consists of:

- a **core product** that can be described in terms of technical and physical qualities (for example, a crystal wine glass consisting of a round base, a long stem and a bell-shaped container, all made of glass)
- a **formal product**, which, in addition to the core product, may also include specific features such as style, quality, brand and packaging (for example, a wine glass with a Vitro trademark packed in a red flannelled carton)
- a **need-satisfying product** comprising further need-satisfying utilities, such as guarantees, installation, repair services and free delivery (for example, glasses guaranteed to have been manufactured by the best artisans)
- the **product image** that gives the product symbolic value by means of the type of marketing message, price and choice of distribution outlet (the Vitro glasses, for example, are sold only at exclusive shops and at a price 50% higher than ordinary wine glasses)
- the **total product** comprising all the above-mentioned components (that is, an expensive wine glass made by the best artisans that is sold only in exclusive shops).

When the concept of the total product is considered, it immediately becomes clear that there are large differences between different consumer products. Consumer products differ in respect of their particular features, their manufacturing and marketing methods, and their purposes. Marketing management consequently has to classify products in more or less homogeneous categories, according to their different qualities.

12.11.3 Classification of consumer products

Consumer products are intended for immediate use by households or consumers. A distinction can be drawn between durable and non-durable consumer products. **Durable consumer products**, such as fridges, cars and furniture, are utilised over a longer period, whereas **non-durable consumer products**, such as cigarettes, chocolate and milk, have a relatively short lifespan. Consumer products can also be classified, on the basis of consumer buying habits, into convenience products, shopping products and speciality products.

- **Convenience products** are products such as sweets, cigarettes, milk, bread and newspapers, which should be within easy reach of the consumer. The qualities and prices of competing convenience products are reasonably homogeneous and the products do not require much explanation to be sold. Furthermore, the retailer does not receive much incentive to "push" one brand in favour of another.
- **Shopping products** are products (for example, clothing and jewellery) for which the consumer wants to compare suitability, quality, price and style before buying. He/she does not have sufficient knowledge of the range of shopping products available and will "shop around" to acquire information. The consumer rarely has enough information and knowledge to visit just one store to buy the product, so he/she shops around to obtain enough

information about the trademark before buying the product. New Balance shoes are examples of shopping products.
- **Speciality products** are products with unique characteristics for which consumers will make a special purchasing effort. A purchaser will often insist on a specific brand. Examples are cars (such as a BMW Z3 sports car), television sets (such as Panasonic) and hi-fi equipment (such as Marantz).

It is important to note that the classification outlined above is based on the purchasing habits of consumers. As consumer purchasing habits differ, the same product (for example, cigars) may be a convenience product for one consumer, a shopping product for another consumer and a speciality product for yet another consumer.

The marketer has to make various product decisions based on the nature of the product to be marketed. One of the most important product decisions is the choice of brand. Almost all the consumer products classified into homogeneous groups have brands distinguishing them from competing products.

12.11.4 Brand decisions

12.11.4.1 The meaning of brands

A brand is a mark that is unique to the product items or ranges produced and marketed by a particular business, and that is chosen to distinguish them from similar competing products. The brand of a product includes the brand name and a specially designed trademark. The **brand name** is a word, a letter or a group of words (for example, Mercedes-Benz). Consumers use this name when they intend to buy the product. The concept of a brand name is therefore much narrower than the concept of a brand (in this case, the three-point star within the circle that typifies the Mercedes-Benz trademark).

Brands can be registered under the Trademarks Act (No. 194 of 1993) (as amended). Such registration protects a business's exclusive right to use a particular brand for a period of ten years.

Figure 12.7 on page 389 shows a number of well-known brands. Some brands consist of only a brand name written in distinctive lettering. Pick n Pay is a good example. Some trademarks are so familiar that the names are almost unnecessary. The distinctive names and trademarks are often used in reminder advertising, for example, on the large billboards (usually positioned right in front of the television cameras) surrounding the field in a soccer stadium.

Figure 12.7 has the names of products in their characteristic lettering as well as their trademarks. In each case, the reader knows what kind of product it is and, in most cases, what the marketing message is, although these are not mentioned.

12.11.4.2 Advantages offered by the use of brands

Well-known brands offer the following advantages to **consumers**:
- They facilitate the identification of products when purchasing.
- They assure consumers of a quality standard they can count on.
- They offer a certain degree of protection to consumers because branded products can be identified with a specific producer.
- They facilitate decision-making because consumers easily recognise the brands they usually buy.
- They serve as a warning against products that do not meet requirements set by consumers.

The use of brands has the following advantages for the **marketer**:
- Brands are the foundation stone of the marketing communication strategy, where the message indicates precisely which product should be purchased.

Figure 12.7: Well-known South African brands

- Brands promote brand loyalty among consumers and make product substitution by the retailer or consumer more difficult. For example, a consumer might insist on buying a Defy oven and perceive no other brand as good enough.
- Brands make price comparison with competing products more difficult and, to a certain extent, protect the retailer against self-destructive price wars. If the consumer wants only a Bosch brand, for example, he/she will not easily buy a cheaper substitute. Price competition is therefore obviated.
- Brands are an inseparable part of the product image and offer the marketer the opportunity of creating the product image. Consider, for example, the connotation generated by the brand name Mercedes-Benz and the three-pointed star in the mind of the ordinary consumer.
- Brands make product differentiation possible and enable the marketer to distinguish his/her product from competing products.
- Brands facilitate the expansion of existing product ranges because consumers tend to accept new additions to an existing range more readily than an unknown product item that is not part of a range. A case in point is the success of Mercedes-Benz's smaller car (the A-series) in the market.

In fact, in a competitive market, it is almost impossible to market a consumer product successfully if it has no brand identification. These days, attempts are increasingly being made to brand products that traditionally have not had brand names, such as milk (Clover) and bread (Albany), to reap the benefits of brand identification.

The manifestation of brand loyalty is closely related to the advantages offered by the use of brands.

12.11.4.3 Brand loyalty

The discussion of the New Balance range of shoes mentioned the brand loyalty of the consumers. Brand loyalty occurs when consumers show loyalty to certain brands. It is the result of good product quality, proven usefulness and repeated marketing communication. A brand that does not meet consumer demands runs the risk of losing the battle against competing brands. A brand that is not introduced properly to consumers will remain unknown and therefore unloved. The consumer gradually moves through three phases of loyalty:

- **Brand recognition.** Consumers recognise the brand and know what it stands for.
- **Brand preference.** Consumers prefer the brand to other competing brands.
- **Brand insistence.** Consumers insist on the specific brand and refuse to accept a substitute.

Marketers naturally aim at achieving brand insistence, because this gives the product speciality value in the eyes of consumers. The consumer will shop around until he/she finds the branded product. In such a situation, a competitor will find it difficult to gain a foothold in the market. However, the marketer still has to advertise the brand and bring it to the attention of consumers, even at this stage.

In a later section of this chapter, the discussion of strategic marketing will refer to the need to maintain long-term relationships with consumers and clients. Brand loyalty is the result of such a long-term relationship. Brand loyalty is possible only if the marketing concept is strictly adhered to.

12.11.4.4 Manufacturer, dealer or generic brands

Manuafacturers usually give their own brands to the products they market, for example, Levi jeans. Large **retailers** or **dealers** also often buy unmarked products from manufacturers and give these products their own brand names. For example, Elements for small children, Free to B for teens and young adults (hip fashion wear) and Merien Hall for stately older adults are used by Edgars for different ranges for different market segments. Then there are the **generic brands**, the so-called no-name brands. The branded products of manufacturers compete directly with dealer and generic brands in what is referred to as the "battle of the brands". It remains to be seen which type of brand will become the most popular. Table 12.3 compares marketing strategies for the three brand types.

A **manufacturer** should decide whether it wants to market its products bearing its own brands or, instead, to market unbranded products directly to dealers. Sometimes large manufacturers have excess manufacturing capacity that they utilise to produce unmarked products for dealers. In such cases, there should be clearly distinguishable market segments at which the market offering can be directed. If this is not the case, the dealer brand will only aggravate the competitive situation by making inroads into the market share of the manufacturer (in other words, cannibalisation).

Compare the divergent characteristics of the three brands mentioned in Table 12.3.

Table 12.3: Manufacturer, dealer and generic brands

Characteristics	Manufacturer brand	Dealer brand	Generic brand
Target market	Quality-conscious buyer, brand loyal	Price conscious, loyal	Price conscious, discriminating buyer, large family, accepts lower quality
Marketing mix			
• Product	Well-known product, strict quality control, clearly distinguishable brands, wide product ranges	Largely the same as for manufacturer brands, but generally less known, limited number of product ranges	Poorer quality, less emphasis on packaging and labelling, few product items
• Price	High price, controlled by manufacturer	Price controlled by retailer	Lower price, controlled by retailer
• Distribution	Generally available at all large retail shops	Generally only available at branches of a specific retailer	The same as for dealer brands
• Marketing communication	Marketing communication campaigns launched by manufacturer	Campaigns launched by relevant retailer, most favourable shelf arrangement	Sales promotion at point of sales

Source: From Houghton Mifflin. 1999. *Management.* 6/E TXT, 1E, p. 663. © South-Western, a part of Cengage Learning, Inc. Reproduced by permission www.cengage.com/permissions.

12.11.4.5 Individual/family brands

Marketing management also has to decide whether it is going to choose an **individual brand** for each product item (for example, Carling Black Label and Hansa Pilsener Beer from SAB) or whether it is going to use a family brand (for example, Kellogg's Rice Krispies, Kellogg's All Bran and Kellogg's Corn Flakes) for the whole range of products. Both decisions have advantages as well as disadvantages.

If a family brand is chosen, the costs of introducing a new product in the range into the market are lower. Spending on marketing communication usually decreases, because consumers are already familiar with the name of the products in the range. The new product can also benefit from the popularity of the other products. The reverse is also true: if one product in such a range performs poorly, the reputation of the other products bearing the same name is damaged. Individual brands are expensive to market because separate marketing communication attempts have to be made for each individual product. An individual brand requires another name, offering the opportunity for originality and aggressive marketing attempts aimed at specific target markets.

12.11.5 Packaging decisions

Packaging can be described as the group of activities concerned with the design, manufacturing and filling of a container or wrapper with the product item so that it can be effectively protected, stored, transported and identified, as well as successfully marketed.

Packaging should be designed so that the product can be handled without damaging the quality of the contents. It is even more important that packaging should promote product sales. The consumer should be able to distinguish the packaging standing on the shelf from the packaging of competing products. The packaging therefore usually has a label bearing the characteristic brand and other important information. Bright colours and striking designs are used on packaging to attract the consumer's attention. The brand-loyal consumer, for example, will recognise from a distance the characteristic packaging of the detergent he/she buys regularly.

New packaging did not stop the demise of old-favourite Lion Lager

Beer aficionados were shocked when SABMiller decided to change the packaging of old-favourite Lion Lager. Gone were the traditional old colours of cream and red, and in their place was a more modern silver colour with blue lettering. The target market was also redefined to include the younger adults (18–24 years) and hip generation of South Africa. The change in packaging and repositioning was not successful, however, and the Lion brand was discontinued in 2003.

12.11.5.1 Different kinds of packaging

Marketing management usually devotes a great deal of attention to choosing packaging and a packaging design that will show off the contents in the best possible way. The different kinds of packaging that can be chosen are the following:

- **Family packaging.** All the products in the range are packed more or less identically. The same packaging material is used and the sizes of packaging are more or less the same. Family packaging is usually related to family brands. (There are, however, exceptions, as in the case of beer, where each kind has an individual brand, but all have more or less similar packaging.) All Koo jams are sold in identical packaging with different labels to indicate the contents. Family brands can facilitate consumer decision-making because the packaging is easily recognisable. It can, however, also be a source of irritation. The consumer may purchase a product that he/she does not really want if the labels and colours resemble each other too closely.

- **Speciality packaging.** This gives an image of exclusivity to the product. Perfume, jewellery and expensive liquor (for example, Chivas Regal whisky in its silver tin box) are often sold in speciality packaging. Such products are popular gifts.
- **Reusable packaging**. This creates the impression that the consumer receives a "free" container if he/she buys the product. The container can be reused for something else later. (An example is the metal container in which Bakers Tennis biscuits used to be sold. The container could be used to store cookies and future packets of Tennis biscuits.) Reusable packaging leads to repeat purchases because consumers tend to collect the containers. The danger is that consumers may stop buying when they have purchased enough containers or if they are reluctant to throw them away when the containers are empty.

12.11.5.2 Choice of packaging design

When it comes to the choice of the packaging design, marketing management has to decide on the kind of packaging material, the shape and size of the packaging, and the graphic design on the label.

The packaging materials (for example, glass bottles, cans, cardboard boxes or plastic tubs) best suited to the product itself are chosen. Glass bottles containing bottled fruit are more attractive than cans, for example, but they are impractical to transport and usually more expensive. Marketers often choose different and better types of packaging material than their competitors in an attempt to differentiate their products from competitors' products. An example is the variety of packaging used for toothpaste. The traditional metal tubes have been replaced by plastic tubes, and there are now also stand-alone dispensers of toothpaste.

The shape of the packaging or container may have a specific functional value, such as reusable plastic tubs for margarine. The shape may also have a symbolic value, which may subconsciously influence buyers. A square shape is supposed to have male connotations, whereas female consumers prefer flowing and round shapes. These types of "male" and "female" shapes for packaging are especially noticeable in the case of toiletries.

Characteristic packaging helps consumers to recognise the product on the shelf, even from a distance. This explains why it is not desirable to change packaging without informing consumers properly. This does not mean that containers should never be modified. Changes are often made in the shapes of packaging and printed matter or labels, either for the sake of improvement, or for functional or aesthetic reasons. Just think how many times the word "new" is used in combination with a new kind of packaging. The product is then advertised in its new packaging to educate consumers about the new look of the packaging.

Packaging sizes are important in that marketing management has to retain the sizes traditionally used in the industry to save money, but in doing so has to forgo the competitive advantage of unusual sizes. Products packaged in unusual sizes draw the consumer's attention, but at the same time make price comparisons difficult.

The label differentiates the product from other similar products, especially if containers have been standardised. The label also serves as the carrier of the marketing message. The colours on the label and the graphic design (letter types and illustration) help to attract and hold the consumer's attention.

Using packaging to sell more wine

In an effort to increase the consumption of wine in South Africa, Distell introduced a six-pack of 250 ml screw-cap bottles to be sold in selected supermarkets in South Africa. The packaging is similar to that in which beer is sold in South Africa. The first brand was Two Oceans Sauvignon Blanc. The objective of the screw-cap bottle is to make wine more accessible to consumers. Consumers can now drink smaller amounts of wine more frequently without any form of waste. The screw cap makes it easy to reseal the wine for another occasion. The six-pack fits easily into any domestic fridge, is very portable and eliminates the need for a corkscrew. Wine producers are using different formats of wine packaging to promote accessibility. Some of the options being used are three-litre bag-in-boxes and wine in a can.

Source: Bizcommunity.com. "Six-pack wines piloting in SA". [Online] Available: http://www.bizcommunity.com/Article.aspx?c=87&l=196&ai=10748 Accessed 4 July 2006.

12.11.6 Product differentiation

Marketing management also has to decide on the way in which the product should be differentiated from other competing products. Product differentiation means that a business distinguishes its product, physically and/or psychologically, from essentially identical competing products, so that the product is regarded as a different product by consumers in a specific target market. Physical and psychological differentiation can take place on the basis of design, quality, colour, taste, size, brand, packaging or any other distinguishing feature, such as price, the marketing communication message or the type of distribution outlet. One of the best examples of differentiation is found in the car market when a new model is added to the range to differentiate the product from competitors' products. Another example is the way in which New Balance's running shoes cater for South African feet by providing comfort for wider feet.

Different kinds of differentiation

- **Differentiation by means of packaging and brand.** The various types of margarine on the market are distinguished by the use of different types of packaging, such as plastic, foil or waxed paper, the brands, the designs on the labels and the colours used.
- **Differentiation by advertising appeals.** Advertising appeals for one brand of detergent emphasise the "enzyme-active ingredients". For another detergent, the "stain-removing power" is underlined and for yet another detergent, the advertising appeals focus on the "clean fresh smell".
- **Differentiation on the basis of price.** There are big differences in the pricing of cosmetic products, for example, Revlon products cost much less than Estée Lauder products. New Balance shoes are known as affordable, which is their point of differentiation.
- **Differentiation on the basis of distribution outlet.** Rolex watches are available only at the biggest and best-known jewellers.

12.11.7 Product obsolescence

An important product decision concerns product obsolescence. A product may intentionally be made technically and/or psychologically obsolete in order to compel the consumer to make repeat purchases. At the technical level, products can be designed to have a specific lifespan. An example is a light bulb. Psychological obsolescence points to the introduction of a new model or style, resulting in the consumer rejecting the "old" product, which may still be completely effective technically. New car models and new fashions are well-known examples of planned psychological obsolescence.

The strategy of planned obsolescence is often criticised because it leads to the waste of scarce resources and aggravates the pollution problem. However, the fact remains that new models are usually technically better than the earlier ones, thereby contributing to greater consumer satisfaction. Planned obsolescence also contributes to economic progress and job creation. An interesting example of planned obsolescence is the Volkswagen Beetle, which made a dramatic comeback a few years ago. The new Beetle doesn't have an air-cooled engine at the back like the original Beetle. Instead it has a two-litre water-cooled engine in the front of the car. Not much of the old Beetle was incorporated in the new version.

12.11.8 Multi-product decisions

Marketing management also has to make decisions on the composition of the product offering (see section 12.11.1). A business seldom manufactures and markets one specific product item only. The product offering usually consists of a product range or even a diversified variety of product items and ranges. The total product offering of a business changes continually. Profitable opportunities occurring in the market are utilised through the development of new products or by takeovers of existing businesses including, naturally, the product items and ranges marketed by those businesses.

Multi-product items in the total product offering reduce the risk of failure and financial loss because the success and profit of one product item can compensate for the poor performance of another product item.

12.11.9 New product decisions

Product decisions also have to be made about the development of new products. Each product starts its life as an idea, conjured up by someone. A sales representative, a dealer, a technician in the manufacturing division or a consumer may suddenly get an idea about a product that will meet specific consumer needs, and that the business should be able to manufacture and market. Successful large businesses often have new-product venture teams, consisting of various functional experts who actively and constantly seek new ideas for new products. In such businesses, top management usually encourages staff to come forward with product ideas. The idea for a new product may be unique and original (an innovation). The product may also be "new" only in the sense that it is an improvement on or a modification of an existing product. The risk of failure and financial loss is usually greater with the marketing of an innovation – a unique, original product – but the possibility of releasing higher profits is also greater. Consider, for example, the introduction of the iPod and the price charged for this new, innovative product.

New product development is planned and executed step by step, and the new product idea goes through various phases until the product is eventually introduced into the market. The phases of new product development are as follows:

- **Phase 1:** Product ideas are developed.
- **Phase 2:** Product ideas are screened according to financial criteria, for example, sales projection and profitability analysis.
- **Phase 3:** Product ideas that do not appear to be viable (profitable) are eliminated.
- **Phase 4:** Physical product development is done by the manufacturing division and a prototype is manufactured.

- **Phase 5:** The marketing strategy is developed. This strategy entails the following:
  - positioning of the product in the market
  - choice of brand
  - design of packaging
  - compilation of the marketing communication message
  - decision on price
  - choice of a distribution outlet.
- **Phase 6:** Test marketing takes place in a specific small segment of the market, for example, in Johannesburg only, to test the market's reaction.
- **Phase 7:** The product is introduced into the market.

Each of the seven phases is preceded by intensive research and several factors can lead to the demise of the product idea. Nonetheless, the continual generation of product ideas remains a priority, for the survival and progress of a business are closely linked to the success achieved by the business in this field.

The introduction of a product into the market (phase 7) is the first phase in a product's life cycle. All four of the phases in a product's life cycle and the integrated marketing strategy during each phase are discussed in the next section.

12.11.10 The nature of the product's life cycle

The product's life cycle, as shown in Figure 12.8, is indicated as a curve in respect of which sales/profits are indicated on the vertical axis and time duration is indicated on the horizontal axis. Four phases are indicated:

- the introductory phase
- the growth phase
- the maturity phase
- the declining phase.

Figure 12.8 also illustrates the sales and profit curves during the four phases of the product's life cycle. The sales curve ascends during the introductory and growth phases, reaching a peak in the maturity phase, and then levelling off (stagnating) and descending during the declining phase. The profit curve

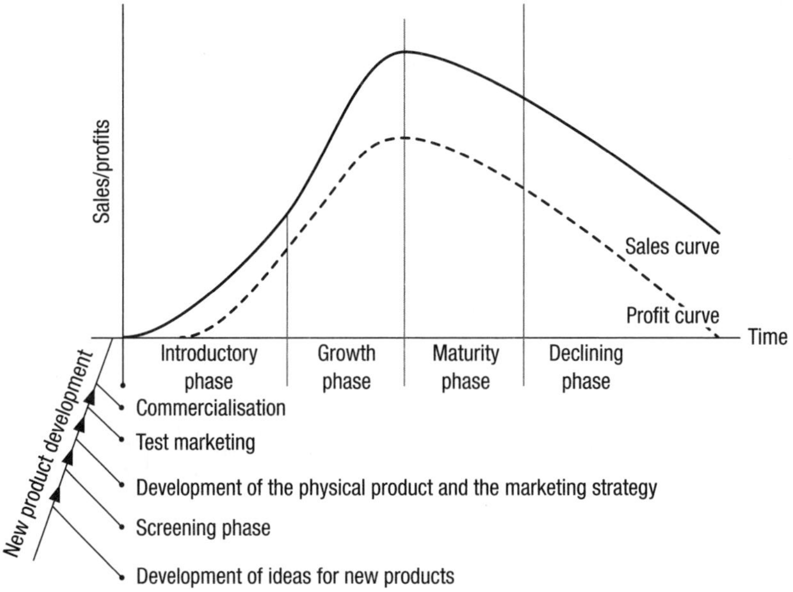

Figure 12.8: Phases in the product's life cycle

looks similar, but starts rising only later in the development phase. The reason is the high costs related to new product development. Costs first have to be recovered before any profit can be made.

The profit curve starts to decline earlier than the sales curve. This is because the product meets keen competition in the maturity phase, causing a price cut (thereby lowering profits).

The marketing communication costs normally rise in this phase, since competition necessitates stimulation of demand. The increased costs naturally affect profits. Marketing management's objective is to sustain the profitable phase of the life cycle for as long as possible. This can be done by constantly modifying the integrated marketing strategy. The declining phase should, at all costs, be avoided.

The curve in Figure 12.8 illustrates the traditional life cycle of a product. Obviously, not all products have identical life cycles. Where an enterprise, for example, markets a whole range of products, each product has its own life cycle. Figure 12.9 illustrates the different life cycles. Although the seven cycles differ, each one reflects a rise, a peak, a stagnation and, in most cases, inevitably a decline. In each of the life-cycle phases, the decisions regarding the price, product, distribution and marketing communication are adjusted. This integrated marketing strategy during the different life-cycle phases is discussed in section 12.11.11.

12.11.11 Marketing strategy during the product life cycle

It has often been stressed that the four marketing instruments have to work together as an integrated whole. They cannot function in isolation. It is marketing management's responsibility to achieve this

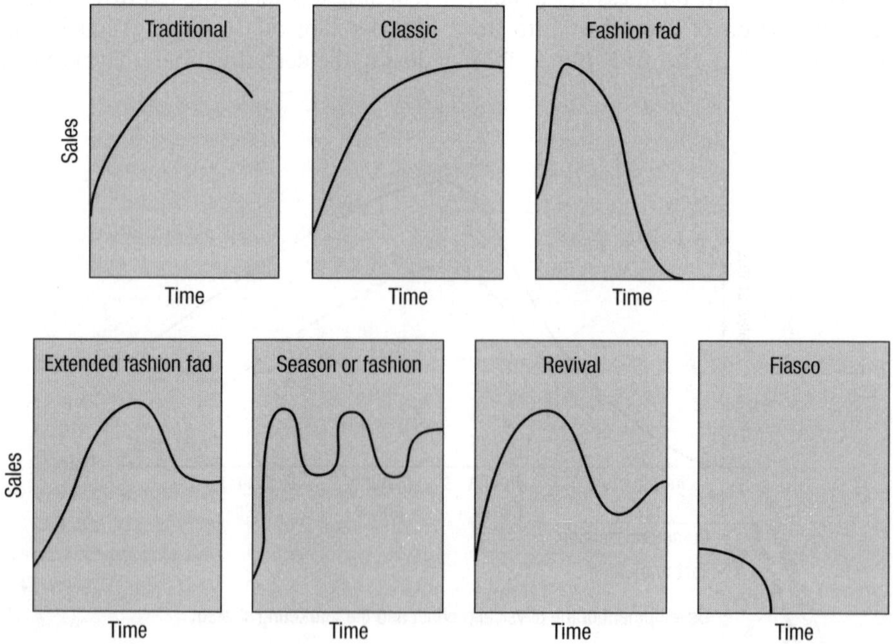

Figure 12.9: Different product life-cycle patterns

Source: Cant, M.C., Strydom, J.W., Jooste, C.J.,Du Plessis,P.J., consulting editor Van der Walt, A. 2006. *Marketing management.* Cape Town: Juta, Chapter 6.

unity because of the numerous variables and because the marketing instruments not only complement each other, but are also mutually interchangeable. The discussion that follows will show how the four marketing instruments can be combined in an integrated marketing strategy during the product's life cycle.

12.11.11.1 Integrated marketing strategy in the introductory phase

The integrated marketing strategy entails the following in the introductory phase:

- **Objective.** The objective is to create a demand. A demand for the product has to be created in the first place because at this stage, consumers are not aware of such a new product (for example, the demand for DVD systems).
- **Target market.** The target market consists of consumers who are adventurous and prepared to try out new things and run risks, for it is possible that the new product may be a great failure.
- **Product decisions.** The product decisions that are taken during product development are implemented (for example, the dimensions and colour of the product).
- **Distribution decisions.** These involve exclusive or selective market coverage. Only a few shops will be prepared to allocate shelf space to the new product.
- **Price decisions.** A high initial price (skimming price) is fixed, since a new product (innovation) usually has a certain degree of prestige value.
- **Marketing communication decisions.** Initially, the business relies heavily on personal selling to dealers. Full-page colour advertisements appear in the more prestigious speciality periodicals. The sales message may contain highly technical information. Publicity is obtained fairly easily because the product usually has news value. Sales promotion techniques can be used to attract attention to the product.

12.11.11.2 Integrated marketing strategy in the growth phase

The integrated marketing strategy entails the following in the growth phase:

- **Objective.** The objective here is to develop a demand. The demand for the specific brand has to be created. At this stage, there are several competing products on the market and the target market is no longer unfamiliar with the product.
- **Target market.** The target market consists of consumers who are less receptive to new things and new ideas. They first want to establish whether the innovators approve of the product.
- **Product decisions.** Minor product modifications are made. The brand is emphasised.
- **Distribution decisions.** This involves selective market coverage.
- **Price decisions.** The price declines because of competition.
- **Marketing communication decisions.** Advertising occurs through the mass media, such as newspapers, radio and television. Sales promotion methods are utilised. All of this is done to promote the specific product and the brand name.

12.11.11.3 Integrated marketing strategy in the maturity phase

The integrated marketing strategy entails the following in the maturity phase:

- **Objective.** The objective is to counteract competition and prolong the life cycle of the product.
- **Target market.** New target markets are sought and exploited because marketing management is aiming at a large market share. Most consumers are aware of the product and its benefits.
- **Product decisions.** Modifications or improvements have to be introduced to differentiate the product from numerous similar products on the market. (Product differentiation is discussed in section 12.11.16). All four marketing instruments should help to achieve product

The growth strategy: Pick n Pay

As mentioned at the beginning of the chapter, Pick n Pay is the largest retail grocery chain in South Africa and it is still following a growth strategy. It has increased its market share in existing markets and its half-year net profit to August 2006 increased by 18,5% to R295 million compared with the same period in 2005.

Pick n Pay intends to introduce new-format hypermarkets, where it intends to invigorate its fresh produce and ready-prepared meals sections, and spruce up departments such as toys and baby products. The first two stores will be introduced at the end of 2006, and two more will be added in 2008. It will also revamp the 14 existing stores that it views as "tired". Pick n Pay will also open six corporate stores, seven Family-franchise stores, as well as five Score Supermarkets and five Boxer Superstores, which are positioned for the lower segments of the market.

In order to grow still further, Pick n Pay also entered a new market segment when it bought the Franklins stores in Australia. In addition to all of this, it diversified by opening its HealthPharm stores (a franchised pharmacy).

Source: "Pick n Pay hypermarkets to take on Woolies", *Business Report*, 18 October 2006 [Online] Available: http://wwwbusrep.co.za/index.php?fSectionID=563&fArticleld=3491317 Accessed 7 November 2006.

differentiation. If this is successful, the product will be perceived as unique by a specific target market. In such a favourable situation, little direct competition will be encountered, even though the product is in the maturity phase. Other product decisions that should receive attention in this phase are the development of new products, extending the product range and product obsolescence. A new product or model starts its life cycle again in the introductory phase.

- **Distribution decisions.** There is intensive market coverage. All suitable dealers with the required facilities are allowed to stock and sell products.
- **Price decisions.** The current market price or market price level should be adhered to unless marketing management has succeeded in differentiating the product successfully. The product is then accepted as unique. Marketing management has price discretion because the consumer perceives the product as unique and does not mind paying more for it.
- **Marketing communication decisions.** There is persuasive advertising through the mass media. The sales message is less technical and more emotional than during the introductory phase. In a television advertisement, for example, children might be depicted as expressing love for their parents because they have bought them a specific brand of DVD player. This type of emotional appeal is often the most important way of differentiating a product from competing products in a highly competitive market.

12.11.11.4 Integrated marketing strategy in the declining phase

The integrated marketing strategy entails the following in the declining phase:

- **Objective.** The objective is either to maintain the market share or to withdraw the product.
- **Target market.** The target market consists of an older, more conservative group of consumers who resist change and avoid innovation.
- **Product decisions.** No modification of the product is considered. Attention is paid to the development of substitute new products or models. The obsolete product is eventually withdrawn from the market.

- **Distribution decisions.** There is limited market coverage and this coverage occurs only in areas where the product is still in demand.
- **Price decisions.** Prices are reduced and the product is offered on sales.
- **Marketing communication decisions.** There is personal selling and advertising only in areas where the product is still in demand.

12.12 Price decisions

12.12.1 The meaning of price

Price may be regarded as the exchange value of a product or service, and it is closely linked to concepts such as benefit and value. The value of a product or service is determined by its benefit to the consumer, and the sacrifice required in terms of money and effort to obtain the product.

Owing to the following factors, it is difficult to describe the concept of "price" and its meaning:

- The marketer and the consumer attach different meanings to the price concept. Marketing management regards price as one of the marketing instruments used to achieve a business's objective. For the consumer, the price he/she pays for a product entails a sacrifice of disposable income. The final price usually represents a compromise between the seller (marketer), who wants to receive as much as possible, and the consumer, who wants to pay as little as possible.
- It is often not possible to specify a single price for a product because of the large number of products, the geographical distribution of consumers and segmentation of the market.
- Price is only one of the four marketing instruments. Should any modification be made to any of the other marketing instruments, costs also change, necessitating a price adjustment. The product price therefore cannot be fixed without considering the influence of the other marketing instruments.

The question now arises as to how the problems mentioned above can be solved, making it possible to determine the final price of a product in such a way that both the marketer and the consumer are satisfied. The answer lies in the process of price determination.

12.12.2 The price-determination process

The price-determination process consists of four phases:

- **Phase 1: Determination of the cost price.** The first step in determining the price of a product is the responsibility of the cost-accounting department and not of marketing management. The unit costs to manufacture and market the product are calculated. The product price cannot be lower than cost because this would entail financial loss, which could ruin the business.
- **Phase 2: Determination of the market price.** The market price is the price the consumer is prepared to pay or the current market price at which competing products are sold. It is marketing management's task to determine the market price. This can be done by launching a market-research project involving consumers or dealers. A survey of the prices of competitors' products can also be undertaken. If the cost price is much higher than the market price, a cost-reduction adjustment has to be made or marketing management has to make a special attempt to convince consumers that the particular product warrants a higher price.
- **Phase 3: Determination of the target price.** The target price is the price that will realise the target rate of return, taking into consideration the cost structure, the business's capital needs and the potential sales volume of the product. One way of

calculating the target price is the cost-plus method. This is done by adding the profit margin to the unit costs of the product. The accepted rate of return determines how large the profit margin will be.

- **Phase 4: Determination of the final price.** This price is the price at which the product is offered to consumers. It is determined through a reconciliation of the market price and the target price. The final price therefore lies somewhere between the market price and the target price. For example, if the market price of an article is R5,00 and the target price is R3,50, then the final price may be set at different levels between R3,50 and R5,00. For various reasons, the final selling price cannot be adjusted further.

12.12.3 Adaptations of the final price

12.12.3.1 Skimming prices

If the product is an innovation and therefore a unique new product, the final price may have a much higher profit margin. Some consumers are prepared to pay the high price because such new inventions usually have prestige value. In fact, if the price is set too low, consumers could possibly doubt the new product's usefulness. For example, electric shavers were priced too low when they were first put on the market. They started to sell only once the price had been almost doubled.

Yet another reason for an innovation to have a high initial price is that marketing management has to recover development costs before a profit can be made. It has already been pointed out that the development of a new invention is an expensive process with great attendant risks. As the product gains popularity, the high initial price can gradually be reduced. The more units that are produced and sold, the lower the costs will be, with the result that the price drops. Of course, competitors find high profits tempting, which mean that marketing management cannot maintain a skimming price for a long time in the face of new competitive products.

12.12.3.2 Market-penetration prices

Marketing management may decide against setting a high skimming price and rather set a **market-penetration price**. Here the initial price of a new product is lower and the marketer hopes to penetrate the market rapidly, discouraging competitors in the process. Competitors may decide that the small profit margin is not worth the effort of marketing a competing product themselves. New Balance followed this approach in pricing its shoes.

12.12.3.3 Market-price level

This strategy is followed if there is keen competition and numerous similar products have to compete against each another. In such a situation, marketers have to maintain the market price. If they set the price of their product higher than the price of their competitors' product, consumers will tend to avoid it. If the price is lower than the prices of competing products, consumers will think there is something wrong with the product. Marketing management can escape the limitations of the market-price strategy only if its product is successfully differentiated and is therefore regarded as unique.

12.12.3.4 Leader prices

Leader pricing concerns special offers. These so-called specials are used by retailers to lure consumers to their shops. Purchasers purchase the low-priced "specials" as well as many other products with a higher profit margin. A very small profit is made on leader-price products. These products are sold at a price lower than the current market price for a limited period only. Manufacturers do not usually like leader pricing. Even though they can sell more products, the profit margin is inadequate and, later, when competitors' products are selected as a leader-price item, sales figures drop. If manufacturers are not prepared to lower their profit margins so that their products can be sold as special offers, the retailer refuses to give them shelf space, giving preference to competing products. The manufacturer is in an unenviable position if the retailer is so large that, as channel captain, the retailer can enforce leader prices. (The question of channel leadership is discussed in greater detail in section 12.13.)

12.12.3.5 Odd prices

Odd prices indicate that the final prices of products have odd numbers. Even prices (for example, R2, R4 and R10) are avoided, and products are rather marked R1,99, R3,79 and R9,95, for example. It is thought that consumers are more likely to accept odd prices and that an odd price looks smaller than an even price.

12.12.3.6 Bait prices

Bait prices are unethical and are therefore avoided by honest retailers. A bait-price item has a particularly low price and is widely advertised. When coming to buy it, purchasers are encouraged to buy a far more expensive item. The retailer does not really intend to sell the bait-price item. Most of the time, it is not even in stock or only one item is available at the low price.

12.13 Distribution decisions

12.13.1 Description of distribution

In an earlier section, marketing was explained as being those activities that have to be carried out to direct the flow of products and services from the business to the consumer in such a way as to satisfy the primary objective of the business and meet the needs of the consumer. It is clear from this definition that a flow or transfer process takes place. Distribution plays an important role here. The transfer takes place along specific distribution channels, which consist of intermediaries (wholesalers and retailers) who are involved in the transfer of products from the manufacturer to the consumer. It is the task of marketing management to link the manufacturer and the various intermediaries in such a way that the product is made available to the consumer in the right place and at the right time.

Distribution entails decision-making about the type of distribution channel. It also entails decisions about the performance of certain activities, for example, physical distribution (also called logistical activities) such as transport-scheduling and stock-keeping.

Later in this section, the various types of distribution channels, the question of channel leadership and the various types of market coverage will be examined. The channel leader or captain is the channel member who may decide which type of channel should be used to achieve the most effective transfer of the product. Distribution decisions also demand that a choice be made regarding the degree of market coverage required.

12.13.2 The choice of the distribution channel

The first decision to be made in respect of **distribution** strategy entails the choice of intermediaries. Five different **distribution channels** are distinguished, as depicted in Figure 12.10 on page 402.

- **Channel 1:** This is also called the direct-distribution channel. Although the intermediary is eliminated, physical distribution activities involved in the transfer of products still have to be performed, in this case by the producer. An example is a vegetable farmer who sells his/her produce at a farm stall. Manufacturers usually sell industrial products directly to other businesses such as factories, which use the products in their manufacturing processes. Door-to-door sales, for example, selling vacuum cleaners, are also an example of direct distribution.
- **Channel 2:** This indirect-distribution channel is found especially in large retail businesses that buy from manufacturers.

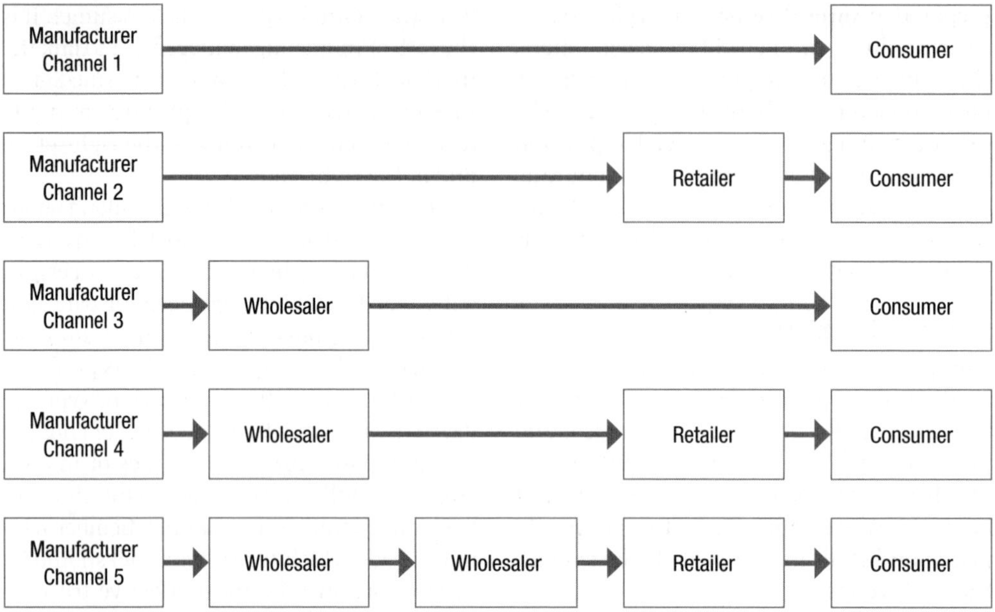

Figure 12.10: The five alternative distribution channels

Pick n Pay, for example, is a large retailer that buys directly from manufacturers and sells to the consumer.

- **Channel 3:** This indirect-distribution channel is often found nowadays. Wholesalers may sell directly to the final consumer, provided these sales constitute less than 50% of their total sales. Examples include Makro and Metro wholesalers.
- **Channel 4:** This is the classic indirect-distribution channel that is still regarded as the most effective by a large number of manufacturers. For example, wholesalers supply stock to the informal retailing sector, such as spaza shops in disadvantaged areas or supermarkets. These shops sell stock on to the final consumer.
- **Channel 5:** In this case, the first wholesaler is usually a speciality wholesaler, which obtains a specific product from numerous producers and then sells it to the second wholesaler, which sells it to the retail trade, which in turn sells it to the consumer. For example, the first wholesaler might be located in a foreign country. This wholesaler would buy products from the manufacturer in that country and deliver them to a wholesaler in South Africa. This wholesaler would then deliver these products to a retailer.

The type of product, the type of market and the existing distribution structure determine which of the channels will offer the greatest advantages. If the product is perishable and the market is localised, direct distribution is the ideal method. A stall next to the road where a farmer sells fresh garden vegetables and milk is an example of a situation in which advantages offered by a direct-distribution channel (channel 1) are utilised. If the product has to be handled and transported in bulk, and the market is such that consumers are widespread, the manufacturer probably has to depend on the specialised knowledge and facilities of intermediaries (such as the wholesaler and retailer, in other words, channel 4) to make the product/s available to consumers. The indirect channel is the ideal choice in such a case.

12.13.3 Channel leadership

Traditionally, the marketing division of a manufacturer of consumer products makes distribution-channel decisions and consequently decides which retail outlets should market the business's products. More recently, however, it is frequently the retailer (for example, Shoprite Checkers) who makes the decisions and therefore controls or dominates the channel. The business that controls or dominates the channel is known as the **channel captain**.

12.13.3.1 The manufacturer as channel captain

If the manufacturer or producer is the channel captain, specific intermediaries often have to be persuaded to distribute the product. The producer may persuade the intermediaries to create a demand for the product by directing intensive marketing communication messages at consumers. This is known as "pull" because the product is "pulled" through the channel by means of consumer demand. (The intermediary is obliged to stock the product because the consumer demands it.) An example of this was Shell Helix oil, which was launched by advertisements aimed directly at the consumer. The consumer asked the retailer to stock the product.

Intermediaries may also be persuaded to "push" a product by actively encouraging sales of products in a store. They may be persuaded to do this by, for example, offering a high profit margin on sales. Demonstration material, shop competitions and special display shelves may also be supplied by the channel captain to encourage the push strategy. Most consumer products such as cooldrinks and coffee are marketed this way. In the marketing of groceries, where competition between different producers is particularly keen, there is often a battle for shelf space. A combination of push and pull is used by the manufacturer as channel captain to persuade the retailer to find shelf space for a particular item between other competing products. It is especially difficult to obtain shelf space for a new competing product. In this case, the manufacturer should create a demand for the new item (pull) by thoroughly informing the consumer about it through advertising. The retailer should then be expected to apply the required push strategy.

12.13.3.2 The retailer as channel captain

If the retailer has a network of branches, enjoys store loyalty and has adequate financial resources, it can take over the channel leadership and lay down its conditions to the producer. An example of this is the Pick n Pay store group, which can be seen as a channel leader. In such cases, the retailer can pull as well as push the product. The retailer advertises the producer's products, actively promoting its sales by granting a price discount to consumers or by means of special exhibits to attract consumers' attention. Special shelf space is also allocated to such products. It is understandable that manufacturers are not very happy with this state of affairs and would rather retain the leadership themselves. If the manufacturer succeeds in obtaining brand loyalty for its products, it is not easy for a retailer to take over the channel leadership. Consumers then look for the specific brand of products and tend to avoid stores that do not stock them. This means that a retailer can be the channel captain for only some of the products in its store.

Here are descriptions and examples of some of the different types of retailer in South Africa:

- **General dealers.** These stores are one of the oldest forms of retailer in South Africa. They offer a wide range of products and operate mostly in rural areas. They sell items ranging from coal stoves to bicycles to clothing to groceries.
- **Department stores.** These large stores sell products in departments, for example, women's clothing, haberdashery and children's clothing. This retailing format is on the decline in South Africa, mainly

because of the introduction of category-killer stores (that is, a retailer, for example, Mr Price, that wants to achieve merchandise dominance by creating narrowly focused, jumbo-sized stores).

- **Speciality stores.** These stores have a narrow but deep product range, for example, jewellery stores.
- **Chain stores.** These stores are similar shops that are found all over the country and are similar in layout and product range. They are centrally controlled by a head office. Woolworths is an example of a chain-store group. The Woolworths head office is situated in Cape Town.
- **Supermarkets.** These stores operate on a self-service basis and sell mostly fast-moving consumer goods (FMCGs) and especially groceries. An example is Shoprite stores.
- **Convenience stores.** These stores are found all over South Africa. Examples are corner cafés, which sell typical convenience products such as bread, milk, newspapers and cigarettes. They are open for extended periods, providing a service to the customer. Another form of convenience store is the forecourt store at petrol-filling stations.
- **Discount stores.** These stores are renowned for a high stock turnover and low prices. They mostly sell shopping products. South African examples include Dion and Game.
- **Hypermarkets.** These stores are larger than supermarkets. In addition to FMCGs, they sell more durable products such as lawnmowers and furniture. They attract people from a large geographical area. South African examples include Pick n Pay hypermarkets.
- **Shopping centres.** Shopping centres are usually found on the periphery of large cities or in suburbs outside the central city. Shopping centres are large buildings that house independent retailers as well as some anchor stores that draw people to the shopping centre. Anchor stores usually include a supermarket, discount store and/or department store. South African examples are Menlyn Retail Park in Pretoria's eastern suburbs, Cavendish Square to the south of Cape Town's city centre and Eastgate in Johannesburg.
- **Mail-order stores.** As the name indicates, these stores sell by mail. For example, Leading Concepts markets its products by sending catalogues to consumers. People then order by mail.
- **Internet stores.**
- **Informal retailers.** Owing to the uniqueness of the South African situation, there are also many informal retailers operating in South Africa. One of the most well-known informal retailers is the spaza shop. The spaza shop is a form of a convenience store found in townships. The shop typically forms part of the home of the entrepreneur. Basic commodities such as bread, milk, cooldrinks and cigarettes are sold through these stores.

12.13.4 Market coverage

The number of intermediaries in the channel is directly linked to the type of market coverage being aimed at. Types of market coverage include intensive, exclusive and selective market coverage.

- **Intensive market coverage** indicates a situation where as many suitable and available intermediaries as possible are utilised, especially by convenience-product producers. An example is Coca-Cola, whose products are distributed through cafés, liquor stores, supermarkets, spaza shops and the forecourt stores at petrol-filling stations.
- **Exclusive market coverage** results when a manufacturer purposely limits the number of people handling its product. Only a few intermediaries obtain exclusive rights to sell the product in a specific geographical area. The intermediaries undertake not to stock other competing products. This type of market coverage is found particularly in

shopping and speciality products such as men's evening clothing and cars.

- **Selective market coverage** refers to the selection of only those intermediaries that will distribute the product efficiently. Selective market coverage lies somewhere between intensive and exclusive market coverage, and can be used by manufacturers of convenience, shopping and speciality products. Medicine, for example, is distributed by pharmacies (chemists) because chemists are the ideal shops to do this efficiently. New Balance follows this market-coverage strategy for its sport shoes.

12.13.5 Physical distribution

A further aspect of the distribution strategy is decision-making about the **physical distribution** activities that have to take place to make a product available to the final consumer. These activities, in order of their relative importance from a cost point of view, include:

- transportation
- storage
- inventory-holding
- receipt and dispatch
- packaging
- administration
- ordering.

The purpose of the physical distribution function is to maintain a specific satisfactory level of service to clients at the lowest possible distribution costs. The optimal service level is that level above which an increase in costs incurred in respect of physical distribution activities will not result in a corresponding increase in sales.

Physical distribution is becoming increasingly important. In earlier times, management was under the impression that physical distribution consisted of transport-scheduling only. However, more attention was paid to this function after managers realised that the effective performance of the physical distribution activities could mean large cost savings for the business and, in addition, could ensure that the product was in the right place at the right time for the convenience of consumers. The three main components of physical distribution are:

- selecting warehouses
- selecting the most suitable mode of transport
- selecting optimal inventory-holding levels.

A compromise between cost and service must be reached in all three components. The most effective performance of physical distribution activities ensures:

- the timeous and reliable delivery of orders

Physical distribution ... helping Coca-Cola to sell into Africa

Coca-Cola uses a unique distribution centre to sell Coke in some of the less-developed African countries. In countries such as Angola, Mozambique, Tanzania and Ethiopia, Coke is sold in areas with poor infrastructure through Manual Distribution Centres (MDCs). This provides a mini-distribution hub to small formal and informal stores in a two- to three-kilometre radius off the beaten track, and creates work for small entrepreneurs. The MDCs are located on truck routes and basically consist of containers holding beverage stock. The small-sales people then come to collect the beverage from the MDC by cart. The MDC also supplies ice to keep the beverage cold for up to 24 hours. There are about 2 500 MDCs in Africa. Together, they offer employment to 12 000 people who support up to 50 000 dependants. The estimated turnover of the MDCs is more than R4 billion per year.

Source: Pressly, D. "Small middlemen have Coke for Africa", *Business Report*, 15 June 2009. [Online] Available: http://www.busrep.co.za index.php?fSectionId=563&fArticleId=5035892 Accessed 22 March 2010.

- adequate inventory so that shortages do not occur
- careful handling of stocks to eliminate damage, perishing and breakage as far as possible.

Physical distribution activities are discussed in greater detail in Chapter 14. As far as marketing is concerned, close liaison between the marketing manager and the purchasing manager is required, and the marketing manager has to be involved in planning and decision-making. If this is not the case, the flow of products from manufacturer to final consumer could be seriously hampered.

12.14 Marketing communication decisions

12.14.1 The nature of marketing communication

The consumer is removed from the manufacturer, intermediaries or point of sale in time and space. Obviously, it is the task of marketing management to communicate with consumers, inform them and make them aware of the variety of products offered on the market. Consumers should also be persuaded by the marketing message to select and buy the producer's product time and again.

Marketing communication can be regarded as the process of **informing**, **persuading** and **reminding** the consumer. Marketing communication comprises six elements that can be used in a specific combination to communicate with consumers. These six elements are:

- advertising
- personal selling
- direct marketing
- sales promotion
- publicity
- public relations.

Figure 12.11 shows the elements of marketing communication. All six elements have to work together to convey the marketing message to the target audience.

Marketing management has to decide on the best combination of the six elements. A marketing communication budget allocates funds to each of the six marketing communication elements. Within the restrictions of this budget, consumers have to be made aware of the business's market offering. They should be persuaded to select and buy product/s, and must be

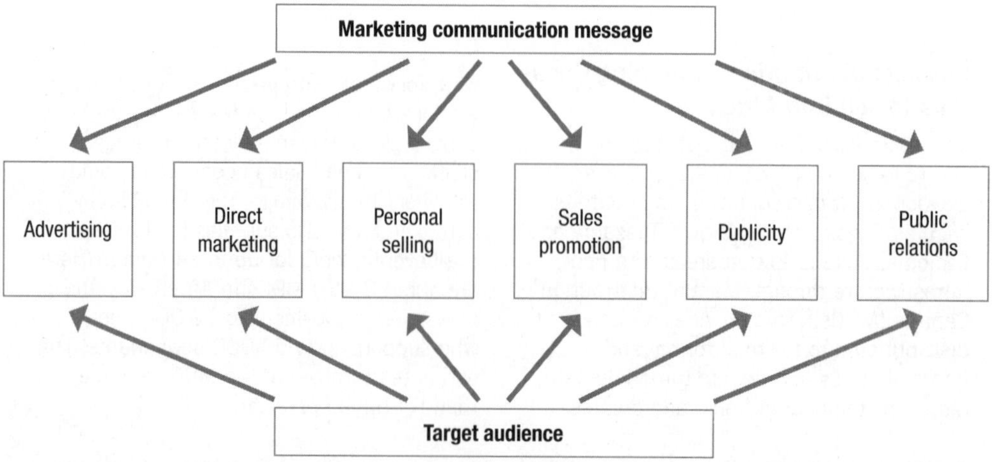

Figure 12.11: Elements of marketing communication

constantly reminded to buy the product/s again. A discussion of the six marketing communication elements follows.

12.14.2 Advertising

Advertising is a controlled and paid-for non-personal marketing communication related to a need-satisfying product and directed by a marketer at a specific target audience.

12.14.2.1 Advertising media

The advertisements that are shown on television or in the movies, broadcast on the radio or placed in magazines and newspapers are examples of advertising. A single placement of such an advertisement is very expensive, hence the need to pay careful attention to both the choice of the media used and to the marketing communication message. Marketing managers should be very sure that their messages will reach the target market (or target audience in this case), and that this audience will notice the message, understand it, accept it and react to it by repeatedly buying the same product.

Outdoor advertising on billboards, posters, bus stops and public-transport vehicles reaches consumers at a time when they are busy with other activities. This is also a good way of reaching a target market that does not read regularly or does not have access to television and the movies. An advertising budget, as part of the marketing communication budget, is prepared to indicate the percentages of the budgeted amount that should be allocated to the various media. Obviously, market research is done to establish the way in which the target market can be reached most effectively.

12.14.2.2 The advertising message

The formulation of the marketing message in advertisements in the different media requires careful consideration. An advertisement in the print media generally consists of three main components: the heading, the illustration and the copy.

The **heading** is supposed to attract the consumer's attention and to deliver the main or most important appeal, or the reason why the product should be bought. The most important message is often repeated at the bottom of the copy. The headline and subheadline are printed in big, bold letters to attract attention.

The **illustration** may be a drawing or a photograph, in black and white or colour. The illustration stimulates interest and invites the reader to read the **copy**, which contains information about the product and the need satisfaction that it can provide. Rational reasons (for example, petrol consumption of 13 km/ℓ in city traffic for the Toyota Yaris car) and emotional reasons (such as a claim that a certain toothpaste will have the effect of all the girls swooning over you) for purchasing the product are given.

The product itself, including the package and the label, should also appear in the illustration. All the components of the illustration itself are chosen to transmit a symbolic message. Models are carefully selected to play a specific role. A homemaker might be chosen to transmit a message about the excellence of a new detergent, while Miss South Africa might be portrayed as a successful user of cosmetics. The intended target audience must be able to relate to or identify with the model in the illustration. (For example, it would be ineffective to use a male as a role model for buying washing powder.) It is important, also, to achieve coherence in all three components. The headline, illustration and copy should not tell conflicting stories.

In radio advertisements, only words and sounds can be used to transmit the advertising message. Music is often used to reinforce the message or to create a specific mood. Jingles and slogans are especially effective in teaching brand names to potential consumers.

Television advertisements are effective because the spoken and written word can be used to spell out the message clearly. Pictorial material, music, jingles and other sounds can be used to reinforce the message. For this reason, television commercials are very expensive and every second counts. Advertisers cannot afford to waste time on irrelevant material. Sometimes television advertisers get so caught up in the entertaining storyline of the television advertisement that they forget what the most important message is: the brand name.

The success of the Red Bull advertising campaign

Red Bull is an energy drink that was launched in South Africa in 1997. The marketing mix used is based on the following:

- The product as an energy drink was new to the market and it worked.
- The packaging was eye catching.
- The distribution channel was good, that is, the product was at the right place at the right time.
- The pricing strategy used was effective (a price-skimming premium strategy, implying that if it is expensive it must work well).

The marketing communications strategy was highly visible. For example, cartoon characters with silly voices were used on TV, providing humour and entertainment value with the slogan "Red Bull – gives you wings!"

12.14.3 Personal selling

Personal selling is a verbal presentation of a product, service or idea to one or more potential purchasers in order to conclude a transaction. Sales representatives are used to inform buyers about a business's product/s and to persuade buyers, through face-to-face communication, to buy the business's products time and again.

Sales representatives of manufacturers visit other businesses and dealers, communicating the marketing message directly. This is the method followed by New Balance to promote sales of its range of shoes. In the same way, wholesalers' sales representatives can be used to visit retailers to try to sell the variety of products handled by the wholesaler. Personal selling between sales representatives and final consumers also takes place. This is known as door-to-door selling (for example, the selling of Tupperware utility plastic containers and the selling of cosmetics from Avroy Shlain). Sales by shop assistants over the counter may also be regarded as personal selling, but normally the retailer does not see it in this light. Retailers usually regard shop assistants as people who help with the physical distribution of the product, that is, people who do not have to be trained in the art of selling.

Example

Cosmetic products are often sold on a door-to-door basis. Avroy Shlain, for example, succeeded in building his extremely successful business by training and motivating his sales representatives to sell his cosmetic products, bearing his own brand name, by means of personal communication.

12.14.4 Direct marketing

Direct marketing uses advertising media (for example, radio and television) to communicate information about a product or service to customers, who can then respond by purchasing the product or service via mail, the telephone or the internet. The benefit of direct marketing is that customers can do the buying from the comfort of their homes, resulting in greater shopping convenience. This benefit ties in with the notion of cocooning, which is prevalent in South Africa today. Cocooning implies that more and more customers create a cocoon in their home. Spending more time at home becomes part of their lifestyle. This is motivated by various factors, including the increase in crime. A recent study found that many internet shoppers do recreational buying. They see this kind of shopping as a pleasurable experience.

Direct marketing has the following benefits:

- A long-term relationship can be developed with the customer.
- The message can be directed at a specific customer.
- A customer database can be developed.
- The results of a direct-marketing campaign can be measured directly.

A number of direct-marketing methods can be used. One example is the use of the internet, where consumers correspond with an organisation such as kalahari.net to order DVDs, CDs and books. Another example is telemarketing, where organisations use the telephone to call the customer at home and offer him/her a product or service. Other examples are direct mail, which solicits the customer to order a product, catalogues that are sent to potential customers and direct-action/response advertising done on TV and in the newspapers, to which customers can respond by phoning and ordering products on a toll-free number. Verimark and Glomail are two South African companies that use direct marketing.

12.14.5 Sales promotion

Sales promotion consists of those marketing communication methods that are not normally classified as advertising, personal selling, direct marketing or publicity, but that complement the other elements in trying to influence consumer behaviour. Examples of such methods are diaries, calendars and T-shirts displaying a brand name and a short sales message. Competitions, demonstrations and the handing out of samples (for example, a small bottle of Handy Andy Micro floor-cleaning liquid) are also examples of sales promotions. Sales promotion has also been used by New Balance in the marketing of its range of shoes.

Sales promotions often have short-term objectives only, for example, to introduce a new product to the market. However, they are valuable methods because they reinforce the effects of the other marketing communication elements. For example, if a consumer has seen a supermarket demonstration of a new pan that browns meat delectably without oil being added (sales promotion), he/she would possibly understand the television advertisement (advertising) better and find it easier to accept the message, especially if he/she has also read an article in a newspaper column (publicity) in which the columnist explained the new cooking method.

12.14.6 Publicity

Publicity is the non-personal stimulation of the demand for a product or service of a business by making its actual current news value available to the mass media to obtain a favourable and "free" media review of the business and its product.

Publicity also interfaces with the business's public-relations function, which is discussed in a later section of this chapter. Should the business or its product receive favourable coverage in the press, on the radio or on television, the publicity (created by the activities of the public-relations division) has a specific marketing communication value for the business.

The distinguishing feature of publicity is that the message to be conveyed should have a certain degree of news value for the audience. Consider, for example, the write-up New Balance received just before the Comrades Marathon in 2006. This is an example of a massive publicity boost to a relative newcomer in this market. Publicity is also more credible than advertising because the audience is more receptive to the message. A further feature of publicity is that marketing management has no direct say in formulating the message because the editors of publications, for example, decide what they want to publish. It is therefore clear that publicity can have a negative effect. (Imagine the negative publicity a motor journalist would give a test car that broke down on a rural road.)

Publicity is not always "free", as is suggested in the definition. A business often has to spend large sums of money on favourable mentions in the press, on radio or on television. Businesses often sponsor sports events or donate large amounts of money to charity. By doing this, a business effectively shows its responsibility towards the community and, in addition, gets free mentions of its name or product in the media. Consumers who notice the hidden message are then more inclined to accept the marketing messages of such a "good" business.

Marketing management should decide which sponsorships or donations could be of benefit to the product/s to be marketed. Top management sometimes decides on sponsorships that are of interest to the top managers personally, notwithstanding the nature of the product or market. In this way, funds are often wasted on matters that do not have sufficient positive marketing communication value and hence will not succeed in demonstrating social responsibility. Specific marketing communication objectives should also be set in respect of sponsorships.

12.14.7 Public relations

12.14.7.1 Defining public relations

Public relations entails decision-making to help an organisation's ability to listen to, appreciate and respond appropriately to those persons and groups whose mutually beneficial relationships the organisation needs to foster as it strives to achieve its mission and vision.

In the light of the discussion on the nature of public relations, the definition[5] that follows explains the main elements of the function. Public relations is the management function that establishes and maintains mutually beneficial relationships between an organisation and its publics. It is a deliberate, planned and sustained process of communication between a business and its publics for the purpose of obtaining, maintaining or improving good strategic relations and mutual understanding between the organisation and its various publics, both internal and external.

The most important elements of this definition of public relations are the following:

- **It is a deliberate activity.** An analysis of the definition given above shows that public relations is a conscious, purposeful activity of business management. Every program is geared to realising clearly formulated objectives. For example, New Balance could set clear goals to establish that its operations were not based on sweatshops and to communicate that fact to all its stakeholders.
- **It is a planned activity.** It is not an incidental process, but an operation that anticipates events, and is prepared for problems and contingencies. It includes a conscious evaluation of all business activities and their influence on the business's image. The management of public relations should act proactively. It should be oriented to the future and should always be ready for any difficulty or emergency.
- **It is a sustained activity.** It takes account of the fact that the public is in a constant process of change, that people have short memories and that amid all the numerous matters competing for their attention, consumers easily forget a business unless they are continually kept informed about it. It therefore has a long-term dimension. For example, New Balance actively communicates with analysts and stakeholders to ensure that they are all aware of the company's stance on ethical production practices in Third World countries. This has become a consistent message from the company's top management teams.
- **It is a communication process.** The term "public relations" pre-supposes communication between individuals and businesses. Establishing communication channels,

especially through the mass media, is therefore a responsibility of public relations. Public-relations management needs to have the necessary communication skills to convey information to the business's various publics so that the members will grasp and accept the message, and ultimately respond as management wishes them to. This means that public-relations management should include communications experts who, in addition to their knowledge of the principles of communication, should also be familiar with the policy and activities of all the functional areas of the business. Public relations should therefore be part of top management. As highlighted above, the top management team of New Balance could communicate the policies and approach of New Balance to ethical practices. For example, it could emphasise its procurement policies on its website.
- **It deals with publics, both internal and external.** A public is any group that influences the organisation or its operations. Internal publics, for example, employees and management, exist within the organisation. External publics exist outside the organisation. Examples of external stakeholders include unions, the media, the community, government, financial institutions and the general public.

Public relations entails creating and maintaining goodwill toward a business. It is clear from the definition that goodwill is the decisive factor. Ill will is something that everyone prefers to avoid, and this applies in business too. The matter of goodwill and ill will occurs in all environmental markets: consumer, labour and financial. Public-relations management concentrates on obtaining goodwill and avoiding ill will in all these markets. It is also important to maintain and improve goodwill once it has been obtained. Sasol has had very good growth lately and has been a good performer in financial terms, yet the numerous accidents that have occurred at its plants have made analysts and governmental safety agencies less than enthusiastic about the performance of the company at times.

12.14.7.2 The public-relations media

Communications media are the channels used to convey the communication message. The spoken word, the printed word, sight and sound symbols, the electronic word, images on the internet and special events are examples of the communications media used by the public-relations department to transmit messages. New Balance could use all of these media to ensure all customers hear the correct message. For example, New Balance could record a television message and distribute it to customers through its website, it could make a radio commercial available to radio stations, it could publish excerpts from speeches in printed material by buying space and placing the excerpts in the media and it could repeat the recorded message at a nationwide roadshow of its new product lines.

The spoken word

The spoken word is used in public relations and face-to-face communication. It is probably the most important method of communication in any business. Both communicator and receiver must speak "the same language" for them to understand each other. In South Africa, effective communication is difficult because there are so many official languages, but even without a language problem, misunderstandings frequently occur because people interpret communication messages differently. This is why the choice of a suitable spokesperson is so important and why ordinary employees cannot be allowed to communicate freely with the media.

The printed media

Newspapers, magazines and company publications are important printed media for the written word. Receivers can read (and try to understand) the message, while carefully selected pictures (illustrations) are used to support and reinforce a non-verbal message. The main types of printed media include:

- **Newspapers.** There are many morning, evening and Sunday papers available in urban and most rural areas. They appear in different languages and are read by a diverse audience. News reports are rigorously selected and it is by no means easy for public-relations departments to get their press releases accepted.
- **Magazines.** There are also a great number and variety of magazines. The following types normally appear weekly, fortnightly or monthly, and are aimed at particular readers:
  - general magazines with articles on a variety of topics of general interest and a wide public readership
  - magazines aimed at a particular section of the public such as men (*Men's Health*) or women (*Bona, Fairlady, True Love*)
  - specialised publications for people who are interested in particular sports, or with specific interests (for example, health-conscious people like to read *Longevity* and outdoor-oriented people read *Getaway*)
  - professional journals read by academics, doctors, lawyers, farmers, engineers and so on (business people, for example, read *Financial Mail*).
- **Company publications.** A wide range of publications are used, for example, handbills, brochures, annual reports, news sheets, books, road maps, guides, directories, recipe books, posters, wall charts, photographs, pictures, pocketbooks, desk diaries and, in some cases, personal newsletters or circulars. Annual reports and newsletters constitute particularly effective ways of conveying news about a business and its activities. It is the job of the public-relations department to issue such publications with the requisite input from other departments. The purpose of these publications is to obtain goodwill or to create a favourable corporate image. For example, New Balance could publish a Code of Ethics that could be placed in both external and internal printed media. The company could also print the code on plastic cards to distribute to each and every New Balance employee around the world.

Sight and sound

The most effective method of conveying a message combines sight and sound. This method allows receivers to see what is happening while sounds (like words and their sound effects) support and reinforce the message. The following media are extremely effective communicators of sight and sound:

- **Radio and television.** Just as the public press is the most important medium for the written word, radio and television are the most important media for sound and picture communications. The public-relations department can use radio and TV as communication media in three ways to transmit messages:
  - It can present prestige advertisements, designed to build a business's image and to make its brands known to the public.
  - It can provide news reports, for example, when there are notable achievements or when newsworthy events take place.
  - A public-relations officer might appear on news reviews or participate in discussion programmes in which newsworthy topics are discussed at length.
- **Films and videos.** Another way of bringing the activities of a business to the attention of the general public is to sponsor documentary films or videos, usually shown on TV or as supporting features in cinemas. Sponsorship of films is not intended as a form of direct-sales promotion, but rather to create a positive and favourable attitude towards the business.

Special events

Visits, receptions, exhibitions and sponsorships are special occasions that present opportunities for communicating messages.

The arrangements for such events are the responsibility of the public-relations department. Crises that occur regularly and unexpectedly are also special events that make substantial demands on the expertise and communication skills of public-relations practitioners. Special events include the following:

- **Press conferences.** Press conferences, usually organised and managed by the public-relations department, are special events that afford the business an opportunity to communicate with the public through the mass media. Both the spoken word and the written word are used at these events. News reporters usually receive a copy of a specially formulated statement made by the spokesperson, after which questions are allowed. This is normally followed by a news report in the mass media. The public-relations officer responsible for addressing the conference must show diplomacy in fielding difficult questions and an ability to encourage further questions by offering positive answers. A press conference on television often causes amusement when an inept spokesperson has to answer embarrassing questions.
- **Visits to the business.** Visits are usually encouraged because they create opportunities for the business to give out information that will foster goodwill. There are usually set visiting times when employees and members of the public are conducted through the premises by somebody with sufficient knowledge of the business to be able to answer any questions. For example, New Balance could encourage independent workers' rights organisations to visit any of its plants to see for themselves the true situation there.
- **Receptions.** Businesses often take advantage of a particular occasion to entertain a select group of people at a luncheon or cocktail party. This is usually accompanied by a speech informing those who are present about particular achievements or developments. This kind of occasion provides an opportunity for hosts and guests to meet and mix informally. Again, the primary objective is to further the image of the business rather than to promote sales, although increased sales may in many cases result from a favourable image.
- **Exhibitions.** Most large businesses have venues in their own buildings that are suitable for holding exhibitions. An exhibition may demonstrate the process a product undergoes through to completion, or what equipment or apparatus is used, or it may provide information, accompanied by photographs, of performances achieved. Practical demonstrations can also be given.
- **Crisis management.** Crises and other unforeseen events constitute threats to the continued survival of a business. The public-relations department must have a crisis plan ready to manage any unfortunate event. A crisis can be caused by a strike, a fire, a big accident on the factory floor, fraud and theft, defective products that threaten danger and even loss of life to consumers, and a whole range of other unexpected and unwelcome events. The purpose of a crisis plan is to limit as far as possible the physical and financial damage caused by the event, and to protect the corporate image. A specially appointed crisis co-ordinator must also be responsible for the following, which relate to internal and external communications:
- compiling a list of persons to be informed about the nature of the crisis
- training of telephone operators to answer enquiries in the correct way
- appointment of a spokesperson
- informing and training employees to act correctly in emergencies (an emergency number should be readily available)
- formulating a message to prevent further possible damage caused by negative rumours.

After the crisis has passed, the public should be reassured that everything is back to normal. In handling a crisis, transparency and honesty should prevail. The Royal Canin product recall, the Sasol plant accidents and the product recall by Mattel toys of some of its toys are recent examples of companies that have had to manage a crisis.

The internet

There is no doubt that the interactive workplace (cyberspace, the internet and the World Wide Web) has affected the way many businesses operate. One of the most important developments is the use of public-relations tools on these channels. Examples of this are the use of podcasts, blogging, web sales, intranet operations and the use of the web to communicate with target publics. These electronic channels will become an increasingly powerful communications tool for public-relations practitioners. Seitel[6] identifies three reasons for this:

- **An increasing consumer demand to be educated as opposed to merely being sold things.** Many consumers and target publics are better educated and know when someone is trying to oversell them. Communications programs should respond by using education-based information instead of blatant promotion. The internet is a good example of the use of such information.
- **Time is of the essence.** The need to move quickly is well known in business, but there is an even greater pressure to operate in a real-time mode. The world has become a global village where immediate communication is possible. The internet and the instantaneous access it provides can be used by public-relations practitioners to respond instantly to any emerging issues or market changes.
- **An increasing need for customisation.** There are more and more choices available to consumers. Compare the limited number of television channels there used to be in South Africa with the current situation. Satellite television has exponentially increased the number of possible channels available to consumers.

This increase in choice means that consumers today have increased expectations. They expect a more focused approach that caters to their specific needs and offers one-to-one communication. Businesses will have to focus on ever-narrower target segments or audiences, and the internet offers the vehicle to do this.

In businesses, electronic mail or e-mail is an increasingly important channel for communication with internal publics or other employees. It has become the preferred choice over traditional print media or fax technology. The advantages of e-mail are that it is more immediate and more interactive. Employees can provide feedback immediately to what they read or hear, and businesses can respond quickly to this feedback. Stormhoek Wine Estate has managed to crack the difficult overseas export market through its creative and innovative use of alternative media such as its blog site to influence the external environment and its external publics. Visit their site at www.stormhoek.co.za and see for yourself. New Balance could release a viral campaign of its Code of Ethics on the internet that could include video clips of the inspection of its production plants around the world, for example. A viral campaign is when the clip is sent by customers who access it to each other, or even place it on a media vehicle such as YouTube to let anyone access it.

12.15 Summary

This chapter focused on the elements of the marketing process. Aspects covered include the definition of marketing, the gradual change in management's approach to marketing, the marketing concept, market research, market segmentation and target-market selection, consumer behaviour and the four marketing instruments.

It was shown that a market-driven organisation is essentially consumer oriented, takes strategic decisions based on pertinent information and maintains close relationships with a view to long-term profitability.

Marketing is a key function of an organisation, as was shown in the sections that dealt with the four marketing instruments that are combined in a marketing strategy. Opportunities in the environment must be met and threats must be dealt with within the framework of an ethical code of conduct, the marketing concept.

The various product decisions (including the product range, the brand, the packaging, the method used to differentiate the product from other products and new product development) were discussed. Product decisions consist of decisions regarding price, distribution and marketing communication or promotion. Distribution decisions entail considering the various distribution channels and the market coverage. It has been shown that a channel captain is able to dominate an entire channel and that large retailers, rather than producers, can act as channel captains. Price decisions are important because a price that is too low may lead to financial loss, perhaps giving the impression that the product is of inferior quality. Prices should be determined in such a way that they stimulate a demand for products. The marketer communicates with consumers through advertising, personal selling, direct marketing, sales promotion and publicity, endeavouring to inform them and persuade them to buy a specific brand repeatedly. Large sums of money are spent on producing effective messages to reach consumers. Public relations is a tool that can be used to support and maintain the positive image of an organisation with its many publics.

To conclude, marketing is a paradox. While it is a simple process, it can, at the same time, be extremely complex. It is at once a philosophy and a dynamic function of a business. It is new, but it is also as old as humankind itself.

Key terms

advertising	market positioning
bait prices	market price
brand	market-price level
brand decisions	market research
brand insistence	market segment
brand loyalty	new product decisions
brand name	odd prices
brand preference	opinion leaders
brand recognition	packaging
buyer	personal selling
channel captain	physical distribution
channel leadership	price
consumer behaviour	product
consumer orientation	product decisions
consumer products	product differentiation
cost price	product diversification
dealer	product items
demographics	product lines
distribution	product obsolescence
distribution channels	product offering
evaluating	product orientation
exclusive market coverage	product-range extensions
family packaging	product ranges
field workers	product recall
final price	profit
generic brands	psychographic
geographic	publicity
group factors	questionnaires
individual factors	reference group
individual/family brands	relationship marketing

intensive market coverage	research methodology
leader prices	retailer
manage	reusable packaging
manufacturer	sales forecasting
market coverage	sales orientation
market forecasting	sales promotion
marketing	segment
marketing communication	segment profile
marketing components	selective market coverage
marketing mix	seller
marketing orientation	services
marketing process	skimming prices
marketing strategy	speciality packaging
marketing thought	target price
market-penetration prices	wholesalers

? Questions for discussion

Reread the case study at the beginning of the chapter and answer the following questions:

1. Why do you think New Balance's marketing campaign was successful despite the fact that the company did not follow the traditional marketing communication approach?
2. Explain how New Balance made use of relationship marketing to build its brand.
3. Do you think New Balance has incorporated the marketing concept into its brand? Explain your answer by referring to each one of the principles of the marketing concept.
4. By referring to the marketing process, indicate how you would compile a marketing strategy for New Balance during the 2010 Comrades event.
5. What are the potential determinants of the buying behaviour of athletes participating in the Comrades?
6. Do you think New Balance has a clear segmented market? Motivate your answer.

? Multiple-choice questions

1. Look at the list of behavioural criteria below.
   i. Product usage
   ii. Brand loyalty
   iii. Post-purchase evaluation
   iv. Reverse price sensitivity

   Now select the combination of behavioural criteria that is relevant in market segmentation.
   a. i, iii
   b. i, ii, iv
   c. ii, iii, iv
   d. i, ii, iii
2. Look at the list of criteria below.
   i. The enterprise must provide the consumer with correct and sufficient information.
   ii. The enterprise must always try to satisfy all of the consumer's needs.
   iii. The enterprise should satisfy the consumer only within the limits of the profit objective.
   iv. The enterprise should contribute to the welfare of the community in which the consumers live.

   Now select the combination of criteria that the enterprise must demonstrate, according to the principle of consumer orientation.
   a. i, ii, iii
   b. i, iii
   c. ii, iii, iv
   d. iii, iv
3. Look at the list of variables known as marketing instruments below.
   i. The product itself
   ii. The distribution of the product
   iii. The marketing communication methods to be used

iv. The price of the product to the consumer
v. Profitability

Now select the combination of variables about which marketing management must take decisions.

a. i, ii, iii, iv
b. i, iii, iv
c. ii, iii, iv, v
d. ii, iii, v

4. Look at the list of variables on a consumer product below.
A consumer product consists of ...
i. a core product.
ii. a formal product.
iii. a need-satisfying product.
iv. the product image.
v. the total product.
Now decide which of these options is wrong.
a. none
b. ii
c. iii
d. iv
e. v

5. __________ mean(s) that an organisation distinguishes its product, physically and/or psychologically, from essentially identical competing products.
a. New product development
b. Product differentiation
c. Multi-product decisions
d. Product obsolescence

Answers to multiple-choice questions

1. b
2. b
3. a
4. a
5. b

References

1. Strydom, J.W., Cant, M.C., Jooste, C.J. & Du Plessis, P.J. 2006. *Marketing Management*. 5th ed. Cape Town: Juta, pp. 19–20.
2. Strydom, J.W., Cant, M.C., Jooste, C.J. & Du Plessis, P.J. 2006. *Marketing Management*. 5th ed. Cape Town: Juta, pp. 20–21.
3. Cant, M.C., Gerber-Nel, C., Nel, D. & Kotze, T. 2005. *Marketing Research*. Pretoria: Van Schaik, pp. 41–55.
4. Cant, M.C., Braink, A. & Brijbal, S. 2006. *Consumer Behaviour*. Cape Town: Juta, p. 2.
5. This definition was adapted from Cutlip, S.M., Center, A.H. & Broom, G.M. 2006. *Effective public relations*. Upper Saddle River: Pearson, p. 5 & Rensburg, R. & Cant, M. 2002. *Public relations: South African perspectives*. Johannesburg: Heinemann, p. 34.
6. Seitel, F.P. 2001. *The practice of public relations*. Upper Saddle River: Prentice-Hall, p. 304.

CHAPTER

13

FINANCIAL MANAGEMENT

The purpose of this chapter

This chapter explains what financial management entails and illustrates financial decision-making.

Learning outcomes

On completion of this chapter you should be able to:

- describe and apply the fundamental principles of financial management
- determine the break-even point of a business organisation
- calculate the present and future value of amounts
- analyse and interpret the financial statements of a business organisation
- understand the financial planning process
- manage the current assets of a business
- evaluate investment decisions
- find financing for a business.

13.1 Introduction

Financial management is the art and science of obtaining enough finance for a business at the lowest cost, investing in assets earning a return greater than the cost of capital, and managing the profitability, liquidity and solvency of the business. In the introductory chapters of this book, the financial function was identified as one of the functional management areas in a business. In this chapter, the nature and meaning of the financial function and its management, in other words, financial management, will be explained. Thereafter, the relationship between financial management, the other functional management areas, related subject disciplines and the environment will be shown. An introduction to a few basic concepts and techniques used by financial management will then follow. The goal and fundamental principles of financial management, including financial analysis, planning and control, will be explained. The chapter also explains how to finance a business and how to evaluate investment decisions.

13.2 The financial function and financial management

A business must have the necessary assets such as land, buildings, machinery, vehicles, equipment, raw materials and trade inventories at its disposal if it is to function efficiently. In addition, business organisations need further resources (such as management acumen and labour) and services (such as a power supply and communication facilities).

A business needs funds, also called **capital**, to obtain the required assets, resources and services. The people or institutions (including the owners) who make funds available to the business lose the right to use those funds in the short or long term, and they also run the risk of losing those funds, or a portion thereof, should the business fail. As a result, suppliers of funds expect compensation for the funds they make available to the business (and also a repayment of funds lent to the business) when it starts to generate funds through the sale of the products or services it produces. Hence, there is a continual flow of funds to and from the business. (See Figure 13.14 on p. 440.)

The **financial function** is concerned with this flow of funds. In particular, it is concerned with the acquisition of funds (known as **financing**), the application of funds for the acquisition of assets (known as **investment**), and the administration of and reporting on financial matters.

Financial management is responsible for the efficient management of all facets of the financial function. Within the broad framework of the strategies and plans of the business, its aim is to make the highest possible contribution to the objectives through the performance of the following tasks:

- financial analysis, reporting, planning and control
- management of the application of funds, also known as the management of the asset structure
- management of the acquisition of funds, also known as the management of the financing or capital structure.

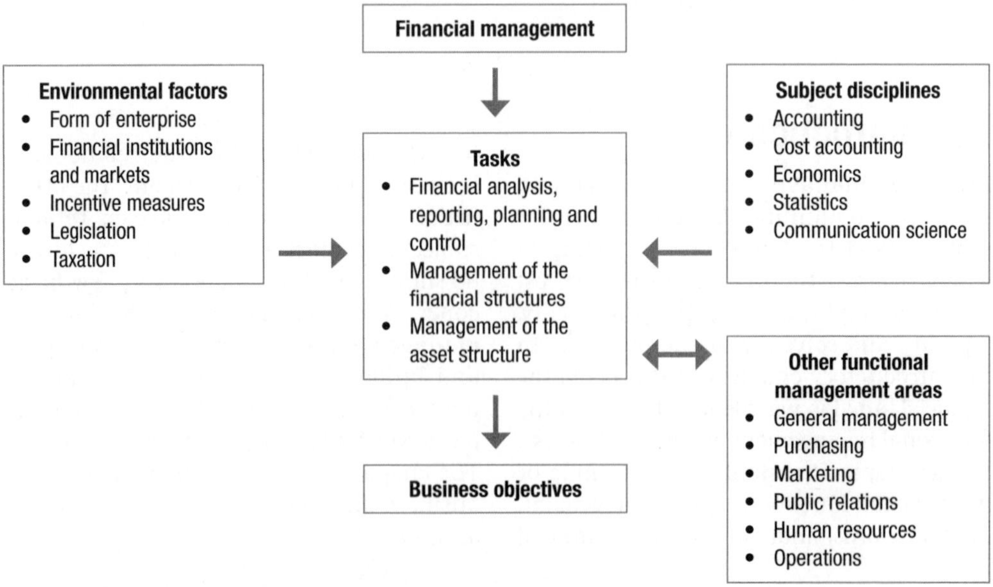

Figure 13.1: The relationship between financial management, other functional management areas, related disciplines and the environment

Financial management cannot function in isolation. Besides the interdependence between the functional management areas (without production and marketing, for example, no funds will be generated, and *vice versa*), financial management should also depend on other related subject disciplines, such as accounting and economics, if it wants to be efficient. As a subsystem of the business, the financial function, and therefore its management, is also influenced by environmental factors. The relationship between financial management, the other functional management areas, related subject disciplines and the environment is illustrated in Figure 13.1 on page 420.

The case study below provides an illustration of how financial management is applied in a real-life situation.

Case study

Financial management in action

Imagine that you own 20 000 shares of a retail firm listed on the JSE. You bought these shares at R5,20 each two years ago, but the price has subsequently declined to R1,90 each. Other firms in the same sector have seen increases in their profitability and share prices.

The annual general meeting (AGM) is scheduled to take place in six weeks' time. From the firm's financial statements, you have determined the information shown in Table 13.1.

Table 13.1: Information determined from the firm's financial statements

Ratio	This year	Average of the previous five years
Gross profit margin	40%	55%
Net profit margin	15%	30%
Return on assets	10%	21%
Return on equity	9%	24%
Earnings per share	45 cents	480 cents
Debt ratio	2%	10%
Current ratio	2,6:1	2:1
Quick ratio	0,8:1	1:1

The economic outlook is positive, interest rates are expected to decline, consumer spending is on the increase and inflation is below 3%. However, the top management seems to be divided about the issues facing the firm.

a. What can management do to improve the firm's profitability?
b. What can the investors (shareholders) do to improve matters?

Answers

a. The actions management could consider for improving the firm's profitability are summarised in Table 13.2 on page 422.
b. An ordinary shareholder of a public company is entitled to vote at the annual

general meeting of the company. The shareholder can improve matters by attending the AGM, and by nominating and voting for new members of the board of directors. If the shareholder cannot attend the meeting him-/herself, he/she can complete a proxy form and nominate someone who will be attending the meeting to vote in a particular manner on his/her behalf. Selling your shares will cause a loss of at least R3,30 per share or a total of R66 000 (R3,30 × 20 000 shares) before any transaction costs are taken into account. It might be worth engaging management and exerting pressure to implement a turnaround strategy that includes the actions described in Table 13.2.

Table 13.2: Actions management could consider for improving a firm's profitability

Ratio	Suggestions
Gross profit margin	1. Increase sales by means of more effective marketing and/or by relaxing the credit standards (increasing credit sales).
	2. Reduce the cost of products sold by buying products at a lower cost from another supplier, stocking products with a faster turnover rate and/or reconsidering products with slow turnover rates.
Net profit margin	1. Increase sales by means of more effective marketing and/or relaxing the credit standards (increasing credit sales).
	2. Reduce the operating expenses and/or improve productivity by means of, *inter alia*, performance-management systems, training and more effective use of technology.
Return on assets	1. Increase sales by means of more effective marketing and/or relaxing the credit standards (increasing credit sales) whilst decreasing expenses or using existing capacity more effectively.
	2. Review assets (disinvest non-core business units, use outsourcing and/or improve productivity).
Return on equity	1. Increase sales by means of more effective marketing, consider relaxing the credit standards (increase credit sales) during periods of possitive economic growth and reducing the cost of products sold. Reduce operating expenses and improve productivity.
	2. Reduce equity (buy back shares and cancel them), borrow to do so (increase the debt ratio).
Earnings per share	1. Improve profitability (as indicated above) by increasing sales and reducing expenses.
	2. Reduce the number of shares (buy back shares and cancel or consolidate shares). Replace this financing with debt financing.

13.3 Concepts in financial management

As in any field of study, it is necessary to describe certain concepts in financial management to present the subject in a meaningful manner.

13.3.1 The balance sheet, asset and financing structure

The **balance sheet** allows the viewer to have an overall grasp of the financial position of a business. It may be diagrammatically represented as in Figure 13.2 on page 423. The balance sheet is also known as the Statement of the Financial Position.

The information in Figure 13.2 is largely self-explanatory. The **asset side** reflects all the possessions of the business, together with their respective values as at the balance-sheet date, and therefore shows the mutual coherence between these possessions. These assets represent the **asset structure** of the business. Assets are normally divided into two broad categories in the balance sheet:

- **fixed assets** (also called non-current assets) such as land, buildings, machinery, vehicles and other equipment
- **current assets** such as cash in the bank, as well as other possessions of the business that will be converted into cash within one year during the normal course of business, such as marketable securities, debtors and all inventories.

The values at which the assets are recorded in the balance sheet differ according to the objectives for drawing up the balance sheet. For this reason, it is essential that the balance sheet should provide an indication of the values at which the assets have been recorded, for example, cost, cost less depreciation or cost plus appreciation.

The **liability** or claims side of the balance sheet reflects the nature and extent of the interests in the assets. In other words, it reflects the mutual coherence of the claims of the persons or institutions that provided funds (capital) for the "purchase" of the assets. Therefore the liability side of the balance sheet shows the **financing** or **capital structure** of the business as at the balance-sheet date.

The liability side of the balance sheet is usually subdivided on the basis of the following two criteria:

- the term for which the funds have been made available
- the source from which the funds have been obtained.

Therefore, the liability side of a company's balance sheet will contain the following details:

- **Long-term funds**. This is also known as non-current liabilities and comprises shareholders' interest and long-term debt.

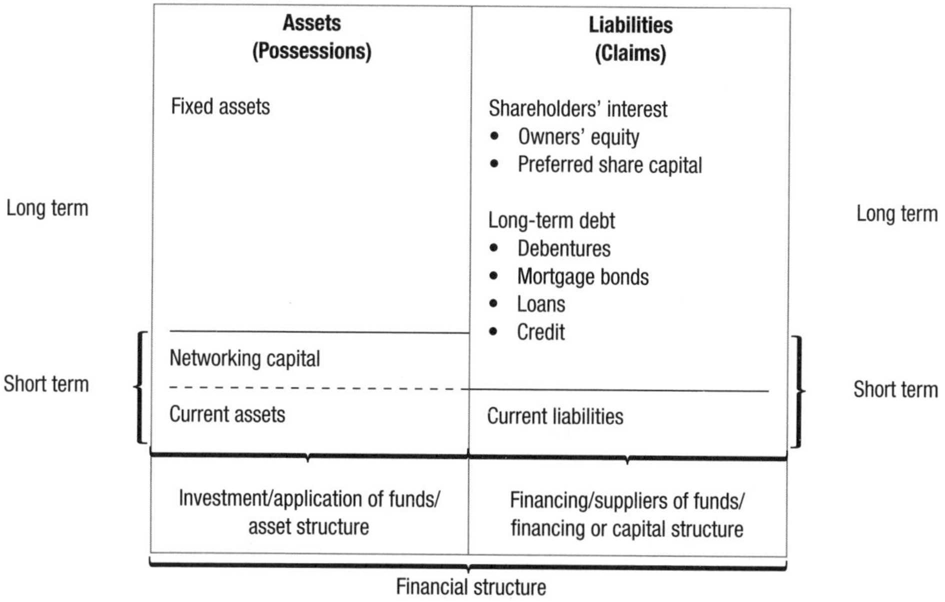

Figure 13.2: A diagrammatic representation of the balance sheet

- **Shareholders' interest** is further subdivided into owners' equity (made up of ordinary share capital, reserves, undistributed or retained profits) and, in some instances, preference-share capital. **Long-term debt** is usually made up of debentures, mortgage bonds, secured loans and long-term credit.
- **Short-term funds**. These are also referred to as current liabilities. They represent all debts or credit that are normally repayable within one year. Examples of these funds are bank overdrafts and trade creditors. The favourable difference between the current assets and the current liabilities represents the net working capital or that portion of the current assets that has been financed from long-term funds.

The shareholders' interest on the liability side of the balance sheet of businesses that do not have ordinary or preference shareholders (for example, sole proprietorships, partnerships and close corporations) is replaced by a capital account that reflects the owners' interest in the business.

13.3.2 Capital

Capital can be described as the accrued power of disposal over the products and services used by a business to generate a monetary return or profit. Stated differently, the capital of a business may briefly be described as the monetary value of the assets of the business at a specific time. The suppliers of capital are shown on the liability side of a balance sheet, as explained in section 13.3.1.

A business needs capital for investment in fixed assets (referred to as the **need for fixed capital**) and capital for investment in current assets (referred to as the **need for working capital**).

A business has a permanent need for a certain minimum portion of working capital. The remaining need for working capital will vary according to factors such as seasonal influences and contingencies that result in an increase or decrease in production activities.

The capital needs of a business can therefore be depicted as in Figure 13.3.

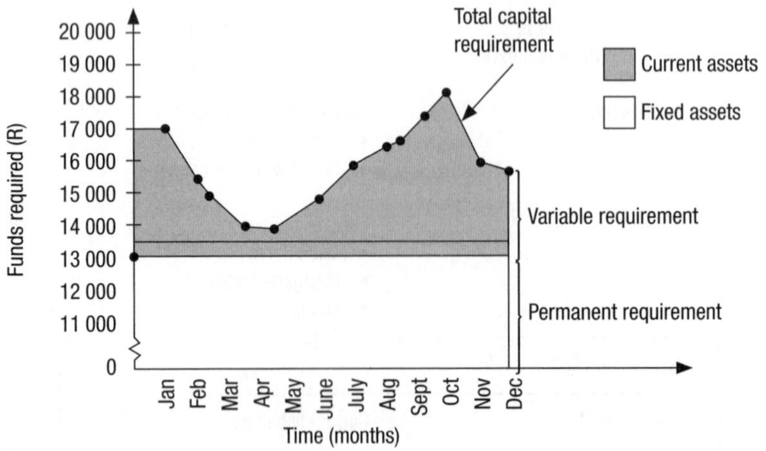

Figure 13.3: The capital requirements of a business

Source: Gitman, L.J. 1991. *Principles of Managerial Finance.* 6th ed., p. 675. Lawrence J. Gitman. Reproduced by permission of Pearson Education, Inc.

13.3.3 Income

The **income** of a business consists primarily of receipts resulting from the sale of its products and/or services. The extent of these receipts for a given period will depend on the quantity of products and/or services sold within that period, and the unit price for which they were sold.

Income = Units sold × Price per unit

The income of the business can also be obtained from other sources, such as interest earned on investments. However, this income will not be taken into account in the discussions that follow.

13.3.4 Costs

Costs can be regarded as the monetary value sacrificed in the production of products and/or services produced for the purpose of resale.

Example: Costs

In a manufacturing firm, cost will consist of used material, rent for a premises and building, depreciation of equipment, wages and salaries for all employees, payment for electricity and communication services, and so on.

Costs are further subdivided according to certain criteria, hence the business has direct costs, indirect costs, overhead expenses, fixed costs and variable costs.

The subdivision of total costs into fixed and variable costs is of particular importance for decision-making purposes. Thus, the remainder of this section will be devoted to this aspect. A further subdivision will be introduced in the discussion of the income statement in section 13.3.6.

Fixed cost is that portion of total cost that remains unchanged (within the boundaries of a fixed production capacity) regardless of an increase or decrease in the quantity of products and/or services produced.

By way of illustration, consider an accountancy practice with production capacity (that is, office space, equipment and permanent staff) to offer accounting services to 100 people. Office rent, depreciation on equipment and staff salaries will not change as long as the clientele does not exceed 100. An increase in the number of clients will necessitate an increase in the staff required. The increase in staff will have an effect on office space and furniture requirements. In this way, a new production capacity is created, which gives rise to a new fixed-cost component.

Total fixed costs as part of total costs for a particular period and capacity can be represented graphically as in Figure 13.4.

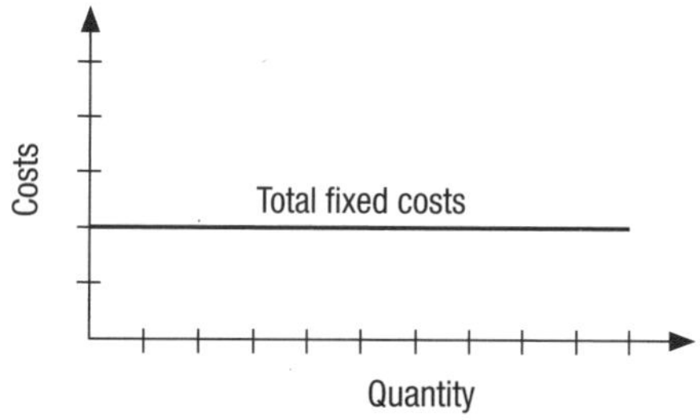

Figure 13.4: A graphical representation of total fixed costs

Total fixed costs are constant, irrespective of the volume produced. Therefore the fixed costs per unit produced will decrease with an increase in the quantity produced, as illustrated in Figure 13.5.

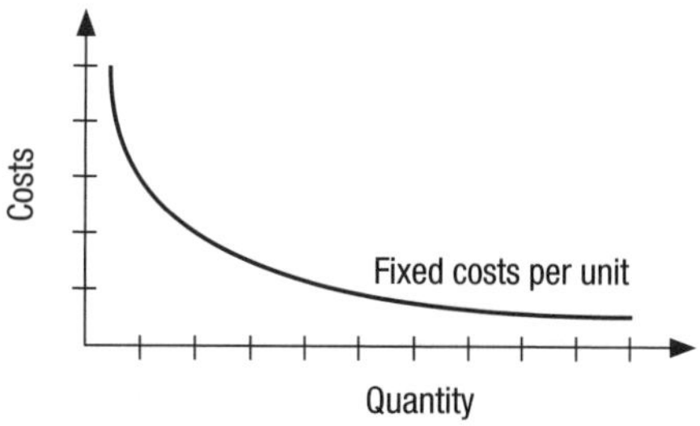

Figure 13.5: A graphical representation of fixed costs per unit

Variable cost is that portion of the total costs that changes according to a change in the volume produced. Some variable cost items, such as manufacturing material costs, can be regarded as pure variable costs because they change in direct proportion to a change in the volume produced. Other variable cost items contain a fixed-cost component, such as the fixed telephone rental. In this instance, there is not a pure linear relationship between these variable cost items and the volume produced. Therefore, these costs are referred to as **semi-variable costs**. Since these semi-variable costs do not have any substantial effect on the principle of fixed and variable costs, a pure linear relationship can, for purposes of illustration, be assumed between total variable costs and volume produced, as represented in Figure 13.6.

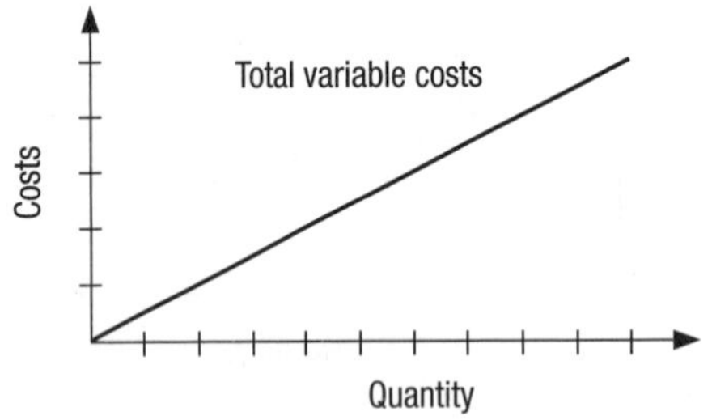

Figure 13.6: A graphical representation of total variable costs

The **variable costs per unit** produced remain more or less constant irrespective of the quantity produced. This point is illustrated in Figure 13.7.

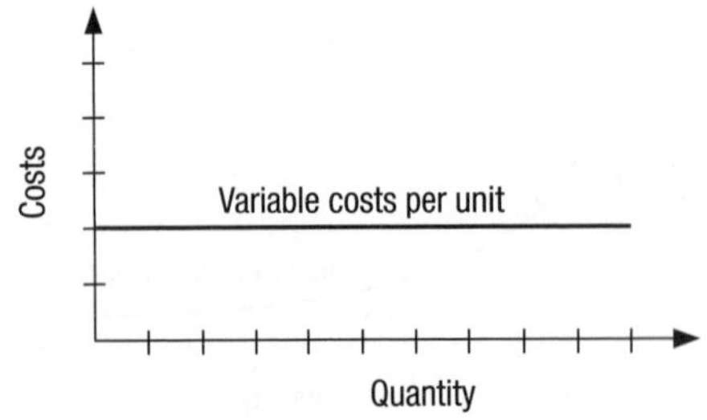

Figure 13.7: A graphical representation of variable costs per unit

The **total costs** involved in the production of a specific number of products produced in a particular period consist of the total fixed costs and the total variable costs incurred in the production of those products. Figure 13.8 graphically illustrates how total costs are arrived at.

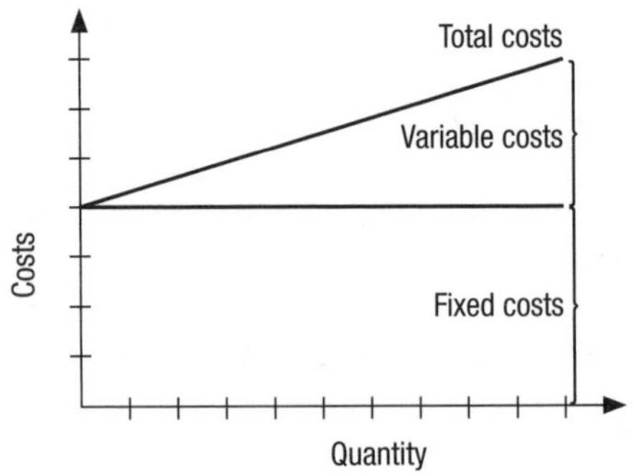

Figure 13.8: A graphical representation of total variable costs

To summarise, it may be stated that the total costs of the business comprise a fixed and a variable component, each of which has a specific relationship with the volume of production. These relationships have a specific influence on the profit made by businesses, as discussed in section 13.5.

13.3.5 Profit

Profit is regarded as the favourable difference between the income earned during a specific period and the **cost** incurred to earn that income. A **loss** results when the cost exceeds the income.

Profit or loss = Income − Cost

or

Profit or loss = (Price × Units sold) − Cost

Although the above comparison applies in general, various profit concepts in the different stages of the profit-determining process may be identified in the income statement.

13.3.6 The income statement

The income statement, one of the annual financial statements of a business, furnishes details about the manner in which the profit or loss for a particular period was arrived at and how it has been distributed. Sometimes the income statement is also referred to as the Statement of Financial Performance.

Figure 13.9 represents, in diagrammatic form, the income statement of a manufacturing business in company form. A numerical example of an income statement of such a business appears in section 13.7.1.1, while certain profit concepts are also further highlighted in Figure 13.14 (see page 440). Note that the income statement of a sole proprietorship, a partnership and a close corporation will in essence differ solely in the division of the net profit.

The information in Figure 13.9 is largely self-explanatory.

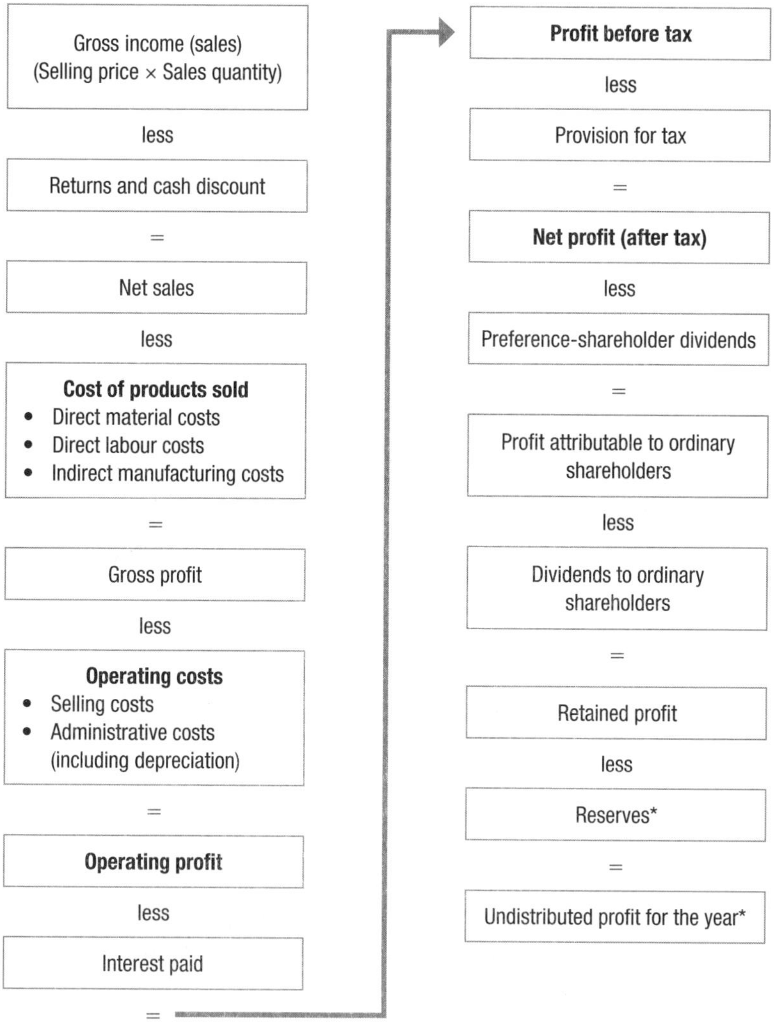

*Appears in the liability side of the balance sheet – see section 13.3.1

Figure 13.9: A diagrammatic representation of an income statement

Note that accountants sometimes use certain terms associated with income statements interchangeably, for example:

- sales/turnover
- operating profit/earnings before interest and tax (EBIT)
- profit/earnings.

13.4 Objective and fundamental principles of financial management[1]

The long-term objective should be to increase the value of the business. This may be accomplished by:

- investing in assets that will add value to the business
- keeping the cost of capital of the business as low as possible.

The short-term financial objective should be to ensure the profitability, liquidity and solvency of the business. Profitability is the ability of the business to generate income that will exceed cost. In order to maximise profit, a firm has to maximise revenue from sales whilst limiting expenses to the essential.

Liquidity is the ability of the business to satisfy its short-term obligations as they become due. In other words, it is the business's ability to pay the trade creditors by the due dates. Liquidity can be improved by accelerating cash inflows (collecting accounts receivable as fast as possible or making cash sales only) and paying creditors as late as possible.

Solvency is the extent to which the assets of the business exceed its liabilities. Solvency differs from liquidity in that liquidity pertains to the settlement of short-term liabilities, while solvency pertains to long-term liabilities such as debentures and mortgage loans.

Financial management is based on three principles: the risk–return principle, the cost–benefit principle and the time value of money principle.

13.4.1 The risk–return principle

Risk is the probability that the actual result of a decision may deviate from the planned end result, with an associated financial loss or waste of funds. Risk differs from uncertainty in that in the case of the latter, there is no probability or measure of the chances that an event will take place, whereas risk is measurable by means of statistical techniques.

Similar to the cost–benefit principle, the **risk–return** principle is a trade-off between risk and return. The greater the risk is, the greater the required rate of return will be.

13.4.2 The cost–benefit principle

Decision-making, which is based on the cost of resources only, will not necessarily lead to the most economic utilisation of resources. Sound financial decision-making requires making an analysis of the total cost and the total benefits, and ensuring that the benefits always exceed the cost. One application of the cost–benefit principle is illustrated in section 13.5 when the cost–volume–profit relationship is explained.

13.4.3 The time value of money principle

The time value of money principle means a person could increase the value of any amount of money by earning interest. If, however, the amount is invested in inventory, equipment, vehicles and so on, then the amount cannot earn interest. This ties up with the previous two principles. From a cost–benefit point of view, the investor has to earn a greater return on the investment in inventory, equipment and vehicles than on the best alternative type of investment. Equally, from a risk–return point of view, the return must compensate adequately for any risk incurred. The time value of money principle will be illustrated in section 13.6.

Applying the concept: Decision time

Someone who invests R500 000 in a business sacrifices the opportunity of earning interest on the amount because it could have been invested in a fixed deposit with less risk to earn 16% interest. The firm must earn a rate of return greater than 16% in order to increase the wealth of the owner.

13.5 Cost–volume–profit relationships

The concepts of costs, fixed costs, variable costs, income and profits, *inter alia*, were explained in section 13.3. In essence, the profitability of a business is determined by the unit selling price of its product, the costs (fixed and variable) of the product and the level of the activity of the business (the volume of production and sales). A change in any one of these three components will result in a change in the total profit made by the business. The components therefore have to be viewed in conjunction with each another and not in isolation. The underlying connection can be explained by means of a simplified numerical example in which only the volume of production and sales changes.

The calculation in the example is referred to as a **break-even analysis**, where the break-even point is reached when total costs are equal to total income. At the break-even point, no profit or loss is realised.

The break-even point in a specific case can be calculated by using the following formula:

$$N = \frac{F}{(SP - V)}$$

N in the formula is the number of units (volume) where no profit or loss is made. The term (SP − V) is referred to as the marginal income or variable profit.

Example: Estimating the profitability

Sales price (SP): R12 per unit
Variable cost (V): R8 per unit
Total fixed cost (FC): R100 000 per annum

Number of units manufactured and sold:
N = 30 000 (case 1)
N = 40 000 (case 2)

Profit = P
From P = Income − Cost

It follows that
P = (N × SP) − [(N × V) + F]

Where
N = 30 000
P is = (30 000 × 12) − [(30 000 × 8) + R100 000
= R360 000 − R340 000
= R20 000

Where
N = 40 000
P is = (40 000 × 12) − [(40 000 × 8) + R100 000]
= R480 000 − R420 000
= R60 000

The break-even analysis can also be done with the aid of a graph, as in Figure 13.10.

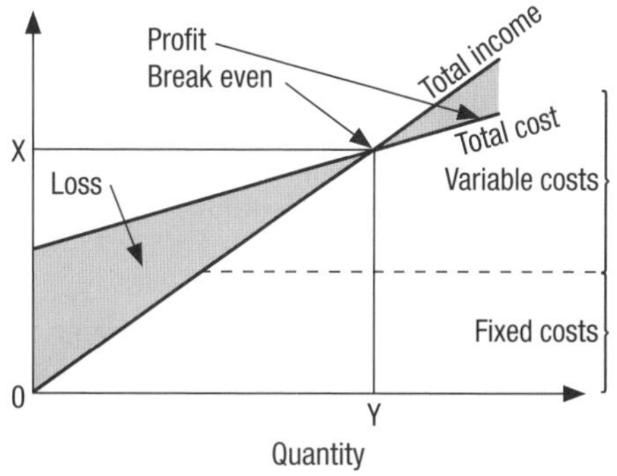

Figure 13.10: A graphical representation of a break-even analysis

The break-even point is reached when the total income and total cost curves intersect, in other words, at a sales and production volume of OY where the total costs and total income equal OX.

In the event of any change in the income as a result of a change in the selling price or a change in variable costs and/or fixed costs, the slope and point of intersection of the curves will change. The new break-even point is then to be obtained accordingly. The profit or loss at any sales volume can also be obtained. These values are the vertical differences between the total-cost and the total-income curves.

Example: Determining the break-even units

$$N = \frac{R100\,000}{(R12 - 8)} = \frac{R100\,000}{4} = 25\,000$$

Replace N = 25 000

P = (25 000 × R12) − [(25 000 × 8) + R100 000]

= 300 000 − R300 000

= R0

From the foregoing examples, it is apparent that the production and sales volumes, the unit selling price, and the fixed and variable costs together have an important effect on the profitability of a business. In practice, this type of analysis is carried out especially in the determination of the minimum size at establishment of a business manufacturing and marketing only one product, and also where the feasibility of potential expansion is concerned. A firm that provides more than one product will have to make use of a budgeted income statement in order to determine its break-even point.

13.6 The time value of money

13.6.1 Introduction

Section 13.2 stated that all businesses require capital. As is evident from the following discussion, the payment or remuneration for the use of money or capital is fundamental to the financial structure of any free-market society. It should be kept in mind in the investment and financing decisions of a business that interest has to be paid for the use of capital. Also, funds or capital are normally required and used for either shorter or longer periods, and the use of capital therefore has a time implication.

Consequently, the purpose of this discussion is to explain the concept of the **time value of money** – the combined effect of both interest and time – in the context of financial decision-making.

Critical thinking

The time value of money influences the way people approach cash flow, as will be illustrated here.

Time value of money and decision-making

What would you choose if you were faced with the choice of receiving a gift of R100 in cash today or the same amount a year from now? Obviously, you would choose to be given the R100 today. Why?

- The R100 received today can be invested to earn interest, resulting in a larger amount after one year, purely because of the time value of money.
- The person who wishes to donate the money may not be able or willing to donate the amount a year from now. To wait causes risk and uncertainty.
- In times of inflation, the real purchasing power of R100 will decline as time goes by.

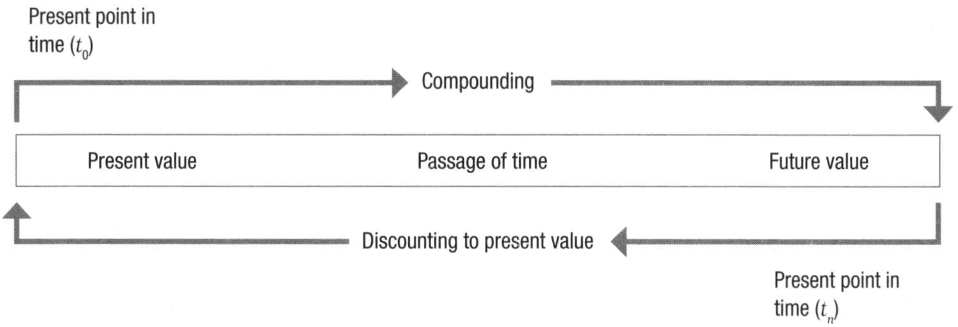

Figure 13.11: The relationship between present value and future value

In principle, the time value of money bears a direct relation to the opportunity of earning interest on an investment. This is the opportunity rate of return on an investment. The opportunity to earn interest in the interim period is foregone if an amount is expected some time in the future rather than being received immediately.

The time value of money can be approached from two different perspectives. On the one hand, the calculation of the **future value** of some given present value or amount is possible, as is, on the other hand, the calculation of the **present value** of some expected future amount.

The processes for the calculation of future values (**compounding**) and for the calculation of present values (**discounting**) proceed in opposite directions, as indicated in Figure 13.11.

13.6.2 The future value of a single amount

The future value of an initial investment or principal is determined by means of **compounding**, which means that the amount of interest earned in each successive period is added to the amount of the investment at the end of the preceding period. Interest in the period immediately following is consequently calculated on a larger amount consisting of capital and interest. Interest is therefore earned on capital and interest in each successive period.

The formula for calculating the future value of an original investment is:

$$FV_n = PV\,(1 + i)^n$$

Where:
- PV is the original investment or present value of the investment.
- FV_n is the future value of the investment after n periods.
- i is the interest rate per period expressed as a decimal number.
- n is the number of discrete periods over which the investment extends.

In fact, these symbols also appear on financial calculators.

The factor $(1 + i)^n$ in the formula is known as the **future-value factor** (FVF) or **compound-interest factor** of a single amount.

The process for future-value calculation is illustrated in Figure 13.12 on page 432.

The future value of an original investment can also be calculated by using tables. An extract from these tables follows.

The example below for a three-year investment at an interest rate of 5% per annum is calculated as follows with the aid of Table 13.5 on page 433:

$$FV_3 = R100\,(1{,}1576)$$
$$= R115{,}76$$

The result is identical to the one obtained by using the formula.

Example

- What is the future value of R100 invested for one year at an interest rate of 5% per annum?

FV_1 = R100 $(1 + 0{,}05)^1$
= R100 (1,05)
= R105

Table 13.3: Calculating future value with a financial calculator (example 1)

Key in	Press	Calculator display	Press
100	±	−100	PV
1	n	1	
5	*I/YR*	5	
	FV	105	

- And if the investment term is three years?

FV_3 = R100 $(1{,}05)^3$
= R100 (1,1576)
= R115,76

Table 13.4: Calculating future value with a financial calculator (example 2)

Key in	Press	Calculator display	Press
100	±	−100	PV
3	n	3	
5	*I/YR*	5	
	FV	115,76	

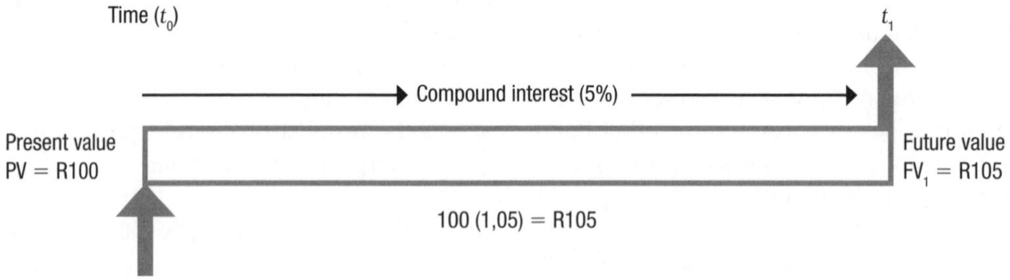

Figure 13.12: Process for future-value calculation

Bear in mind that the future-value factor $(1 + i)^n$ is an exponential function, which means that the initial amount will grow exponentially over time.

The higher the interest rate is, the faster the future value will grow for any given investment period as a result of the compounding effect and, consequently, interest is earned on interest in each successive period. The concept of the compound interest rate as a growth rate is of vital importance in financial management.

The values of any of the four variables in the equation for the calculation of the future value can be determined if the values of the remaining three variables are known, as shown below.

Example

$FV_n = PV(1 + i)^n$

- Future value
- Present value
- Compound interest rate
- Duration

Table 13.5: Extract from a table used to calculate future value of an original investment

	Future-value factors $(1 + i)^n$		
Periods (n)	**5%**	**10%**	**15%**
1	1,0500	1,1000	1,1500
2	1,1025	1,2100	1,3225
3	1,1576	1,3310	1,5209
4	1,2155	1,4641	1,7490
5	1,2763	1,6105	2,0114
6	1,3401	1,7716	2,3131
7	1,4071	1,9487	2,6600
8	1,4775	2,1436	3,0590
9	1,5513	2,3579	3,5179
10	1,6289	2,5937	4,0456

13.6.3 Present value

13.6.3.1 The present value of a single amount

The present value is also based on the principle that the value of money is, *inter alia*, affected by the timing of receipts or disbursements, as in the case of the future value.

If it is accepted that a rand today is worth more than a rand expected at some future date, what would the present value be now of an amount expected in future? The answer to this question revolves around the following:

- investment opportunities available to the investor or recipient
- the future point in time at which the money is expected.

An amount of R105 that is expected one year from now will have a present value of R100, provided the opportunity exists to invest the R100 today (time t_0) at an interest rate of 5% per annum.

The interest rate, which is used for discounting the future value of R105 one year from now to a present value of R100,

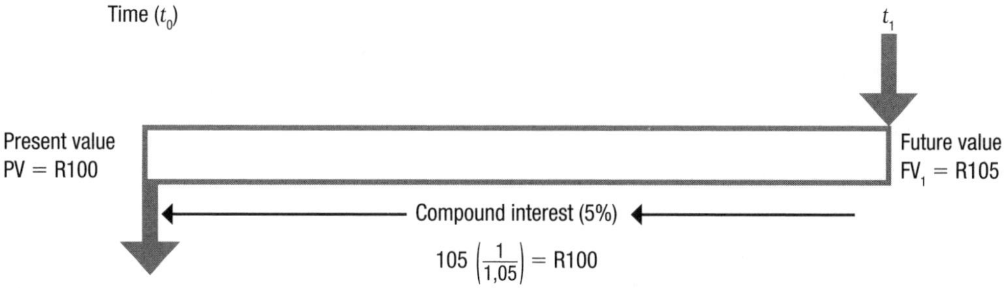

Figure 13.13: Process for calculating the present value of a single amount

reflects the time value of money and is the key to the present-value approach. This interest rate or opportunity rate of return is the rate of interest that could be earned on alternative investments with similar risks if the money had been available for investment now. Stated differently, it is the rate of return that would be foregone by not utilising the investment opportunity. The process of discounting is explained by means of the time line in Figure 13.13 on page 433.

The **discounting process** is the reciprocal of the compounding process.

Consequently, the formula for the calculation of the present value of a future single amount is:

$$PV = FV_n \left(\frac{1}{(1+i)}\right)^n$$

The factor $\left(\frac{1}{(1+i)}\right)^n$ is known as the **present-value factor** or **discounting factor** for a future single amount.

Tables have also been compiled for the calculation of present values. An extract from these tables follows.

Example: Calculating present values

- What is the present value of R105 expected one year from now if the investor's opportunity cost (discount rate) is 5% per annum?

$$PV = FV_1 \left(\frac{1}{(1+0{,}05)}\right)^1$$

$$= R105 \left(\frac{1}{(1{,}05)}\right)^1$$

$$= R100$$

Table 13.6: Calculating present value with a financial calculator (example 1)

Key in	Press	Calculator display	Press
105		105	FV
1	N	1	
5	I/YR	5	
	PV	−100	

(The minus sign in front of the R100 can be ignored here. It is displayed purely as a result of the convention of financial calculators in order to distinguish between cash inflows and cash outflows, where negative figures normally indicate cash outflows).

- What is the present value of R115,76 invested under the same circumstances and expected in three years' time?

$$PV = R115{,}76 \left(\frac{1}{(1+0{,}05)}\right)^3$$

$$= R115{,}76\ (0{,}8638)$$

$$= R100$$

Table 13.7: Calculating present value with a financial calculator (example 2)

Key in	Press	Calculator display	Press
115,76		115,76	FV
3	N	3	
5	I/YR	5	
	PV	−100	

Table 13.8: Extract from a table used to calculate present values

	Discouting factors $\frac{1}{(1+i)^n}$		
Periods (n)	**5%**	**10%**	**15%**
1	0,9524	0,9091	0,8696
2	0,9070	0,8264	0,7561
3	0,8638	0,7513	0,6575
4	0,8227	0,6830	0,5718
5	0,7835	0,6209	0,4972
6	0,7462	0,5645	0,4323
7	0,7107	0,5132	0,3759
8	0,6768	0,4665	0,3269
9	0,6446	0,4241	0,2843
10	0,6139	0,3855	0,2472

In the example on page 434, the present value of R115,76 expected three years from now is calculated as follows, with the aid of Table 13.8, at an opportunity rate of return or discounting rate of 5%.

$$\begin{aligned} PV &= R115{,}76\ (PVF_{5,3}) \\ &= R115{,}76\ (0{,}8638) \\ &= R100 \end{aligned}$$

The present value of a single amount is, accordingly, defined as follows:

> The **present value (PV)** of a future **FV$_n$** is the monetary amount that can be invested today at a given interest rate i per period in order to grow to the same future amount after n periods.

As illustrated in the example on page 434, as long as the opportunity for investment at 5% per annum exists, the investor should be indifferent to a choice between R100 today or R115,76 in three years' time.

Closer investigation of the preceding discounting factors reveals that the values of these factors decrease progressively as i or n, or both, increase. The exceptionally high decrease in the discounting factor with relatively high interest rates and long time periods means that:

- The higher the interest rate is, the smaller the present value of a given future amount will be.
- The further in the future an amount is expected, the smaller its present value at a given interest rate will be.

Interestingly, the present-value factor $PVF_{10,10} = 0{,}3855$ implies that the present value of R1,00 expected in ten years is only 38,55 cents today, if the R1,00 could have been invested today at 10% for ten years. If an investment opportunity at 15% should exist (which is not unrealistic), the present value of R1,00 expected ten years from now is only 24,72 cents ($PVF_{15,10} = 0{,}2472$). Put differently, this also means that the value or purchasing power of R1,00 will decline to 24,72 cents over the next ten years if the average annual inflation rate is to be 15% a year over this period.

The present-value factors and the future-value factors (as well as the tables for these factors) are based on the assumption that any funds generated in any period over the total duration of the investment or project (such as annual interest receipts) are reinvested at the same interest rate for the remainder of the total investment period.

The values of any one of the four variables in the equation for the calculation of the future value can be determined provided that the values of the three remaining variables are known.

Example

$$PV = FV_n\left(\frac{1}{1+i}\right)^n$$

- Present value
- Future value
- Opportunity rate of return or discounting rate
- Duration

13.6.3.2 The present value of an uneven cash-flow stream

The determination of the present value of a series of unequal cash-flow amounts is approached in the same way as one would approach a single amount, irrespective of the total duration or the number of time periods involved. As in all applications of the time value of money, the timing of the cash receipts or disbursements is of crucial importance. This is evident from the following example of the calculation of the present value of an uneven cash-flow stream at an interest rate or discounting rate of 10%.

The appropriate discounting factors are found in Table 13.8.

$$\begin{aligned} PV &= R1\,000\ (0{,}9091) + R500\ (0{,}8264) + 0 \\ &\quad + R4\,500\ (0{,}6830) + R6\,000\ (0{,}6209) \\ &= R909{,}10 + R413{,}20 + 0 \\ &\quad + R3\,073{,}50 + R3\,725{,}40 \\ &= R8\,121{,}20 \end{aligned}$$

Example

Year (t)	Annual cash inflow (Cf_t)
1	R1 000
2	R500
3	R0
4	R4 500
5	R6 000
Total	R12 000

The calculation can be done by means of a financial calculator as shown in Table 13.9.

Table 13.9: Calculating present value of a mixed stream with a financial calculator (example 3)

Key in	Press	Calculator display
0	CF	0
1 000	CF	1 000
500	CF	500
0	CF	0
4 500	CF	4 500
6 000	CF	6 000
10	I/YR	10
	NPV	8 121,40

Notes:

1. Financial calculators assume the first cash flow (Cf) for this type of calculation occurs in time period 0. The figures in the table above indicate that the first cash inflow of R1 000 only occurred in period 1. Thus the cash inflow of R0 for time period 0, followed by the R1 000 of time period 1 and the subsequent cash inflows.
2. The NPV procedure by means of a financial calculator does not require that the number of periods (n) be keyed in.
3. Financial calculators use up to ten digits in order to perform calculations. Financial tables normally indicate only three or four digits. This leads to different answers when time value of money calculations are performed. In the above example, the financial calculator produced an answer of

R8 121,40 compared to the answer of R8 121,20 produced by means of financial tables. Note that no cash flow occurs at the end of the third period, and no contribution to the total present value at time t_0 therefore originates from that period. The cash-flow amounts at the end of the first, second, fourth and fifth years respectively are multiplied by the respective discounting factors $PVF_{10,1}$, $PVF_{10,2}$, $PVF_{10,4}$ and $PVF_{10,5}$. The present values of the individual cash amounts are eventually added to obtain the total present value for the above uneven cash-flow stream at time t_0. Capital investment decisions in particular require the calculation of the present value of uneven cash-flow streams.

This brief overview of the present-value approach is deemed sufficient for the purposes of this discussion. However, in practice, interest on savings accounts and deposits are often calculated biannually, quarterly, monthly, weekly and even daily. This could apply to both future-value and present-value applications, and is known as intra-year compounding and discounting.

13.6.4 Conclusion

The principles and application of compounding and the time value of money as a basis for the determination of present values as well as future values have been explained in this section. The present-value approach is an indispensable aid in financial management, particularly for a large business and listed company, where the majority of investment and financing decisions are taken in accordance with the goal of the maximisation of the value of the business. Even for small business organisations, a basic knowledge of compound-interest methodology and unsophisticated discounted cash-flow applications could be invaluable for capital investment decisions.

The most important implications of time value of money are as follows:

- Inflow must be accelerated. (Encourage debtors to pay their accounts as soon as possible.)
- Outflow should be delayed without damaging the firm's credit record. (Pay creditors as late as possible.)
- Manage inventory as optimally as possible because it represents capital that does not earn a return before it is sold.

13.7 Financial analysis, planning and control[2]

In section 13.2, effective financial analysis, planning and control were identified as tasks of financial management. In this section, a short review of these related tasks is given.

13.7.1 Financial analysis

Financial analysis is necessary to monitor the general financial position of a business and, in the process, to limit the risk of financial failure of the business as far as possible. Financial analyses will reveal certain trends, and also the financial strengths and weaknesses of the business so that corrective measures, if necessary, can be taken in time. To help it with its financial analyses, financial management have the following important aids at their disposal:

- the income statement
- the balance sheet
- the funds-flow statement
- financial ratios.

The sections that follow will focus on the various statements and the calculation of certain financial ratios.

13.7.1.1 The income statement

The income statement has already been described in section 13.3.6 and diagrammatically represented in Figure 13.9 on page 427. Consequently, a numerical example of a manufacturing company's abridged income statement (see Table 13.10 on page 438) will suffice for the purposes of this section.

Table 13.10: An example of an abridged income statement (rand values)

Abridged income statement of ABC Limited for the year ended 28 February 2009		
Net sales		R3 000 000
Less cost of sales (cost of products sold)		2 250 000
• Direct labour costs	1 000 000	
• Direct material costs	900 000	
• Indirect manufacturing costs	350 000	
Gross profit		750 000
Less operating costs		400 000
• Selling expenses	150 000	
• Depreciation	80 000	
• Administrative costs	170 000	
Operating profit		350 000
Less interest paid		30 000
Profit before tax		320 000
Tax (29%)		92 800
Net profit after tax		227 200
Less dividends to preference shareholders		5 000
Profit attributable to ordinary shareholders		222 200
Less dividends to ordinary shareholders		75 000
Retained profit (earnings)		147 200
Less reserves		–
Undistributed profit for the year		147 200

13.7.1.2 The balance sheet

The balance sheet of a **company** and the most important balance-sheet items have already been discussed in section 13.3.1 and represented diagrammatically in Figure 13.2 (see page 423). Thus, a numerical example of a company's balance sheet will suffice for the purposes of this section (see Table 13.11).

Table 13.11: An example of a company balance sheet

Balance sheet of ABC Limited at 28 February 2009

Assets (Employment of capital)				**Equity and liabilities (Capital employed)**		
			R			**R**
Fixed assets			800 000	**Shareholder's capital**		
Lands and buildings (cost price)		200 000		Authorised and issued – ordinary shares (200 000 at R1 each)		200 000
Plant and equipment (cost price)	1 200 000					
Less				**Distributable reserves**		
Accumulated depreciation	600 000	600 000		Capital reserves	300 000	
				Undistributed profit	350 000	650 000
Other assets				*Owners' equity*		850 000
Investments			–	Preference-share capital		50 000
Total long-term assets			800 000	*Shareholders' interest*		900 000
Current assets			550 000	**Long-term debt**		
Cash		60 000		Debentures		200 000
Marketable securities		30 000		*Total long-term liabilities*		1 100 000
Debtors (net)		220 000				
Inventory		200 000		**Current liabilities**		250 000
Pre-paid expenses		40 000		Trade creditors	100 000	
				Bank overdraft	100 000	
				Arrear expenses	50 000	
			1 350 000			1 350 000

13.7.1.3 The flow of funds in a business

A business has to make optimum use of its limited funds to achieve its objectives. It is therefore necessary to conduct an analysis of how the capital of the business is employed and supplied. This analysis involves the flow of funds in the business.

The flow of funds of a firm is a continuous process and, following on the previous explanations of the balance sheet and income statement, can be represented as in Figure 13.14.

The following points are apparent from Figure 13.14:

- The business obtains funds in the financial market and utilises these funds at a cost to produce products and/or services.
- The business sells these products and/or services at a price higher than the production costs and therefore shows an operating profit.
- Interest is paid to the suppliers of loan capital from the operating profit. This means an outflow of funds from the business.
- The profit remaining after the interest has been paid is taxable. This means a further outflow of funds from the business.
- The profit remaining after tax can be applied to preference and ordinary shareholders' dividends (outflow of funds), reserves and undistributed profits, resulting in a reinvestment in the production process.

It is clear from Figure 13.14 that there is a continuous flow of funds to and from the business. If the sales value of the products and/or services produced by the business exceeds the costs incurred in the production of those products and/or services, including the depreciation on equipment, the business will show a profit. A portion of the profit, after payment of interest and tax, is normally distributed among the preference and ordinary shareholders in the form of

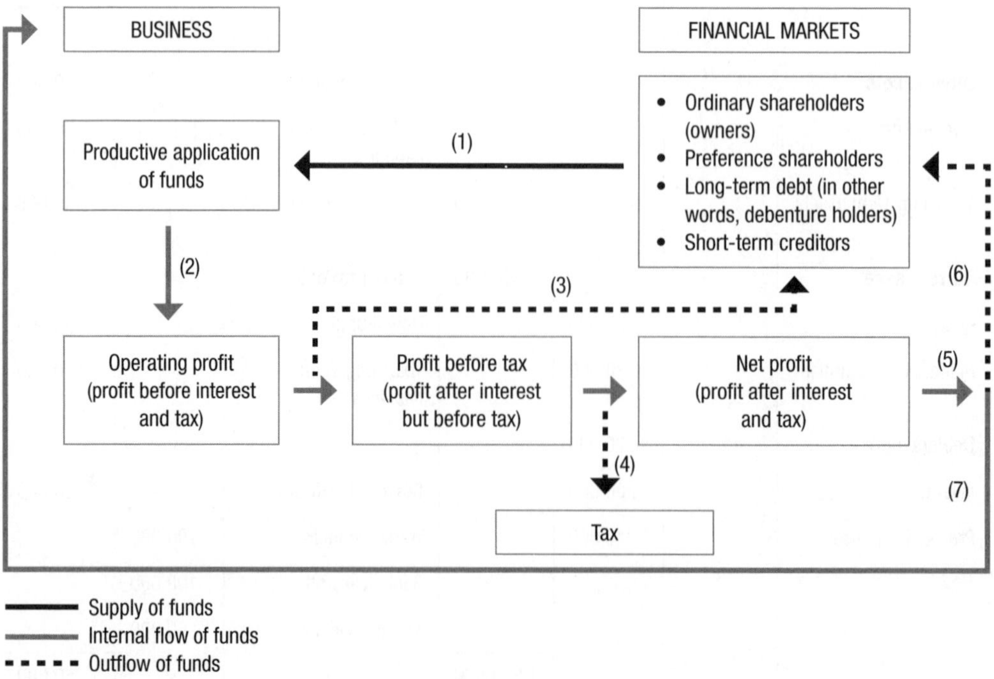

Figure 13.14: A simplified diagrammatical representation of the flow of funds of a business

dividends. The remaining profit is reinvested in the business. The reinvestment leads to an increase in the available funds of the business.

13.7.1.4 The funds-flow statement

The funds-flow statement helps with the analysis of the changes in the financial position of the business between two consecutive balance-sheet dates and, in the process, reflects the net effect of all transactions for a specific period on the financial position of the business. With this in mind, the balance sheets at the beginning and end of the period under review, as well as the income statement for the same period, are used.

The funds-flow statement is based on the self-explanatory point of departure that the employment of funds depends on the availability of funds. In other words, before funds can be applied, they have to be obtained from some source.

There are two approaches to drawing up a funds-flow statement:

- according to changes in the net working capital
- according to changes in the cash position, including the current bank account.

Both approaches have their merits. However, the remainder of the discussion of the funds-flow statement will be based on the second approach, simply because funds-flow statements drawn up according to this method contain more information than those drawn up using the first approach.

The funds-flow statement that is drawn up on a cash basis contains a summary of the sources from which cash has been generated between two consecutive balance-sheet dates, as well as a summary of the purposes for which cash has been used during the same period. If more cash has been generated than employed during the period under review, the cash available to the business will increase, and *vice versa*.

Funds-flow statements drawn up according to this approach can be presented in various forms. Table 13.12 on page 442 represents one of the forms that can be adopted.

An analysis of the funds-flow statement offers many advantages, including the following:

- It gives an indication of whether the cash dividends are justified in terms of the cash generated by the business activities (profit).
- It gives an indication of how the growth in fixed assets has been financed.
- It gives an indication of possible imbalances in the application of funds.
- It helps financial management to analyse and evaluate the financing methods of the business.

13.7.1.5 Financial ratios

As mentioned earlier, financial ratios are one of the aids that financial management can employ in the process of effective financial analysis and control.

A financial ratio gives the relationship between two items (or groups of items) in the financial statements (especially the income statement and the balance sheet). It also serves as a performance criterion to point out potential strengths and weaknesses of the business.

However, it must be emphasised that financial ratios do not identify the reasons for the strengths and weaknesses. They only indicate symptoms that need to be further diagnosed by financial management.

The financial ratios of a business are used by the following interested parties:

- **financial management**, with a view to internal control, planning and decision-making
- the **suppliers of borrowed capital**, to evaluate the ability of the business to pay its debt and interest
- **investment analysts**, to evaluate the business as an investment opportunity
- **labour unions**, with a view to salary negotiations.

Table 13.12: A framework for a funds-flow statement on cash use

Funds-flow statement for the period 1 March 2008 to 28 February 2009

Source of funds	**R**	**R**	**Application of funds**	**R**	**R**
Profit before tax		....	*Loss*		....
			Depreciation in share and preference-share capital		....
			Income tax paid		....
Depreciation[1]		....			
Increase in share and preference-share capital		....	Cash dividends		....
Increase in debt (excluding bank overdraft and provisions)			*Decrease in debt* (excluding bank overdraft and provisions)		
• Trade creditors	....		• Trade creditors	....	
• Arrear expenses	....		• Arrear expenses	....	
• Long-term loans	....	....	• Long-term loans	....	....
Decrease in assets (excluding cash in bank and on hand)			*Increase in assets* (excluding cash in bank and on hand)		
• Debtors	....		• Debtors	....	
• Stocks	....		• Stocks	....	
• Pre-paid expenses	....		• Pre-paid expenses	....	
• Sales of fixed assets[2]	....	....	• Sales of fixed assets[3]	....	....
Subtotal			Subtotal		
Balance (decrease in cash)[4]		(X)	Balance (increase in cash)[4]		(X)
		XXX			XXX

Notes:

1. Depreciation is deducted as a cost in order to calculate the profit (loss) before tax. Because it actually represents a non-cash cost, depreciation has to be added back to reflect the actual cash position.
2. Shown at net selling price.
3. At cost.
4. If the total source of funds exceeds the total application of funds, the difference will mean an increase in cash, and *vice versa*. The balances have to tally with the difference in cash between the opening and closing balance sheet.

Financial ratios as such have little, if any, usage value, and must be viewed against certain significant standards or norms to give them usage value. Three types of comparisons are significant in this regard:

- a comparison of the current financial ratios of the business with the corresponding ratios of the past and/or expected future ratios with a view to revealing a tendency
- a comparison of the financial ratios of the business with those of other similar businesses
- a comparison of the financial ratios of the business with the norms for the particular industry as a whole.

There are many different kinds of financial ratio and various classification methods. In this section, only a few kinds are mentioned without paying attention to their respective merits. The calculations of the various ratios are explained by using the information given in the previous income statement (see Table 13.10 on page 438) and balance sheet (see Table 13.11 on page 439).

Liquidity ratios

Liquidity ratios provide an indication of the ability of a business to meet its short-term obligations as they become due without curtailing or ceasing its normal activities. Providers of loan capital are interested in liquidity ratios because they give an indication of the degree to which a business can meet its debt obligations fully and punctually in the normal course of events.

Two liquidity ratios are of importance: the current ratio and the acid-test ratio.

The current ratio

The **current ratio** reflects the relationship between the value of the current assets and the extent of the current liabilities of a business.

$$\text{Current ratio} = \frac{\text{Current assets}}{\text{Current liabilities}}$$

Using the figures of ABC Limited contained in Table 13.11 on page 439 results in a current ratio of 2,2:1, calculated as follows:

$$\text{Current ratio} = \frac{\text{Current assets}}{\text{Current liabilities}}$$

$$= \frac{550\ 000}{250\ 000}$$

$$= 2{,}2:1$$

This means that the business had R2,20 of current assets available for each R1 of its current liabilities (short-term obligations). The smaller the ratio is, the greater the possibility that the business will not be able to meet its debt obligations fully and punctually without curtailing or ceasing its normal activities. Traditionally a current ratio of 2:1 is recommended.

The acid-test ratio

Since inventory cannot always be readily converted into cash in the short term, it may be misleading to evaluate the liquidity position of a business simply on the basis of the current ratio. The **acid-test ratio** should therefore be used in combination with the current ratio as a criterion for evaluating liquidity.

$$\text{Acid-test ratio} = \frac{\text{Current assets} - \text{Inventory}}{\text{Current liabilities}}$$

Using the figures of ABC Limited contained in Table 13.11 on page 439 results in an acid-test ratio of 1,4:1, calculated as follows:

$$\text{Acid-test ratio} = \frac{\text{Current assets} - \text{Inventory}}{\text{Current liabilities}}$$

$$= \frac{550\ 000 - 200\ 000}{250\ 000}$$

$$= \frac{350\ 000}{250\ 000}$$

$$= 1{,}40:1$$

This shows that for each rand's worth of current liabilities, the business had R1,40 of current assets, excluding inventory. As in the case of the current ratio, a larger ratio reflects a healthier liquidity position than a smaller ratio. Normally, a minimum acid-test ratio of 1:1 is recommended.

Liquidity ratios should be evaluated with caution. The **nature** and **condition** of the current assets and the "correctness" of the **values** at which they were recorded in the balance sheet can cause the actual liquidity position to differ radically from that which is reflected by the liquidity ratios.

Although it is important for a business to be liquid, it is also possible to be excessively liquid. A current ratio of, for example, 5:1 could be an indication that the firm is carrying too much inventory, selling too much on credit, collecting accounts receivable too slowly and/or has too much cash on hand. An acid-test ratio of, for example, 3:1 could be an indication that the firm is selling too much on credit, collecting accounts receivable too slowly and/or has too much cash on hand. In such a case, funds are not being used optimally, but are confined to unproductive use in current assets. It is therefore important to realise that one should not strive unrestrictedly towards an improvement in the liquidity ratios.

Solvency ratios

Solvency ratios indicate the ability of a business to repay its debts from the sale of the assets on cessation of its activities. Capital lenders usually show strong interest in solvency ratios because these indicate the risk level of an investment in the business. Seen from another angle, it gives the business an indication of the extent to which it will have access to additional loan capital and the extent of its risk in its current financing.

There are two particularly important solvency ratios: the debt ratio and the gearing ratio.

The debt ratio

The **debt ratio** may be calculated using the following equation:

$$\text{Debt ratio} = \frac{\text{Debt}}{\text{Assets}} \times \frac{100}{1}$$

Using the figures of ABC Limited contained in Table 13.11 on page 439 results in a debt ratio of 37%, calculated as follows:

$$\text{Debt ratio} = \frac{\text{Debt}}{\text{Assets}} \times \frac{100}{1}$$

$$= \frac{500\,000}{1\,350\,000} \times \frac{100}{1}$$

$$= 37\%$$

This means that 37% of the assets were financed by debt (including preference shares if they are callable). A lower percentage reflects a more favourable position than a higher percentage, and a maximum debt ratio of 50% is normally required.

The gearing ratio

The **gearing ratio** may be calculated using the following equation:

$$\text{Gearing ratio} = \frac{\text{Owners' equity}}{\text{Debt}}$$

Using the figures of ABC Limited contained in Table 13.11 on page 439 results in a gearing ratio of 1,7:1, calculated as follows:

$$\text{Gearing ratio} = \frac{\text{Owners' equity}}{\text{Debt}}$$

$$= \frac{850\,000}{500\,000}$$

$$= 1{,}7:1$$

This indicates that for each R1 of debt (including preference shares), the business had R1,70 of owners' equity. (The value of preference shares in the balance sheet should be regarded as debt if the preference shares are callable). A larger ratio once again reflects a more favourable situation than a smaller ratio, and a minimum gearing ratio of 1:1 is normally required.

The following aspects concerning solvency ratios need to be emphasised:

- The solvency ratios illustrate the same situation as seen from different angles. To evaluate the solvency situation of a

business, it is therefore necessary to use only one of these ratios.
- Solvency ratios should not simply be accepted at face value. What constitutes a safe ratio for a particular business depends on various factors such as the risks to which it is subject, the nature of the assets and the degree to which creditors will be accommodating in emergency situations.

Profitability, rate of return or yield ratios

Firms strive to achieve the greatest possible profitability. They therefore also wish to achieve the greatest profitability ratios. To achieve this, they must maximise their income and limit cost (expenses) to the essential. Sound profitability not only enables the firm to survive financially, but it also enables the firm to obtain financing relatively easier. The share prices of listed companies normally increase in reaction to announcements of good profitability figures.

Gross profit margin

The **gross profit margin** may be found by:

$$\frac{\text{Gross profit}}{\text{Sales}} \times \frac{100}{1}$$

The gross profit margin indicates how profitable sales have been. The gross profit also gives an indication of the mark-up percentage used by a firm. A firm with a gross profit margin of 50% uses (on average) a mark-up of 100%, as will be illustrated here. Assume sales equal R200 and the cost of products sold equals R100. This yields a gross profit of R100 and a gross profit margin of 50%:

$$\text{Gross profit margin} = \frac{\text{Gross profit}}{\text{Sales}} \times \frac{100}{1}$$

$$= \frac{\text{R200} - \text{R100}}{\text{R200}} \times \frac{100}{1}$$

$$= 50\%$$

Using the figures of ABC Limited contained in Table 13.10 on page 438 and Table 13.11 on page 439 results in a gross profit margin of 25%:

Gross profit margin

$$= \frac{\text{Gross profit}}{\text{Sales}} \times \frac{100}{1}$$

$$= \frac{3\,000\,000 - 2\,250\,000}{3\,000\,000} \times \frac{100}{1}$$

$$= 25\%$$

Firms prefer to achieve the greatest possible gross profit margin. In the case of ABC Ltd, the 25% gross profit margin indicates that the firm uses a mark-up percentage of approximately 33%. In other words, products manufactured or bought at, for example, R100 are sold at R133:

$$\text{Gross profit margin} = \frac{133 - 100}{133} \times \frac{100}{1}$$

$$= 25\%$$

A firm aiming to improve its gross profit margin will have to improve its marketing efforts in order to increase sales whilst simultaneously reducing the cost of products sold. The firm could, for example, reconsider aspects of the marketing instruments (product, price, promotion and distribution) and make suitable adjustments, which would in turn require adjustments to the manufacturing process (if it is a manufacturing firm) and/or procurement. Firms intent on reducing cost should, however, do so with care in order not to sacrifice quality and alienate clients in the process. In this respect, firms normally prefer to improve product features (including quality) in order to justify a price increase.

Net profit margin

The **net profit margin** gives an indication of the overall profitability of the firm and management's ability to control revenue and expenses.

Net profit margin may be found by:

$$\frac{\text{Net income}}{\text{Sales}} \times \frac{100}{1}$$

Using the figures of ABC Limited contained in Table 13.10 on page 438 and Table 13.11 on page 439 results in a net profit margin of 7,57%:

$$\text{Net profit margin} = \frac{227\ 200}{3\ 000\ 000} \times \frac{100}{1}$$

$$= 7{,}57\%$$

In order to improve profitability, management needs to consider the measures already suggested for improving the gross profit margin and focus on operating expenses. Productivity will have to be evaluated and, if necessary, will have to be improved. Firms could calculate annually or quarterly the percentage of sales each operating expense (for example, salaries) constitutes. Management can compare these figures with those of previous years in order to identify deviations.

Return on total capital

This ratio may be computed as follows:

$$\text{Return on total capital} = \frac{\text{Operating profit} - \text{Tax}}{\text{Total capital}} \times \frac{100}{1}$$

Using the figures of ABC Limited contained in Table 13.10 on page 438 and Table 13.11 on page 439 results in a return on total capital (after tax) of 19,1%, calculated as follows:

Return on total capital

$$= \frac{350\ 000 - 92\ 800}{1\ 350\ 000} \times \frac{100}{1}$$

$$= 19{,}1\%$$

A firm wishing to improve its return on total capital needs to consider the same measures as those proposed in respect of the gross profit margin and net profit margin. Since the total capital (capital employed) is equal to the total assets (employment of capital), the firm needs to investigate whether it could function with less capital and/or improve the productivity (if possible) of its assets. A firm can reduce its capital by paying off long-term loans quicker (especially during periods of rising interest rates), by paying greater dividends (if the profitability and cash flow permit it) or a portion of the firm's shares could be repurchased and cancelled. The firm also needs to review its core business. Parts of the firm that cannot be regarded as core business can be sold (for example, company houses that are let to employees).

Return on shareholders' interest

The return on shareholders' interest may be calculated using the following equation:

$$\frac{\text{Net profit after tax}}{\text{Shareholders' interest}} \times \frac{100}{1}$$

Using the figures of ABC Limited contained in Table 13.10 on page 438 and Table 13.11 on page 439 results in a return on shareholders' interest of 25,2%, calculated as follows:

Return on shareholders' interest

$$= \frac{227\ 200}{900\ 000} \times \frac{100}{1}$$

$$= 25{,}2\%$$

A firm wishing to improve its return on shareholders' funds should consider the same measures as those proposed for the profitability ratios discussed so far

Return on owners' equity (ROE)

The **return on owners' equity** may be calculated using the following equation:

ROE

$$= \frac{\text{Net income}}{\text{Sales}} \times \frac{\text{Sales}}{\text{Total assets}} \times \frac{\text{Total assets}}{\text{Owners' equity}}$$

A firm's return on equity (ROE) therefore depends on the firm's net profit margin, asset turnover and financial leverage.

The ROE can be reduced to:

$$\text{ROE} = \frac{\text{Net income}}{\text{Owners' equity}} \times \frac{100}{1}$$

Using the figures of ABC Limited contained in Table 13.10 on page 438 and Table 13.11

on page 439 results in a return on owners' equity of 26,1%, calculated as follows:

$$ROE = \frac{222\ 200}{850\ 000} \times \frac{100}{1}$$

$$= 26{,}1\%$$

An increase in ROE can be achieved by means of an increase in the net profit margin, asset turnover and financial leverage. Financial leverage can be attained by using more long-term borrowed funds and less ordinary-share capital. A firm could, for example, borrow money in order to buy back its own ordinary shares and cancel the shares that have been bought back. Such an approach can be applied relatively safely during periods of declining interest rates, but is risky during periods of rising interest rates.

The ROE, in turn, has an important influence on the sustainable growth rate (g) of a firm. The sustainable growth rate is found by:

$$g = ROE \times \text{Retention ratio}$$

$$\text{where Retention ratio} = \frac{\text{Retained earnings}}{\text{Net income}}$$

Example: Calculating the growth rate

ABC Ltd achieved a ROE of 26,1% and R75 000 of the net income was paid out as dividends. The retained earnings is equal to R222 200 − R75 000 = R147 200, representing a pay-out ratio of 33,8% or a retention ratio of 66,2%.

Retention rate

$$= \frac{R147\ 200}{R222\ 200} \times \frac{100}{1}$$

$$= 66{,}2\%$$

Given a ROE and a retention rate of 66,2%, the form's sustainable growth rate is equal to:

$$g = 26{,}1\% \times 0{,}662 = 17{,}278\%$$

So far, liquidity, solvency and profitability ratios have been described. As described earlier, normally an increase in profitability of a listed company leads to an increase in the share price of such a firm. Since the long-term goal of the firm is to increase the value of the firm, management should also focus on measures of economic value.

Measures of economic value[3]

Measures of economic value are the economic value added (EVA) and market value added (MVA). These measures can best be applied to public companies, in other words, companies listed on a securities exchange such as the Johannesburg Securities Exchange (JSE), the London Stock Exchange (LSE) and the New York Stock Exchange (NYSE).

Economic value added (EVA)

EVA is defined as:

$$EVA = EBIT(1 - T) - \text{Cost of capital expressed in rand}$$

where EBIT = earnings before interest and tax
T = tax rate

Example: Calculating the EVA

Assume a firm has achieved an EBIT of R2 400 000 and is subject to a tax rate of 29%. The firm's balance sheet shows owners' equity at R8 000 000 and debt at R2 000 000. The firm's weighted average cost of capital (WACC) is 16%.

$$\begin{aligned} EVA &= R2\ 400\ 000\ (1 - 0{,}29) - 0{,}16\ (R800\ 000 + R200\ 000) \\ &= R2\ 400\ 000\ (0{,}71) - 0{,}16\ (R1\ 000\ 000) \\ &= R1\ 704\ 000 - R160\ 000 \\ &= R1\ 544\ 000 \end{aligned}$$

Market value added (MVA)

A positive EVA is an additional contribution to shareholders' wealth made during the year. The market value of a public company's equity is simply the number of shares that has been issued times the price of the share. If this market value is greater than the book value of the shares, then the value added is called market value added (MVA)[4].

Example: Market value added

Assume the ordinary shares of Telkom Ltd were issued at R10 each (the par value). A year later, these shares trade at R79,15 each. The R69,15 difference is regarded as the MVA of the share.

13.7.1.6 Concluding remarks

The preceding explanation offered a brief survey of the financial-analysis task of financial management. From the explanation, it is apparent that the income statement, balance sheet, funds-flow statement and financial ratios are important aids in the performance of this task.

In the section that follows, the focus is on financial planning and control on the basis of this planning.

13.7.2 Financial planning and control

Financial planning forms an integral part of the strategic planning of a firm. Top management has to formulate the vision and mission for the firm, analyse the strengths and weaknesses of the firm, and identify opportunities and threats in the external environment. The probability of successfully implementing the strategy that top management has decided on depends on the extent to which the firm has suitable human and financial resources at its disposal, or can attract such resources.

Financial planning and control are done in most business organisations by means of budgets.

A budget can be seen as a formal written plan of future action, expressed in monetary terms and sometimes also in physical terms, to implement the strategy of the business and to achieve the goals with limited resources. As such, budgets are also used for control purposes. Control is done by comparing the actual results with the planned (budgeted) results periodically or on a continuous basis. In this way, deviations are identified and corrective action can be taken in time.

This section provides a brief overview of the following issues:

- the focal points of budgets in the control system of a manufacturing business
- an integrated budgeting system for a manufacturing business
- zero-base budgeting
- the balanced-scorecard (BSC) approach.

13.7.2.1 The focal points of budgets in a control system

Control systems are devised to ensure that a specified strategic business function or activity (for example, manufacturing or sales) is carried out properly. Consequently, control

Critical thinking

The link between profitability and share prices

Will the share price of a company (listed on a securities exchange) increase if the firm's profitability increases?

Normally, yes. Keep in mind, however, that a good company is not necessarily a good investment. The reason for this is that those who have superior information anticipate the improved profitability of the firm better than the uninformed investor. Once the information about improved profitability is announced in the media, the share price would already reflect such information. An investor buying these shares at that point in time would be buying a fully priced or overpriced share and will not necessarily achieve a high rate of return from the investment.

systems should focus on, and budgets should be devised for, various responsibility centres in a business. A responsibility centre can be described as any organisational or functional unit in a business that is headed by a manager responsible for the activities of that unit. All responsibility centres use resources (inputs or costs) to produce something (outputs or income). Typically, responsibility is assigned to income, cost (expense), profit and/or investment centres.

- In the case of an **income centre**, outputs are measured in monetary terms, though the size of these outputs is not directly compared with the input costs. The sales department of a business is an example of such an income centre. The effectiveness of the centre is not measured in terms of how much the income (units sold × selling prices) exceeds the cost of the centre (for example, salaries and rent). Instead, budgets in the form of sales quotas are prepared and the budgeted figures are compared with actual sales. This provides a useful picture of the effectiveness of individual sales personnel or of the centre itself.
- In the case of a **cost centre**, inputs are measured in monetary terms, though outputs are not. The reason for this is that the primary purpose of such a centre is not the generation of income. Good examples of cost centres are the maintenance, research and administrative departments of a business. Consequently, budgets should be developed only for the input portion of these centres' operations.
- In the case of a **profit centre**, performance is measured by the monetary difference between income (outputs) and costs (inputs). A profit centre is created whenever an organisational unit is given the responsibility of earning a profit. In this case, budgets should be developed in such a way that provision is made for the planning and control of inputs and outputs.
- In the case of an **investment centre**, the monetary value of inputs and outputs is again measured, but the profit is also assessed in terms of the assets (investment) employed to produce this profit.

It should be clear that any profit centre can also be considered as an investment centre because its activities require some form of capital investment. However, if the capital investment is relatively small or if its manager/s have no control over the capital investment, it is more appropriate from a planning and control point of view (and thus also from a budgeting point of view) to treat it as a profit centre.

13.7.2.2 An integrated budgeting system for a manufacturing business

In essence, an integrated budgeting system for a manufacturing business consists of two main types of budget:

- operating budgets
- financial budgets.

Figure 13.15 on page 450 shows the operating and financial components of an integrated budgeting system of a manufacturing business diagrammatically.

Operating budgets parallel three of the responsibility centres discussed earlier:

- **Cost budgets.** There are two types of cost budgets: manufacturing-cost budgets and discretionary-cost budgets. Manufacturing-cost budgets are used where outputs can be measured accurately. These budgets usually describe the material and labour costs involved in each production item, as well as the estimated overhead costs. These budgets are designed to measure efficiency. If the budget is exceeded, it means that manufacturing costs were higher than they should have been. Discretionary-cost budgets are used for cost centres in which output cannot be measured accurately (for example, administration and research). Discretionary cost budgets are not used to assess efficiency because performance standards for discretionary expenses are difficult to devise.

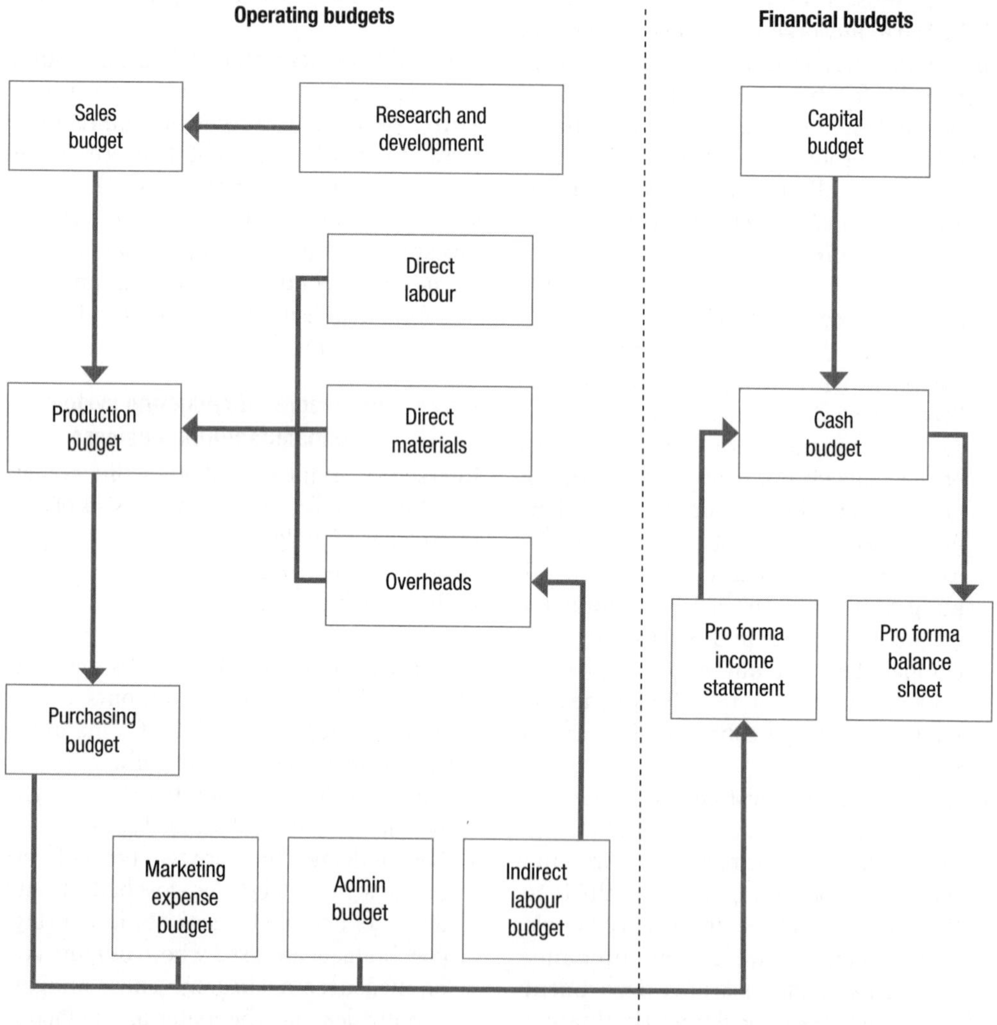

Figure 13.15: The operating and financial components of an integrated budgeting system

Source: Marx, J. 2009. *Finance for non-financial managers*. 2nd ed. Pretoria: Van Schaik, p. 60. Used by permission of Van Schaik Publishers.

- **Income budgets.** These budgets are developed to measure marketing and sales effectiveness. They consist of the expected sales quantity multiplied by the expected unit selling price of each product. The income budget is the most critical part of a profit budget, yet it is also one of the most uncertain because it is based on projected future sales.
- **The profit plan or profit budget.** This budget combines cost and income budgets, and is used by managers who have responsibility for both the expenses and income of their units. Such managers frequently head an entire division or business.

Financial budgets, which are used by financial management for the execution of the financial planning and control task, consist of capital-expenditure, cash, financing and balance-sheet budgets. These budgets, prepared from information contained in the operating budgets, integrate the financial planning of the business with its operational planning. Financial budgets serve three major purposes:

- They verify the viability of the operational planning (operating budgets).
- They reveal the financial actions that the business must take to make the execution of its operating budgets possible.
- They indicate how the operating plans of the business will affect its future financial actions and condition.

If these future actions and conditions are undesirable (for example, over-borrowing to finance additional facilities), appropriate changes in the operating plans may be required.

The **capital expenditure budget** indicates the expected (budgeted) future capital investment in physical facilities (buildings, equipment and so on) to maintain its present capacity or expand the future productive capacity.

The **cash budget** indicates:

- the extent, time and sources of expected cash inflows
- the extent, time and purposes of expected cash outflows
- the expected availability of cash in comparison with the expected need for it.

The **financing budget** is developed to assure the business of the availability of funds to meet the budgeted shortfalls of receipts (income) relative to payments (expenses) in the short term, and to schedule medium-term and long-term borrowing or financing. The financing budget is therefore developed in conjunction with the cash budget to provide the business with the funds it needs at the times it needs them.

The **budgeted balance sheet** brings together all the other budgets to project how the financial position of the business will look at the end of the budget period if actual results conform to planned results. An analysis of the balance-sheet budget may suggest problems (for example, a poor solvency situation owing to over-borrowing) or opportunities (for example, excessive liquidity, creating the opportunity to expand) that will require alterations to the other budgets.

13.7.2.3 Traditional budgeting

Traditional budgeting involves using the actual income and expenditure of the previous year as a basis and making adjustments for expected changes in circumstances. The projected sales serve as the point of departure for the budgeting process. Information must be gathered in order to determine which factors will lead to an increase or decline in sales, as well as factors that will influence cost. Examples of these are inflation, interest rates, exchange rates, wage demands, the actions of competitors and changes to tax legislation.

Applying the concept: What to expect in tough times

Retail firms (for example, Edgars) can expect that during times of inflation accompanied by increases in interest rates, the firm's sales could decline, bad debts could increase, the collection of debt could slow down and/or the cost of collecting outstanding debt could increase (as a result of follow-up work). At the same time, the firm has to pay more interest on its loans, pay increased rent on hired retail space and face wage demands. The opposite can be expected during times of declining inflation and interest rates.

The firm's plans and budgets are usually negotiated and finalised during a time-consuming process. A lack of insight into and commitment to the firm's strategy can cause managers to pursue the interests of their own departments only during this phase, instead of thinking enterprise-wide. Such behaviour leads to suboptimum budgets.

One of the disadvantages of the traditional budgeting approach is that some managers continue the same activities year after year without critically re-evaluating priorities and possible changes in the external and internal environments. This managerial challenge can be handled using either zero-base budgeting or the balanced-scorecard approach.

13.7.2.4 Zero-base budgeting

In contrast with traditional budgeting, zero-base budgeting enables the business to look at its activities and priorities afresh on an annual basis. In this case, historical results are not taken as a basis for the next budgeting period. Instead, each manager has to justify anew his/her entire budget request.

In theory, zero-base budgeting leads to a better prioritisation of resource allocations and more efficient businesses. In practice, however, it may generate undue amounts of paperwork, and demoralise managers and other employees who are expected to justify their activities and expenses, and in essence, therefore, their existence, on an annual basis.

13.7.2.5 The balanced-scorecard approach[5]

The balanced-scorecard (BSC) approach was introduced by Kaplan & Norton (1996). The balanced-scorecard approach enables managers to align their departments' budgets with the firm's vision and mission. This approach suggests that strategy be implemented from four perspectives (each with its own goals, measures, targets and initiatives):

- **Financial.** What do investors expect from the firm in order to evaluate it as financially successful?
- **Customers.** What do customers expect from the firm in order to see it as fulfilling its vision?
- **Internal processes.** Which processes must be excellent in order to satisfy customers and shareholders?
- **Learning and growth.** How will the ability of the firm to change and improve be maintained in order for the firm to reach its vision?

The BSC approach improves the budgeting process. It makes it essential for management to identify and focus on relevant information in order to budget effectively. From a planning point of view, it exposes the internal and external challenges that management is confronted with. Managers must then consider the best measures to deal with these challenges. The allocation of resources is linked to specific measures

> **Critical thinking**
>
> **The budget dilemma**
>
> Is it better for a manager at the middle management level to exceed his/her cost budget at the end of a financial year, or is better to have funds to spare?
>
> Both are problematic. Exceeding a cost budget could be interpreted as a lack of planning and control on the part of the manager (although there might be valid reasons for exceeding the budget, for example, an increase in activity). Funds to spare are sometimes regarded by middle management as proof to the top management of how sparingly it has used the firm's resources under its control. However, surplus funds at the end of the financial year may also indicate that the manager intentionally over-estimated costs to create the impression that his/her budget is managed well. It may, however, be an indication that the manager did not achieve all the objectives that had been set at the beginning of the year. Unspent funds at the end of a financial year may also result in a reduction of the manager's budget for the following year.

of the scorecard. This approach offers a uniform way according to which departments can achieve their goals in respect of finances, customers, processes and growth perspectives[6].

This approach requires that managers review the scorecard on a monthly or quarterly basis. In contrast with other approaches to budgeting, BSC enables managers to make adjustments to their budgets during a financial year to enable them to achieve their goals.

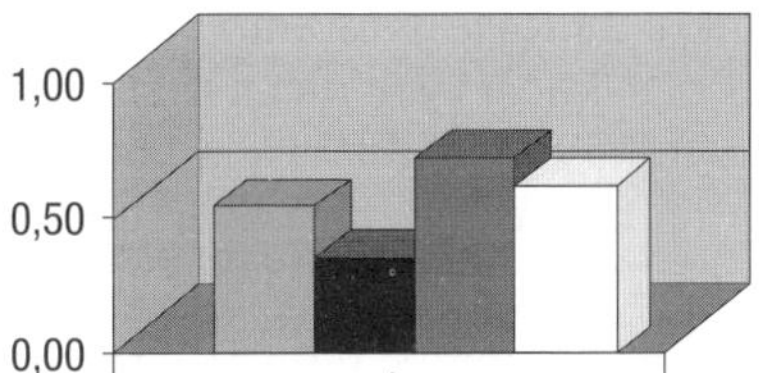

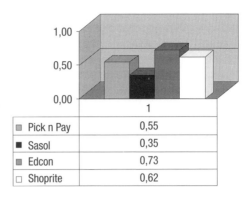

	1
Pick n Pay	0,55
Sasol	0,35
Edcon	0,73
Shoprite	0,62

Figure 13.16: The ratio of current assets to total assets for selected South African companies (2009)

Sources: Edcon. Annual report 2009. [Online] Available: http://www.edcon.co.za Accessed 21 March 2010.
Pick n Pay. Annual report 2009. [Online] Available: http://www.picknpay-ir.co.za/financials Accessed 21 March 2010.
Sasol. Annual report 2009. [Online] Available: http://www.sasol.com Accessed 21 March 2010.
Shoprite. Annual report 2009. [Online] Available: http://www.shopriteholdings.co.za Accessed 21 March 2010.

13.8 Asset management: The management of current assets

Current assets include items such as cash, marketable securities, debtors and inventory. These items are needed to ensure the continuous and smooth functioning of the business. Cash, for example, is needed to pay bills that are not perfectly matched by current cash inflows, while an adequate supply of raw materials is required to sustain the manufacturing process. Sales may be influenced by the credit the business is prepared to allow.

Current assets are therefore a necessary and significant component of the total assets of the business. Figure 13.16 shows that the ratio of current to total assets may vary from company to company. A retailer such as Pick n Pay has a large ratio of current to total assets compared to, say, Sasol, which is listed under the JSE Oil and Gas Exploration and Production sector, and produces fuels and chemicals for the chemical industry. Pick n Pay's large ratio of current to total assets occurs because most of the assets of retail stores are in the form of inventory (current assets). Its main business is trading in inventory, not manufacturing. The chemical industry, in contrast, has large investments in plant and other fixed assets.

In managing current assets, management should always keep in mind the consequences of having too much or too little invested in them. Two factors play a role: cost and risk.

An over-investment in current assets means a low degree of risk, in that more-than-adequate amounts of cash are available to pay bills when they fall due, or sales are amply supported by more-than-sufficient levels of inventory. However, over-investment causes profits to be less than the maximum, firstly because of the cost associated with the capital invested in additional current assets, and secondly because of income foregone that could have been earned elsewhere (the so-called opportunity cost of capital). The funds invested in excess inventory could, for example, have been invested in a short-term deposit earning interest at the prevailing interest rate.

An under-investment in current assets, however, increases the risk of cash and inventory shortages, and the costs associated with these shortages, but it also decreases the opportunity cost. For example, a business that is short of cash may have to pay high interest rates to obtain funds on short notice, while a shortage of inventory may result in a loss of sales, or even mean that the business has to buy inventory from competitors at high prices to keep customers satisfied. The optimal level of investment in current assets is a trade-off between the costs and the risks involved.

As can be seen from the graph in Figure 13.16 on page 453, companies differ in their holdings of current assets as a percentage of total assets. Some differences are due to the type of industry. For example, it is evident that Sasol has a very low percentage of current assets compared to Edcon. Sasol is in the petroleum and related industries, while Edcon is mostly in clothing retail, with companies such as Edgars, Jet and CNA. Pick n Pay and Shoprite are predominantly supermarket retailers and have a slightly lower holding of current assets than Edcon. Pick n Pay also differs from Shoprite in its holdings since it has a lower holding of current assets. This can be attributed to its broader diversification of businesses that have more non-current assets than Shoprite.

Applying the concept: Risks and costs of investing in current assets

The example below illustrates that cost and risk are of prime importance in the management of current assets.

Table 13.13: Balance sheets and operating profit (after tax)

	Business	
	A	B
Cash	1 000	1 000
Marketable securities		10 000
Debtors	19 000	19 000
Inventory	30 000	30 000
Current assets	50 000	60 000
Fixed assets	100 000	100 000
Total	150 000	160 000
Current liabilities	20 000	20 000
Debt (long-term)	30 000	30 000
Shareholders' funds	100 000	110 000
Total	150 000	160 000
Operating income (after tax)	15 000	15 300*

*B earns 6% on an investment of R10 000 in marketable securities. At a tax rate of 50%, the income after tax is R300.

$$\text{Current ratio} = \frac{\text{Current assets}}{\text{Current liability}}$$

Business A	Business B
$\frac{50\,000}{20\,000} = 2{,}5{:}1$	$\frac{60\,000}{20\,000} = 3{:}1$

$$\text{Rate of return (after tax)} = \frac{\text{Operating income (after tax)}}{\text{Total capital}}$$

Business A	Business B
$\frac{15\,000}{150\,000} = 10\%$	$\frac{15\,300}{160\,000} = 9{,}6\%$

B is more liquid than A (current ratio of 3:1 compared to a ratio of 2,5:1 for A) and therefore also less risky than A. The rate of return of B, however, is less than that of A (a rate of return of 9,6% compared to that of a rate of return of 10%). See section 13.7.1.5 for a discussion and a definition of the current ratios and rate of return (after tax).

Case study

Sound financial management and its link with shareholder value

Table 13.14 shows an extract of the balance sheet of ABC Limited, and indicates how proper management of current assets and non-current assets can translate into good business management and lead to an increase in shareholder value.

Table 13.14: Extract of ABC Limited Balance Sheet as at 31 December 2009

Assets	Value	Link to value creation
Current assets		
Stock or inventories	950 500	Inventories normally form the core of the day-to-day trade of the business. For a clothing retailer such as Edgars, examples are shoes, clothes and bedding. Inventories are purchased from a supplier at a particular price and the merchant then adds a mark-up to cover the cost of running the business, as well as provide for a profit margin. This is usually referred to as the mark-up. For example: Purchase price for one pair of shoes: R45,00 per pair Mark-up of 50% (50% × R45): R22,50 per pair Selling price per pair: R67,50 per pair
Debtors or receivables	450 250	Edgars sells most of its inventories on credit to its customers. These customers are then referred to as debtors. A customer who buys on credit would be expected to pay the company over 30 days or more. This presents a problem to Edgars since it does not receive cash immediately, and yet has had to pay for the inventories from its supplier. If the customer pays on the due date, then Edgars can manage and plan for cash-flow movement. If the customer defaults on payments, this can present a cash-flow squeeze, which can lead to reduced profits and/or possibly a loss for the company. This loss is normally deducted from the shareholders' funds.
Cash and cash equivalents	250 950	That cash and cash equivalents need to be managed as cash is the key in managing the business on a day-to-day basis. Cash is used to settle creditors and for purchasing inventories, as well as settling overheads. While it is important to have adequate cash resources, managers should remember that holding too much cash can lead to low returns (low shareholder value).
Total current assets	**1 651 700**	
Non-current assets		
Land and buildings	450 000	These are long-term assets that provide the basis for production and for long-term value of the business. It is a well-documented fact that land and buildings generally appreciate over time, meaning that their value always increases. Managers should, however, be careful not to invest too much in unnecessary land and buildings, since cash is then tied up in non-core business. For Edgars, it might be a better strategy to lease or rent its properties (this also has a tax advantage as lease/rental payments qualify for tax deduction, which leads to increased tax savings).

Equipment and machinery	250 000	These form part of the productive capacity of the business. Machinery that is under-utilised is very costly to the business. Not only does it cost the company in terms of maintenance, but it also loses value by depreciation on an annual basis. An example is a fork-lift truck used in stacking up inventories in a warehouse. This equipment is vital for the business, but having too many fork-lift trucks does not add value to the business.
Vehicles	455 000	Most vehicles are used for deliveries and for collections of inventories. Issues regarding machinery also apply to vehicles, but are even more important here since vehicles generally lose their value (depreciate) within a period of three to five years.
Equity investments	450 000	These are investments by a company in other businesses. The company would therefore receive a return on its investment via a dividend payout. The choice of an equity investment is important since it should always be compared to the returns the company receives from its own operations. For example, if Edgars receives 25% return from R1 invested in Edgars operations, it should ensure that it receives at least the same return or more from outside equity investments. There are exceptions, for example, when the equity investment is made for strategic reasons. For Edgars, this could be an investment in a company that supplies it with scarce raw material for the production of clothes. (Silk production could be a good example.)
Goodwill	356 250	Goodwill is an intangible asset that a company receives when it acquires another business. For example, if Edgars were to acquire Truworths assets valued at R7 million, but pay a price of R12 million, the difference of R5 million represents an asset called goodwill. This arises from a number of sources, for example, favourable location, strong management talent, skilled workers, a stable brand name on the market and so forth. This asset can be used by Edgars as a tax deduction on an annual basis. For example, after a profit of R712 500, Edgars could write off the goodwill of R356 250 as an expense called amortisation. This would reduce the taxable profit by half, leading to lower taxes being paid, and thereby leading to more cash flow being available to Edgars.
Non-current assets	**1 961 250**	
TOTAL ASSETS	**3 612 950**	

13.8.1 The management of cash and marketable securities

Cash is the money (currency and coin) the business has on hand in petty-cash drawers, in cash registers, and in current and savings accounts with financial institutions.

The costs of holding cash are:

- **Loss of interest.** Cash in the form of notes and coins, and even money in a current account at a bank, earns no interest.
- **Loss of purchasing power.** During a period of inflation, there is an erosion in the value of money. This becomes even more serious if no interest is earned on that money.

The costs of little or no cash are:

- **Loss of goodwill.** Failure to meet financial obligations on time due to cash shortages will seriously affect the relationship between the company and its employees,

Critical thinking

The mark-up percentage does not necessarily translate to a similar profit margin.

Mark-up versus profit margins

Using information from Table 13.14 on page 455, discuss the following questions:

- A mark-up of 50% on cost implies that the price of a product will be calculated as follows:
  Cost price × (1 + 0,50)
  This means that ABC Limited will make a net profit margin of 50%. Is this true? Discuss.
- The following financial statements represent a firm's actual position as of December 31 2010. In this situation, what will the ending current liabilities account for 2011 be?

Balance sheet	2010	2011
Cash	250 950	
Receivables	450 250	
Net fixed assets	1 861 250	
Current liabilities		
Common equity	1 000 000	
Income statement		
Sales	1 000 000	
Gross profit	600 000	
Operating profit	200 000	
Net income (after tax)	120 000	

Assumptions:

A. Sales are expected to increase by 20% in 2011.
B. Gross profit, operating profit, net income, current assets and current liabilities will be the same percentage of sales in 2011 as they were in 2010.
C. Depreciation in 2011 will be R25 000.
D. Dividends will be R50 000.
E. Gross fixed assets will remain constant.

creditors, and suppliers of raw materials and services.

- **Loss of opportunities.** Cash shortages will make it impossible to react quickly to a lucrative business opportunity.
- **Inability to claim discounts.** Discounts for prompt and early payment are very advantageous in percentage terms. Cash shortages may preclude the claiming of such discounts.
- **Cost of borrowing.** Shortages of cash may force a business to raise money at short notice at expensive rates.

Marketable securities are investment instruments on which a business earns a fixed interest income. They can easily be converted into cash and are therefore also referred to as near-cash assets. An example of a marketable security is a short-term treasury bill issued by the government.

There are three reasons for a business having a certain amount of cash available:

- **The transaction motive.** The transaction motive exists primarily because receipts and disbursements are not fully synchronised. Expenses must often be paid before any cash income has been received. The business needs to have sufficient cash available to meet normal current expenditures such as the payment of wages, salaries, rent and creditors.

- **The precautionary motive.** The precautionary motive entails the keeping of cash, in addition to that prompted by the transaction motive, for contingencies. Contingencies are unexpected events such as a large debtor defaulting on its account or employees making an unexpected wage demand that may strain the financial position of the business. These funds are usually held in the form of marketable securities or money-market funds that can easily be converted into cash.
- **The speculative motive.** The speculative motive implies that the business must be able to capitalise on good opportunities such as unexpected bargains and bulk purchases. Additional funds for this purpose are usually also held in the form of marketable securities. A competitor may, for example, be declared insolvent and its inventory sold at bargain prices. The business can capitalise on this opportunity only if it has extra cash available to take advantage of the opportunity.

Cash management is essential to obtain the optimal trade-off between the liquidity risk and the cost of being too liquid. This is achieved by focusing on the **cash budget** and the **cash cycle**. These two aspects of cash management will now be considered in more detail.

13.8.1.1 The cash budget

Determining the cash needs of a business is an important aspect of cash management. Unutilised cash surpluses or cash shortages result in the cost and risk of the cash investment increasing unnecessarily. Cash-flow problems were advanced as the primary cause of the demise of several large real-estate development companies, such as Corlett Drive Estates, in the early 1970s.

The cash budget facilitates the planning and control of cash. Its purpose is to identify future cash shortages and cash surpluses. The cash budget is therefore a detailed plan of future cash flows for a specific period. It is composed of the following three elements:

- **Cash receipts.** These originate from cash sales, collections from credit sales and other sources such as cash injections in the form of, for example, bank loans.
- **Cash disbursements.** These are broadly categorised as cash paid for purchases of merchandise, raw materials and operating expenses such as salaries.
- **Net changes in cash.** These represent the difference between cash receipts and cash disbursements.

The cash budget serves as a basis for determining the cash needs of a business and indicates when bridging finance will be required. The example that follows shows how the cash budget is used to determine cash needs.

It is clear that the cash budget can be used to identify temporary cash shortages and that this information can be used to arrange bridging finance timeously. It also indicates excess liquidity. This information can also be used to plan temporary investments in marketable securities.

The cash budget for Save Retailers in the box on page 459 shows, for example, that bridging finance will have to be arranged for April and May, and that arrangements will have to be made to invest the cash surplus that will arise during June.

Quote the banker, "Watch cash flow."

Though my bottom line is black, I am flat upon my back,
My cash flows out and customers pay slow.
The growth of my receivables is almost unbelievable;
The result is certain unremitting woe!
And I hear the banker utter an ominous low mutter,
"Watch cash flow."

Source: Bailey, S.H. 1975. "Quote the banker: Watch cash flow", *Publishers Weekly*, 13 January.

Applying the concept: The cash budget

For Save Retailers there is a 30-day collection period on debtors, which means that there is a lag of 30 days between a credit sale and the receipt of cash. Consequently, cash collections in any month equal the credit sales one month prior. Purchases on credit must also be paid within 30 days.

Table 13.15: Save Retailers

	March	April	May	June
1. CASH ON HAND (A)	0	20	(32)	(13)
2. CASH RECEIPTS				
(a) Cash sales	25	23	30	50
(b) Collections from debtors	225	200	270	450
TOTAL CASH RECEIPTS (B)	250	223	300	500
3. CASH DISBURSEMENTS				
(a) Creditors	144	144	144	144
(b) Wages	60	60	66	66
(c) Overheads	26	26	26	26
(d) Owners' withdrawal	0	45	45	43
TOTAL CASH DISBURSEMENTS (C)	230	275	281	279
4. NET CASH POSITIONS (A + B – C)	20	(32)	(13)	208

Although one assumes that profit equals an amount held in cash, this is almost never the case. The difference between profit and cash flow is illustrated in the example on page 460. This example shows that a profitable business may not be able to continue its operations owing to a cash shortage. The shortage arises despite growing sales and the accumulation of profits.

13.8.1.2 The cash cycle

The cash cycle in a manufacturing business, as illustrated in Figure 13.17, indicates the time it takes to complete the following cycle:

- investing cash in raw materials
- converting the raw materials to finished products
- selling the finished products on credit
- ending the cycle by collecting cash.

Figure 13.17: The cash cycle in a business

Example: Profits and cash flow

Suppose a company has a product that costs R75 to manufacture and is sold for R100. Payment is received within 30 days of sale. Production is based on the expected sales of the following month. Sales for the next three months, January to March, are expected to increase. Production costs are paid during the month in which production takes place. From December to April, the course of events is as follows:

December 1 500 units were sold on credit. Debtors on 1 January amount to R150 000 and 1 500 units were in stock.

January

1 January:	CASH	R 75 000
	Inventory (1 500 @ R75)	R112 500
	Debtors (1 500 @ R100)	R150 000

During January, 2 000 units are sold and 2 500 are manufactured to keep one month's sales (1 500 + 2 500 − 2 000 = 2 000) in stock.

Profit for January: 2 000 units × (R100 − 75)
= 2 000 × R25
= R50 000

February

1 February: CASH

Opening balance	R 75 000
Plus: Received from debtors	R150 000
Minus: Production costs (2 500 × R75)	R187 500
Closing cash balance	R 37 500

Inventory (2 000 units @ R75) R150 000

Opening balance	1 500
Plus: Manufactured	2 500
Minus: Sales	2 000

Debtors (2 000 @ R100) R200 000

During February, sales increase to 2 500 units, and in preparation for sales expected in March, 3 000 units are produced.

Profit for February: 2 500 units × (R100 − 75)
= 2 500 × R25
= R62 500

Cumulative profit = R50 000 + R62 500
= R112 500

March

1 March: CASH

Opening balance	R 37 500
Plus: Received from debtors	R200 000
Minus: Production costs (3 000 × R75)	R225 000
Closing balance	R 12 500

Inventory (2 500 units @ R75) R187 500

Opening balance	2 000
Plus: Manufactured	3 000
Minus: Sales	2 500

During March, sales increase to 3 000 units, and in preparation for sales expected in April, 3 500 units are produced.

Profit for March: 3 000 units × (R100 – 75)
= 3 000 × R25
= R75 000

Cumulative profit: R50 000 + R62 500 + R75 000
= R187 500

April

1 April: CASH

Opening balance	R 12 500
Plus: Received from debtors	R250 000
Minus: Production costs (3 500 × R75)	R262 500
Closing cash balance	R0

Inventory (3 000 units @ R75) R225 000

Opening balance	2 500
Plus: Manufactured	3 500
Minus: Sales	3 000

Debtors: (3 000 @ R100) R300 000

Notwithstanding a total net profit of R187 500 after three months on April 1, the business is without cash and production cannot be continued.

Wholesalers and retailers are not involved in the second step, but are rather concerned with directly converting cash into inventory. Businesses that offer no credit have no conversion from debtors to cash. As a rule, cash is available only after money has been collected from debtors.

The cash cycle is a continuous process. It should be clear that the demand for cash can be greatly reduced if the cycle is speeded up. This is achieved by rapid cash collections and by proper management of debtors and stock (inventory).

13.8.2 The management of debtors

Debtors arise when a business sells on credit to its clients. Debtors have to settle their accounts in a given period (usually within 30 or 60 days after date of purchase). Credit may be extended to either an individual or a business. Credit granted to an individual is referred to as consumer credit. Credit extended to a business is known as trade credit. Debtor accounts represent a considerable portion of the investment in current assets in most businesses and obviously demand efficient management.

Credit sales increase total sales and income. As pointed out in the management of cash, debtor accounts have to be recovered as soon as feasible to keep the cash requirements of the business as low as possible. Once again, an optimal balance has to be struck between the amount of credit sales (the higher the credit sales, the higher the income and, it is hoped, the profitability) and the size of debtor accounts (the greater the size of debtor accounts and the longer the collection period, the higher the investment and cash needs of the business will be, and the lower the profitability).

In any business, the three most important facets of the management of debtor accounts are:

- the credit policy
- the credit terms
- the collection policy.

The **credit policy** contains directives according to which it is decided whether credit should be granted to clients and, if so, how much. Essentially, this involves an evaluation of the creditworthiness of debtors based on realistic credit standards. Realistic credit standards revolve around the four Cs of credit:

- **character** – the customer's willingness to pay
- **capacity** – the customer's ability to pay
- **capital** – the customer's financial resources
- **conditions** – current economic or business conditions.

These four general characteristics are assessed from sources such as financial statements, the customer's bank and credit agencies. Credit agencies specialise in providing credit ratings and credit reports on individual businesses.

Credit terms define the credit period and any discount offered for early payment. They are usually stated as "net *t*" or "*d*/*t*1, *n*/*t*". The first (*t*) denotes that payment is due within *t* days from when the goods are received. The second (*d*/*t*1, *n*/*t*) allows a discount of *d*% if payment is made within *t*1 days; otherwise the full amount is due within *t* days. For example, "3/10, *n*/30" means that a 3% discount can be taken from the invoice amount if payment is made within 10 days; otherwise, full payment is due within 30 days.

The **collection policy** concerns the guidelines for the collection of debtor accounts that have not been paid by due dates. The collection policy may be applied rigorously or less rigorously, depending on circumstances. The level of **bad debts** is often regarded as a criterion of the effectiveness of credit and collection policies.

The costs of granting credit include the following:

- **Loss of interest.** Granting credit is similar to granting interest-free loans. This means that interest is lost on the amount of credit advanced to trade debtors.
- **Costs associated with determining the customer's creditworthiness.** The procedure

to determine the creditworthiness of a customer costs money, but fortunately this cost only needs to be incurred once. After the initial screening procedure, the company reassesses the customer on its own experience of the customer's track record of payment.

- **Administration and record-keeping costs.** Most companies that grant credit find it necessary to employ people to administer and collect trade debts.
- **Bad debts.** Unless a company adopts an extremely cautious credit-granting policy, it is almost inevitable that some trade debts will not be paid. Although this risk can be insured against, it still remains a cost to the company.

The costs mentioned above must be considered against the loss of goodwill if credit is denied in a competitive market where customers may obtain the same products on credit terms elsewhere.

> Saying "no" to a customer may be an easy answer, but your competitors may gain a profitable sale. This is not the way to increase turnover and profit.
>
> ***Source:*** Posner, M. 1990. *Successful credit control*, New York: BSP Professional Books, p. 1.

13.8.3 The management of stock (inventory)

The concept "inventory stock" includes raw and auxiliary materials, work in progress, semi-finished products, trading stock and so on, and, like debtors, represents a considerable portion of the investment in working capital. In inventory management, there is once again a conflict between the profit objective (to keep the lowest-possible supply of stock, and to keep stock turnover as high as possible, in order to minimise the investment in stock, as well as attendant cash needs) and the operating objective (to keep as much stock as possible to ensure that the business is never without, and to ensure that production interruptions and therefore loss of sales never occur).

It is once again the task of financial management to combine the relevant variables in the framework of a sound purchasing and inventory policy optimally in order to increase profitability without subjecting the business to unnecessary risks.

The costs of holding inventory stock are:

- **Lost interest.** This refers to the interest that could have been earned on the money that is tied up in holding inventory stock.
- **Storage cost.** This cost includes the rent of space occupied by the inventory stock and the cost of employing people to guard and manage the stock
- **Insurance costs.** Holding inventory stock exposes the business to risk of fire and theft of the stock. Insurance will provide cover against these losses, but this will involve an additional cost in the form of premiums that have to be paid to the insurance company.
- **Obsolescence.** Stocks can become obsolete. For example, they may go out of fashion. Thus, apparently perfectly good inventory stock may be of little more value than scrap.

The cost of holding little or no inventory stocks are:

- **The loss of customer goodwill.** Failure to be able to supply a customer owing to insufficient stock may mean the loss of not only that particular order, but of other orders as well.
- **Production interruption dislocation.** Running out of stock can be very costly for certain types of companies. For example, a motor manufacturer that runs out of a major body section has no choice but to stop production.
- **Loss of flexibility.** Additional stock-holding creates a safety margin whereby mishaps of various descriptions can be accommodated without major and costly repercussions. Without these buffer inventory levels, the company loses this flexibility.

- **Re-order costs.** A company existing on little or no stock will be forced to place a large number of small orders with short intervals between each order. Each order gives rise to costs, including the cost of placing the order and the cost of physically receiving the goods.

Critical thinking

It is crucial that businesses estimate their expected cash flows as accurately as possible.

Determining cash flows

A company collects R1 million per month in October, November and December. The company's cash payments represented 85% of October's receipts, 120% of November's receipts and 95% of December's receipts. On 1 October, the company had a cash balance of R100 000, which also represented its minimum operating needs.

1. Which of the following methods would be used to forecast this company's cash position?
   a. Distribution
   b. Percentage of sales
   c. Time series
   d. Receipts and disbursements
2. Which of the following represents the company's ending cash position for November?
   a. (R200 000)
   b. (R50 000)
   c. R50 000
   d. R100 000
3. In addition to short-term investments, which of the following provides liquidity reserve?
   i. Long-term investments
   ii. Unused short-term borrowing
   iii. Unused long-term borrowing
   a. i only
   b. ii only
   c. ii and iii only
   d. i, ii and iii

13.8.4 Final comments on the asset side of the balance sheet

The discussion of the asset side of the balance sheet has given only a brief overview of the management of current assets. Only a few fundamental financial implications have been discussed to show how complex the management of current assets is.

13.9 Asset management: Long-term investment decisions and capital budgeting

13.9.1 The nature of capital investments

Capital investment involves the use of funds of a business to acquire fixed assets such as land, buildings and equipment, the benefits of which accrue over periods longer than one year.

Long-term investment decisions determine the type, size and composition of a business's fixed assets, as well as the amount of permanent working capital required for the implementation and continued operation of capital-investment projects.

The importance of capital investments and the capital-investment decision-making process cannot be over-emphasised.

Table 13.16 on page 465 gives the three major capital-expenditure projects in South Africa with estimated completion dates after 2009.

The success of large businesses ultimately depends on their ability to identify capital-investment opportunities that will maximise shareholders' wealth. Conversely, examples abound of business failures because businesses failed to identify opportunities or invested in unprofitable projects.

The importance of capital-investment projects is reflected by the following three factors:

Table 13.16: Three major capital-expenditure projects

Project	Company	Value (R billion)	Estimated completion date
Coal power generation project	Eskom	150	2012
Power supply infrastructure	Eskom	150	2012
Airports upgrade	Airports Company SA	20	2010

- **The relative magnitude of the amounts involved.** The amounts involved in capital investment are much larger than those relating to, for example, decisions about the amount of credit to be extended or purchasing inventory.
- **The long-term nature of capital-investment decisions.** The benefits from capital-investment projects may accrue in periods varying from two or three years to as much as 30 or 40 years.
- **The strategic nature of capital investment projects.** Investment decisions of a strategic nature, such as the development of an entirely new product, the application of a new technology, the decision to diversify internationally or the decision to embark on rendering a strategic service could have a profound effect on the future development of a business. For example, Honda's decision to branch out from motorcycles to passenger vehicles entirely changed the strategic direction of the company.

13.9.2 The evaluation of investment projects

The basic principle underlying the evaluation of investment decision-making is cost–benefit analysis, in which the cost of each project is compared to its benefits (see Figure 13.18). Projects in which benefits exceed the costs add value to the business and increase stakeholders' wealth.

Two additional factors require further consideration when comparing benefits and costs. Firstly, benefits and costs occur at different times. Any comparison of benefits

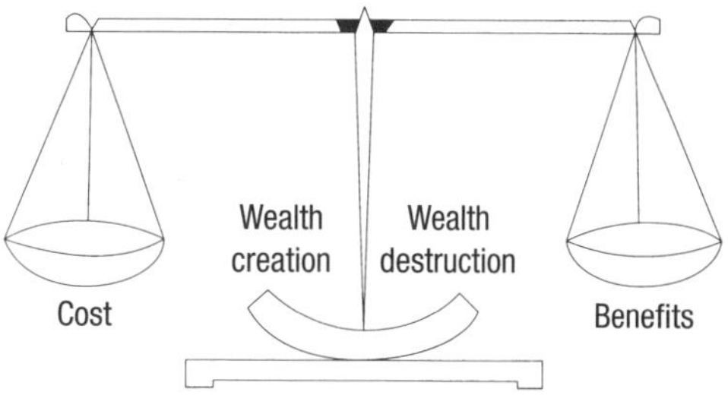

Figure 13.18: A cost–benefit representation of investment decision-making

Source: Adapted from Kolb, B.A. 1983. *Principles of financial management.* Plano, Texas: Business Publications, p. 323.

and costs should therefore take the time value of money (discussed earlier in this chapter) into account.

Secondly, "cost" and "benefits" (income) are accounting concepts that do not necessarily reflect the timing and amounts of payments to the business. The concept "cash flow", which minimises accounting ambiguities associated with concepts relating to income and costs, is therefore used instead.

13.9.2.1 Cash-flow concepts[7]

Cash flow represents cash transactions. The net effect of cash revenues (sources of cash) and cash expenses (uses of cash) is the net cash flow.

Net cash flow =
Cash revenues − Cash expenses

Table 13.17 on page 467 provides examples of transactions that result in cash inflows (sources of cash) and cash outflows (uses of cash).

Examples: The challenges Eskom and ACSA face

Despite a massive effort by Eskom involving more than R150 billion of capital expenditure over the next five years, electricity-supply security will remain inadequate and reserve margins will be paper thin. Eskom is probably doing all it can to restore supply security. Its current installed net generation capacity of about 37 000 MW will be boosted by the return to service of about 3 500 MW of old coal-fired stations, about 2 000 MW of new open-cycle gas turbines, a small 100 MW wind farm and a massive new coal plant of about 4 200 MW (the so-called Alpha and Charlie projects).

Source: Eberhard, A. "Faults in plan for supply security". *Business Day Internet Edition*. [Online] Available: http://www.businessday.co.za/articles/topstories.aspx?ID=BD4A419095 Accessed 29 March 2007.

Eskom will bump up its capital expenditure to generate additional capacity to a massive R150 billion over the next five years, which could see the cost of generating and distributing electricity rise as much as 34%. This is an increase of 55% on the R97 billion projected five-year expenditure to upgrade SA's power supply infrastructure announced only last year. The latest figure emerged from a briefing note to Eskom executives on the plan, which has already been approved by Eskom's board. Half of the material increase in capital expenditure will be funded by Eskom and the balance will be funded through internationally raised debt.

Source: Le Roux, M. 2007. "Eskom growth 'ends cheap power'". [Online] Available: http://www.dpe.gov.za/parliamentary-295 Accessed 21 March 2010.

The decision of the Ford Motor Company during the 1950s to manufacture and market the Ford Edsel required an investment of USD250 million. With losses amounting to USD200 million in the first two-and-a-half years of the project, it was "... in all, a USD450 million mistake".

Source: 1959. "The Edsel dies and Ford regroups survivors". *Business Week*, 28 November, p. 27.

Three of Eskom's power stations were closed down in 1988. Together they had given 153 years of service. They had burnt 144 million tons of coal and produced 140 000 million kilowatt hours of electricity.

Source: 1988. "Three oldest power stations closed down". Eskom Annual Report, p. 29.

Airports Company SA (ACSA) has ramped up its capital expenditure to R19,3 billion to meet expected growth in passenger traffic beyond 2010, says Transport Minister Jeff Radebe. Addressing the annual conference of the Board of Airline Representatives of SA in Hermanus on Friday, Radebe said ACSA expected to handle 31 million passengers at its nine airports by 2010 when SA hosts the Soccer World Cup. ACSA's previous capital-expenditure figure mentioned last month was R5,2 billion. Later in the month, the company announced it would go to the bond market to raise R12 billion for investment in airport capacity. It completed its first, over-subscribed bond issue of R2 billion earlier this month with another planned for later this year.

Source: Phasiwe, K. 2007. "Acsa to roll out R19bn upgrade for SA airport infrastructure". *Business Day*, 17 August. [Online] Available: http://www.businessday.co.za/Articles/Content.aspx?id=35442 Accessed 22 March 2010.

Table 13.17: Examples of the sources and uses of cash

Sources of cash	Uses of cash
A decrease in assets	An increase in assets
An increase in liabilities	A decrease in liabilities
Cash sales	Credit sales
Investment income	Dividend payments to shareholders

Cash flow differs from profit shown on the income statement in that the latter also includes non-cash costs such as depreciation.

Example: Depreciation

Assume that a printing business, ABC Litho Printing, buys a printing machine that will last for ten years. The business spends a large sum of money to acquire the machine, but will not spend any significant amounts until the end of the tenth year, when the machine has to be replaced.

It does not make sense to assume that the business makes profits during years one to nine and then incurs a large loss in year ten when it has to replace the machine. The machine will be used for the entire period, and not only in year ten.

The net profit of the business is adjusted for the use of the machine in years one to nine by deducting depreciation from income. The amount of depreciation is determined by depreciation rules laid down by the tax authorities, as tax is levied on profits after depreciation has been deducted.

However, the cash-flow amount the business has available for reinvestment is equal to the profit after tax plus the depreciation. This amount is the net cash flow into the business.

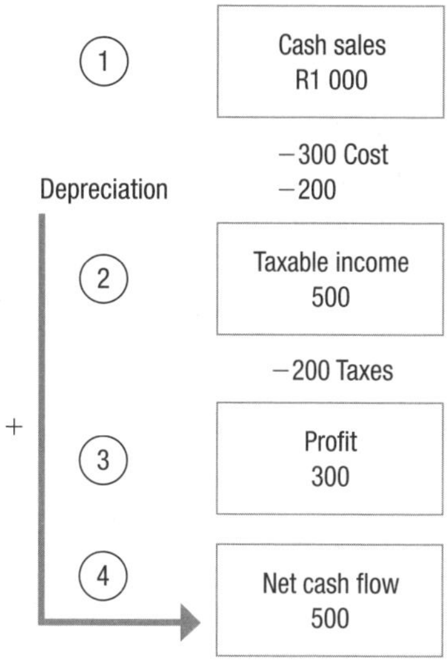

Figure 13.19: Profit and cash flow for ABC Litho Printers

As shown in the representation of the cash flow for ABC Litho in Figure 13.19, the net cash flow is the difference between cash income and cash expenditures. If the net cash flow is positive, it means an inflow of cash and it is referred to as a net cash inflow. However, cash expenditures can also exceed cash income. This results in a negative cash flow and it is then referred to as net cash outflow.

The following three cash-flow components are distinguished for capital-budgeting purposes:

- **The initial investment.** This is the money paid at the beginning of a project for the acquisition of equipment or the purchase of a production plant. The net cash flow during this phase is negative and represents a net cash outflow.
- **The expected annual cash flows over the life of the project.** The annual net cash flow can be positive or negative. The net cash flow is positive when cash income exceeds cash disbursements. This represents a cash inflow for the business. The opposite is true when cash disbursements exceed income. This may happen, for example, when expensive refurbishing is required after a number of years of operation and cash income is insufficient to cover these cash expenses.

- **The expected terminal cash flow, related to the termination of the project.** This terminal net cash flow is usually positive. The plant is sold and cash income exceeds cash expenses. It may happen, however, that the cost of cleaning up a site is so high that the terminal net cash flow is negative. Think, for example, of a nuclear power plant where the terminal value of the plant is low because of its limited use, but where the cost of disposing of the enriched uranium is very high.

The **magnitude of the expected net cash flows** of a project and **the timing of these cash flows** are crucial in the evaluation of investment proposals on the basis of the present value or discounted cash-flow approach, where the **net cash flow (the cash inflow minus cash outflow) can occur during a specific period or at a specific time.**

For evaluation purposes, it is therefore imperative to approach potential projects in a future-oriented time framework and to present the expected cash-flow stream of a potential project on a time line, as illustrated in Figure 13.20.

The annual **net cash flows** are normally calculated as the profit after interest and tax, plus any non-cash cost items such as depreciation minus the cash outflows for the particular year.

- The **initial investment** (C_0) is the net cash outflow at the commencement of the project at time t_0, usually for the acquisition of fixed assets and required current assets.
- The **annual net cash flows** (operating cash flows) (CF_t) are the net cash flows after tax that occur at any point during the life of the project minus cash outflow for the year. A positive net cash flow means that the cash inflow exceeds the cash outflow. A negative net cash flow implies the opposite.
- The **life of the project** (n periods or years), also referred to as the economic life of the project, is determined by the effects of physical, technological and economic factors.
- The terminal cash flow (TCF) is the expected net cash flow after tax, which is related to the termination of the project, such as the sale of its assets and the

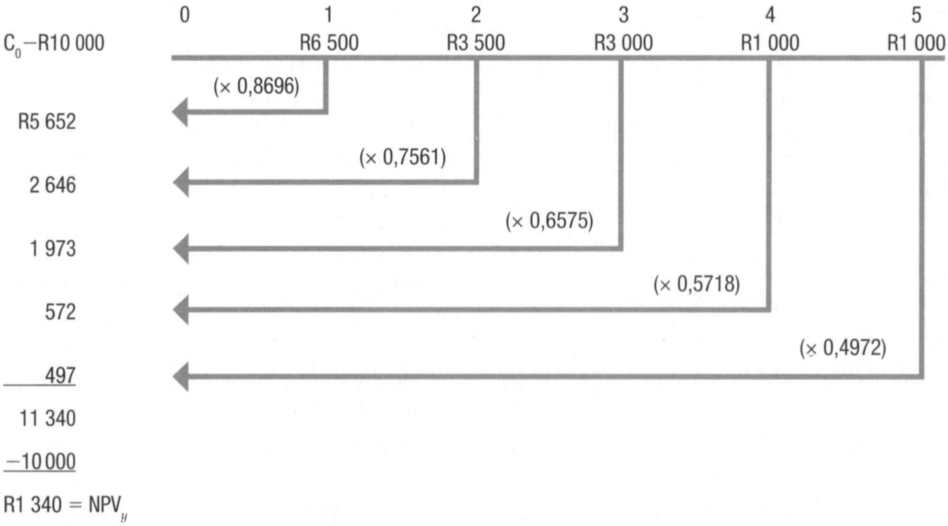

Figure 13.20: A time line for project Y

recovery of the working capital that was initially required. Depending on circumstances, the terminal net cash flow can again be positive or negative if it occurs only at the end of the final year of the life of the project life. This is indicated by TCF_n.

13.9.2.2 The net present value (NPV) and internal rate of return (IRR) methods[8]

NPV and IRR are **discounted cash-flow** (DCF) methods. They involve discounting estimated future cash flows to their present values, and take the magnitude and timing of cash flows into account.

The NPV is the difference between the present value of all net cash inflows (after tax) and the present value of all cash outflows (usually the initial investment) directly related to the project.

The formula for the calculation of NPV is as follows:

NPV = Present value of net cash inflows − Initial investment

The application of NPV involves the following:

- forecasting the three components of project cash flows (the initial investment, the annual net cash flows and the terminal cash flow) as accurately as possible
- deciding on an appropriate discounting rate
- calculating the present values of the above three project cash-flow components for a project determining the NPV of the project (the difference between the present value of the net cash inflows and that of the net cash outflow). The NPV may be positive or negative. The decision criterion is that positive NPVs may be acceptable projects because they will add value to the business.
- accepting all projects with a positive NPV and rejecting all those with a negative NPV in accordance with NPV decision criteria.

We shall explain the NPV method by means of a practical example by comparing investment proposals X and Y. The information about these projects appears in Table 13.18.

Assuming that the business's cost of capital is given as 15%, determining the

Table 13.18: Information about potential projects X and Y

Relevant information: initial investment (C_0)		Project X	Project Y
		R10 000	R10 000
Year	Time	Net cash flow (CF_t)	Net cash flow (CF_t)
1	$t = 1$	R2 800	R6 500
2	$t = 2$	R2 800	R3 500
3	$t = 3$	R2 800	R3 000
4	$t = 4$	R2 800	R1 000
5	$t = 5$	R2 800	R1 000

Notes:

1. The initial investment C_0 at time t_0 is the same for both projects, namely R10 000.
2. In this example, it is assumed that the net cash flow at the end of year five in both cases comprises only annual cash flows and not terminal cash flow.

NPV for project Y, for example, involves discounting the estimated net cash inflows at a discounting rate of 15% and subtracting the net cash outflow of R10 000 from the sum of the present value of the inflows.

To form a better idea of the cash flow at each point in time (year-end) over the entire project life, the total cash flows for project Y can be presented on a time line, as illustrated in Figure 13.20 on page 468.

In addition to a **time line**, NPV_x and NPV_y can also be determined by using a tabular format as illustrated in Table 13.18 on page 469 at a discount rate of 15%. See Table 13.19 for the discounting factors.

At a discount rate of 15%, NPV_x is negative and NPV_y is positive.

The **decision criteria** for the NPV are as follows:

- **Accept** projects with a positive NPV (NPV > 0). A positive NPV means that both the initial investment amount and all financing costs, as well as an addition to the value of the business (equal to the amount of the positive NPV) are sustained by the net cash flow of the project. In the case of project Y in the example that follows (see Table 13.20), an investment of

Table 13.19: Discounting factors

Period (*n*)	Discount rate	
	10%	**15%**
1	0,9091	0,8696
2	0,8264	0,7561
3	0,7513	0,6575
4	0,6830	0,5718
5	0,6209	0,4972

Table 13.20: Calculation of the NPV for projects X and Y

Year (*t*)	Project X			Project Y		
	Net cash inflow (CF_t) (1)	15% discounting factor ($PVT_{15,t}$) (2)	Present value (PV) (1) × (2)	Net cash inflow (CF_t) (1)	15% discounting factor ($PVT_{15,t}$) (2)	Present value (PV) (1) × (2)
1	R2 800	0,8696	R2 435	R6 500	0,8696	R5 652
2	2 800	0,7561	2 117	3 500	0,7561	2 646
3	2 800	0,6575	1 841	3 000	0,6575	1 973
4	2 800	0,5718	1 601	1 000	0,5718	572
5	2 800	0,4972	1 392	1 000	0,4972	497
		Total present value	9 386			11 340
		Minus: investment (C_0)	−10 000			−10 000
		NPV_x =	**−614**		NPV_y =	**1 340**

Notes:
- Since the initial investment C_0 occurs at time t_0, it represents a present value and requires no discounting.
- The NPVs for projects X and Y are: NPV_x = −R614; NPV_y = R1 340.

R10 000 will increase in value to R11 340 in present-value terms.

- **Reject** projects with a negative NPV (NPV < 0). In the case of the example in Table 13.20, the negative NPV of project X means that the net cash flow discounted at a rate of 15% is insufficient to redeem the initial investment amount and the related financing costs. Such a project would consequently have an adverse effect on the value of the business because additional funds (cash) would have to be found elsewhere to meet the shortfall. In the case of project X in Table 13.20, an investment of R10 000 will decrease to R9 386 in present-day terms.
- Projects with NPV = 0 make **no contribution** to value and are usually **rejected.** For a project with NPV = 0, the given project net cash flow, discounted at the business's cost of capital, is just sufficient to repay both the financing costs of the project and the total amount of financing.

The following questions might now be asked: How should the NPV as a criterion for decisions on investment possibilities be interpreted? and: In short, what does NPV mean in this context?

The IRR is that discount rate that equates the present value of cash inflows with the initial investment. The decision criterion when using the IRR is as follows: if the IRR is greater than the discount rate (normally the cost of capital), the project will add value (and *vice versa*).

In the case of the example given in Table 13.21, the IRR of project X is 12,38%, which is lower than 15%. This confirms the finding of the NPV method: project X will not add value. In the case of project Y, the IRR of 23,02% is greater than 15%, also confirming the finding of the NPV method: project Y will add value.

Table 13.21: Calculating NPV and IRR by means of a financial calculator

Project X		
Key in	**Press**	**Calculator display**
−10 000	CF	−10 000,00
2 800	CF	2 800,00
2 800	CF	2 800,00
2 800	CF	2 800,00
2 800	CF	2 800,00
15	I/YR	15,00
	NPV	−613,97
	IRR	12,38
Project Y		
Key in	**Press**	**Calculator display**
−10 000	CF	−10 000,00
6 500	CF	6 500,00
3 500	CF	3 500,00
3 000	CF	3 000,00
1 000	CF	1 000,00
1 000	CF	1 000,00
15	I/YR	15,00
	NPV	1 340,16
	IRR	23,02

13.9.2.3 Risk and uncertainty

The limitation of the above analysis of new investments is that it does not take risk into account.

Risk is defined as any deviation from the expected outcome. Such deviations may or may not occur. Managers are therefore not sure that they will occur, but managers are able to identify the size of the deviations and even the likelihood that they will occur.

Example: Probabilities and risk

Throwing the dice is an example of something involving risk. The person throwing knows that the outcome must be a number from one to six. He/she also knows that each number has the same chance of occurrence (one in six), but does not know which number will come up in any particular throw.

Uncertainty, in contrast to risk, describes a situation where managers are simply unable to identify the various deviations and are unable to assess the likelihood of their occurrence. Most business decisions have an element of uncertainty, but since there is no formal way of dealing with uncertainty, managers focus only on taking risk into account when making capital investment decisions.

Sensitivity analysis as one method for taking risk into account in capital investment decisions will now be discussed by referring to a practical example. Other methods will be discussed later in the chapter.

As was indicated earlier, investment decisions based on the NPV criterion are made on the basis of "best" predictions of the various cash flows. Sensitivity analysis takes each cash flow and determines by how much the estimate of that factor could be incorrect before it would affect the decision.

Example: Calculating NPV

Assume that Khumbali Resources is considering investing in a mineral-extraction process. The demand for the product is 5 000 tons for five years. The following data relates to this decision:

- The plant is expected to cost R500 000 and it has no resale value.
- The investment in the plant has to be paid immediately.
- The selling price of the product is R100 per ton.
- The cost of producing one ton of the product is R70.
- The cost of capital for Khumbali Resources is 10%.
- Tax is ignored.

Requirements:

- an assessment of the project by using the NPV method
- a sensitivity analysis of the project.

Solution:

The cash flow of the project will be as follows:

- Year 0: (500 000)
- Year 1: 5 000 × (100 − 70) = R150 000
- Year 2: 5 000 × (100 − 70) = R150 000
- Year 3: 5 000 × (100 − 70) = R150 000
- Year 4: 5 000 × (100 − 70) = R150 000
- Year 5: 5 000 × (100 − 70) = R150 000.

The NPV is equal to

$-500\ 000 + (150\ 000 \times PVIF_{10,1}) + (150\ 000 \times PVIF_{10,2}) + (150\ 000 \times PVIF_{10,3}) + (150\ 000 \times PVIF_{10,4}) + (150\ 000 \times PVIF_{10,5})$

$= -500\ 000 + (150\ 000 \times 0{,}909) + (150\ 000 \times 0{,}826) + (150\ 000 \times 0{,}751) + (150\ 000 \times 0{,}683) + (150\ 000 \times 0{,}621)$

$= -500\ 000 + 136\ 350 + 123\ 900 + 112\ 650 + 102\ 450 + 93\ 150$

$= 68\ 500$

- PVIF = Present value interest factor

The project should therefore be accepted on the NPV. The NPV is positive.

Sensitivity analysis determines how sensitive the project is to deviations in any of the cash flows. Our discussion of sensitivity analysis is limited to the sensitivity of the following factors whose estimates were used in calculating the NPV:

- original investment (−I)
- annual demand (V)
- net cash flow per ton (C).

In terms of the above, the NPV of the project is given by:

$(-I) + (V \times C \times PV_{r,1}) + (V \times C \times PV_{3,2}) + (V \times C \times PV_{r,3}) + (V \times C \times PV_{10,4}) + (V \times C \times PV_{10,5})$

$= (-I) + (5\,000 \times 30 \times PV_{10,1}) + (5\,000 \times 30 \times PV_{10,2}) + (5\,000 \times 30 \times PV_{10,3}) + (5\,000 \times 30 \times PV_{10,4}) + (5\,000 \times 30 \times PV_{10,5})$

- **The original investment.** The present value of the cash inflows amounts to R568 500. This means that the original investment could increase by R68 500 before the project might become marginal.
- **Annual demand (V).** For the NPV to equal zero, the annual demand has to decrease to:

$(-I) + (V \times 30 \times 0{,}909) + (V \times 30 \times 0{,}826) + (V \times 30 \times 0{,}751) + (V \times 30 \times 0{,}683) + (V \times 30 \times 0{,}621) = 0$

That is:

$0 = -500\,000 + 27{,}27V + 24{,}78V + 22{,}53V + 20{,}49V + 18{,}63V$

$113{,}7V = 500\,000$

$V = 500\,000 \div 113{,}7 = 4\,397{,}53$

This means that demand can decrease to 4 397 tons before the project becomes marginal.

- **Net cash flow per ton.** For the NPV to equal zero, the net cash flow has to decrease to:

$(-I) + (5\,000 \times C \times 0{,}909) + (5\,000 \times C \times 0{,}826) + (5\,000 \times C \times 0{,}751) + (5\,000 \times C \times 0{,}683) + (5\,000 \times C \times 0{,}621) = 0$

That is:

$0 = -500\,000 + 4545C + 4\,130C + 3\,755C + 3\,415C + 3\,105C$

$18\,950C = 500\,000$

$C = 500\,000 \div 18\,950 = 26{,}38$

The net cash flow can therefore decrease from R30 to R26,38 before the project becomes marginal.

The results can be tabulated as in Table 13.22.

The results in Table 13.22 show at a glance how sensitive the NPV is on the basis of the original estimates to changes in the variables used in the decision. This gives some indication of the riskiness of the project.

Table 13.22: The sensitivity analysis of the Khumbali Resources project

Factor	Original estimate (R)	Value to give NPV of zero (R)	Difference as percentage of original estimate (%)
Original investment (I)	500 000	568 500	13,7
Annual demand (V)	5 000	4 397	12,1
Net cash flow (C)	30	26,38	12,1

13.9.2.4 Final comments on the evaluation of investment projects

This section has considered the most important aspects of fixed-asset management: the evaluation of potential capital-investment projects and decisions on the desirability of such projects. After briefly looking at the importance of capital investments, the net present value method (NPV) and internal rate of return (IRR) for the evaluation of capital-investment proposals and the riskiness of projects were described.

The NPV is a discounted cash-flow method that takes the timing and the magnitude of cash flows into account. Investment decision-making based on the NPV therefore maximises stakeholders' wealth.

Sensitivity analysis can be used to assess the riskiness of the factors that are used to determine the NPV.

Critical thinking

Consider the payback period, NPV and IRR techniques.

Capital budgeting

1. A company is considering the purchase of land and the construction of a new factory. The land, which would be bought immediately, has a cost of R200 000 and the building, which would be erected at the end of the year, would cost R1 000 000. It is estimated that the firm's after-tax cash flow would be increased by R200 000, beginning at the end of the second year, and that this incremental flow would increase at a 10% rate annually over the next ten years. What would be the payback period correct to the nearest number of years?
2. What is the difference between the net present value (NPV) and the internal rate of return (IRR)?

13.10 Financing

As indicated earlier, the management of the financing structure is one of the tasks of the financial manager. This entails making decisions about the forms of financing (types of finance) and the sources of finance (the suppliers of finance) to minimise the cost and risk to the business.

In this section, financial markets and the sources and forms of short-term finance will be examined. This will be followed by a discussion of the sources and forms of long-term finance, as well as the cost of long-term capital.

13.10.1 Financial markets

Financial markets and financial institutions play an important role in the financing of businesses. The section that follows explains their role.

At a given point in time, an economic system consists of individuals and institutions with surplus funds (the savers) and individuals and institutions with a shortage of funds. Growing businesses require funds for new investments or to expand their existing production capacity. These businesses have a shortage of funds, and to grow, they must have access to the funds of individuals and institutions that do not have an immediate need for them.

- Financial markets are the channels through which holders of surplus funds (the savers) make their funds available to those who require additional finance.
- Financial institutions play an important role in this regard. They act as intermediaries on financial markets between the savers and those with a shortage of funds. This financial service is referred to as **financial intermediation**.
- Financial intermediation[9] is the process through which financial institutions pool funds from savers and make these funds available to individuals and institutions requiring finance.

Through financial intermediation, the individual saver with relatively small savings is given the opportunity to invest in a large capital-intensive business such as a chemical plant. The saver who invests in a business is referred to as a financier. The business rewards the financier for the use of the funds so that the financier shares in the wealth created by the business.

The financier receives an asset in the form of a financial claim in exchange for his/her money. Financial claims have different names and characteristics, and include savings and cheque (call) accounts, fixed deposits, debentures, and ordinary and preferred shares. In everyday usage, these financial claims are referred to as securities or financial instruments.

13.10.1.1 Primary and secondary markets

As indicated above, a saver receives an asset in the form of a financial claim against the institution to which money was made available. These claims are also referred to as securities. New issues of financial claims are referred to as issues on the primary market.

Some types of financial claims are negotiable and can be traded on financial markets. Trading in these securities after they have been issued takes place in the secondary market. This means that a saver who needs money can trade the claim on the secondary market to obtain cash. The Johannesburg Securities Exchange (JSE) is an example of a market where savers can convert their investments to cash virtually immediately. The tradeability of securities ensures that savers with surplus funds continue to invest. Once issued, they can be traded on the market and the holder may again obtain cash.

Company shares and debentures are examples of negotiable financial instruments, and savings and call accounts are non-negotiable claims.

13.10.1.2 Money and capital markets

The money market is the market for financial instruments with a short-term maturity. Funds are borrowed and lent in the money market for periods of one day (that is, overnight) or for months. The periods of the transactions depend on the particular needs of savers and institutions with a shortage of funds. The money market has no central physical location and transactions are conducted from the premises of the various participants, for example, banks, using telephones or online computer terminals.

Funds required for long-term investment are raised and traded by investors on the capital market. In South Africa, much of this trading takes place on the Johannesburg Securities Exchange. However, long-term investment transactions are also done privately. An investor may, for example, sell shares held in a private company directly to another investor without channelling the transaction through a stock exchange.

13.10.1.3 Types of institutions

As indicated previously, financial institutions interpose themselves as intermediaries between savers and institutions with a shortage of funds by rendering a service to both. Financial institutions are divided into two broad categories: deposit-taking institutions and non-deposit-taking institutions.

Deposit-taking institutions

- The South African Reserve Bank is South Africa's central bank. It acts as a banker to the central government, keeps the banking accounts of government departments and advances loans to the state. It also regulates private banks so that government monetary policy is adhered to and it has the sole right to issue bank notes. Its most important liability is the bank notes and coins in circulation. For example, a R50 note in circulation means that the Reserve Bank owes the holder an amount of R50.
- The Land and Agricultural Bank (Land Bank) grants loans to farmers and agricultural co-operatives.
- The Corporation for Public Deposits (CPD) accepts surplus funds from departments,

institutions and organisations in the public sector. It is owned by the Reserve Bank. It accepts short-term deposits, pays interest on them and repays the deposits on demand.

- Private-sector banks, as a group, are the single largest type of financial intermediary in the financial system. Banks take deposits from individuals and organisations with surplus funds and lend them to others with a shortage of funds. In addition to this function, they provide financial services such as insurance-broking and administering estates. They also facilitate foreign trade.
- The Post Office Savings Bank accepts deposits from the public, but does not grant credit or offer cheque facilities. The government is ultimately responsible for its solvency. In contrast to other banks, the Post Office Savings Bank is therefore not regulated by the Banks Act (No. 94 of 1990).

Non-deposit-taking institutions

Non-deposit-taking institutions are considered in three categories: public sector, private sector and other.

Public-sector institutions

- **Public Investment Commissioners (PIC).** The PIC operates as an investment intermediary for long-term public funds. It administers and invests the public sector's retirement schemes, provident schemes and social security funds, for example, the Workmen's Compensation Fund. The funds it administers amount to approximately one-third of the total administered by all private insurers and retirement funds.

Private-sector institutions

- **Life assurers, pension and provident funds.** The main purpose of these institutions is the payment of lump sums to beneficiaries at death, on retirement or at the attainment of a certain age. They provide people with income after retirement until death. To fulfill this function, life assurers collect premiums from policyholders, and pension and provident funds receive monthly contributions from employers and employees. The premiums and contributions received are made available to institutions until required by the insurance company or pension fund.
- **Short-term insurers.** Short-term insurers provide cover against accidental losses caused by fire, theft, storms and so on. The premiums received are sufficient to cover the risk for a particular year. These premiums are also made available to borrowers by investing them on the money market.
- **Collective investment schemes (also known as unit trusts).** These schemes provide small investors with the opportunity to invest their surplus funds in large companies. The administrators of unit trusts invest funds received in, for example, a number of companies listed on the JSE. The fund is divided into small affordable units and each investor receives an allocation of units according to his/her investment. The funds are managed by professional investment managers.

Other institutions

- **Industrial Development Corporation (IDC).** The main purpose of the IDC is to promote industrial development by assisting the private sector in financing new businesses and expanding existing ones. It extends credit, takes up shares and facilitates the financing of expansion of industrial businesses. For example, it helped to finance Sasol.
- **Khula Enterprise Finance Limited (Khula).** Khula was established to provide wholesale finance for new small businesses and for the expansion of existing businesses. For example, a person wishing to start a panel-beating business may approach Khula through its retail financial intermediaries (RFIs) for funds.
- **Ntsika Enterprise Promotion Agency (Ntsika).** Ntsika's role is to render an

efficient and effective promotion and support service to small, medium and micro-enterprises (SMMEs) in order to contribute towards equitable economic growth in South Africa. Ntsika provides wholesale non-financial support services for SMME promotion and development. It also provides funding to organisations providing approved services.
- **Development Bank of South Africa (DBSA).** The purpose of the DBSA is to promote development in areas not served by the private sector. It provides finance for infrastructure projects such as roads, dams and telecommunications.

13.10.2 Short-term financing

The short-term financing decision requires finding the optimal combination of long-term and short-term financing to finance current assets.

As in the management of current assets, risks and costs must be weighed against each other when making this decision. This section introduces different forms of short-term financing. It is followed by a discussion of the implications of a combination of long-term and short-term financing for the financing of current assets.

The following are the most common forms of short-term financing:
- trade credit
- accruals
- bank overdrafts
- factoring.

Each of these forms of financing will now be discussed.

13.10.2.1 Trade credit

Trade credit is an important form of finance for businesses and is mainly in the form of suppliers' credit. This means that a supplier does not take payment from the business when products or services are purchased. The business is expected to pay only after 30, 60 or 90 days, depending on the credit terms.

When Pick n Pay, for example, purchases cereal on credit from Tiger Oats (the supplier), it implies that Tiger Oats finances the purchase for Pick n Pay for the period for which the supplier's credit is granted, namely 30, 60 or 90 days.

As shown in Figure 13.21, wholesalers and retailers such as Pick n Pay make extensive use of trade credit as a form of finance because of the nature of their business. Smaller businesses also rely on trade credit because they find it more difficult to obtain funds on money and capital markets. As a rule, trade credit can be obtained quite readily by any business with a reasonable financial record.

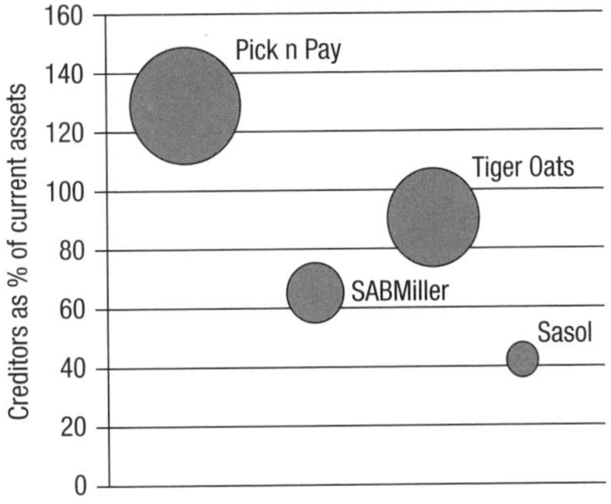

Figure 13.21: The use of trade credit as a form of finance – selected listed companies

To ensure prompt payment, the supplier often offers a cash rebate for early payment. This rebate applies only if the buyer pays before a stated date, which precedes the due date of the account.

How do we calculate the advantage of the cash rebate? The following formula can be used:

Cost of not accepting the rebate

$$= \frac{(\%\ \text{Rebate})}{100\% - \%\ \text{Rebate}} \times \frac{365}{(\text{Additional number of days after rebate period for which funds are available})}$$

Management may also decide to delay payment within certain limits. Funds are consequently available to the business for a longer period, which decreases its additional cash needs. This is risky, as the consequence of such a decision could be that the creditworthiness of the business is jeopardised and suppliers may refuse to supply it in future.

Trade credit offers the following advantages as a source of short-term funds[10]:

- It is readily available to businesses that pay their suppliers regularly and is also a source of spontaneous financing, which is explained in the example that follows.
- It is informal. If a business currently pays its bills within the discount period, additional credit can simply be obtained by delaying payment until the end of the net period at the cost of forgoing the discount.
- Trade credit is more flexible than other forms of short-term financing because the business does not have to negotiate a loan agreement, provide security or adhere to a rigid repayment schedule.

Example: Trade credit

Simeka Retailers purchases an average of R50 000 a day on terms of "net 30" from Mega Wholesalers. That is, the goods must be paid for within 30 days of the invoice date. This means Mega Wholesalers provides R50 000 × 30 = R1 500 000 in short-term financing to Simeka. Now assume that Simeka's sales – and therefore purchases – double. The trade credit that Mega extends to Simeka also doubles to R3 000 000. Simeka obtains this additional amount of financing virtually automatically, in other words, it is obtained spontaneously.

13.10.2.2 Accruals

As with trade credit, accruals are also a source of spontaneous finance. The most common expenses accrued are wages and taxes.

Accrued wages represent money that a business owes its employees. Employees provide part of the short-term financing for the business by waiting a month or a week to be paid, rather than being paid every day.

Accrued tax is also a form of financing. The level of financing from accrued taxes is determined by the amount of tax payable and the frequency with which it is paid.

Accruals have no associated cost. They are therefore a valuable source of finance because they are cost-free substitutes for otherwise costly short-term credit.

13.10.2.3 Bank overdrafts

An overdraft facility is an arrangement with a bank that allows a business to make payments from a cheque account in excess of the balance in the account. The purpose of an overdraft is to bridge the gap between cash income and cash expenses. An overdraft usually increases through to the month-end, when the clients of the business pay their accounts.

An overdraft arrangement is reviewed annually, usually when the annual financial statements become available, so that the bank can evaluate the current financial position of the business. The interest charged on an overdraft is negotiable and relates to the risk profile of the borrower.

Interest is charged daily on the outstanding balance. This means that the borrower only pays interest on that part of the overdraft that is being used. In contrast to other forms of financing, a bank overdraft is repayable on demand. This means that the bank may cancel the facility at any time.

An overdraft is a flexible form of short-term financing. It is cost effective if used correctly.

13.10.2.4 Debtor finance

Debtor finance consists of factoring and invoice discounting. In contrast to a bank overdraft, debtor finance is, strictly speaking, not borrowing. It is not a loan secured by the book debts of the business. Instead, it involves the sale of debtors to a debtor-financing company.

Invoice discounting is the sale of existing debtors to a debtor-financing company. This company then converts credit sales to cash sales and provides the business with a cash injection by releasing funds that were tied up in working capital. Invoice discounting is usually confidential. In other words, debtors are not advised of the arrangement between the business and the finance company.

Factoring is similar to invoice discounting, but it goes one step further. With factoring, the financier also undertakes to administer and control the collection of debt. In contrast to invoice discounting, debtors are aware of the agreement between the business and the financier.

The financier to whom the debtors are sold is known as the factor. The factor buys approved debtors from the business after carefully examining each account individually. The factor receives commission and interest on amounts paid to the business before the expiry date of the debt. The factor usually pays the business 70% to 80% of the amount outstanding from debtors immediately and the remainder when the debtor pays.

Two common types of factoring practice are:

- **Non-recourse factoring.** The factor buys the debtors outright and bears the risk of bad debts. The factor accepts responsibility for credit control, debt collection and sales records. Customers pay the factor direct.
- **Recourse factoring.** In recourse factoring, the factor provides the same services as in non-recourse factoring, but the seller guarantees that debts are recoverable. The factor recovers any bad debt from the seller.

Factoring of debtor accounts has the following advantages:

- The cost of debtor administration is transferred to the factor.
- The turnover of current assets is increased and less capital is required to finance debtors.
- Liquidity ratios improve.
- More cash is available for other purposes.

The cost of factoring fluctuates according to the conditions laid down by the factor. In considering factoring, the cost should be compared to the savings achieved through not having the administrative liability of debt collection.

13.10.2.5 The short-term financing decision

The cost of short-term funds is generally lower than that of long-term funds. One reason is that trade credit does not really involve a cost. From a cost or profit point of view, it is advantageous for a business to make use of short-term funds for the financing of

Case study

Factoring: A new financing alternative for small companies

Factoring, where companies sell their book of debtors to a bank or a factoring company to obtain cash immediately, has traditionally only been available to large companies. Small- to medium-sized enterprises (SMEs) find it difficult to obtain working capital from banks. However, a South African company has developed a world first by allowing small- to medium-sized enterprises the opportunity to factor their invoices. This will provide them with an entirely new form of financing that they could not access previously.

Source: Masango, G. 2007. "Black like Me". *Finweek*, 23 August, p. 12.

its current assets, but too heavy a dependence on them increases the risk of finance not being available when required.

Consider, for example, a financial manager who relies on having short-term debt rescheduled. There is an unforeseen economic downturn, the financial position of the business deteriorates and the bank manager refuses to renew the business's overdraft. It is clear that the financial manager is faced with a liquidity crisis. A plan will have to be devised to meet the crisis.

The more frequently a business has to refinance its debt, the greater the risk of becoming illiquid. This risk therefore increases as the period for which the debt is granted decreases.

The use of long-term funds to satisfy working-capital requirements has exactly the opposite implications for a business. From a cost point of view, it is disadvantageous because long-term funds are generally more expensive than short-term funds. They will also be under-utilised because of the variable nature of portions of working-capital requirements. On the other hand, if more long-term funds are used, there is less risk of funds not being available if and when required.

Figure 13.22 illustrates the following three approaches to the short-term financing problem:

- The **matching approach** (also referred to as the hedging approach) involves matching the period for which finance is obtained with the expected life of the asset. Financing arranged for periods longer than the life of an asset is costly because it is not utilised for the entire period. However, if finance is arranged for a period shorter than the life of the asset, there will be additional transactional costs to arrange for new short-term finance repeatedly. According to this approach, fixed assets and permanent current assets are financed with long-term financing and temporary current assets are financed with short-term funds.
- In the **aggressive approach**, the financial manager uses more short-term financing than is needed with the matching approach. Permanent current assets are partially financed with short-term funds, instead of using only long-term funds as in the case of the matching approach.
- In the **conservative approach**, the financial manager uses more long-term funds than with the matching approach. The temporary current-asset requirement is financed with long-term funds. This plan is conservative because it involves the use of a relatively large proportion of long-term funds, which is less risky.

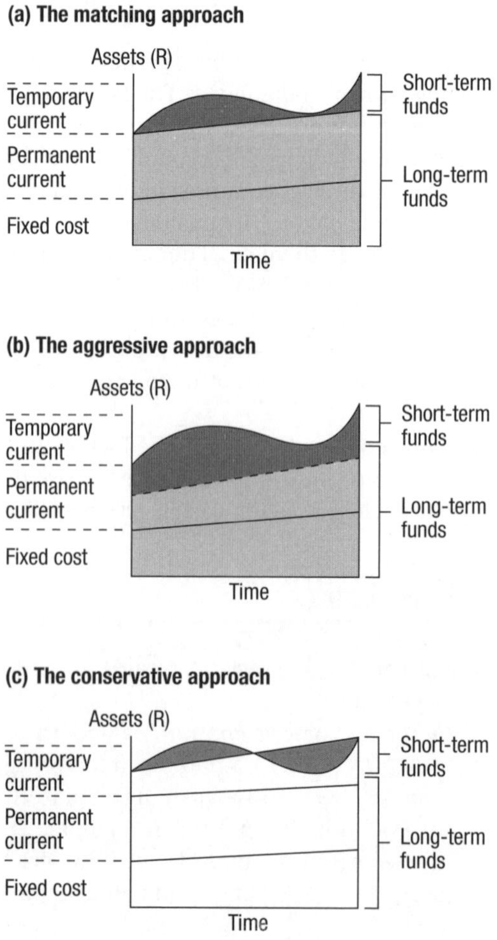

Figure 13.22: Short-term financing plans

13.10.2.6 Concluding remarks

The choice of a financing plan for a business's current assets entails a trade-off between risk and return. From a cost point of view, it is preferable to finance current assets needs with short-term funds, while risk considerations demand the use of long-term funds.

> **Critical thinking**
>
> The cost and risk associated with financing need to be considered carefully.
>
> **Deciding about finance**
>
> Assume that Thabeng Enterprises is running into cash-flow problems. It is a privately owned company. Thabeng can finance its working capital by extending its bank loan or by factoring debtors. Taking risk considerations into account, which would be the most appropriate form of financing for Thabeng?

13.11 Long-term financing

This section focuses on the characteristics of the various forms of long-term financing and the implications of the various sources of financing for businesses.

This is followed by a discussion of the cost of capital and the establishment of an optimal capital structure, with specific reference to financial gearing.

13.11.1 Shareholders' interest

Shareholders' interest in a company is subdivided into owners' equity and preference-shareholders' capital.

13.11.1.1 Owners' equity

Owners' equity consists of the funds made directly available by the legal owners (ordinary shareholders) in the form of share capital, as well as indirect contributions in the form of profit retention as reserves and undistributed profits.

- The **ordinary share**. Ordinary shareholders are the true owners of a business. An ordinary share therefore gives right of ownership (right of possession). Shareholders receive share certificates in exchange for the money they make available to the business.
- There are two types of ordinary shares: **par value shares** and **non-par value shares**. Par value shares all have the same value, while the value of non-par value shares differs. A business can only issue one of the two types of shares, not both.
- A co-owner of the business, the ordinary shareholder, has a claim to profits. The portion of profit paid to ordinary shareholders is known as a dividend. It is paid out in proportion to the shareholding of each ordinary shareholder. The following are important characteristics of the ordinary share:
  - The liability of ordinary shareholders is limited to the amount of share capital they contributed to the business. This means that if the business is liquidated, shareholders may lose this money, but may not otherwise be held liable for its debts. That is why we add the word "Limited" to the name of a public or private company.
  - Shareholders have no certainty that the money paid for the shares will be recouped, for this depends on the success of the business.
  - Ordinary shares in a listed company (in other words, a public company traded on the stock exchange) can be traded on a stock exchange.
  - Ordinary shareholders are the owners of the business and usually have full control of it in that they can vote at general meetings to appoint directors of the company and on such matters as the amount of dividends to be paid to shareholders. Voting rights are usually in proportion to shareholdings.
  - In contrast to interest payable on borrowed capital, a business has no

legal obligation to reward ordinary shareholders in the form of dividends for their investment in shares.
  - Share capital is available to the business for an unlimited period. Ordinary share capital does not have to be repaid. Shareholders may, however, convert their investments into cash by selling their shares to another investor. South African companies listed on the JSE are allowed to buy back their own shares.
- The issue of additional ordinary shares by an existing company may have the following disadvantages:
  - The earnings per share (profit attributable to ordinary shareholders divided by the number of issued shares) of existing shareholders may decrease because the profit attributable to ordinary shareholders does not immediately increase in relation to the increase in the number of issued shares. This phenomenon is known as the dilution of existing shareholders' earnings.
  - Existing shareholders may lose control because voting rights are linked to shareholdings, and people other than existing shareholders may take up new shares and become majority shareholders. This danger applies not only to the issue of new shares, but generally also to a business whose shares are listed on a stock exchange and can therefore easily be obtained by others, including competitors.
  - The cost of issuing new ordinary shares and the riskiness of an investment in ordinary shares may result in the cost of ordinary share capital being higher than that of other forms of financing.
- Ordinary shares, however, hold some advantages for a business, the following being the most important:
  - There is no risk involved for the business because payment of dividends and redemption of capital are not compulsory.
  - Additional ordinary shares serve as security for attracting additional borrowed capital, which provides greater flexibility for capital structure decisions. The base of shareholders' capital gives the financial manager the additional flexibility to use a combination of share capital and debt to finance the business.
- Retained profit consists of reserves and undistributed profit, and represents amounts that would otherwise have been paid out to shareholders as dividends. Retained profit is also referred to as self-financing or internal financing. As a form of financing, it holds various advantages for a business:
  - No issue costs are involved so it is cheaper than the issuing of additional ordinary shares.
  - Capital is immediately available for use.
  - It lends flexibility to the capital structure because it serves as security for attracting additional borrowed capital.
  - In contrast to the issue of new shares, there are no control implications for existing shareholders.
  - It serves as an alternative form of financing if conditions are unfavourable in the capital market as a result of, for example, high interest rates.
  - It entails no interest or redemption obligations.

Internal financing is consequently an easy and inexpensive form of financing for a business. However, from the point of view of the owners (ordinary shareholders), it has a serious short-term disadvantage because the retention of profit means the forfeiting of dividends.

13.11.1.2 Preference-shareholders' capital

Preference shares fall somewhere between debentures (discussed later) and ordinary shares in terms of risk. They have some

Table 13.23: Sources and forms of long-term financing for a business in the form of a company

	Source	Balance-sheet classification	Form
1	Owners or ordinary shareholders	Owner's equity or own capital	• Ordinary shares • Reserves • Undistributed profit • Preference shares
2	Preference shareholders	Preference-shareholders' capital	
1 + 2	Share capital	Shareholders' interest	Total of the above
3	Suppliers of debt capital/credit suppliers	Long-term or borrowed capital over a long-term period	• Debentures • Bonds • Registered term loans • Financial leases
1 + 2 + 3		Total long-term capital	

Notes:
The sources and forms of long-term financing for other forms of businesses differ only in some respects from those for a company:
1. Other forms of business do not have any preference shareholders, and therefore there are no preference shares and no preference-shareholders' capital.
2. The own capital or owner's equity comprises funds that the owner/s contribute to the business, as well as profits that are not withdrawn by the owners. The owners' equity is included in a capital account in the balance sheet.
3. Other forms of business do not make use of debentures.

characteristics of both debentures and ordinary shares. If a business is doing poorly, it will first pay debenture holders their required interest and then pay dividends to preference shareholders. Anything left goes to ordinary shareholders.

Two forms of preference shares are distinguished: the ordinary preference share and the cumulative preference share. In the case of the ordinary preference share, shareholders forfeit a dividend if the directors decide not to declare one in a particular year. Cumulative preference shareholders retain the right to receive an arrear dividend in the following year.

A preference share has the following characteristics:

- It has a preferential claim over an ordinary share on profit after tax. In contrast to the dividend on an ordinary share, however, a preference-share dividend is limited to a certain maximum. For example, the holders of a 10% preference share will never receive more than a 10% return on their investment, but could in bad times receive no dividend, or one of less than 10%.
- It has a preferential claim over ordinary shares on the assets of the business in the case of liquidation.
- The term of availability is unlimited.
- Authority can vary between full voting rights and no voting rights at all, but usually an ordinary preference share provides no voting rights.

From the viewpoint of the business, preference shares have an advantage over ordinary shares in that their cost is usually lower. For the shareholder, ordinary shares are more risky because preference shareholders have a priority claim on net profit after tax and on assets in the case of liquidation.

13.11.2 Long-term debt

Long-term debt generally refers to debt that will mature (has to be repaid) in a year or more, and can usually be obtained in two ways:

- through a loan
- through credit.

A loan is a contract in which the receiver of funds (the borrower) undertakes to make interest payments at specified times to the supplier of funds (the lender) and to redeem the total principal sum in payments over an agreed period or on a specific due date.

With credit, the supplier of credit (the supplier of capital) provides the business (the receiver of capital) with power of disposal over an asset and receives extended payments in return, consisting of a principal sum and an interest component. Financial leasing (discussed later) is an example of credit financing.

Some debt instruments (such as debentures, which are discussed later) bear a fixed rate of interest for the period of the debt. In other cases, for example, mortgage bonds, the interest rate is not fixed, but fluctuates with market forces. This is known as variable interest.

Debt that is secured on one or more assets of the business is known as secured debt. In the event of liquidation of the business, the proceeds from the secured assets would be used first to satisfy the claim of the secured supplier of credit. For example, the holder of a mortgage bond that is secured on any property must be repaid on liquidation before the proceeds from the sale of the property may be used to satisfy the claims of other creditors.

In the case of unsecured debt, a creditor does not have any preferential claim on the assets of a business.

In practice, there are various forms of long-term debt. The most important forms of long-term debt are discussed below.

13.11.2.1 Loans

The following types of loans are of special importance:

- **Debentures** are the most common form of long-term debt in the case of companies. The business (the borrower) issues a certificate to the lender showing the conditions of the loan. This certificate is negotiable, which means that it can be traded on financial markets. Payment of the loan, consisting of a principal sum plus interest, is made to the presenter of the certificate. A debenture has a fixed interest charge and the loan is available to the business over a specified term.
- **Bonds** are secured loans and are issued with fixed assets such as fixed property as security (mortgage bonds). The amount that can be raised depends primarily on the value of the property. Typically, a mortgage bond will not exceed 75% of the value of the property.
- **Registered-term loans** are unsecured loans and, in contrast to debentures, are not freely negotiable. The name of the lender and the credit conditions are recorded in the books of the lender (business).

For a business, loans have the following advantages:

- Costs are limited in that they are determined by the loan interest rate.
- Interest payments are deductible for tax purposes.
- The control of the owners is usually not influenced by the issue of more loans.
- Loans do not dilute the earnings of ordinary shares.

A disadvantage is that the fixed interest obligations and the priority claims of loans in the case of liquidation increase the risks inherent in the business to its owners.

13.11.2.2 Financial leasing

A financial lease is a contract that provides the right to the use of an asset, legally owned by the lessor, in exchange for a specified rental paid by the lessee. The lessor is the party who promises to make the asset available for use by the lessee.

A financial lease is a form of credit-financing that should not be confused with an operating lease. In contrast to an operating lease, financial leasing gives the lessee the opportunity of owning the asset at the end of the lease. An operating lease can be terminated by giving the required notice, but a financial lease is a non-terminative agreement between the lessee and the lessor. Hence it is a financing agreement (lease) and not an operating-lease agreement.

Two basic forms of financial leasing are the following[11]:

- **Direct financial leasing** of operating equipment such as motor vehicles and computers. In direct leasing, the lease amount, which is repayable in regular instalments, is determined in such a way that the value of the asset, plus an interest charge, is paid back by the end of the term of the lease, which is usually related to the lifespan of the asset. Maintenance and insurance of the asset are normally the responsibility of the lessee. Financial leases are used to finance motor vehicles, plant and equipment.
- **Leaseback agreements** involve assets of a more permanent nature. In leaseback agreements, certain assets that the business owns are sold to the credit supplier and at the same time leased back by the business according to a long-term agreement. Leaseback agreements are usually entered into by businesses that need to raise funds. The assets are generally of a highly specialised nature. The business obtains cash without losing the use of property or equipment through the leaseback arrangement. For example, a dentist may decide to obtain additional funds by financing his/her equipment on a leaseback arrangement. The lease payments of a financial lease are deductible for tax purposes. When the advantages of financial leasing are weighed against ownership through purchase with loan capital, the after-tax costs have to be compared. One should therefore bear in mind that in the case of ownership through the use of loan capital, depreciation, investment rebates and interest payments contribute to tax savings.

13.11.3 Sources of financing for small businesses

It is always sad to see a new business with great profit potential fall by the wayside only because it was not properly financed from the beginning. This happens too often among the thousands of new small businesses started in this country every year. The error comes from either not knowing the total financial needs of the business or failing to provide for those needs in the planning stage.

No business should ever be started without a clear and positive understanding of where its total capital needs are coming from. As has been seen in previous chapters, a very important phase of the entire planning process is to determine what assets will be needed and how they are to be provided. When the amount of the net ownership capital needed has been determined, the proprietors turn to the problem of making sure that the entire amount is available. The total sum should preferably be deposited in the company's bank account before any commitments are made by the new owners.

When several sources of capital are available, the planners must remember that all sources may not be equally desirable. Borrowed capital is shown on the balance sheet as a liability. It must be paid back at specific periods. These repayments of principal amounts are not operating expenses, which are deducted on the income statement before planned profits are produced. They are payments for the provision of investment capital and are to be paid out of the profits shown on the income statement. Many researchers have found that failure to recognise this basic fact is the most common cause of financial strain among small businesses. It is important, therefore, to consider the repayment schedules when choosing among sources of financing.

The various types of financing available to small businesses usually have a similar classification to those of a company, with a few differences and additions. A few of these forms of financing a small business will be discussed in the sections that follow.

Two things should be recognised when one is faced with the problem of obtaining outside capital assistance:

- An established business with a good record of operations usually has better access to available sources of capital than a new business.
- Some personal capital available for investment in the business by the owner is almost always essential to obtaining any type of outside assistance.

The possibilities of each of the sources of funds listed will be investigated against this background.

13.11.3.1 Personal funds

Whenever potential creditors, partners or shareholders are invited to invest in or lend financial assistance to a business, their first question is, "How much does the owner have invested?" Every business contains an element of risk and outsiders who invest in a new business wish to be sure that such risk is shared by the owner. Trading on "too thin an equity base" means that the owner's investment is too small relative to the investment of outsiders. A financing plan that indicates that the business is starting out on this basis does not usually invite confidence from creditors. As seen in the previous section on capital structure, this does not always mean that the new owners must have 50% of the total capital needs to invest, but it does mean that they should look to other ownership capital rather than only to creditor capital in their financial plan. In any event, it is important that the owners have assets of their own to invest in the business. The closer to 50% of the total capital needs that can be provided, the greater will be their independence and share of net profits.

13.11.3.2 Loans from relatives and friends

Although this type of borrowing to provide original investment capital is generally frowned upon by experienced business operators, it remains a prominent device used in the financial planning of small businesses. Many owners are encouraged in their enterprise by parents, relatives or friends who offer to supply loans to the business to get it started. Quite often, no other sources are available after normal trade credit and supplier contracts have been utilised.

It is unfortunate, however, that many otherwise successful businesses have been beset by troubles because relatives or friends interfered with the operations. Mixing family or social relationships with business can be dangerous. Many such situations might have been averted if the terms of the loans had been more clearly specified, including the rights of the lenders to insist upon making operational policy. The best way to avoid subsequent problems is to make sure that loans are made on a businesslike basis. They should be viewed as business dealings. The right of the owner to make decisions should be respected by all parties involved. Arrangements for retiring such loans, including any options for early payment and the procedure if loans become delinquent, should be clearly understood and set out in writing. The owner should be sure such loans are properly presented on the balance sheet. Payments due in one year are current liabilities; the others are fixed liabilities.

13.11.3.3 Trade credit

Trade credit is the financial assistance available from other businesses with whom the business has dealings. Most prominent are the suppliers of an inventory that is constantly being replaced. It has previously been noted that wholesalers who desire a retailer's business, for example, will offer generous terms for payment of invoices. Manufacturers will do the same for wholesalers whose business they desire. Financing the opening inventory usually represents one of the larger investments in a typical small business. If a R20 000 inventory can be purchased for a R10 000 down payment and the balance in 30 days, the wholesaler has virtually provided R10 000 of the required capital to open the business. The owner then has an opportunity to sell that inventory at a profit and thus to have the funds to pay off the original balance. As a record for successful operation is established, even more attractive terms may be offered on subsequent purchases. A grocer may have several such suppliers. Other businesses may have only one or two major suppliers. The inducement of a sales discount for prompt payment of invoices should always tempt the owner to pay within the maximum discount period.

13.11.3.4 Loans or credit from equipment sellers

This type of financial aid is often considered another form of trade credit. It does, however, have distinct characteristics. The small business may need counters, shelves, display cases, delivery trucks and other equipment such as air conditioning, refrigeration units and food counters. These, too, are a large investment for the new small business and are recognised as such by the major suppliers of items like these. The purchases, it is hoped, are not made on a regular basis, but represent a large part of the capital needed to get started. The suppliers usually offer good credit terms with a modest down payment and a contract for the balance spread over one, two or three years.

This type of credit, when financing charges are reasonable, can be most helpful to the planner. The caution is in its over-use, remembering, again, that the principal payments must be paid out of profits anticipated. Any principal repayments of this type, too, are for the provision of capital and are not operating expenses. Too much of this type of financing can distort the current and acid-test ratios, and upset the business's financial liquidity. Many cases are on record where the monthly payments on such fixed assets exceed the profits earned from sales in the month.

13.11.3.5 Mortgage loans

If the small-business owners own a commercial building, they can normally secure a mortgage on it with payments over as many as 20 years. This may, for example, be the building in which the new business will operate. In that case, the planners will be making mortgage payments instead of rental payments to a landlord. They may wish to risk a mortgage on their homes. Even second mortgages are sometimes used, although this is not recommended. When profits are uncertain, caution is advised in committing any assets to mortgage claims. As a clear profit pattern becomes more stable and predictable, the use of mortgage credit becomes less risky.

13.11.3.6 Commercial bank loans

Historically, a line of credit at a chartered bank was designed to enable a merchant to purchase an inventory of merchandise. When the merchandise was sold at a profit, the bank was paid its loan. This situation is still followed by many banks. This use of bank credit is still the best way to establish credit with a commercial bank. Since the relaxation of bank restrictions in recent years, however, many other types of loans and financing are now available to qualified applicants. In fact, we now have banks that advertise: "If you are planning to go into business, come see us." The cold, hard facts of economic reality will be faced in such a visit, but the prospective business owner with an otherwise-sound financing plan, a reputation for integrity and a business deemed likely to succeed may still establish some bank credit in the planning stage. Short-term loans are usually considered loans over a period not exceeding one year. If adequate collateral is available, longer-term loans may be obtained. Getting influential or wealthy friends to co-sign notes may also be helpful.

The policies of several of the chartered banks should always be checked in the planning stage. Many small-business owners with experience have long described banks as "a place where you can borrow money when you prove that you don't need it". Some banks are earnestly trying to remove that image today. In keeping with the previously noted axiom that rewards must be commensurate with cost and risk, however, interest rates charged by banks to small businesses are significantly higher than the rates charged to large businesses.

13.11.3.7 Small-business loans

The proprietor of a small business enterprise or a person who is about to establish a new business may borrow funds under this program for the acquisition of fixed assets, modernisation of premises (leasehold improvements), or the purchase of land or buildings necessary for the operation of the business. The loans are usually provided and administered by the chartered banks and other designated lending institutions such as Khula Enterprise Finance Limited. The loans have fixed terms of repayments of the principal, typically five years. The interest charged on these loans is fluctuating (floating). This rate is usually one or more percent higher than the commercial bank's prime lending rate.

13.11.3.8 Taking in partners

Despite all the necessary precautions, raising capital often necessitates taking one or more partners into the business. If more than one manager is not needed, the new partners may not be employed in the business, but may hold full partner status as a result of their investment in the business. The partnership agreement is important here. Inducements can be offered to such a finance partner, but the duties, responsibilities and authority of each partner must be clearly understood. (At this point, the partnership is being considered only from the standpoint of providing a source of investment funds.)

13.11.3.9 Selling capital shares

Aside from the technical, legal and operational advantages of the corporate form of legal organisation, its advantages are greater than the disadvantages as a device for raising capital. Many small-business owners seem to believe that the corporate form was designed only for very large businesses. This is false, however. It is true that this legal form has not been as widely used as it might be, but this is believed to be the result of a lack of knowledge of its advantages.

Consider a new-business planner who needs R100 000 in ownership capital, but has only R30 000 to invest. Would it not be desirable for him/her to go to a local investment dealer as a corporation and request the sale of R50 000 of 7% preference shares and R50 000 of common shares? The owner takes title to R30 000 of the voting common shares and can hold the unsold shares in the business for possible future financing for expansion. The preference share is given a priority of dividends and may not have voting privilege. Usually only the common share has voting power. The owner still owns a majority of the common shares outstanding and has no problem of control. The investment dealer sells the shares to customers who are probably unknown. A detailed study of the plans of the business is contained in a prospectus, which the investment dealer will prepare. The business planner does not have to pursue relatives or plead with friends for financial "favours", does not have to take in undesired partners to raise capital, has assured a financial plan for expansion, and has all the protection of the corporate form of organisation. The investment dealer will charge for this service. The charge will be higher if the dealer guarantees the sale of the full amount and less if the shares are sold on a "best-efforts" basis. The investment dealer's fee is chargeable to organisation expense and can be amortised over the succeeding five to ten years. This procedure is followed by the most informed new business planners who desire growth. It should be investigated for appropriateness by many new businesses.

The raising of funds described above is called "private placement" of limited share distribution. When stock-market conditions are depressed, this financing route can be an important alternative to the public distribution of the company's shares, also known as "going public".

13.11.3.10 Venture-capital funding

Small businesses may sometimes (albeit not too often) qualify for investment funds from venture-capital businesses. These companies provide equity and loan capital to potentially high-growth small companies. An example is Khula Equity Scheme. Khula has set up regional venture-capital companies to invest a minimum of R1 million in small businesses needing significant equity investment.

When applying to a venture-capital business, it is absolutely essential to provide it with a comprehensive business plan. If this plan passes the first screening, the venture capitalist will investigate further and examine "with due diligence" the product, the technology, potential market share, competitive situation, financial requirements and projections, and, most importantly, the competence of management. After the venture capitalist decides to make an investment, it will usually do so in return for part ownership in the business (common or preference shares) and/or by the provision of a direct loan with share-purchase options. Typically, a venture-capital business will not seek a controlling interest in the business. However, it will try to protect its investment by being able to assume control if the small business gets into financial trouble.

13.11.4 Concluding remarks

In the discussion above, the forms and sources of long-term financing available to a business were briefly analysed. The question that now arises is how the financial management of a business can combine the various forms of financing in the most efficient way. This consideration will now receive attention.

13.12 The cost of capital

Profitable and growing businesses continually need capital to finance expansion and new investment. Because of the costs involved in using capital (dividends to shareholders and interest paid to credit suppliers), financial management must ensure that only the necessary amount of capital is obtained, and that the cost and risk are kept to a minimum.

In attracting capital (one of the main tasks of financial management), the various forms of financing must be combined in a mix that results in the lowest-possible cost and lowest risk for the business.

The cost of capital is of crucial importance in both capital-investment decisions and financing decisions:

- In capital-investment decisions, the cost of capital serves as a benchmark for investment proposals. The cost of capital was assumed as given in the calculation of the net present value (NPV) in this chapter.
- In financing decisions, the various types of capital earmarked for financing the investments of a business should be combined so that the cost of capital to the business is kept to a minimum.

It is clear from the above that investment and financing decisions should be considered simultaneously because in practice, they cannot really be separated.

Capital structure refers to the combination of forms of long-term financing (ordinary and preference shares and debt) to finance the business.

The weighted average cost of capital, k_a, is determined by weighting the component cost of each type of long-term capital in the capital structure by its proportion to the total. This involves the following three steps:

- Calculate the after-tax cost of each individual form of capital (for example, ordinary shares, preference shares and long-term debt).
- Calculate the proportion or weight of each form of capital in the total capital structure.
- Combine the costs of the individual forms of capital and the corresponding weights of each of these forms to determine the weighted average cost of capital.

For privately owned businesses and small businesses, it is extremely difficult to arrive at a reliable cost of capital figure, primarily because of a lack of information. The inherent uncertainty in small businesses has resulted in relatively high rates of return being required by those investing in such businesses.

13.12.1 Risk

For an investor, risk consists of two components:

- the possible loss of the principal sum (the original amount invested)
- the possibility that no compensation will be paid for the use of the capital (no interest or dividend payments).

Any action that increases the possibility that the principal sum might be forfeited (as in the case of liquidation) or that compensation (in the form of dividends) will not be paid increases the risk for the supplier of capital. The use of borrowed capital such as debentures increases the possibility that dividends might not be paid and therefore increases the risk to ordinary shareholders.

13.13 Summary

This chapter began by examining the nature of the financial function and the tasks of financial management, as well as the relationship between financial management, the other functional management areas, related subject disciplines and the environment. Thereafter, various concepts generally used in financial management, as well as certain techniques employed by financial management, were explained. The goal and fundamental principles of financial management were also explained. Finally, one of the tasks of financial management, namely financial analysis, planning and control, was outlined.

Secondly, the chapter explained the management of the asset structure of a business, in other words, short-term investment decisions (managing current assets) and long-term capital-investment decisions. Rational and purposeful decisions in these areas ensure to a large extent that the goals of the business are pursued as effectively as possible. Some important guidelines and techniques for both types of investment decisions were presented, bearing in mind that current and fixed-asset management are totally integrated in practice.

Thirdly, the nature and characteristics of the various forms of long-term capital were discussed. This was followed by a discussion of the factors involved in establishing the cost of capital. The long-term financing decision based both on the various forms of long-term capital and also on the risk involved was explained.

This brief overview of financial management aimed to put into perspective the interesting and important facets of financial management, as well as the challenges and complexities of this functional area of management. Bear in mind, however, that the various aspects of financial management are all interrelated and integrated in the course of business operations, and that the function of financial management should be performed with full awareness and in the context of all other functions of the business.

Key terms

accruals	financial gearing
assets	financial institutions
bad debt	future value
balance sheet	income
break-even analysis	income statement
budgeting	internal rate of return
capital	net present value
cash flow	opportunity cost
cost of capital	ordinary shares
current asset	preference shares
current liability	present value
current ratio	profit
debt	risk–return
default	shareholders' interest
equity	time value of money
expenses	working capital

Questions for discussion

1. How would you respond if you were the owner and manager of a business and the quarterly financial reports started showing your firm was making a loss?
2. Looking at the financial statements of your firm, you notice the net profit is not equal to your bank balance on 28 February. How do you explain this?
3. How would you determine whether it is financially viable to start your own business?
4. A group of managers discuss financial planning. "Compiling a budget is a waste of time. The business environment is simply too unpredictable," says one manager. Another manager responds, "You must work according to a plan. Yes, your results will not match the budgeted figures 100%, but failing to plan is planning to fail". What is your view?
5. One of your fellow students remarks that you can be a good financial manager only if you are a chartered accountant (CA). Would you agree or disagree? Why?
6. Two of the ratios that are used to evaluate the management of current assets are the current ratio and acid-test ratio. Assume a firm has a current ratio of 4:1 and an acid-test ratio of 3:1. Are these ratios indicating that the firm is managing its current assets well or could they possibly be indicating some problems?
7. Should a firm increase its sales for credit rather than for cash during periods of recession? Why not?
8. What alternatives could a firm's management pursue if the firm's cash budget indicates a negative cash flow during the following six months?
9. What other alternatives are there for evaluating risk whilst doing capital budgeting?
10. During periods of rapid economic growth, interest rates are relatively low compared to relatively high interest rates during periods of recession. How would this influence the feasibility of capital expenditures?
11. What factors affect the level of gearing at which your organisation operates?
12. Explain what you understand the term "cost of capital" to mean.
13. Determine the cost of capital for your own organisation.
14. What would you take into consideration if choosing between preference and ordinary shares when selecting financing for your company?
15. Briefly explain the meaning of the term "financial intermediation".

? Multiple-choice questions

1. You are to receive an amount of R1 000 two years from now. However, if you had received the amount today and invested it, you would have been able to earn 10% interest per annum on the amount. What would the amount be worth if you could receive it now instead of waiting two years?
   a. R785
   b. R805
   c. R826
   d. R854

2. Gunn & Moore manufactures cricket bats at one of its plants. The fixed cost amounts to R1 600 000 per annum. The bats are sold at R400 each and the variable cost per unit amounts to R150. The break-even point of this plant is __________ units.
   a. 2 909
   b. 2 300
   c. 4 000
   d. 6 400

Use the following information to answer Question 3 and Question 4:

Income statement for the year	
Sales	6 543 876
Less cost of goods sold	4 384 396
Gross profit	2 159 480
Less operating expenses	1 190 653
Operating profits	968 827
Less interest expense	98 400
Net profit before tax	870 427
Less tax (28%)	243 720
Net profit after tax	626 707
Distributed as follows:	
Dividends to preference shareholders	0
Dividends to ordinary shareholders	250 683
Retained earnings	376 024
	626 707
Additional information:	
Number of ordinary shares	2 506 830
Current price of share	500 cents

Balance sheet at year end			
Fixed assets	8 000 000	Shareholders' interest:	
Current assets:		Ordinary shares	7 100 000
Cash	1 000	Retained earnings	700 000
Accounts receivable	191 000	Long-term debt	640 000
Inventory	358 000	Current liabilities:	
		Accounts payable	110 000
	8 550 000		8 550 000

3. The firm's return on investment (ROI) is equal to ...
   a. 7,33%.
   b. 8,03%.
   c. 9,58%.
   d. 10,9%.
4. The firm's current ratio is equal to __________ and shows __________ management of the liquidity, because it __________ be able to pay its creditors promptly.
   a. 1,7:1, good, will
   b. 2,0:1, reasonable, should
   c. 5,0:1, good, might
   d. 5,0:1, poor, might not
5. ABIL Ltd has made an initial investment requiring R4 210 879. The firm's cost of capital is 14% and the net annual cash inflow is expected to be R1 453 644 per annum for five successive years. The net present value of the investment is closest to ...
   a. R201 357.
   b. R499 048.
   c. R779 599.
   d. R2 757 235.

Answers to multiple-choice questions

1. c
2. d
3. a
4. d
5. c

References

1. Marx, J., De Swardt, C.J., Beaumont-Smith, M. & Erasmus, P.D. 2010. *Financial management in Southern Africa.* 3rd ed. Cape Town: Pearson.
2. Partially based on Gitman, L.J. 2010. *Principles of Managerial Finance.* 1st ed. Cape Town: Pearson Education, pp. 91–142.
3. Stern, J. [Online] Available: http://www.sternstewart.com Accessed 26 January 2010.
4. Marx, J., De Beer, J.S., Mpofu, R.T., Nortje, A & Van de Venter, T.W.G. 2009. *Investment management.* 3rd ed. Pretoria: Van Schaik, p. 155.
5. Kaplan, R. & Norton, D. 1996. "Balanced Scorecard Basics". [Online] Available: http://www.balancedscorecard.org/BSCResources/AbouttheBalancedScorecard/tabid/55/Default.aspx Accessed 27 January 2010.
6. Frye, CD. "Improve budgeting using balanced scorecards". [Online] Available: http://office.microsoft.com/en-us/excel/HA011929941033.aspx Accessed 27 January 2010.
7. Du Toit, G.S., Oost, E. & Neuland, E.W. 1997. *Investment decisions: Principles and applications.* Pretoria: University of South Africa, pp. 77–83.
8. McLaney, M. 1991. *Business finance for decision makers.* London: Pitman Publishing, p. 92.
9. Kohn, M. 2004. *Financial institutions and markets.* New York: Oxford, p. 142.
10. Damadoran, A. 2001. *Corporate finance: Theory and practice.* New York: Wiley, p. 140.
11 ABSA Bank. 1996. *Principles of finance and your business.* Johannesburg: ABSA, p. 23.

Websites: www.finforum.co.za/markets
www.BFA.co.za
www.24.com
www.khula.org.za

CHAPTER

14

PURCHASING AND SUPPLY MANAGEMENT[1]

The purpose of this chapter

The purpose of this chapter is to place the purchasing or sourcing function and its role in an organisation into perspective, and to explain the management, process and most important activities of the function.

Learning outcomes

On completion of this chapter you should be able to:

- place the purchasing and supply function, and the nature of purchasing and supply activities in an organisation in perspective
- explain the role and importance of the purchasing and supply function in the success and efficiency of a business
- explain the application of the management tasks of planning, organising and control in the purchasing and supply function
- illustrate and explain the logical steps to be followed in a purchasing and supply transaction
- indicate the role of the purchasing and supply function in quality decisions
- explain the role of quantity decisions in the purchasing and supply process
- give an overview of the selection and management of suppliers
- pinpoint certain aspects of pricing as purchasing and supply activity
- place the right time for purchasing and supply in perspective.

14.1 Introduction

Consumers need to make purchases almost on a daily basis to satisfy their day-to-day needs. They make large purchases, such as buying a motor car or a house, to satisfy their long-term needs. In the same way, a business also has to make purchases to meet its daily and long-term needs. Because people make purchases almost every day, the value of the **purchasing and supply function** in business is often under-estimated. There is a perception that anyone is capable of making purchases for a business.

However, purchasing and supply in a business entail far more than merely comparing the prices of two or more competitive bids and then buying material from the supplier that offers the best prices and service. Buyers in a manufacturing business buy a great variety of materials. These materials range from stationery, cleaning agents, cafeteria services and globes to bulk fuel, strategic material (which is sometimes difficult to obtain) for production processes, and equipment for office and production processes. Buyers are also involved in the purchase of capital goods, for example, robot-controlled processing equipment and complicated computer systems.

Buyers are expected to keep abreast of better substitute materials, new developments and technology in the market. A buyer's expertise can improve the progressiveness, productivity and profitability of a business. Buyers often have to make trips abroad or develop local **suppliers** because of the lack of existing sources. They also have to ensure that materials purchased meet quality requirements because this has an effect on the quality of the business's final product (in the case of a manufacturer) and the quality of products resold (in a retail business). Buyers need to be aware of market trends, seasons and the state of the market. They should, for example, know how many suppliers and how many buyers are present in a particular market, as this has a crucial effect on the purchase price of materials, the way in which suppliers should be approached and the type of relationship required.

Organisations make different kinds of purchases. For example, Eskom purchases coal, water, copper cable, poles, materials, parts and services (for example, civil and electrical engineering, cleaning and security services) for the construction and maintenance of power plants and office buildings, motor vehicles, computer systems, office equipment, stationery, legal services, training services and transport services, and consumables such as toilet paper, cleaning materials and refreshments. Woolworths purchases merchandising and materials-handling equipment (for example, shelves, trolleys, baskets and refrigerators), products for selling in its retail shops, for example, perishable products (fruit, meat and dairy products), groceries, clothing products, home products (crockery, cutlery, curtains and bedding), computer systems, office equipment, stationery, legal services, training services and transport services, and consumables such as toilet paper, cleaning materials and refreshments.

The **purpose** of the purchasing and supply function is not only to provide the right materials, services and equipment, but also to ensure that they are purchased at a reasonable price, satisfy quality requirements and are received in the correct quantities at the right place and time. The activities of the purchasing and supply function are derived from this.

The purchasing and supply function should:

- select suppliers
- purchase and arrange for the transport of materials to the business
- decide what prices to accept
- determine the quantity and quality of materials or services
- expedite and receive materials
- control warehousing and inventory-holding
- determine the timing of purchases.

To perform these activities optimally, the purchasing and supply function needs to be managed, that is, planned, organised and controlled.

Purchasing and supply management

Purchasing and supply management entails the planning, organising, leading and controlling of all activities relating to the purchase of materials and services from an external source. It is aimed at maintaining and increasing the business's profitability and efficiency of customer service.

14.2 The importance of the purchasing and supply function to the business

The importance of the purchasing and supply function differs from one business to the next, but in most businesses, purchasing has a profound influence on profit and other aspects of the business, which are discussed below.

14.2.1 Greatest expenditure for the business

Purchasing costs are a business's biggest expense, especially in businesses where final products are purchased and no actual value is added to the product. Figure 14.1 illustrates the share of purchasing in the spending of each available rand in various businesses. In retailing businesses such as Spar or Edgars, for example, up to 90% of each available rand may be spent on purchases. It therefore stands to reason that purchasing costs is an area where cost savings can make a vital contribution to the business's profits, since profit can be expressed as the favourable difference between income and expenditure.

Applying the concept: The scope of purchasing costs

Purchasing costs contribute to more than 80% of a Honda motor car's final price. The cost of steel, tyres, glass, paint, fabric, aluminium, copper and electronic components represents more than 60% of the final price of the motor vehicle. Purchasing costs contribute 65% of the price of a bottle of Coca-Cola. These include the cost of bottles, caps, cans, packaging materials and transportation.

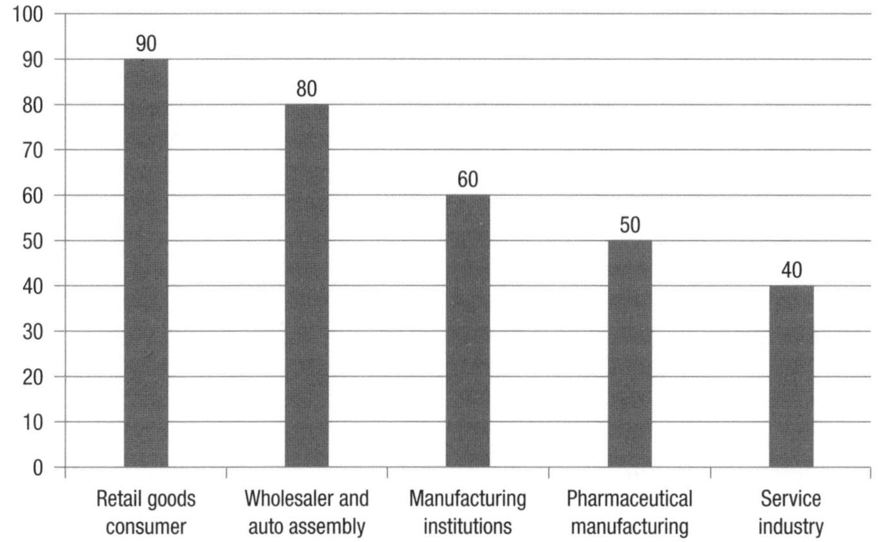

Figure 14.1: The share of purchasing cost of each rand income in various businesses

Sources: Compiled from Leenders, M.R., Fearon, H.E., Flynn, A.E. & Johnson, P.F. 2002. *Purchasing and supply management.* 12th ed. New York: McGraw-Hill, p. 13 & Hugo, W.M.J., Badenhorst-Weiss, J.A. & Van Biljon, E.H.B. 2006. *Purchasing and supply management.* 5th ed. Pretoria: Van Schaik, p. 11.

14.2.2 Inventory-holding

Stock is held to prevent disruptions in the transformation process (production or operational) that would be caused by an interruption in the flow of materials to a business. The aim of **inventory management** is to keep inventory levels as low as possible without risking an interruption in the operational process (as a result of an out-of-stock situation). The reason for this is that large sums of operating capital are tied up in inventory. This capital could be applied elsewhere to earn revenue. If too much capital is tied up in inventory, a business could encounter cash-flow problems (discussed in Chapter 13). Besides cash-flow problems, warehousing costs are a big cost element, usually ranging from 10% to 25% of total investment in inventory[2].

Warehousing costs include the costs (interest) of financing warehousing, warehouse staff, insurance and obsolescence. Effective purchasing and supply management can reduce inventory-holding by ensuring an uninterrupted flow of materials of the right quality to the production process at the time when they are needed. The more reliable the provision or purchase of materials is, the smaller the amount of inventory that needs to be stored. Inventory and inventory-holding are discussed in more detail later in the chapter.

14.2.3 Profit leverage

The profit-leverage effect means that if purchasing costs constitute a major portion of the total cost of a business, a saving in purchasing costs has greater profit potential than a similar increase in sales. For example, a 4% reduction in purchasing costs can make the same contribution to profitability as an increase of 20% in sales would make.

The contribution of the purchasing and supply function to profitability differs from business to business and from sector to sector. Effective purchasing normally has a greater profit potential in a commercial organisation than in a manufacturing business, as can be inferred from section 14.2.1. In the pharmaceutical industry, for example, where the value of patent medicine content is very low compared to the research and marketing costs of the product, saving on purchasing costs does not have such a profound effect on profit. However, in the motor-assembly industry, any saving on purchasing costs, where material costs are very high, has a decisive effect on the business's profitability, as illustrated in the Honda example on page 497.

Purchasing as a factor in profitability is also more critical when a business frequently changes its suppliers, if the price of materials fluctuates continually, where fashion is concerned and where markets for the final product are highly competitive, for example, in the case of everyday consumer articles. The contribution of purchasing to profitability is less critical but still important where prices and suppliers are relatively stable and where the industry is not characterised by innovation[3].

14.2.4 Contributions to the marketing of products

By purchasing materials of the right quality and price at the right time, a manufacturer can make final products available in the right quantities at a competitive price at the right time to its customers (for example, retailers or the final consumer). A retail buyer has a greater and more direct influence on the marketing of merchandise (for example, clothing) where the availability of the right product (type, quality, style and brand) at the right time in the right quantities is an important consideration in successful marketing. Effective purchasing can therefore facilitate the marketing of a business's products and contribute indirectly to profit through the marketing function.

14.3 The management task of the purchasing and supply manager

In Part 2 of this book, you were introduced to the general management principles of planning, organising and control. As was mentioned earlier, purchasing and supply, like all other functional areas (marketing, finance, operations and so on), must be managed to ensure that the purchasing and supply function operates effectively and makes the best possible contribution to the profit of the business and efficient client service. In the sections that follow, the application of the main management elements of the purchasing and supply function (planning, organising and control) will be addressed without discussing the principles in detail.

14.3.1 Purchasing and supply planning

Essentially, the planning of the purchasing and supply function means "managing the purchasing and supply function for the future". Purchasing and supply-planning entails formulating purchasing and supply objectives, which the purchasing and supply function should strive to reach by a particular future period, and drawing up purchasing and supply plans to achieve these objectives. These plans should include the optimal application of resources (people, physical facilities and funds) to achieve the objectives.

The planning of the purchasing and supply function, like planning in the business itself and other functional management areas, takes place at the following levels (see Chapter 6):

- **Strategic level.** At this level, planning entails the purchasing and supply manager providing input to business planning. The elements of strategic purchasing and supply planning differ from one business to the next. Where the purchasing and supply function is deemed to be less important and merely involves a clerical function, the purchasing and supply function is not involved in strategic planning. When a business has accepted the supply-chain management approach, purchasing and supply will be involved in strategic planning. Planning at strategic level is normally of a long-term nature. It is aimed

Strategic level	Tactical management level	Operational level
Supplier alliances	Systems integration	Communication with suppliers' operational staff
Supplier development	Negotiation	Expediting
Supply-chain integration	Interface development	File and system maintenance
Long-term planning	Human-resources development	Enquiries and quotations
Availability forecasting	Total quality management	Pricing
Policy formulation	Contracting	Returns and recycling
In/outsourcing decisions	Cost-reduction techniques	

Figure 14.2: Levels of purchasing and supply planning

Source: Baillie, P., Farmer, D., Crocker, B., Jessop, D. & Jones, D. 2005. *Purchasing principles and management.* 9th ed. Harlow: Financial Times/ Prentice Hall (Pearson Education Ltd), p. 36.

at safeguarding materials provision, developing supplier sources and maintaining the competitive position of the business. Typical strategic planning elements are supplier alliances, supplier development, supply-chain process integration, availability forecasting, and purchasing and supply policy.

- **Tactical or middle-management level.** This type of planning may cover the medium-term needs of the business, including budgeting, the purchasing and supply system and organisation, purchasing and supply methods, negotiation, development of human resources, interface development with other functions and suppliers (by means of cross-functional teams), contracting and employing cost-reduction techniques.
- **Operations level.** At the lowest operations level, plans are formulated to allow the daily functioning of the purchasing and supply function to proceed as smoothly as possible. This benefits the business as a whole, as well as other functions serviced by the purchasing and supply function. Planning at this level is of a short-term nature. It includes planning the tasks of expediting, keeping records, maintaining the purchasing and supply system, invoice clearance, handling of requisitions, enquiries and quotations, and pricing decisions[4].

The levels of purchasing and supply planning are depicted in Figure 14.2 on page 499.

The formulation of objectives is one of the most important planning tasks. Table 14.1 provides an indication of the purchasing and supply objectives that can be derived from the business's objectives.

14.3.2 Organising the purchasing and supply function

Chapter 7 has an in-depth discussion of organising as an element of management. The focus in this section is merely on the application of organising in the purchasing and supply function.

Purchasing and supply organisation

Purchasing and supply organisation involves the creation of a structure of responsibility and authority for the purchasing and supply function, and the organisation of purchasing and supply activities to realise purchasing and business objectives.

There are four main issues that need to be addressed in organising the purchasing and supply function:

- the place of the purchasing and supply function in the organisational structure

Table 14.1: Purchasing and supply objectives derived from the business's objectives

Business objectives	Purchasing and supply objectives
• To retain the market share	• To search for more unique products in the supplier market
• To move from the speciality market to the general market	• To seek new and larger suppliers, and develop a new-materials flow system to handle larger quantities and a greater variety of items while keeping total inventory volume as low as possible
• To develop specific new products and services	• To seek or develop new suppliers
• To develop an overall production capacity plan, including an overall make-or-buy policy	• To develop systems that integrate capacity planning and purchasing and supply planning, together with a policy of make-or-buy
• To initiate a cost-reduction plan	• To standardise materials and reduce suppliers

- the internal organisation of the purchasing and supply function
- co-ordination with other functional management areas
- cross-functional teams (organising the purchasing and supply function according to the supply-chain management approach).

14.3.2.1 The place of the purchasing and supply function in the organisational structure

The place of the purchasing and supply function in the business is affected by two elements: **centralisation** or **decentralisation**, and the hierarchical level of the purchasing and supply function in the organisational structure of the business.

Centralisation or decentralisation

In a business with a centralised purchasing and supply function, the purchasing and supply manager and his/her personnel have the authority and are responsible for the purchasing and supply function. In an organisation with a single business unit, this is the obvious organisational structure. However, if an organisation has a head office with different business units, branches or plants, there are various options, including the following:

- a centralised purchasing and supply function, situated at head office, is responsible for purchasing
- each plant or branch does its own purchasing, which means that the purchasing

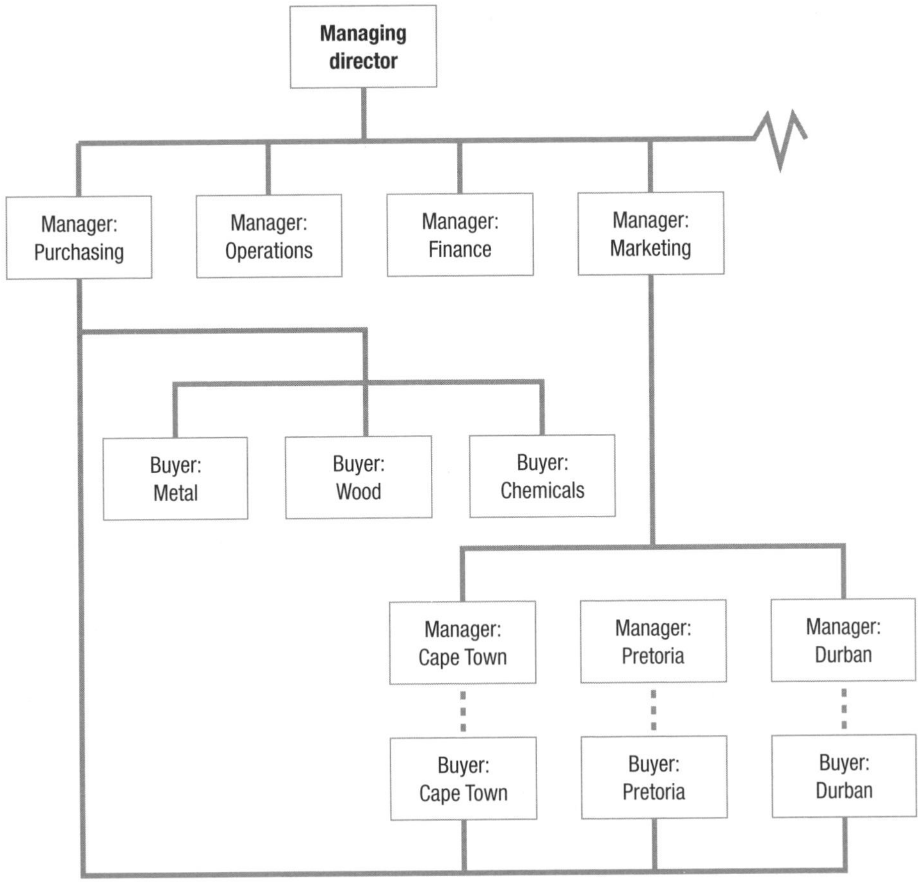

Figure 14.3: Business with a centralised purchasing and supply structure

and supply function is organised on a decentralised basis
- a combination of centralised and decentralised functions, where some materials and services are bought on a centralised basis and other materials are bought on a decentralised basis.

A **centralised purchasing and supply structure** has certain advantages. One advantage is that the standardisation of purchasing and supply procedures as well as materials or services purchased is possible. Standardisation has great cost-saving advantages. For example, a greater volume of materials of one kind being purchased from a supplier results in lower inventory levels and lower prices because of better discounts for volume orders. Because of volumes, purchasing and supply personnel can concentrate on buying a specific commodity (material or service), which makes specialisation possible. A centralised purchasing and supply organisation is especially suitable if the needs of different business units, plants or branches are much the same, as is the case, for example, with all Pick n Pay hypermarkets. If the greatest proportion of a business's purchases is made from a single supplier or a few suppliers, and if the material is of strategic importance to the continuation of the business's activities, it is preferable to purchase on a centralised basis. Figure 14.3 on page 501 illustrates a centralised purchasing and supply structure for a multi-plant business.

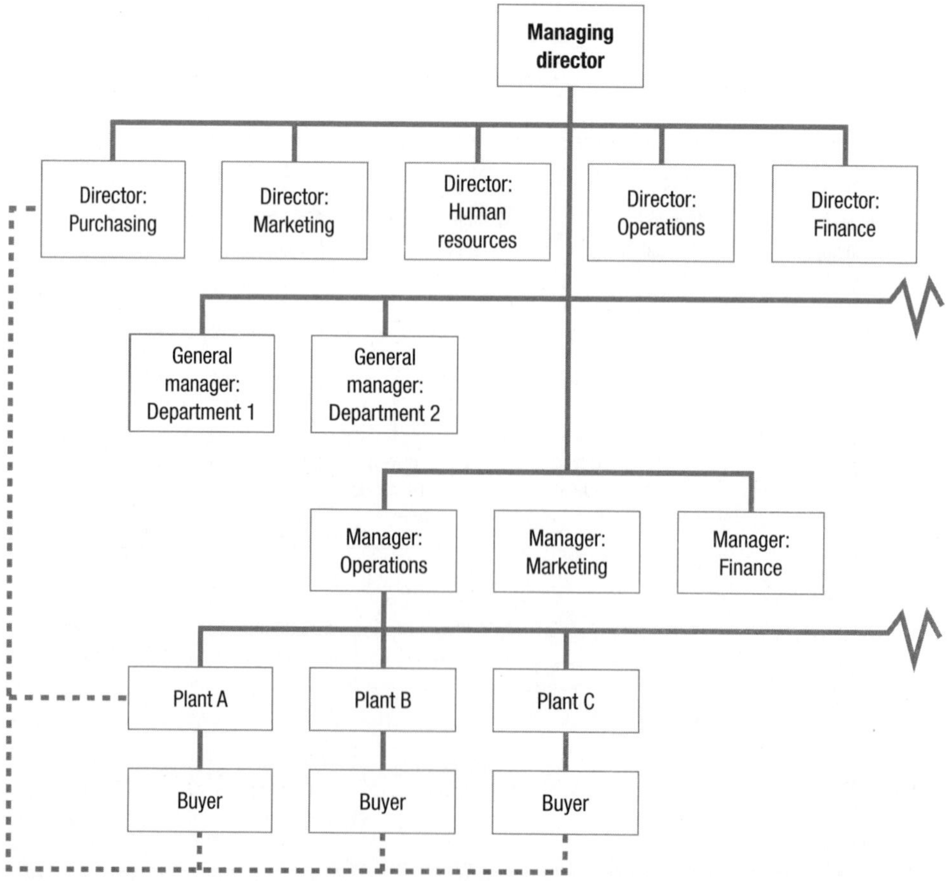

Figure 14.4: Business with a decentralised purchasing and supply structure

A **decentralised purchasing and supply structure** is particularly suited to a business comprising geographically dispersed plants whose purchases are made from a number of their local suppliers. Also, if the plants perform divergent activities and therefore have unique needs in terms of purchases, decentralisation is the obvious choice. Where the different decentralised plants are regarded as profit centres, it is necessary for each plant to have autonomy over its own expenditure, hence, in this case, decentralisation of purchasing and supply is the right option. A decentralised purchasing and supply structure has the advantage that buyers have closer contact with users (users of the purchased products and services in the business) and local suppliers, and reaction times to the requests of users are quicker. Figure 14.4 on page 502 depicts a decentralised purchasing and supply structure in a business with various plants.

A **combination of centralisation and decentralisation** is a useful middle course. In this application, the centralised purchasing office purchases collective requirements, enters into long-term contracts on behalf of the whole business, purchases capital equipment, formulates purchasing and supply policy and strategies, trains buyers, and evaluates decentralised purchasing and supply performance. Decentralised purchasing and supply provides for the specialised needs and small purchases of the plant. The buyers report directly to the head of the plant, but operate within the parameters of policy laid down by the centralised purchasing and supply authority. Figure 14.5 shows a centralised/decentralised purchasing and supply structure.

Applying the concept: A combination of centralised and decentralised purchasing and supply

At Telkom, the head office negotiates large contracts with suppliers of copper cable, optic fibre and microwave dishes. Decentralised regional offices buy non-strategic items such as tools, maintenance materials and services from local suppliers.

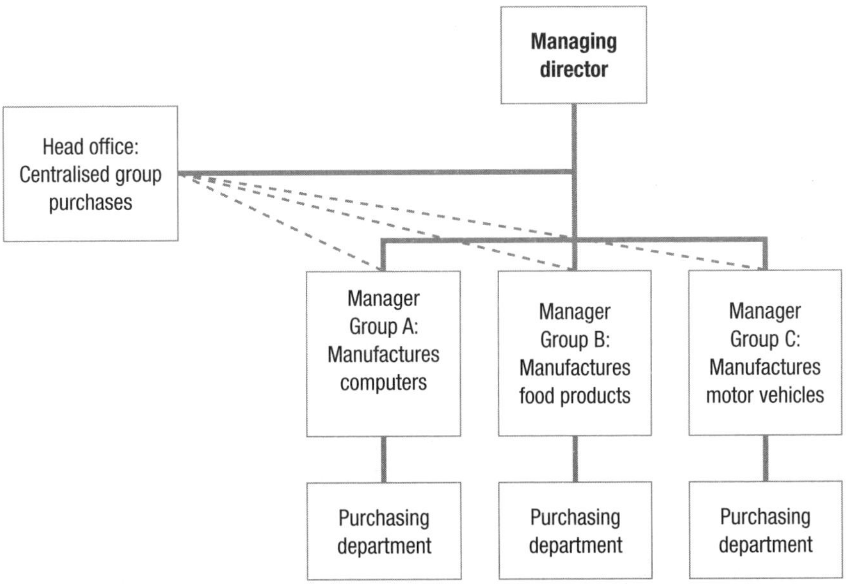

Figure 14.5: Business with a centralised/decentralised purchasing and supply structure

The hierarchical level of the purchasing and supply function in the organisational structure

The hierarchical level of the purchasing and supply function is primarily determined by the importance of the purchasing and supply function to the business. The importance of the function is determined by the following factors, among others:

- **The value of the purchased materials in relation to the total expenditure of the business.** The greater purchasing's share of total expenditure, the more important the purchasing and supply function is. If only this factor is taken into consideration, one could say that purchasing and supply is more important in a retail organisation than in a manufacturing business. However, it is not the only factor that determines the importance of purchasing and supply.
- **The situation in the supplier market.** If the supply market is a monopoly (only one supplier) or an oligopoly (only a few suppliers), as is the case in certain markets in South Africa, negotiation should take place at a high level to negotiate the best value for the business. Purchasing and supply is important here, and the head of the purchasing and supply function should put forward proposals and operate at a high level in the business.
- **The size of the business.** In larger businesses, the purchasing and supply manager is usually placed on the same level as other functional managers, such as the marketing manager, the financial manager and the operations manager. In smaller businesses, the purchasing and supply function often falls under the financial manager or the marketing manager.
- **The nature of the materials purchased and the specialised knowledge and skills of buyers.** This determines the status of buyers and the purchasing and supply manager in the business. For example, in the purchase of technologically advanced custom-made materials, the buyer needs in-depth technical knowledge, as well as negotiating and commercial skills. However, when it comes to purchasing cleaning agents and stationery, no special knowledge or skills are required.
- **Top management's perception.** The top management's perception of the importance of the purchasing and supply function will determine its status in the organisation.

14.3.2.2 Internal organisation of the purchasing and supply function

The purchasing and supply function can be organised internally in a variety of ways. The organisation may consist of an **informal structure** in which buyers purchase any material or service and process whatever requisitions or enquiries are placed on their desks. In such a case, the buyer is responsible for the whole spectrum of activities, from asking for quotations or calling for tenders to the expediting and receipt of the product. Conversely, the function can be divided into **specialist groups** in which each person takes responsibility for buying a specific material or service. In a larger business, the function can be split so that a buyer is responsible for all the purchases from a specific supplier, especially in the case of strategic materials.

In the case of the purchase of a specific commodity or material, the buyers concerned may develop into specialists who come to know the product and supplier market extremely well, thus bringing large-scale cost benefits for the business. A buyer who is responsible for purchasing from a specific supplier can build up a long-term relationship with that supplier. Developing open and personal relationships with suppliers of scarce or strategic materials is especially important.

14.3.2.3 Co-ordination with other functional management areas

Traditionally, co-ordination was regarded as a management task. However, this book follows the latest trends and sees co-ordination as part of organising. Therefore, little mention is made here of co-ordination.

However, because the purchasing and supply function has a support role and function, co-ordination with other functions in the business and with suppliers is important. The purchasing and supply function cannot make an optimal contribution to the objectives of the business and the supply chain in isolation. Co-ordination of the purchasing and supply function occurs at three levels:

- Various purchasing and supply activities must be co-ordinated internally in the purchasing and supply function.
- The purchasing environment (suppliers) must be co-ordinated with purchasing and supply activities.
- The purchasing and supply function must be co-ordinated with other functional management areas such as finance, marketing and production, and eventually with the needs of the final consumer.

Purchasing and supply co-ordination

Purchasing and supply co-ordination may be regarded as the conscious effort to harmonise the activities of the purchasing and supply function, the activities of other functional areas and the activities of suppliers in ways to ensure full co-operation in the pursuit of purchasing and supply objectives.

Open communication, conscious motivation, and standardisation of specifications, procedures and documentation are aids to improve co-ordination internally in the purchasing and supply function, in the business itself and externally with suppliers. Strategic alliances with suppliers and integrated systems are important aids for co-ordination. The just-in-time (JIT) system, the materials-requirements planning system (MRP) and other systems plan and control the inventory and materials-flow process. They are also important co-ordinating instruments within the purchasing and supply function and the business, and with suppliers.

14.3.2.4 Cross-functional sourcing teams

Cross-functional sourcing teams

A cross-functional sourcing team consists of personnel from at least three functions brought together to execute a purchasing-related (materials or services) assignment or solve a purchasing-related problem.

The use of cross-functional sourcing or purchasing teams is an important practice in purchasing and supply. The purchaser co-operates on a team with colleagues in other functional management areas to perform numerous tasks, which include supplier selection, negotiating corporate-wide purchasing agreements, developing cost-reduction strategies, developing sourcing strategies, developing suppliers and the evaluation of suppliers' performance. Purchasers are also involved in other teams that have been assigned specific tasks such as value analysis and the development of new products.

The objectives of using cross-functional sourcing teams are to obtain a wide perspective on problems, to stimulate innovative thinking and to obtain the best value for the organisations and the customers. The teams may be permanent, or they may exist only for a specific period or until a specific task has been completed. Suppliers can be included in a functional team for certain tasks such as new-product development or the establishment of quality standards. To be a member of a cross-functional team, a buyer must have the ability to work with groups and display leadership qualities.

14.3.3 Control in the purchasing and supply function

Purchasing and supply control, like control in other functional management areas of a business, is the measure adopted to ensure that purchasing and supply objectives are pursued within acceptable and accepted standards or norms and guidelines. This is done according to a specific policy established during purchasing and supply planning. Purchasing and supply planning, and, more specifically, the formulation of objectives, is therefore the first step in the control process. The steps comprise setting objectives, setting criteria and norms, measuring actual performance, comparing actual performance with the norms, studying deviations and taking corrective measures (if necessary). The steps in the control process were discussed in detail and illustrated in Chapter 9. Areas of control in the purchasing and supply situation, however, require further investigation. The management task in the purchasing and supply function, and the performance of purchasing and supply activities, need to be evaluated (controlled).

14.3.3.1 The assessment of purchasing and supply management

The **management** performance of the purchasing and supply function should be evaluated just like other activities of the purchasing and supply function, because management can influence the overall job performance and achievement of the purchasing and supply function and, ultimately, the performance of the business. Management is intangible and difficult to measure quantitatively. Therefore, there is a certain amount of subjectivity in measuring management.

An evaluation sheet or questionnaire can be used to assess management performance in purchasing[5]. This may include aspects such as:

- the leadership shown in the introduction of new ideas, systems, approaches or strategies
- the number or percentage of purchasing contracts established
- the knowledge and skills to lead the purchasing and supply function in an increasingly complex purchasing environment
- the relationships established with strategic suppliers
- the adequacy of performance appraisal and control systems in the purchasing and supply function
- the contribution to cross-functional teams
- the role in the establishment and management of supply chains
- the effectiveness of the use of the total purchasing leverage of the firm
- the appropriateness of purchasing and supply policies, procedures and practices.

14.3.3.2 The assessment of purchasing and supply activities

As was mentioned earlier, the aim of the purchasing and supply function is to supply the business in the most effective way with the right materials of the desired quality, quantities and price at the right place and time. To realise this objective, the purchasing and supply function has to perform certain activities. Control is necessary to ascertain whether these activities are being performed **effectively**. The following control points or criteria can be used to gauge the effectiveness of purchasing and supply activities[6]:

- **price proficiency**, by, for example, comparing actual prices with planned or market prices, the number and value of discounts negotiated for a specific period, and determining which part of every rand turnover constitutes purchasing costs
- **supplier performance**, by, for example, noting rejected orders, orders received late and the number of times it was necessary to expedite the process
- **timeliness**, by, for example, noting the number of orders indicated as urgent and the number of operations interrupted or rescheduled as a result of shortages
- **cost-saving**, by, for example, comparing costs with those of previous periods
- **workload**, by, for example, looking at the number of orders and requisitions
- **purchasing costs**, by expressing administrative purchasing costs as a percentage of the monetary value of purchases

- **inventory-holding**, by calculating inventory turnover, and making further enquiries into inventory losses and obsolescence of stock
- **relationship performance with suppliers**, by means of a survey or scrutiny of supplier turnover, or number of alliances formed
- **relationship with other functional-management areas**, by monitoring the diligent execution of requests to the purchasing and supply function, and the contribution purchasers make in cross-functional teams.

Once these measurement criteria have been laid down, the actual results can be measured and compared with a standard or norm such as past performance or the results of similar businesses. A report on performance and problem areas should be compiled and submitted to top management with the necessary recommendations. (See again the steps in the control process in Chapter 9.)

14.4 Purchasing process and activities

Although each purchasing and supply activity is discussed separately in this chapter, this does not mean that purchasing and supply activities exist or are performed in isolation. In fact, the different purchasing and supply activities are often executed simultaneously and are interdependent. Price and quality, price and time, price and choice of suppliers, and time and quantity are inseparably intertwined. The practical execution of purchasing and supply activities is clear from the discussion of the stages in the purchasing and supply process or cycle.

The case study on page 508 provides insight into how a purchasing and supply-related problem can have a negative effect on many participants in a supply chain.

14.4.1 The purchasing process

The discussion of the purchasing and supply process or cycle in this section provides a clear picture of the steps in the purchasing and supply transaction, how the steps follow each other logically, who in the business is involved in each step and the documentation involved in each step. Not all the steps are necessarily taken in each purchasing and supply transaction, and some steps may take place simultaneously.

A large number of businesses in South Africa have computerised their purchasing and supply process. Computerised systems are also based on the purchasing and supply cycle discussed here. Computerisation expedites the process considerably and usually reduces the documentation involved.

Figure 14.6 on page 509 reflects the basic steps in the purchasing and supply cycle, the functional management areas involved and the documentation used.

The steps of the purchasing and supply cycle are explained in more detail below:

- **Development and description of a need.** Because of the activities of other functional-management areas such as marketing and operations (also called "users" or "consumers"), there is a need for materials and services. The need is conveyed by means of a requisition, order card, or materials and specification list to the purchasing and supply function. To ensure that the desired materials or services are purchased, the buyer must take careful note of the specification, which is actually a description of the need. The specification describes the material and the required quality of that material. The buyer should also look closely at the quantities specified and the date on which the material or service is required. In a manufacturing business, the greatest need is for materials and services in the production or operational function. In a

Case study

Cooldrinks lose their fizz

While the world worries about an oversupply of carbon dioxide caused by increasing emissions, in South Africa, we've almost run out of carbon dioxide (CO_2) to put into soft drinks.

The national CO_2 shortage has affected normal production of Coca-Cola brands in the past four weeks and it is likely to persist into the new year.

Sasol and PetroSA, the primary suppliers of CO_2, closed their plants for routine maintenance earlier this year. Consequently, they were not able to meet commitments to Afrox, which supplies Amalgamated Beverage Industries (ABI) with gas. ABI bottles Coca-Cola in South Africa. Since the shortage, ABI has only been able to meet about 60% to 75% of the normal demand. In November and December, however, demand is 150% higher than usual, resulting in a significant shortfall.

Retailers, general dealers and neighbourhood supermarkets throughout the country are affected. The company has more than 43 000 customers who supply soft drinks to consumers. ABI is planning to import about 20 million soft-drink cans during November and December, said company spokesperson Michael Farr, but the usual variety of brands and sizes will not be available.

"We are expecting our first shipment from the United Kingdom and Singapore this week," he confirmed. He said ABI would focus on Coca-Cola core brands, which include Coca-Cola, Sprite and Fanta. These soft drinks make up about 80% of what is currently consumed in the market. However, lower-volume brands such as Fanta Pine and Fanta Grape, Sprite Zero and Tab will remain in short supply for the next four months.

ABI says it hopes the shortage will be under control by January 2007, but it could ease in a matter of days. Farr said the company is expecting a full supply of food-grade CO_2 from Afrox next week. "We are working flat out to normalise supplies as soon as we can and, in the short term, we are doing our best to ensure that all our customers receive the maximum stock that we are able to provide," said Farr. He added that fair supply to customers is currently done on the basis of how much the customers need and that ABI has an obligation to meet this need. But at least we still have alcohol. Contrary to earlier reports, SABMiller has confirmed that beer production won't be affected, as its breweries are self-reliant as far as CO_2 is concerned.

PetroSA spokesperson Butana Nkosi said it would be able to supply CO_2 by next Friday. Sasol spokesperson Marina Bidoli said the company's Sasolburg plant had been shut down last month, resulting in a 12-day CO_2 shortage. However, the plant has been operating at full production since October 27.

Shoprite spokesperson Brian Weyers said the shortage was unpredictable and that all areas would not be affected in the same way. "Should a shortage of carbonated soft drinks arise, it is expected that consumers will switch to alternative products in the beverage category, such as cordials, nectars and fruit juices."

But spaza-shop owner Tshepo Tshikane of Mogale City felt betrayed by ABI for failing to communicate the CO_2 shortage to informal-business-sector players. He explained that carbonated drinks make up half of his income in summer and that limited stock could damage his business. "Why can't these people come up with alternatives, such as importing carbon dioxide?" he asked.

Source: Dibetle, M. 2006. "Cooldrinks lose their fizz". *Mail & Guardian.* [Online] Available: http://www.mg.co.za/article/article/2006-11-17-cooldrinks-lose-their-fizz Accessed 26 January 2010.

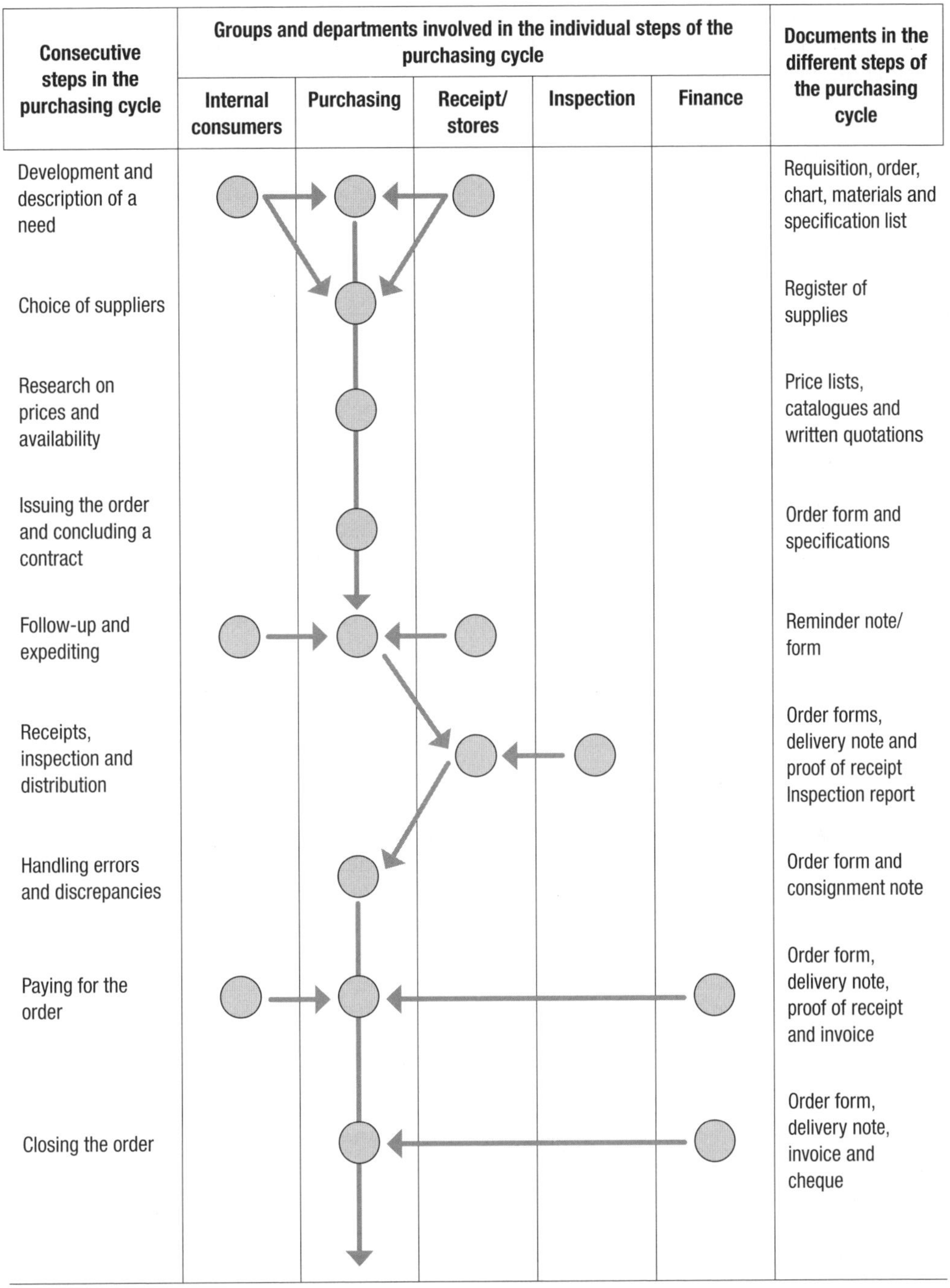
Consecutive steps in the purchasing cycle
Groups and departments involved in the individual steps of the purchasing cycle
Internal consumers
Purchasing
Receipt/ stores
Inspection
Finance
Documents in the different steps of the purchasing cycle
Development and description of a need
Requisition, order, chart, materials and specification list
Choice of suppliers
Register of supplies
Research on prices and availability
Price lists, catalogues and written quotations
Issuing the order and concluding a contract
Order form and specifications
Follow-up and expediting
Reminder note/ form
Receipts, inspection and distribution
Order forms, delivery note and proof of receipt Inspection report
Handling errors and discrepancies
Order form and consignment note
Paying for the order
Order form, delivery note, proof of receipt and invoice
Closing the order
Order form, delivery note, invoice and cheque

Figure 14.6: Steps in the purchasing and supply cycle of a commercial business

Source: Adapted from Hugo, W.M.J., Badenhorst-Weiss, J.A. & Van Biljon, E.H.B. 2006. *Purchasing and supply management.* 5th ed. Pretoria: Van Schaik, p.16.

retail organisation, the greatest need is for materials and services in the marketing function (merchandising).

> **Critical thinking**
>
> What would happen if the consumer or functional departments did not describe their needs for materials or services clearly on a requisition? What would happen if a purchaser did not analyse the requisition carefully?

- **Choice of suppliers.** The choice of the right supplier is the principal activity of the purchasing and supply function. This choice is discussed in more detail later. The complexity of the decision depends on various factors, for example, whether it is a new purchase or a repurchase, whether a contract needs to be entered into or already exists, or whether standard or specialised materials are required. Depending on the factors, the buyer will use documents such as the register of suppliers, order forms, contracts, price lists, quotations or tenders. In a new buying situation, especially where a contract has to be drawn up, determining the present and future availability of the materials or services is a vital consideration in the choice of supplier. Determining the future availability of materials or services is no easy task. A study of the technical, managerial and financial abilities of suppliers, their progressiveness, idle capacity and past performance (if the business has used that supplier previously) is necessary. This is done by analysing the financial statements of suppliers, making personal visits and conducting interviews with their staff and management, and obtaining credit-bureau reports. It is important to note that user functions (for example, marketing or production) may make recommendations about a particular supplier, but the final choice rests with the purchasing and supply function.

> **Critical thinking**
>
> How would the decision process on suppliers differ if a construction firm purchased maintenance materials, iron rods, cement and consulting engineering services?

- **Research on prices and availability.** This is actually part of the previous step. The prices of standard materials or services and materials or services with a low monetary value are determined with the aid of price lists and telephonic, verbal or written quotations. Because standard materials or services are available everywhere, prices are in fact determined by competition. The prices of non-standard, specialised materials or custom-made items are often determined by tender or quotation in conjunction with negotiations.
- **Issuing the order and concluding a contract.** The order and the contract are important documents because they spell out unequivocally to the supplier the needs of the business and the conditions of the purchasing transaction. They also constitute a legally valid contract to which both parties are bound by law. The order or contract should contain specific conditions for the transaction in respect of quantities, quality, prices, discounts, delivery dates, customs clearances and exchange-rate clearances.
- **Follow-up and expediting.** The purchasing and supply function's task is completed only when materials or services of the right quality and quantity have been received at the right place, and, most importantly, at the right time. One of the administrative tasks in the purchasing and supply function is to determine whether materials

are received or services are performed in good time. If not, or if they are overdue, the supplier should be reminded (by letter, fax, telephone or electronically if a computer system links the business and its suppliers) that it has not adhered to the clauses of the contract and that it should concentrate on the speedy delivery of required materials. The importance of this task is often under-estimated. If a supplier is late with deliveries, this can interrupt the production or operational process in a manufacturing business, or leave a retailer with empty shelves. This can also have serious implications for supplier relations and the continued use of a specific supplier.

- **Receipts, inspection and distribution.** Stores reception (as a subfunction of purchasing and supply) is responsible for checking the quantities and conditions of materials when they are received. The delivery note of the supplier is signed and is proof that the materials were received. Inspection (a subfunction of purchasing and supply) checks the quality of the materials and compiles an inspection report. The materials are sent to the users (that is, the functions that requested the products) with a copy of the order or they are taken up as inventory in the stores. In the case of services, the specific users who requested the services need to compile a report on the performance of the service provider.
- **Handling errors and discrepancies.** Communication and keeping good relations with suppliers are important tasks of the purchasing and supply function. If defective materials are received or services are performed poorly, the purchasing and supply function should communicate with the suppliers concerning these in a way that will prevent future defective consignments, but still ensure good relations.

> **Critical thinking**
>
> Explain how the handling of errors would differ if a furniture-maker received unacceptable consignments of the following materials:
> - wood
> - screws.

- **Paying for the order.** It is the task of purchasing and supply to prepare authorisation for payment of the supplier. The purchasing and supply function checks the delivery note, the inspection report, the invoice and the order to confirm that the quantities, quality, price and discounts are correct, and to verify the calculations. It then authorises the finance function to pay the supplier. The purchasing and supply function should execute this task carefully and quickly so that suppliers are paid in accordance with the payment policy of the business.
- **Closing the order.** Once the supplier has been paid, the purchasing and supply function must file all documents pertaining to the particular transaction or incorporate them into a system for future reference. This is a crucial part of the evaluation of a supplier's performance. It also constitutes an assessment of the purchasing and supply function's performance.

> **Critical thinking**
>
> Think about the case study on the shortage of CO_2 in the soft-drink industry. Where in the purchasing process did the most crucial problems occur?

This discussion of the purchasing and supply cycle has placed in perspective the principal purchasing and supply activities: decisions about quality and quantities, choosing and managing suppliers, pricing, decisions about purchasing, and supply times. The next step is to examine these activities in greater depth.

14.4.2 Quality decisions as a purchasing and supply activity

14.4.2.1 The role of quality in purchasing

The four main factors in each purchasing and supply decision are quality, supplier service, delivery and price. Quality is probably the most important of these factors. Even if the price and the service that a supplier offers are outstanding, material or services will not be bought from the supplier if the quality is in any way lower than required because the material or service will not perform the function for which it was purchased.

Quality is an inseparable part of other purchasing and supply activities. Top quality is normally associated with high prices and *vice versa*. Quality also determines the number of suppliers. The higher the quality requirements are, the fewer suppliers there will be to satisfy such requirements. Quality of materials also influences inventory-holding or the quantity to be purchased. In the case of high-quality requirements, a reliable supplier that can meet the specification and deliver on time will be chosen. Smaller volumes of materials can therefore be kept in stock because fewer materials will be rejected during inspection. In fact, continuous high quality is an absolute necessity in stockless systems such as **just-in-time (JIT)** and **materials-requirements planning (MRP)**, which are discussed in section 14.4.3.3.

The quality of purchased products and services rests on the following considerations, which will be discussed in the next section:

- determining the right quality for a given goal
- describing quality so that both the buyer and seller understand it clearly
- controlling quality to ensure that requirements are met.

14.4.2.2 Determining the right quality

A buyer has a different perspective of the concept "the right quality" from the perspective of a technical person. From a purchasing and supply perspective, the right quality can be defined as follows:

> **Definition**
> The right quality is that quality that is purchased at the lowest price, which satisfies a specific need and performs the function for which it was purchased.

For **engineers and designers**, technical considerations such as job performance and reliability are often the only factors that are important. It frequently happens that engineers and designers request the purchase of the highest- or best-quality materials or services without any commercial considerations, when lower-quality materials or services would do the job just as well. Buyers are more attuned to commercial considerations such as the right quality, availability, price and delivery. A buyer should therefore have the right to question technical requirements or to request that **specifications** be reconsidered on the strength of commercial considerations.

The best quality is therefore not necessarily the right quality. The right quality for a specific purchase is determined by balancing suitability (technical requirements), availability and cost (commercial requirements).

The **end-user** and/or the **marketing function** also often provide input on suitable quality, since the right quality materials not only increase the productivity of the user, but also influence the quality and price of the final product to be marketed. The quality of products is important for marketing as well as for public relations because quality influences the image the business wants to project and is decisive in determining which customers wish to associate with the business and its products. After-sales service, a policy on taking back materials or service of a poor quality and the provision of guarantees by the supplier are important considerations that tie in closely with decisions pertaining to quality. Suppliers also play a vital role in determining suitable quality because they are often in a position to recommend alternative materials or services.

> **Critical thinking**
>
> Would purchasers in the motor-assembly industry query the quality of parts to be installed in the engine of a motor car?

14.4.2.3 Description of quality

Quality refers to measurable qualities, a condition or characteristics of materials or service usually expressed according to grade, class, brand or specifications. It should be possible to describe the desired quality, otherwise the person requisitioning the material or service cannot communicate clearly with a buyer, or the buyer cannot communicate with a supplier, about what exactly is required. (For communication purposes, the description of quality is entered on the requisition and order.) The description of quality is also important because it serves as a measure for judging the quality of incoming materials by means of inspection or the evaluation of services performed. The following methods and forms should be noted:

- **Specifications are the most general method of describing quality.** A specification is a description of non-standard materials or services that are able to perform a certain function. Specifications for materials can be drawn up according to dimensions or physical features such as tolerance, work ability, uniformity and chemical composition. For services, other dimensions will be used, such as the nature of the service and a step-by-step exposition of actions, time lines and required outcomes for each step.
- **Standardisation is a further aid in describing quality.** It is, in effect, the process of making materials, methods, practices and techniques uniform. Standardisation can be set by a business or organisation, or nationally or internationally by an industry, and it has several advantages. If a business or organisation standardises materials, total inventory can be reduced because fewer kinds and qualities are kept. Standardisation also improves collaboration between the user and buyer in a business, and communication between the buyer and supplier. Industrial and international standards make possible the mass production of products. Because many suppliers manufacture standard products and standard materials can be bought everywhere, competition in the market is increased, and the purchasing and supply price of the product is reduced.
- **Other forms of quality description are market grades, brands, SABS (South African Bureau of Standards) standards, engineering drawings and samples.**

> **Critical thinking**
>
> What is the value of standardisation in a franchise group such as Steers? Has standardisation any value in a ladies' fashion boutique? If so, in what way does it have value?

14.4.2.4 Control of quality

It is imperative to control the quality of incoming materials and purchased services. Poor-quality materials and services interrupt the manufacturing process, expose workers to danger, have a detrimental effect on the final product, and ultimately reduce the satisfaction of end-users and alter the perception they have of the business and its products.

Inspection is the normal process used to control quality. It is a method that ensures that the measurement, design, job performance and quality of materials or services received satisfy the standards or specifications on the order. It also ensures that products or services are suitable for the purpose for which they have been ordered. Inspection is a technical process. It is not the task of purchasers, but must be carried out by the quality-control function or the function where purchased services are performed.

During inspection by quality controllers, samples of delivered materials or services are subjected to tests. However, inspection *per se* is not enough to guarantee the quality of incoming materials or services. If the purchasing and supply function buys from a supplier that has maintained top-quality standards for years, it is unnecessary to inspect its products or services. In such a case, the business can negotiate **a supplier-certification agreement** with the supplier. Based on agreed terms, the supplier and the buyer's quality-control functions work together for a specific time. The materials and operation processes are subject to intensive inspection for a certain period. After this, the supplier is certified and it becomes responsible for quality assurance.

The SABS has a certification scheme whereby enterprises are encouraged and supported in endeavours to establish and operate quality-control systems or quality-assurance programs. Part of the certification scheme of the SABS is the well-known ISO 9000 to 9004 and ISO 14000 international standards. The establishment and operation of such programs by suppliers is extremely costly. Since the quality of materials or services is assured, buyers will be prepared to pay high prices, particularly when high quality is crucial.

> **Critical thinking**
>
> Think about the case study on the shortage of CO_2 in the soft-drink industry. Do you think that Sasol, PetroSA, Afrox and ABI have quality-assurance programs and implement ISO standards? Give reasons for your answer.

14.4.3 Deciding on purchasing and supply quantities

14.4.3.1 The need for inventory-holding

The purchasing and supply function would be able to buy the exact quantity of materials required at a certain time if all of the following criteria were met:

- The operations function was 100% certain of the quantity of materials to be used in the manufacturing process.
- The marketing function was 100% certain about how many products are going to be sold.
- There were no supply problems in the supplier market.
- The incoming materials completely satisfied quality requirements.

Unfortunately, such a situation simply does not exist in practice. Marketing and production or operations budgets are based solely on estimates. The supplier market in South Africa tends to be unreliable with regard to delivery and quality. Consequently, the buyer has to purchase more materials than required to prevent a possible shortage when the materials are needed. The result is that inventory-holding becomes necessary. Inventory-holding is therefore inextricably intertwined with the tasks of a buyer.

During the sanctions era prior to 1994, it was normal practice for South African businesses to keep large stocks, especially in the case of businesses importing materials from abroad. After South Africa's readmission to normal world trade, however, the worldwide trend of keeping minimum inventory also took root in South Africa. The reason for this trend is that inventory-holding generates considerable costs and ties up large amounts of operating capital. One of the main aims of contemporary approaches such as supply-chain management and the concomitant enablers (for example, supplier alliances, JIT, MRP, **enterprise resource planning** (ERP), **efficient consumer response**

(ECR), **automatic replenishment** (AR), **quick response** (QR) and e-procurement) is to limit **inventory-holding** to the minimum.

If the holding of inventory is so unpopular, why should inventory be held at all? There are two major reasons for this:

- Inventory-holding helps to ensure that the operations process (or the marketing process in a retailing organisation) can continue without interruptions resulting from shortages of materials.
- It allows businesses to utilise cost savings through longer production runs and volume discounts.

It is therefore clear that too little or too much inventory is undesirable. Both conditions have certain cost implications or disadvantages. Table 14.2 provides a summary of some of the implications of too little or too much inventory.

> **Critical thinking**
>
> Why should fuel companies keep more stock rather than less stock? Why should a retailer such as Edgars or Fruit & Veg City not keep too much stock?

14.4.3.2 Inventory costs

Certain costs increase when large quantities of stock are purchased, while other costs increase with the purchase of small quantities. It is necessary to categorise these cost elements and examine them more closely to determine optimal inventory quantity, that is, the inventory quantity that results in the lowest total cost of inventory.

Inventory-carrying costs are those costs that are involved in keeping inventory. They include the cost of storage, salaries of warehouse staff, insurance, property tax, obsolescence, wear and tear, theft, interest charges (for the financing of inventory) and opportunity costs (loss of income from investment in alternative profit-bearing projects, as capital has been invested in inventory). Larger order quantities cause larger inventory levels and therefore higher inventory-carrying costs. The opposite applies to small quantities and lower inventory levels.

Inventory-ordering costs are the costs of placing an order. Ordering costs include the salaries of purchasing and supply and expediting personnel, stationery, telephone and fax costs, online (e-procurement) costs and postage. Larger purchasing and supply quantities result in fewer orders being placed and a decline in ordering costs.

Total inventory costs consist of the sum total of inventory-carrying costs and inventory-ordering costs. Ordering costs decline and carrying costs increase as order quantities increase. Ordering costs increase (because more orders have to be made) and carrying costs decrease as order quantities decrease. The influence of quantity on the two

Table 14.2: Implications of inventory positions

Disadvantages of too much inventory	Disadvantages of too little inventory
• Operating capital is tied up, with the resultant opportunity and interest costs • Losses in terms of depreciation, obsolescence, damage and theft • Costs in terms of storage space (rental or interest), more warehouse staff and equipment, and bigger insurance premiums	• Higher unit prices as a result of smaller orders • More urgent orders with concomitant higher order and transport costs, and strained relations with suppliers • Cost of production or job interruptions and the accompanying strained relations with users or marketers in the business • Lost sales because of empty shelves in the retail organisation and the resultant negative impact on the business's image

cost categories is indicated in Figure 14.7. The lowest total inventory cost is achieved where the two curves (carrying cost and ordering cost) intersect, in other words, when ordering costs are equal to carrying costs. The number of units opposite the lowest total inventory cost on the graph is the most **economic order quantity** (EOQ).

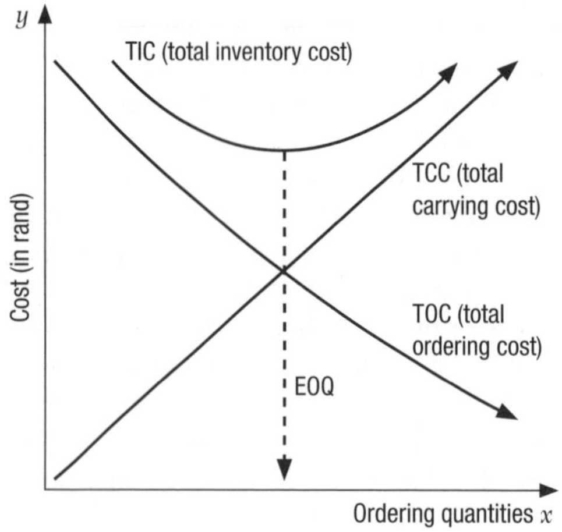

Figure 14.7: The economic order quantity

14.4.3.3 Inventory-control systems

Inventory should be managed and controlled so that optimal inventory levels can be maintained. This means that inventory should be kept at such a level that the best service can be rendered to the user or customer at the lowest possible cost. The quantities that are ordered each time should keep inventory at this optimal level. Most inventory-control systems are based on the principles of one of the systems described below.

The system of fixed-order quantities

This system is based on the principle that each time new inventory is required, a fixed quantity (the EOQ) is ordered. The system is represented visually in Figure 14.8.

The EOQ is ordered once inventory reaches a certain level (order point B) as a result of the use or selling of inventory items (A to B). Inventory is then replenished by ordering the EOQ to reach the maximum inventory level. The order level is determined in such a way that inventory does not become depleted during the delivery period of the order (lead time).

The system is advantageous because attention is focused only on a specific item when the inventory level reaches the ordering point and the same quantity is ordered every time. However, the system is unsuitable for items whose consumption or lead times are unreliable.

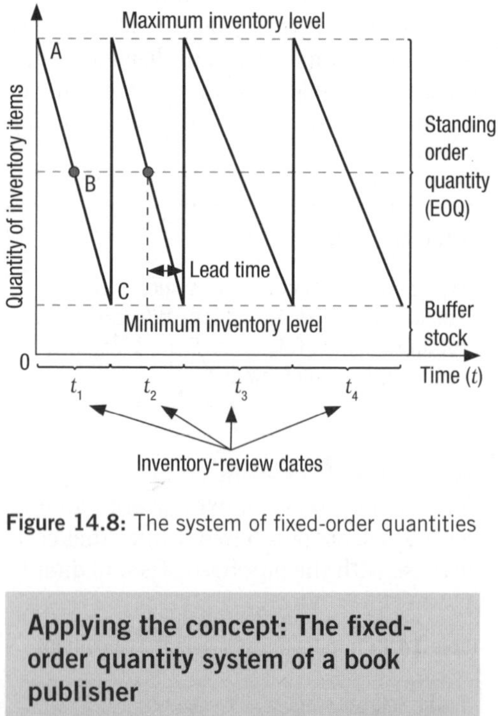

Figure 14.8: The system of fixed-order quantities

> **Applying the concept: The fixed-order quantity system of a book publisher**
>
> A publisher may decide that when there are only 100 copies of a certain book in stock (level B), 3 000 copies need to be printed (that is, a fixed-order quantity) to bring inventory up to level A. A buffer stock (for example, 50 books) is also kept as a precaution against unforeseen and exceptional circumstances.

> **Critical thinking**
>
> Decide which of the following two situations the **fixed-order quantity** method would be more suitable for:
> - a security-gate manufacturer who delivers standardised security gates for large retail groups such as Makro and Builder's Warehouse
> - a retail shop such as Foschini.

The cyclical-ordering system

According to this system, each item in the inventory is checked or reviewed at fixed intervals and is supplemented by an order to bring the inventory level to its maximum level again. Thus the ordering times are fixed, but the order quantity varies, as shown in Figure 14.9. The system is suitable for seasonal materials or materials that are used on an irregular basis, but where the acquisition of such materials can be planned far in advance on the basis of sales forecasts, for example, in a clothing store. This system is used in grocery stores where, at the end of every week or month, stock-taking is done for each product on the shelves and the order quantities are adjusted to the quantity on the shelves. Thus, for example, more soft drinks are ordered every week or month during summer than in winter.

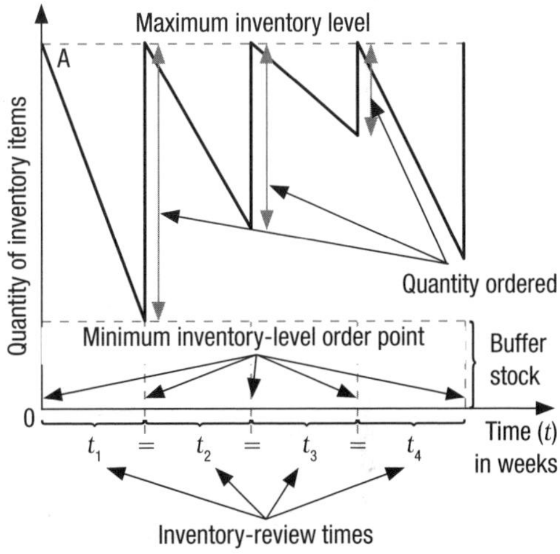

Figure 14.9: The cyclical-ordering system

The materials-requirements planning (MRP) system

MRP is a computer-assisted system where the aim is to maintain minimum inventory levels. The system uses a computer to calculate the total need for materials that may be required by an operations process in a given period. The planned quantity of final products to be manufactured during the production or operations process in the given period is broken down into components and materials by the computer. It then determines the total need for each type of raw material and component, with due consideration for lead times, so that materials or components are received when the production process needs them. The advantage of the system is that inventory levels are low. However, the system works only if suppliers are extremely reliable with their delivery and quality. Contracts with suppliers are usually needed to keep this system going.

> **Critical thinking**
>
> Can MRP work if certain materials used in the production process need to be imported? What influence will the importation have on the inventory (stock) levels of the specific materials?

The just-in-time (JIT) system

This is in fact a production- or operations-scheduling system and not an inventory system. It virtually eliminates the holding of inventory. Its operation is based on requiring suppliers to deliver materials of the right quality to the business on the day they are needed and where they are needed – in other words, just in time. The system requires regular deliveries and quantities should correspond exactly to needs. In other words, it is not the inventory system that determines the quantities to be purchased or to be delivered, but the operations or production system. Therefore, purchasing and supply has little or no influence on the quantities to be purchased. It is imperative for purchasing and supply to work closely with operations management because the purchasing and supply function needs to be fully conversant with the changing needs of the operations system.

The JIT system works properly only if the supplier is extremely reliable and is integrated into the business's production or operations system. Supplier alliances are needed to make JIT work. The JIT system cannot satisfy all the needs of the business. Only materials used in the operations process are purchased according to the JIT approach. Requirements that do not relate to the manufacture of the business's final product (for example, office and operations equipment and maintenance materials) obviously do not justify the use of the sophisticated JIT system and concomitant attention to the supplier base.

The quick-response (QR) and automatic-replenishment (AR) systems

QR is defined as a vertical strategy in the supply chain in which the manufacturer strives to provide products and services to its retail customers in exact quantities on a continuous basis with minimal lead times, resulting in minimum inventory levels throughout the retail apparel supply chain. QR can be regarded as the retail version of the manufacturing JIT concept. The system aims to deliver materials or merchandise to areas in the exact amount required at the precise time they are needed. With JIT, the use of raw materials pulls raw materials into the production process. With QR, merchandise is pulled by customer sales. In both cases, information about the production rate or the sales figures is substituted with materials or merchandise.

AR is an integral part of any QR program. AR can be defined as an exchange relationship in which the supplier replenishes or restocks inventory based upon actual product usage and stock-level information provided by the retail buyer. AR therefore provides the final customer (consumer) with the desired product and service in a timely fashion. The goal of AR is to manage inventory levels effectively. With AR, as already indicated, information is substituted for inventory or merchandise[7].

The efficient consumer response (ECR) system

ECR was developed for the grocery industry and is based on the same principles as QR. ECR calls for the creation of a timely, accurate and paperless flow of information. It relies heavily on electronic data interchange (EDI) and strategic alliances between supply-chain members. The goal of ECR is to eliminate costs such as inventory-holding and ordering costs in an entire supply chain. The underlying objectives are to reduce cycle time (time from placing the order to receiving the goods) in the supply chain, reduce inventories, avoid duplications in logistics costs and increase customer service[8].

> **Critical thinking**
>
> Think about the case study on the shortage of CO_2 in the soft-drink industry. Do you think that Afrox and ABI keep sufficient stock of CO_2? Suppose they had kept two-weeks usage of CO_2. Do you think they could have prevented the crises in the consumer market? In view of the seasonal nature of demand for carbonated soft drinks, which inventory-holding technique would you recommend to Afrox and ABI for CO_2?

14.4.4 The selection and management of suppliers

14.4.4.1 The importance of selecting the right suppliers

Effective purchasing and supply rely on the selection of the right suppliers, particularly in the supply of strategic materials or services. As a result, the selection of suppliers is one of the most vital tasks of the purchasing and supply function. Competitive prices, reliable quality, timely deliveries, technical support and good after-sales service are determined primarily by the choice of the right supplier. Hence, it is essential for the purchasing and supply function to proceed systematically and objectively in selecting suppliers. An important consideration when making this choice is that a long-term relationship with suppliers of strategic products or services is necessary to ensure effective purchasing and supply at all times. Important components of such a relationship are honesty, fairness and frankness.

14.4.4.2 The selection process

Supplier selection is an ongoing process. Existing suppliers have to be constantly reconsidered with each new purchase, especially in view of changing circumstances and needs. Past performance of an existing supplier obviously counts a great deal in the selection process. However, the care taken in the selection process will be determined by the scope of the transaction, the availability of materials, the strategic value of materials and whether they are standard or custom made. Custom-made items are items for a specific purpose and are therefore not generally available in the market. Standard items, however, are freely available at more or less the same quality and price, and in this case the choice of suppliers is not particularly important.

The process starts with the compilation of a list of suppliers that may be able to satisfy the need. The list can be compiled from various sources, including own supplier register, industrial advertisements, the Yellow Pages, trade guides, open tenders, shows and exhibitions. The list is then reduced to a short list, taking into account factors such as location, progressiveness, general reputation, and financial and technical ability. Suppliers on the short list are then requested to give a quote or negotiations are conducted with them. The aim is to obtain the best value (in respect of price, quality, service and delivery) for the business. The final choice of a supplier is based on considerations such as past performance, quality, price, delivery, technical support, progressiveness and reliability.

Once the choice has been made, the next step is the continuous evaluation of the performance of the supplier to ensure that it conforms to expectations. Unsatisfactory suppliers must be eliminated. The objective evaluation of supplier performance is important for the following reasons:

- Ineffective or unreliable suppliers are identified.
- It leads to an improvement in supplier performance.
- It serves as a guideline for the development of suppliers.

14.4.4.3 Developing suppliers

Purchasing and supply functions may become involved in the development of suppliers for various reasons. Suppliers may be developed for black economic empowerment purposes or to improve their performance as a result of performance appraisals, or if materials or services do not exist in the (local) market.

Black economic empowerment (BEE) through purchasing

In the spirit of reconstruction and development, and setting right inequalities, there is increasing pressure on South African businesses to give disadvantaged suppliers who show potential an opportunity to enter the market. Large organisations can help these suppliers develop, over time, into fully fledged independent suppliers. BEE purchasing and supply may be done in the following ways:

- When comparing quotations (prices) of the different suppliers, a certain percentage may be subtracted from the quoted prices of independent disadvantaged suppliers in order to benefit them.
- Specific pre-identified materials and services may be purchased from disadvantaged suppliers with potential, and such suppliers may be supported for adhering to the contract and executing orders. Support

given to disadvantaged suppliers may be in the form of managerial and technical assistance, making facilities available, staff training and advancing operating capital.
- Products and services that were formerly produced by the business may be subcontracted or outsourced to disadvantaged suppliers. Management of a business may, for example, decide to sell catering services to employees in the cafeteria, which then functions as a separate business, rendering services on a contract basis.
- A certain preference percentage can be accorded when comparing prices to other suppliers who, in turn, commit to making a certain percentage of their purchases from suppliers (second-tier suppliers) from disadvantaged groups.

Materials or service not available

If a firm has a need for a particular material or service that is not available in the market, it can enter into a contract with a chosen supplier of another material or service to manufacture this material (product) or provide this service. Assistance to such a supplier may be in the form of staff training, the reconstruction or expansion of facilities, or the implementation of new facilities. A joint venture can be formed with the supplier. In any case, a long-term agreement with the supplier would be a prerequisite.

Normal performance appraisal

Normal performance appraisals can contribute to the development of suppliers by identifying their weaknesses and encouraging them to perform better. This is an important factor in establishing successful long-term ties with suppliers.

14.4.4.4 Long-term relationships with suppliers

The nature of the relationships that organisations have with their suppliers varies. Some relationships are distant and formal, while other relationships are closer and more personal. An organisation will have little involvement with suppliers of standard, easy-to-get products or services, but a great deal of involvement with suppliers of strategic scarce materials or highly complicated, unique services. An alliance or a partnership is a high-involvement relationship. Attributes of strategic-supplier alliances are trust and co-operation, interdependence, joint quality-improvement efforts, information (and systems) sharing, risk and benefit sharing, and joint problem-solving.

Critical thinking

Think about the case study on the shortage of CO_2 in the soft-drink industry.
- Do you agree that CO_2 is a strategic material for ABI?
- Why can one make such a supposition?
- What kind of relationship should exist between ABI, Afrox, Sasol and PetroSA?
- Do you think that all the expectations and requirements of such a relationship were met in this case?
- Identify the cause of the problems in this case.

14.4.5 Pricing decisions

14.4.5.1 The "best" price

Price has traditionally been regarded as the decisive factor in awarding orders. However, low prices go hand in hand with higher costs in other areas. These include the costs and risks attached to low quality and high inventory, when low prices (as a result of quantity discounts) are linked to quantity. The right price is not necessarily the lowest one. The total or final costs should rather be seen as the decisive factor in awarding orders. In other words, price should be regarded as only one of the components of value, together with quality, delivery and cost of use. A buyer should always strive to obtain the highest value for the business.

On the one hand, the price paid for materials or services must be reasonable and should enable the purchasing enterprise to make its own product or service competitive in the market. On the other hand, a reasonable price should also be fair to the supplier to ensure that a supplier sells its materials or service at a price that will ensure its profitability and survival. The price should therefore be fair to the purchasing firm and the supplier in terms of profitability and value.

14.4.5.2 Price determination

The methods used to determine purchasing prices depend on the nature of the materials and the value of the transaction. Published price lists and available market information, including catalogues, brochures and advertisements in trade journals, are most suitable for the purchase of standard materials and orders of a low monetary value (for example, when purchasing screws and stationery). Other methods of price determination are quotations and tenders (also called "bids" or "bidding"). When a business uses this method of price determination, it asks suppliers to make an offer. The purchaser sometimes calls for open tenders by publishing the invitation to tender. Any supplier can make an offer. The trend, however, is to issue a request to tender to a number of known suppliers. These "closed tenders" are most suitable for purchasers with a complete list of suppliers.

Quotations are quick and informal. They can be made by telephone, by fax or electronically. Quotations are used when standard materials are purchased, but they are also suitable for non-standard or custom-made materials with a high monetary value (for example, custom-made equipment that performs a unique function). Tenders are accompanied by a drawn-out procedure that has to be followed to the letter. The modern trend is to limit the use of tenders to the minimum. Tenders are usually suitable for the purchase of custom-made materials with a high monetary value, when there is plenty of time for the process and when there are many suppliers in the market in active and serious competition with each other (for example, in the construction of buildings).

Tenders and quotations are also used as a basis for post-tender negotiations. Post-tender negotiations take place between purchaser and tenderer/s if none of the tenders received is deemed acceptable, or where a supplier is chosen above another for certain reasons, but the price or other conditions are unacceptable. Negotiation often gives a buyer the best results. However, successful negotiation requires careful preparation by an experienced negotiation team. Negotiation entails a personal meeting between buyer and seller with a view to reaching a compromise and concluding a deal. It is an expensive method that is justified only in transactions with a high monetary value, where contract conditions are complex, when the execution of the contract stretches over a long period and when business is conducted with the only suppliers in the market (a monopoly) or a supplier in a strong market position.

Although tenders and negotiations have been discussed as pricing methods, it is important to emphasise that they are also used to determine quality, service and delivery of purchased materials or services.

> **Critical thinking**
>
> Why were tenders used as a method of selecting suppliers and determining prices for the Gautrain project?

14.4.6 Timing of purchases

14.4.6.1 The "right" time to buy

The time at which purchases are made often determines the price paid for materials. In the same way, time and price determine the quantity to be purchased.

The aims of buying at the right time are:

- to ensure that the business is supplied on an ongoing basis with the materials and services required for it to operate without interruptions

- to reduce the risk of price fluctuations
- to keep inventory-holding at an optimal level.

To realise these aims, a buyer should have a sound knowledge of the market and trends.

14.4.6.2 Factors influencing the scheduling of purchases

Various internal and external factors influence the time at which purchases (and obviously their quantity) should be made. Internally, business policy may prevent buyers from buying speculatively, so that they are unable to make use of bargain offers. Furthermore, the availability of funds in the business determines when products are purchased. Changes in the marketing and operations requirements may influence the time at which purchases are made because most purchases are made for these functions. Physical facilities such as storage space are another factor that influences the timing of purchases.

The first external factors to determine the time of purchases are market conditions (supply and demand) and government regulations. During recessions, there is a favourable buyers' market and materials can be bought at lower prices because of the decrease in demand for materials resulting from fewer economic activities. During these periods, it is advisable to buy large quantities of materials. Obviously a business can benefit from such market conditions only if it has the necessary funds, and provided that its economic activities and demand for the final product or service are expected to increase. In a boom period, economic activities are high and the demand for suppliers' products increases. Prices increase and service to the purchaser tapers off. During such periods, it is wise to buy early at lower prices. Buyers should, as far as possible, avoid making purchases when prices are high. If the boom is expected to level out (prices are expected to decrease), it is wise to buy at the last minute (within the limits of lead times) and in small quantities.

Lead times and the reliability of suppliers are additional external factors that determine the timing of purchases. Government restrictions are another consideration in that they place limitations on organisations conducting business with foreign suppliers. A buyer in South Africa will, for example, have difficulty in obtaining permission to purchase materials overseas if South Africa's foreign money supply is limited or if local suppliers' continued existence is at risk (for example, the textile industry in South Africa).

> **Critical thinking**
>
> If petroleum companies in South Africa obtain information about a future meeting of crude-oil producers in the Middle East and expectations are that these producers will decrease their barrel output in order to increase prices, what will the South African companies do? What will the advantages and disadvantages of their action be?

14.5 Summary

The purchasing and supply function is an important one for the following reasons:

- It has a significant influence on the profitability of the business.
- It is often the greatest spender of business revenue.
- This function makes it possible for the business to sell its final products at competitive prices.

The purchasing and supply function, like all other functions in the business, should be planned, organised and controlled to ensure that it helps achieve the objectives of the business. This chapter has provided some insight into the management of the purchasing and supply function.

The main purchasing activities of quality, quantity, price, supplier selection and timing were discussed. It was emphasised that the different purchasing and supply activities do not occur in isolation, but on an integrated basis. The integration of the purchasing function with other functions of the business to enable the system to operate as a whole was also emphasised.

Key terms

automatic replenishment	negotiations
centralisation	post-tender negotiations
cross-functional sourcing teams	profit-leverage effect
decentralisation	published price lists
developing suppliers	purchasing and supply cycle
economic order quantity	purchasing and supply function
efficient consumer response	quick response
enterprise resource planning	quotations
fixed-order quantities	specifications
inventory-carrying costs	speculative purchasing
inventory-holding	standardisation
inventory management	supplier performance
inventory-ordering costs	suppliers
just-in-time	tenders
materials-requirements planning	

Questions for discussion

Reread the case study on page 508 and answer the following questions:

1. List all the materials and services purchased by Amalgamated Beverage Industries (ABI).
2. Explain the importance of the purchasing and supply (procurement) function for ABI.
3. Make conclusions about the way procurement is managed (planned, organised and controlled) at ABI.
4. List the steps in the purchasing cycle and use the case of ABI as an example to explain the steps the business will follow when purchasing CO_2.
5. Explain the possible quality-description methods ABI will use to order CO_2.
6. Use the ABI case study to explain and illustrate the disadvantages of holding too much and too little inventory.
7. Explain the fixed-order quantities and cyclical-ordering systems. Which system is the most appropriate for ABI to use for CO_2?
8. What alternatives does ABI have to prevent the shortage of CO_2 in the future?

Multiple-choice questions

1. Look at the list of details that follows.
   i. Quality specifications
   ii. Supplier
   iii. Delivery time
   iv. Price
   v. Quantity of items
   Now decide what combination of details will appear on the requisition.
   a. i, ii, iii, iv, v
   b. i, iii, v
   c. i, iii, iv, v
   d. ii, iii, iv
2. When an organisation purchases an important strategic item, which of the following qualities will it regard as most important when deciding on a supplier?
   a. Price, quality and delivery
   b. Location, cost and value
   c. Financial stability, managerial and technical ability, and capacity
   d. Technical ability and quality
3. Quality of products ...
   i. is directly associated with price.
   ii. determines the number of potential suppliers.
   iii. influences inventory-holding.

   iv. should be in line with the function the item needs to perform.

   Now decide what combination of statements is correct.

   a. i, ii, iii, iv
   b. i, ii
   c. i, ii, iii
   d. iii, iv

4. Which of these statements is incorrect?
   a. Both QR and JIT rely on minimum lead times.
   b. AR can be regarded as the retail version of JIT.
   c. Supplier alliances are necessary to make JIT and ECR work.
   d. With AR, information is substituted for inventory.
5. Which of the following actions would you recommend to ABI to prevent future shortages of CO_2?
   a. Become more involved in BEE purchasing.
   b. Award a low mark to Afrox with supplier-performance evaluation.
   c. Conclude a supplier alliance with Afrox.
   d. Find or become involved in the development of another supplier who can also provide CO_2.

Answers to multiple-choice questions

1. b
2. c
3. a
4. b
5. d

References

1. "Purchasing" is also known as "procurement". "Supply" is added because purchasing or procurement is no longer seen as a reactive service function of organisations. In modern firms, it is acknowledged that purchasing makes a strategic contribution. Purchasing management is involved in processes, both in the firm and at suppliers, to ensure the efficient flow of materials and services in the right quantity and of the right quality at the right time to the organisation and through the supply chain as a whole at the lowest possible total cost. For example, the purchasing function studies the supply market of strategic commodities and develops supply strategies accordingly. When the purchasing or procurement function is on such a level that it makes a strategic impact (when "supply" is added), companies (for example, Mittal Steel and SABMiller) often call the function the "commercial function".
2. Baillie, P., Farmer, D., Crocker, B., Jessop, D. & Jones, D. 2008. *Purchasing principles and management*. 10th ed. Essex, England: Prentice Hall (Pearson Education), p. 162.
3. Lysons, K. & Farrington, B. 2006. *Purchasing and Supply Chain Management*. 7th ed. Essex: Prentice Hall (Pearson Education), p. 20.
4. Hugo, W.M.J., Badenhorst-Weiss, J.A. & Van Biljon, E.H.B. 2006. *Purchasing and supply management*. 5th ed. Pretoria: Van Schaik, pp. 27–32.
5. Hugo, W.M.J., Badenhorst-Weiss, J.A. & Van Biljon, E.H.B. 2006. *Purchasing and supply management*. 5th ed. Pretoria: Van Schaik, p. 45.
6. Supply-chain management is an extension of the systems approach. According to the systems approach, the internal functions of the business (marketing, finance, purchasing and supply, production, human resources and so on) are managed as an integrated whole. In the supply-chain management approach, the integration extends beyond the individual business. The "system" in supply-chain management consists of managing, in an integrated fashion, the flow of materials in all the linked organisations, from the raw material stage through all the stages of transformation to delivery of the final product to the end-user (consumer). The intention is that businesses in the supply chain co-operate in networks with mutual long-term agreements to deliver the end product to the final consumer in the most effective way and at the lowest cost. This is achieved by sharing information, know-how and even facilities, and by eliminating waste between the various stages of the transformation process.
7. Hugo, W.M.J., Badenhorst-Weiss, J.A. & Van Biljon, E.H.B. 2004. *Supply chain management: Logistics in perspective*. Pretoria: Van Schaik, pp. 349–350.

8. Hugo, W.M.J., Badenhorst-Weiss, J.A. & Van Biljon, E.H.B. 2004. *Supply chain management: Logistics in perspective.* Pretoria: Van Schaik, pp. 350–352.

PART 4

Business

STRATEGY AND DECISION-MAKING

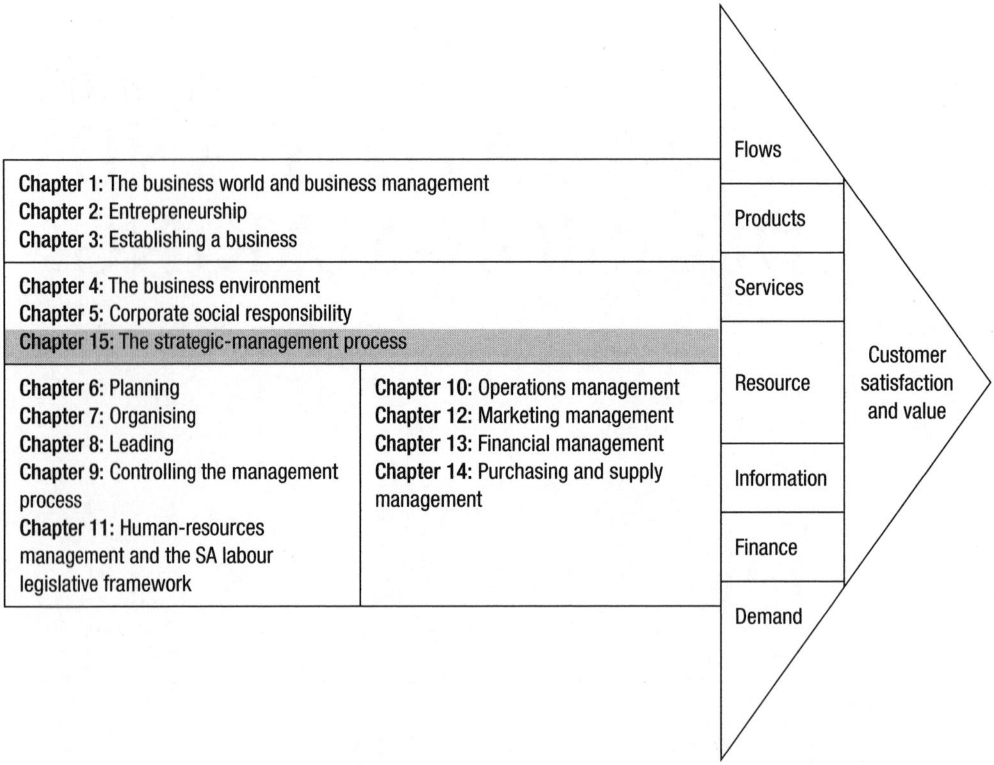

Source: Adapted from Mentzer, T. J. (ed.). 2001. *Supply Chain Management.* London: Sage, pp. 22–23.

CHAPTER

15

THE STRATEGIC-MANAGEMENT PROCESS

The purpose of this chapter

This chapter introduces you to two key management concepts: the strategic-management process and management intelligence systems. The strategic-management process is a comprehensive management approach that encompasses and directs management activities at all levels of the organisation. Strategic management and management in general rely on information and intelligence sourced by management intelligence systems, which play a critical role in any organisation.

Learning outcomes

On completion of this chapter you should be able to:

- distinguish between corporate level, business level and functional strategies and operations
- explain the strategic-management process
- discuss the role of strategic management in the management of the organisation
- explain the role of information and intelligence systems in the strategic-management process.

15.1 Introduction

While the book so far has focused on the management process, it is important to understand that there is a bigger management picture called strategic management. **Strategic management** considers the organisation's environment (internal and external) to identify opportunities and threats, as well as internal strengths and weaknesses. It provides direction and intent to the organisation, and identifies the most suitable ways of creating value for stakeholders. It also provides a system for co-ordinating management activities throughout the organisation. In this process, intelligence is indispensible. Understanding the internal and external environments is a key part of the organisational planning processes. By constantly obtaining feedback from operations and the external environment, the organisation can ensure that it adapts to fundamental changes in the environment or gets failing initiatives back on track. Consider how

Dell co-operates with business partners and customers to ensure that the company retains a competitive advantage in the case study that follows.

Case study

Managing velocity: Dell Computer Corporation

Dell Computer gains time (and money) by using technology and information to blur traditional boundaries between a company and its customers.

Michael Dell began in 1984 with a simple business insight: he could bypass the dealer channel through which personal computers were then sold. Instead, he would sell directly to customers and build customised products to order. In one swoop, Dell eliminated the reseller's mark-up, and the costs and risks associated with carrying large inventories of finished goods. The formula became known as the direct business model, and it gave Dell a substantial cost advantage. Dell's product line has expanded over the years. In addition to desktop personal computers, the company now sells a broader range of hardware: laptops, servers and workstations. But make no mistake, Dell sells physical things, manufactured goods that must be assembled and transported and delivered and serviced with a staff of about 22 000 worldwide and a base in Round Rock, Texas.

Is Dell, then, stuck in the past of material goods and physical flows? Or is it part of the so-called "new economy", creating wealth through "intangible streams of data, images and symbols"? In fact, Dell is both.

Companies have always thrived by offering customers superior value, giving them more for less. For the most part, they offer better value by shrinking the time and the resources consumed in meeting customers' needs. But like many other companies today, Dell is harnessing the tools of the knowledge economy – information and technology – to bring new levels of efficiency and productivity to the old world of tangible goods. Consider all the activities and resources that go into making and selling a computer. As a small start-up, Dell simply couldn't afford to create every piece of that value chain. Instead, its strategy has been to build systems from components made by other companies. Let them invest in R&D and in factories. For each component, Dell evaluates the field and picks the best to be its suppliers. Dell then works so closely with them that they become, in Dell's words, "virtually integrated". While they remain independent companies, each free to focus on what it does best, they share information and co-ordinate their activities as if they were part of one vertically integrated company.

Real-time information-sharing with suppliers is the key to just-in-time assembly. Instead of having suppliers make periodic deliveries to a warehouse, Dell tells them the exact number of components it needs, at what hour of the day, delivered to which loading dock at its factory. This is precisely the kind of information a company would freely share with an internal supplier.

Dell's rule in working with partners is to have as few as possible, and to keep them as long as they maintain their technological and quality leadership. Managed this way, supplier partnerships give Dell the flexibility to respond to changes in the market. Doing so can dramatically speed time to market, thus creating substantial value that the buyer and supplier can share. Speed is critical for two reasons. First, in the computer business, the cost of components goes down as much as 50% a year. The company with two or three months of inventory will be at a significant cost disadvantage to the company with eleven days because its products were built with more expensive parts. Second, in technology markets with frequent product transitions, it's easy to get stuck holding obsolete inventory or to be late to market with the hottest new products.

Co-ordination between companies is not new to the knowledge economy. However, such tight co-ordination would not be possible without sophisticated data exchange. Managing velocity is about managing information, using a constant flow of information to drive operating practices. In essence, Dell substitutes information for inventory. The result is that Dell turns its inventory over thirty times per year, an extraordinary feat given the complexity of its product line. But without credible information about what customers are actually buying, says Dell: "Trying to manage eleven days of inventory would be insane. We couldn't do it without customers who work with us as partners."

Working closely with customers is critical to the Dell strategy. Ninety per cent of Dell's sales go to institutions – business or government – and 70% to very large customers that buy at least USD1 million in PCs a year. With those large customers, Dell maintains an on-site team that functions less as a vendor and more as the customer's information-technology department for PCs. The team will typically be involved in planning the customer's PC needs and the configuration of their network. Thus Dell's sales-account managers have unusually good information on what each customer intends to buy. Smaller customers buy direct from Dell over the telephone. Not only can Dell compile real-time data about what's selling, but its salespeople can also steer customers, while they're on the phone, toward product configurations that are available, further using information to fine-tune the balance between supply and demand.

In short, by eliminating the middleman, Dell captures valuable information from customers, which it uses to lower its inventory, its costs and its risks. Information from the customer flows all the way through manufacturing to Dell's suppliers, making the whole an efficient and flexible system. In this way, the direct model allows Dell to build computers to meet real demand from real end customers.

Beyond substituting information for inventory, Dell combines technology and information to blur the traditional boundaries that separate a company from its customers. Consider technical support. Dell has made it possible for its customers to access its internal support tools online in the same way as Dell's own technical support teams do. In effect, Dell is enabling the customer to service itself, saving time and money on both sides.

Dell has done something analogous with its selling function. It has developed customised intranet sites called Premier Pages for well over 400 of its largest global customers, giving them direct access to purchasing and technical information. A customer can allow its thousands of employees to use the Premier Page as a kind of interactive catalogue of all the model configurations that the company authorises. Employees can then price and order the PC they want. Employees are happy to have some choice, and Dell and the customer both eliminate all the paperwork and sales time normally associated with corporate purchasing.

Beyond Dell's mechanisms for sales and support, the company has set up a number of forums to exchange information with the customer. Platinum Councils, for example, are regional meetings – in Asia-Pacific, Japan, the US and Europe – of Dell's largest customers. In these meetings, Dell's senior technologists share their views on where the technology is heading over the next two years and listen to customers talking about their needs. Helping the customer anticipate the flow of new technology helps Dell, as well, in thinking about new product offerings and in forecasting demand.

Most of the managerial challenges at Dell Computer have to do with speeding the pace of every element of its business. Life cycles are measured in months, not years, and companies must move fast to stay in the game. In a world where customer needs and technologies change quickly, managers must sense and respond to rapid shifts, process new information very quickly and make decisions in real time.

Source: Magretta, J. 1998. "Managing velocity: Dell Computer Corporation" from "The Power of Virtual Integration: An Interview with Dell Computer's Michael Dell". *Harvard Business Review*, March/April.

15.2 Strategic management

Before we explore the definition of strategy, it is important to note that strategic management involves different levels of the organisation (see Table 15.1 on page 533). At the highest level of strategy, corporate-level strategy is concerned with managing the multi-business corporation and is the domain of the corporate board of directors. At the next level, it is the imperative of the management of each of the strategic business units to seek sources of sustainable competitive advantage. This provides the framework for functional managers to develop and implement functional strategies. At the lowest level of the organisation, it is the responsibility of supervisors or first-line management to manage from day to day in line with the overall strategic direction of the organisation.

The overall purpose of strategic management is to ensure consistency in the management of the organisation (see Figure 15.1). In the first instance, the selected strategies have to be consistent with the opportunities and threats presented by the external environment. Secondly, the selected strategies have to be consistent with the core and distinctive capabilities (strengths and weaknesses) of the organisation. As these may change over time, and may accordingly prompt changes in strategy and sources of competitive advantage, it can also be seen as dynamic consistency. For example, in its early years, micro-processor producer Intel's time to market was consistently faster than all its competitors, providing it with a series of competitive advantages. However, as competitors caught up with Intel, it changed its competitive advantage to a strong brand (think about the "Intel Inside" sticker you see on many personal and portable computers) and strong relationships with leading producers. Finally, there needs to be consistency between the selected strategies and the internal environment. For example, policies and procedures have to be aligned with the chosen strategic direction of the organisation.

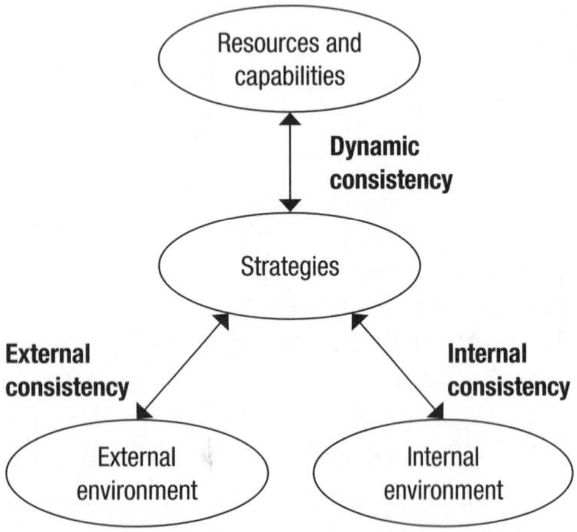

Figure 15.1: Strategic management as the quest for consistency

Table 15.1: Management at different organisational levels

Level of management	Description	Organisational unit	Time frame	Responsibility	Goal	Example
Corporate	Decisions on the scope of the corporation (what businesses to be in)	Multi-business corporation or single business looking to expand	Three to five years or longer	Board of directors	Creating shareholder value	Woolworths alliance with Engen Quick-Shops
Business	Decisions on how to compete in an industry	Strategic business unit (for example, division or subsidiary)	Three to five years	Managing director or CEO	Establishing sustainable competitive advantage	Woolworths competing on quality (differentiation)
Functional	Decisions on how best to implement business strategy	Functional department (for example, marketing)	One year	Functional manager (for example, marketing manager)	Effective implementation of business strategy	Woolworths campaign to increase environmentally friendly packaging
Operations	Decisions on best ways to implement functional strategies	Operational section (for example, quality-control section)	Day to day	First-line management	Production efficiency	Woolworths promise to keep in-store queue times to a minimum

From the previous discussion, it may be concluded that a good strategic-management process leads to three outcomes:

- It optimises consistency between the different levels of management.
- It optimises consistency between the organisation and its internal and external environments.
- It leads to sustained performance higher than the industry norm. In other words, it leads to **sustainable competitive advantage**.

15.3 The strategic-management process

There are many different versions and depictions of the strategic-management process, but most of these approaches have certain common characteristics. Figure 15.2 on page 534 is a simplified version of the strategic-management process, depicting the most common characteristics of a good strategic-management process.

- The first step in the strategic-management process is the establishment of **strategic direction**. This usually consists of a vision and mission statement that provides impetus and direction to the organisation. This is discussed in section 15.3.1.
- From the strategic direction, more specific **strategic objectives** can be derived. These are typically long term in nature (typically a three-to-five-year focus) and are measurable outcomes. This is also discussed in section 15.3.1.
- The purpose of the **external environmental analysis** is to identify opportunities and threats in the macro- and market

environments (see Chapter 4) that may influence the objectives and choice of strategies to attain objectives. This is discussed in section 15.3.2.

- The purpose of the **internal analysis** is to identify and appraise the resources and capabilities of the organisation (the micro-environment, see Chapter 4) in order to identify key strengths and weaknesses that may affect the strategic goals and choice of strategies. This is discussed in section 15.3.3.
- The **choice of strategies** should be determined in such a way as to attain the strategic goals most effectively and efficiently. However, this is often constrained or enabled by external and internal environmental conditions. For example, after the global financial crisis, even brilliant strategies may be constrained by the organisation's inability to raise funds in tough economic conditions. This is discussed in section 15.3.4.
- One of the most difficult yet important aspects of the strategic-management process is the ability to implement selected strategies successfully. Without **strategy implementation**, even the most brilliant strategies are worthless. This is discussed in section 15.3.5.
- **Strategic control** is required to ensure that the implementation of strategy remains on track and also to ensure that environmental changes are picked up early enough to take evasive action if required. Ideally, it provides feedback to the entire process. It is highly dependent on actionable management intelligence. This is discussed in section 15.3.6.

By now, some similarities between the strategic-management process and the generic management process should be emerging. Determining strategic direction and strategic goals, internal and external environmental analysis and **strategic choice** forms part of the

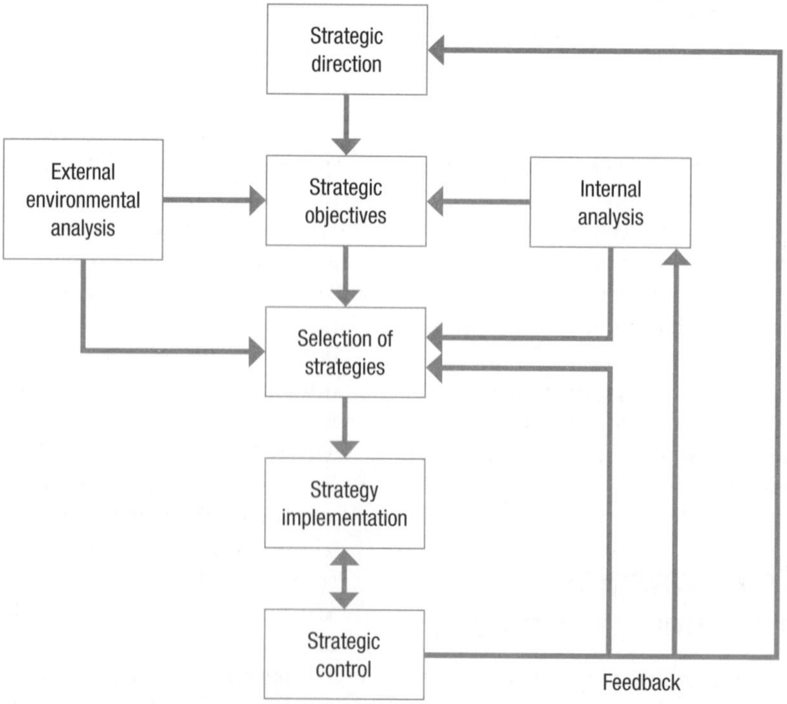

Figure 15.2: The strategic-management process

planning elements of strategic management, and is also known as strategy formulation. Strategy implementation corresponds with the **organising** and **leading** elements of the management process, while strategic control is fairly obviously similar to other generic management **control** processes.

15.3.1 Strategic direction and strategic objectives

The strategic direction of the organisation most commonly consists of a vision and a mission statement. While the vision is quite often the original dream of the founder, the mission is generally a more grounded expression of the overall purpose of the organisation.

Gamble and Thompson[1] describe the vision as the long-term future view of top management of the product-customer-market-technology focus of the organisation.

Here are some examples of vision statements.

Standard Bank (retail bank)

We aspire to be a leading emerging markets' financial services organisation.

Source: Standard Bank. 2009. [Online] Available: http://www.standardbank.com/VisionAndValues.aspx Accessed 22 December 2009.

MTN Group Vision (mobile telecommunications operator)

MTN's vision is to be the emerging markets' leading telecommunications provider. Our strategy is built on three pillars: consolidation and diversification; leveraging our footprint and intellectual capacity; and convergence and operational evolution.

Source: MTN. 2009. [Online] Available: http://www.mtn.com/AboutMTNGroup/VisionAndStrategy.aspx Accessed 22 December 2009.

University of South Africa (comprehensive open-distance learning institution)

"Towards *the* African university in the service of humanity"

Source: UNISA. 2009. [Online] Available: http://www.unisa.ac.za/default.asp?Cmd=ViewContent&ContentID=3 Accessed 22 December 2009.

City Lodge Hotels Vision (hotel group)

We will be recognised as the preferred southern African hotel group.

Through dedicated leadership and teamwork we will demonstrate our consistent commitment to delivering caring service with style and grace.

We will constantly enhance our guest experience through our passionate people, ongoing innovation and leading-edge technology.

Our integrity, values and ongoing investment in our people and hotels will provide exceptional returns to stakeholders and ensure continued, sustainable growth.

Source: The City Lodge Family of Hotels. 2009. [Online] Available: http://www.citylodge.co.za/hotelgroup.htm Accessed 22 December 2009.

Considering the role of the vision statement as a forward-looking statement of future direction, we could identify some characteristics of a useful vision statement:

- It should serve as an inspiration to the stakeholders of the organisation and should be written in a such a way that it inspires commitment and confidence.
- It should be short enough to remember easily, yet it should contain enough information to direct activities. If written too broadly and generically, it will not guide management decisions.
- It should be closely identified with the organisation. In the worst instances,

visions end up being so generic that if you took away the company name, the vision could apply to any organisation in any industry.
- It contains some indication of the future direction of the organisation. In other words, it is forward looking and indicates some future state.

The mission, on the other hand, is an expression of the current focus and long-term purpose of the organisation.

Here are some examples of mission statements.

Pick n Pay (retailer)

We serve
With our hearts we create a great place to be
With our minds we create an excellent place to shop

Source: Pick n Pay. 2009. [Online] Available: http://www.picknpay.co.za/static/section/index.php?page_id=984 Accessed 22 December 2009.

Multichoice (digital media)

To bring digital media entertainment, content and services to subscribers through multiple devices.

Source: Multichoice. 2009. [Online] Available: http://www.multichoice.co.za/multichoice/view/multichoice/en/page35 Accessed 22 December 2009.

South Africa Revenue Service (SARS) (government department)

To optimise revenue yield, facilitate trade and enlist new tax contributors by promoting awareness of the obligation to voluntarily comply with South African tax and customs laws, and to provide a quality and responsive service to the public.

Source: SARS. 2009. [Online] Available: http://www.sars.gov.za/home.asp?pid=201 Accessed 22 December 2009.

One of the ways in which strategic direction contributes to strategic success is by providing a mechanism for ensuring internal consistency. Ideally, all objectives and strategies in the rest of the organisation should link in some way to the stated strategic intent of the organisation. The first step in this process is to develop strategic objectives. These are typically long-term objectives, but should (like all other objectives) be SMART (specific, measurable, attainable, realistic and timed). It is also important to ensure that these objectives are not only financial, but also cover other important areas. The balanced scorecard (see Chapter 13) was developed specifically with this in mind. It provides a mechanism for developing a more balanced portfolio of strategic objectives, addressing financial objectives, customer objectives, internal processes, and learning and growth[2]. At the next level, functional objectives are set, typically with a one-year time frame, while operational targets are the day-to-day production guidelines that support the functional objectives. Figure 15.3 depicts this hierarchy of objectives.

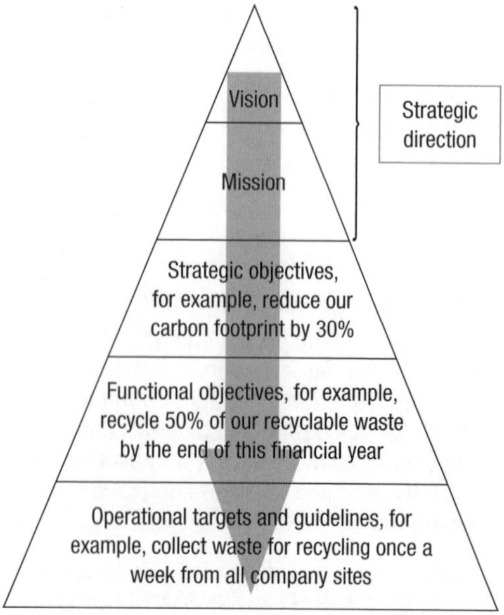

Figure 15.3: The hierarchy of objectives

15.3.2 External environmental analysis

The purpose of external environmental analysis is to identify opportunities and threats. (You will find a more complete discussion of the external environment in Chapter 4.) Opportunities are those forces or events that will allow the organisation to meet or exceed its strategic objectives, while threats will constrain the ability of the organisation to attain its strategic objectives. In severe cases, threats may potentially threaten the existence of an organisation. For example, labour brokers are currently in danger of being banned by the government.

15.3.3 Internal analysis

The purpose of the process of internal analysis is to discover what the organisation is better at than its competitors, and also to uncover key weaknesses that could prevent it from attaining its objectives or could make it vulnerable to competition. In understanding the strategic sources of competitive advantage, the role of resources and core capabilities has become increasingly important. This approach suggests that organisations can be successful by exploiting their assets and capabilities. Take, for example, MTN and Vodacom. These organisations started around the same time and yet they have ended up in very different places (see the case study that follows). It could be argued that MTN used the organisational capabilities that it had developed in the South African market very well to expand into other countries. These "hubs" (like Nigeria and then Iran) were then used as a basis for expansion into other countries in the region. This is an example of a strategy where key strengths were used as a basis for competitive advantage. Figure 15.4 on page 538 depicts the use of resources and capabilities (using MTN as an example) as bases for competitive advantage. Organisations typically have a wide range of resources (tangible, intangible and human). However, resources on their own are of little value. It is how these resources are combined into organisational capabilities that provides an organisation with a competitive advantage.

Case study

Vodacom and MTN in Africa

Despite Vodacom and MTN starting out as the only two licensed cellular operators, MTN currently leads the African cellular market with approximately 74,1 million subscribers by 30 June 2008, compared to Vodacom's 34 million subscribers (as at 31 March 2008). Vodacom had a presence in five African countries and dominated the South African cellular market, while MTN had a presence in 21 countries, five of these in the Middle East. By this time, it was clear that MTN was aiming to become a leading player in developing countries rather than only in Africa.

MTN was clearly much more aggressive than Vodacom in entering the African market. MTN entered its first international market, Rwanda, in 1997. In 1998, it won licences in Uganda and Swaziland, while in 2000 it purchased a stake in Cameroon's state-owned GSM network. In 2001, the company obtained a GSM licence in Nigeria. After a three-year break, MTN entered further African markets in 2005, including Ivory Coast, Zambia, Congo and Botswana. In the same year, it also made an acquisition in Iran, its first market outside Africa. Since then, MTN has established operations in Cyprus, Syria, Afghanistan and Yemen.

Vodacom executives clearly felt some frustration about investing in Africa, and because of this, there was a concern that the best opportunities in Africa had come and gone. Perhaps it was not surprising then that Vodacom seemed to refocus its energies on dominating even more in South Africa by expanding its focus beyond mobile services. In his farewell as CEO in the *Vodaworld* magazine, Alan Knott-Craig summarised this new aggressive growth strategy for Vodacom: "From now on we plan to lead in all areas of electronic communications technology: network infrastructure, voice and non-voice services, especially data communication." In August 2008, Vodacom announced its intention to acquire Gateway Communications SA (Pty) Ltd, the largest independent provider of satellite and terrestrial interconnection services in Africa. Vodacom had taken its biggest step so far outside of its familiar cellular communications territory.

Sources: Compiled from information sourced from the websites of MTN, Vodacom and it news AFRICA [Online] Available: http://www.mtn.com; http:// www.vodacom.com; http:// www.itnewsafrica.com Accessed 22 December 2009 & Knott-Craig, A. 2008. "New leadership will continue the Vodacom way". *Vodaworld*. Spring 2008, p. 6.

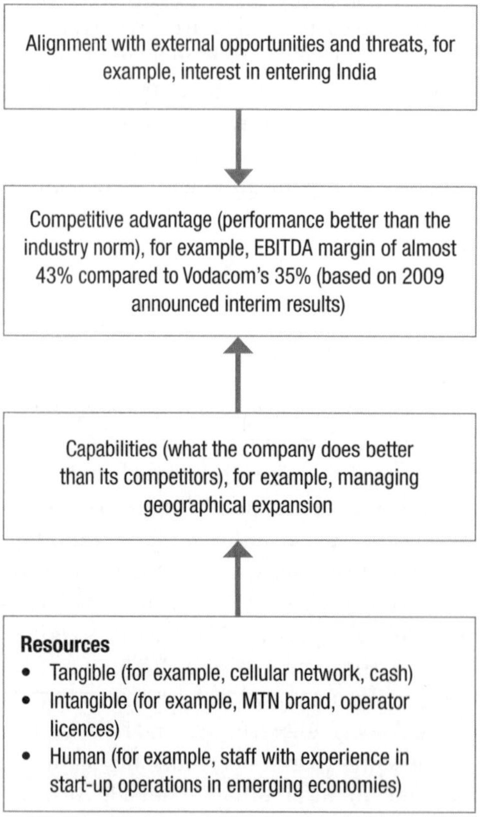

Figure 15.4: Resources and competitive advantage

15.3.4 Strategic choice

In this phase of the strategic-management process, the organisation goes about selecting those strategies that will best help it attain its strategic objectives. In this section, the role of strategies as a course of action to align the organisation's strengths, weaknesses, opportunities and threats is examined. The SWOT matrix depicted in Figure 15.5 on page 539 serves to assist managers in generating strategic options that best align the internal and external environments.

Although there are many different strategic options to choose from, Michael Porter developed the notion of generic strategies. He suggested that there are three basic generic strategies, and that any one of these strategies or a combination of strategic options is generally available to the strategic business unit. The generic strategies are differentiation, cost leadership and focus.

- In **differentiation** strategies, the organisation's competitive advantage stems from the higher prices that customers are willing to pay for the perceived quality of the product. For example, the Apple iPod and Apple iPhone sell at a significant premium compared to other MP3 players and smart cellphones, leveraging Apple's

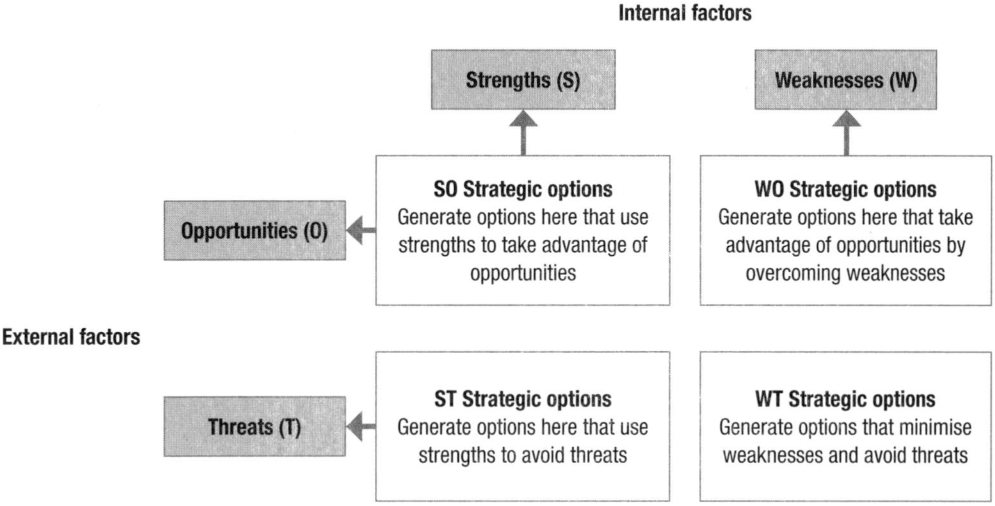

Figure 15.5: The SWOT matrix

Source: Johnson, G., Scholes, K. & Whittington, R. 2008. *Exploring corporate strategy.* 8th ed. Essex: Prentice Hall, p. 347.

brand, its reputation for sleek, high-quality design and its loyal core customer base.

- In **cost leadership** strategies, the organisation's competitive advantage stems from its ability to produce its products and services at a significantly lower production cost than its competitors. Note that cost leadership does not necessarily imply the lowest or even a low price, since competitive advantage would more likely derive from producing at lower cost but selling at comparative prices to the market average. Low-cost airlines such as kulula.com produce their service at a lower cost than full service airlines by, for example, using cheaper airports (like Lanseria), reducing onboard service (for example, no free food and drinks) and using technology to minimise and streamline pre-flight service (for example, online booking and check-in, and boarding passes can be printed beforehand).
- In a **focus** strategy, the organisation attempts to gain dominance in a narrow segment of the market, either though differentiation or cost leadership in that segment. For example, Mont Blanc pens are targeted firmly at the narrow but lucrative high-income segment of the market.

15.3.5 Strategy implementation

Strategy implementation is the "doing" part of the strategy, where the organising and leading take place to ensure that strategies are implemented effectively and efficiently. During this phase, the strategy is aligned with the internal environment. This alignment takes place around three key aspects: the alignment of business and functional strategies, the alignment of leadership and culture, and the creation of technology systems and organisational processes to support the strategy[3]. These aspects are discussed below and are depicted in Figure 15.6 on page 540. See also the Telkom case study on pages 542–543 for examples of some of the elements of strategy implementation in action.

15.3.5.1 Alignment of business and functional strategies

This takes place through the hierarchy of objectives (see Figure 15.3 on page 536), but also by ensuring that functional strategies

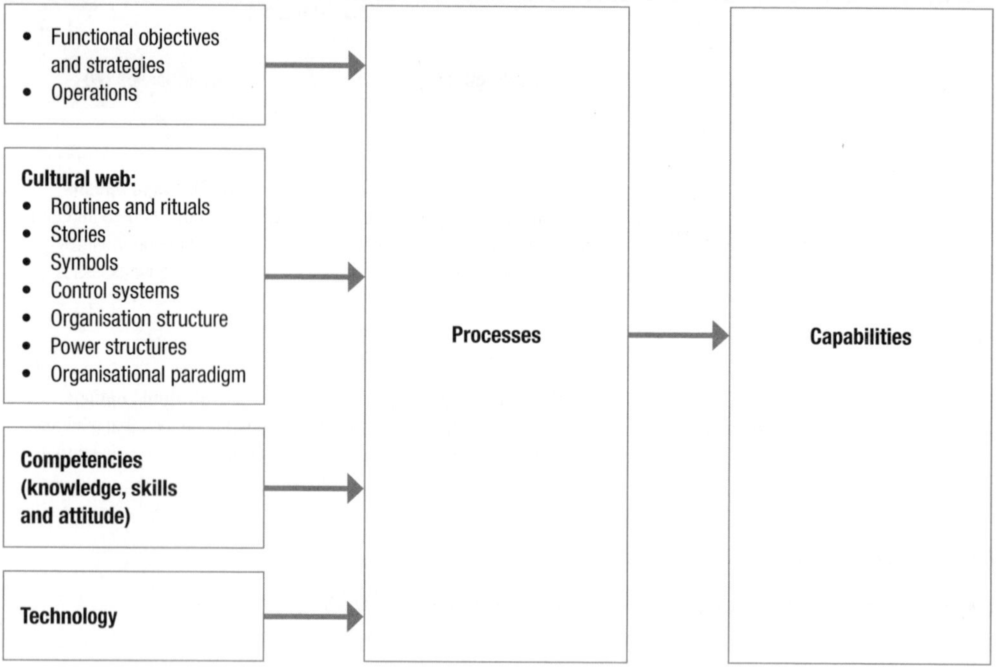

Figure 15.6: The elements of strategy implementation

support the business level strategy directly or indirectly. Table 15.2 on page 541 provides some examples of how functional strategies can support cost leadership and differentiation strategies respectively.

15.3.5.2 Leadership and culture

The leaders of the organisation play a critical role in ensuring that the culture of the organisation is aligned with the strategic direction. This is no easy task, since culture does not change overnight. However, it is important, since a strong culture can be a source of competitive advantage in its own right. Rather than being just one thing, culture can be seen as a number of interlinking aspects, as described in the notion of a cultural web[4]. The cultural web consists of the following elements that are all interlinked:

- **Routines** describe "the way we do things around here", those behaviours that members of the organisation display towards people inside and outside the organisation. These can, of course, be positive or negative in nature. The ideal is to reinforce positive behaviour that supports strategic direction.
- **Rituals** are those activities or events through which the organisation reinforces its values and "the way we do things around here". These can be formal or informal, and again they can be positive or negative. Lunchtime gatherings in the canteen to complain about customers and co-workers, for example, are also a ritual!
- The organisational culture is also reinforced by the **stories** that are told inside and outside the organisation about events and individuals. Rather than only being touching or amusing, these stories also highlight what is important to the organisation.
- The organisation's **symbols**, such as logos, buildings, vehicles and other physical manifestations, even the language used, provide a "shorthand" description of the nature of the organisation. Think, for

Table 15.2: Business and functional strategies

Functional area	Differentiation strategy	Cost-leadership strategy
Marketing	High investment in branding, creating perception of quality	Focus on mass marketing through competitive pricing and pervasive distribution
Operations	High levels of quality control and production quality	Focus on mass production and standardisation
Finance	Manage and maximise margins	Focus on cost control
Research and Development	Relatively high investment in this area to innovate and improve products and service	Will rather imitate than innovate when it comes to product development
Human Resources	Incentives based on quality of products and service	Incentives based on quantity of production and cost control

example, how customers are described in your organisation. If they are often described in negative terms, this communicates something about how you feel about serving customers.

- The dominant **power structures** in the organisation influence the way the organisation thinks about its environment and its business. These power structures can be formal or informal, and can come from many sources. Examples of these sources include expertise (for example, accountants, lawyers or engineers), bargaining forums (for example, trade unions) or strong individuals (for example, the CEO).
- **Control systems** are those measurement and reward systems that help shape behaviour in the organisation. For example, if managers are rewarded for short-term financial results, this is what they will generally focus on in their functional strategies and operations.
- The **organisation structure** reflects the network of formal relationships and power structures in the organisation, and should ideally be designed to facilitate the strategic direction of the organisation. It happens quite often that organisation structure gets in the way of the organisation's strategy implementation. For example, customer-service representatives may be unable to deliver good customer service because too much of their decision power rests with their supervisors or other managers.
- The organisation's **paradigm** is the overall picture of how the employees think about their organisation. This reflects and is linked to the other elements of the cultural web.

Because culture is dependent on the behaviour and attitudes of individuals, it is very difficult to change and virtually impossible to control. Leaders play a key role in establishing the culture of the organisation. Some key reasons why culture is so often misaligned with the strategic efforts of the organisation include the following issues:

- Sometimes leaders do not embody the culture that best fits the strategic direction. This is often a reason why leadership changes when strategy changes fundamentally.
- Some leaders follow a "Do as I say, don't do as I do" attitude. In other words, they do not lead by example. Perhaps even worse are leaders who are completely absent or so weak that they exert little influence over behaviour. These are leaders who do not lead.

- There is often an excessive focus on "hard systems" like organisation structure and control systems at the expense of "soft systems" like routines and rituals, or *vice versa*.

The best way to address these shortcomings is to manage change considering all elements of organisation culture, to understand the present situation and what needs to change.

15.3.5.3 Competencies, technology and processes

In addition to the behavioural and structural elements making up the cultural web, there are three additional aspects that directly influence the implementation of strategy: competencies, technology and processes.

- The organisation needs to ensure that individuals have the right **competencies**, which consist of the right knowledge, skills and attitudes. For example, when Vodacom decided to become a "total telecommunications provider", it recruited individuals with skills in managing data networks and converged ICT services.
- Different types of **technology** can play a key role in strategy implementation. Production technologies and information and communication technologies (ICT) are of particular importance. Low-cost airlines, for example, make extensive use of online technology for bookings, payment and check-in as a means of reducing their costs. It also provides a useful mechanism for linking to service partners such as car-rental companies.
- All the elements discussed above and in the two previous sections mean little unless they are integrated in **processes** to deliver results. For example, project-management processes will combine behaviour, organisation structure, control and reward systems, competencies and technologies to manage key projects. More importantly, processes form the basis for organisational **capabilities** that might ultimately become the basis for competitive advantage.

Case study

Telkom's radical change

Mr. Reuben September, CEO of Telkom, says that the commitment of his leadership team to reposition the company to compete aggressively in the South African and African market is building up momentum, despite greater challenges.

Because of increasing competition, Telkom is making itself leaner and more flexible.

"We are diving deeply into the business. The deeper you dive, the longer it takes to surface again," he says. "That does not mean we are drowning." Results will also not be visible overnight.

In a panel discussion yesterday, management indicated that "strategic partnerships" are being investigated. The possible partners for data centres and fixed-line and mobile services possess the necessary scale and expertise, and have a successful track record.

The mobile services division will be established with the help of these partners, and in the case of Nigerian Multi-Links, there is even the possibility of a consolidation.

With the launch of its interim results to the end of September yesterday, the group announced that a business plan for the mobile division has been approved. It will cost about R6 billion over the next five years to develop this division. This service will be available in 2010.

Management feels that the many growth opportunities place the group in an exciting position. "Some of the opportunities have been created by the company itself. But that does not guarantee success," September says.

Mobile services, broadband and the expansion of its data centres will generate new income streams.

The group has also been reducing cost drastically for some time now; it is aiming for 10% by 2011.

Nombulelo "Pinky" Moholi, managing director of Telkom South Africa, says research is supporting the creation of a fourth mobile-service provider. According to Moholi, mobile services will be a logical extension of the organisation.

Telkom also has factors in its favor, like the competencies that have already been developed, its sales channel and the distribution network already created. It was, for example, involved in building the networks of Vodacom, Cell C and MTN.

But Telkom is hesitant to enter this playing field too hastily – too many others have perished before. "The key is not to have a service, but the customer service afterwards," Moholi says.

In the end, a company is being built to meet all customers' needs. September says people are looking for simplicity in their lives, like receiving accounts from one service provider instead of from several different ones.

Source: Sake24.com. 2009. [Online] Available: http://www.sake24.com/articles/default/display_article.aspx?Channel=News_Maatskappye&ArticleId=6-100_2562677&IsColumnistStory=False Accessed 22 December 2009.

15.3.6 Strategic control

Strategic management is a complex and ongoing process, suggesting that strategic control needs to reflect these complexities. In order to address the need to monitor and evaluate strategic management fully, strategic control needs to:

- be forward looking as well as backward looking
- have internal and external focus
- be able to manage by exception, in other words, it must be able to focus on the "big issues"
- be actionable, in other words, it must be able to support strategic decision-making
- be systematic, in other words, it must be a continuous process.

Strategic management is thus highly dependent on the ongoing generation of information about the organisation, its environment and its performance relative to competitors. Figure 15.7 on page 544 is a typical strategic information system. Typical organisations engage in environment-scanning activities (commonly known as **competitive intelligence**) that focus on the external environment and generate unstructured data about competitors and other external factors. On the other hand, internal information systems (commonly known as **business intelligence systems**) provide information on the organisation's performance. By their nature, business intelligence systems (BIS) provide structured, often quantitative and historical information. The information obtained from these two streams is often disparate and fundamentally different. Consequently, the organisation often requires **integrating mechanisms** to analyse and integrate information, and present it in a more actionable format. These mechanisms can be people, processes or technologies that add value to information. These mechanisms can also help to reduce the information overload that many managers have to deal with every day and improve information quality.

An abundance of information does not guarantee quality or strategic value. Information value needs to satisfy quality criteria: richness (how should it look?), reach (who is it intended for?) and affiliation (where does it come from?). The ultimate goal of information is to provide strategic just-in-time decision support. Its value lies in the quality of the information. There are two categories of quality:

- **Form, content and time.** In other words, information is only valuable if it is in the right format for use, is appropriate for use and is available when required. Thus the information should be obtained and developed for a specific purpose and used in a specific context.
- **Richness and reach of information.** In other words, the information developed should be meaningful and evocative enough to respond to (and exceed) the need, and its source should be trustworthy.

Each of these aspects and their role in strategic control is examined in more detail below.

15.3.6.1 Competitive intelligence

Competitive intelligence (CI) refers to those environmental-scanning activities that the organisation undertakes constantly to monitor its external environment. This process can help the organisation to answer the following questions in relation to the strategic-control process:

- Are the assumptions that we made when formulating our strategy still valid, and how might it change? For example, if an organisation with international business ties is highly exposed to foreign exchange rates, the organisation needs to monitor the events that may cause these rates to fluctuate.
- Are there opportunities and threats in our future that we may need to be aware of, even if they are "weak signals" at this point, and how might they affect us?
- When potentially catastrophic events occur (for example, the global financial crisis in 2008), what could the impact be on our chosen strategy, and how should we change it?

Because of the vast amount of information that is available in the external environment, the CI process is often focused on **key intelligence topics**. These are specific themes identified by the management of the organisation to help direct its environmental scanning efforts.

The most important sources of CI are discussed below.

Information in the public domain

The internet has had a massive effect on the availability of intelligence in the public

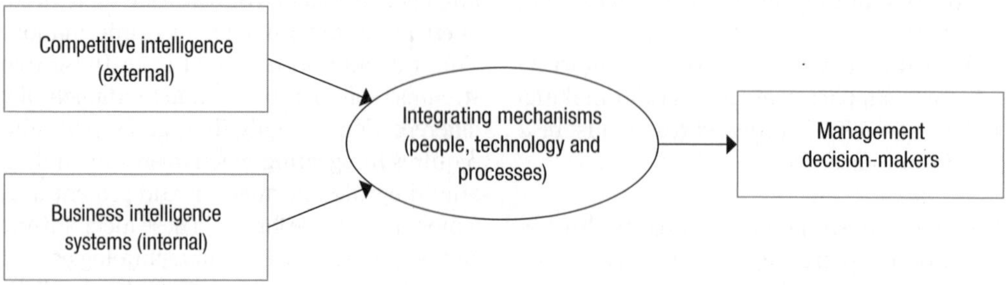

Figure 15.7: Strategic information systems

domain. For example, annual reports of listed companies are now easily available for downloading, whereas they were mailed to shareholders in the past. There is also a plethora of useful publications (either for free or for sale), both online and in physical format, that can be of great use. In addition, useful government information such as patent registrations can be a great source of intelligence. However, it should be remembered that intelligence in the public domain is available to everyone. As such, it does not necessarily provide any particular advantage.

Human intelligence

Human intelligence is obtained from human contacts inside or outside the organisation. Some analysts have observed that up to 80% of what an organisation needs to know can be found inside the organisation. It therefore makes sense to develop internal sources as a means of scanning the environment or obtaining more information on a specific key intelligence topic. For example, think about your organisation's sales team. They are in contact with customers and compete head-on with your competition every day. Who better to ask about a specific competitor's strategy? In addition to internal sources, external human sources such as investment analysts, journalists, competitors' employees and suppliers can also be targeted. Unlike public domain sources, human sources are unique and dependent on the quality of relationships you have with your sources. It is important to point out at that CI does not involve "spying" and it should be done according to ethical principles. (See the box alongside for the Code of Ethics of the Society of Competitive Intelligence Professionals.)

Customers

Although customers are also human sources of intelligence, they are a special class of source, which can be involved in many different ways. For example, customers can be asked about their service experiences, how they perceive your organisation and its products compared to your competitors, and they can be involved in product-development processes as a means of ensuring that products meet customer needs. Best practice suggests that organisations need a constant dialogue with their customers on key issues. See, for example, the role of Platinum Councils in the Dell case study at the beginning of the chapter.

The SCIP Code of Ethics for CI Professionals

The Code of Ethics of the Society of Competitive Intelligence Professionals (SCIP) urges members to follow these principles:

- to strive continually to increase the recognition and respect of the profession
- to comply with all applicable laws, domestic and international
- to disclose all relevant information accurately, including one's identity and organisation, prior to all interviews
- to avoid conflicts of interest in fulfilling one's duties
- to provide honest and realistic recommendations and conclusions in the execution of one's duties
- to promote this code of ethics within one's company, with third-party contractors and within the entire profession
- to adhere to and abide by one's company policies, objectives and guidelines faithfully.

Source: SCIP. 2009. "SCIP Code of Ethics for CI Professionals". [Online] Available: http://www.scip.org/About/content.cfm?ItemNumber=578&navItemNumber=504 Accessed 22 December 2009. © 2007 Society of Competitive Intelligence Professionals.

15.3.6.2 Business Intelligence Systems (BIS)

Business Intelligence Systems integrate various (often disparate) information systems with a view to making the information available to decision-makers in the organisation.

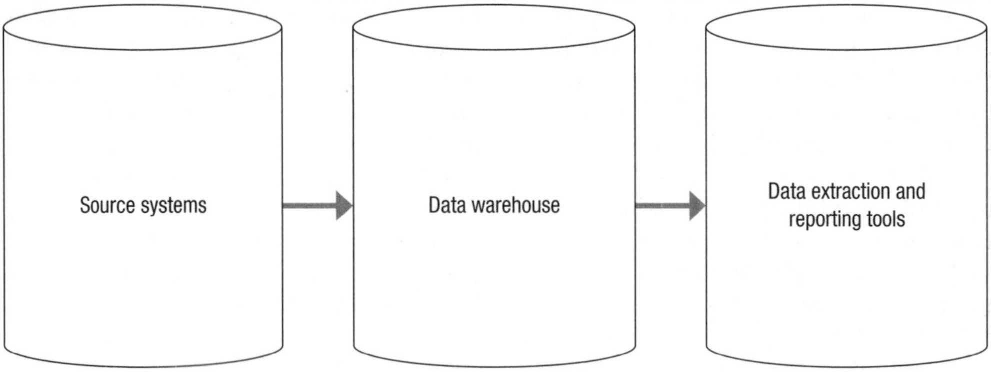

Figure 15.8: A simplified view of business intelligence systems

Figure 15.8 presents a simplified view of BIS for the purpose of this discussion.

The BIS requires data from its source. This could be from a number of different systems that record transactional data, such as point-of-sale systems, customer relationship management and enterprise resource planning systems (for example, SAP). The data is brought together in a central storage facility, generally referred to as a data warehouse, from where it can be extracted for use by managers using tools like online analytical processing (OLAP), data mining and executive information systems (including dashboards). These are briefly discussed below.

Online analytical processing (OLAP) provides a means for users to view data from a data warehouse in a multi-dimensional format. For example, OLAP allows users to compare data based on criteria such as geographical areas, product lines and time.

The concept of **data mining** is becoming increasingly popular as an analytical process consisting of statistical techniques, artificial intelligence and database research. It is designed to explore data (usually large amounts of business or market-related data) in search of consistent patterns and/or systematic relationships between variables. The ultimate goal is prediction. For example, retailers may use data mining to analyse shopping patterns and to predict what products are likely to be bought at the same time. This helps to optimise the shop layout and merchandising.

Executive information systems (EIS) refers to operational data presented in the form of charts, tables and reports for the use of managers[5]. One particularly useful development in this regard has been the use of **management dashboards** as a way to present layered information in a simple, actionable format. Like a car's dashboard or control panel, a software (digital) dashboard provides decision-makers with the input necessary to "drive" the business. Dashboards allow managers to monitor the contribution of the various departments in their organisation using a few key indicators. To gauge exactly how well an organisation is performing overall, dashboards allow users to capture and report specific data points from each department within the organisation, thus providing a "snapshot" of performance. Digital dashboards offer the following benefits to users:

- a visual presentation of performance measures
- the ability to identify and correct negative trends
- measurement of efficiencies/inefficiencies
- the ability to generate detailed reports showing new trends
- the ability to make more informed decisions based on collected business intelligence

- alignment strategies and organisational goals
- time-saving when running multiple reports
- total visibility of all systems instantly.

The use of BIS is a key aspect of strategic monitoring and control, since it provides a means of tracking strategy implementation and ensuring strategic alignment between different levels of strategy[6]. In addition, it provides a way to identify opportunities for improving efficiency and effectiveness. Although BIS have promised the integration of structured internal data with external, unstructured data, in practice this does not happen without the intervention of people, processes or technology.

Business **strategy alignment** refers to the alignment of business-unit functions with the functions of information for the effective use of information (see Figure 15.9). Any business should ensure that all information (internally and externally) is captured in a central hub where it can be stored, distributed and retrieved when needed.

There should be clear alignment between all levels of strategy and, at all levels, there should be inclusion of the information and knowledge strategy. An organisation's information strategy is linked to its human-resources management through its knowledge system. It is not easy to align something that up to now has merely been an operational function of an organisation. However, if information and knowledge become the main drivers, they should become the main items of strategy. In doing this, the organisation should ensure the following conditions:

- Information and knowledge are represented at board level.
- There is adequate governance of IS in place.
- There is adequate technological capability.
- There is adequate human capability.
- Information and knowledge become part of the value management.
- All process and systems are designed around information.

15.3.6.3 Integrating mechanisms

The role of integrating mechanisms is to ensure that all available data is integrated, analysed and presented to management decision-makers in such a way that it supports the decision-making process. Integration can be done by people, processes or technologies, often in combination.

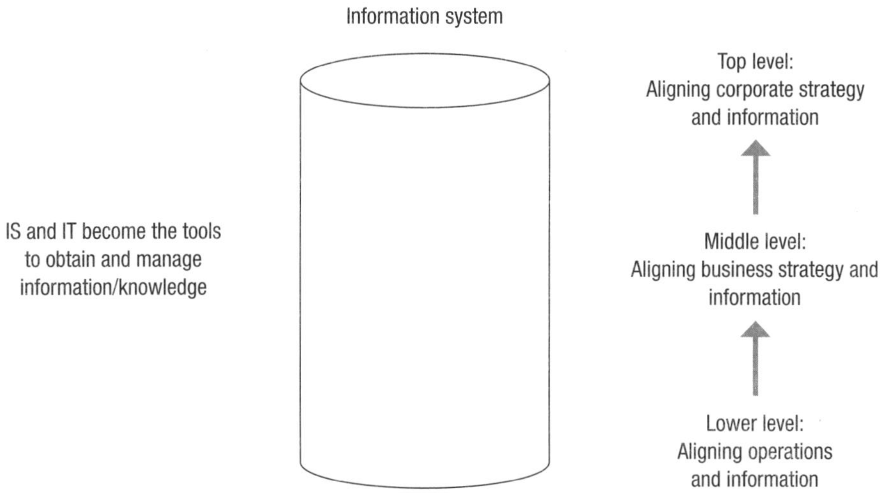

Figure 15.9: Information strategy as information hub carrying all information that drives strategy

- CI officers or analysts, chief information officers and market researchers are all examples of positions that have been created to assist decision-makers to obtain and analyse information for decision support. Multi-disciplinary intelligence teams can also play a key role in presenting a comprehensive understanding of a competitor, an issue or a situation.
- Processes like scenario analysis and planning, business war-gaming and strategic-planning workshops can be used to develop a more comprehensive and actionable view from existing information.
- Technology (most often specialist software) can support people and processes in generating actionable information. For example, business simulation software can be used to support business war-gaming and provide a way for managers to examine the possible outcomes of their decisions.

15.4 Summary

Strategic management provides an overarching process that directs and contains all management decisions and actions. Many systems exist to help organisations scan their environments, identifying strengths, weaknesses, opportunities and threats that form the basis of strategic decision-making. To this end, it is important to understand the role of information in strategic management as a means to monitor, evaluate and control constantly.

Information is not merely an operational tool; it belongs to the organisation (leadership and all levels of management down to the shop floor) and should be entrenched in strategy.

Key terms

business intelligence	strategic direction
competitive intelligence	strategic management
environmental analysis	strategic objectives
strategic alignment	strategic implementation
strategic choice	

Questions for discussion

Reread the case study about Dell Computers at the beginning of the chapter and answer the following questions:

1. What is Dell's core business? Justify your answer.
2. How would you describe Dell's business strategy?
3. Give five examples of strategy implementation initiatives from the case study.
4. How does Dell use CI and BIS in its strategy? Is this appropriate?

Multiple-choice questions

1. "To be the leading provider (as measured by share of revenue) of mobile data services in the southern African consumer market by 2015" is an example of a ...
   a. functional objective.
   b. mission.
   c. strategic objective.
   d. vision.
2. Volvo's strategy is to focus on safety as a means to create willingness amongst consumers to pay more for their cars. This is an example of a ... strategy at the business level.
   a. niche
   b. cost-leadership
   c. quality
   d. differentiation

3. Which one of the following elements is not a mechanism for strategy implementation?
   a. rituals and routines
   b. functional strategies
   c. organisation structure
   d. mission statement
4. Which one of the following is not an application of strategic information?
   a. dashboards
   b. data mining
   c. databases
   d. BI
5. As CIO, you want to align your organisation's strategy and information. Which one of the following is not critical to this task?
   a. Information and knowledge are represented at board level.
   b. There is adequate governance in place.
   c. There is enough information available.
   d. There is adequate human capability.

Answers to multiple-choice questions

1. c
2. d
3. d
4. c
5. c

References

1. Gamble, J.E. and Thompson, A.A. Jr. 2009. *Essentials of Strategic Management: The quest for Competitive Advantage*. New York: McGraw-Hill Irwin, p. 15.
2. Gamble, J.E. and Thompson, A.A. Jr. 2009. *Essentials of Strategic Management: The quest for Competitive Advantage*. New York: McGraw-Hill Irwin.
3. Porter, M. 1985.
4. Johnson, G., Scholes, K. & Whittington, R. 2008. *Exploring corporate strategy*. 8th ed. Essex: Prentice Hall.
5. Daniel, E., Wilson, H. & McDonald, M. 2001. "Towards a map of marketing information systems: An inductive study". *European Journal of Marketing*. 37(5/6), pp. 821–847.
6. This discussion is based on Venkatraman, N., Henderson, J.C & Oldach, S. 1993. "Continuous Strategic Alignment: Exploiting information technology capabilities for competitive success". *European Management Journal*. June, 11(2), pp. 139–149.

Websites: www.valuebasedmanagement.net
www.acm.org/constitution/code
www.computer.org/tab/code11
www.icann.org/
www.scip.org/

INDEX

Page numbers in **bold** refer to figures and tables.

D

G

Q

R